J. Stanley Warford

Computing Fundamentals

The Efficiency of Theorem Proving Strategies
by David A. Plaisted and Yunshan Zhu

Applied Pattern Recognition
by Dietrich W. R. Paulus and Joachim Hornegger

SAP® R/3® Interfacing using BAPIs
by Gerd Moser

Scalable Search in Computer Chess
by Ernst A. Heinz

The SAP® R/3® Guide to EDI and Interfaces
by Axel Angeli, Ulrich Streit and Robi Gonfalonieri

**Optimising Business Performance
with Standard Software Systems**
by Heinz-Dieter Knöll, Lukas W. H. Kühl,
Roland W. A. Kühl and Robert Moreton

ASP – Application Service Providing
by SCN Education B.V.

Customer Relationship Management
by SCN Education B.V.

Data Warehousing
by SCN Education B.V.

Electronic Banking
by SCN Education B.V.

Mobile Networking with WAP
by SCN Education B.V.

Efficient eReporting with SAP EC®
by Andreas H. Schuler and Andreas Pfeifer

Interactive Broadband Media
by Nikolas Mohr and Gerhard P. Thomas

Sales and Distribution with SAP®
by Gerhard Oberniedermaier and Tamara Sell-Jander

Efficient SAP R/3-Data Archiving
by Markus Korschen

Computing Fundamentals
by J. Stanley Warford

J. Stanley Warford

Computing Fundamentals

The Theory and Practice of Software Design with BlackBox Component Builder

Edited by Karlheinz Hug

vieweg

Bibliographic information published by Die Deutsche Bibliothek
Die Deutsche Bibliothek lists this publication in the Deutsche Nationalbibliographie;
detailed bibliographic data is available in the Internet at <http://dnb.ddb.de>.

1st edition December 2002

Vieweg is a company in the specialist publishing group BertelsmannSpringer.
www.vieweg.de

Cover design: Ulrike Weigel, www.CorporateDesignGroup.de
Printing and binding: Lengericher Handelsdruckerei, Lengerich
Printed on acid-free paper.
Printed in Germany

ISBN 3-528-05828-5

Foreword

The world of computing has always had one corner stone of particular interest to many, from educators to practitioners: languages. And programming languages in particular. Over the years, we have seen new languages come—and, much less frequently, old languages go. It is always tempting to focus on "the one" language of fashion of the day. In this very readable and instructive textbook, Stan Warford has done the unusual—and risky—by taking the programming language Component Pascal that is far from mainstream, although it does have roots that are among the strongest in the field.

Given that the concept of formal language, whether at the level of architecture, design, or implementation language, is central to our discipline, it is important that students continue to be exposed to a wide variety of languages. No single language does everything perfectly, or even well, and students need to understand this fundamental tradeoff. The same holds for frameworks and programming models that need to be designed to allow harmony between the natural ways of a language and the needs to a framework for a particular domain.

I had the privilege of being one of the key designers of this language, together with my friends at Oberon microsystems. One thing we knew back the early 1990s, when we started this effort, was that a language alone wasn't any good anymore. So we co-designed the language Component Pascal and the environment BlackBox Component Builder, which unites an application framework, a development environment, and an application runtime environment—in many ways bringing together the advantages of highly dynamic languages and systems like Lisp or Smalltalk and those of statically checked languages like Modula-2, Oberon, Java, and now C#.

Stan succeeds in providing a highly original introduction to programming. One that alternates between the high-level aspects of immediate user impact, such as dialogs and views, and the low-level concepts of core programming, such as loops and recursion. As a result, students are always able to anchor what they learn in application scenarios that make immediate sense. The ability to create functional programs quickly, while not deviating to adopt an arsenal of "dirty tricks", will help keep students motivated. The clean underlying approach and overall structure will at the same time lead to a deep understanding of principles and rigor.

Clemens Szyperski
Redmond, July 2002

Editor's Note

What do you say after "Hello World"? Everyone who teaches programming has an answer. For Stan Warford, the question is meaningless, because in his book and lectures, he does not start with "Hello World" or even sequential IO. Rather, he starts with modules, interfaces, and the construction of dialog boxes. Yet his book is not one of those "click-here-and-then-click-there" lightweights, which merely describe the user interface of some currently popular development system. He sticks to all the classical topics—like structured algorithms, searching and sorting, stacks, lists, and trees—which should be part of any serious course in computing. However, he does not do this job in an old-fashioned way but with a unique approach introducing all the modern things we did not have ten years ago (at least not in introductory books): GUIs, components, frameworks, UML, design by contract, design patterns. He gets all this together with solid theoretical basics like grammars, EBNF, verification, GCL, complexity. He explains every notion and every line of his example programs thoroughly. The text—simple, clear sentences—is accompanied by numerous figures drawn carefully, so that every student will easily understand even complicated facts.

These are only a few reasons why I like Stan's book. I liked it since I first saw a preliminary version. At that time I was working on my own book "Module, Klassen, Verträge", which is the first German language book using Component Pascal and BlackBox. I even considered abandoning my book, because what could I say that Stan did not already say in his? Fortunately, with the help of my colleague Helmut Ketz at Reutlingen University, I found an approach for my book that complements Stan's approach. Then I got a chance to help publish this book, for which I am most grateful. Thank you Cuno Pfister and Wolfgang Weck at Oberon microsystems and Reinald Klockenbusch at Vieweg!

Now this is the first English language book using Component Pascal and BlackBox. Since both our books fit together well, we have prepared an online service for the readers of both books, which is available at

```
http://userserv.fh-reutlingen.de/~hug
```

It includes a glossary in English and German covering topics of both books. May it serve you well!

Karlheinz Hug
Reutlingen, September 2002

Preface

This book is the outgrowth of an introductory computer science course taught at Pepperdine University. The course, as well as the book, is primarily for majors in computer science who intend a more in-depth study later, and secondarily for non-majors who desire a strong background in computers so they can deal with them effectively in their chosen fields.

For years we had followed the common practice of basing the course on the programming language Pascal. The emergence of many ideas in the field of software engineering led us to reevaluate the goals of the introductory course and how they could be effectively achieved. Rather than to simply append the new ideas onto the old approach we found that a paradigm shift was necessary, which had the effect of changing both the content and the organization of the course. Those ideas as reflected in this book include:

The ideas behind this book

- Frameworks

- Graphical user interfaces

- Object-oriented languages

There is an interrelationship between all these ideas. Each idea gains a measure of force in conjunction with the others, so that the whole is more than the sum of its parts.

Frameworks

A framework consists of a complete programming environment including a text editor and all the other tools needed to write and execute programs. The BlackBox framework is an exceptionally powerful but simple framework for software development. Power and especially simplicity are desirable attributes for teaching introductory programming. Like all good frameworks, BlackBox is platform independent, so that students and teacher need not complete their work with the same operating system. Furthermore, the cost of the framework for academic use is free, with the complete development system available for downloading from the Internet.

A framework is more than a collection of code libraries that provide an application programming interface for the developer. Like many development environments, the BlackBox framework does not require the programmer to write the event loop for the graphical user interface (GUI). Unlike most systems, however, which generate the event loop with code skeletons for the programmer to fill in to handle interaction events, the BlackBox framework *is* the main program and the programmer's application is simply an extension of the framework. The event loop is hidden and there is no handwaving to explain confusing code skeletons. The benefit of this arrangement is that students learn distributed control from the outset, which is an important aspect of object-oriented programming.

Distributed control

Another advantage of the BlackBox framework for teaching programming principles is its use of design by contract, which is also prominent in the Eiffel system. The idea is that every service provided by a method or procedure has preconditions that must be satisfied by the client. If the preconditions are met the method or procedure is guaranteed to function correctly, satisfying the postcondition. The documentation of the framework reflects this philosophy by specifying preconditions and postconditions for its services. Furthermore, the ASSERT statement is a primitive in the programming language, so that students can specify their own pre- and postconditions in their programs. There is a correspondence between pre- and postconditions of the framework and the Hoare triple of formal methods. Our introductory sequence requires a concurrent course in formal methods and integrates those topics with the programming course based on this book. The formal methods material is segregated in optional starred sections for the benefit of those whose curriculum does not include this requirement.

Optional starred sections for formal methods material

Graphical user interfaces

Using an object-oriented framework in the first year caused a reassessment of the entire issue of input/output. As it turns out, there is a natural one-to-one replacement of old topics with new ones. In place of interactive I/O, where the program prompts the user for input with a command line interface, is dialog box I/O. In place of file I/O is window I/O.

The BlackBox framework provides a Forms subsystem, which enables the student to program a GUI. A form is a component that is implemented with the model-view-controller (MVC) design pattern to produce a dialog box. The beauty of the framework is that students can begin programming immediately with dialog boxes without having to know the details of the MVC design pattern. The services provided by the Forms subsystem are so simple and so powerful that the programs we formerly assigned using Pascal with interactive input are longer than the equivalent programs with a dialog box. Programming with a GUI from the outset in the introductory course motivates students, because they learn how to produce programs with a professional appearance.

Dialog boxes

The simplicity of using the Forms subsystem with BlackBox is in marked contrast to the equivalent task of programming with Java's AWT or Swing library of classes. Programming with the Forms subsystem requires no concept of listeners or of layout management. An input field of a dialog box is simply mapped by the framework to an exported variable. Consequently, the chapter on dialog boxes can immediately follow the chapter on variables.

In BlackBox, files take a secondary role to the GUI and are available at a lower level of abstraction than are windows. Although it is possible to perform file I/O in BlackBox this text replaces it with scanning from and writing to the focus window. The user achieves the corresponding file operation by selecting Open or Save from the File menu, which hides the mechanisms of file I/O. BlackBox provides a scanner

Window I/O

that is powerful for experienced programmers to use but proved too difficult to understand for beginners. This book uses a scanner designed for the introductory course that can scan integers, reals, characters, strings, one-dimensional arrays of integers and reals, and two-dimensional arrays of integers and reals. Window I/O requires slightly more understanding of the MVC design pattern and is introduced later than dialog boxes.

Object-oriented languages

There is a debate among computer science educators about the placement of object-oriented (OO) programming in the first year of instruction. Some argue that students should program with objects from the outset even to the exclusion of procedural programming, while others advocate a more gradual mixed approach. To a certain extent, the choice is dictated by the language and development environment chosen to teach the concepts. For example, if you teach Java, which attempts to be purely OO, in the introductory course then it is impossible to construct a function that is not also a method even if inheritance or polymorphism are not used. Languages like C++ or Ada are, by design, mixed languages. That is, they are not pure OO languages but have procedural features as well.

The BlackBox framework is based on a new language named Component Pascal. Because it is a derivative of Oberon/L, much evolution has occurred since Pascal was designed. The pedigree of the language is

Pascal → Modula → Oberon → Oberon-2 → Oberon/L → Component Pascal

Unlike C++ and Ada, which added object-orientation onto an existing procedural language, Component Pascal is designed with no backward-compatibility requirements. However, like C++ and Ada, Component Pascal is by design a mixed-paradigm language with procedural and OO features.

The BlackBox framework lends itself to a gradual, mixed approach in the exposition of software design. For example, the dialog boxes provided by the Forms subsystem require procedural programming even though the subsystem is itself based heavily on objects. The approach taken in this book is more evolutionary than revolutionary. Its goal is to move the student through successively higher levels of abstraction, starting with procedural programming and concluding with OO programming.

The goal of this book

Some computer science educators claim that it is harmful to teach procedural decomposition to beginning programmers. They maintain that all data structures should be objects and that a pure object-oriented (OO) language should be used. Otherwise, you force students into the dreaded paradigm shift experienced by seasoned professionals when they switch to object orientation. Whether the dreaded paradigm shift occurs depends on how late in the student's academic career the shift is required. When recursion was new, we taught it late, and it was a shift. Now we teach it the first year and it is simply another tool. Scheme advocates maintain that recursion, along with the functional paradigm, should be taught at the outset, though most others incorporate it as one of many tools.

Certainly, object orientation belongs in the first year so the dreaded paradigm shift will not occur. But whether inheritance and polymorphism (which are the tools of OO design) should be taught at the outset is debatable. This book has abstraction as a theme, and students progress from lower levels of abstraction (procedural) to higher (OO). This progression has the advantage of teaching the abstraction process, which is a more general concept than object orientation. OO programming is still taught in the first year, minimizing the paradigm shift. In my experience, students can learn procedural programming first without harm as long as they are not steeped in it for an extended period of time before progressing to OO.

Like most languages designed by Niklaus Wirth, Component Pascal is small, simple, elegant, yet powerful. Component Pascal has many features to recommend it:

- Modules—The module is the basic unit of compilation. Variables can be global to a module, which eliminates the necessity of the confusing static feature of C++ and Java.

- Interfaces—Unlike header files in C++, the interface is created automatically by the compiler. The framework automatically keeps track of consistency between compiled and recompiled modules.

- Memory protection—The C++ language provides explicit pointers but cannot insure against memory leaks. The Java language does not provide explicit pointers, but guarantees memory protection with its automatic garbage collection. Component Pascal is unique in that it provides both explicit pointers as well as automatic garbage collection.

- Object-oriented—Component Pascal is fully object-oriented with polymorphism and single inheritance.

- Dynamic linker/loader—The compiler generates fast native code. There is no virtual machine or byte code intermediate language. Modules are loaded on demand within the framework.

Unfortunately, Component Pascal also has one major weakness that prevents its widespread use as a language in the typical introductory Computer Science course. Namely, C++ is entrenched in the professional software development world, Java is entrenched in the Web world, and universities are pressured to produce graduates with specific skills in those two languages. The pressure in the introductory course comes internally from teachers of the upper-level courses who want their students to already have C++ and Java skills. Those teachers get the pressure externally from industry, which wants university graduates with those skills.

There was a time in computer science education when programming languages for the introductory course were determined not by industry pressure but by pedagogical and technical considerations. Whether those days are gone forever or will reappear after the supply of computer science graduates finally matches the extreme employment demand remains to be seen.

At Pepperdine University, students study Component Pascal during the first year—that is, two semesters—from this book. The second year they study C++ — again for two semesters. The third year they are introduced to the functional paradigm with Common Lisp, the declarative paradigm with Prolog, and the concurrent paradigm with Java. Java is the primary language of instruction throughout the third and fourth years. This curriculum provides the benefit of Component Pascal in the introductory course while at the same time giving students the skills demanded by industry.

Resources

One of the best features of BlackBox is that the complete development system is available from Oberon microsystems at

```
http://www.oberon.ch/
```

and is free for educational use. The on-line documentation contains the defining language report and a sequence of tutorials (although geared to the experienced programmer, not the typical introductory computer science student). The educational version has the full programming capability of the developer version. At the time of this writing, Oberon microsystems does not supply the current 1.4 version of Black-Box for Macintosh operating systems. However, an older Macintosh version is still available at Oberon microsystems' ftp server

```
ftp://www.oberon.ch/BlackBox/Mac/REL132/BB132A.HQX
```

Note that the above URL begins with `ftp://` instead of the usual `http://`. Support for the Macintosh development environment is no longer available, and some interfaces have been changed in the transition from the 1.3 family to 1.4. However, none of the programs in this book use any of the changed interfaces, and all programs work as described on both MSWindows and MacOS. Documents are fully exchangeable between installations of the two releases.

All the programs in this book, as well as a set of lecture slides in PDF format, are available electronically at

```
ftp://ftp.pepperdine.edu/pub/compsci/comp-fund
```

Also at this site is a paper presented at an ACM SIGCSE conference that gives a few more details of our experience using BlackBox in the first-year course.

Acknowledgments

The designers of the BlackBox framework deserve congratulations for the sheer technical excellence of their product. Many people contributed useful suggestions and corrections to this manuscript in its various stages of development including Bill Bunch, Leighton Cowart, Reinhard Dietrich, Peter Fogg, Stephan Gehring, Dominik Gruntz, Rick Miltimore, Bernhard Treutwein, Wolfgang Weck, Russ Yost, and Brennan Young, as well as countless students at Pepperdine University who endured previous beta versions. I especially thank two individuals who had a large influence on the content—Professor John Motil, whose constructive criticisms of early versions of the scanners in the PboxMappers module improved them considerably, and Professor Dung "Zung" Nguyen, who provided many of the ideas for the data structure specifications and the object-oriented design patterns. At Vieweg, Professor Karlheinz Hug has been most helpful in the publication process.

Stan Warford
Malibu, July 2002

Contents

 Chapter *1*

The BlackBox Framework

Computers, as useful as they are, have no innate intelligence. Any intelligent behavior that a computer exhibits is a reflection of the program that resides in its memory. That program was conceived, designed, and written by one or more human beings. How friendly a program is to the user, or how useful, or how frustrating is determined largely by the quality of the program design. When we marvel at the power of computers we are paying tribute to programs that are designed well. And when we blame the computer for making a mistake that blame must inevitably fall on a person—either the designer, the programmer, or someone who earlier entered incorrect data into the system. Computers are so new to the human scene that getting them to work efficiently and effectively is a great challenge. Reports of computer failure in the popular press attest to the fact that developing computer systems that are both error free and easy to use is difficult.

The software design problem

The BlackBox system provides the human software designer a tool to develop such systems. This chapter introduces the BlackBox framework and its text subsystem and shows how to encode your BlackBox documents for electronic transmission.

The purpose of the BlackBox system

The BlackBox framework

The BlackBox framework is a powerful tool based on modern software design principles. The framework has many characteristics, four of which are:

- The Component Pascal language
- Cross-platform capability
- Graphical user interface
- Object-oriented language and system

Four characteristics of the BlackBox framework

A framework consists of a complete programming environment including a text editor and all the other tools needed to write and execute programs. Part of the framework is a programming language. In the BlackBox framework, the programming language is Component Pascal. The Component Pascal language is nearly identical to the Oberon-2 language, which is used in systems other than BlackBox. This book is an introduction to both the BlackBox framework and the Component Pascal language.Those features of the language that you will learn will be applicable to other systems that incorporate Oberon-2. However, much of the power of the programming environment is derived from the framework. Although they will be similar, the features of the framework that you learn will not in general be applicable to other programming environments.

The Component Pascal language

The programming language Component Pascal is the newest descendent in the Algol family of languages. Algol stands for *algo*rithmic *l*anguage. It was designed in 1960 and had a major impact on programming languages. Although several short-comings surfaced later after extensive experience, it quickly gained a reputation as a simple and elegant language. Two members of the committee that designed the language were John Backus and Peter Naur. They devised a method for specifying the grammatical rules of the language. Their specification method is still used for many programming languages including the Component Pascal language.

The Algol language

Another member of the Algol design committee was Niklaus Wirth, a professor of computer science at ETH Zürich, the Swiss Federal Institute of Technology. He proposed some changes to the language that were eventually incorporated into a dialect called Algol-W. He made more substantial changes in that language with his design in 1970 of the popular Pascal programming language. Wirth named Pascal after Blaise Pascal, a French religious thinker, mathematician, and physician who lived in the seventeenth century. Pascal is credited with inventing the Pascaline, a calculating machine that used gears and dials to represent and manipulate numeric values. Wirth's two design goals for the Pascal language were that it be a good vehicle for teaching structured programming and that it be easy to implement on the computers of that day. He was especially successful in meeting the teaching goal for the language, because it quickly gained widespread use in universities around the world.

The Pascal language

Not content with the success of Pascal, Niklaus Wirth improved on his design in 1979 with the language Modula-2, so called because of its ability to subdivide a program into modules. With Pascal, a large program must be written as if it were a single document. The concept of dividing a program into modules is like the concept of dividing a book into chapters. In the same way that a chapter of a textbook collects similar topics under one subheading, a module collects similar program parts under one "compilation unit". To show the power of Modula-2 Wirth designed an entire computer, which he called Lilith, based solely on that language.

The Modula-2 language

The Oberon project was begun in 1985 at ETH. By this time computer hardware and its associated software had become powerful and complex. With the complexity came difficulty in software design and programming. A primary goal of the Oberon project was to develop a programming language that would be simple to learn and use, but powerful enough to solve complex problems. Wirth's philosophy of programming languages is that a complex language is not required to solve a complex problem. On the contrary, he believes that languages containing complex features whose purposes are to solve complex problems actually hinder the problem solving effort. The idea is that it is difficult enough for a programmer to solve a complex problem without having to also cope with the complexity of the language. Having a simple programming language as a tool reduces the total complexity of the problem to be solved.

The Oberon language incorporated a modern software design technique known as object-oriented programming, while maintaining the successful features of modularity from Modula-2 and structure from Pascal. In 1992, Wirth and H. P. Mössenböck added a few features to the original Oberon language which resulted in the language Oberon-2, named after the second largest moon of the planet Uranus. Inspiration for the name came from the Voyager 2 space probe whose small computer controlled the spacecraft's data acquisition and transmission system.

The Oberon-2 language

In 1997, the Oberon microsystems company made a few additional changes to Oberon-2, some of which make the language more consistent with the popular Java language, and some of which made the language more useful in a framework environment. They named the new language Component Pascal. The word "component" in the name of the language is to emphasize the suitability of the language for writing objects that are components of containers. An example of a component is a spreadsheet object that is contained in a word processing container. Because this is an introductory book, it will not be able to delve into those advanced features of component programming. But it is good to know that with Component Pascal you will be learning a language that is capable of solving industrial strength problems. Unlike Pascal, the primary goal of Component Pascal is not a teaching goal. However, Component Pascal has its roots in Pascal, and because of that it is an excellent language to learn principles of software development. Because the difference between Oberon and Component Pascal is so small, Niklaus Wirth is considered to be the designer of Component Pascal.

The Component Pascal language

Niklaus Wirth is the designer of the Component Pascal language

If you have experience with Pascal you will notice many similarities with Component Pascal. There may even be a few features that you miss. If so, remember that missing features do not equate to less power. If you have no prior programming experience you will surely not miss a thing, and you may even have the advantage of not having to unlearn some old ways of thinking.

Cross-platform capability

Imagine a country in which the same company that owned the local electrical power plant also owned the local appliance factory. The company designs the electrical wall outlet to accommodate the appliances that it makes in its factory. If you buy a toaster from the company there is no problem plugging it into the electrical outlet, because the same company that makes the outlet makes the appliance, and it designs the plug on the toaster to fit the outlet on the wall.

Suppose that another company moves into the neighborhood and sets up a competing electrical power plant and a competing appliance factory. The new company thinks that it can provide a better wall outlet and corresponding plug in its appliances, so it makes them differently from the first company. Unfortunately, a plug from the first company will not fit a wall socket from the second company and vice versa. This situation forces people to choose who they will get their electric power from and commits them to buy their appliances from the same company.

The compatibility issue

Now suppose that a third company moves to town and is not interested in setting up a local power plant, but is only interested in making appliances to sell to customers of both the other companies. To do so this third company will have to design its appliances to be compatible with both types of outlets. Each appliance will come in two models—one model with a plug compatible with the first company's outlet and another model with a plug compatible with the second company's outlet.

The scenario described above is certainly not optimal for the third company. If the first two competing companies would simply standardize on their outlet design the third company would only need to manufacture one model of its appliance, which it could sell to either type of customer. Manufacturing costs would be lower because of increased economy of scale and customers would benefit from the lower prices.

This scenario is not much different from the world of computing today. Every computer is controlled by an operating system. Like the wall outlet designed by the power plant, each operating system has its own standards to which applications must adhere. There are at least three different widespread operating systems with three different standards—various Microsoft Windows operating systems, MacOS, and UNIX. The standard specified by an operating system is called an *application programming interface*, or API for short. An operating system's API is a specification to which programmers must adhere if they want their programs to operate with that operating system. The API of each of these operating systems is different from the others. Consequently, if you write a program that you want to use with Windows98 it will not work on a computer that is running the MacOS or UNIX.

The application programming interface (API)

A remarkable feature of the BlackBox framework is its cross-platform capability. Of all the software development environments on the market at the time of this writing, BlackBox and the various Java systems are the most successful in providing a programmer with the ability to write a complex general-purpose program that will work with little or no modification on any of the above three operating systems. It is as if an additional company moved into town and supplied a converter to be positioned between the wall socket and the appliance plug.

Cross-platform capability

The appliance company is now free to make only one kind of appliance that will work with both customers. It only needs to include the converter with its appliance. Similarly, the programmer is now free to write only one program that will work with any operating system. The BlackBox framework is the converter between the computers as shown in Figure 1.1.

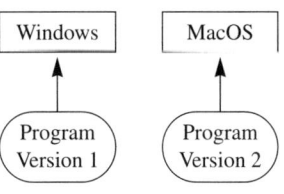

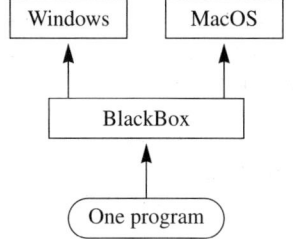

Figure 1.1
The cross-platform capability of BlackBox.

(a) Multiple versions without the BlackBox framework.

(b) One program with the BlackBox framework.

Graphical user interface

The cross-platform capability of BlackBox would not be that remarkable if it were confined to the programming language Component Pascal. Programs written in all the older languages mentioned previously have the capability to run on different computers with their different operating systems. However, such portable programs based on a language instead of a framework do not have the capability of providing the user with the *graphical user interface* (GUI) of modern operating systems. Instead, such programs execute in what is called a command-line interface. If you have experience with the DOS operating system you know how a command line interface works. The user is presented with a prompt character on the left side of the screen—usually the % character—and must type a command to instruct the operating system to perform a task.

The graphical user interface (GUI)

The GUI was invented by the Xerox company and later popularized by Apple with its Macintosh computer. A GUI is characterized by input that is controlled by a mouse as well as the keyboard. Rather than having to memorize and enter commands from the keyboard the user simply makes selections from a menu bar at the top of the screen or from a dialog box that pops up in the middle of the screen. Each operating system has its own GUI with its own look and feel.

The real advance made by the BlackBox framework is not just its portability across operating systems, but the fact that its portability adopts the GUI of the host operating system and is not limited to a command-line interface. This book assumes you have access to and are familiar with either the Microsoft Windows operating system or the Macintosh. The BlackBox system can be installed under either system and every program described in this book will run under both MSWindows and the MacOS. BlackBox is impressive because the same program will produce a dialog box that conforms to the MSWindows GUI if it is executed on a MSWindows machine and to the MacOS GUI if it is executed on a Macintosh. Figure 1.2 shows an example of dialog boxes that were developed on a Macintosh and a MSWindows machine. Each dialog box maintains the style of its host GUI. Furthermore, the program that performs the processing for both dialog boxes is identical. The programmer who develops a program for one machine need not change the program for it to run on the other machine.

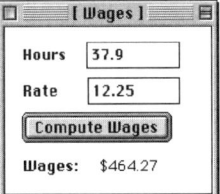

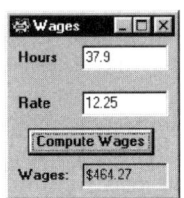

Figure 1.2
The same dialog box with two different operating systems.

(a) A Macintosh dialog box developed in the BlackBox framework.

(b) A MSWindows dialog box developed in the BlackBox framework.

Object-oriented language and system

Object-oriented languages are based on the concept of abstraction. In computer science, abstraction is the subdivision of a system into layers in which the details of one layer of abstraction are hidden from layers at a higher level. A computer scientist uses abstraction as a thinking tool to understand a system, to model a problem, and to master complexity.

Abstraction is the hiding of details.

An example of levels of abstraction that is closely analogous to computer systems is the automobile. Like a computer system, the automobile is a man-made machine. It consists of an engine, a transmission, an electrical system, a cooling system, and a chassis. Each part of an automobile is subdivided further. The electrical system has, among other things, a battery, headlights, and a voltage regulator.

People relate to automobiles at different levels of abstraction. At the highest level of abstraction are the drivers. Drivers perform their tasks by knowing how to operate the car: how to start it, how to use the accelerator, and how to apply the brakes, for example. At the next lower level of abstraction are the backyard mechanics. They understand more of the details under the hood than the casual drivers do. They know how to change the oil and the spark plugs. They do not need this detailed knowledge to drive the automobile. At the next lower level of abstraction are the master mechanics. They can completely remove the engine, take it apart, fix it, and put it back together again.

The history of the development of programming languages is a progression from lower levels of abstraction to higher levels. Early programming languages required the programmer to know details of the computer system that are hidden from the programmer using modern programming languages. Object-oriented languages are the latest step in this evolution. In the same way that automobile drivers no longer need to be master mechanics to use their automobiles, programmers can use the capabilities of software objects to produce graphical user interfaces without knowing many of the details that would be visible in older languages.

Programming languages have evolved through four levels of abstraction.

- Type and Statement abstraction
- Structure and Procedure abstraction
- Class abstraction
- Behavior abstraction

The four levels of abstraction in programming languages

The last two levels encompass object-oriented programming. Chapter 23 describes each of the levels in detail. This book mirrors the historical development of programming languages. It presents software design first using type and statement abstraction, then structure and procedure abstraction, then class abstraction, and finally behavior abstraction. Component Pascal is a particularly good language to learn for this journey, because it provides all four levels of abstraction in one language.

Project folders

All software development systems have some pattern of organization for storing program and documentation files. These patterns vary from one framework to the next. This section describes the way you should organize your files in the BlackBox framework in order to work the problems in this book. It assumes you know the commands to create directories or folders on the hard drive in your computer.

The first task in setting up the BlackBox framework is to acquire it and install it. Fortunately, this powerful system is available free for personal and educational use from the Swiss company Oberon microsystems. The Preface gives instruction for downloading it from the World Wide Web.

After downloading the software, execute the installation program. Then, simply follow the installation instructions on the screen, which should result in a folder named BlackBox on your hard drive.

The BlackBox folder will have many subfolders within it, including folders named Form, Text, and Sql, which are examples of subsystems of the framework. Form is the subsystem that enables you to write dialog boxes, Text makes possible the creation and modification of text documents such as program listings and documentation, and Sql is a database subsystem that you may wish to investigate, but which is beyond the scope of this book. You can see that there are many other subsystems that have been installed in the BlackBox folder.

To hand in the problems from this book to your instructor, you need to establish your own project folder alongside Form, Text, and Sql. Assume that the typical class contains fewer than 100 students. Each student is assigned a unique two-digit number. Say you are the 99th student on the roster and are assigned the number 99 on the first day of class. You should then create a new project folder named Hw99 within the BlackBox folder. Hw stands for homework, and Hw99 is the folder that will contain your homework assignments. (The folder names described here may differ somewhat from the names your instructor prefers.) Figure 1.3 shows the placement of this project folder among some other folders.

Now that you have created your Hw99 project folder, you should create six subfolders named Code, Docu, Mod, Rsrc, Sym, and Enc. The first five names are special names that the BlackBox framework recognizes. Their contents will be as follows.

- Mod—the programs you write with the text editor

- Code—the machine language version that the Component Pascal translator will create from your programs in Mod

- Sym—the symbol table that the Component Pascal translator will create from your programs in Mod

- Docu—the documentation you write with the text editor that accompanies the programs in the Mod folder

- Rsrc—the resources that you create with the Form subsystem that accompany the programs in the Mod folder

Folder names with special meaning to the BlackBox framework

The last folder, Enc, is not standard for the BlackBox framework but is recommended for completing the programs in this book. Enc stands for encode. As explained later in this chapter, to hand in your homework electronically you will need to store your work in a standard encoded form. Enc will be a convenient folder in which to place your encoded assignments before transferring them electronically to your instructor.

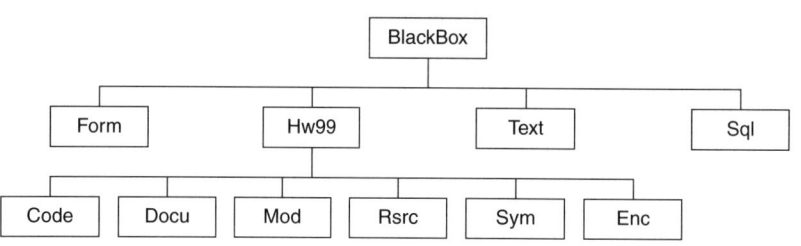

Figure 1.3
The homework project folder.

The text subsystem

After creating your project folder with its subfolders, you should execute the Black-Box program and explore its on-line help system. You may notice that when you execute BlackBox, a window labeled Log is displayed. You will normally want to keep the Log window visible as you work. In the help system you will find a table of contents of the help subjects that are available for your perusal. Locate the topic named User Manuals, which contains the following links, similar to links on a World Wide Web browser: Framework, Text Subsystem, Form Subsystem, Dev Subsystem, and Custom Commands. Clicking on one of these links will bring up a documentation window appropriate to the topic on which you clicked. You can click on the Text Subsystem link to learn how to use the text editor to create and modify documents. Its capabilities are similar to those of word processors.

This book will use the same notation that the on-line help system uses to indicate a menu selection. A right arrow will indicate the selection of a topic from a list of menu items from the menu bar at the top of the window. For example, to create a new text document, you select the New command from the menu bar item labeled File. The arrow notation indicates this selection as File→New. Another documentation convention is the definition of the modifier key. If you are using a MSWindows machine the modifier key is the key labeled *Ctrl*. If you are using a MacOS machine the modifier key is the key labeled *option*.

The right arrow menu convention

The modifier key

Two features of the text subsystem are especially nice for writing programs—the Undo command and the Drag and Drop feature. After you have performed several operations such as inserting and deleting text in a text document experiment with Edit→Undo and Edit→Redo. You will discover that the Undo command can reverse not only the previous operation, but all operations up to the one after the most recent File→Save command.

Figure 1.4 shows the Drag and Drop feature. Figure 1.4(a) shows the selection of a stretch of text, which you are probably familiar with from your word processing experience. With Drag and Drop, you can put the arrow cursor in the selection, press the mouse button, and while the button is pressed drag the selected text to an insertion point at some other part of the document. Figure 1.4(b) shows the result of dragging the text to the second line and releasing the mouse button. Note that the original text has been moved from the first line and no longer appears there. If you want to duplicate the selected text, press the modifier key as you are releasing the mouse button. Figure 1.4(c) shows the result of this action. Note that the first line contains the original selection of text, which has been duplicated on the second line. This feature is useful in programming when you must type several lines of text that are identical except for a few small differences. After typing the first line you can simply duplicate the whole line and enter the difference on the duplicated lines rather than type them all from scratch.

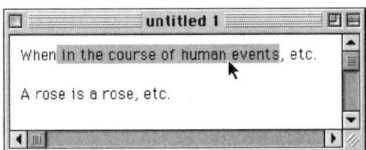

(**a**) Selecting a stretch of text.

Figure 1.4
The Drag and Drop feature.

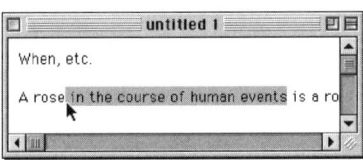

(**b**) Drag and drop the selection.

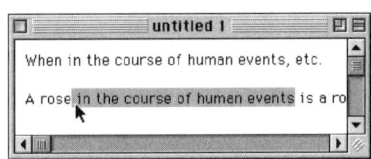

(**c**) Drag and drop with copy.

Encoding BlackBox documents

You will eventually use the text subsystem to create programs written in the Component Pascal language. After you write your programs and test them, you will need to hand them in to your instructor electronically. Before you hand them in you must encode them in a format that is safe for transmission via email over a network. The BlackBox framework has a special encoding feature that is designed for such transmissions. To describe how to use the encoding system, this section will explain how to encode a document that you create with the text subsystem.

Suppose you have a document such as a personal letter that you have entered using the features of the text editor. Select File→Save As to save your document. In the dialog box from the Save As command, manipulate the controls so the document will be saved in the folder named Docu within the folder named Hw99 (assuming your assigned number is 99) that you have previously installed in your BlackBox folder. If you are using MacOS, check the dialog box to make sure the Format control specifies Document. If you are using MSWindows, check the dialog box to make sure the Save As type control specifies Document. Unlike the MacOS system, MSWindows will append the suffix .odc to the end of a document file. Make up a name for your document and save it. Let us suppose for the time being that you name your document Letter. Figure 1.5 shows the dialog box just before the save.

Now that you have saved the document close the document window. The Log window should still be showing somewhere on the screen. If you have previously closed the Log window you can bring it back up again by selecting Info→Open Log.

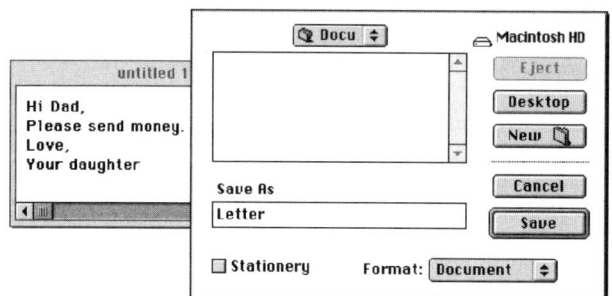

(a) MacOS.

Figure 1.5
Saving a document.

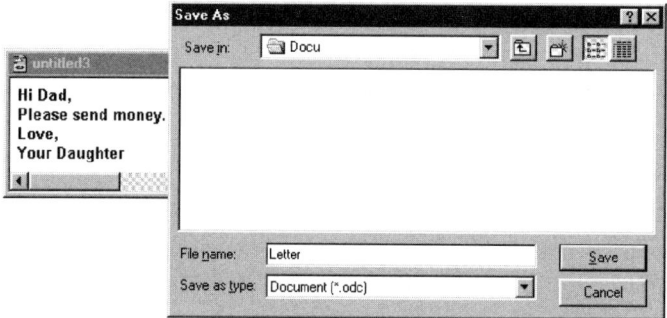

(b) MSWindows.

Now click on the Log window to make sure it is the active window. An active window such as this is called the focus window. Enter the following line of text in the Log:

The focus window

Hw99/Docu/Letter

if you are using a Macintosh or

Hw99/Docu/Letter.odc

if you are using a MSWindows machine. If you are an experienced MSWindows user you may be tempted to substitute back slash characters for the forward slashes shown above. Resist that temptation. The forward slash will work fine even with MSWindows and the back slash character will cause grief for users of other systems when you exchange documents between your computers. Now select that line of text in your Log as shown in Figure 1.6.

Do not use the back slash character.

With the text highlighted, select Tools→Encode File List. There are other encode options under the Tools menu, but in a class based on this book you should never select them. To grade your homework efficiently, your instructor always needs you

Always select Encode File List

Figure 1.6
Entering a file list to be encoded.

to select the Encode File List option. If you select any of the other encode options you will probably be giving your instructor extra unnecessary work. If you have made all the correct entries so far, the result of selecting Tools→Encode File List will be a new window that contains the encoded file similar to that shown in Figure 1.7.

Figure 1.7
The result of selecting Tools→Encode File List.

The first line of the encoded file should begin with

StdCoder.Decode

and the last line should be

--- end of encoding ---

If your encode window does not begin and end with these lines, you need to review the above procedure and try it again.

Now it is time to save your encoded file. With the encode window similar to Figure 1.7 in focus, select File→Save As. In the dialog box from the Save As command, manipulate the controls so the document will be saved in the folder named Enc within the folder named Hw99. If you are using MacOS, verify that the Format control specifies Text. If you are using MSWindows, verify that the Save As type control specifies Plain Text. Select a name for your encoded file according to the guidelines specified by your instructor. For example, she may assign a two-digit number to each assignment. If this document is to be handed in as the first assignment she may specify that you name the document A01 as Figure 1.8 shows.

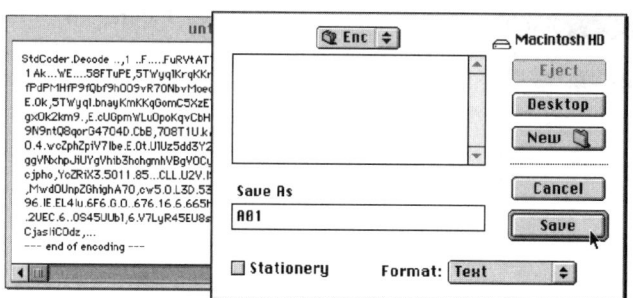

Figure 1.8
Saving the encoded
document.

(a) MacOS.

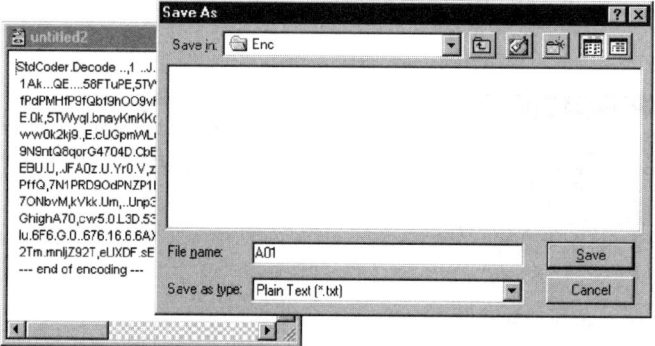

(b) MSWindows.

It is possible to encode many documents into one file. To encode several documents simply list the name of each one you want to include in the Log window. Separate the names with spaces or tabs, or put each name on a separate line. Then, instead of highlighting a single file name as in Figure 1.6, highlight the entire list of names. When you select Tools→Encode File List, all the listed files will be encoded into one window, which you can then save to a file. This technique will be useful for your homework submissions because you will typically need to hand in more than one file for each assignment.

Now that the document is saved in your Enc folder you will need to hand it in electronically. The procedure for doing this will vary depending on the particular networks and computer systems that are used at your institution.

If you ever receive an encoded document you must first open it. Select File→Open. If you are using MacOS, put a check in the check box labeled "more files". If you are using MSWindows, change the control labeled Files of type: to specify All Files. These settings will make the encoded files visible in the dialog box. When you open the encoded file a window should appear similar to Figure 1.7. With that window in focus, select Tools→Decode. The files will be decoded and

Decoding a document

placed in folders with the same names as the ones they came from. If you do not have folders in your BlackBox folder with the same names from which the encoded files come, the decode command will create folders with those names on your disk before storing the files. For example, when you encoded

Hw99/Docu/Letter

you specified that the file named Letter in the folder named Docu in the folder named Hw99 was to be encoded. When the recipient decodes your file, his disk may not have a folder named Hw99 in his BlackBox folder. When he selects Tools→Decode the framework will create a new folder named Hw99 in his BlackBox folder, and will create a new folder named Docu in the Hw99 folder. It will then decode the file and place it in the Docu folder, giving it the name Letter.

Exercises

At the end of each chapter in this book is a set of exercises and problems. Work the exercises on paper by hand. The problems are programs to be entered into the computer and submitted electronically.

1. Identify the following acronyms.

    (a) Algol   **(b)** ETH   **(c)** API   **(d)** GUI

2. **(a)** Who devised a method for specifying the grammatical rules of the Algol language?
    (b) How did the Pascal language get its name?
    (c) How did the Oberon-2 language get its name?
    (d) Who designed the Component Pascal language?
    (e) What is the significance of the name Component in Component Pascal?

Problems

3. Create the project folder for the problems you will write for this book. Create the six subfolders within the project folder as described in this chapter. Read briefly the documentation in the on-line help titled Text Subsystem in the User's Guide. Write a document with the BlackBox text editor. Include your name, address, and a description of your favorite hobbies. Include more than one font style and more than one color of text. Experiment with the drag-and-drop and multiple undo features of the text subsystem. Store your document in your Docu folder. Use the Encode File List command to encode your document. Store the encoded document in your Enc folder. Submit your assignment electronically as specified by your instructor.

4. Your instructor has placed an encoded document for you to retrieve electronically. Retrieve it, decode it, read it, and follow the instructions contained in the document.

Chapter *2*

Languages and Grammars

Two attributes of a programming language are its syntax and semantics. A computer language's syntax is the set of rules that a program listing must obey to be declared a valid program of the language. Its semantics is the meaning or logic behind the valid program. When you begin your study of the Component Pascal programming language in the next chapter you will need to know the language's syntax to be able to write programs that the computer will accept.

Syntax and semantics

Three common techniques to describe a language's syntax are:

Techniques for describing a language's syntax

- Grammars

- Regular expressions

- Finite state machines

This chapter introduces grammars. A variation of a grammar is used to describe the syntax of Component Pascal. Space limitations preclude a presentation of regular expressions and finite state machines. Later sections present finite state machines in a context other than describing a language's syntax.

Languages

Every language has an alphabet. Formally, an *alphabet* is a finite, nonempty set of characters.

An alphabet

Example 2.1 The alphabet for the language of real numbers that are not written in scientific notation is the set

{0, 1, 2, 3, 4, 5, 6, 7, 8, 9, +, -, .}

When you write a real number, such as -23.7, you use only the characters from the alphabet. If you attempt to write a real number using some other character not in the alphabet, such as -2y.7, then the sequence of characters that you write cannot be a valid real number. ∎

Example 2.2 Another example of a language is the language of expressions that you are familiar with from algebra. Examples of some valid algebraic expressions are:

a × b	c × (x + y)	c × y + x
(x − y) × (x + y)	(x − y) / (x + y)	(− (− (− ((b)))))

The expression a @ b is not valid because the character @ is not in the alphabet of the language of algebraic expressions. The alphabet for the language of algebraic expressions using only lowercase variable letters is:

{a, b, c, d, e, f, g, h, i, j, k, l, m, n, o, p, q, r, s, t, u, v, w, x, y, z, (,), +, −, ×, /}   ∎

The alphabet specifies which characters are legal to use in the language. To make a sentence in the language you join two or more characters together to form a string. The operation of joining them together is called *concatenation*. In Example 2.1 the string -23.7 is the concatenation of the individual characters -, 2, 3, ., and 7.

Concatenation

Concatenation applies not only to individual characters in an alphabet to construct a string, but also to strings to construct bigger strings. In Example 2.2 the string c × y is concatenated with the string + x to produce the string c × y + x.

The *length* of a string is the number of characters in the string. The string c × y + x has a length of five. The string of length zero, called the empty string, is denoted by the Greek letter ε to distinguish it from the English characters in an alphabet. Its concatenation properties are

The length of a string

$$\varepsilon x = x\varepsilon = x$$

The empty string

where x is a string. The empty string is useful for describing syntax rules.

In mathematics terminology, ε is the identity element for the concatenation operation. In general, an *identity element*, i, for an operation is one that does not change a value, x, when x is operated on by i.

Identity elements

Example 2.3 One is the identity element for multiplication because

$$1 \cdot x = x \cdot 1 = x \qquad \blacksquare$$

If T is an alphabet, the *closure* of T, denoted T^*, is the set of all possible strings formed by concatenating elements from T. T^* is extremely large. For example, if T is the set of characters and punctuation marks of the English alphabet, T^* includes all the sentences in the collected works of Shakespeare, in the English Bible, and in all the English encyclopedias ever published. It includes all strings of those characters ever printed in all the libraries in all the world throughout history, and then some. Not only does it include all those meaningful strings, it includes meaningless ones as well.

The closure of an alphabet

Example 2.4 Here are some elements of T^* for the English alphabet:

To be or not to be, that is the question.
Go fly a kite.
Here over highly toward?
alkeu jfoj ,9nm20mfq23jk l?x!jeo   ∎

Example 2.5 Some elements of T^* where T is the alphabet of the language for real numbers are

```
-2894.01
24
+78.3.80
--234--
6
```
∎

You can easily construct many other elements of T^* with any of the alphabets in the previous examples. Because strings can be infinitely long, the closure of any alphabet has an infinite number of elements.

What is a language? In the examples of T^* that were just presented, some of the strings are in the language and some are not. In Example 2.4, the first two strings are valid English sentences; that is, they are in the language. The last two strings are not in the language. A *language* is a subset of the closure of its alphabet. Of the infinite number of strings you can construct from concatenating strings of characters from its alphabet, only some will be in the language.

A language

Example 2.6 Consider the following two elements of T^* where T is the alphabet for Example 2.2.

a × b   c × ((x + y)

The first element of T^* is in the language of algebraic expressions, but the second is not, because it has a syntax error. It is illegal to have a left parenthesis without a matching right parenthesis. ∎

Grammars

To define a language, you need a way to specify which of the many elements of T^* are in the language and which are not. A grammar is a system that specifies how you can concatenate the characters of alphabet T to form a legal string in a language. Formally, a grammar contains four parts:

- N, a nonterminal alphabet
- T, a terminal alphabet
- P, a set of rules of production
- S, the start symbol, an element of N

The four parts of a grammar

An element from the nonterminal alphabet, N, represents a group of characters from the terminal alphabet, T. A nonterminal symbol is sometimes a single descriptive word that begins with an uppercase letter to distinguish it from a terminal symbol. You see the terminals when you read the language. The rules of production use the nonterminals to describe the structure of the language, which may not be readily apparent when you read the language.

Example 2.7 In the English language, the nonterminals include Verb, Adverb,

Noun, Adjective, Preposition, and Subject among others. A valid English sentence is

Computer science is fun.

The word is is a Verb. Because Verb is a nonterminal you do not see it in the sentence. In other words, even though is is a Verb you would never see the sentence

Computer science Verb fun.   ∎

Every grammar has a special nonterminal called the start symbol, *S*. Notice that *N* is a set, but *S* is not. *S* is one of the elements of set *N*. The start symbol, along with the rules of production, *P*, enables you to decide whether a string of terminals is a valid sentence in the language. If, starting from *S*, you can generate the string of terminals using the rules of production, then the string is a valid sentence.

The start symbol

A grammar for identifiers

The Component Pascal programming language has a rule for naming things. The rule is that the first character of the name must be a letter or underscore character and the remaining characters, if any, can be letters, or digits, or underscores in any combination. The name is called a Component Pascal identifier. Grammar A in Figure 2.1 specifies these rules for a Component Pascal identifier. Even though an identifier can use any uppercase or lowercase letter, or digit, or the underscore character, to keep the example small this grammar permits only the letters a, b, and c and the digits 1, 2, and 3.

N = {Identifier, Letter, Digit}
T = {a, b, c, 1, 2, 3}
P = the productions
       1. Identifier → Letter
       2. Identifier → Identifier Letter
       3. Identifier → Identifier Digit
       4. Letter → a
       5. Letter → b
       6. Letter → c
       7. Digit → 1
       8. Digit → 2
       9. Digit → 3
S = Identifier

Figure 2.1
Grammar A for Component Pascal identifiers.

This grammar has three nonterminals, namely, Identifier, Letter, and Digit. The start symbol is Identifier, one of the elements from the set of nonterminals. The rules of production are of the form

The rules of production

$A \rightarrow w$

where *A* is a nonterminal and *w* is a string of terminals and nonterminals. The symbol → means "produces." You should read production rule number 3 in this grammar as, "An identifier produces an identifier followed by a digit."

The grammar specifies the language by a process called a *derivation*. To derive a valid sentence in the language, you begin with the start symbol and substitute for nonterminals from the rules of production until you get a string of terminals.

Derivations

Example 2.8 Here is a derivation of the identifier cab3 from Grammar A:

Identifier	⇒ Identifier Digit	Rule 3
	⇒ Identifier 3	Rule 9
	⇒ Identifier Letter 3	Rule 2
	⇒ Identifier b 3	Rule 5
	⇒ Identifier Letter b 3	Rule 2
	⇒ Identifier a b 3	Rule 4
	⇒ Letter a b 3	Rule 1
	⇒ c a b 3	Rule 6

Next to each derivation step is the production rule on which the substitution is based. For example, Rule 2,

Identifier → Identifier Letter

was used to substitute for Identifier in the derivation step

Identifier 3 ⇒ Identifier Letter 3

The symbol ⇒ means "derives in one step." You should read this derivation step as "Identifier followed by 3 derives in one step Identifier followed by Letter followed by 3."

Analogous to the closure operation on an alphabet is the closure of the derivation operation. The symbol ⇒* means "derives in zero or more steps." You can summarize the previous eight derivation steps as

Closure of the derivation operation

Identifier ⇒* c a b 3

This derivation proves that cab3 is a valid identifier, because it can be derived from the start symbol, Identifier. A language specified by a grammar consists of all the strings derivable from the start symbol using the rules of production. The grammar provides an operational test for membership in the language. If it is impossible to derive a string, the string is not in the language.

A grammar for signed integers

Grammar B in Figure 2.2 defines the language of signed integers, where d represents a decimal digit. The start symbol is I, which stands for integer. F is the first character, which is an optional sign, and M is the magnitude.

N = {I, F, M}
T = {+, -, d}
P = the productions
      1. I → F M
      2. F → +
      3. F → -
      4. F → ε
      5. M → d M
      6. M → d
S = I

Figure 2.2
Grammar B for signed
integers.

Sometimes the rules of production are not numbered and are combined on one line to conserve space on the printed page. You can write the rules of production for this grammar as

I → F M
F → + | - | ε
M → d | d M

where the vertical bar, |, is the alternation operator and is read as "or." Read the last line as "M produces d, or d followed by M."

Example 2.9 Here are some derivations of valid signed integers in this grammar:

I ⇒ F M	I ⇒ F M	I ⇒ F M
⇒ F d M	⇒ F d M	⇒ F d M
⇒ F d d M	⇒ F d d	⇒ F d d M
⇒ F d d d	⇒ d d	⇒ F d d d M
⇒ - d d d		⇒ F d d d d M
		⇒ F d d d d
		⇒ + d d d d

Note how the last step of the second derivation used the empty string to derive dd from Fdd. It used the production F → ε and the fact that εd = d. This production rule with the empty string is a convenient way to express the fact that a positive or negative sign in front of the magnitude is optional.

Some illegal strings from this grammar are ddd+, +-ddd, and ddd+dd. Try to derive these strings from the grammar to convince yourself that they are not in the language. Can you informally prove from the rules of production that each of these strings is not in the language?

The productions in both of the example grammars have recursive rules in which a nonterminal is defined in terms of itself. Rule 3 of Grammar A defines an Identifier in terms of an Identifier as

Identifier → Identifier Digit

and Rule 5 of Grammar B defines M in terms of M as

M → d M

Recursive rules produce languages with an infinite number of legal sentences. To derive an identifier, you can keep substituting Identifier Digit for Identifier as long as you like to produce an arbitrarily long identifier. Like all recursive definitions, there must be an additional nonrecursive rule to provide the basis for the definition. Otherwise the sequence of substitutions for the nonterminal could never stop. The nonrecursive rule M → d provides the basis for M in Grammar B.

A context sensitive grammar

The production rules for the previous grammars always contained a single nonterminal on the left side. Grammar C in Figure 2.3 has some production rules with both a terminal and nonterminal on the left side.

N = {A, B, C}
T = {a, b, c}
P = the productions
     1. A → a A B C
     2. A → a b C
     3. C B → B C
     4. b B → b b
     5. b C → b c
     6. c C → c c
S = A

Figure 2.3
Grammar C, a context sensitive grammar.

Example 2.10 Here is a derivation of a string of terminals with this grammar:

A	⇒ a A B C	Rule 1
	⇒ a a A B C B C	Rule 1
	⇒ a a a b C B C B C	Rule 2
	⇒ a a a b B C C B C	Rule 3
	⇒ a a a b B C B C C	Rule 3
	⇒ a a a b B B C C C	Rule 3
	⇒ a a a b b B C C C	Rule 4
	⇒ a a a b b b C C C	Rule 4
	⇒ a a a b b b c C C	Rule 5
	⇒ a a a b b b c c C	Rule 6
	⇒ a a a b b b c c c	Rule 6

An example of a substitution in this derivation is using Rule 5 in the step aaabbbCCC ⇒ aaabbbcCC. Rule 5 says that you can substitute c for C, but only if the C has a b to the left of it. ∎

In the English language, to quote a phrase out of context means to quote it without regard to the other phrases that surround it. Rule 5 is an example of a context-sensitive rule. It does not permit the substitution of C by c unless C is in the proper context, namely, immediately to the right of a b.

Loosely speaking, a *context-sensitive grammar* is one in which the production rules may contain more than just a single nonterminal on the left side. In contrast, grammars that are restricted to a single nonterminal on the left side of every production rule are called context-free. (The precise theoretical definitions of context-sensitive and context-free grammars are more restrictive than these definitions. For the sake of simplicity, this chapter will use the previous definitions, although you should be aware that a more rigorous description of the theory would not define them as we have here.) *Context sensitive grammars*

Some other examples of valid strings in the language specified by this grammar are abc, aabbcc, and aaaabbbbcccc. Two examples of invalid strings are aabc and cba. You should derive these valid strings and also try to derive the invalid strings to prove their invalidity to yourself. Some experimentation with the rules should convince you that the language is the set of strings that begins with one or more a's, followed by an equal number of b's, followed by the same number of c's. Mathematically, this language, L, can be written

$$L = \{a^n b^n c^n \mid n > 0\}$$

which you should read as "The language L is the set of strings $a^n b^n c^n$ such that n is greater than 0." The notation a^n means the concatenation of n a's.

The parsing problem

Deriving valid strings from a grammar is fairly straightforward. You can arbitrarily pick some nonterminal on the right side of the current intermediate string and select rules for the substitution repeatedly until you get a string of terminals. Such random derivations can give you many sample strings from the language.

Suppose we turn the problem around, however, and start with some given string of characters from the language's alphabet that is supposed to represent a valid sentence. You must determine if the string of terminals is indeed valid. But, the only way to determine if a string is valid is to derive it from the start symbol of the grammar. So, you must attempt such a derivation. If you succeed, you know the string is a valid sentence. The problem of determining whether or not a given string of terminal characters is valid for a specific grammar is called parsing, and is illustrated schematically in Figure 2.4.

Parsing a given string is more difficult than deriving an arbitrary valid string. The parsing problem is a form of searching. The parsing algorithm must search for just the right sequence of substitutions to derive the proposed string. Not only must it find the derivation if the proposed string is valid, but it must also admit the possibility that the proposed string may not be valid. If you look for a lost diamond ring in your room and do not find it, that does not mean the ring is not in your room. It may simply mean that you did not look in the right place. Similarly, if you try to find a derivation for a proposed string and do not find it, how do you know that such a derivation does not exist?

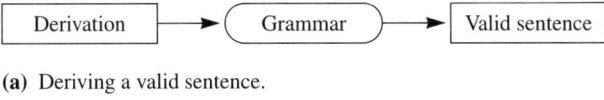

(a) Deriving a valid sentence.

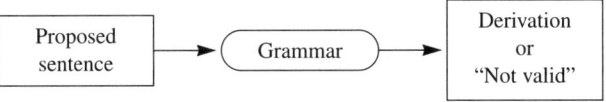

(b) The parsing problem.

Figure 2.4
The difference between
deriving an arbitrary sentence
and parsing a proposed
sentence.

A grammar for algebraic expressions

To see some of the difficulty a parser may encounter, consider Grammar D in Figure
2.5, which describes an algebraic expression. Nonterminal E represents the expression. T represents a term and F represents a factor.

N = {E, T, F}
T = {+, ×, (,), a}
P = the productions
      1. E → E + T
      2. E → T
      3. T → T × F
      4. T → F
      5. F → (E)
      6. F → a
S = E

Figure 2.5
Grammar D, a grammar for
algebraic expressions.

Suppose you are given the string of terminals

(a × a) + a

and the production rules of this grammar and are asked to parse the proposed string.
The correct parse is

E	⇒ E + T	Rule 1
	⇒ T + T	Rule 2
	⇒ F + T	Rule 4
	⇒ (E) + T	Rule 5
	⇒ (T) + T	Rule 2
	⇒ (T × F) + T	Rule 3
	⇒ (F × F) + T	Rule 4
	⇒ (a × F) + T	Rule 6
	⇒ (a × a) + T	Rule 6

$\Rightarrow (a \times a) + F$ Rule 4
$\Rightarrow (a \times a) + a$ Rule 6

The reason this could be difficult is that you might make a bad decision early in the parse that looks plausible at the time, but which leads to a dead end. For example, you might spot the "(" in the string that you were given and choose Rule 5 immediately. Your attempted parse might be

$E \Rightarrow T$ Rule 2
$\quad \Rightarrow F$ Rule 4
$\quad \Rightarrow (E)$ Rule 5
$\quad \Rightarrow (T)$ Rule 2
$\quad \Rightarrow (T \times F)$ Rule 3
$\quad \Rightarrow (F \times F)$ Rule 4
$\quad \Rightarrow (a \times F)$ Rule 6
$\quad \Rightarrow (a \times a)$ Rule 6

Until now, you have seemingly made progress toward your goal of parsing the original expression, because the intermediate string looks more like the original string at each successive step of the derivation. Unfortunately, now you are stuck, because there is no way to get the + a part of the original string. After reaching this dead end, you may be tempted to conclude that the proposed string is invalid, but that would be a mistake. Just because you cannot find a derivation, does not mean that such a derivation does not exist.

One interesting aspect of a parse is that it can be represented as a tree. The start symbol is the root of the tree. Each interior node of the tree is a nonterminal, and each leaf is a terminal. The children of an interior node are the symbols from the right side of the production rule substituted for the parent node in the derivation. The tree is called a syntax tree, for obvious reasons. Figure 2.6 shows the syntax tree for $(a \times a) + a$ with Grammar D, and Figure 2.7 shows it for dd with Grammar B.

Figure 2.6
The syntax tree for the parse of $(a \times a) + a$ in Grammar D.

Extended Backus-Naur form

The technique of using a grammar to specify the syntax rules of a programming language is sometimes called Backus-Naur Form (BNF) after John Backus and Peter Naur who developed it in the late 1950's. Backus was instrumental in the design of the Fortran language as was Naur for the Algol 60 language. An extended version of the system for specifying language syntax has come into use that is called Extended Backus-Naur Form (EBNF). The production rules are a bit simpler when written with EBNF because there is no need for the empty string ε, and there are usually not so many recursive production rules.

A minor difference in notation is that the equals sign = is sometimes used in place of the right arrow $\rightarrow$ when writing the production rules. An alternate notation is to use the two colons followed by the equals sign ::= to signify the same thing. More significantly, however, EBNF adds the following three operations:

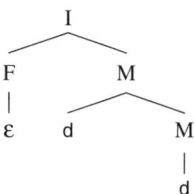

Figure 2.7
The syntax tree for the parse of dd in Grammar B.

■ Alternation—select one of several alternatives

■ Optional—include zero or one time

■ Repetition—include zero or more times

The alternation symbol is the vertical bar |. The vertical bar was used previously to select between two complete productions of the grammar. However, in EBNF the bar is used within a single production rule. The notation for specifying that a symbol is optional is to enclose it in square brackets [ ]. To specify that it can be included even more than once enclose it in curly braces { }.

Example 2.11   The second and third production rules of Grammar A are recursive. That is, Identifier appears on both sides of the production arrow and is thus defined in terms of itself.

1. Identifier → Letter
2. Identifier → Identifier Letter
3. Identifier → Identifier Digit

As shown in Example 2.8 in the derivation of cab3, the effect of the recursive definition is to allow an unlimited number of letters or digits in the identifier. From the first production rule, Identifier must begin with Letter. These three production rules can be written in EBNF with one rule as

Identifier → Letter {Letter | Digit}

In English, you should read this as, "An identifier is a Letter followed by zero or more occurrences of a Letter or a Digit."   ∎

Example 2.12   The production rules of Grammar B included one with the empty string to signify that the leading + or - sign is optional. The six production rules

1. I → F M
2. F → +
3. F → -
4. F → ε
5. M → d M
6. M → d

can be conveniently written in only one EBNF rule as

I → [+ | -] d { d }

which you should read in English as, "An I is an optional + or -, followed by one d, followed by zero or more occurrences of d."   ∎

Component Pascal syntax

The Component Pascal syntax is specified by EBNF and is given in Appendix A. It is also available in the BlackBox on-line documentation under Component Pascal Language Report.

There are a few notational differences from the above examples. The production arrow → is written as an equals sign =. A more significant difference follows from the problem that the square brackets [ ], curly braces { } and vertical bar | used in the EBNF system are all valid characters in the language. So there must be some way to distinguish whether, for example, a square bracket [is an EBNF optional operator or a Component Pascal terminal symbol. The report makes the distinction by enclosing the symbol in double quotes " " if it is a Component Pascal terminal. Other terminals in the language are the words written in all uppercase letters.

Example 2.13 Referring to the production rules in Appendix A, here is a derivation that proves the string of terminals

IF alpha < 3 THEN DoBeta END

is a valid Statement. The derivation assumes that alpha and DoBeta have previously been shown to be valid Ident's, and that 3 has previously been shown to be a valid Integer.

$$
\begin{aligned}
\text{Statement} \Rightarrow{}& \text{IF Expr THEN StatementSeq END} \\
\Rightarrow{}& \text{IF SimpleExpr Relation SimpleExpr THEN StatementSeq END} \\
\Rightarrow{}& \text{IF Term Relation SimpleExpr THEN StatementSeq END} \\
\Rightarrow{}& \text{IF Factor Relation SimpleExpr THEN StatementSeq END} \\
\Rightarrow{}& \text{IF Designator Relation SimpleExpr THEN StatementSeq END} \\
\Rightarrow{}& \text{IF Qualident Relation SimpleExpr THEN StatementSeq END} \\
\Rightarrow{}& \text{IF Ident Relation SimpleExpr THEN StatementSeq END} \\
\Rightarrow^*{}& \text{IF alpha Relation SimpleExpr THEN StatementSeq END} \\
\Rightarrow{}& \text{IF alpha < SimpleExpr THEN StatementSeq END} \\
\Rightarrow{}& \text{IF alpha < Term THEN StatementSeq END} \\
\Rightarrow{}& \text{IF alpha < Factor THEN StatementSeq END} \\
\Rightarrow{}& \text{IF alpha < Number THEN StatementSeq END} \\
\Rightarrow{}& \text{IF alpha < Integer THEN StatementSeq END} \\
\Rightarrow^*{}& \text{IF alpha < 3 THEN StatementSeq END} \\
\Rightarrow{}& \text{IF alpha < 3 THEN Statement END} \\
\Rightarrow{}& \text{IF alpha < 3 THEN Designator END} \\
\Rightarrow{}& \text{IF alpha < 3 THEN Qualident END} \\
\Rightarrow{}& \text{IF alpha < 3 THEN Ident END} \\
\Rightarrow^*{}& \text{IF alpha < 3 THEN doBeta END}
\end{aligned}
$$

Figure 2.8 shows the corresponding syntax tree for this derivation. The dashed line from Ident to alpha indicates that more than one derivation step is hidden in the tree and corresponds to ⇒* in the above derivation. ∎

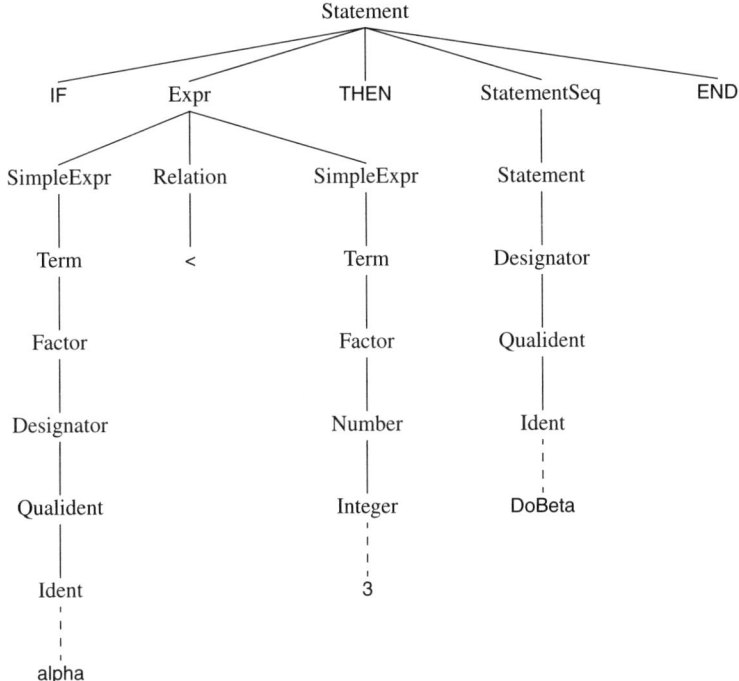

Figure 2.8
The syntax tree for the derivation in Example 2.13.

Unlike Grammar C, the production rules in Appendix A always have a single nonterminal on the left side. So it would appear from the production rules that the Component Pascal language is context free. However, it is not. The language report contains additional rules that must be followed to write a valid Component Pascal program. Following the grammar rules is a necessary but not sufficient condition for writing a valid program. That is, if you write a valid program you must conform to the grammar rules. But if you follow the grammar rules it does not automatically follow that you have written a valid program.

Exercises

1. What is the identity element for the addition operation on integers?

2. Derive the following strings with Grammar A in Figure 2.1 and draw the corresponding syntax tree.

   (a) abc123   (b) a1b2c3   (c) a321bc

3. Derive the following strings with Grammar B in Figure 2.2 and draw the corresponding syntax tree.

   (a) -d   (b) +ddd   (c) d

4. Derive the following strings with Grammar C in Figure 2.3.

   (a) abc   **(b)** aabbcc   **(c)** aaaabbbbcccc

5. For each of the following strings, state whether it can be derived from the rules of Grammar D in Figure 2.5. If it can, draw the corresponding syntax tree.

   (a) a + (a)   **(b)** a × (+ a)   **(c)** a × (a + a)
   (d) a × (a + a) × a   **(e)** a − a   **(f)** (((a)))

6. For the grammar of Component Pascal in Appendix A, draw the syntax tree for StatementSeq from the following strings, assuming that *S1*, *S2*, *S3* and *S4* are each valid Statements and *C1* and *C2* are each valid Exprs.

(a)	**(b)**	**(c)**	**(d)**
IF *C1* THEN	IF *C1* THEN	IF *C1* THEN	*S1* ;
S1	*S1* ;	IF *C2* THEN	WHILE *C1* DO
END ;	IF *C2* THEN	*S1*	IF *C2* THEN
S2	*S2*	ELSE	*S2*
	ELSE	*S2*	END ;
	S3	END ;	*S3*
	END	*S3*	END
	END ;	ELSE	
	S4	*S4*	
		END	

7. For the Component Pascal grammar in Appendix A, draw the syntax tree for Statement.

   (a) Alpha := 1
   (b) Alpha := Alpha * 3
   (c) Alpha := (Beta < 1)
   (d) Alpha := ((Beta < 1) or (Gamma > 24))
   (e) Alpha (Beta)
   (f) Alpha (Beta, 24)

Chapter *3*

Modules and Interfaces

The BlackBox framework consists of tools to help the software designer write application programs. Typical applications present dialog boxes and menu options to the user. When the user enters data into a dialog box and clicks a button with the mouse or makes a menu selection, a program that the software designer wrote is activated. The framework maintains the necessary connections between the programs and the actions of the user. To accomplish the required connections the BlackBox framework uses three collections:

- Modules
- Classes
- Procedures

Each of these collections groups various items together into a single unit. This chapter shows how to organize simple procedures into modules. Later chapters show how to use classes.

Modules

The *module* is the outermost collection of classes, procedures, and data. Every Component Pascal program you write must be contained within a module, which is also known as a *compilation unit*. Figure 3.1 shows one possible organization of a module. It is a collection of some data, a procedure, and a class. A procedure groups data and program statements together.

In Figure 3.1, the word Data1 represents data that is contained in the module but is not contained in a procedure. Data that is not contained in a procedure or a class is called *global* data in contrast to *local* data, which is. Data3 is local to Class3, and Data3a is local to Procedure3a.

The two lines in Procedure2 represent program statements. The program statements are grouped so they can be executed as if they were a single statement. A class can collect several procedures together as well as data. Many combinations of collections are possible. Figure 3.1 shows that some procedures may have data while others may not. You can also put procedures inside other procedures, but we will not have occasion to do so in this book. Putting procedures inside a class is the organization required for the design technique called *object-oriented programming* (OOP). The latter part of this book describes principles of OOP.

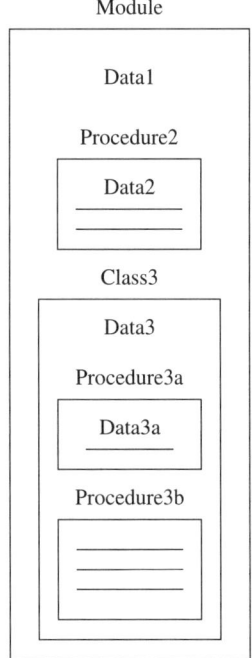

Figure 3.1
A module containing a procedure and an object.

Interfaces

The BlackBox framework is a collection of modules that you will use to write your programs. Your programs will consist of procedures that are contained within a module that you will write. The modules of the framework all fit together and cooperate to provide services for the programmer's module. A programmer thinks of a particular module in the framework as providing a service for him in much the same way that a professional, say an attorney, provides a service for her customers. The terminology from the commercial world is often carried over to computer science. In the same way that the attorney provides a service to her clients, a module in the framework is a *server* that provides a service to the programmer's module, which is the *client*.

The client/server view

Figure 3.2 shows the relationship between the client module, which you will write, and the server module, which is provided by the framework. The interaction between the two modules is governed by specific rules or protocols that are defined by the server module in its interface. The *interface* of a module is a list of all the items that are exported by the module. Its purpose is to describe the rules that a client module must follow to use its services. You should develop the skill of reading the interface of a module to determine the rules to be followed when requesting its services.

The interface and its purpose

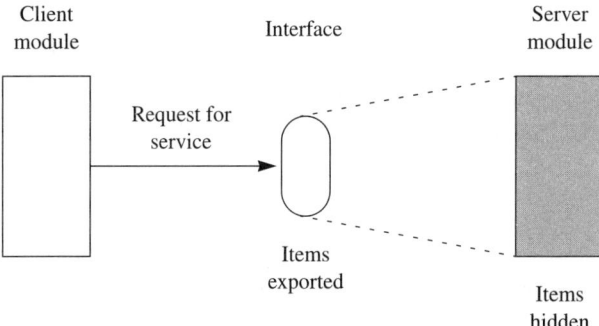

Client module   Interface   Server module

Request for service

Items exported

Items hidden

Figure 3.2
The interface between a client module and a server module.

The server module can export many kinds of items including data, procedures, and classes. The client module has access to the items exported by the server. Any items that are not exported by the server are hidden from the client and are not accessible. If the server is written well, knowledge about the items that are hidden will not be needed anyway by the client to perform its task. The hiding of detail is the essence of *abstraction*, and is an important idea in software design. The server module is darkly shaded in Figure 3.2 to indicate that its details cannot be seen by the client. This concept is so important that the representation of a server module as a "black box" whose details are hidden is the inspiration for the name of the Black-Box framework.

The essence of abstraction

If you want to use a module but you are not sure of the exported items, the framework provides a convenient way for you to view the module's interface. You simply type the name of the module, highlight it in a stretch of text, and select Info→Interface from the menu bar. For example, Figure 3.3 shows how you could view the interface of a module named StdLog, which you will use for your first program. The name of the module, StdLog, has been typed in the Log and selected. With this stretch of text in the focus window, Info→Client Interface is selected from the menu bar. The result is a new window with the text shown in Figure 3.4.

You can always tell when you are inspecting an interface by the first word DEFI-NITION in the listing. The items listed between DEFINITION and END are the items exported by the module. This module exports many items, six of which are shown here—the procedures Bool, Char, Int, Ln, Real, and String. Your first program will use procedure String from module StdLog.

```
DEFINITION StdLog;

    PROCEDURE Bool (x: BOOLEAN);
    PROCEDURE Char (ch: CHAR);
    PROCEDURE Int (i: LONGINT);
    PROCEDURE Ln;
    PROCEDURE Real (x: REAL);
    PROCEDURE String (IN str: ARRAY OF CHAR);

END StdLog.
```

Compilers

A computer can directly execute statements only if they are written in the language that the machine can understand. Languages for machines are written in a complex code that is difficult for humans to read or write. The code is called machine language. So a Component Pascal statement must first be translated to machine language before executing. The function of the *compiler* is to perform the translation from a program written in Component Pascal to machine language. The compiler also generates the interface between the program and the rest of the framework. Running a program is a three-step process:

- Write the program in Component Pascal, called the *source program.*

- Invoke the compiler to translate, or compile, the source program from Component Pascal to machine language. The machine language version is called the *object program* and is stored in the code file. The interface is stored in the symbol file.

- Execute the object program.

If you want to execute a program that was previously compiled, you do not need to translate it again. You can simply execute the object program directly. If you ever delete the object program from your disk you can always get it back from the source program by compiling again. But the translation can only go one way. If you ever delete the source program you cannot recover it from the object program.

The Component Pascal compiler is software, not hardware. It is a program that is stored in a file on your disk. In the BlackBox framework, the compiler is located in the development subsystem, abbreviated Dev. Like all programs, the compiler has input, does processing, and produces output. Figure 3.5 shows that the input to the compiler is the source program and the output is the object program and the interface.

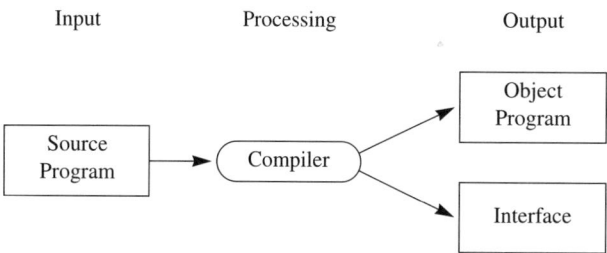

Input   Processing   Output

Figure 3.5
The compiler as a program.

When you write the source program, it will be saved in a file on disk just like any other document would be. The text files you wrote in the first chapter were saved in files stored in the Docu folder. You should save your Component Pascal source programs in the Mod folder. When you invoke the compiler, it will produce the code file for the object program, and the framework will save it in the Code folder. The compiler will also produce the interface, which the framework will save in the Sym folder. Both the object program and the interface are created automatically by the compiler from your source program. Most other programming languages require the programmer to write not only the source program, but the interface as well. If you have used such a language before, having the interface produced automatically might take some getting used to. The way in which BlackBox manages the interfaces of the modules is a major benefit over other development systems.

Programs

Figure 3.6 is a program that outputs a message to the Log. To run this program, you should first select File→New and type the listing in the untitled document window as it is shown in the figure. Be particularly careful about the punctuation marks. There are several differences in the program that you should type compared to the program in Figure 3.6.

Every module must have a name. In Figure 3.6 the name of the module is Hw90Pr0380. When you develop software for a large project that requires many modules, it is important to have a consistent naming convention for your modules and your files. In the process of studying from this book, you will be writing many modules and so will need a consistent naming system. The guidelines for naming the modules in this chapter are a system that is appropriate for programs that are written as assignments in a class. Your instructor may have different guidelines for you to follow.

MODULE Hw99Pr0380;
(* Stan Warford *)
(* June 12, 2002 *)

    IMPORT StdLog;

    PROCEDURE **PrintAddress***;
    BEGIN
        StdLog.String("Mr. K. Kong"); StdLog.Ln;
        StdLog.String("Empire State Building"); StdLog.Ln;
        StdLog.String("350 Fifth Avenue"); StdLog.Ln;
        StdLog.String("New York, NY 10118-0110"); StdLog.Ln
    END PrintAddress;

END Hw99Pr0380.

Figure 3.6
Sending output to the Log.

Chapter 1 described a system where each student in the class is assigned a unique two-digit number. The name of the module in Figure 3.6 is appropriate for a student who has been assigned the number 99. The first part of the name Hw99 consists of the letters Hw, which stands for homework, followed by the assigned student number. The second part of the name Pr0380 assumes that this program is a homework assignment as specified in Chapter 3, Problem 80. You must be careful to distinguish between uppercase and lowercase letters. In the name Hw99Pr0380, H and P are uppercase, while w and r are lowercase. When you type a program for an assignment use your assigned number in place of 99, the chapter from which the assignment is taken in place of 03, and the problem number in place of 80.

After you have entered the text, select File→Save As to save the file as a document (not Ascii or Plain Text). Manipulate the controls of the dialog box so the document will be saved in the folder named Mod within the folder named Hw99 that you previously installed in your BlackBox folder. Name the file Pr0380 when you save it. Note that the first part of the module name Hw99 is the name of your folder contained in the BlackBox folder, while the second half of the module name Pr0380 is the name of the file that is within the Mod folder that is within your folder.

You can see from Appendix A how Figure 3.6 conforms to the structure for a module. The EBNF syntax rule for Module from the appendix is

MODULE Ident " ; " [ImportList] DeclSeq [BEGIN StatementSeq] [CLOSE StatementSeq] END Ident " . "

In this program Ident is Hw99Pr0380, there is an ImportList containing StdLog, the declaration sequence DeclSeq corresponds to the procedure named PrintAddress with its own BEGIN and END, there is no BEGIN StatementSeq part, and there is no CLOSE StatementSeq part. Notice how the module must terminate with a period.

Comments

The documentation section at the beginning of the module in Figure 3.6 is enclosed in comment brackets, (* and *). The compiler ignores everything between the brackets. The only purpose of the documentation section is to provide information to a human reader. The comments in this module list the programmer's name and the date the program was written. You can write a comment anywhere that a blank space can occur and not affect the program execution. All your modules should contain a documentation section with at least your name and the date you wrote the program. In the BlackBox framework, documentation about how to use a module is placed in the Docu file, which is described later.

Reserved words

Figure 3.6 has five reserved words—MODULE, IMPORT, PROCEDURE, BEGIN, and END. Reserved words have special meaning to the Component Pascal compiler. The reserved word MODULE indicates to the compiler the start of a Component Pascal module. The reserved word IMPORT tells the compiler that another module, StdLog in this case, will be used by this module. PROCEDURE indicates the beginning of a procedure declaration. BEGIN indicates the start of a list of Component Pascal statements, and END indicates the end of the list. Component Pascal has 40 reserved words. They are:

ABSTRACT	ELSIF	LIMITED	RECORD	*Component Pascal's reserved*
ARRAY	EMPTY	LOOP	REPEAT	*words*
BEGIN	END	MOD	RETURN	
BY	EXIT	MODULE	THEN	
CASE	EXTENSIBLE	NIL	TO	
CLOSE	FOR	OF	TYPE	
CONST	IF	OR	UNTIL	
DIV	IMPORT	OUT	VAR	
DO	IN	POINTER	WHILE	
ELSE	IS	PROCEDURE	WITH	

These are terminal symbols in the grammar in Appendix A.

Identifiers

The name of the module is Hw99Pr0380 and the name of the procedure in the module is PrintAddress. Both names are Component Pascal identifiers determined arbitrarily by the programmer. You could just as easily call the procedure OutputName instead of PrintAddress. In that case, the first line of the listing after the documentation section would be

PROCEDURE **OutputName***;

Items other than modules and procedures can be named by Component Pascal identifiers. Regardless of the item named, you must follow the rules for devising an identifier. Component Pascal identifiers may contain only letters, digits, and underscore characters, and they must start with a letter or underscore character. The EBNF syntax rule for Ident from the appendix is

(Letter | " _ ") {Letter | " _ " | Digit}

An identifier can consist of more than one word, but the words may not be separated by a space. If an identifier contains more than one word you should capitalize the first letter of the word to make it easily readable.

Example 3.1   Here are five legal Component Pascal identifiers:

NewYork   DC9   quantityOnHand   i   hoursWorked

Notice how much easier it is to read the identifier quantityOnHand instead of quantityonhand.

■

Component Pascal distinguishes between uppercase and lowercase characters in identifiers or reserved words. So, hours and Hours would be detected by the compiler as different identifiers. Reserved words may not be used as Component Pascal identifiers.

Example 3.2   Here are some illegal Component Pascal identifiers:

7Eleven   Tax%   home-Address   TO

The first is illegal because it does not begin with a letter. The second and third have characters other than letters or digits. The last is illegal because it is a reserved word.

■

Unlike Standard Pascal and Oberon-2, Component Pascal allows the underscore character in its identifiers. The rule to allow the underscore character is provided mainly for compatibility with the widespread Java and C++ programming languages.

Example 3.3   Here are some legal Component Pascal identifiers that use the underscore character.

new_york   quantity_on_hand   hours_worked   ■

To write a Component Pascal program you must make up identifiers to name items. You should get in the habit of using mnemonic identifiers, that is, identifiers that remind the human reader about the meaning of the item you are naming. PrintAddress is a good name for the procedure in module Hw99Pr0380 because the program prints an address on the Log. The program would execute exactly the same if you wrote

PROCEDURE **Xyz***;

But that would be horrible style, because the identifier indicates nothing about what the program does. Even worse would be

PROCEDURE **Payroll***;

for this module, because that would indicate to the human reader that the program has something to do with a payroll problem, which it does not. When you use a program from this book as a model for your own program, do not blindly copy the identifiers if they are not appropriate to your problem. Instead, make up your own mnemonic identifiers.

Exporting and importing procedures

In the same way that a large company is subdivided into several departments, a large software project is subdivided into several modules. For a company to function effectively, people within a department must be able to communicate with people in other departments. Similarly, for a large program to function effectively, communication must take place between entities in different modules. It is the responsibility of the software designer to specify how the communication between modules is to take place.

To maintain an orderly flow of work, most companies place some restriction on the lines of communication between departments. For example, a manufacturing worker usually is not allowed to walk in to the legal department and ask the company's attorneys about the latest legal issues the company is dealing with. Indeed, some of the information in the legal department might be privileged information that should be kept hidden from production workers.

In the same way that information is hidden between departments of a company, information can be hidden within a module. In Component Pascal, hiding information within a module is the default rule. That is, all items are hidden within a module and are not accessible to other modules unless the programmer makes them accessible. When a module *exports* an item, it gives permission for another module to use it. If a module wants to use an item that another module has exported, it must *import* the item.

The line

IMPORT StdLog;

in Figure 3.6 indicates to the compiler that module Hw99Pr0380 wants to import all of the items exported by module StdLog. Module StdLog, whose interface is shown in Figure 3.4, contains a collection of procedures that output messages to the Log.   *Importing a module*

The asterisk after the name of the procedure PrintAddress* is called an *export mark*. The asterisk indicates to the compiler that this procedure is to be made available to other modules that want to import it. We will see later that items other than procedures can be exported and imported.   *Exporting a module*

Statements

The statement

StdLog.String("Mr. K. Kong")

causes the phrase Mr. K. Kong to be printed on the Log. This statement is using the procedure named String from the module named StdLog. If module Hw99Pr0380 had not imported module StdLog, this statement would produce an error. To execute a procedure from an imported module, you must type the name of the module followed by a period followed by the name of the procedure you want to execute.

Following the name of the procedure String are a pair of parentheses ( ). Within the parentheses is the parameter "Mr. K. Kong". The procedure prints the content between the double quote to the Log. It is permitted to use single quotes instead of double quotes. Hence the statement

StdLog.String('Mr. K. Kong')

would produce the same output to the Log. If you want a double quote to be printed to the Log you must enclose the phrase by single quotes and vice versa.

Example 3.4   The statement

StdLog.String('He said, "Hello". How are you?')

prints the phrase

He said, "Hello". How are you?

to the Log.   ∎

The statement

StdLog.Ln

executes the procedure named Ln from the module StdLog. Unlike procedure String from the same module, this procedure has no parameter. Procedure Ln sends the cursor in the Log to the beginning of the next line, which causes the second Std-Log.String to place its parameter below the first one.

You can see from Figure 3.4 that module StdLog exports six procedures. Module Hw99Pr0380 uses two of them—String and Ln. There are no parentheses following Ln indicating that this procedure has no parameters. String does have parentheses following it. The item

IN str: ARRAY OF CHAR

that is contained between parentheses is called the *signature* of procedure String. str is the name of the parameter and ARRAY OF CHAR is its type. str is called the *formal* parameter. It matches the *actual* parameter "Mr. K. Kong" in the procedure call.

Signatures, formal parameters and actual parameters

The meaning of IN in the signature is described later. The parameters in the interface are guidelines for the use of the procedure in the importing module. The type ARRAY OF CHAR in the formal parameter list indicates that the actual parameter must be an array of characters, which is what "Mr. K. Kong" is.

You can get more extensive information about a documented module from the framework by highlighting the module name and selecting Info→Documentation. You should try this now to inspect the documentation of module StdLog.

All the lines between BEGIN and END in module Hw99Pr0380 are called executable statements, because they perform an operation when the program executes. Component Pascal has the following 11 executable statements:

assignment	if	return
case	loop	while
exit	procedure	with
for	repeat	

We will consider them in later chapters. The StdLog.String statement is an example of a procedure statement, or procedure call. IMPORT is an example of a nonexecutable statement. It has an effect during the compile phase as opposed to the execute phase.

You may have noticed in procedure PrintAddress that a semicolon appears after each StdLog statement except for the last one. This production rule from Appendix A for a statement sequence

StatementSeq = Statement { " ; " Statement}

shows that semicolons are used to separate two statements. For example, use the semicolon after the first StdLog.String statement to separate it from the following StdLog.Ln statement. Then use the semicolon after the StdLog.Ln statement to separate it from the following StdLog.String. The reserved word END, however, is not a statement. Therefore, you do not need a semicolon separator after the last StdLog.Ln. The general rule to remember is

■ Do not place a semicolon before an END.

Syntax errors

Now that the program has been written and saved in the Mod folder, it is time to attempt a compile. With the source window in focus select Dev→Compile And Unload to translate the program. If your program has no errors, the compiler will create the object program and the interface and store them on your disk. But how does the compiler determine where to store them? It examines the name of the module, scanning it from left to right. It assumes the first letter of the module name is the first letter of the project folder. Then it assumes that every letter and digit after the first character up to but not including the first uppercase letter is also part of the project folder. The rest of the module name is taken to be the name of the file where the object program and the interface are to be stored. The object file is stored in the Code folder and the interface is stored in the Sym folder.

How to compile a Component Pascal program

Example 3.5 The module in Figure 3.6 is named Hw99Pr0380. The programmer saved it in the file BlackBox/Hw99/Mod/Pr0380. When this module was compiled by selecting Dev→Compile And Unload, the compiler scanned the name Hw99Pr0380 from left to right until it reached the uppercase P. It determined that the project folder was Hw99 and that the name of the file is Pr0380. Therefore, it stored the object file in BlackBox/Hw99/Code/Pr0380 and the interface in BlackBox/Hw99/Sym/Pr0380. In the end there were three files, all named Pr0380, in three different folders—the source file in the Mod folder, the object file in the Code folder, and the interface in the Sym folder. ∎

When you try to execute a program, two types of errors are possible:

- Syntax error—The program does not compile.

- Logical error—The program compiles but produces incorrect results.

The production rules of the grammar can only indicate possible sources of syntax errors, not logical errors. Remember from Chapter 2 that they are not even perfect at specifying all the syntax rules of the Component Pascal language.

Figure 3.7 illustrates a syntax error. When a program does not compile, no object program can be generated, and it is impossible to test for logical errors. Errors, whether syntax or logical, are called bugs. Getting the errors out of your program is called debugging. Can you spot the bug in Figure 3.7?

```
MODULE Hw99Pr0381;
(* Stan Warford *)
(* June 12, 2002 *)

    IMPORT StdLog;

    PROCEDURE PrintAddress*
    BEGIN
        StdLog.String("Mr. K. Kong"); StdLog.Ln;
        StdLog.String("Empire State Building"); StdLog.Ln;
        StdLog.String("350 Fifth Avenue"); StdLog.Ln;
        StdLog.String("New York, NY 10118-0110"); StdLog.Ln
    END PrintAddress;

END Hw99Pr0381.
```

Figure 3.7
This procedure has a bug.

If you try to compile this module the following error message will be printed on the Log:

```
compiling "Hw99Pr0381"
one error detected
```

The compiler will also place a marker symbol in the window of your source text that indicates where it detected the error and will give a more detailed description of the error. Clicking the error marker causes the marker to expand to reveal an error message. On MSWindows, the error message is also displayed at the bottom of the window. You can then figure out what the error was and make the correction with your text editor. After you make any changes you should select File→Save to save your changed file then Dev→Compile And Unload again. It is not necessary to remove the error marker symbols in your text before attempting another compile. The compiler automatically removes all error markers before it attempts a translation. Repeat the correction process until you get a successful compilation. When you succeed, a message on the Log will inform you of the translation it made.

Documentation files

Now that you have a program written and translated, you need to provide a way for the user to execute your program. In the BlackBox framework, user documentation is stored in the Docu folder. Figure 3.8 shows the documentation for module Hw99Pr0380.

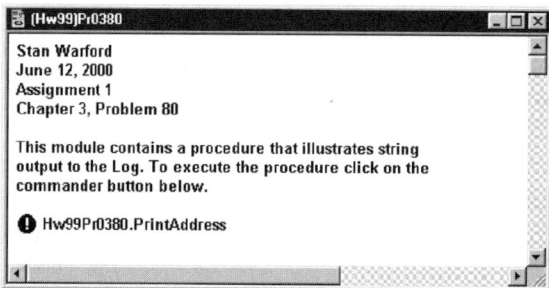

Figure 3.8
Documentation for module Hw99Pr0380, It is stored as file Pr0380 in the Docu folder.

To create user documentation you select File→New and enter a description of the program and instructions for the user on how to use it. The document in Figure 3.8 is not compiled. So, the comments contained in it do not need to be enclosed in comment brackets (* and *) as are the comments in the source listing.

Do not use comment brackets in your Docu file.

The instructions for the user shown in the figure include a commander button that the user should click to execute the program. Many of the programs you will write with this book can be conveniently executed by providing the user with a *commander button* in the user documentation. To insert the commander button select Tools→Insert Commander with your insertion cursor in your documentation window at the location where you want the button. (Be careful to *not* select the option Controls→Insert Command Button, which sounds similar but is quite different.)

The commander button

Following the commander button you place the command to be executed. A command is a procedure that is exported by a module. The syntax is identical to that used in a module to execute an imported procedure. Namely, following the commander button you place the name of the module followed by a period followed by the name of the exported procedure.

This documentation should be saved as a file named Pr0380 in BlackBox/Hw99/Docu. We now have four files all named Pr0380 stored in four different folders as shown in Figure 3.9. You write and save the source program in the Mod folder and the documentation in the Docu folder. The BlackBox system creates and stores the object program in the Code folder and the interface in the Sym folder.

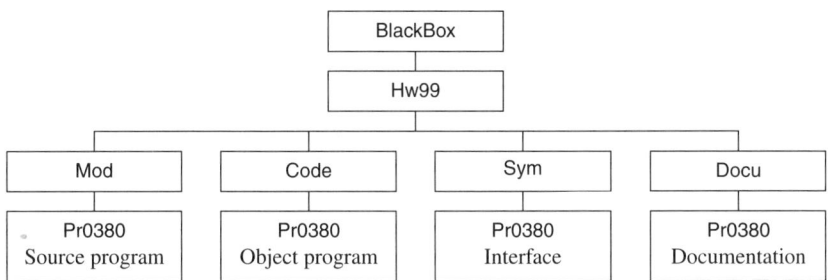

Figure 3.9
The files associated with a
BlackBox program.

When you click the commander button the following text should appear on the Log.

Mr. K. Kong
Empire State Building
350 Fifth Avenue
New York, NY 10118-0110

Even the modules that you write have interfaces. Figure 3.10 shows the interface for module Hw99Pr0380. As the programmer of the module Hw99Pr0380, you do not write the interface. The compiler produces it automatically. The interface in Figure 3.10 was produced by highlighting the text Hw99Pr0380 in some document and selecting Info→Interface (after the module was compiled). You do not need to type the name of the module in the Log to select it. For example, you can select the name of your module in your source code document to bring up its interface. The export marks are omitted in the interface because they would be redundant. Every item listed in the interface is an exported item.

DEFINITION Hw99Pr0380;

    PROCEDURE PrintAddress;

END Hw99Pr0380.

Figure 3.10
The interface for the program
in Figure 3.6.

Program style

Some computer languages are line-oriented, that is, each statement must be written on a separate line. Listing 3.11 shows that Component Pascal is not line-oriented. The behavior of the object program does not depend on the spacing or indentation style of the source program. The program in Listing 3.11 produces the same output as the one in Listing 3.6.

MODULE Hw99Pr0382;
(* Stan Warford *)
(* June 18, 2002 *)

IMPORT StdLog;

PROCEDURE **PrintAddress**   *;
BEGIN StdLog.**String**   ("Mr. K. Kong"); StdLog.Ln;
StdLog.String
("Empire State Building");   StdLog.Ln
; StdLog.String   ("350 Fifth Avenue"); StdLog.Ln;
StdLog.String
("New York, NY 10118-0110"); StdLog.Ln
END PrintAddress; END *Hw99Pr0382.*

Figure 3.11
This module compiles
without error.

One good habit to cultivate when learning to program is to adhere to a consistent standard of style. You should follow either the style of the programs in this book, the style specified by your instructor or employer, or a consistent style from some other source. The document titled Programming Conventions in the BlackBox on-line help system has detailed guidelines for Component Pascal programming style. The style conventions in this book have only a few differences from the published guidelines. The most noticeable difference is that the guidelines specify that all comments be in italic. Both this book and the published guidelines recommend that all exported procedures in a module be in a bold font.

The computer does not require such neatness for the program to work. However, just getting the program to work correctly is not sufficient. Good style is necessary because people, as well as computers, must read your programs. You would not write a business letter without the paragraphs indented consistently. Nor should you write a program that way. Although you may want to rebel at first against such seemingly trivial details, you will find in the long run that they are not restrictive at all. In fact just the opposite is true—these rules are liberating.

The importance of good style

The situation is similar to that of a new driver on the road for the first time. Think of how many restrictive rules there are—speed limits, yield signs, stop signals, and so on. New drivers may feel hampered and may worry about all the rules they need to remember. But experienced drivers do not even consciously try to remember the rules. They know them subconsciously. What's more, the rules liberate them from fear of an accident. Programming standards will liberate your mind to think constructively. The standards will take care of the details, freeing you to take care of the problem.

Proper procedures

The next two modules introduce the concept of a programmer-defined procedure, which will be discussed in more detail in later chapters. Procedures are useful when your program has a task that it needs to perform more than once. Programmers working with procedures must first define the task in the procedure declaration part then invoke or call the procedure when the task needs to bc executed. The program in Figure 3.12 outputs a pattern on the Log.

```
MODULE Hw99Pr0383;
  IMPORT StdLog;

  PROCEDURE PrintPattern*;
  BEGIN
    StdLog.String("@"); StdLog.Ln;
    StdLog.String("@ @"); StdLog.Ln;
    StdLog.String("@ @ @"); StdLog.Ln;
    StdLog.String("@ @ @ @"); StdLog.Ln;
    StdLog.String("@"); StdLog.Ln;
    StdLog.String("@ @"); StdLog.Ln;
    StdLog.String("@ @ @"); StdLog.Ln;
    StdLog.String("@ @ @ @"); StdLog.Ln;
    StdLog.String("@"); StdLog.Ln;
    StdLog.String("@ @"); StdLog.Ln;
    StdLog.String("@ @ @"); StdLog.Ln;
    StdLog.String("@ @ @ @"); StdLog.Ln
  END PrintPattern;

END Hw99Pr0383.
```

Figure 3.12

This procedure prints three triangles to the Log.

The exported procedure PrintPattern in Figure 3.12 outputs a pattern of asterisks without using another procedure. The pattern is a repetition of three smaller patterns in the shape of a triangle. The module in Figure 3.13, on the other hand, collects the statements that print a single triangle into another procedure that is not exported. The programmer declared the procedure and gave it the name PrintTriangle. She then called the procedure three times to produce the final pattern.

In Figure 3.13, PrintTriangle is an identifier that names the procedure. Figure 3.14 shows that procedures PrintTriangle and PrintPattern are both nested in module Hw99Pr0384. The StdLog.String statements in region (1) belong to procedure Print-Triangle. The procedure call statements in region (2) belong to the procedure Print-Pattern.

When PrintPattern is invoked the first statement in region (2) is executed. It is a call to procedure PrintTriangle defined earlier in the listing, and causes execution to jump to the first statement of region (1). The computer then executes all the statements of region (1). After it executes the last statement of region (1), it transfers execution to the statement after the one that made the call in the calling procedure. At this point the first triangle has been printed.

```
MODULE Hw99Pr0384;
  IMPORT StdLog;

  PROCEDURE PrintTriangle;
  BEGIN
    StdLog.String("@"); StdLog.Ln;
    StdLog.String("@ @"); StdLog.Ln;
    StdLog.String("@ @ @"); StdLog.Ln;
    StdLog.String("@ @ @ @"); StdLog.Ln
  END PrintTriangle;

  PROCEDURE PrintPattern*;
  BEGIN
    PrintTriangle;
    PrintTriangle;
    PrintTriangle
  END PrintPattern;

END Hw99Pr0384.
```

Figure 3.13
This procedure prints three triangles to the Log using a procedure.

Next, the computer executes the second statement in region (2), which is another call to procedure PrintTriangle. So, the statements in region (1) execute again. Similarly, the third statement in region (2) makes them execute a third time. In general, a procedure call causes control to jump to the previously defined procedure. After the procedure executes, control returns to the statement after the calling statement. Figure 3.15 shows the order in which statements are executed in a module that has ProcedureP2, which is exported, making two procedure calls to ProcedureP1, which is not exported.

Because PrintTriangle is an identifier, the programmer determined it arbitrarily. The program would produce the exact output if the programmer wrote

PROCEDURE WriteTriangle

in the definition of the procedure, and then called it with

WriteTriangle

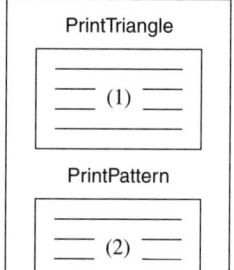

Figure 3.14
Procedures PrintPattern and PrintTriangle nested in module Hw99Pr0384.

in the main program. The only requirement is that the name in the procedure definition match the name in the procedure call. Of course, the identifiers you choose for the names of your procedures should be mnemonic.

Procedures are useful when you need to perform the same task at several different points in a program. They are also useful in structuring a program into levels of abstraction, even if the task is only performed once. Although this program uses a procedure to output text to the Log, later programs will use procedures to process data as well.

The StdLog.String and StdLog.Ln statements are procedure calls. They differ from PrintTriangle in two respects. First, they are imported from a framework module as opposed to being user-defined procedures. Their declaration part is hidden

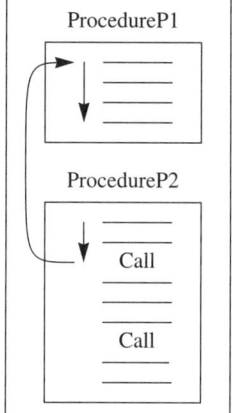

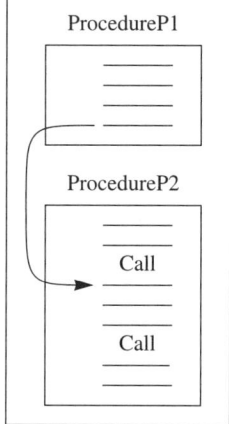

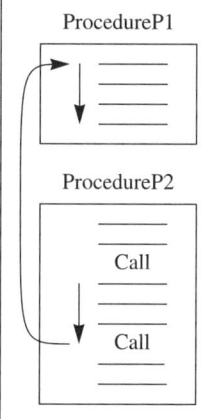

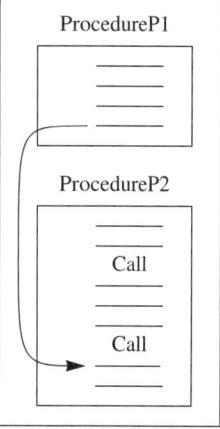

(a) The first call transfers control to the procedure. The procedure executes.

(b) The procedure returns control to the statement following the first call.

(c) The second call transfers control to the procedure. The procedure executes again.

(d) The procedure returns control to the statement following the second call.

Figure 3.15
The order of execution when a procedure has two procedure calls.

from the programmer, although their interface is available on-line. This is in contrast to a programmer-defined procedure, which must be declared within the programmer's module.

Second, StdLog.String calls include a string parameter enclosed in parentheses. The declaration part needs this information to do its task. It needs the string to know what to output to the Log. Programmer-defined procedures can also have parameters. Later chapters will explain how to define procedures with parameters.

Figure 3.16 shows the interface for module Hw99Pr0384. Only the exported procedure PrintPattern shows in the interface. Because procedure PrintTriangle is not exported, it does not appear in the interface.

```
DEFINITION Hw99Pr0384;

    PROCEDURE  PrintPattern;

END Hw99Pr0384.
```

Figure 3.16
The interface for the module in Listing 3.13.

Exercises

1. Define the following terms.

    (a) module   **(b)** global data   **(c)** local data

2. What is an interface? What is its purpose?

3. What is the essence of abstraction?

4. What is the function of a compiler?

5. State whether each of the following Component Pascal identifiers is valid. For those that are not valid, explain why they are not.

    (a) hourlyWage   **(b)** last 1   **(c)** WITH
    (d) one Name   **(e)** 1stOne   **(f)** %Profit
    (g) Acme-Tool   **(h)** A

6. State whether each of the following Component Pascal identifiers is valid. For those that are not valid, explain why they are not.

    (a) amountOnHand   **(b)** 2Day   **(c)** superCallifragillistic
    (d) BY   **(e)** Soc-Sec-Num   **(f)** John Smith
    (g) tools/Bolts   **(h)** i

7. Find all the syntax errors in the following Component Pascal procedure. Assume that module StdLog has been imported correctly.

    ```
    PROCEDURE PrintString; *
    BEGIN
        StdLog.String ('Is this wrong?'); StdLog.Ln;
        StdLog.String ('Maybe it's right'); StdLog.Ln
    END;
    ```

8. Find all the syntax errors in the following Component Pascal procedure. Assume that module StdLog has been imported correctly.

    ```
    PROCEDURE PrintString *;
    BEGIN
        StdLog.String ("This can't be wrong!); StdLog.Ln;
        StdLog.String ("Or can it?"); StdLog.Ln
    END;
    ```

9. Inspect the interface of module TextViews, and answer the following questions about the procedures that are listed in it.

    (a) Does procedure SetCtrlDir have a parameter list?
    (b) Does procedure Deposit have a parameter list?
    (c) What is the signature of procedure SetDir? What is the name of its formal parameter? What is its type?

Problems

10. Write a Component Pascal program to output the following two-line message on the Log:

She said, "Hi there.
What's up?"

Use two StdLog.String procedure calls for the second line to print both the single and the double quote marks. Test your program by inserting a commander button in a documentation file to execute the procedure.

11. Write a Component Pascal program to output to the Log your name and address suitable for use as a mailing label. Test your program by inserting a commander button in a documentation file to execute the procedure.

12. Using a procedure that is not exported to output a single pattern, write a Component Pascal program to output the following triple pattern on the Log:

```
+
+++
+++++
+++
+
+
+++
+++++
+++
+
+
+++
+++++
+++
+
```

Test your program by inserting a commander button in a documentation file to execute the exported procedure.

 Chapter *4*

Variables

Every Component Pascal variable has three attributes:

- A name
- A type
- A value

The three attributes of a variable

A variable's name is an identifier determined arbitrarily by the programmer. A variable's type specifies the kind of values it can have. Variable names and types are declared in the declaration sequence, which must be placed before the executable statements of a procedure. Unlike a variable's name and type, a variable's value does not in general appear in a program listing. The value is contained in main memory during execution of the program.

Real variables

Figure 4.1 shows how to declare real variables in a program. The output of procedure Rectangle is:

```
The width is 3.6
The length is 12.4
```

```
MODULE Pbox04A;
   IMPORT StdLog;

   PROCEDURE Rectangle*;
   VAR
      width: REAL;
      length: REAL;
   BEGIN
      width := 3.6;
      length := 12.4;
      StdLog.String("The width is "); StdLog.Real(width); StdLog.Ln;
      StdLog.String("The length is "); StdLog.Real(length); StdLog.Ln
   END Rectangle;

END Pbox04A.
```

Figure 4.1
A procedure that sets the value of two real variables and outputs them to the Log.

The modules in Chapter 3 have names that begin with Hw99 to illustrate how you should name your modules if you are student number 99 in a class of many students. Beginning with this chapter, most modules will be named according to the chapter number of the book. Hence, the name of the module in Figure 4.1 is Pbox04A, where Pbox04 represents Chapter 4 of programming with BlackBox using *Computing Fundamentals*, and A is the first program in the chapter. Pbox04B will be the name of the next module in this chapter, and so on. If you are studying this book as part of a class, you should continue to use your assigned number with the convention you learned in Chapter 3.

As Figure 4.1 shows, the declaration sequence begins with the reserved word VAR and contains a list of all variables used in the procedure. width is the first variable's name, and REAL is its type. The type REAL means the variable's value will be a real number, with a fractional part indicated by a decimal point. The name and type of a variable are separated by a colon.

Variables of type REAL

Notice how semicolons are used in a declaration sequence. One of the EBNF alternatives for a declaration sequence is

VAR {VarDecl " ; "}

which shows that semicolons serve to terminate a variable declaration. They do not separate one variable declaration from the following variable declaration. The semicolon that terminates the variable declaration

length: REAL;

is necessary even though it occurs before BEGIN, which is not a statement.

Assignment statements

Unlike names and types, the values of the variables are usually not visible in the program listing (although they are in this program). Instead, they exist in main memory during program execution. An assignment statement sets the value of a variable. The assignment statement

width := 3.6;

sets the value of the variable width to 3.6. The := symbol is called the *assignment symbol*. You should read this statement in English as "width gets 3.6." Do not say "width equals 3.6." The equals symbol, =, has a different meaning in Component Pascal from the assignment symbol, :=.

The assignment symbol is pronounced "gets".

The name of a variable must be on the left side of the assignment symbol, and an expression must be on the right side. A numeric value such as 3.6 is an example of a real expression.

Real output

Figure 3.4 shows the interface for the StdLog module. The specification for procedure Real in the StdLog module is

PROCEDURE Real (x: REAL);

The parameter x in the interface is the formal parameter. It has type REAL. The types of the formal parameters tell you what is allowed in the actual parameters. In the program in Figure 4.1 the first call to StdLog.Real is

Formal parameters

StdLog.Real(width)

The actual parameter in the procedure call is width. Actual parameter width corresponds to formal parameter x. The procedure call adheres to the specification given in the interface, because the type of actual parameter width corresponds to the type of formal parameter x—both are REAL. The value for x that you give to procedure Real is the value that you want to print on the Log.

Actual parameters

Real expressions

The four real operations in Component Pascal are addition, subtraction, multiplication, and division, indicated symbolically by +, -, *, and / as summarized in Figure 4.2. They have the same precedence you are familiar with from algebra. The operators * and / have a higher precedence than + and -. When parentheses are present in the expression, the contents of the parentheses are evaluated first.

Operator	Meaning
+	Addition
-	Subtraction
*	Multiplication
/	Division

Figure 4.2
The real operators.

Example 4.1 Two examples of expressions and their evaluations without parentheses are

```
4.0 * 5.5 + 6.0          4.0 + 5.5 * 6.0
22.0 + 6.0               4.0 + 33.0
28.0                     37.0
```

The multiplication operation is performed first because it has higher precedence than addition.   ∎

Example 4.2 An example with parentheses is

4.0 * (5.5 + 6.0)
4.0 × 11.5
46.0

The addition is performed before the multiplication because the addition is within parentheses. ∎

An operator ρ is associative if $(a \, \rho \, b)\rho \, c \equiv a \, \rho(b \, \rho \, c)$. For example, + is associative, because $(a+b)+c \equiv a+(b+c)$. However, − is not associative, because it is not the case that $(a-b)-c \equiv a-(b-c)$. If two operators of the same precedence are adjacent, the evaluation is done from left to right. This rule makes a difference if an operator is not associative. *Associative operators*

Left-to-right rule

Example 4.3 Two examples of the left-to-right rule are

11.5 - 3.0 - 4.5   25.0 / 10.0 / 5.0
8.5 − 4.5   2.5 / 5.0
4.0   0.5

Notice the difference that this rule makes in the results. If you first subtract 4.5 from 3.0 to get −1.5, and then subtract that from 11.5, you get 13.0, which is different from the correct value of 4.0. Similarly, if you first divide 10.0 by 5.0 to get 2.0, and then divide 25.0 by 2.0, you get 12.5, which is different from the correct value of 0.5. ∎

```
MODULE Pbox04B;
   IMPORT StdLog;

   PROCEDURE Rectangle*;
   VAR
      width, length: REAL;
      area, perim: REAL;
   BEGIN
      width := 3.6;
      length := 12.4;
      StdLog.String("The width is "); StdLog.Real(width); StdLog.Ln;
      StdLog.String("The length is "); StdLog.Real(length); StdLog.Ln;
      area := width * length;
      perim := 2.0 * (width + length);
      StdLog.String("The area is "); StdLog.Real(area); StdLog.Ln;
      StdLog.String("The perimeter is "); StdLog.Real(perim); StdLog.Ln
   END Rectangle;

END Pbox04B.
```

Figure 4.3
Using real expressions in a program.

Figure 4.3 shows how to use a real expression in a complete program. The output on the Log of this program is

The width is 3.6
The length is 12.4
The area is 44.64
The perimeter is 32.0

Integer variables

Figure 4.4 shows how to declare an integer variable in a program. You should check the interface for module StdLog to see the specification for procedure Int. The output of the program is:

You have 39 cents in change.

```
MODULE Pbox04C;
   IMPORT StdLog;


   PROCEDURE Change*;
   VAR
      cents: INTEGER;
   BEGIN
      cents := 39;
      StdLog.String("You have "); StdLog.Int(cents);
      StdLog.String(" cents in change."); StdLog.Ln
   END Change;

END Pbox04C.
```

Figure 4.4
A procedure that sets the value of an integer variable and outputs it to the Log.

Computers store integer values in main memory differently from real values. To store an integer, the computer has two storage compartments—one for the sign of the number and one for its magnitude. However, to store a real value, the computer uses binary scientific notation with four storage compartments—one for the sign of the exponent (the power of 2), one for the exponent, one for the sign of the value, and one for the magnitude.

Because of this difference in the way the computer stores integer and real values, Component Pascal puts some restrictions on how you use them in a program. The procedure in Figure 4.5 illustrates the fact that you cannot assign a real value to an integer variable. The procedure has an assignment incompatibility error and will not compile.

You can, however, assign an integer value to a real variable. Component Pascal will convert the integer value to the corresponding equal real value before making the assignment.

Example 4.4   If you declare x to have type real then the assignment statement

x := 5

is legal even though 5 is an integer value. Component Pascal converts the integer value 5 to the real value 5.0 before making the assignment to x.   ∎

```
MODULE Pbox04D;
   IMPORT StdLog;

   PROCEDURE Error*;
   VAR
      i: INTEGER;
   BEGIN
      i := 2.7;
      StdLog.String("The value of i is "); StdLog.Int(i); StdLog.Ln
   END Error;

END Pbox04D.
```

Figure 4.5
A procedure that tries to assign a real value to an integer variable. This procedure has a bug.

Integer expressions

Integer values, which do not have fractional parts, are used for counting whole objects. For example, if you need to keep track of the number of employees who work for your company, you could have a variable, numEmpl, of type integer whose value represents the number of workers the company has. numEmpl could never have a value like 234.6, because you cannot have 0.6 of an employee. Figure 4.6 summarizes the integer operations.

Operator	Meaning
+	Addition
-	Subtraction
*	Multiplication
DIV	Division
MOD	Modulo

Figure 4.6
The integer operators.

Addition, subtraction, and multiplication for integer values are similar to the same operations for real values, but division is different. In integer division, denoted by the operator DIV, a fractional part cannot be included in the result. Instead, the fractional part is discarded, or truncated.

Example 4.5 The real expression 14.0 / 3.0 evaluates to 4.667, but the integer expression 14 DIV 3 evaluates to 4. Further examples of DIV are:

```
15 DIV 3 = 5
14 DIV 3 = 4
13 DIV 3 = 4
12 DIV 3 = 4
11 DIV 3 = 3
```

Another integer operator related to integer division is the MOD operator. MOD stands for modulus, which is the remainder when you divide one integer by another.

Example 4.6 The expression 14 MOD 3 evaluates to 2, because you get a remainder of 2 when you divide 14 by 3. Further examples of MOD are:

15 MOD 3 = 0
14 MOD 3 = 2
13 MOD 3 = 1
12 MOD 3 = 0
11 MOD 3 = 2   ∎

The DIV and MOD operators of Component Pascal are related by a mathematical equation. The equation is based on the following two facts.

- m div n is the quotient of $m \div n$.

- m mod n is the remainder of $m \div n$.

Let q represent the quotient and r represent the remainder, so that

$$q = m \text{ div } n$$
$$r = m \text{ mod } n$$

Then the relationship between div and mod is expressed mathematically as

$$m = q \cdot n + r \qquad 0 \le r < n$$

Example 4.7 For $m = 14$ and $n = 3$ as in Example 4.5 and Example 4.6 above, q and r are calculated as

$$q = m \text{ div } n = 14 \text{ div } 3 = 4$$
$$r = m \text{ mod } n = 14 \text{ mod } 3 = 2$$

The mathematical relationship with these numbers is

$$14 = 4 \cdot 3 + 2 \qquad 0 \le 2 < 3$$

You can see that for the given divisor $n = 3$, the remainder r will always satisfy the inequality $0 \le r < 3$. In Example 4.6, the remainders when you divide by 3 are limited to the values 0, 1, and 2, which are all less than 3.   ∎

The relationship between div and mod as expressed by the equation and the accompanying inequality assumes that neither the dividend m nor the divisor n are negative. If either or both of them are negative, then one or the other (or both) of the quotient q and remainder r will be negative as well. Component Pascal has a rule that describes precisely the results of the operations in that case. However, as programs in this book never use negative quotients or divisors you can safely ignore that situation.

The procedure in Figure 4.7 uses integer expressions to compute the change in dimes, nickels, and pennies for a given number of cents with American currency. (There are 100 cents in a dollar, a dime is a 10-cent coin, a nickel is a five-cent coin, and a penny is a one-cent coin.) Integer variables are appropriate for this problem, because you cannot have a fraction of a coin. The output to the Log from procedure MakeChange is

```
You have 39 cents in change.
Dimes: 3
Nickels: 1
Pennies: 4
```

```
MODULE Pbox04E;
   IMPORT StdLog;

   PROCEDURE MakeChange*;
   VAR
      cents: INTEGER;
      dimes, nickels, pennies: INTEGER;
   BEGIN
      cents := 39;
      StdLog.String("You have "); StdLog.Int(cents);
      StdLog.String(" cents in change."); StdLog.Ln;
      dimes := cents DIV 10;
      cents := cents MOD 10;
      nickels := cents DIV 5;
      pennies := cents MOD 5;
      StdLog.String("Dimes: "); StdLog.Int(dimes); StdLog.Ln;
      StdLog.String("Nickels: "); StdLog.Int(nickels); StdLog.Ln;
      StdLog.String("Pennies: "); StdLog.Int(pennies); StdLog.Ln
   END MakeChange;

END Pbox04E.
```

Figure 4.7
The number of dimes, nickels, and pennies required for a given amount of change.

The first assignment statement computes the number of dimes by dividing the amount of change by 10 with the DIV operator. Notice that DIV does not round off the value to 4, which would be the incorrect number of dimes for the change. The second assignment statement gives cents a new value, the remainder of the change after the three dimes have been accounted for. The values for nickels and pennies are computed similarly.

Component Pascal provides two procedures for processing integers—INC and DEC, which stand for increment and decrement respectively. INC(v) adds 1 to integer variable v, INC(v, n) adds n to variable v, DEC(v) subtracts 1 from variable v, and DEC(v, n) subtracts n from variable v. Figure 4.8 summarizes the equivalent assignment statements.

You might be wondering why you would bother with these functions when it would be just as easy to use the assignment statements directly. The reason is that

Procedure	Meaning
INC(v)	v := v + 1
INC(v, n)	v := v + n
DEC(v)	v := v - 1
DEC(v, n)	v := v - n

Figure 4.8
The increment and decrement
functions for integers.

the functions are designed to make use of special increment and decrement features of the computer hardware. The equivalent assignment statements may require more storage for the object program and the resulting object program may run slower than if you use the increment and decrement functions.

Mixed expressions

Component Pascal numeric expressions are similar to the mathematical expressions that you learned in algebra, but they have one important difference. Algebra usually makes no distinction between expressions for real values and expressions for integer values. However, because computers store integer values and real values with different internal codes, Component Pascal makes an important distinction between real and integer expressions.

Component Pascal permits you to use integer values in real expressions, though it does not permit you to use real values in integer expressions. This feature is another example of automatic conversion from integer to real values, as described in the discussion of Figure 4.5. When you use an integer value in a real expression, the compiler converts it to the equivalent real value before translating the expression to machine language.

Example 4.8 Suppose dollars is a real variable and cents is an integer variable. The assignment

dollars := dollars + cents / 100.0

is legal even though dollars and 100.0, which are real, are in the same expression as cents, which is integer. Because the division operator is /, not DIV, the compiler expects both operands to be real. Though the 100.0 operand is already real, the cents operand is integer, so the compiler converts it to real. Then the addition takes place between the two real operands. ∎

Example 4.9 The expression

dollars MOD 100

would be illegal if dollars is a real variable, because MOD expects its operands to be integers. There is no automatic conversion from real to integer, only from integer to real. ∎

These ideas may be a little confusing at first because the symbols for addition, subtraction, and multiplication are the same for real expressions as they are for integer expressions. (However, the symbols for division are different.) Whether an expression with +, -, or * is an integer expression or a real expression depends on its operands. If one or both of its operands is real, the result is real. If both operands are integers, the result is integer. Figure 4.9 summarizes the types of results for the arithmetic operations.

Operator	Operation	Type of operands	Type of result
+	Addition	Both integer	Integer
		At least one real	Real
-	Subtraction	Both integer	Integer
		At least one real	Real
*	Multiplication	Both integer	Integer
		At least one real	Real
/	Real division	Integers or reals	Real
DIV	Integer division	Integers	Integer
MOD	Modulus	Integers	Integer

Figure 4.9
Types of results for the arithmetic operations.

Example 4.10 Here are two examples of legal mixed expressions:

14.0 / (12 DIV 5)   98 / 3
14.0 / 2   98.0 / 3.0
14.0 / 2.0   32.667
7.0

In each example, Component Pascal recognizes that / is a real operator and converts the operands to real values if necessary. ∎

ABS(x) is a Component Pascal function that returns the absolute value of x. It is *The ABS function* unusual because the type that it returns depends on the type of the parameter x. If the type of x is integer the type of the returned value is integer, and if the type of x is real the type of the returned value is real.

Example 4.11 The function ABS(-3) returns integer 3, ABS(3) returns integer 3, and ABS(-3.7) returns real 3.7. ∎

In mathematics, there is no largest integer. There is no upper limit on the value that an integer variable can have. But all computers have finite storage capacity for storing numeric values. Fortunately, Component Pascal allows you to store fairly large values in your numeric variables. An value of type INTEGER can store values in the range

–2,147,483,648 .. 2,147,483,647

If you ever need to store values larger than two billion you have the option of declaring a variable of type LONGINT, which can store values in the range

–9,223,372,036,854,775,808 .. 9,223,372,036,854,775,807

You can assign an integer expression to a long integer variable. Component Pascal will provide automatic conversion from integer to long integer similar to how it provides automatic conversion from integer to real. But you cannot assign a long integer expression to an integer variable.

Example 4.12 If myInt is an integer variable, and myLongInt is a long integer variable, then

myInt := myLongInt

is not legal, but

myLongInt := myInt

is legal. ∎

If you ever have a long integer value that you need to assign to an integer variable you can use the SHORT(x) function to do the conversion. If the type of x is long integer, then SHORT returns the equivalent integer.

The SHORT function

Example 4.13 The following expression is legal.

myInt := SHORT(myLongInt) ∎

If you have a real value that you need to use in an integer expression, Component Pascal provides a function called ENTIER(x). It takes a real value for x and returns a long integer value as the truncated value of x.

The ENTIER function

Example 4.14 If dollars is a real variable and bigBills is a long integer variable, then

bigBills := ENTIER(dollars)

truncates the value of dollars, converts it to a long integer, and assigns it to bigBills. If dollars has the value 4.95, then bigBills gets 4. You must write

bills := SHORT(ENTIER(dollars))

if bills is an integer variable. ∎

If you ever need to use the maximum value of an integer, you do not need to remember the 10-digit sequence. MAX is a built-in function that takes a type for the actual parameter and returns the maximum value for that type. Similarly, the MIN function returns the minimum value for a type.

The MAX and MIN functions for types

Example 4.15 The statements

```
StdLog.String("MAX(INTEGER) = "); StdLog.Int(MAX(INTEGER)); StdLog.Ln;
StdLog.String("MIN(INTEGER) = "); StdLog.Int(MIN(INTEGER)); StdLog.Ln;
```

produce the following output on the Log:

```
MAX(INTEGER) = 2147483647
MIN(INTEGER) = -2147483648
```
∎

MAX and MIN can be used with types other than integer. If you output the maximum value of the real type, you will discover that it is about 1.798×10^{308} .

MAX and MIN are unusual on two counts. First, most functions take variables or constants for their actual parameters, while MAX and MIN take a type. Second, there is another form of MAX and MIN that does take variables and constants. If you supply the MAX function with two actual parameters, it will return the larger of the two. Similarly, MIN will return the minimum of two actual parameters.

The MAX and MIN functions for variables and constants

Example 4.16 If myData is an integer variable, the statements

```
myData := 7;
StdLog.String("The larger is"); StdLog.Int(MAX(myData, 5)); StdLog.Ln;
```

produce the following output on the Log:

```
The larger is 7
```

because 7 is greater than 5. In this example, MAX has variable myData for the first actual parameter and constant 5 for the second. ∎

Function procedures

BlackBox provides module Math, a standard library that is documented on-line. A few of the many functions from the interface are listed in Figure 4.10. Math.Pi() always returns the value of π. Math.Exp(x) raises the base of the natural logarithms, e, to the power specified by the parameter x. Math.Ln(x) returns the natural logarithm of x, and Math.Log(x) returns the base-10 logarithm. The angles of the trigonometric functions are always expressed in radians, not degrees.

DEFINITION Math;

    PROCEDURE Pi (): REAL;

    PROCEDURE Sqrt (x: REAL): REAL;
    PROCEDURE Exp (x: REAL): REAL;
    PROCEDURE Ln (x: REAL): REAL;
    PROCEDURE Log (x: REAL): REAL;
    PROCEDURE Power (x, y: REAL): REAL;
    PROCEDURE IntPower (x: REAL; n: INTEGER): REAL;

    PROCEDURE Sin (x: REAL): REAL;
    PROCEDURE Cos (x: REAL): REAL;
    PROCEDURE Tan (x: REAL): REAL;
    PROCEDURE ArcSin (x: REAL): REAL;
    PROCEDURE ArcCos (x: REAL): REAL;
    PROCEDURE ArcTan (x: REAL): REAL;

END Math.

Figure 4.10
Some of the math functions from the interface of the Math module.

Proper procedures and function procedures

Component Pascal provides two types of procedures—proper procedures and function procedures. The procedures in module StdLog shown in its interface in Figure 3.4 are all proper procedures. The procedures listed in the interface for module Math are all function procedures. You can tell from an interface whether a procedure is a function procedure by inspection of its formal parameters. If the formal parameters include a colon : followed by a type to the right of the parentheses ( ), the procedure is a function procedure. Otherwise it is a proper procedure.

Function procedures are similar to functions in mathematics, where $f(x)$ usually means a function of x. If you supply a value for x, the function will return a value for $f(x)$. In the specification of a function procedure, the type following the parentheses is the type of the value returned by the function procedure.

Example 4.17   The interface for function procedure IntPower

PROCEDURE IntPower (x: REAL; n: INTEGER): REAL

specifies that the first parameter must be compatible with real, the second parameter must be compatible with integer, and the value returned by the function will have type real. If alpha has type real, then the assignment

alpha := Math.IntPower(2.4, 3)

is legal. The function procedure returns the real value 13.824, which is then assigned to alpha. The assignment would not be legal if alpha had type integer because you cannot assign a real value to an integer variable.   ▌

In the same way that you can assign an integer value to a real variable because of the automatic conversion from integer to real, you can supply an integer actual parameter to a real formal parameter. But you cannot supply a real actual parameter to an integer formal parameter.

Example 4.18   The assignment statement

alpha := Math.IntPower(2, 3)

is legal even though 2 is an integer and x is a real. However, the assignment statement

alpha := Math.IntPower(2, 3.0)

is not legal because 3.0 is a real but n is an integer.   ∎

Loosely speaking, an arithmetic expression is a combination of real values, integer values, variable identifiers, operators, functions, and parentheses. The exact syntax is specified in Appendix A. However, your experience from mathematics is probably sufficient to recognize an illegal expression.

Example 4.19   The following examples are valid expressions, assuming that a and b are real variables, and i and j are integer variables.

a * (b + 4.7)   2 * (3 + 4 * (i + 1))
2.1   -3.4 * Math.Sin(ABS(b))
j   Math.Cos(Math.Pi() / 4.0)   ∎

Example 4.20   An example of an illegal expression is

a * ((b + 4.7)

because one of the left parentheses does not have a matching right parenthesis.   ∎

Character variables

Component Pascal has several types that are not numeric, one of which is CHAR. CHAR stands for character. A variable that has type CHAR can have a value that is a single letter or punctuation mark or digit, not limited to the English alphabet. The possible values include characters from most of the languages in the world, as specified by the Unicode character standard. The character values are the ones that are printed on the keycaps of the keyboard. Example of character values are: R, r, E, e, $, and 4. In a Component Pascal program listing, character values are enclosed in single quote or double quote marks.

Example 4.21   You could declare the following variables in a procedure

char1, char2, char3: CHAR;

A valid sequence of assignment statements would then be

char1 := 'b'; char2 := 'u'; char3 := 't'

The following output statements

StdLog.Char(char3); StdLog.Char(char2); StdLog.Char(char1)

would then produce the output

tub

on the Log.

The decimal digits are included in the Unicode character set. There is a difference between the character '4' and the integer 4.

Example 4.22 In the previous example, the assignment statement

char1 := '4'

would be legal, but the assignment statement char1 := 4 would not, because char1 has type CHAR and 4 has type INTEGER.

It is occasionally useful to process characters with the arithmetic operators. Because the arithmetic operators cannot operate on characters directly, Component Pascal provides a means for transforming between characters and integers. To perform an arithmetic operation on a character, you first convert it to an integer, then perform the operation on the integer, then convert the integer back to a character. The transformation between characters and integers is based on the fact that each character has a place on the integer number line. Figure 4.11 shows the characters below the number line with their associated integer values above the line.

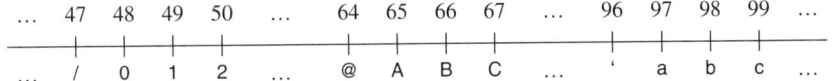

Figure 4.11
The number line for some of the character values.

The integer above a character is called its ordinal value. For example, the ordinal value of the character 'B' is 66, and the ordinal value of the character '1' is 49. The two functions that Component Pascal provides for converting between characters and integers are ORD and CHR. ORD takes a character for its actual parameter and returns its corresponding ordinal value. CHR takes an integer for its actual parameter and returns the corresponding character.

Example 4.23 Suppose myCh is a variable that has type character and myInt is a variable that has type integer. You want to change myCh to have the value of the next letter in the alphabet. This operation corresponds to adding 1 to the character, but

Component Pascal does not permit addition on characters. The following statements perform the conversion using ORD and CHR:

```
myInt := ORD(myCh);
INC(myInt);
myCh := CHR(myInt)
```

A more economical way to do the same thing is to dispense with the integer variable altogether and write the single statement

```
myCh := CHR(ORD(myCh) + 1)
```

In either case, if myCh has the value S before execution it will have the value T after execution.
∎

The PboxStrings module

The BlackBox framework provides a module called Strings that has several procedures for operating on characters. Some of the procedures in Strings, however, are difficult for beginning programmers to use. Consequently, this author has written a module called PboxStrings that contains procedures similar to those contained in Strings. The procedures are easier to use than those in Strings and are designed as an aid to presenting the material in this book. The PboxStrings module is contained in the Pbox project folder, which is not part of the standard BlackBox distribution. Your instructor can give you a copy of the Pbox modules, or you can obtain them from the author over the Internet. The URL for the World Wide Web site is

`ftp://ftp.pepperdine.edu/pub/compsci/prog-bbox/` *The URL for the Pbox project*

Note that this URL begins with `ftp://` and not the usual `http://`. The site contains not only the Pbox project folder, but also the source code for every program in this book. You should be aware that any software you develop with the Pbox modules will not be usable on a computer that does not have the Pbox project installed.

Figure 4.12 is the interface for PboxStrings. It includes function Lower, which converts a character to lowercase, and Upper, which converts to uppercase.

```
DEFINITION PboxStrings;

    PROCEDURE Lower (ch: CHAR): CHAR;
    PROCEDURE Upper (ch: CHAR): CHAR;
    PROCEDURE ToLower (from: ARRAY OF CHAR; OUT to: ARRAY OF CHAR);
    PROCEDURE ToUpper (from: ARRAY OF CHAR; OUT to: ARRAY OF CHAR);
    PROCEDURE IntToString (n, minWidth: INTEGER; OUT s: ARRAY OF CHAR);
    PROCEDURE RealToString (x: REAL; minWidth, dec: INTEGER; OUT s: ARRAY OF CHAR);

END PboxStrings.
```

Figure 4.12
The interface for PboxStrings.

Example 4.24 If myCh is a variable that has type character and value 'B', then the statement

myCh := PboxStrings.Lower(myCh)

changes its value to 'b'. If the same variable has a lowercase value, say 'h', before execution of the statement, its value will not be changed when the statement executes. ∎

Character arrays

Characters are more useful when you string them together to form words and sentences. In Component Pascal, you can string values together with a construction called an *array*. An array is simply a collection of values, all of which must have the same type. A character array can have a value that is a string. Figure 4.13 is an example of a procedure that declares variable message to have type character array. Procedure PrintString prints the text What's up, Doc? to the Log.

An array is a collection of values, all with the same type.

```
MODULE Pbox04F;
   IMPORT StdLog;

   PROCEDURE PrintString*;
   VAR
      message: ARRAY 128 OF CHAR;
   BEGIN
      message := "What's up, Doc?";
      StdLog.String(message); StdLog.Ln
   END PrintString;

END Pbox04F.
```

Figure 4.13
A procedure that declares a variable with string type.

The individual characters that form a string are stored consecutively in the memory of the computer. A special character, written 0X in Component Pascal, is also stored after the last character to serve as a marker for the end of the string. When procedure PrintString declares the variable message to be an array of 128 characters, it is declaring that the string value of message can have as many as 127 characters, because one spot in the array must contain the last 0X character. Figure 4.14 shows how the characters in variable message are stored.

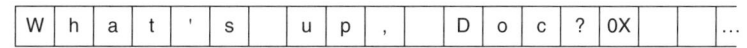

Figure 4.14
Storage of a string value in an array of characters.

When you declare a variable to be an array of characters you must decide how many characters to allocate. The size of the array should be a bit larger than the longest string you would expect to store in the variable. If you make all your arrays excessively large you will be wasting memory. For example, if the array is to store the last name of a person, 128 characters would be way too many. Perhaps 32 would be more reasonable, because few people have last names with more than 31 characters.

The procedure StdLog.String can take as its actual parameter a variable of type character array as well as a string. In Figure 3.6 the actual parameter of Std-Log.String is the string "Mr. K. Kong", but in Figure 4.13 the actual parameter of Std-Log.String is the variable message that has type character array.

Chapter 2 introduced the concatenation operation on strings of letters. Component Pascal uses the + symbol for concatenation when it is placed between strings or character arrays. Figure 4.15 shows a procedure whose output is identical to that of the procedure in Figure 4.4. It uses the + symbol to concatenate several strings.

The + symbol for concatenation

```
MODULE Pbox04G;
   IMPORT StdLog, PboxStrings;

   PROCEDURE Change*;
   VAR
      cents: INTEGER;
      centString: ARRAY 16 OF CHAR;
      message: ARRAY 64 OF CHAR;
   BEGIN
      cents := 39;
      PboxStrings.IntToString(cents, 1, centString);
      message := "You have " + centString + " cents in change.";
      StdLog.String(message); StdLog.Ln
   END Change;

END Pbox04G.
```

Figure 4.15
A procedure that uses the + operator to concatenate strings. It imports the PboxStrings module.

Figure 4.12 shows the interface for PboxStrings. Proper procedure IntToString has three formal parameters—n, minWidth, and s. Notice that s is preceded by the reserved word OUT. A formal parameter preceded by OUT is designed to change the value of its actual parameter. In this program, the actual parameter is centString. Procedure IntToString will change the value of centString when it executes.

The meaning of OUT in a formal parameter list

Here is how the program works. The variable declaration in procedure Change of Figure 4.15 declares cents to have type INTEGER. During execution, the first assignment statement gives the value 39 to cents. Then the IntToString statement makes a string image of the value. The second parameter in an IntToString call specifies the minimum field width. This IntToString call specifies a minimum field width of one because the value displayed on the Log will appear in the middle of a sentence. Because the field width will expand, if necessary, to fit all the digits into the display, this technique guarantees proper spacing within the sentence. Figure 4.16 shows the value of centString after the call to IntToString is completed.

The next statement concatenates the string "You have " with the value of cent-String, then concatenates that with the string " cents in change.", and assigns the result to the character array message. Finally, StdLog.String prints the value of mes-

| 3 | 9 | 0X | | | | | | | | | | | | | | |

Figure 4.16
The value of centString.

sage to the Log.

Suppose you specify a field width of 2, anticipating that the value of the variable will require exactly two digits to display. If the value is 39, as in Figure 4.15, the output will be unchanged. But if the value is 8 instead of 39 and you still specify a field width of 2, the output would be

You have   8 cents in change.

with an extra space before the 8. If you specify a field width of 1, the spacing will always be correct in the sentence regardless of how many digits are required to display the value.

Procedure RealToString works like IntToString except that it has four parameters instead of three—x, minWidth, dec, and s. x is the real value for which you want the string display. minWidth and s are the minimum field width and the resulting string as with procedure IntToString. dec allows you to specify how many places past the decimal point you want to include. RealToString rounds off fractional values as you would expect.

Example 4.25 Suppose amtOwed is a variable that has type real and value 84.376. It represents a dollar amount, and you want to display the value to the nearest cent, which is two places past the decimal point. Assuming that message and dollarString are arrays of characters, the following statements

```
PboxStrings.RealToString(amtOwed, 1, 2, dollarString);
message := "You owe " + dollarString + " dollars.";
StdLog.String(message); StdLog.Ln
```

will produce

You owe 84.38 dollars.

on the Log.   ∎

It is sometimes necessary to assign one character array that has a string value to another character array. Component Pascal executes the assignment by copying every value in the array regardless of the number of characters in the string.

Example 4.26 Suppose myString and yourString are both declared as follows.

```
VAR
    myString, yourString: ARRAY 16 OF CHAR;
```

If myString has previously been given the value "Short", then the assignment statement

yourString := myString

makes 16 copies as shown in Figure 4.17(a), even though the string has only five characters. ∎

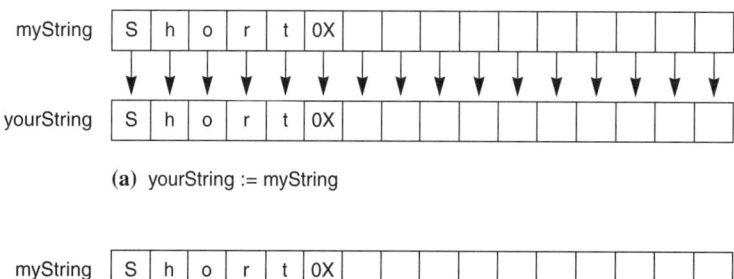

myString | yourString

(a) yourString := myString

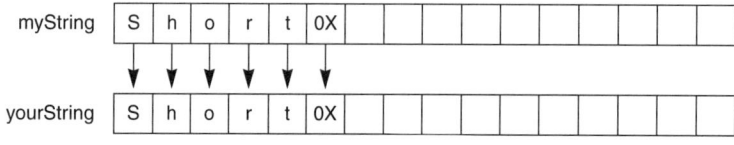

(b) yourString := myString$

Figure 4.17
Character array assignments.

The problem of unnecessary character copies occurs because you must allocate more memory than is required by most of the string values stored in the array. Component Pascal provides a $ selector that you can use to eliminate the unnecessary character copies during array assignment. Appending the $ selector to the name of a character array changes its designation to include only the characters from the first position up to and including the 0X.

The $ selector

Example 4.27 With myString and yourString declared as in Example 4.26, the name myString$ designates the five characters "Short" plus the 0X character. The assignment

yourString := myString$

makes only six copies as shown in Figure 4.17(b). ∎

★ Guarded command language

The starred sections of this book are for those who have studied, or are currently studying, formal methods. Formal methods are the mathematical foundation of most programming languages, including Component Pascal and are increasingly important in the field of software engineering. If you have not yet learned formal methods you may omit these sections.

The goal of the starred sections is to show the application of formal methods to computing practice with Component Pascal. The goal is not to teach principles of

The purpose of GCL

formal methods, which is outside the scope of this book. A common language used to analyze algorithms with formal methods is the guarded command language, which this book abbreviates as GCL. This section introduces GCL and shows the relationship between GCL and Component Pascal (CP).

One difference between GCL and CP are the goals and intended use of each language. The goal of GCL is to provide a convenient mathematical notation for proving the correctness of programs. It is typically used by hand with pencil and paper. The notation is, therefore, short and succinct to minimize the amount of handwriting. Variable names are purposely kept short, typically only one letter long. Such a practice is preferred in GCL but discouraged in CP where the services of a document editor permit longer, more descriptive names to be used with ease to enhance readability.

GCL does not require a separate VAR section to declare the type of a variable. Instead, you simply write the variable followed by a colon, followed by the symbol for its type from Figure 4.18.

CP	GCL
INTEGER	$\mathbb{Z}$
REAL	$\mathbb{R}$

Figure 4.18
Specifying type in GCL.

Example 4.28 A CP program that contains the variable section

```
VAR
    cents: INTEGER;
    dollarAmount: REAL;
```

would be written in GCL as

c: $\mathbb{Z}$
d: $\mathbb{R}$

where the single variable name c is used in place of the longer, more descriptive name cents and similarly with d for dollarAmount. ∎

Fortunately, the assignment statement := is the same in both CP and GCL. The state of a computation is a list of the variables and their values. The effect of an assignment statement is to change the state of the computation by changing the values.

Assignment in GCL

Example 4.29 With the variables declared as in Example 4.28, suppose the state of the computation is $(c, 47), (d, 89.60)$. The assignment statement to add 5% to dollarAmount in CP

```
dollarAmount := dollarAmount * 1.05
```

is written

$d := d * 1.05$

in GCL and changes the state to $(c, 47), (d, 94.08)$. ∎

In GCL, you can combine the type information for a variable with any expression. This technique saves a little extra writing.

Example 4.30 The type declaration of Example 4.28 could be combined with the assignment statement of Example 4.29 as

$d: \mathbb{R} := d * 1.05$

Alternatively, the type information could be combined with the initial state as

$(c: \mathbb{Z}, 47), (d: \mathbb{R}, 89.60)$ ∎

As in CP, the semicolon in GCL represents a sequence of statements. That is, the statements are executed in order not simultaneously.

Example 4.31 The assignment statements from Figure 4.7 are written in GCL as

$d := c$ div $10; c := c$ mod $10; n := c$ div $5; p := c$ mod 5 ∎

Multiple assignment

In addition to sequencing statements with the semicolon symbol, you can perform multiple assignments in GCL, a feature that is not available in CP. With multiple assignments, the values are changed simultaneously. To translate between multiple assignments in GCL and sequential assignments in CP you can sometimes simply make the multiple assignments sequential and the computations will be equivalent. However, if the first assignment in a sequence changes the value of a variable that is in turn used in an expression on the right side of a later assignment, the translation will be incorrect. In such a case, you will need to resort to a temporary variable in the sequential version.

Example 4.32 The multiple assignment in GCL

$c, n := c$ mod $10, c$ div 5

is not equivalent to the CP sequence

```
cents := cents MOD 10;
nickels := cents DIV 5
```

If the initial state is $(c, 39), (n, ?)$, then the final state after the multiple assignment will be $(c, 9), (n, 7)$, because 39 div 5 is 7. However, the final state after the sequential assignment will be $(c, 9), (n, 1)$, because 9 div 5 is 1. On the other hand, the multiple assignment

$d, c := c$ div $10, c$ mod 10

is equivalent to

```
dimes := cents DIV 10;
cents := cents MOD 10
```
∎

Example 4.33 If you want to exchange the values of x and y in GCL you can simply write the multiple assignment

$x, y := y, x$

which, for example, would change the state $(x, 3), (y, 14)$ to $(x, 14), (y, 3)$. However, the corresponding sequence in CP

x := y; y := x

would change the state $(x, 3), (y, 14)$ to $(x, 14), (y, 14)$, because the modified value of x is assigned to y instead of the original value of x. To exchange the values requires a temporary variable, say t, to store the original value of x so that it can be assigned to y.

t := x; x := y; y := t   ■

Exercises

1. Inspect the interface of module TextViews on-line in BlackBox using the technique of Figure 3.3, and answer the following questions about the procedures that are listed in it.

   (a) How many modules are listed in the IMPORT list of TextViews?
   (b) State whether each of the following is a proper procedure or a function procedure: Deposit, Focus, ShowRange, ThisRuler.
   (c) How many parameters does ShowRange have? What are their names?
   (d) How many parameters does ThisRuler have? What is the type of its returned value?

2. Evaluate the following expressions. Indicate real results in your answer with a decimal point and integer results by not including a decimal point. If the expression is illegal, explain why.

(a) 5.0 / 2.0	**(b)** 5 / 2	**(c)** 5 DIV 2
(d) 5.0 DIV 2.0	**(e)** 5 MOD 2	**(f)** 5.0 MOD 2
(g) ENTIER(8.3)	**(h)** ENTIER(8.7)	**(i)** ABS(-6.8)
(j) ABS(6)	**(k)** Math.IntPower(3.0, 2)	**(l)** Math.IntPower(3.0, 2.0)
(m) Math.Sqrt(16.0)	**(n)** Math.Sqrt(16)	**(o)** Math.Sin(0.0)
(p) Math.Exp(1.0)	**(q)** Math.Ln(Math.Exp(4.7))	

3. Evaluate the following expressions. Indicate real results in your answer with a decimal point and integer results by not including a decimal point. If the expression is illegal, explain why.

(**a**) 7.0 / 3.0   (**b**) 7 / 3   (**c**) 7 DIV 3

(**d**) 7.0 DIV 3.0   (**e**) 7 MOD 3   (**f**) 7.0 MOD 3

(**g**) ENTIER(7.3)   (**h**) ENTIER(7.9)   (**i**) ABS(-4.8)

(**j**) ABS(4)   (**k**) Math.IntPower(4.0, 2)   (**l**) Math.IntPower(4.0, 2.0)

(**m**) Math.Sqrt(9.0)   (**n**) Math.Sqrt(9)   (**o**) Math.Sin(0.0)

(**p**) Math.Exp(1.0)   (**q**) Math.Ln(Math.Exp(5.1))

4. Evaluate the following expressions. Indicate a character result in your answer by enclosing it in quotes. If the expression is illegal, explain why.

(**a**) ORD('b')   (**b**) CHR(50)   (**c**) @ + 1

(**d**) '@' + 1   (**e**) ORD('@' + 1)   (**f**) ORD(@) + 1

(**g**) ORD('@') + 1   (**h**) CHR(ORD('@') + 1)   (**i**) 'a' - 'A'

(**j**) CHR(ORD('D') + ORD('a') - ORD('A'))

5. Evaluate the following expressions. Indicate a character result in your answer by enclosing it in quotes. If the expression is illegal, explain why.

(**a**) ORD('B')   (**b**) CHR(49)   (**c**) / + 1

(**d**) '/' + 1   (**e**) ORD('/' + 1)   (**f**) ORD(/) + 1

(**g**) ORD('/') + 1   (**h**) CHR(ORD('/') + 1)   (**i**) 'a' - 'A'

(**j**) CHR(ORD('E') + ORD('a') - ORD('A'))

6. i and j are integer variables, and x is a real variable. Determine the values of each of the variables after the sequence of assignments statements executes. Indicate real values with a decimal point and integer values by not including a decimal point.

(**a**)	(**b**)	(**c**)
i := 18;	j := 14;	i := 3;
j := i DIV 7;	i := j MOD 5;	j := 18;
x := 4.5;	x := 2.7;	x := 7.9;
INC(i);	INC(j);	i := j;
x := x + i * 2	x := x + j * 2	j := i

7. Write the mathematical relation between DIV and MOD, including the inequality, for dividend 27 and divisor 6.

8. In Example 4.17, (**a**) is x a formal parameter or is it an actual parameter? (**b**) is 2.4 a formal parameter or is it an actual parameter?

9. If myMessage and yourMessage are both declared to be ARRAY 128 OF CHAR, and myMessage has the string value "Look out!", (**a**) how many characters are copied with the assignment yourMessage := myMessage? (**b**) How many with the assignment yourMessage := myMessage$?

10. Write the equivalent CP program statements for the following GCL statements. For each part, write the final state if the initial state is $(x, 1), (y, 2), (z, 3)$.

(**a**) $x, y := x + z, y * x$
(**b**) $x, y, z := x + z, y + x, z + y$
(**c**) $x, y, z := y + 4, y + x, z + y$

Problems

11. Write a procedure with integer variable feet and real variables inches and meters. Assign feet and inches values and compute the equivalent length in meters. One inch is exactly 0.0254 meters and one foot is exactly 12 inches. Use StdLog.Int and StdLog.Real to output the values identified appropriately. Here is a sample output to the Log.

Feet: 4
Inches: 3.8
Meters: 1.31572

12. Work Problem 11, but display the computed value for meters to two places past the decimal. Use StdLog.Int and StdLog.Real for feet and inches and PboxStrings.RealToString with a character array variable for meters.

13. Write a procedure with two real variables for the temperature in Fahrenheit and Celsius. Assign a value to the variable for Fahrenheit and compute the equivalent temperature in Celsius. Show both temperatures on the Log with their values identified appropriately as the values are in Problem 11.

14. Work Problem 13, but display the computed value for Celsius to one place past the decimal. Use StdLog.Real for the Fahrenheit value and PboxStrings.RealToString with a string variable for the Celsius value.

15. Write a procedure with two real variables for the lengths of two perpendicular sides of a right triangle and a third variable for the length of the hypotenuse. Assign values to the variables for the sides and compute the value for the hypotenuse. Show all three lengths on the Log with their values identified appropriately as the values are in Problem 11.

16. Work Problem 15, but display the computed value for the hypotenuse to one place past the decimal. Use StdLog.Real for the side values and PboxStrings.RealToString with a string variable for the hypotenuse value.

17. Write a procedure with a real variable for the radius of a circle and two additional real variables for its circumference and area. Assign values to the variables for the radius and compute the values for the circumference. Import the value of π from module Math for your computations. Show all three measures on the Log with their values identified appropriately as the values are in Problem 11.

18. Work Problem 17, but display the computed values for the circumference and area to one place past the decimal. Use StdLog.Real for the radius value and PboxStrings.RealToString with a string variable for the circumference and radius values.

19. Modify the program in Figure 4.7 to make change for quarters as well as dimes, nickels, and pennies. (A quarter is a 25-cent coin.)

20. Write a procedure with three integer variables for the number of hours, days, and weeks. Assign a value to the variable for hours and compute the equivalent number of days, weeks, and hours. Show all time measures on the Log with their values identified appropriately as the values are in Problem 11. For example, if the variable for hours is assigned 4123, the output should be

Total hours: 4123
Number of weeks: 24
Number of days: 3
Number of hours: 19

Chapter *5*

Dialog Boxes

In a graphical user interface, the user typically decides what action to execute by selecting an option from a list of menu items at the top of the screen. If the action to be performed requires a data value to be processed, the user is prompted to enter the data value by entering it in a dialog box. Menu items and dialog boxes are the predominant GUI methods for interacting with human users. This chapter shows how to construct dialog boxes that manage the input, execution, and output of the program. The dialog boxes in this chapter are activated by the commander button. Later chapters will describe how to install menu items, which, when selected by the user, can initiate procedures or activate dialog boxes.

Numeric input from a dialog box

This section shows how to link elements in a Component Pascal module with a dialog box. The dialog box allows the user to input a value in a rectangular input area called a field. A button will be provided in the dialog box, which will cause an exported procedure to be executed when pressed.

The process of programming a dialog box requires the following steps:

- Decide which elements belong in the dialog box.

- For each input/output element, determine the type of the corresponding variable.

- For each button, determine what processing must be performed.

- Write a module with each of the variables and procedures exported. Compile the module.

- Select Controls→New Form… and link the module to the dialog box.

- Fine tune the layout of the elements of the form.

- Write a Docu document with a commander to activate and test the dialog box.

The design process for programming with dialog

These steps will be illustrated by an example similar to the module in Figure 4.7 in the previous chapter. Procedure MakeChange in that program assigns the value 39 to the variable cents, then computes the corresponding number of dimes, nickels, and pennies, which it displays on the Log. Such a program is not too useful because the same output is produced every time it executes. To get the number of coins for a different value of cents you would have to modify the source program by changing 39 to whatever value you want, recompile the program, then execute it again.

It would be much better if you could present the user with a dialog box in which she could enter the number of cents in change. Figure 5.1 shows the desired dialog box for the user. The rectangular box, called a text field, is the input area. The user enters the number of cents in change into the box then clicks the button labeled Compute. Clicking the button with the mouse causes the program to print the number of dimes, nickels, and pennies onto the Log.

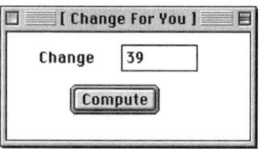

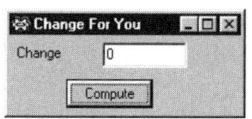

(a) MacOS.   (b) MSWindows.

Figure 5.1
The dialog box for inputting an integer value shown in mask mode.

In this problem, we want three elements in the dialog box—the label Change that identifies the text field, the text field for the user input, and the button that causes the computation to commence. The next step in the design process is to write a program that contains variables and procedures that correspond to the elements of the desired dialog box. In the dialog box of Figure 5.1, the label Change and the input text field correspond to a single element of type INTEGER. It is an integer element because the user should not enter a value with a decimal point. The button labeled Compute corresponds to a procedure.

The module in Figure 5.2 illustrates the next step in the design process. It is a program containing an exported variable named change that corresponds to the label Change and the input text field, and an exported procedure named MakeChange that corresponds to the button labeled Compute. Later in the design process, we will link the variable change to the text field of the dialog box. When the user enters an integer in the text field of the dialog box, the BlackBox framework automatically assigns that integer value to change. We will also link the procedure MakeChange to the button labeled Compute in Figure 5.1. When the user clicks the button with the mouse, MakeChange will execute.

Variable change is located within module Pbox05A but outside procedure Make-Change, unlike variable cents, which is located within procedure MakeChange. Variables that are located within a module and not within a procedure are called *global* variables, in contrast to those that are within a procedure, which are called *local* variables. Variable cents is local to procedure MakeChange, while variable change is global.

Global and local variables

In Component Pascal, variables that correspond to elements of a dialog box must be global. An attempt to export cents will cause the compiler to protest with the error message, Illegally marked identifier. The reason for the restriction on the exporting of variables is that local variables exist only during execution of their procedures, while global variables exist as long as their modules are *loaded* into main memory. When the dialog box of Figure 5.1 is activated, the framework loads the module linked to it into main memory. When the user enters a value, and before she clicks the Compute button, change gets the value she enters. At this point in time, variable cents does not even exist, because procedure MakeChange is not executing.

Loading modules into main memory

It is only when the user clicks the Compute button triggering the execution of MakeChange that variables cents, dimes, nickels, and pennies come into existence.

```
MODULE Pbox05A;
   IMPORT StdLog;

   VAR
      change*: INTEGER;

   PROCEDURE MakeChange*;
      VAR
         cents: INTEGER;
         dimes, nickels, pennies: INTEGER;
   BEGIN
      cents := change;
      dimes := cents DIV 10;
      cents := cents MOD 10;
      nickels := cents DIV 5;
      pennies := cents MOD 5;
      StdLog.String("You have "); StdLog.Int( change);
      StdLog.String(" cents in change."); StdLog.Ln;
      StdLog.String("Dimes: "); StdLog.Int(dimes); StdLog.Ln;
      StdLog.String("Nickels: "); StdLog.Int(nickels); StdLog.Ln;
      StdLog.String("Pennies: "); StdLog.Int(pennies); StdLog.Ln
   END MakeChange;

BEGIN
   change := 0
END Pbox05A.
```

Figure 5.2

A module for constructing a dialog box to input an integer value.

Module Pbox05A has an initialization part with an assignment statement

change := 0

This statement belongs to the module and is not part of a procedure. The question naturally arises, When does this statement execute? Until now, all executable statements belonged to procedures, and an exported procedure began execution in response to the click of a commander by the user. Such is not the case with the statements in the initialization part of a module. Instead, they are executed once when the module is loaded from disk into main memory. Figure 5.3 illustrates the loading process for this program.

Before a procedure can execute, the entire module in which it is contained must be placed in the main memory of the computer. Figure 5.3(a) shows the situation after the source program has been written and compiled. The compiler creates the object program, which it stores on disk in the Code folder, and the interface, which it stores on the disk in the Sym folder. When the user first activates the dialog box linked to a module, the framework loads the object program for the module into main memory. Figure 5.3(b) shows the loading into main memory that must take

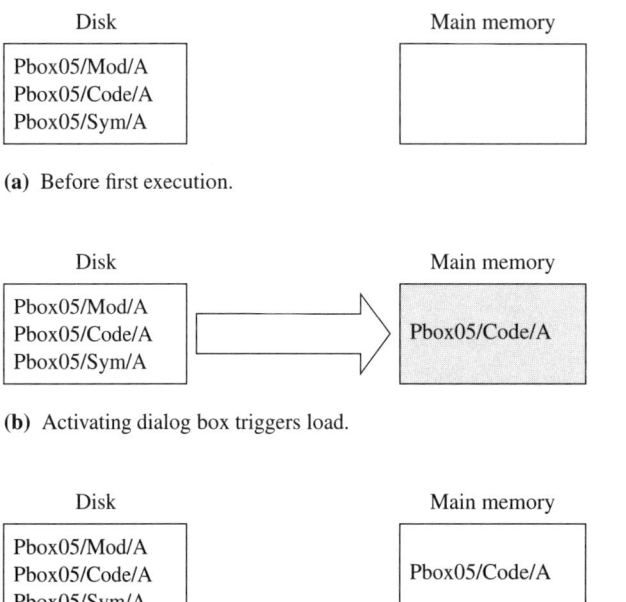

Figure 5.3
Dynamic loading in the
BlackBox framework.

Disk

Pbox05/Mod/A
Pbox05/Code/A
Pbox05/Sym/A

Main memory

(a) Before first execution.

Disk

Pbox05/Mod/A
Pbox05/Code/A
Pbox05/Sym/A

Main memory

Pbox05/Code/A

(b) Activating dialog box triggers load.

Disk

Pbox05/Mod/A
Pbox05/Code/A
Pbox05/Sym/A

Main memory

Pbox05/Code/A

(c) Subsequent executions do not require load.

place before the first execution of any procedure. Subsequent executions of the procedure do not require loading, as shown in Figure 5.3(c).

The statement in the initialization part of the module is executed once when the module is loaded and before any procedures in the module are executed. The statement

change := 0

assigns zero to change so it will have a default value when the dialog box is displayed for the first time

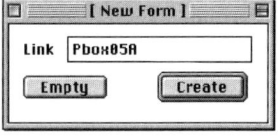

Figure 5.4
The result of selecting
Controls→New Form... .

(a) MacOS.

(b) MSWindows.

The fourth step in the design process is to select Controls→New Form…, which you should attempt only after you get your program compiled. A dialog box will appear as shown in Figure 5.4. It asks the programmer for a link to the desired dialog box. In this example, the programmer entered Pbox05A. If you have not compiled your program, the framework will have no object file with the information it needs to make the link to the exported record. After you enter the link, click the Create button to create the dialog box for the program.

Figure 5.5 shows the box as it appears in layout mode when it is created by selecting Controls→New Form... . Layout mode is for constructing a dialog box instead of using it. For example, if the dialog box is in mask mode, as it is in Figure 5.1, and you click the button then the procedure that the button is linked to will execute. But if the dialog box is in layout mode and you click the button then the button is simply selected and can be repositioned or resized by dragging it with the mouse. You can distinguish visually between the modes by the background grid that appears in layout mode but is absent in mask mode.

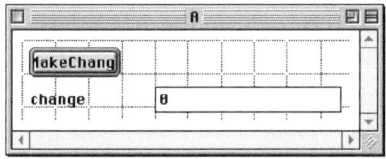

(a) MacOS.

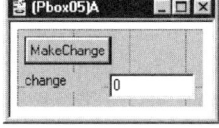

(b) MSWindows.

Figure 5.5
The dialog box shown in layout mode.

When you select Controls→New Form... and click the Create button the Black-Box framework inspects the interface of the module to which the new dialog box is linked. It inserts objects into the dialog box based on the types of the items exported by the module. The objects in a dialog box are called controls, because they allow the user to control the action of the computer by interacting with them via the mouse and keyboard. In this example, the framework inspected two exported items and as a result inserted three controls into the dialog box. The exported variable, change of type INTEGER, caused the framework to insert two controls—a caption control that appears as the word change in the dialog box of Figure 5.5, and a text field control that appears as the rectangular input area. The exported procedure MakeChange caused the framework to insert one control—a command button that appears at the top of the dialog box.

A new dialog box created by the framework is not usually suitable for immediate use. In this example, you would need to spruce up the appearance by capitalizing the c in change for the caption control and changing the wording in the command button control. In layout mode the attributes of a control are inspected and changed by selecting the control then choosing Edit→Part Info... (Macintosh) or Edit→Object Properties... (Windows) from the menu. Figure 5.6 shows the resulting dialog box, called the Inspector, when the caption control is selected.

The five primary attributes of a control as displayed in Figure 5.6 are (a) the control type, (b) how the control is linked, (c) the label for the control, (d) the guard for the control, and (e) the notifier for the control. The figure shows that (a) the type of the control is caption, (b) the control is linked to Pbox05A.change, (c) the control's label is change, (d) there is no guard, and (e) there is no notifier. The label of the caption is what appears to the user. To spruce up this control you would capitalize c

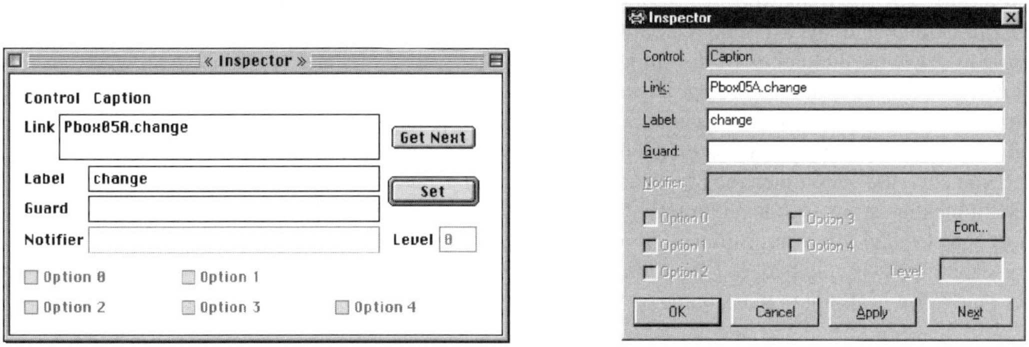

(a) MacOS.

(b) MSWindows.

Figure 5.6
The dialog box for editing a
control's attributes.

in change in the label field and click the Set button to set the change. Because the
purpose of a caption control is to simply display the label in the dialog box, the link
field of a caption control serves no apparent purpose. You could eliminate the link
field in this caption control with no adverse affect on your program.

A similar inspection of the attributes of the rectangular input area shows that it is
of type text field, it is linked to Pbox05A.change, and it has no label, guard, or notifier. With this control, the link is crucial. When the user enters text into the rectangular input area and clicks the compute button the framework recognizes the link
between the dialog box and the exported variable. It converts the text value entered
by the user into an integer value, which it gives to the integer change. The label
attribute does not apply to a text field control.

The push button, which is a command button control, uses both the link and the
label attributes. The link specifies the procedure to be executed when the button is
pressed and the label specifies the text to be displayed on the face of the button. To
spruce up this control you would change the label to Compute.

Another way of sprucing up the box when it is in layout mode is to use the commands of the Layout menu, which permit you to align the controls in various ways.
Normally, a dialog box cannot be resized when it is in mask mode and the user is
entering data. In layout mode you can resize the window that contains the dialog
box, but the size of the window in layout mode does not affect the size of the dialog
box. To change the size of the dialog box you must be in layout mode and choose
Edit→Select Document. The entire dialog box is then selected with handles for
resizing with the mouse.

When you have finished sprucing up your dialog select File→Save As... to save
it. Dialog forms should always be saved in layout mode. You must save it in the Rsrc
folder of your project. Rsrc stands for resource, and the folder contains various programming resources for a project. As an example, the dialog box of Figure 5.5 was
saved with name DlgA in the Rsrc folder that was itself in the project folder named
Pbox05. Dialog boxes are stored as standard BlackBox compound documents. If
you ever want to modify the dialog box simply open the document as you would any
other file and edit it. And when you save it, be sure that it is in layout mode.

The last step in the design process is to create documentation, which is stored in

*Always save dialog forms in
layout mode.*

the Docu folder as usual. The commander should be followed by a procedure from the StdCmds module instead of a procedure from your module. Figure 5.7 shows the documentation for this program.

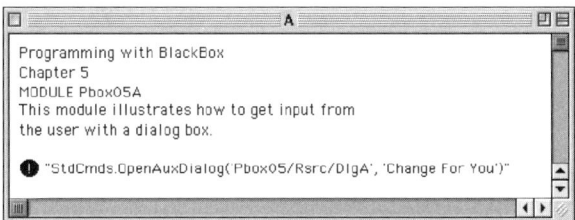

Figure 5.7
The documentation for the module in Listing 5.2

In this example the commander was followed with the string

"StdCmds.OpenAuxDialog('Pbox05/Rsrc/DlgA', 'Change For You')"

The StdCmds module contains the procedure OpenAuxDialog, whose purpose is to open a dialog box in mask mode. It requires two parameters, each of which is a string. The first parameter 'Pbox05/Rsrc/DlgA' specifies the file that is to be opened, and the second parameter 'Change For You' specifies the title to appear in the title bar of the dialog box. Figure 5.1 shows this title.

Numeric output to a dialog box

The previous example showed how to input an integer value into a dialog box. The output was sent to the Log. The Log is for development and debugging. A commercial application would not use the Log for output. It is more common for the results of a computation to be shown in a dialog box or in some other document such as a spreadsheet document or a word processing document. Figure 5.8 shows a dialog box that displays the output from the computation.

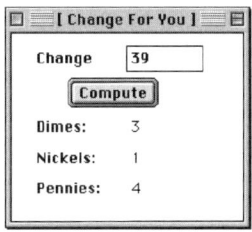

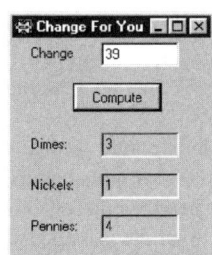

(a) MacOS.   **(b)** MSWindows.

Figure 5.8
A dialog box that displays output as well as input.

The dialog box in Figure 5.8 is a bit more complex than the one in Figure 5.1. It has nine controls, eight of which are linked to four variables and one of which is linked to a procedure. Figure 5.9 shows the corresponding module.

```
MODULE Pbox05B;
   IMPORT Dialog;

   VAR
      d*: RECORD
         change*: INTEGER;
         dimes-, nickels-, pennies-: INTEGER
      END;

   PROCEDURE MakeChange*;
      VAR
         cents: INTEGER;
   BEGIN
      cents := d.change;
      d.dimes := cents DIV 10;
      cents := cents MOD 10;
      d.nickels := cents DIV 5;
      d.pennies := cents MOD 5;
      Dialog.Update(d)
   END MakeChange;

BEGIN
   d.change := 0;
   d.dimes := 0; d.nickels := 0; d.pennies := 0
END Pbox05B.
```

Figure 5.9
Sending output to a dialog box.

Records

It would be possible for the module in Figure 5.9 to declare four global variables using the same technique as does the previous module. However, when more than one variable is to be linked to a dialog, the preferred programming style is to group them together in a record. A *record* is similar to an array in that both are collections of values. They are different in that the collection of values in an array must all have the same type. For example, variable message in Figure 4.13 is an array of characters. Every element of the array must be a character because that is a property of arrays.

A record is a collection of values, which need not have the same type.

The module in Figure 5.9 has a single exported record named d for dialog box. As is the case for all records, the type of this variable begins with the reserved word RECORD and ends with the word END. Between these words is a collection of four *fields*, each with a name and a type. The first field is named change, has type integer, and is exported with the familiar asterisk * export mark. The next three fields are named dimes, nickels, and pennies, also have type integer, but have a different kind of export mark. The hyphen - indicates *read-only export* and is for displaying values in a dialog box that the user is not allowed to change. You can see from the dialog

The fields of a record

Read-only export

box in Figure 5.8 that the user enters a value for Change and the computer calculates the proper number of dimes. Because the user does not enter a value for dimes, field dimes is exported read only. Note that export marks are required for both the variable d and its fields. To emphasize the difference between exporting with * and with -, exporting with * is called *read/write export*.

Read/write export

You refer to a field in a record in the same way that you refer to a procedure in a module. Namely, you write the name of the record followed by a period followed by the name of the field in the record. For example, you refer to field change in record d by writing d.change. Records are used to group values other than those for dialog boxes. When used for values in a dialog box, the record is known as an interactor, because of its role in the interaction between the user and the program.

Referencing a field in a record

An interactor is a record linked to a dialog box.

As before, the button labeled Compute is linked to MakeChange. In this program, procedure MakeChange computes the coins for the change and assigns those values to d.dimes, d.nickels, and d.pennies. However, simply changing the value of an interactor's field does not automatically transmit that change to the visual appearance of an open dialog box on the screen. Procedure Dialog.Update has the ability to transmit the change to the screen. It is only when Dialog.Update(d) executes that the changes to the values of d.dimes, d.nickels, and d.pennies are displayed in the dialog box.

Figure 5.10 shows the initial dialog box in layout mode when Controls→New Form… is selected and linked to Pbox05B. When you group variables together into a record the BlackBox forms creator inserts a control element called a group box that surrounds the elements. The default value for the label of the group box is the name of the record, which is d in the figure. Because a group box was not desired in the final dialog box it was simply deleted while in layout mode. If you want a group box in your dialog box you can use the Inspector to change the text that appears to the user. You can also resize the box, and move the controls around to include or exclude any controls you wish.

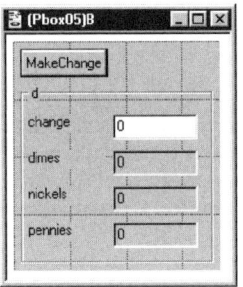

(a) MacOS. **(b)** MSWindows.

Figure 5.10
The default form produced by the forms creator for the module of Figure 5.9.

You should experiment with the Layout menu options, which provide many useful tools for creating precisely positioned elements. For example, if you highlight several controls and select Layout→Align Left all the controls you highlighted will shift horizontally to the left until their left sides are all aligned. Another handy feature that is not evident from the Layout menu selections is called Drag and Pick. Say you have resized several controls and you now want them to be all the same size. Highlight several controls that have different sizes, hold down the command key (MacOS) or the alt key (MSWindows), and then drag to another destination control. When you release the mouse, all selected views will be made the same size as the destination control.

String output to a dialog box

In the previous example, the interactor contained an integer field change for input and integer fields nickels, dimes, and pennies for output. Input and output with real variables is similar. Sometimes it is desirable to use string output to display the result in a way that is more conventional for the user.

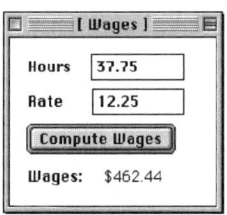

Figure 5.11
A dialog box with string output for Listing 5.12.

For example, suppose you want to include a dollar amount as the output. You want to prefix the value with a dollar sign $ and have the value displayed to the nearest cent, which is two places past the decimal point. To make the output look this nice requires you to convert the real value to a string with the desired format. Figure 5.11 shows a dialog box for such a scenario.

Figure 5.12 (page 85) shows the program corresponding to the dialog box of Figure 5.11. Even though the output appears to be a real value, the program shows that it is a string, because the type of d.result is an array of 16 characters. When procedure ComputeWages executes, it calculates wage, which is a real variable, as the product of d.hours and d.rate. With the input shown in Figure 5.11, wage would get the real value 462.4375. The program then calls procedure RealToString from module PboxStrings to convert the real value to a string value with two places past the decimal point. In the actual parameter list of RealToString, 1 is the field width, which will expand to accommodate any real value, and 2 is the number of places past the decimal. This procedure call gives the string value "462.44" to d.result. The next statement concatenates the dollar sign to the beginning of d.result, which finally gets displayed with the call to Dialog.Update.

Problems

1. Design a dialog box to input an integer value for the number of feet and a real value for the number of inches. When the user clicks a button in the dialog box, compute the equivalent length in meters and output the results of the computation to the Log. One inch is exactly 0.0254 meters and one foot is exactly 12 inches. Here is a sample output to the Log.

   Feet: 4
   Inches: 3.8
   Meters: 1.31572

2. Work Problem 1, but display the computed value for meters in the dialog box.

3. Work Problem 1, but display the computed value for meters in the dialog box to two places past the decimal point. Use string output as in the program of Figure 5.12.

```
MODULE Pbox05C;
   IMPORT Dialog, PboxStrings;

   VAR
      d*: RECORD
         hours*, rate*: REAL;
         result-: ARRAY 16 OF CHAR
      END;

   PROCEDURE ComputeWages*;
      VAR
         wage: REAL;
   BEGIN
      wage := d.hours * d.rate;
      PboxStrings.RealToString(wage, 1, 2, d.result);
      d.result :="$" + d.result;
      Dialog.Update(d)
   END ComputeWages;

BEGIN
   d.hours := 0.0; d.rate := 0.0;
   d.result := ""
END Pbox05C.
```

Figure 5.12
A program that produces string output to a dialog box.

4. Design a dialog box to input a real value for the temperature in Fahrenheit. When the user clicks a button in the dialog box, compute the equivalent temperature in Celsius and show both temperatures on the Log with their values identified appropriately as are the values in Problem 1.

5. Work Problem 4, but display the computed value for the Celsius temperature in the dialog box.

6. Work Problem 4, but display the computed value for the Celsius temperature in the dialog box to one place past the decimal point. Use string output as in the program of Figure 5.12.

7. Design a dialog box to input two real values for the lengths of two perpendicular sides of a right triangle. When the user clicks a button in the dialog box, compute the length of the hypotenuse and show all three lengths on the Log with their values identified appropriately as are the values in Problem 1.

8. Work Problem 7, but display the computed value for the length of the hypotenuse in the dialog box.

9. Work Problem 7, but display the computed value for the length of the hypotenuse in the dialog box to one place past the decimal point. Use string output as in the program of Figure 5.12.

10. Design a dialog box to input a real value for the radius of a circle. When the user clicks a button in the dialog box, compute the circumference and area and show all three mea-

sures on the Log with their values identified appropriately as are the values in Problem 1. Import the value of π from module Math for your computations.

11. Work Problem 10, but display the computed values for the circumference and area in the dialog box.

12. Work Problem 10, but display the computed values for the circumference and area in the dialog box to one place past the decimal point. Use string output as in the program of Figure 5.12.

13. Design a dialog box to input an integer value for the total number of hours. When the user clicks a button in the dialog box, compute the equivalent number of days, weeks, and hours. Show all time measures on the Log as in the following sample.

Total hours: 4123
Number of weeks: 24
Number of days: 3
Number of hours: 19

14. Work Problem 13, but display the computed values for the number of weeks, days, and hours in the dialog box.

15. Construct a five-function integer calculator as shown in the dialog box of Figure 5.13. The result from the dialog box is shown just after the user pressed the button labeled *. You will need to export five procedures, one for each button.

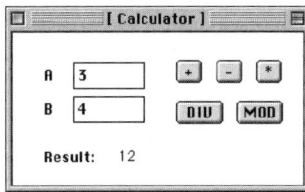

Figure 5.13
The dialog box for Problem 15.

16. Construct a four-function real number calculator similar to the integer calculator of Problem 15. Allow the user to add, subtract, multiply or divide two real numbers. You will need to export four procedures, one for each button.

 Chapter *6*

Selection

Some problems can be solved by a fixed computation. For example, to compute the area of a rectangle you always multiply the length by the width. Many problems, however, cannot be solved by a fixed computation. For instance, some businesses sell their products at a price that depends on the quantity of the order. They charge a lower price per ball for an order of 200 golf balls than for an order of 10 golf balls. A program to calculate the total dollar amount of an order cannot simply multiply the quantity by a fixed unit price if the unit price itself depends on the quantity.

This chapter describes boolean expressions and IF statements. Together these features of the Component Pascal language permit the programmer to alter, or select, the computation depending on the outcome of a test on one or more data values.

Boolean expressions and types

Boolean expressions always have one of two values, either true or false. The simplest boolean expressions use the relational operators of Figure 6.1. In mathematics notation, the "less than or equal to" operator is ≤. This symbol is not available on most keyboards, so Component Pascal programs require that you write "less than or equal to" as the two symbols <= without a space between them. The same idea applies to the "greater than or equal to" operator. The "not equal to" sign # resembles the mathematical symbol ≠.

Operator	Meaning
=	Equal to
<	Less than
<=	Less than or equal to
>	Greater than
>=	Greater than or equal to
#	Not equal to

Figure 6.1
The relational operators.

Example 6.1   An example of a boolean expression is

income > 2400

where income is an integer variable. This expression is either true or false, depending on the value of income. If income has the value 2500, the expression is true. If it has the value 2300 or even 2400, the expression is false.   ∎

Example 6.2   In contrast to the previous example, the expression

income >= 2400

evaluates to true if income has the value 2400.   ∎

Variables of type boolean are declared in the variable declaration part similarly to the way numeric and character variables are declared. A boolean variable can have one of two values, true or false.

Example 6.3   The following variable declaration part declares rich to be a boolean variable.

VAR
   rich: BOOLEAN;

The assignment statement

rich := income > 2400

gives rich the value true if income has value greater than 2400, and gives the value false otherwise.   ∎

The ODD function is a built-in Component Pascal function that takes an integer parameter and returns true if the value of the integer is odd. There is no corresponding even function.

Example 6.4   Suppose that i is a variable of type integer that has the value 14. Then the boolean expression

ODD(i)

has the value false, and the expression

ODD(i + 1)

has the value true.   ∎

Boolean expressions may contain the AND operator, written &. Suppose *p* is the statement "The sky is green," which is obviously false, and *q* is the statement "Computer science is fun," which is obviously true. Then, *p* & *q* is the statement "The sky is green and computer science is fun," which is false. For the entire statement *p* & *q* to be true, *p* must be true apart from *q*, and *q* must be true apart from *p*. If either or both are false, then the entire statement is false. Figure 6.2(a), the truth table for the & operator, summarizes these ideas.

Boolean expressions may also contain the OR operator, written OR. With *p* and *q* representing the same statements about the sky and computer science, *p* OR *q* is the statement "The sky is green or computer science is fun." This time, the entire statement is true. *p* OR *q* is true if *p* is true, if *q* is true, or if they are both true. Figure 6.2(b), the truth table for the OR operator, summarizes these ideas.

One other boolean operator is the NOT operator, written ~. If *p* is the statement "The sky is green," which is false, then ~ *p* is the statement "The sky is not green," which is true. Figure 6.2(c) is the truth table for the ~ operator.

Figure 6.2
Truth tables for the boolean operators.

p	*q*	*p* & *q*
TRUE	TRUE	TRUE
TRUE	FALSE	FALSE
FALSE	TRUE	FALSE
FALSE	FALSE	FALSE

(a) The & operator.

p	*q*	*p* OR *q*
TRUE	TRUE	TRUE
TRUE	FALSE	TRUE
FALSE	TRUE	TRUE
FALSE	FALSE	FALSE

(b) The OR operator.

p	~ *p*
TRUE	FALSE
FALSE	TRUE

(c) The ~ operator.

Example 6.5 Suppose that i is a variable of type integer that has the value 8. Then the boolean expression

~ODD(i)

has the value true. ∎

Sometimes it is possible to simplify a boolean expression that contains the ~ operator with a relational operator.

Example 6.6 The boolean expression

~(numSides > 8)

first evaluates the boolean expression (numSides > 8). If numSides has the value 10, then (numSides > 8) is true, and ~(numSides > 8) is false. A simpler way to write an equivalent boolean expression is

numSides <= 8

Suppose again that numSides has the value 10. Then numSides <= 8 is false, as it was in the previous expression. The two boolean expressions are the same regardless of the value of numSides. ∎

This example demonstrates that the <= operator is the inverse of the > operator. Figure 6.3 shows the relational operators and their inverses.

Operator	Inverse Operator
=	#
<	>=
<=	>

Figure 6.3
The inverses of the relational operators.

Example 6.7 You could write the expression

~(numTrials = maxTrials)

more simply as

numTrials # maxTrials

because the # operator is the inverse of the = operator. ▌

A common mistake you should avoid is putting the ~ operator next to a relational operator. A relational operator must be placed between two integers, reals, or characters and cannot be next to a ~.

Example 6.8 The compiler will not accept the expression

numTrials ~= maxTrials

because the equals operator cannot have the NOT operator to its left. ▌

Another error you should avoid is combining two relational operators with one variable, as is frequently done in mathematics. The mathematical expression

$5 \leq n < 10$

means that *n* is greater than or equal to 5 and less than 10. Such expressions are common in mathematics. However, they are illegal in Component Pascal.

Example 6.9 To test if the variable numTrials is greater than or equal to 5 and less than 10, you may be tempted to write the boolean expression as

5 <= numTrials < 10

This expression is illegal, because the same operand, numTrials, is used by both operators. You should write it with the & operator as follows:

(5 <= numTrials) & (numTrials < 10)

If numTrials has the value 6, this boolean expression evaluates to true AND true, which is true. ∎

Two other rules, known as De Morgan's laws, can sometimes help to simplify boolean expressions. Suppose that *p* and *q* are boolean expressions. De Morgan's laws are

~(*p* OR *q*) = ~*p* & ~*q*
~(*p* & *q*) = ~*p* OR ~*q*

Example 6.10 As an example of the first of De Morgan's laws, you can write the boolean expression

~((slope >= 1.0) OR (length <= 0.0))

more simply as

(slope < 1.0) & (length > 0.0)

because < is the inverse of >=, and > is the inverse of <=. ∎

When the Component Pascal compiler encounters a boolean expression in your program, it gives the NOT operator the highest precedence, the AND operator the next highest precedence, and the OR operator the lowest precedence of the three. Figure 6.4 summarizes these precedence rules and also compares the precedence of the boolean operators to the relational and arithmetic operators.

Operator	Precedence
~	Highest
&, DIV, MOD, /, *	
OR, +, -	
=, #, <, >, <=, >=	Lowest

Figure 6.4
Precedence of the Component Pascal operators.

Example 6.11 The Component Pascal compiler interprets the boolean expression

~ p & q

as (~p) & q rather than ~(p & q). ∎

Example 6.12 If alpha, beta, and gamma are integer variables, the boolean expression alpha < beta & gamma = 0

is illegal because the compiler groups beta & gamma first. The & operator expects boolean operands, but beta and gamma are integers. You should write the expression as

(alpha < beta) & (gamma = 0)

which is now a legal boolean expression.

IF statements

IF statements allow you to solve problems that are not based on fixed computations. The idea is to evaluate a boolean expression, and if that expression is true, perform a computation. Figure 6.5 shows an example of such a conditional computation. The dialog box is for computing the wages for an employee who may have worked overtime. Customarily, weekly wages are computed as the hourly rate times the number of hours worked, as long as the employee does not work more than 40 hours. If the employee works more than 40 hours, then the number of hours in excess of 40 are paid at time and a half. That is, the hourly rate for those hours beyond 40 is 1.5 times the normal rate.

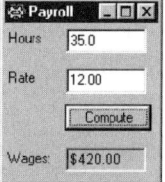

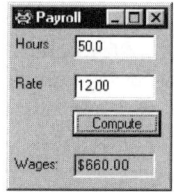

(a) Without overtime.   (b) With overtime.

Figure 6.5
The dialog box for a payroll calculation.

The listing in Figure 6.6 shows an implementation of the dialog box for calculating the payroll. The assignment statement

wages := d.hours * d.rate

computes wages as the product of d.hours and d.rate assuming no overtime. When the input is 50 for the hours worked and 12 for the hourly rate as shown in Figure 6.5(b), wages gets the value 600.00. This value is not yet correct because the 10 hours beyond 40 were computed at straight time, not time and a half.

```
MODULE Pbox06A;
   IMPORT Dialog, PboxStrings;
   VAR
      d*: RECORD
         hours*, rate*: REAL;
         message-: ARRAY 32 OF CHAR
      END;

   PROCEDURE ComputeWages*;
      VAR
         wages: REAL;
         wageString: ARRAY 32 OF CHAR;
   BEGIN
      wages := d.hours * d.rate;
      IF d.hours > 40.0 THEN
         wages := wages + (d.hours - 40.0) * 0.5 * d.rate
      END;
      PboxStrings.RealToString(wages, 1, 2, wageString);
      d.message := "$" + wageString;
      Dialog.Update(d)
   END ComputeWages;

BEGIN
   d.hours := 0.0; d.rate := 0.0;
   d.message := ""
END Pbox06A.
```

Figure 6.6

A payroll calculation program. It uses an IF statement without an ELSE part.

The words IF and THEN are Component Pascal reserved words. When an IF statement executes, it first evaluates the boolean expression following the reserved word IF. If the boolean expression is true, it executes the statement sequence between the reserved word THEN and the reserved word END. Otherwise, it skips the statement sequence. In this example, after Wages is computed as d.hours * d.rate, the IF statement evaluates the boolean expression

d.hours > 40.0

which is true, because the value of d.hours is 50. So the assignment statement following the IF statement

wages := wages + (d.hours - 40.0) * 0.5 + d.rate

executes. The value of wages is increased to reflect the extra amount (at half time) earned in overtime.

Appendix A shows that the EBNF syntax for an IF statement is

IF Expr THEN StatementSeq {ELSIF Expr THEN StatementSeq} [ELSE StatementSeq] END

The IF statement in Listing 6.6 does not have an ELSIF part, nor does it have an ELSE part.

Flowcharts

You can visualize the action of an IF statement with a flowchart. Figure 6.7 shows some of the more common flowchart symbols. The start symbol corresponds to the reserved word BEGIN, which starts the executable statements of a Component Pascal procedure. The stop symbol, which is the same shape as the start symbol, corresponds to the reserved word END. The parallelogram corresponds to input and output statements. Rectangles correspond to processing, performed by the assignment statement in Component Pascal. The hexagon is a symbol that indicates the test of some condition. It is used in several Component Pascal statements, including the IF statement. The symbol that looks like a hamburger corresponds to the CASE statement, a selection statement described later in this chapter. The circle is the collector symbol for joining lines from other flowchart symbols.

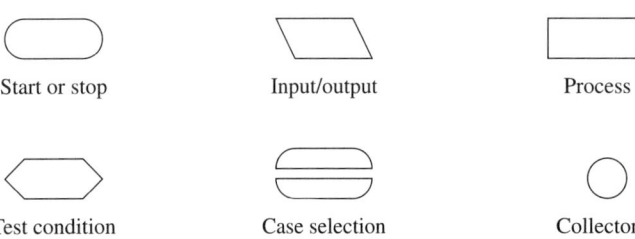

Start or stop Input/output Process

Test condition Case selection Collector

Figure 6.7
The flowchart symbols.

Figure 6.8 is the flowchart for an IF statement without an ELSE part. The incoming arrow from the top points to the test condition box, which represents the boolean expression of the IF statement. If the boolean expression is true, control branches to the left to the processing box, which represents the statement sequence after the reserved word THEN. If the boolean expression is false, control branches to the right, skipping execution of the statement sequence after the reserved word THEN. The two branches of the IF statement join at the collector symbol corresponding to the reserved word END. Figure 6.9 is the program of Figure 6.6 in flowchart form.

Flowcharts are useful for visualizing the logic of a program. They used to be considered helpful in software design, but have fallen out of favor for several reasons. Flowcharts are fine for small programs but they require huge pages of paper for large programs. They also require artwork and are consequently more difficult to modify than the programs they represent. This book presents flowcharts to help you visualize the behavior of some Component Pascal statements. As you gain experience writing Component Pascal programs, however, you will not need to rely on flowcharts to design your software.

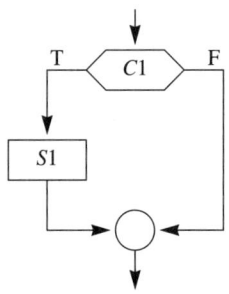

Figure 6.8
The flowchart for an IF statement without an ELSE

IF statements with an ELSE part

The listing in Figure 6.10 presents a different way to compute the wage correctly. Its output is identical to the output of Figure 6.6.

The program uses an IF statement with an ELSE part. If the boolean expression in the IF statement is true, the statement sequence following the THEN part

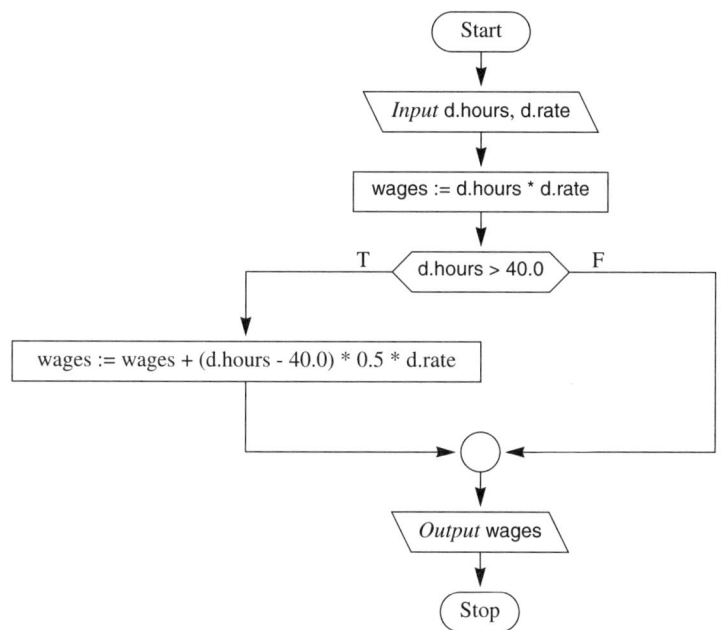

Figure 6.9
The flowchart for the program
of Figure 6.6.

wages := d.hours * d.rate

executes. After it executes, the statement sequence after the reserved word ELSE

wages := 40.0 * d.rate + (d.hours - 40.0) * 1.5 * d.rate

is skipped. If, on the other hand, the boolean expression in the IF statement is false, the THEN part is skipped, and the ELSE part executes. The effect of the IF statement is to select one of the two statements to execute.

There is no semicolon after the statement following the reserved word THEN. You can see in Appendix A that there are no semicolons in the syntax definition for an IF statement. Then why is there a semicolon after the reserved word END? That semicolon is there to separate the entire IF statement from the following Pbox-Strings.RealToString. These statements are part of the statement sequence of the body of the procedure. The EBNF description of a procedure declaration is

PROCEDURE [Receiver] IdentDef [FormalPars] "; " DeclSeq [BEGIN StatementSeq] END Ident.

and the EBNF description of a statement sequence is

Statement {"; " Statement}.

```
MODULE Pbox06B;
  IMPORT Dialog, PboxStrings;
  VAR
    d*: RECORD
      hours*, rate*: REAL;
      message-: ARRAY 32 OF CHAR
    END;

  PROCEDURE ComputeWages*;
    VAR
      wages: REAL;
      wageString: ARRAY 32 OF CHAR;
  BEGIN
    IF d.hours <= 40.0 THEN
      wages := d.hours * d.rate
    ELSE
      wages := 40.0 * d.rate + (d.hours - 40.0) * 1.5 * d.rate
    END;
    PboxStrings.RealToString(wages, 1, 2, wageString);
    d.message := "$" + wageString;
    Dialog.Update(d)
  END ComputeWages;

BEGIN
  d.hours := 0.0; d.rate := 0.0;
  d.message := ""
END Pbox06B.
```

Figure 6.10
A payroll calculation program that uses an IF statement with an ELSE part.

So, the statements in the statement sequence between the BEGIN and END of the procedure are separated by semicolons. We now have three general rules for placing semicolons:

- Do not place a semicolon after a THEN.

- Do not place a semicolon before an END.

- Do not place a semicolon before an ELSE.

Figure 6.11 shows the flowchart for an IF statement with an ELSE part. It is similar to the flowchart for an IF statement without an ELSE part in two respects. Both flowcharts have exactly one collector, and both have exactly one arrow coming in at the top and one arrow going out at the bottom.

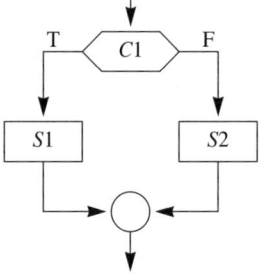

Figure 6.11
The flowchart for an IF statement with an ELSE part.

Boolean variables

Figure 6.12 shows the dialog box for the next program. The program determines whether a customer qualifies for a 15% airline discount. If the customer qualifies, it computes the discounted fare. Otherwise, it states that the customer does not qualify. A customer qualifies by having made more than 4 flights during the previous 12 months and being 65 years of age or older.

The dialog contains a control called a check box. The user can check the square

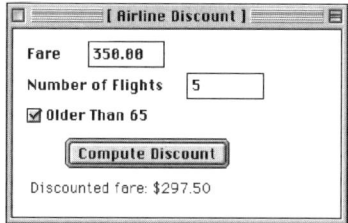 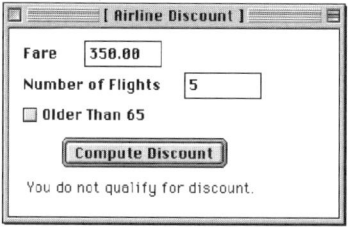

(a) Fare with discount.   **(b)** Fare without discount.

Figure 6.12
The dialog box for computing
a possible discount for an
airline fare.

input field to indicate whether she is older than 65. It is clear that the input field for Fare is linked to a variable of type real, and the input field for the number of flights is linked to a variable of type integer. But what is type of the variable to which the check box is linked? There are two possibilities for the input of this field. Either the box is checked or it is not checked. So, the variable to which it is linked has type boolean. If the box is checked the boolean variable gets the value true, and if it is not checked the variable gets the value false. The listing in Figure 6.13 shows the program for this dialog box.

Constants

The constant section is similar to the variable section, except that an equal sign follows the identifier instead of a colon. Another difference is that in the variable section a type is associated with each identifier, while in the constant section a value is associated with each identifier. Constants are similar to variables in that you refer to them by their names, which are Component Pascal identifiers. However, you cannot change the value of a constant the way you can the value of a variable.

Example 6.13   The assignment statement

discount := 0.20

would be illegal in this program, because discount is a constant.   ∎

Procedure FlightDiscount defines the identifier discount to be the constant 0.15 and flightLimit to be 4. The program would produce exactly the same result without the constant section and with the expression in the IF statement changed from

IF (d.numFlights > flightLimit) & d.olderThan65 THEN

to

IF (d.numFlights > 4) & d.olderThan65 THEN

and the computation for the fare changed from

fare := (1.0 - discount) * d.fare;

```
MODULE Pbox06C;
  IMPORT Dialog, PboxStrings;
  VAR
    d*: RECORD
      fare*: REAL;
      numFlights*: INTEGER;
      olderThan65*: BOOLEAN;
      message-: ARRAY 64 OF CHAR
    END;

  PROCEDURE FlightDiscount*;
    CONST
      discount = 0.15;
      flightLimit = 4;
    VAR
      fare: REAL;
      fareString: ARRAY 32 OF CHAR;
  BEGIN
    IF (d.numFlights > flightLimit) & d.olderThan65 THEN
      fare := (1.0 - discount) * d.fare;
      PboxStrings.RealToString(fare, 1, 2, fareString);
      d.message := "Discounted fare: $" + fareString
    ELSE
      d.message := "You do not qualify for discount."
    END;
    Dialog.Update(d)
  END FlightDiscount;

BEGIN
  d.fare := 0.0; d.numFlights := 0;
  d.olderThan65 := FALSE;
  d.message := ""
END Pbox06C.
```

Figure 6.13
A program to compute the discount on an airline ticket.

to

fare :— 0.85 * d.fare;

So, what is the advantage of a constant section? One advantage is the ease with which you can modify the program. This program is short, and it is easy to locate the assignment statement where it computes the discount. If you wanted to modify the program to change the discount to 20% instead of 15%, you could find the assignment statement with your text editor and change the 0.85 to 0.80. But in a large program, the statement that performs the computation may be difficult to locate. Also, more than one computation may need to be modified to make one change.

The advantages of a constant

For example, suppose you write a big tax computation program in which a tax rate for both businesses and individuals is 20%. These rates are used in many different computations. You do not use a constant definition part, so that the value 0.20 is scattered in various expressions throughout the program. Now suppose that a new tax law changes the rate for businesses to 30% but leaves the rate for individuals unchanged. To modify the program you cannot simply use your text editor to change every occurrence of 0.20 to 0.30, because that would change the rate for individuals as well.

On the other hand, suppose you write the program with a constant section that defines

```
CONST
   businessRate = 0.20;
   individualRate = 0.20;
```

and use these identifiers in the appropriate expressions in the program. Then, if the tax law changes the business rate to 30% you only need to change one value at the beginning of the program to modify it correctly.

Another advantage of constants is the increased readability that identifiers provide. In this program, the expression

```
(1.0 - discount) * d.fare
```

represents the meaning of the computation better than the expression

```
0.85 * d.fare
```

The presence of identifier discount tells the reader explicitly that a discounted fare is being computed.

Selection with strings

Component Pascal provides a convenient feature for testing strings according to alphabetic order. Consider the problem to determine whether string "berry" comes before "bear" in alphabetic order. The proper algorithm compares the first two letters. Because the first b in "berry" equals the first b in "bear", you must compare the second letters. Alas, the e in "berry" equals the e in "bear" as well, so you must go to the third letter. Finally, the third letters are not equal. Because a is less than r, as shown on the number line for the character values in Figure 4.11, "bear" is less than "berry" and so comes first in alphabetic order regardless of the letters beyond the third. Of course, the algorithm must handle words of unequal length as well. Which comes first in alphabetic order, "batter" or "bat"?

The alphabetizing algorithm

With Component Pascal, you can use the relational operators of Figure 6.1 to compare not only integers, reals, and individual characters, but strings of characters as well. The comparison of two strings takes complete account of the above algorithm, including the case where two strings are of unequal length. Figure 6.14 shows a dialog box, which is implemented by the program of Figure 6.15, to compare two strings entered by the user. Regardless of whether the user enters "bear" or "berry" first, the output indicates which comes first in alphabetic order. It also correctly handles the case of unequal word lengths.

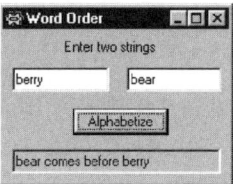

(a) First "berry", then "bear".

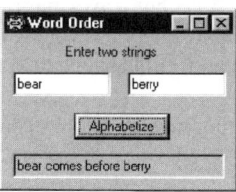

(b) First "bear", then "berry".

Figure 6.14
A dialog box for comparing strings in alphabetic order.

```
MODULE Pbox06D;
   IMPORT Dialog;
   VAR
      d*: RECORD
         string1*, string2*: ARRAY 16 OF CHAR;
         message-: ARRAY 64 OF CHAR;
      END;

   PROCEDURE Alphabetize*;
   BEGIN
      IF d.string1 < d.string2 THEN
         d.message := d.string1 + " comes before " + d.string2
      ELSE
         d.message := d.string2 + " comes before " + d.string1
      END;
      Dialog.Update(d)
   END Alphabetize;

BEGIN
   d.string1 := ""; d.string2 := ""
END Pbox06D.
```

Figure 6.15
A program to compare two strings.

Although this program correctly alphabetizes strings whose letters are all lowercase or all uppercase, it will not always work correctly if the user enters strings that contain both upper- and lowercase letters. Figure 6.16 shows what happens when the user enters "bear" and "Berry". The output erroneously claims that "Berry" comes before "bear". The origin of the problem lies in the ordering of the characters on the number line in Figure 4.11. All the uppercase characters lie to the left of all the lowercase characters. Therefore, the character B is less than the character b, and the alphabetizing algorithm blindly concludes that "Berry" is less than "bear" without even considering the characters beyond the first one in the string. Because every uppercase letter is less than every lowercase letter, the program will even claim that "Zebra" comes before "antelope"!

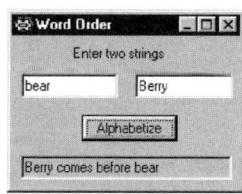

Figure 6.16
Erroneous output from the program of Figure 6.15.

This program needs to be improved, and it can be with the help of module PboxStrings, whose interface is listed in Figure 4.12. The module contains procedure ToLower, which is listed as

PROCEDURE ToLower (from: ARRAY OF CHAR; OUT to: ARRAY OF CHAR);

You supply an actual parameter for from that has already been given a string value, and a variable for to that is initially undefined. When you call ToLower, the procedure will copy all the characters from from to to, converting any uppercase letters to lowercase. Recall that OUT specifies call by result, which has the effect of changing your actual parameter.

How does this procedure help solve the problem? You can declare two local variables, say lower1 and lower2, in procedure Alphabetize and use ToLower to give them the lowercase versions of d.string1 and d.string2 respectively. In the IF statement, compare lower1 with lower2 instead of d.string1 with d.string2. Because lower1 and lower2 will contain only lowercase characters, the comparison will be correct. Of course, all this manipulation should take place behind the scenes unknown to the user. If the user enters "bear" and "Berry" the message on the dialog box should read

Berry comes before bear

and not

berry comes before bear

Implementation of this improvement is a problem at the end of the chapter.

Using IF statements

This section points out some aspects of IF statements that tend to give beginning programmers problems. Some are style guidelines that have been mentioned previously, while others are unique to IF statements. In the following discussion and throughout the remainder of the book, we will sometimes use the word *code*. One meaning for code is what a programmer writes in a program listing. Coding an algorithm means writing a program in some programming language that will execute the algorithm on a computer. A code fragment is a few lines of code from a program listing.

The word code

A common tendency with boolean variables is to use a redundant computation with the equals operator. A boolean variable is a special case of a boolean expression, and so can be used alone as a boolean expression in an IF statement.

Example 6.14 In the listing of Figure 6.13, you could write the test for the IF statement as

IF (d.numFlights > flightLimit) & (d.olderThan65 = TRUE) THEN

With this test the program still works correctly, because the expression d.olderThan65 = TRUE evaluates to true when d.olderThan65 has the value true and to false when d.olderThan65 has the value false. But this is bad style because it contains a redundant computation. The more straightforward test

IF (d.numFlights > flightLimit) & d.olderThan65 THEN

presented in Listing 6.13 is better.   ▌

Boolean variables are useful because they allow Component Pascal IF statements to be written similar to English phrases whose meaning is close to the effect of the Component Pascal statement. In the previous example, IF (d.numFlights > flightLimit) & d.olderThan65 THEN is much like an English phrase. You should name your boolean variables so that the test of an IF statement corresponds to the way you would phrase the test in English.

Example 6.15   Suppose that exempt is a boolean variable that indicates whether a taxpayer is exempt from a tax. Instead of writing the test

IF exempt = FALSE THEN

you should write the equivalent test

IF ~exempt THEN

because this corresponds more closely to the way you would state the test in English.   ▌

It is worth repeating a point here that was made in a previous chapter: do not save typing time by choosing extremely short identifiers at the expense of program readability.

Example 6.16   In the previous example, if you choose e for the identifier instead of exempt, the test of the IF statement becomes

IF ~e THEN

which would be more difficult for a human reader to understand.   ▌

Our last problem area concerns the unnecessary duplication of code. Suppose you write an IF statement with an ELSE part that has the following form:

```
IF Condition 1 THEN
    Statement 1 ;
    Statement 2
ELSE
    Statement 3 ;
    Statement 2
END
```

where Statement 2 is the same statement in both alternatives of the IF statement. Condition 1 is a boolean expression. If it is true, Statement 1 executes, followed by Statement 2. Otherwise, Statement 3 executes, followed by Statement 2. Regardless of whether Condition 1 is true or false, Statement 2 executes. It is simpler to write

```
IF Condition 1 THEN
    Statement 1
ELSE
    Statement 3
END;
Statement 2
```

which executes like the previous code but does not duplicate Statement 2 in the code fragment.

Radio buttons

Each test in an IF statement evaluates a boolean expression, which can have the values true or false. So every test selects between two alternatives. A single CASE statement, however, can select between more than just two alternatives. The type of the expression to be tested cannot be a boolean because more than two alternatives are possible. Its type is usually integer.

Radio buttons are common controls in dialog boxes when the user is required to make one of several choices. They are a generalization of check boxes, which require that the user select one of two choices—either checked or not checked. Radio buttons always come in sets of two or more. Figure 6.17 shows a dialog box with four radio buttons. The dialog box requests that the user answer a multiple choice question about U.S. history. It provides four choices, only one of which is correct. A CASE statement is an appropriate way to analyze the input from this set of radio buttons because more than two alternatives is possible.

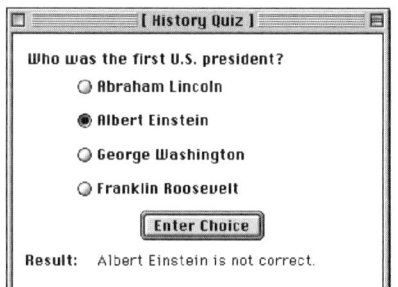 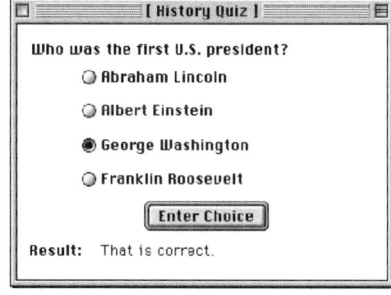

Figure 6.17
A dialog box with a set of four radio buttons.

The controls are called radio buttons because of their similarity to the push buttons on old automobile radios for tuning in stations. You can only have one station tuned in at a time. If you change the setting to a new radio station by pushing a button, then any button that was previously pressed is released. Similarly, in a dialog box with radio buttons if one button is pressed, as indicated by the solid circle, then any button that was previously pressed is released, as indicated by the open circles.

Until now, each input/output control in a dialog box has been linked to a variable in an exported record that has consistently been named d. It would appear from Figure 6.17 that we would need five fields in d—one for each of the four radio buttons and one for the result. Such is not the case, however. Instead, all four radio buttons are linked to a single integer variable in d. The listing in Figure 6.18 shows this integer as multipleChoice.

```
MODULE Pbox06E;
    IMPORT Dialog;
    VAR
        d*: RECORD
            multipleChoice*: INTEGER;
            message-: ARRAY 64 OF CHAR
        END;

    PROCEDURE PresidentQuiz*;
    BEGIN
        CASE d.multipleChoice OF
        0:
            d.message := "Abraham Lincoln is not correct." |
        1:
            d.message := "Albert Einstein is not correct." |
        2:
            d.message := "That is correct." |
        3:
            d.message := "Franklin Roosevelt is not correct."
        END;
        Dialog.Update(d)
    END PresidentQuiz;

BEGIN
    d.multipleChoice := 0;
    d.message := ""
END Pbox06E.
```

Figure 6.18
A module that takes its input from a set of radio buttons. It uses a CASE statement.

The radio buttons are linked such that when the button for Abraham Lincoln is pressed the value of d.multipleChoice is 0, when the button for Albert Einstein is pressed its value is 1, when the button for Washington is pressed its value is 2, and when the button for Roosevelt is pressed its value is 3.

It is a bit cumbersome to set up the links for radio buttons compared to setting up the links for the other controls. The problem is that when you declare multipleChoice to be an integer in record d and create a new form linked to it by choosing Controls→New Form… the BlackBox system will supply an integer input field instead of a set of four radio buttons. You must delete the integer input field, insert four radio buttons, then set up their proper links manually. Figure 6.19 shows this process.

Figure 6.19(a) shows the controls that are provided by the BlackBox forms generator when you create a new form by selecting Controls→New Form… and link it to Pbox09A.d. The forms generator inserts an integer input field for the integer d.multipleChoice. Part (b) of the figure shows the result of selecting the input field and deleting it by pressing the delete key. Part (c) shows how to enlarge the forms document to make room for the radio buttons. Choose Edit→Select Document to select the forms document for enlarging. Part (d) shows the result of choosing Controls→Insert Radio Button. A radio button control is inserted in the forms document

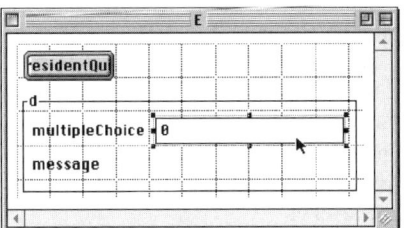

(a) Select the integer field provided by the forms generator.

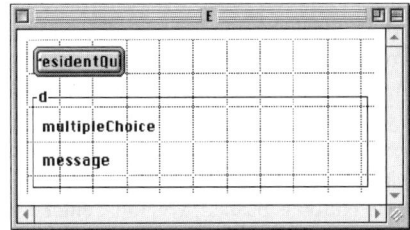

(b) Delete the integer field by pressing the delete key.

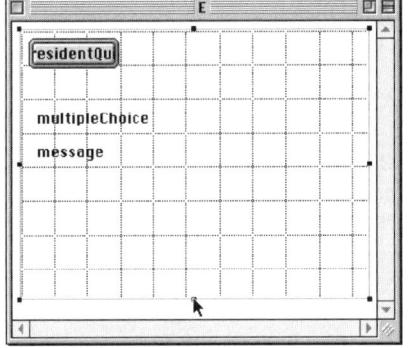

(c) Select the document and enlarge it to make room for the radio buttons.

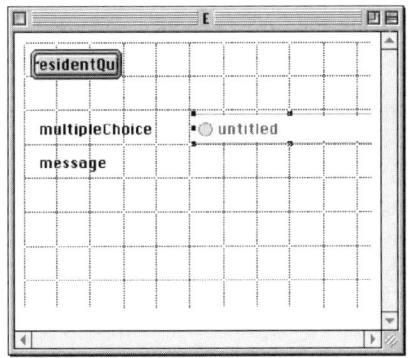

(d) Insert the first radio button by selecting Controls→Insert Radio Button.

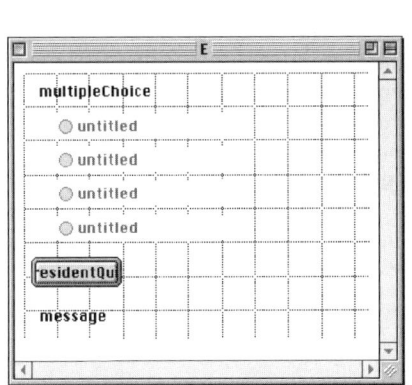

(e) Insert three more radio buttons and arrange them.

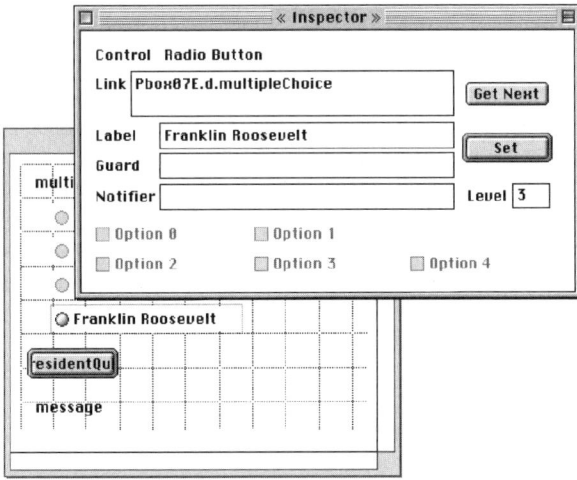

(f) Set the proper links manually with the component Inspector.

at some random location. Part (e) shows the dialog box after arranging the radio button where you want it and inserting and arranging the other three radio buttons.

The last step is to set the proper links with the component inspector as shown in Figure 6.19(f). The figure shows the settings for the fourth radio button. You must manually enter the link to the exported integer, which in this case is Pbox09A.d.mutipleChoice. Enter the text that you want to appear next to the radio button in the label field, which in this case is Franklin Roosevelt. Because you want the value of d.multipleChoice to be 3 when this radio button is pushed, you must enter 3 for the level of the control as shown in the inspector in part (f).

The CASE statement

The listing in Figure 6.18 shows how the CASE statement can select from more than just two alternatives. The Component Pascal syntax for a CASE statement is

CASE Expr OF Case {" | " Case} [ELSE StatementSeq] END

In this program, the expression Expr between reserved words CASE and OF is simply d.multipleChoice. Following OF is a list of one or more cases, each case separated by a vertical bar |. This program has four cases separated by three vertical bars. It does not have the optional ELSE part.

The Component Pascal syntax for an individual Case is

[CaseLabels {" , " CaseLabels} " : " StatementSeq]

Each Case consists of one or more CaseLabels separated by commas followed by a colon followed by our familiar StatementSeq. In this program, the case label for the second case is 1, and the statement sequence is the single assignment statement

d.message := "Albert Einstein is not correct."

When the user selects one of the radio buttons in the dialog box of Figure 6.17 and presses the button labeled Enter Choice, procedure PresidentQuiz executes. The first statement in the procedure is the CASE statement, which evaluates the expression d.multipleChoice. Execution then skips directly to the statement sequence of the corresponding case label skipping all other cases. Following execution of that statement sequence, execution skips directly to the end of the CASE statement again skipping all other cases. In this program, suppose the user has clicked the fourth radio button corresponding to Roosevelt. This selection causes d.mutipleChoice to have the value 3. When the CASE statement executes, it skips directly to the assignment statement

d.message := "Franklin Roosevelt is not correct."

skipping all other cases.

If the value of the expression does not occur as a label of any case, the statement sequence following the ELSE is selected, if there is an ELSE. Otherwise, the program is aborted with a trap. This program does not require an ELSE part if the levels for the radio buttons are set up correctly. Because each level is set to have a value of 0, 1, 2, or 3 we are guaranteed that d.multipleChoice can have no other value.

Figure 6.20 shows the flowchart for the module in Figure 6.18. Note how the case selection symbol has more than one alternative arrow leaving it compared to the IF hexagon flowchart symbol that always has two arrows leaving it.

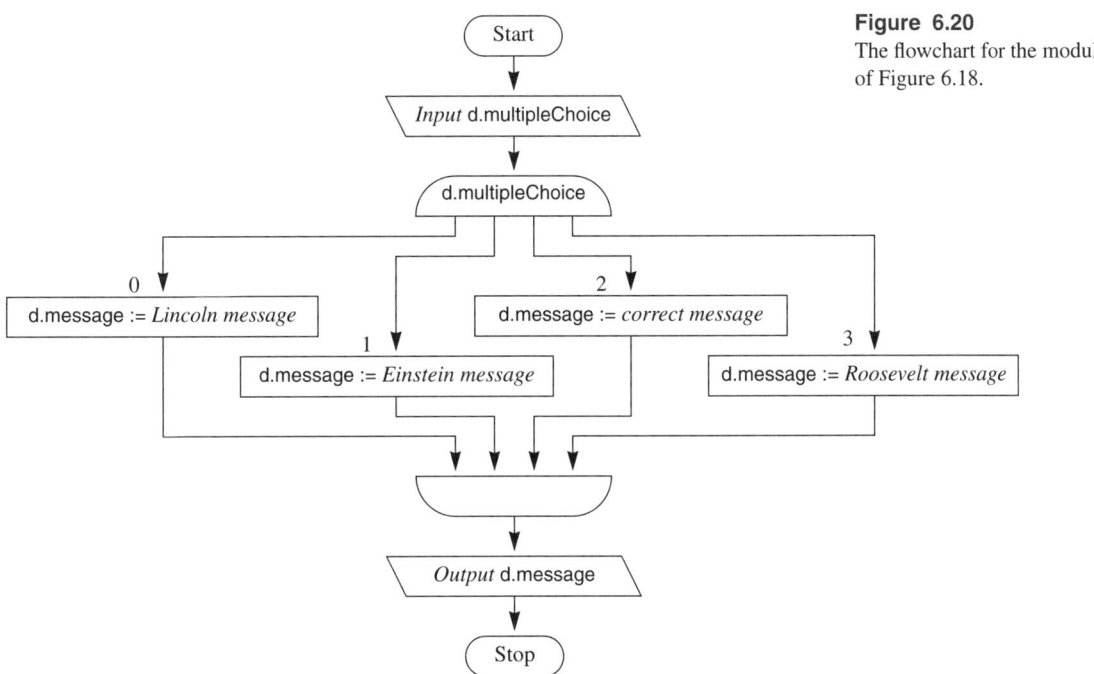

Figure 6.20
The flowchart for the module of Figure 6.18.

★ Guarded commands

The Component Pascal (CP) operations of &, OR, and ~ correspond directly to the Guarded Command Language (GCL) operators of conjunction, disjunction, and negation as Figure 6.21 shows. Not only are the symbols different but the precedence is different as well. In CP, ~ has the highest precedence, & has the second highest, and OR has the lowest of the three. But in GCL, ∧ and ∨ have the same precedence, although ¬ has higher precedence than both as in CP. Consequently, you must be careful to place parentheses in a GCL statement where you might not need it in a CP one.

CP	GCL
&	∧
OR	∨
~	¬

Figure 6.21
The boolean operators in GCL.

Example 6.17 The CP boolean expression

(sum < 100) OR (a < b) & (b < c)

causes the & operation to execute first followed by the OR operation. However, the equivalent boolean expression in GCL is

$$(sum < 100) \lor ((a < b) \land (b < c))$$

where the parentheses are required to indicate that the $\land$ operation occurs first. ∎

The guarded command language is so called because several of its statements, including the **if** statement, contain a phrase of the form $B \rightarrow S$ known as a guarded command. B is a boolean condition that must be true in order for statement S to execute. In the same way that semicolons separate statements, the symbol ▯ separates guarded commands. In CP, every IF statement terminates with an END. In GCL, every **if** statement terminates with **fi**, which is **if** spelled backward. Another difference between GCL and CP is that there is no phrase corresponding to ELSE in GCL. Instead, a guarded command is used for the ELSE part. If there is no ELSE part in the CP statement, you must use a guarded command with the **skip** statement, which does nothing when it executes.

Example 6.18 In Figure 6.6, using w for wages, h for d.hours, and r for d.rate the CP statements

```
IF d.hours > 40.0 THEN
    wages := wages + (d.hours - 40.0) * 0.5 * d.rate
END
```

are written in GCL as

if $h > 40.0 \rightarrow w := w + (h - 40.0) * 0.5 * r$
▯ $h \leq 40.0 \rightarrow$ **skip**
fi ∎

If there is an ELSE part in the CP statement, you still specify what happens in the false alternative with a guarded command in GCL.

Example 6.19 In Figure 6.7, again using w for wages, h for d.hours, and r for d.rate the CP statements

```
IF d.hours <= 40.0 THEN
    wages := d.hours * d.rate
ELSE
    wages := 40.0 * d.rate + (d.hours - 40.0) * 1.5 * d.rate
END
```

are written in GCL as

if $h \leq 40.0 \rightarrow w := d * r$
▯ $h > 40.0 \rightarrow w := 40.0 * r + (h - 40.0) * 1.5 * r$
fi ∎

From these examples, you can see that GCL requires the programmer to be more explicit in the precondition that must be true for one of the alternatives of an **if** statement to execute. In Example 6.19, you cannot tell simply by reading the code what must be true for the false alternative to execute. You must deduce that for the false alternative to execute the boolean expression

d.hours <= 40.0

must be false, and from that fact reason that d.hours > 40.0 must be true. On the other hand, in GCL the guard tells you explicitly what must be true for the else part to execute.

Exercises

1. State whether the boolean expression

    ODD(num1) & (num2 <= 10)

    is true or false for each of the following sets of values for the integer variables num1 and num2.

    (**a**) num1 = 6, num2 = 10
    (**b**) num1 = 5, num2 = 11
    (**c**) num1 = 5, num2 = 10

2. State whether the boolean expression

    (num1 >5) OR (num2 <= 12)

    is true or false for each of the following sets of values for the integer variables num1 and num2.

    (**a**) num1 = 20, num2 = 12
    (**b**) num1 = 7, num2 = 8
    (**c**) num1 = 2, num2 = 13

3. Write the equivalent of the following IF tests without using the ~ operator.

    (**a**) IF ~(num < 16) THEN
    (**b**) IF ~((num1 < 20) OR (num2 >= 10)) THEN
    (**c**) IF ~((num1 = 20) & (num2 > 10)) THEN

4. Predict the output of the program in Figure 6.6 for the following inputs.

    (**a**) d.hours = 38.0, d.rate = 4.75
    (**b**) d.hours = 50.0, d.rate = 5.00
    (**c**) d.hours = –2.0, d.rate = 10.00

5. Predict the output of the program in Figure 6.10 for the following inputs.

(a) d.hours = 36.0, d.rate = 5.00
(b) d.hours = 48.0, d.rate = 6.00
(c) d.hours = −1.0, d.rate = 10.00

6.   Predict the output of the program in Figure 6.13 for the following inputs.

(a) d.fare = 100.00, d.numFlights = 9, d.olderThan65 = false
(b) d.fare = 100.00, d.numFlights = 19, d.olderThan65 = true
(c) d.fare = 100.00, d.numFlights = 14, d.olderThan65 = true

7.   Draw the flowcharts for the procedures in **(a)** Figure 6.10 and **(b)** Figure 6.13.

8.   Draw the flowcharts for the following code fragments.

(a)	**(b)**
IF *Condition 1* THEN	IF *Condition 1* THEN
Statement 1	*Statement 1*
ELSE	ELSE
Statement 2 ;	*Statement 2*
Statement 3	END;
END	*Statement 3*

9.   Simplify the following code fragment. Assume that none of the statements change the variables in Condition 1.

IF *Condition 1* THEN
    Statement 1 ;
    Statement 2
ELSE
    Statement 1 ;
    Statement 3
END

10. Rewrite the following code fragments with the correct indentation and draw their flow-charts.

(a)	**(b)**
Statement 1 ;	*Statement 1* ;
IF *Condition 1* THEN	IF *Condition 1* THEN
Statement 2	*Statement 2*
ELSE	ELSE
Statement 3	*Statement 3* ;
END;	*Statement 4*
Statement 4 ;	END;
Statement 5	*Statement 5*

11. Translate the following code fragments from CP to GCL.

(a)
```
IF d.age > 65 THEN
    rate := 0.2 * d.wages
ELSE
    rate := 0.3 * d.wages
END
```

(b)
```
IF d.xCoordinate > 1000 THEN
    d.xCoordinate := d.xCoordinate - 1000
END
```

12. Translate the following code fragments from GCL to CP.

(a)
if $a \geq b \rightarrow a, b := b, a$
 ⫿ $a < b \rightarrow$ **skip**
fi

(b)
if $j > 100 \rightarrow m :=$ "large"
 ⫿ $j \leq 100 \rightarrow m :=$ "small"
fi

Problems

13. A salesperson's commission is computed as 15% of the sales that exceed $1000. Write a Component Pascal program to input a sales figure from a dialog box and output the salesperson's commission in a dialog box message. Use an IF statement without an ELSE part.

14. In a bowling tournament, participants bowl three games and receive a consolation prize of $15 regardless of their score. Those bowlers whose three-game average exceeds 200 get an additional prize of $50. Write a program to input a bowler's three scores from a dialog box and output his prize earnings in a dialog box message.

15. Write a Component Pascal program to input two integer values from a dialog box and output them in numeric order in a dialog box message.

16. A student gets on the dean's list if her grade point average (GPA) is at least 3.5 (based on a scale of 4.0 for an A, 3.0 for a B, etc.). Write a program that implements a dialog box with input fields for the number of A's, B's, C's, D's, and F's a student earned during a given semester and with output fields for her GPA and a message telling whether she made the dean's list.

17. Design a dialog box with an integer input field for "Age" and a check box for "Dependent". If the age field is less than 21 and the check box is checked output the message, "You qualify.", otherwise, "You do not qualify." in an output field in the dialog box.

18. Make the improvement described in the text to the program of Figure 6.15.

19. A person's last initial determines her registration period, as the table in Figure 6.22(a) shows. Write a program using a CASE statement that asks a user to select the initial of her last name as shown in the dialog box of Figure 6.22(b) and output the registration period.

Last initial	Registration period
A, B, C	9:00
D, E, F, G	10:00
H, I, J, K, L	11:00
M, N, O, P	12:00
Q, R, S	1:00
T, U, V, W	2:00
X, Y, Z	3:00

(a) Table of registration periods.

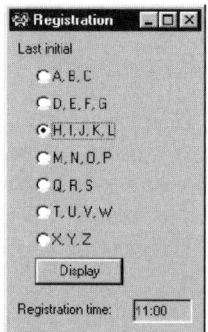

(b) Dialog box.

Figure 6.22
The information for Problem 19.

Chapter *7*

Abstract Stacks and Lists

The concept of abstraction is pervasive in many of the sciences. Although abstraction has many nuances, one that is of primary importance in computer science is the idea of hidden detail. The modules of Component Pascal provide abstraction for the programmer. The interface of a module shows those elements of the module that are exported and therefore available for other modules to import. All parts of the module that are not exported are hidden details.

Abstraction as hidden detail

Two abstractions that a module can supply are the abstract data structure (ADS) and the abstract data type (ADT). A module that supplies an ADS contains an entity that is useful for the programmer to manipulate. An example of an ADS that your programs have manipulated is the Log. The module StdLog permits you to send strings, integer values, and real values to the Log. The details of how the information gets displayed on the Log are hidden. The programmer only needs to know how to use procedures such as String and Int that are listed in the interface of StdLog. One characteristic of an ADS is that only one entity or data structure is provided by the exporting module. There is only one Log in the BlackBox system.

Abstract data structures

In contrast to a module that supplies an ADS, a module that supplies an ADT exports a type. Modules that use an ADT can declare variables to be of that type. Because a module is free to declare more than one variable to be of the exported type, it can have more than one data structure.

Abstract data types

The BlackBox framework provides the programmer both kinds of entities—ADSs and ADTs. Whether it provides an ADS or an ADT depends on whether it is designed to provide one data structure for the programmer to manipulate, or a type so the programmer can create and manipulate as many data structures needed to solve the problem at hand.

When to use an ADS versus an ADT

This chapter describes two abstractions—stacks and lists. For each of these two abstractions, it illustrates how it could be provided as an ADS and as an ADT. These abstractions are not part of the standard BlackBox distribution, but are contained in the Pbox project for use with this book. This chapter shows the power of abstraction by allowing you to use the data structures without knowing the details of how they are implemented. After you learn more about the Component Pascal language, later chapters will reveal the details that are hidden behind the interfaces for these abstractions.

Stacks

A stack is also called a last in, first out (LIFO) list. It is a structure that stores values. *The LIFO property of a stack* Two operations access the values stored on a stack—push and pop. You can visualize a stack as a spring-loaded stack of dishes in a restaurant. When the busboy puts a clean dish on top of the stack, the weight of the dish pushes the stack. If he puts yet another dish on top, it will push down the stack a bit further. If a waitress needs a dish, she takes one from the top of the stack. In other words, the last dish put on the stack is the first one out when someone retrieves a dish.

In abstract form, a stack is a list of values with the operations *push* for storage *The push and pop operations* and *pop* for retrieval. Figure 7.1 shows a sequence of operations on a stack in abstract form. In the figure, the push operation places a value on the stack. d.x is a real variable that is not a part of the stack. The pop operation gives the value to d.x from the top of the stack.

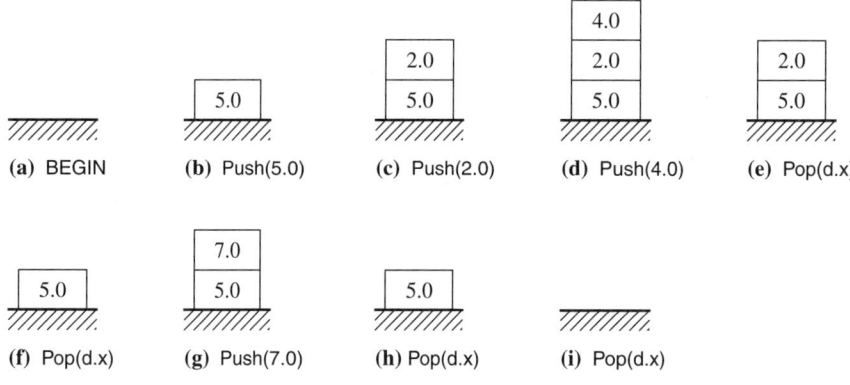

Figure 7.1
A sequence of operations on a stack.

The figure shows the values 5.0, 2.0, and 4.0 pushed onto the stack. The first pop operation in (e) gives the value of 4.0 to d.x. Because 4.0 was the last value in, it is the first value out. Figure 7.1(f) shows the stack partially empty, with only 5.0. Then 7.0 is pushed onto the stack. The next pop operation in (h) gives 7.0 to d.x. Because 7.0 was the last value in, it is the first value out.

Evaluating postfix expressions

Stacks are common in computer systems. One application of stacks is in the processing of arithmetic expressions. When you write a Component Pascal expression such as 3 + 5 in a program, the Component Pascal compiler must translate it to machine language. Then the machine language program executes.

There are three kinds of arithmetic notation:

- Infix   3 + 5
- Prefix   + 3 5
- Postfix   3 5 +

Infix notation is the notation you learned as a child. The plus operator is between the operands 3 and 5. In prefix notation, the operator precedes its operands, and in postfix notation, the operator follows its operands.

The expressions you write in a Component Pascal program are infix expressions. Unfortunately, infix expressions are difficult to evaluate when the program executes in machine language. It is easier for the computer to evaluate a postfix expression. Component Pascal compilers convert infix expressions to postfix. Then, when the machine-language version of the program executes, it evaluates the postfix expression.

The evaluation of a postfix expression requires a stack of operands. The algorithm for evaluating a postfix expression is

- Scan the postfix expression from left to right.

- If you encounter an operand, push it onto the stack.

- If you encounter an operator, apply the operator to the top two operands of the stack. Replace the two operands with the result of the operation.

- After scanning the entire postfix expression, the stack should have one item, the value of the expression.

The algorithm for evaluating a postfix expression

Example 7.1   Here is a trace of the evaluation for the postfix expression

1 6 + 5 2 – ×

In this trace, the bottom of the stack is on the left.

Stack	Expression
empty	1 6 + 5 2 – ×
1	6 + 5 2 – ×
1 6	+ 5 2 – ×
7	5 2 – ×
7 5	2 – ×
7 5 2	– ×
7 3	×
21	empty

The algorithm first pushes 1, then 6. It encounters the plus operator and applies it to 1 and 6, replacing them with 7 on the stack. It pushes 5 and 2, encounters the minus operator and replaces the 5 and 2 with their difference on the stack. Then it encounters the multiply operator. It applies it to 7 and 3, producing the final result of 21. ∎

Translation from infix to postfix

A computer system must solve two basic problems to process an expression from a Component Pascal program. First, it must translate the infix expression to postfix, and second, it must evaluate the postfix expression. The previous algorithm showed the evaluation of a postfix expression. The following discussion shows how to translate from infix to postfix.

Example 7.2   Five examples of infix expressions and their corresponding postfix expressions are

Infix	Postfix
2 + 3	2 3 +
2 × 5 + 3	2 5 × 3 +
2 + 5 × 3	2 5 3 × +
2 × 3 + 5 × 4	2 3 × 5 4 × +
2 + 3 × 5 + 4	2 3 5 × + 4 +

You can verify that they are equivalent by evaluating the postfix expression according to the evaluation algorithm. ∎

Two different postfix expressions can be equivalent to the same infix expression.

Example 7.3   The postfix expressions

5 3 × 2 +

and

2 5 3 × +

are both equivalent to the infix expression

2 + 5 × 3

However, the operands of the first postfix expression (5, 3, 2) are in a different order from the operands of the infix expression (2, 5, 3). ∎

One property of the postfix expressions in Example 7.2 is that their operands are all in the same order as the operands of the equivalent infix expressions. The translation algorithm that follows has the same property.

Maintain the order of the operands.

A characteristic of infix that is not shared by postfix is the precedence of the operators. In the infix expression 2 + 5 × 3, the multiplication is performed before the addition because multiplication has a higher precedence than addition. In postfix, however, there is no operator precedence. The order in which an operation is performed is determined strictly by the position of the operator in the postfix expression. That is one reason computers can evaluate postfix expressions more easily than infix expressions.

Postfix has no operator precedence.

In the translation of the preceding expressions from infix to postfix, only the placement of the operators is different. In fact, the multiplication operators occur before the addition operators, because multiplication has a higher precedence than addition in the infix expression. An algorithm that translates from infix to postfix only needs to shift the operators to the right and possibly reorder them. The order of the operands remains unchanged.

The following algorithm for translating an expression from infix to postfix uses a stack to temporarily store the operators until they can be inserted further to the right into the postfix expression.

- Scan the infix expression from left to right.

- If the item is an operand, move it directly to the postfix expression.

- If the item is an operator, compare it with the operator on top of the stack:

  ▲ If the operator on top of the stack has a precedence lower than that of the item just encountered in the infix expression or if the stack is empty, push the item just encountered onto the stack.

  ▲ If the operator on top of the stack has a precedence higher than or equal to that of the item just encountered in the infix expression, pop items off the stack. Place them in the postfix expression until either the precedence of the top operator is less than the precedence of the item or the stack is empty. Then push the item onto the stack.

- After the entire infix expression has been scanned, pop any remaining operators left on the stack and put them in the postfix expression.

The algorithm for translating from infix to postfix

Because the operands pass directly to the postfix expression, they will maintain their order. The algorithm allows an operator to be pushed onto the stack only if the stack top contains an operator of lower precedence. Therefore, the stack will always have the operators with the highest precedence near the top.

Example 7.4   Here is a trace of the translation process according to the previous algorithm:

Postfix output	*Stack*	*Infix input*
empty	empty	2 + 3 × 5 + 4
2	empty	+ 3 × 5 + 4
2	+	3 × 5 + 4
2 3	+	× 5 + 4
2 3	+ ×	5 + 4
2 3 5	+ ×	+ 4
2 3 5 ×	+	+ 4
2 3 5 × +	empty	+ 4
2 3 5 × +	+	4
2 3 5 × + 4	+	empty
2 3 5 × + 4 +	empty	empty

When the algorithm gets the multiplication operator, it compares it with the addition operator on top of the stack. Multiplication has a higher precedence than addition. Therefore, it puts the multiplication operator on the stack. After it sends the 5 operand to the postfix expression, the multiplication operator follows it. So when you evaluate the postfix expression, you will multiply 3 by 5 before adding the result to 2. ▮

Another reason why postfix expressions are easier to evaluate than infix expressions is that postfix expressions have no parentheses. Infix expressions can have parentheses. When they do, all of the operations inside the parentheses must be performed before the operations outside. Converting an infix expression with parentheses is only slightly more complicated than converting an expression without

Postfix expressions have no parentheses.

parentheses.

Example 7.5 Here are some examples of infix expressions with parentheses and the corresponding postfix expressions.

Infix	*Postfix*
2 × (7 + 3)	2 7 3 + ×
2 × (7 + 3 × 4)	2 7 3 4 × + ×
2 × (7 × 3 + 4)	2 7 3 × 4 + ×
2 + (7 × 3 + 4)	2 7 3 × 4 + +
2 × (7 × (3 + 4) + 5)	2 7 3 4 + × 5 + ×

Again, the order of the operands is the same. You should evaluate these expressions to convince yourself that they are equivalent. ∎

When a left parenthesis is detected in the left to right scan, it marks the starting point of a substack within the main stack. It is as if a new expression is to be evaluated, the expression within the parentheses. The algorithm pushes the left parenthesis onto the stack to mark the beginning of the substack. It converts the subexpression using the substack. When it encounters the matching right parenthesis, it pops the operators off the substack and places them in the postfix expression until it reaches the left parenthesis. It discards the pair of parentheses and continues converting.

Example 7.6 Here is an example of the translation process for an infix expression containing parentheses:

Postfix output	*Stack*	*Expression*
empty	empty	2 × (7 + 3 × 4) + 6
2	empty	× (7 + 3 × 4) + 6
2	×	(7 + 3 × 4) + 6
2	× (	7 + 3 × 4) + 6
2 7	× (	+ 3 × 4) + 6
2 7	× (+	3 × 4) + 6
2 7 3	× (+	× 4) + 6
2 7 3	× (+ ×	4) + 6
2 7 3 4	× (+ ×	) + 6
2 7 3 4 ×	× (+	) + 6
2 7 3 4 × +	× (	) + 6
2 7 3 4 × +	×	+ 6
2 7 3 4 × + ×	empty	+ 6
2 7 3 4 × + ×	+	6
2 7 3 4 × + × 6	+	empty
2 7 3 4 × + × 6 +	empty	empty

When the algorithm encounters the left parenthesis, it simply pushes it onto the stack with the multiplication operator. It continues the conversion, placing the addi-

tion and multiplication operators on the stack. When it encounters the right parenthesis, the algorithm knows it is at the end of the subexpression between the two
parentheses. It pops the multiplication and addition operators off the stack. Then the
algorithm discards the pair of parentheses and continues the conversion. ∎

The stack abstract data structure

Figure 7.2 is the interface of the stack data structure provided by module PboxStack-
ADS. It contains five exported items—one constant and four procedures. The constant is named capacity and gives the maximum number of items that can be stored
on the stack. Constants are similar to variables except that their values cannot be   *You cannot change the value*
changed with an assignment statement.   *of a constant.*

```
DEFINITION PboxStackADS;

    CONST
        capacity = 8;

    PROCEDURE Clear;
    PROCEDURE NumItems (): INTEGER;
    PROCEDURE Pop (OUT val: REAL);
    PROCEDURE Push (val: REAL);

END PboxStackADS.
```

Figure 7.2
The interface of the stack
abstract data structure.

As usual, you can view the interface by highlighting PboxStackADS in a display
of text on some window and selecting Info→Interface. The interface gives you the   *Inspecting the interface*
names of all the items exported by the module. For the procedures, it gives you the
formal parameters including their types, so you will know what type the corresponding actual parameters must have.

The interface does not provide you with a description of what each procedure
does, although you can usually surmise that from its name. For example, it is obvious from its name that procedure Pop pops a value off a stack. In case you need
more information about the items exported from a module than what is supplied in
its interface, you can highlight the module name and select Info→Documentation. If   *Inspecting the documentation*
the programmer of the module has supplied corresponding documentation in the
Docu folder, a window will open the documentation in browser mode. The documentation fragments in the following discussion are available on-line by highlighting PboxStackADS and selecting Info→Documentation.

Here is the documentation for capacity.

CONST capacity
The maximum number of real values in the stack.

There is a limit to how many items the user can put on this stack. You can see from
the interface that a maximum of eight real values are allowed.

Procedure Clear has this documentation.

PROCEDURE **Clear**
Post
The stack is cleared to the empty stack.

The word Post in the documentation indicates a postcondition. In general, the documentation of a procedure in BlackBox consists of the procedure's preconditions and postconditions. A precondition states what must be true *before* the procedure executes in order for it to execute correctly. A postcondition states what must be true *after* the procedure executes if all its preconditions were true beforehand. Procedure Clear has no preconditions and one postcondition, which specifies that regardless of the initial state of the stack it will be empty after procedure Clear executes.

Preconditions and postconditions

The specification for procedure NumItems is

PROCEDURE **NumItems** (): INTEGER
Post
Returns the number of elements in the stack.

You can tell from its signature that it is a function procedure, not a proper procedure, and it has no parameters in its formal parameter list. When you execute NumItems, it returns the number elements in the stack regardless of the initial state of the stack.

Procedure Pop has a precondition as well as a postcondition.

PROCEDURE **Pop** (OUT val: REAL)
Pre
0 < NumItems()   20
Post
An item is removed from the top of the stack and val gets its value.

The precondition requires that the number of elements in the stack be greater than 0 in order to guarantee the post condition after you execute Pop. This is a reasonable precondition, because how can you pop an element off a stack if there are no elements in the stack to begin with? The integer 20 that follows the precondition is an error number that is displayed if the precondition is ever violated. One of the programming style convention for Component Pascal in the BlackBox framework is that the error numbers for precondition violations begin with integer 20. The next section gives an example that shows what happens when you violate a precondition.

A precondition programming style

The specification for procedure Push reveals that it also has a precondition.

PROCEDURE **Push** (val: REAL)
Pre
NumItems() < capacity   20
Post
val is pushed onto the top of the stack.

The precondition states that the number of items on the stack must be less than the maximum number allowed. That is, there must be room for at least one more item if you want to push an item onto the top of the stack.

Formal parameters val in Pop and val in Push show that each of these procedures expects a single real actual parameter. The word OUT before a formal parameter in

OUT parameters

the parameter list of a procedure indicates two things:

- The value of the parameter is considered to be undefined when the procedure is called.
- The procedure will change the value of the actual parameter.

Figure 7.1(e) illustrates these two points. Before the pop operation, the value of actual parameter val is considered undefined. After the pop operation, val has the value 4.0 from the top of the stack. Procedure Pop changes the value of val to 4.0.

Figure 7.3 shows a dialog box that illustrates the use of the stack ADS provided by PboxStackADS. To push a value onto the stack, the user enters a real value in the text field and then pushes the button labeled Push. To pop a value off the stack, the user pushes the button labeled Pop, after which the dialog box displays the value popped in the region to the right of the Pop button. The dialog box shows the current number of items on the stack after each push and pop operation. The button labeled Clear Stack removes all items off the stack. The box in Figure 7.3 shows the result of pressing the Pop button after pushing 5.0, 2.0, and 4.0. It corresponds to the state of the stack in Figure 7.1(e).

Figure 7.4 is the listing of a program that implements the dialog box of Figure 7.3. It imports PboxStackADS and contains the usual record named d whose fields are linked to the dialog box. The initialization part of the module assigns the appropriate procedures to the procedure fields of d. Rather than initialize the default values of the remaining fields of d individually, the initialization part of the module simply calls procedure Clear, which initializes the stack and sets the proper default values.

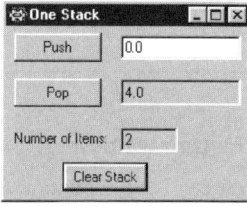

Figure 7.3
The dialog box that goes with the program in Figure 7.4.

Figure 7.4
A program that uses the stack abstract data structure.

```
MODULE Pbox07A;
  IMPORT Dialog, PboxStackADS;

  VAR
    d*: RECORD
      valuePushed*, valuePopped-: REAL;
      numItems-: INTEGER;
    END;

  PROCEDURE Push*;
  BEGIN
    PboxStackADS.Push(d.valuePushed);
    d.numItems := PboxStackADS.NumItems();
    Dialog.Update(d)
  END Push;

  PROCEDURE Pop*;
  BEGIN
    PboxStackADS.Pop(d.valuePopped);
    d.numItems := PboxStackADS.NumItems();
    Dialog.Update(d)
  END Pop;
```

```
PROCEDURE ClearStack*;
BEGIN
   PboxStackADS.Clear;
   d.valuePushed := 0.0; d.valuePopped := 0.0;
   d.numItems := 0;
   Dialog.Update(d)
END ClearStack;

BEGIN
   ClearStack
END Pbox07A.
```

Figure 7.4

Continued.

The trap window

You can easily violate a precondition with the dialog box in Figure 7.3 by simply pressing the button labeled Clear Stack followed by pressing the button labeled Pop. Because Clear Stack makes the stack empty, when you attempt to execute procedure Pop its precondition

0 < NumItems()

will be false, because NumItems will return 0. BlackBox responds to this condition with the trap window, whose purpose is to provide information to the programmer about the cause of some error condition. Figure 7.5 shows the top part of the trap window generated from the above scenario.

The purpose of the trap window

Link to global variables

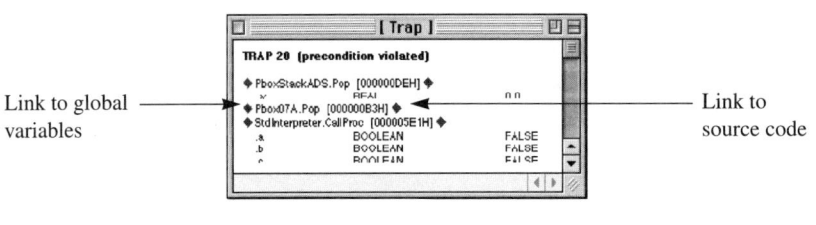

Link to source code

(a) MacOS

Figure 7.5

A trap window for the stack ADS program.

Link to global variables

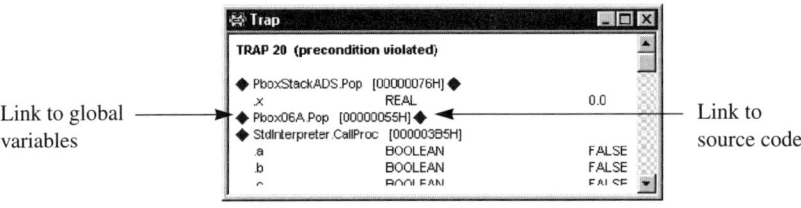

Link to source code

(b) MSWindows

The first line of the trap window gives a description for the cause of the trap. In this case the cause is that a precondition was violated, specifically the precondition with error number 20. The lines with the diamond marks in front of them are the names of the procedures that are executing when the trap occurs. You can see from the second line in the trap window that procedure PboxStackADS.Pop was executing when its precondition was violated. It was called by Pbox07A.Pop, which was in turn called by StdInterpreter.CallProc, and so on. If you scroll down the trap window you can see that the procedures you write are the last of a long line of procedures that the framework calls before eventually calling yours. Information in the lower procedures is useful only to the programmers of the BlackBox framework and can be ignored.

If you ever get a trap window with a precondition violation, it is easy to read the corresponding documentation. Simply highlight the top procedure name in the trap window (which is possible even though the trap window is in browser mode) and select Info→Documentation. If the programmer has supplied a corresponding Docu file, the framework will open the documentation and you can read the specification. In Figure 7.5, if you highlight PboxStackADS.Pop and select Info→Documentation you will see the specification that describes the precondition for procedure Pop.

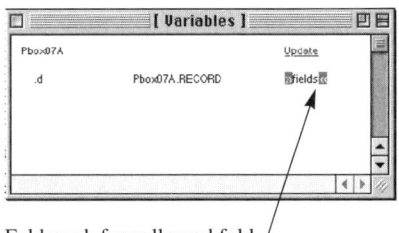

Fold mark for collapsed fold

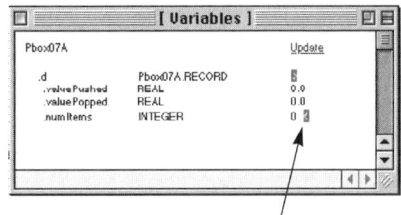

Fold mark for expanded fold

(a) MacOS

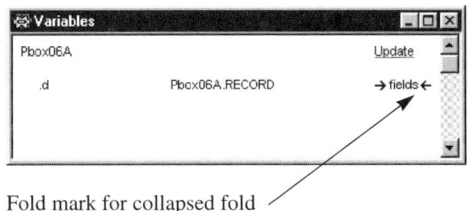

Fold mark for collapsed fold

Fold mark for expanded fold

(b) MSWindows

Figure 7.6
Global variables generated from the trap window of Figure 7.5.

Each procedure that is executing when the trap occurs has a leading mark, which links to the global variables of the module, and a trailing mark, which links to the source code of the executing procedure. When you click on the leading mark a new

window is activated that shows the values of any global variables. Clicking on the *Link to global variables*
leading mark of Pbox07A.Pop shown in Figure 7.5 produces the window shown in
Figure 7.6. The global variable in Pbox07A is record d, the interactor for the dialog
box.

Recall that a record is a collection of values, not necessarily of the same type.
Record d has three values—valuePushed of type real, valuePopped of type real, and
numItems of type integer. When the window that displays d is activated you cannot
see the three fields that comprise d because they are contained in a collapsed fold. A *Folds*
fold is a section of text enclosed by fold marks. When the fold is expanded the text is
visible. When it is collapsed the text is invisible. You can expand and collapse the
text between fold marks by clicking on the marks. Figure 7.6 shows the fold marks
for the collapsed fold and the expanded fold which results from clicking on the
mark. You can see by inspecting the values in the expanded fold that the type of
numItems is integer and its value was 0 when the trap occurred.

Before you experiment with the link to the source code in Figure 7.5, you should
insure that the window for the source code of module Pbox07A is *not* opened. When
that is the case and you click on the link to the source code in the trap window, *Link to source code*
BlackBox will open a window with the source code in it. It will highlight the statement that was executing when the trap occurred. Figure 7.7 shows the result of
clicking the link to the source code in Figure 7.5. You can see from the figure that
not only is the window opened, but the text PboxStackADS.Pop(d.valuePopped) is
highlighted. The highlighting shows you that the call to procedure Pop was executing when the trap occurred.

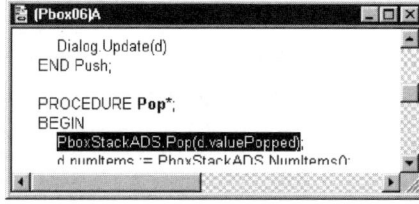

Figure 7.7
Source code window opened
by the link to the source code
in Figure 7.5.

The trap window not only gives you links to global variables and source code, it
also gives you the types and values of formal parameters and local variables. Unlike
global variables and source code, formal parameters and local variables are not
accessed via links, but are provided directly in the trap window. Figure 7.5 shows a
value of 0 for formal parameter x in procedure PboxADS.Pop. Local variables
include a and b in StdInterpreter.CallProc, as well as many others not shown in the
figure. Much of this information is helpful when you encounter errors in your program. You should develop skill in using the information provided by the trap window to correct your programs.

The stack abstract data type

Previous chapters showed how to program with several types, such as INTEGER and
REAL. Because these types are provided by the Component Pascal language, they

are also known as *primitive* types. Component Pascal requires that all primitive types be indicated by spelling them with all uppercase letters. Most programming language designers recognize that programmers will frequently need types other than those provided by the language. Therefore, they provide a facility for programmers to define their own types, known as *programmer-defined* types. The style convention for programmer-defined types is to capitalize the first letter.

Primitive types

Programmer-defined types

The dialog box for the stack abstract data structure provided only one stack for the user to manipulate. The distinguishing feature of an abstract data *type* in contrast to an abstract data *structure* is that a module with an ADT exports a type. Hence, the importing module can declare several variables of the exported type, and therefore have several data structures to manipulate. The listing in Figure 7.8 shows the interface of a module that provides a stack ADT.

```
DEFINITION PboxStackADT;

    CONST
        capacity = 8;

    TYPE
        Stack = RECORD END;

    PROCEDURE Clear (VAR s: Stack);
    PROCEDURE NumItems (IN s: Stack): INTEGER;
    PROCEDURE Pop (VAR s: Stack; OUT val: REAL);
    PROCEDURE Push (VAR s: Stack; val: REAL);

END PboxStackADT.
```

Figure 7.8
The interface of the stack abstract data type.

The interface of the stack ADT shows the same constant for the capacity of a stack and the same four procedures—Clear, NumItems, Pop, and Push. However, an additional item is exported—the type Stack. The interface shows that the type stack is a record, but it appears to have no fields. If you examine MODULE PboxStackADT, you will undoubtedly see some fields in the record for the type. However, none of them are exported. This is yet another example of hidden detail in the concept of abstraction. The interface hides the details of the implementation of the stack. As a programmer who wants to use the type Stack, you only need to be concerned with the behavior of the procedures, and the specifications for using the parameters in the parameter lists.

If you inspect the documentation of module PboxStackADT you will find that the description of Stack is

TYPE Stack
The stack abstract data type supplied by PboxStackADT.

Stack is a programmer-defined type supplied by the module for client modules to use. In the same way that you can declare a real variable in Component Pascal with the code fragment

```
VAR
    myReal: REAL;
```

you can declare a stack variable with the code fragment

```
VAR
    myStack: Stack;
```

The parameter lists for the stack ADT procedures are identical to those for the stack ADS except for the addition in each one of a formal parameter of type Stack. The additional parameter is necessary because a module that uses this ADT may have more than one stack variable. If you want to push a value onto a stack, you must give not only the value you want to push but the stack on which you want to push it. Here are the specifications for Clear and Pop, which describe how formal parameter s is used by the client module.

```
PROCEDURE Clear (VAR s: Stack)
Post
Stack s is cleared to the empty stack.
```

```
PROCEDURE Pop (VAR s: Stack; OUT val: REAL)
Pre
0 < NumItems(s)   20
Post
An item is removed from the top of stack s and val gets its value.
```

Specifications for the other procedures are similar.

The formal parameters of the stack ADT show four different calling modes that Component Pascal provides:

- Default Call by value
- IN   Call by constant reference
- OUT   Call by result
- VAR   Call by reference

The four calling modes of Component Pascal

Parameter val in Push uses the default call by value. Parameter s in NumItems uses the IN mode known as call by constant reference. Parameter val in Pop uses the OUT mode known as call by result. And parameter s in ClearStack uses the VAR mode known as call by reference.

There are some subtle differences between these four modes that later chapters investigate. For now, you should recognize one important property of these modes:

- In call by value (default) and call by constant reference (IN), the procedure does *not* change the value of the actual parameter.

- In call by result (OUT) and call by reference (VAR), the procedure *does* change the value of the actual parameter.

Changing versus not changing the value of the actual parameter.

You can understand how this property applies to the parameters of the procedures in the stack ADT. When you call procedure Push, you give a value for val that you want to be pushed onto the stack. You do *not* want the procedure to change the value of val. When you call procedure Numltems, you give a stack for which you want the number of items. You do *not* want the procedure to change the stack. These two modes are call by value and call by constant reference, in which the actual parameter does not change.

When you call procedure Pop, you provide a variable to receive the popped value. You *do* want the procedure to change the value of the variable you provide. When you call procedure ClearStack, you provide the stack variable that you want to be cleared. You *do* want the procedure to change the stack. These two modes are call by result and call by reference, in which the actual parameter does change.

Figure 7.9 shows a dialog box that illustrates the facility of multiple data structures with the stack ADT. It lets the user manipulate two stacks labeled Stack A and Stack B. After the user enters a value in the text box he has the option of pushing the value onto Stack A or onto Stack B. Similarly, the box has two buttons for the pop operation—one for popping from Stack A and one for popping from Stack B—and two displays for the number of items in each of the stacks. The clear button clears both stacks.

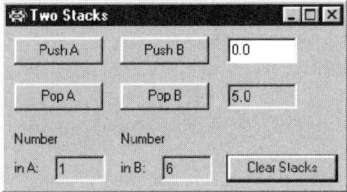

Figure 7.9
The dialog box for manipulating two stacks.

Figure 7.10 shows a program for the dialog box of Figure 7.9. As usual, the box for user input of a real value corresponds to a real exported field valuePushed in the interactor d. The real value popped and the integer number of items in stack A and B are exported read-only, because the program computes their values.

In contrast to the program that used the stack ADS, this program includes two global variables in addition to the interactor d. StackA and StackB are both declared to be of type PboxStackADT.Stack. This is possible only because the interface of Figure 7.8 shows that Stack is a type exported by module PboxStackADT. Note how the stacks themselves are contained in module Pbox07B as global variables, while there is no global stack in module Pbox07A. The procedures in module Pbox07A manipulate one stack that is contained in PboxStackADS.

Now, what happens when the user wants to push the value 3.5 onto stack A? She enters 3.5 into the input text box and presses the button labeled Push A. The programmer has linked this button to procedure PushA in module Pbox07B. The first statement of this procedure is the call

PboxStackADT.Push(stackA, d.valuePushed)

the actual parameter stackA corresponds to formal parameter s, and actual parameter d.valuePushed corresponds to formal parameter val. So, the value 3.5 is pushed onto stackA. Remember that val is called by value. This operation does *not* change the value of d.valuePushed. Also, s is called by reference. This operation *does* change stackA, because it now has 3.5 on its top whereas before the call it did not.

```
MODULE Pbox07B;
   IMPORT Dialog, PboxStackADT;

   VAR
     d*: RECORD
        valuePushed*, valuePopped-: REAL;
        numItemsA-, numItemsB-: INTEGER;
     END;
     stackA, stackB: PboxStackADT.Stack;

   PROCEDURE PushA*;
   BEGIN
     PboxStackADT.Push(stackA, d.valuePushed);
     d.numItemsA := PboxStackADT.NumItems(stackA);
     Dialog.Update(d)
   END PushA;

   PROCEDURE PushB*;
   BEGIN
     PboxStackADT.Push(stackB, d.valuePushed);
     d.numItemsB := PboxStackADT.NumItems(stackB);
     Dialog.Update(d)
   END PushB;

   PROCEDURE PopA*;
   BEGIN
     PboxStackADT.Pop(stackA, d.valuePopped);
     d.numItemsA := PboxStackADT.NumItems(stackA);
     Dialog.Update(d)
   END PopA;

   PROCEDURE PopB*;
   BEGIN
     PboxStackADT.Pop(stackB, d.valuePopped);
     d.numItemsB := PboxStackADT.NumItems(stackB);
     Dialog.Update(d)
   END PopB;

   PROCEDURE ClearStacks*;
   BEGIN
     PboxStackADT.Clear(stackA);
     PboxStackADT.Clear(stackB);
     d.valuePushed := 0.0; d.valuePopped := 0.0;
     d.numItemsA := 0; d.numItemsB := 0;
     Dialog.Update(d)
   END ClearStacks;

BEGIN
   ClearStacks
END Pbox07B.
```

Figure 7.10
A program that uses the stack abstract data type.

The second statement in procedure PushA is

d.numItemsA := PboxStackADT.NumItems(stackA)

The statement calls function NumItems, which returns the number of items in the stack specified by its parameter, stackA in this case. d.numItemsA gets the value returned. Function NumItems in module PboxStackADS has no parameters, because there is only one stack in an abstract data structure. When the programmer requests the number of items in a stack, it is understood to be the number of items in the one stack supplied by the ADS. With the abstract data type in module PboxStackADT, however, the programmer must specify the stack for which the number of elements is desired.

The last statement in procedure PushA is

Dialog.Update(d)

which, as usual, makes the change to d.numItemsA visible in the dialog box.

Figure 7.11 illustrates the difference between the stack ADS of Pbox07A and the stack ADT of Pbox07B. With the ADS, there is only one data structure, and it is contained in the exporting module. When the importing procedure manipulates a stack it always manipulates this one data structure. With the ADT, the exporting procedure exports a type, and the data structures are contained in the importing module. When the importing module manipulates a stack, it must specify via a parameter which stack is to be manipulated.

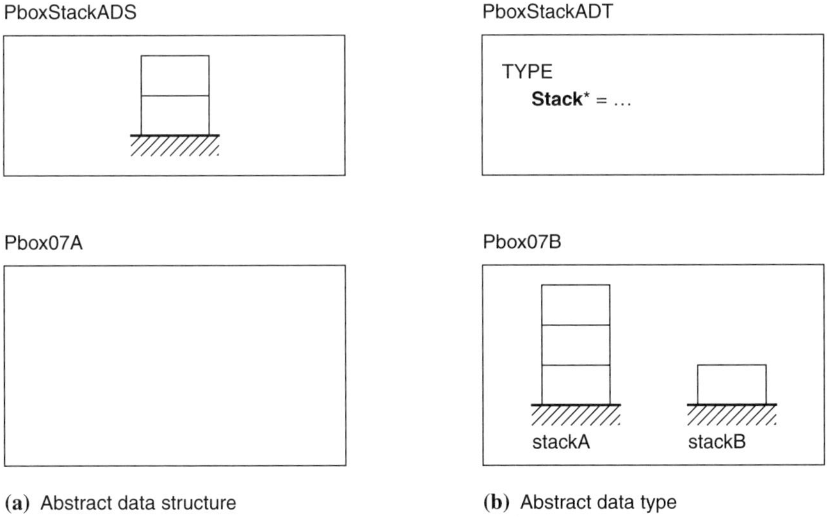

PboxStackADS

PboxStackADT

Figure 7.11
The difference between an abstract data structure and an abstract data type.

TYPE
 Stack * = …

Pbox07A

Pbox07B

stackA   stackB

(a) Abstract data structure

(b) Abstract data type

The list abstract data structure

Like a stack, a list is a data structure that stores values. A list, however, is more flexible than a stack, because when you store an element in a list you are not limited to storing it at one end of the structure. Furthermore, when you remove an element from a list, you can remove it from any location as well. To have the capability of storing and retrieving from any location in a list, you must have a means of specifying an arbitrary location in the list. Each element has associated with it an integer called its *position*. The position of the first element of a list is 0. Figure 7.12 shows the container for a list of at most eight elements. The first element is stored at position 0, and if the list were full the last element would be stored at position 7. The previous sections described stacks as containers of real numbers. In practice, data structures can store values of any type. In this and the following sections, the list data structures will store values of type string.

Figure 7.13 is the interface for the list abstract data structure. As with the stack, the list is not part of the standard BlackBox system and must be accessed from the Pbox project. The interface contains a constant capacity of eight, which is the maximum number of elements in the list. Even though this is an ADS as opposed to an ADT, a type is nevertheless exported. However, type T is *not* the type of the list. It is the type of each *element* in the list. In this interface, type T appears as a type of some formal parameters.

0	trout
1	tuna
2	cod
3	salmon
4	
5	
6	
7	

Figure 7.12
A list that contains a maximum of eight strings.

```
DEFINITION PboxListADS;

    CONST
       capacity = 8;
    TYPE
       T = ARRAY 16 OF CHAR;

    PROCEDURE Clear;
    PROCEDURE Display;
    PROCEDURE GetElementN (n: INTEGER; OUT val: T);
    PROCEDURE InsertAtN (n: INTEGER; IN val: T);
    PROCEDURE Length (): INTEGER;
    PROCEDURE RemoveN (n: INTEGER);
    PROCEDURE Search (IN srchVal: T; OUT n: INTEGER; OUT fnd: BOOLEAN);

END PboxListADS.
```

Figure 7.13
The interface of the list abstract data structure.

The ADS could have been written without T by writing ARRAY 16 OF CHAR everywhere T appears in a parameter list. One advantage of using T is that the parameter lists are shorter because of the abbreviation that T provides. Another, more important, advantage is for the programmer of the ADS. To change the type of the elements stored in the list you would need to change only one line of code. For example, to store a list of reals you would need to change only the line

T = ARRAY 16 OF CHAR;

to

T = REAL;

The documentation for T is

TYPE **T**
The type of each element in the list.

The specification for procedure Clear is

PROCEDURE **Clear**
Post
The list is initialized to the empty list.

It has no precondition. The post condition is that the list is cleared.

Example 7.7 If you execute Clear when the list has the four elements as in Figure
7.12, then all four elements will be removed from the list.   ∎

Procedure Length is a function that returns the length of the list. Its specification
is

PROCEDURE **Length** (): INTEGER
Post
Returns the number of elements in the list.

Example 7.8 If you call Length() when the list has the elements as in Figure 7.12,
the function will return 4, because there are four elements in the list.   ∎

Procedure InsertAtN inserts an element at position n, shifting the elements below
to make room for the new element. It has two preconditions.

PROCEDURE **InsertAtN** (n: INTEGER; IN val: T)
Pre
0 <= n   20
Length() < capacity   21
Post
val is inserted at position n in the list, increasing Length() by 1.
If n > Length(), val is appended to the list.

The first precondition states that the value you supply for n cannot be negative. This
is a reasonable precondition, because n is the position in the list at which element val
is inserted. Because there are no negative positions, you are not allowed to provide a
negative position. The second precondition states that the length of the list must be
less than its maximum capacity. This is a reasonable precondition, because if the list
is already filled to capacity there will be no room for an additional element.

Example 7.9 If the list has the elements as in Figure 7.12, and you execute

InsertAtN(2, myString)

where myString has the value "bass", then the list will be changed as in Figure 7.14(a). If instead you execute

InsertAtN(0, myString)

then the list will be changed as in Figure 7.14(b). And if instead you execute

InsertAtN(7, myString)

a precondition is not violated. Element "bass" is inserted at position 4 at the end of the list as shown in Figure 7.14(c).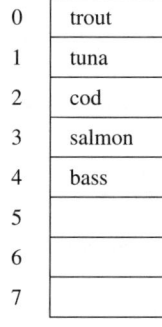

0	trout
1	tuna
2	bass
3	cod
4	salmon
5	
6	
7	

(a) After inserting at position 2.

0	bass
1	trout
2	tuna
3	cod
4	salmon
5	
6	
7	

(b) After inserting at position 0.

0	trout
1	tuna
2	cod
3	salmon
4	bass
5	
6	
7	

(c) After inserting at position 7.

Figure 7.14
The list of Figure 7.12 after executing the statements of Example 7.9.

Procedure RemoveN removes the element from position n, shifting the elements below to take up the room vacated by the removed element. Here is its specification.

PROCEDURE **RemoveN** (n: INTEGER)
Pre
0 <= n   20
Post
If n < Length(), the element at position n in the list is removed.
Otherwise, the list is unchanged.

The precondition does not allow you to supply a negative value for position n.

Example 7.10 If the list has the elements as in Figure 7.12, and you execute

RemoveN(2)

then the list will be changed as in Figure 7.15(a). If instead you execute

RemoveN(0)

then the list will be changed as in Figure 7.15(b). And if instead you execute

RemoveN(7)

a precondition is not violated. The list simply remains unchanged as shown in Figure 7.15(c). ∎

0	trout
1	tuna
2	salmon
3	
4	
5	
6	
7	

(a) After removing from position 2.

0	tuna
1	cod
2	salmon
3	
4	
5	
6	
7	

(b) After removing from position 0.

0	trout
1	tuna
2	cod
3	salmon
4	
5	
6	
7	

(c) After removing from position 7.

Figure 7.15
The list of Figure 7.12 after executing the statements of Example 7.10.

Procedures InsertAtN and RemoveN alter the content of the list. The list ADS provides two procedures that allow you to query the list without altering its content. With procedure GetElementN, you supply a position n, and it gives you the element at that position. Procedure Search does the reverse. You give it an element, and it returns the position of that element in the list. It includes a boolean parameter fnd, which is set to FALSE if the element is not found in the list. In that case, the value returned for n is not defined. Here are the specifications of GetElementN and Search.

PROCEDURE **GetElementN** (n: INTEGER; OUT val: T)
Pre
$0 <= n$ 20
$n <$ Length()   21
Post
val gets the data value of the element at position n of the list.
Note: 0 is the position of the first element in the list.

PROCEDURE **Search** (IN srchVal: T; OUT n: INTEGER; OUT fnd: BOOLEAN)
Post
If srchVal is in the list, fnd is set to TRUE and n is set to the first position where srchVal is found. Otherwise, fnd is set to FALSE and n is undefined.

Example 7.11   If the list has the elements as in Figure 7.12, and you execute

GetElementN(2, myString)

then myString will get the value "cod". Execution of

GetElementN(4, myString)

violates a precondition and generates a trap.   ∎

Example 7.12   If the list has the elements as in Figure 7.12, myString has value "cod", position is an integer variable, found is a boolean variable, and you execute

Search(myString, position, found)

then found will get TRUE and position will get the value 2. If you execute the same statement when myString has value "catfish", found will get FALSE and position will get some undefined value. Note that the position of the last element, "salmon", is 3, not 4, because the position of the first element, "trout", is 0, not 1.   ∎

The specification of procedure Display is

PROCEDURE **Display**
Post
The list is output to the Log, one element per line with each element preceded by its position.

Display has no preconditions.

Example 7.13   If the list has the elements as in Figure 7.12, and you execute procedure Display, the following text will be printed on the Log.

```
0 trout
1 tuna
2 cod
3 salmon
```
                                                                                ∎

Figure 7.16 shows a dialog box that allows the user to manipulate a list of strings. The state of the dialog box corresponds to a list that contains four elements as in Figure 7.12. The user has previously entered the elements by pressing the Insert button. She queried the list by asking for the location of element "salmon", which the dialog box gives as position 3, and for the retrieval of the element at position 1, which the dialog box gives as "tuna". With each insert and deletion of an element the current number of items is displayed.

The listing in Figure 7.17 is a program that implements the dialog box in Figure 7.16. It is a straightforward mapping from input and output values of the dialog box to variables in the d interactor, and from the buttons of the dialog box to exported procedures in the module.

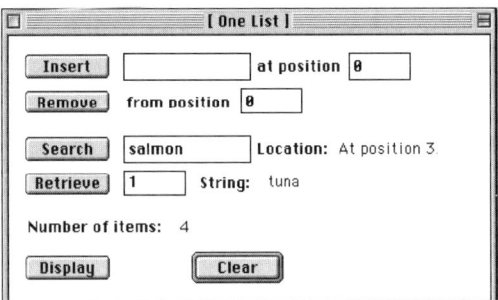

Figure 7.16
The dialog box for
manipulating a list.

```
MODULE Pbox07C;
    IMPORT Dialog, PboxListADS, PboxStrings;

    TYPE
        String32 = ARRAY 32 OF CHAR;

    VAR
        d*: RECORD
            insertT*: PboxListADS.T; insertPosition*: INTEGER;
            removePosition*: INTEGER;
            searchT*: PboxListADS.T; searchPosition-: String32;
            retrievePosition*: INTEGER; retrieveT-: PboxListADS.T;
            numItems-: INTEGER;
        END;

    PROCEDURE InsertAt*;
    BEGIN
        PboxListADS.InsertAtN(d.insertPosition, d.insertT);
        d.numItems := PboxListADS.Length();
        Dialog.Update(d)
    END InsertAt;

    PROCEDURE RemoveFrom*;
    BEGIN
        PboxListADS.RemoveN(d.removePosition);
        d.numItems := PboxListADS.Length();
        Dialog.Update(d)
    END RemoveFrom;
```

Figure 7.17
A program that uses the list
abstract data structure to
implement the dialog box of
Figure 7.16.

Figure 7.17
Continued.

```
PROCEDURE SearchFor*;
VAR
    found: BOOLEAN;
    position: INTEGER;
BEGIN
    PboxListADS.Search(d.searchT, position, found);
    IF found THEN
        PboxStrings.IntToString(position, 1, d.searchPosition);
        d.searchPosition := "At position " + d.searchPosition + ".";
    ELSE
        d.searchPosition := "Not in list.";
    END;
    Dialog.Update(d)
END SearchFor;

PROCEDURE RetrieveFrom*;
BEGIN
    PboxListADS.GetElementN(d.retrievePosition, d.retrieveT);
    Dialog.Update(d)
END RetrieveFrom;

PROCEDURE DisplayList*;
BEGIN
    PboxListADS.Display;
    Dialog.Update(d)
END DisplayList;

PROCEDURE ClearList*;
BEGIN
    PboxListADS.Clear;
    d.insertT := ""; d.insertPosition := 0;
    d.removePosition := 0;
    d.searchT := ""; d.searchPosition := "";
    d.retrievePosition := 0; d.retrieveT := "";
    d.numItems := PboxListADS.Length();
    Dialog.Update(d)
END ClearList;

BEGIN
    ClearList
END Pbox07C.
```

As an example of the mapping, consider the first line of the dialog box that allows the user to insert an element into the list. The user must enter a string into the first box and an integer representing the location of where to insert the string into the second box. These two values require two fields in the d interactor, both exported read-write because the user enters the values. The corresponding fields in the d inter-actor are

insertT*: PboxListADS.T; insertPosition*: INTEGER

The type of insertT is PboxListADS.T, which we know from the interface in Figure 7.13 is the same as **ARRAY 16 OF CHAR**. This type permits the user to enter a string of up to 15 characters. The button labeled Insert is obviously linked to the procedure named InsertAt.

How does this procedure work? Suppose that the list has the elements as in Figure 7.12 and the user has entered bass in the first box and 2 in the second box. These actions give the value "bass" to d.insertT and 2 to d.insertPosition. When the user clicks the button labeled Insert, procedure InsertAt executes because that is the procedure to which the button is linked.

The first statement of procedure InsertAt is

PboxListADS.InsertAtN(d.insertPosition, d.insertT)

Actual parameter d.insertPosition corresponds to formal parameter n in the interface of Figure 7.13, and actual parameter d.insertT corresponds to formal parameter val. The procedure inserts "bass" before the element at position 2, as shown in Figure 7.14(a).

Because of this change in the list, the number of elements needs to be updated. The second statement of procedure InsertAt is

d.numItems := PboxListADS.Length()

which changes the value of d.numItems to 5 to reflect the new length of the list. This new value does not become visible to the user until the third statement of procedure InsertAt

Dialog.Update(d)

executes.

As another example, consider execution of procedure SearchFor. Suppose the user enters "salmon" in the input field adjacent to the button labeled Search as in Figure 7.16. When she presses the button, procedure SearchFor executes. Its first statement

PboxListADS.Search(d.searchT, position, found)

is a call to procedure Search in module PboxListADS with actual parameters d.searchT, position, and found. Before the procedure call, d.searchT has the value "salmon", and position and found are local variables that have undefined values. During execution, procedure Search gives found the value TRUE and position the value 3, because it found the string "salmon" at position 3 of the list. The next statement in procedure SearchFor is the IF statement

```
IF found THEN
    PboxStrings.IntToString(position, 1, d.searchPosition);
    d.searchPosition := "At position " + d.searchPosition + "."
ELSE
    d.searchPosition := "Not in list."
END
```

Its purpose is to set the value of d.searchPosition, whose type is String32.

The programmer defined the type String32 earlier in the listing

TYPE

   String32 = ARRAY 32 OF CHAR;

Defining character array
types

to be an array of 32 characters. String32 is a Component Pascal identifier chosen by the programmer. The module would have worked just as well had the programmer not defined the String32 type and declared d.searchPosition directly as

searchT*: PboxListADS.T; searchPosition-: ARRAY 32 OF CHAR

Although there is no advantage in this program to declare the String32 type, in certain situations when arrays of characters are assigned to each other or compared to each other it is necessary to do so. This book generally follows the practice of defining such types from now on.

Because found has value TRUE, the THEN part of the IF statement executes and the ELSE part is skipped. The two statements in the THEN part

PboxStrings.IntToString(position, 1, d.searchPosition);
d.searchPosition := "At position " + d.searchPosition + "."

convert the integer value 3 to the string value "3", storing the string value in d.searchPosition, then convert the string value "3" to the string value "At position 3.", which gets stored in d.searchPosition. Finally, the last statement of SearchFor

Dialog.Update(d)

makes the value of d.searchPosition visible in the dialog box.

The workings of the other buttons are similar. You can view the dialog box as the specification of the program. The way to specify what a program should do is to sketch the dialog box first. You then set up the input and output values in the box to correspond to fields of the interactor d, and the buttons of the dialog box to correspond to exported procedures. In the program of Figure 7.17, there is a close correlation between the task that must be accomplished by a button and the services provided by the server module PboxListADS. The program consists of simply linking the controls of the dialog box correctly and calling the appropriate exported procedure.

The list abstract data type

The listing of Figure 7.18 is the interface for the list abstract data type. You have surely surmised by now that the difference between a list ADS and a list ADT is that the list ADT exports the list type, which permits the importing module to declare more than one list data structure.

DEFINITION PboxListADT;

Figure 7.18
The interface of the list
abstract data type.

    CONST
      capacity = 8;

    TYPE
      List = RECORD END;
      T = ARRAY 16 OF CHAR;

    PROCEDURE Clear (VAR lst: List);
    PROCEDURE Display (IN lst: List);
    PROCEDURE GetElementN (IN lst: List; n: INTEGER; OUT val: T);
    PROCEDURE InsertAtN (VAR lst: List; n: INTEGER; IN val: T);
    PROCEDURE Length (IN lst: List): INTEGER;
    PROCEDURE RemoveN (VAR lst: List; n: INTEGER);
    PROCEDURE Search (VAR lst: List; IN srchVal: T; OUT n: INTEGER; OUT fnd: BOOLEAN);

END PboxListADT.

Comparing Figure 7.18 with Figure 7.13, the list ADT exports the additional type

List = RECORD END

that is not exported by the list ADS. This is the type of the list itself. You can tell from the interface that a list is a record, that is, a collection of values which do not necessarily have identical types. However, the fields of the exported record are not shown in the interface. They are hidden in the black box of the implementation—yet another example of the pervasive concept of abstraction. At this stage of our understanding, we do not need to know how the list is implemented. We only need to know how to use the procedures.

Apart from the type of the list that is exported, every other item in the list ADT of Figure 7.18 is identical in name and purpose to the corresponding item in the list ADS. The only difference in the parameter lists of the procedures in the ADT is the addition of a formal parameter to specify on which list the operation is to be performed. For example, the specification of procedure InsertAtN for the list ADS is

PROCEDURE **InsertAtN** (n: INTEGER; IN val: T)
Pre
0 <= n   20
Length() < capacity   21
Post
val is inserted at position n in the list, increasing Length() by 1.
If n > Length(), val is appended to the list.

while the specification of procedure InsertAtN for the list ADT is

PROCEDURE **InsertAtN** (VAR lst: List; n: INTEGER; IN val: T);
Pre
0 <= n   20
Length(lst) < capacity   21
Post
val is inserted at position n in list lst, increasing Length(lst) by 1.
If n > Length(lst), val is appended to lst.

You can see that the precoditions and postconditions are identical, except that the postcondition for the list ADS says that val is inserted in *the* list, whereas the postcondition for the list ADT says that val is inserted in list lst. The pre- and postconditions for the other procedures of the list ADT are similar in the same way to those of the list ADS.

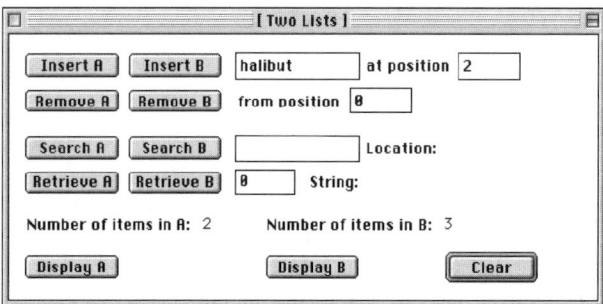

Figure 7.19
The dialog box for manipulating two lists.

Figure 7.19 shows a dialog box that allows the user to manipulate two lists. The listing in Figure 7.20 is an implementation of the dialog box based on the list ADT.

```
MODULE Pbox07D;
    IMPORT Dialog, PboxListADT, PboxStrings;

    TYPE
        String32 = ARRAY 32 OF CHAR;

    VAR
        d*: RECORD
            insertT*: PboxListADT.T; insertPosition*: INTEGER;
            removePosition*: INTEGER;
            searchT*: PboxListADT.T; searchPosition-: String32;
            retrievePosition*: INTEGER; retrieveT-: PboxListADT.T;
            numItemsA-, numItemsB-: INTEGER;
        END;
        listA, listB: PboxListADT.List;
```

Figure 7.20
A program that uses the list abstract data type

```
PROCEDURE InsertAtA*;
BEGIN
    PboxListADT.InsertAtN(listA, d.insertPosition, d.insertT);
    d.numItemsA := PboxListADT.Length(listA);
    Dialog.Update(d)
END InsertAtA;

PROCEDURE InsertAtB*;
BEGIN
    PboxListADT.InsertAtN(listB, d.insertPosition, d.insertT);
    d.numItemsB := PboxListADT.Length(listB);
    Dialog.Update(d)
END InsertAtB;

PROCEDURE RemoveFromA*;
BEGIN
    PboxListADT.RemoveN(listA, d.removePosition);
    d.numItemsA := PboxListADT.Length(listA);
    Dialog.Update(d)
END RemoveFromA;

PROCEDURE RemoveFromB*;
BEGIN
    PboxListADT.RemoveN(listB, d.removePosition);
    d.numItemsB := PboxListADT.Length(listB);
    Dialog.Update(d)
END RemoveFromB;

PROCEDURE SearchForA*;
VAR
    found: BOOLEAN;
    position: INTEGER;
BEGIN
    PboxListADT.Search(listA, d.searchT, position, found);
    IF found THEN
        PboxStrings.IntToString(position, 1, d.searchPosition);
        d.searchPosition := "At position " + d.searchPosition + ".";
    ELSE
        d.searchPosition := "Not in list.";
    END;
    Dialog.Update(d)
END SearchForA;
```

Figure 7.20
Continued.

```
PROCEDURE SearchForB*;
VAR
   found: BOOLEAN;
   position: INTEGER;
BEGIN
   PboxListADT.Search(listB, d.searchT, position, found);
   IF found THEN
      PboxStrings.IntToString(position, 1, d.searchPosition);
      d.searchPosition := "At position " + d.searchPosition + ".";
   ELSE
      d.searchPosition := "Not in list."
   END;
   Dialog.Update(d)
END SearchForB;

PROCEDURE RetrieveFromA*;
BEGIN
   PboxListADT.GetElementN(listA, d.retrievePosition, d.retrieveT);
   Dialog.Update(d)
END RetrieveFromA;

PROCEDURE RetrieveFromB*;
BEGIN
   PboxListADT.GetElementN(listB, d.retrievePosition, d.retrieveT);
   Dialog.Update(d)
END RetrieveFromB;

PROCEDURE DisplayListA*;
BEGIN
   PboxListADT.Display(listA);
END DisplayListA;

PROCEDURE DisplayListB*;
BEGIN
   PboxListADT.Display(listB);
END DisplayListB;

PROCEDURE ClearLists*;
BEGIN
   PboxListADT.Clear(listA); PboxListADT.Clear(listB);
   d.insertT := ""; d.insertPosition := 0;
   d.removePosition := 0;
   d.searchT := ""; d.searchPosition := "";
   d.retrievePosition := 0; d.retrieveT := "";
   d.numItemsA := 0; d.numItemsB := 0;
   Dialog.Update(d)
END ClearLists;

BEGIN
   ClearLists
END Pbox07D.
```

Figure 7.20
Continued.

The structure of the module is characteristic of those that import a type. There are two global variables, listA and listB, that correspond to the two lists that are manipulated by the user. They are declared as

listA, listB: PboxListADT.List;

That is, each list has the type that is exported by module PboxListADT. When the user clicks the button labeled Insert A, procedure InsertAtA executes. Its first statement is

PboxListADT.InsertAtN(listA, d.insertPosition, d.insertT)

The first actual parameter listA corresponds to the first formal parameter lst. This is how the calling procedure tells the called procedure on which list the operation is to be performed.

Queues

A queue is also called a first in, first out (FIFO) list. It is similar to a stack in that it stores values in a list in the order it receives them, but different in that data is retrieved from the opposite end of the list. The two operation on a queue are *enqueue* and *dequeue*, which correspond to push and pop for a stack.

The FIFO property of a queue

You can visualize a queue as a line of people at a ticket window. When another person comes to buy a ticket, she goes to the back of the line, corresponding to the enqueue operation. When the clerk at the window can serve another person he helps the person from the front of the line, corresponding to the dequeue operation. The first person to enter the queue is the first one to be served.

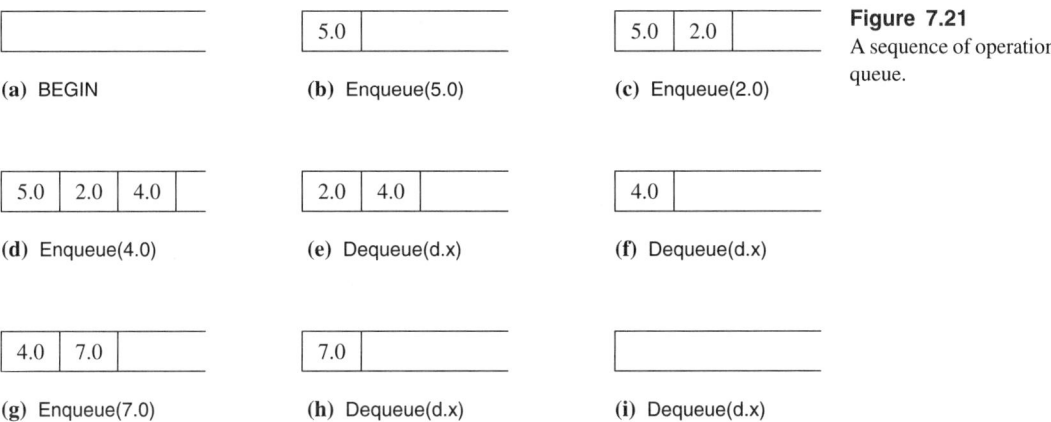

Figure 7.21
A sequence of operations on a queue.

Figure 7.21 shows a sequence of operations on a queue in abstract form. It corresponds to the sequence in Figure 7.1 for a stack, but Push is replaced by Enqueue and Pop is replaced by Dequeue. In the figure, values 5.0, 2.0, and 4.0 are added to the queue. The first delete operation gives the value of 5.0 to val. Contrast this with the first pop operation in Figure 7.1, which gives 4.0 to val. In Figure 7.21, because 5.0 was the first value in, it is the first value out.

The Pbox project does not provide a queue for you to manipulate. However, you can simulate the behavior of a queue with the list ADS or ADT provided by Pbox. The implementations of the queue ADS and ADT are problems at the end of this chapter.

Design by contract

Most of the programming problems in the early part of this book require you to write client modules. Later problems near the end require you to write server modules as well. Sometimes in a commercial software development environment, the same programmer writes the client module and the server module. However, for large projects, it is more common for one person to program the server modules that are imported by a different client programmer. In that situation, the interface becomes a *contract* between the two programmers. The interface specifies the name of the procedures and the number and types of their parameters. The documentation, which always includes the interface, also states any preconditions that must be satisfied if the procedure is to execute correctly. As with all written contracts, the specification of the precondition is in the form of a guarantee. The programmer of the server module is making a guarantee that *if* the programmer of the client ensures that the precondition is not violated *then* the procedure will execute correctly.

A common use of the IF statement is to prevent a trap from ever occurring in a user's program. Such programs are sometimes called *bulletproof*. You have probably *Bulletproof programs* experienced commercial programs that are not bulletproof. The fortunate user gets a dialog box with a message like, "Your application program has terminated because an error of type -781 has occurred," or something else equally meaningless. The unfortunate user must restart the computer. Programmers of client modules make their programs bulletproof by reading the contract suppled by the interface and using the IF statement to ensure that their programs never violate the contract. Problem 27 requires you to make the program of Figure 7.4 bulletproof using IF statements in the client module. Such a program will prevent the user from ever experiencing the trap window of Figure 7.5.

Chapter 17 shows how the ASSERT procedure implements the precondition in the server module by bringing up the trap window when the precondition is violated. Later in this book, you will learn how to program server modules that are imported by client modules. When you work those problems, you will also be writing the client modules that import the server modules. You may be tempted to simplify your programming by putting IF statements that make the program bulletproof in your server module. That is a bad habit. You should always keep in mind that in a commercial software development environment, the programmer of the server is usually not the same person as the programmer of the client.

It is the job of the programmer of the server to establish the contract in the interface with preconditions for the procedures. She implements the preconditions with the ASSERT procedure. It is the job of the programmer of the client to make the application program bulletproof. He makes it bulletproof with the IF statement. This software practice is summarized by the design-by-contract rule, which states

- IF in the client.

- ASSERT in the server.

The design-by-contract rule

It may seem unnecessarily complicated for you to do in two places what you could more easily do in one place. But, because the programmer of the server is usually not the same person as the programmer of the client, you should get into the habit of writing your modules according to the design-by-contract rule.

★ Formal specifications

The preconditions and postconditions for procedures in BlackBox documentation correspond to the preconditions and postconditions for the *Hoare triple* of formal methods. Formally, the three parts of a Hoare triple are:

The Hoare triple

- the precondition, P

- the statement, S

- the postcondition, Q

which is usually written $\{P\}S\{Q\}$ in formal methods notation. The precondition and postcondition are conditions that can be either true or false. The interpretation of Hoare triple $\{P\}S\{Q\}$ is, "If P is true and you execute S, then Q is guaranteed to be true." The statement S can represent a single programming statement or, more generally, a sequence of statements. In this chapter, S represents the sequence of programming statements in the implementation of the procedure. Because the interface hides the implementation, you cannot see S from any of the program listings in this chapter.

The interpretation of a Hoare triple

Sometimes the sequence of statements that S represents is supposed to change some value, or set of values, or data structure. To indicate what is to be changed, S is written as if it were a single assignment statement, even though it still represents a set of statements in general. The left side of the assignment is a variable or set of variables to be changed and the right side of the assignment is a question mark. The question mark signifies that the formal specification does not state how the values of the variables are to be changed. It only states which variables are to be changed.

Example 7.14 The documentation of RemoveN for the list ADT

```
PROCEDURE RemoveN (VAR lst: List; n: INTEGER)
Pre
0 <= n   20
Post
If n < Length(lst), the element at position n in list lst is removed.
Otherwise, the list is unchanged.
```

is written formally as

$$\{0 \le n \wedge Length(lst) = \mathbf{L}\}$$
$$lst := ?$$
$$\{(n < \mathbf{L} \Rightarrow \text{Element at } n \text{ is removed} \wedge Length(lst) = \mathbf{L} - 1) \wedge (n \ge \mathbf{L} \Rightarrow lst \text{ is unchanged})\}$$

The letter $\mathbf{L}$, called a rigid variable, is used to save the initial value of the function *Length(lst)* in the Hoare triple. If n is less than the initial length of the list, whatever the length is before execution of the procedure, and the preconditions are satisfied, then after execution the length of the list will be its initial value minus one. *S* is the expression *lst := ?*, which indicates that *lst* is the data structure to be changed. ∎

Rigid variables

If the documentation has no precondition, then the formal precondition is the weakest possible precondition, namely *true*.

The weakest possible precondition is true.

Example 7.15   The documentation of Length for the list ADT

PROCEDURE **Length** (IN lst: List): INTEGER
Post
Returns the number of elements in list lst.

is written formally as

$$\{true\}S\{Length(lst) = \text{The length of } lst\}$$ ∎

In the previous examples of the Hoare triple, the symbol *S* stands for the statements in the implementation of the procedure. The abstraction of the interface hides the details of the statements from the client program. A Hoare triple $\{P\}S\{Q\}$ consisting of a given precondition *P* and postcondition *Q*, but an unknown *S*, is called a *formal specification*. The software designer who writes the procedure treats the formal specification as a contract. She assumes that the client program will insure that the precondition is true, then writes the statements that will make the postcondition true after the procedure executes.

Formal specifications

Another use of the Hoare triple is to define the assignment statement. When used this way, *S* is not hidden as it is in a formal specification, but is the assignment statement. Formally, the assignment statement is defined in terms of the Hoare triple and textual substitution, which also uses the := symbol. If *E* is an expression and *R* is a postcondition, then the assignment statement $x := E$ is defined as the Hoare triple

$$\{R[x := E]\}x := E\{R\}$$

Formal definition of assignment

where the := symbol in the precondition signifies textual substitution. Textual substitution of *E* for *x* in the postcondition produces the weakest precondition for the Hoare triple.

Example 7.16   The definition of $x := x + 2$ for the postcondition $x > 0$ is the Hoare triple

$$\{x + 2 > 0\}\, x := x + 2 \,\{x > 0\}$$

You can see that this Hoare triple is valid because if $x + 2 > 0$ is true before the assignment statement executes, that is, if $x > -2$, then the postcondition $x > 0$ is guaranteed to be true afterwards. Of course, many other Hoare triples have this same property. For example, the Hoare triple

$$\{x - 1 > 0\}\, x := x + 2 \,\{x > 0\}$$

is also valid, because if $x - 1 > 0$ is true before execution then the postcondition $x > 0$ is guaranteed to be true afterwards. Even though the second Hoare triple is valid, it is not useful in defining the assignment statement. The precondition of the first Hoare triple $x + 2 > 0$ is weaker than that of the second $x - 1 > 0$ because it puts less of an initial restriction on x. It only requires that x be greater than -2, while the other precondition requires that x be greater than 1. ∎

Exercises

1. Evaluate the following postfix expressions.

   (a) 2 5 1 3 + − ×
   (b) 2 5 1 + 3 − ×
   (c) 2 5 + 1 − 3 ×
   (d) 1 1 1 1 1 1 − − − − −

2. Convert the following infix expressions to postfix.

   (a) $a + b - c \times d$
   (b) $x \times (z - y) / w$
   (c) $F - G \times (H + I \times J)$
   (d) $p \times (q \times (r + s / t) + u) + v$

3. Trace the execution of the algorithm for converting the following infix expression to postfix. Show the contents of the stack at each step of the conversion as in Example 7.6.

   (a) $5 + 2 - 6 \times 4$
   (b) $2 \times (3 + 4 \times 5 + 6)$

4. Inspect the documentation of module TextModels and answer the following questions about procedure Delete.

   (a) What does procedure Delete do?
   (b) How many preconditions does it have?
   (c) What is the first precondition?
   (d) How many postconditions does it have?

5. What two things does the word OUT signify when it is placed before a formal parameter?

6. Identify whether each of the following parameter passing indicators is call by value, call by result, call by reference, or call by constant reference.

   (a) IN   **(b)** OUT   **(c)** default   **(d)** VAR

7. Complete the following statements by choosing the correct option in parentheses.

   (a) In call by value the procedure (does / does not) change the value of the actual parameter.
   (b) In call by result the procedure (does / does not) change the value of the actual parameter.
   (c) In call by reference the procedure (does / does not) change the value of the actual parameter.
   (d) In call by constant reference the procedure (does / does not) change the value of the actual parameter.

8. Suppose PboxStackADS were written as a stack of strings instead of a stack of reals. Use the style of the interface in Figure 7.13 to write the interface for such a stack.

9. Suppose PboxStackADT were written as a stack of strings instead of a stack of reals. Use the style of the interface in Figure 7.18 to write the interface for such a stack.

10. What is the design-by-contract rule?

11. **(a)** What is the interpretation of the Hoare triple $\{P\}S\{Q\}$? **(b)** What is a formal specification?

12. Write the formal specification for **(a)** PboxListADT.Clear, **(b)** PboxStackADT.Pop. For part (b) you will need to use two rigid variables, one to save the initial value of the number of elements in the stack and one to save the initial value of the top of the stack. You may use $TopOf(s)$ in the precondition to indicate the value of the top of stack s. Note that PboxStackADT.Pop changes both s and val.

13. What is the weakest precondition for the assignment statement $x := x - 5$ whose post-condition is $x < 20$?

Problems

14. Construct a four-function reverse polish notation (RPN) real calculator as shown in the dialog box of Figure 7.22. The calculator has an internal stack and uses postfix notation to evaluate the result. When the user presses the Enter button push the value onto the stack and display the value in the field labeled Top. The button labeled "-" pops one item off the stack into a temporary variable, then pops a second item off the stack into another temporary variable. It subtracts the first from the second (notice the order), pushes the difference onto the stack, and displays it in the field labeled Top. For example, to evaluate the postfix expression 2 3 4 + × you would perform the sequence: type 2, press Enter, type 3, press Enter, type 4, press Enter, press +, press *. The figure shows the dialog box just before pressing * in the above sequence. Use the abstract data structure PboxStackADS.

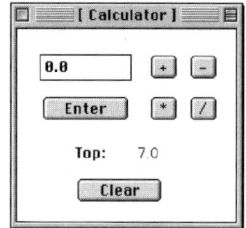

Figure 7.22
The four-function RPN calculator for Problem 14.

15. Do Problem 14, but use the abstract data type from PboxStackADT.

16. Expand your program of Problem 14 to make it a full-featured scientific calculator. Include the trigonometric functions sine, cosine, tangent and their inverses, and the natural logarithm and its inverse. Include a button for the user to enter π and compute the

square and the square root. Get the value of π from the Math module. Use the abstract data structure PboxStackADS.

17. Do Problem 16, but use the abstract data type from PboxStackADT.

18. The abstract list is more general than the abstract stack, because you can insert and remove from any location instead of only from the top. In PboxListADS, if you call procedure InsertAtN and give n the value 0 then the item will always be prepended to the front of the list. Furthermore, if you call procedure RemoveN and give n the value 0, then the item will always be removed from the front of the list. Write a program that implements a dialog box that looks and behaves exactly like Figure 7.3, but import PboxListADS instead of PboxStackADS. To pop a value with the procedures of Pbox-ListADS you will need to get the value with procedure GetElementN before you remove it with RemoveN.

19. The abstract list is more general than the abstract stack, because you can insert and remove from any location instead of only from the top. In PboxListADT, if you call procedure InsertAtN and give the n the value 0 then the item will always be prepended to the front of the list. Furthermore, if you call procedure RemoveN and give n the value 0, then the item will always be removed from the front of the list. Write a program that implements a dialog box that looks and behaves exactly like Figure 7.9, but import PboxListADT instead of PboxStackADT. To pop a value with the procedures of Pbox-ListADT you will need to get the value with procedure GetElementN before you remove it with RemoveN.

20. Implement a dialog box that looks and behaves like Figure 7.9, but with one additional button labeled "A to B". When the user presses this button an item should be popped off of Stack A and pushed onto Stack B. The text fields for Push and Pop should not change. Only the fields for the number of items in Stacks A and B should change. Use a temporary variable called temp in your procedure AToB to store the value between the pop and push operations.

21. Implement a dialog box that looks and behaves like Figure 7.3, but with one additional button labeled "Swap Top". If the stack contains two or more items when the user presses this button, the top two items on the stack should be exchanged. Otherwise, the stack should remain unchanged. The text fields for Push and Pop should not change, nor should the field for the number of items change. Use two temporary variables called temp1 and temp2 in your procedure SwapTop to store the two values between the pop and push operations. Import module PboxStackADS.

22. Work Problem 21, but import module PboxStackADT.

23. Implement a dialog box that looks and behaves like Figure 7.16, but with one additional button labeled "Front to Back". If the list contains two or more items when the user presses this button, the item at the front of the list should be moved to the back of the list. Otherwise, the list should remain unchanged. All the text fields for the dialog box should not change, nor should the field for the number of items change. Use a temporary variable called temp in your procedure FrontToBack to store the front values between the remove and insert operations. Import module PboxListADS.

24. Work Problem 23, but import module PboxListADT.

25. In PboxListADS, if you call procedure InsertAtN and give the n the value PboxList-ADS.capacity then the item will always be appended to the rear of the list. Furthermore, if you call procedure RemoveN and give n the value 0, then the item will always be removed from the front of the list. Write a program that implements a dialog box that looks exactly like Figure 7.3, but with the Push button relabeled Enqueue, the Pop button relabeled Dequeue, the Clear Stack button relabeled Clear Queue, and the window title relabeled One Queue. The buttons must implement the FIFO policy as shown in Figure 7.21. The type of the values stored should be PboxListADS.T instead of REAL.

26. In PboxListADT, if you call procedure InsertAtN and give the n the value PboxList-ADS.capacity then the item will always be appended to the rear of the list. Furthermore, if you call procedure RemoveN and give n the value 0, then the item will always be removed from the front of the list. Write a program that implements a dialog box that looks exactly like Figure 7.9, but with the Push buttons relabeled Enqueue, the Pop buttons relabeled Dequeue, the Clear Stacks button relabeled Clear Queues, and the window title relabeled Two Queues. The buttons must implement the FIFO policy as shown in Figure 7.21. The type of the values stored should be PboxListADT.T instead of REAL.

27. Inspect the preconditions of all the procedures that are called in module Pbox07A of Figure 7.4 for the stack ADS and modify the module to insure that a trap can never occur. If the user enters a value in a dialog box that would violate a precondition when a button is pressed, the program should simply do nothing to the stack or the dialog box.

28. Do Problem 27 but with module Pbox07B in Figure 7.10 for the stack ADT.

29. Do Problem 27 but with module Pbox07C in Figure 7.17 for the list ADS.

30. Do Problem 27 but with module Pbox07D in Figure 7.20 for the list ADT.

Chapter *8*

Nested Selections

Nested boxes consist of an outer large box, inside which there is another box, inside which there is another box, and so on to the innermost box. Figure 3.1 is a set of nested boxes that illustrates how procedures are nested in modules, and data is nested in procedures and modules. Nesting is closely related to the concept of abstraction. If the outer large box has a lid, it hides the details of the remaining boxes that are within it. And hiding detail is the essence of abstraction.

The concept of nesting

Nested IF statements

Figure 6.11 shows that an IF statement selects one of two alternative statement sequences, depending on the value of a boolean expression. Component Pascal allows either of those alternative statements to contain another IF statement. An IF statement contained in one of the alternatives of another IF statement is called a nested IF statement.

Figure 8.1 shows the dialog box for a program that inputs a salary and calculates an income tax from it. There is no tax at all if the salary is less than or equal to $10,000. Otherwise, the tax is 20% on the salary between $10,000 and $30,000 and 30% on the salary that is in excess of $30,000. You can see from the figure that a single IF statement is not sufficient to compute the tax, because there are three possible outcomes and the single IF statement shown in Figure 6.11 has only two alternatives.

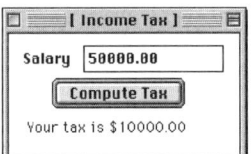
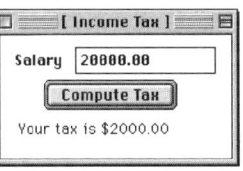
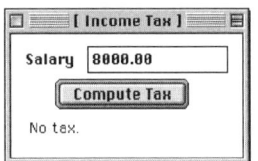

Figure 8.1
A dialog box that requires more than two alternative computations.

The program in Figure 8.2 implements the dialog box with a nested IF statement. After the user enters that value for d.salary and clicks the compute button, the outer IF statement in procedure IncomeTax executes. If its boolean expression,

d.salary > minTaxable

is false, which it will be if the value of d.salary is less than or equal to 10,000.00, the statement sequence containing the nested IF statement is skipped, and the message string is set to the "no tax" message.

```
MODULE Pbox08A;
   IMPORT Dialog, PboxStrings;
   VAR
      d*: RECORD
         salary*: REAL;
         message-: ARRAY 64 OF CHAR
      END;

   PROCEDURE IncomeTax*;
      CONST
         lowRate = 0.20;
         highRate = 0.30;
         minTaxable = 10000.00;
         maxTaxable = 30000.00;
      VAR
         tax: REAL;
         taxString: ARRAY 32 OF CHAR;
   BEGIN
      IF d.salary > minTaxable THEN
         IF d.salary <= maxTaxable THEN
            tax := (d.salary - minTaxable) * lowRate
         ELSE
            tax := (maxTaxable - minTaxable) * lowRate + (d.salary - maxTaxable) * highRate
         END;
         PboxStrings.RealToString(tax, 1, 2, taxString);
         d.message := "Your tax is $" + taxString
      ELSE
         d.message := "No tax."
      END;
      Dialog.Update(d)
   END IncomeTax;

BEGIN
   d.salary := 0.0;
   d.message := ""
END Pbox08A.
```

Figure 8.2

An income tax computation with a nested IF statement.

If the boolean expression is true, the nested IF executes. It evaluates the boolean expression

d.salary <= maxTaxable

If this boolean expression is true, it computes the tax according to the low rate, and if it is false according to the high rate on the excess beyond maxTaxable.

Figure 8.3 is the flowchart for the listing in Figure 8.2. It shows the inner IF statement nested in the true alternative of the outer IF statement. You can see from the

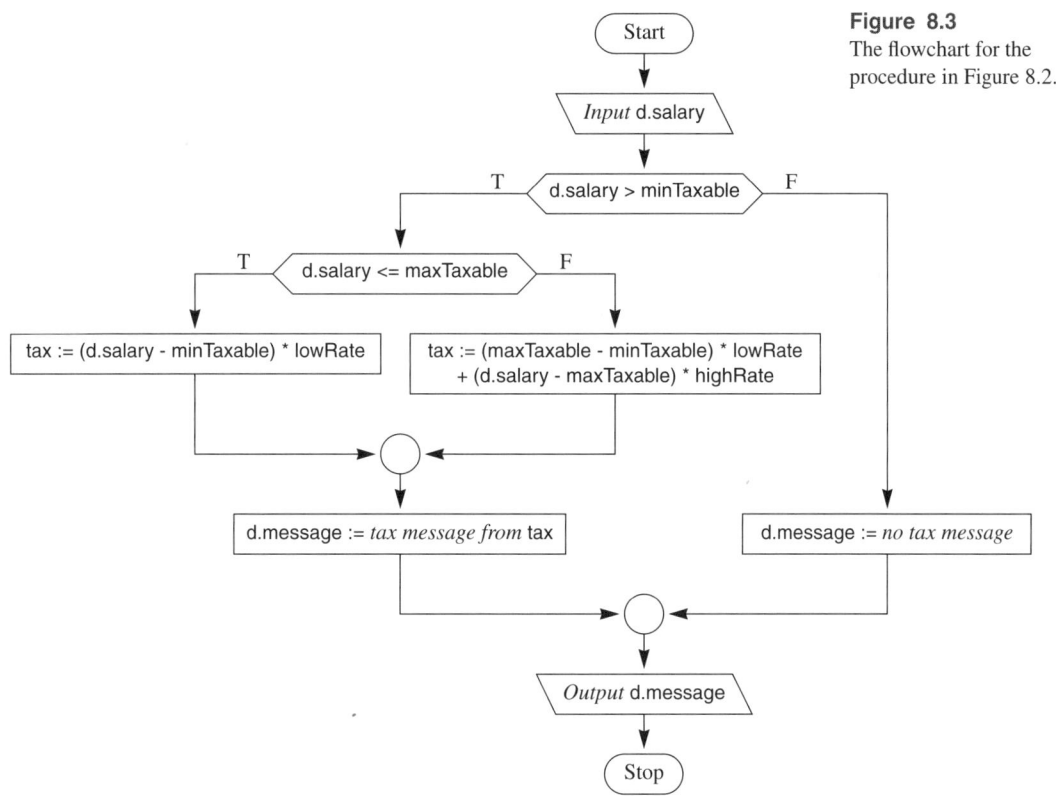

Figure 8.3
The flowchart for the
procedure in Figure 8.2.

flowchart that the nested condition

d.salary <= maxTaxable

will never be evaluated if the outer condition is false. The flowchart also shows that each IF statement terminates with the circular collector symbol aligned vertically with its condition. Because this program contains two IF statements, its flowchart contains two circular collector symbols.

IF statements with an ELSIF part

The previous program had the nested IF statement in the true alternative of the outer IF statement. Component Pascal allows you to nest an IF statement in either the true alternative or the false alternative of the outer IF statement. Figure 8.4 shows a dialog box that computes the letter grade from an integer score according to the traditional 10-point criteria. That is, a score of 90 or more is an A, between 80 and 89 is a B, between 70 and 79 is a C, between 60 and 69 is a D, and less than 60 is an F. The program shown in Figure 8.5 implements this dialog box using IF statements that are nested inside the false alternatives of the outer IF statements.

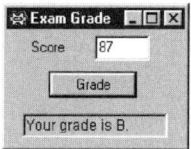
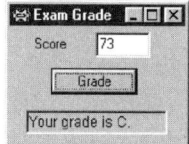
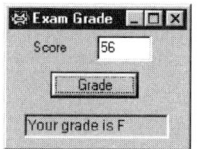

Figure 8.4
A dialog box for computing a letter grade from an exam score.

```
MODULE Pbox08B;
    IMPORT Dialog;
    VAR
        d*: RECORD
            score*: INTEGER;
            message-: ARRAY 64 OF CHAR
        END;

    PROCEDURE TestGrade*;
    BEGIN
        IF d.score >= 90 THEN
            d.message := "Your grade is A."
        ELSE
            IF d.score >= 80 THEN
                d.message := "Your grade is B."
            ELSE
                IF d.score >= 70 THEN
                    d.message := "Your grade is C."
                ELSE
                    IF d.score >= 60 THEN
                        d.message := "Your grade is D."
                    ELSE
                        d.message := "Your grade is F."
                    END
                END
            END
        END;
        Dialog.Update(d)
    END TestGrade;

BEGIN
    d.score := 0;
    d.message := ""
END Pbox08B.
```

Figure 8.5
Conversion of an integer exam score into a letter grade.

You can nest IF statements to any level. The last IF statement in this program is nested three levels deep. Each IF statement is nested in the ELSE part of its outer IF statement.

Suppose the value of Score is 93. The boolean expression of the outer IF statement d.score >= 90

would be true, and the "Grade of A" message would be output. The ELSE part of the outer IF statement would be skipped. Because the ELSE part is a single large nested IF statement, none of the other boolean expressions is ever tested.

Suppose the value of d.score is 70. The boolean expression of the outer IF statement would be false, and the ELSE part of the outer IF statement would execute. Now the boolean expression

d.score >= 80

of the second IF statement would be tested as false. So the ELSE part of the second IF statement would execute. This time, the boolean expression

d.score >= 70

would be true, and the "Grade of C" message would be output. The ELSE part of the third IF statement is skipped. Therefore, the D and F messages are not output.

This pattern of a succession of IF statements nested in the false alternatives occurs so frequently in practice that Component Pascal has a special ELSIF option to perform the equivalent processing with a single IF statement. The same procedure can be written with a single IF statement as:

```
PROCEDURE TestGrade*;
BEGIN
   IF d.score >= 90 THEN
      d.message := "Your grade is A."
   ELSIF d.score >= 80 THEN
      d.message := "Your grade is B."
   ELSIF d.score >= 70 THEN
      d.message := "Your grade is C."
   ELSIF d.score >= 60 THEN
      d.message := "Your grade is D."
   ELSE
      d.message := "Your grade is F."
   END;
   Dialog.Update(d)
END TestGrade;
```

You can think of ELSIF and the last ELSE as a list of conditions that starts with the first IF condition. The boolean expressions in the list are evaluated in order, starting with the first. When a boolean expression is false, the next one in the list is tested. The first boolean expression that tests true causes its alternative to execute and the rest of the ELSIF alternatives in the list to be skipped.

When deciding whether to use this feature of the IF statement, you must be careful to distinguish between nested IF statements and sequential IF statements, which are not nested. The following IF statements are sequential:

```
IF d.score >= 90 THEN
   d.message := "Your grade is A."
END;
IF d.score >= 80 THEN
   d.message := "Your grade is B."
END;
IF d.score >= 70 THEN
   d.message := "Your grade is C."
END;
IF d.score >= 60 THEN
   d.message := "Your grade is D.";
ELSE
   d.message := "Your grade is F.";
END
```

In this code fragment, suppose that d.score gets the value 70 from the dialog box. The first two boolean expressions would be false and the third one would be true. But after d.message gets the C message, the next IF statement would execute. Because d.score >= 60 is true, d.message would get the D message destroying the previously stored C message. The net result would be an erroneous output of

Your grade is D.

Figure 8.6 shows the difference in flow of control between three sequential IF statements and an IF statement with two ELSIF parts.

Assertions and invariants

When complex IF statements are nested it is sometimes helpful to formulate assertions to keep track of what is happening in the program. An *assertion* is a condition *Assertions* that is assumed to be true at a given point in a program. One example of an assertion is the precondition P in the Hoare triple $\{P\}S\{Q\}$. It is a condition that is assumed to be true for statement S to execute correctly. If P is true, then after S executes, Q is guaranteed to be true.

Another example of an assertion is the *invariant*. It differs from a precondition *Invariants* only by its physical placement in a program and by its use in program design. Whereas preconditions are assertions placed at the beginning point of a procedure, invariants are typically placed within procedure code. Furthermore, preconditions are frequently provided in the documentation of server modules as guidelines for use by client programmers. They are especially valuable if the programmer of the server is a different individual from the programmer of the client. Invariants, however, are usually intended as guidelines for a single programmer within a single procedure. They are hidden from the user of the module that contains the procedure.

Component Pascal provides assertions with the ASSERT procedure. ASSERT *The ASSERT procedure* takes two parameters, a condition and an error number. The condition is a boolean expression. That is, it is an expression that evaluates to one of two possible values, true or false. When you execute ASSERT, it evaluates the condition. If the condition is true nothing happens and the program continues as if the ASSERT statement were not in the program. If the condition is false, however, the program terminates with a

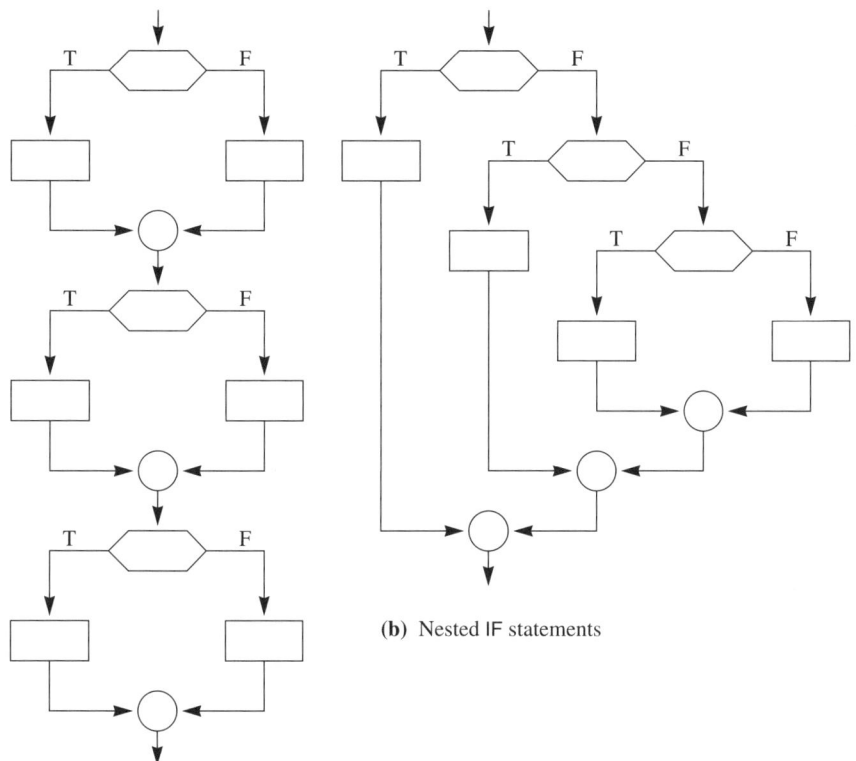

Figure 8.6
Flowcharts for sequential IF statements versus a single IF statement with two ELSIF parts.

(b) Nested IF statements

(a) Sequential IF statements

trap. The error number is the number that appears in the trap window.

With Component Pascal, you can use the ASSERT procedure to implement pre-conditions and invariants. Recall from Chapter 7 that one of the programming style conventions for Component Pascal in the BlackBox framework is that the error numbers for precondition violations begin with integer 20. Similarly, error numbers for invariant violations should begin with integer 100.

Example 8.1 The following code fragment is the nested IF statement of Figure 8.2 with invariants. Note that the pseudocode statements in italic may summarize several statements from the original program.

```
IF d.salary > minTaxable THEN
    IF d.salary <= maxTaxable THEN
        ASSERT((minTaxable < d.salary) & (d.salary <= maxTaxable), 100);
        tax := (d.salary - minTaxable) * lowRate
    ELSE
        ASSERT(d.salary > maxTaxable, 101);
        tax := (maxTaxable - minTaxable) * lowRate + (d.salary - maxTaxable) * highRate
    END;
    d.message := tax message from tax
ELSE
    ASSERT(d.salary <= minTaxable, 102);
    d.message := no tax message
END;
```

To see how invariants are formulated, we will begin with the simplest invariant, which can be found just before the statement

d.message := *no tax message*

What condition must be true at this point in the program? In other words, what condition must be true just before this assignment statement executes? The boolean expression of the outer IF statement must be false. But if the expression

d.salary > minTaxable

is false, the expression

d.salary <= minTaxable

must be true, which is the invariant shown in the code fragment.

The next invariant we will consider is the one just before the statement

tax := (d.salary - minTaxable) * lowRate

Why must d.salary be greater than minTaxable and less than or equal to maxTaxable at that point in the program? Because to arrive at that point, the boolean expression of the outer IF statement must be true. Then the boolean expression of the nested IF statement also must be true. The invariant

(minTaxable < d.salary) & (d.salary <= maxTaxable)

is simply reflecting those two conditions.

The remaining invariant is just before the statement

tax := (maxTaxable - minTaxable) * lowRate + (d.salary - maxTaxable) * highRate

To arrive at this point, the boolean expression of the outer IF statement must be true and the boolean expression of the nested IF statement must be false. Therefore, to get to this point in the program, d.salary must satisfy (d.salary > minTaxable) & (d.salary > maxTaxable)

So why does the implementation of the invariant in the code fragment

ASSERT(d.salary > maxTaxable, 101)

seem to ignore the fact that d.salary must be greater than minTaxable?

The answer to this question involves the concept of strong versus weak invariants. One invariant is stronger than another if it places greater limits on the possible *Strong invariants* values of a variable. In general, stronger invariants are more helpful in analysis of logic than weaker ones, because they give you more information. Suppose you ask your teacher for your score on an exam. If she says, "You scored between 50 and 80," she is not giving as much information as if she says, "You scored between 73 and 75." The second statement places a greater limitation on the possible values of your exam score and, therefore, gives you more information.

In this example,

d.salary > minTaxable

is a valid invariant, because it is a condition guaranteed to be true at this point in the program. However,

d.salary > maxTaxable

is stronger because it places a greater limitation on the possible values of d.salary.

One way of visualizing strong invariants is with the number line. Figure 8.7 shows the regions of the real number line corresponding to each of the preceding conditions. Recall from mathematics that the AND operation corresponds to the intersection of the regions, while the OR operation corresponds to the union of the regions. The intersection of these two regions is simply the region for

d.salary > maxTaxable

by itself, which is the stronger invariant.

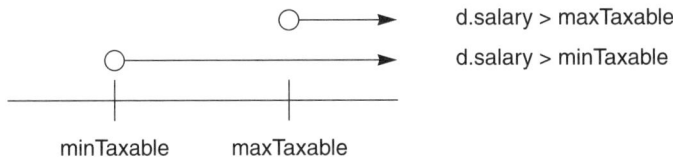

d.salary > maxTaxable
d.salary > minTaxable

Figure 8.7
The real number line showing the conditions d.salary > maxTaxable and d.salary > minTaxable.

One purpose of an invariant is to document your analysis of what condition you calculate should be true at a given point of your program. If your analysis is correct, a call to the ASSERT procedure should do nothing. That is, in fact, what the ASSERT procedure does. If the boolean condition in the ASSERT procedure call is true, nothing happens and the program continues to execute. If the boolean condition is false, however, the ASSERT procedure causes the program to abort with a trap. Why would a programmer ever want his program to abort with a trap? He never would! So why would anyone ever put an ASSERT call in his program?

The primary purpose of a call to ASSERT to implement an invariant is for testing the correctness of your program. If the analysis of your program is correct, your assertions will never trigger a trap and all will be well for you and the users of your software. But if you make an error in your analysis you will have an error in your program and it will not execute correctly. The trap will show you where your analysis of what should be true at that point of the program is not true after all. You can then correct the program. Better to have a controlled abort of your program when you are testing it than to release it for the users with an error in the program.

The purpose of a call to ASSERT to implement an invariant

To write programs that work correctly, you must be able to analyze the logic of the statements you write. Invariants will help you to think through the logic of your programs. In the beginning, it may seem that invariants make things more complicated than necessary. But after some practice, you will find that you can formulate invariants in your mind as you write your programs. That ability will make it easier for you to write correct programs. Occasionally, it may help to write an ASSERT call in a program to make the program easier to understand.

Example 8.2 Consider the following code fragment, where age is a variable of type INTEGER.

```
IF age > 65 THEN
    Statement 1
ELSIF age > 21 THEN
    Statement 2
ELSE
    Statement 3
END
```

The logic in this code is identical to that in Figure 8.6(b), where the nesting was consistently in the false part of the IF statements. What are the strongest invariants you can formulate before each statement?

For Statement 1, the condition age > 65 must be true. That is the strongest invariant you can formulate at this point of the program.

For Statement 2, the boolean expression of the outer IF statement, age > 65 must be false. In other words, age <= 65 must be true. Furthermore, the boolean expression of the ELSIF condition, age > 21, also must be true. So the strongest invariant at this point is

(21 < age) & (age <= 65)

which corresponds to the intersection of the two regions in Figure 8.8.

For Statement 3, both boolean expressions must be false; that is, age <= 65 and age <= 21 must be true. The strongest invariant is

Age <= 21

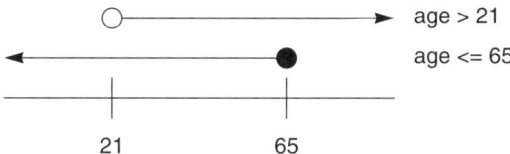

Figure 8.8
The number line showing the two conditions age > 21 and age <= 65.

which corresponds to the intersection of the two regions in Figure 8.9. The final code fragment that implements the strongest invariants is

```
IF age > 65 THEN
    ASSERT(age > 65, 100);
    Statement 1
ELSIF age > 21 THEN
    ASSERT((21 < age) & (age <= 65), 101);
    Statement 2
ELSE
    ASSERT(age <= 21, 102);
    Statement 3
END
```

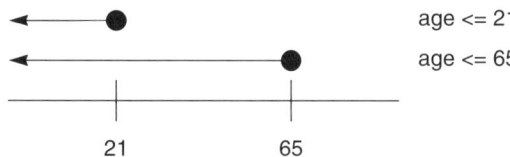

Figure 8.9
The number line showing the two conditions age <= 21 and age <= 65.

Dead code

Something to avoid when you write nested IF statements is dead code. *Dead code* is a statement that cannot possibly execute. If you ever discover dead code in your own program or in a program that someone else wrote, you can be sure that it was unintentional. Because dead code never executes, there is never a reason to put it in a program except by mistake. Formulating the strongest invariant can help you discover dead code.

Dead code

Component Pascal provides a procedure that we will use to indicate dead code. When you execute procedure HALT, the program always terminates with a trap, regardless of the value of any boolean expression. Like the ASSERT procedure, the HALT procedure is used for testing large programs. If a programmer wants to view the values of the variables at a given point of a program, she can insert a call to HALT. When the program reaches that point, it will terminate and show the trap window including the values of all the variables at the time the program was interrupted.

Typical purpose of a call to HALT

The procedure call

HALT(100)

is logically equivalent to

ASSERT(FALSE, 100)

Because the boolean expression in the above ASSERT call is always false, its execution would always generate a trap. But this is precisely the behavior of the call to HALT. The following examples use a call to HALT to indicate the strongest invariant of dead code. In the same way that an ASSERT call with the strongest invariant will not affect the execution of a program, a HALT call with dead code will not affect a program. Because dead code never executes, the HALT procedure will never be called.

The purpose of a call to HALT in this chapter

Keep in mind, however, that this use of HALT would never be found in production code because a programmer would never willfully have dead code in her program. The following examples are designed to teach you skill in identifying dead code, so you can root it out of your programs.

Example 8.3   Consider the following code fragment:

```
IF quantity < 200 THEN
    Statement 1
ELSIF quantity >= 100 THEN
    Statement 2
ELSE
    Statement 3
END
```

Statement 3 can never execute regardless of the value of quantity. To see why, try to formulate a strong invariant at the point just before Statement 3. To get to that point in the program, you must have quantity >= 200 because the first boolean expression must be false. You must also have quantity < 100 because the second boolean expression also must be false. But it is impossible to have quantity greater than or equal to 200 and less than 100 at the same time. So Statement 3 can never execute and is dead code. The code fragment with the strongest invariants implemented using calls to ASSERT and HALT is

```
IF quantity < 200 THEN
    ASSERT(quantity < 200, 100);
    Statement 1
ELSIF quantity >= 100 THEN
    ASSERT(quantity >= 200, 101);
    Statement 2
ELSE
    HALT(102);
    Statement 3
END
```

Do not conclude from this example that dead code is always the last statement in a sequence of ELSIF parts. You must analyze each situation afresh. The general strategy to determine the strongest invariant at a given point is to list the boolean conditions that must be true. This may involve taking the NOT of some expressions if the nesting is in the false part of an IF statement. The intersection of the corresponding regions represents the strongest invariant. If the intersection at a given point is empty, the statement at that point is dead code.

Example 8.4 Consider the following code fragment, where n has type INTEGER.

```
IF (15 <= n) & (n < 20) THEN
    IF (n > 10) THEN
        Statement 1
    ELSE
        Statement 2
    END
ELSE
    Statement 3
END
```

What is the strongest invariant you can formulate at each statement? The first step is to draw a sketch of the number line with the integer values in their proper order, as in Figure 8.10.

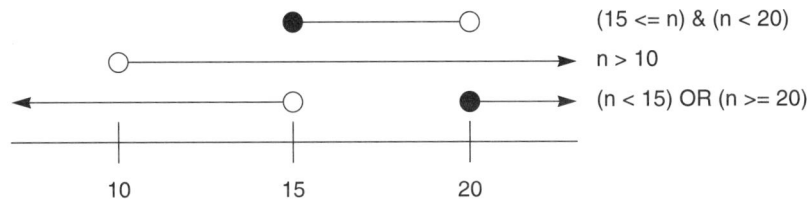

(15 <= n) & (n < 20)

n > 10

(n < 15) OR (n >= 20)

Figure 8.10
The number line for Example 8.4.

For Statement 1, you can see from the figure that the intersection of the top two lines corresponds to both boolean expressions being true. The strongest invariant is

(15 <= n) & (n < 20)

For Statement 2, n must be less than or equal to 10 and between 15 and 20, which is impossible. So Statement 2 is dead code.

For Statement 3, the first boolean expression must be false. From De Morgan's law it follows that the strongest invariant is

(n < 15) OR (n >= 20)

This corresponds to the third region of Figure 8.10, which is that part of the number line not included in the first region. The code with all the invariants implemented with calls to ASSERT and HALT is

```
IF (15 <= n) & (n < 20) THEN
   IF (n > 10) THEN
      ASSERT((15 <= n) & (n < 20), 100);
      Statement 1
   ELSE
      HALT(101);
      Statement 2
   END
ELSE
   ASSERT((n < 15) OR (n >= 20), 102);
   Statement 3
END
```
∎

Using nested IF statements

One of the most common problems beginning programmers have is a failure to recognize the appropriateness of the logic characterized by a sequence of ELSIF parts in an IF statement.

Example 8.5 Suppose you need to perform three different computations depending on the value of weight, a real variable. The following code:

```
IF weight > 150.0 THEN
   Statement 1
END;
IF (weight > 50.0) & (weight <= 150.0) THEN
   Statement 2
END;
IF (weight <= 50.0) THEN
   Statement 3
END
```

is not as efficient as the equivalent IF statement with a sequence of ELSIF parts:

```
IF weight > 150.0 THEN
   Statement 1
ELSIF weight > 50.0 THEN
   Statement 2
ELSE
   Statement 3
END
```

For example, suppose weight has a value of 200.0. In the first code fragment, every boolean expression must be evaluated because the IF statements are sequential. But in the second fragment, only the first boolean expression is evaluated because the sequence of ELSIFs is skipped. ∎

Another tendency when programming with ELSIF logic is to include an unnecessary redundant test at the end.

Example 8.6 The following code fragment has a redundant test.

```
IF price > 2000 THEN
    Statement 1
ELSIF price > 1000 THEN
    Statement 2
ELSIF price <= 1000 THEN
    Statement 3
END
```

The last boolean expression is redundant. In the following code fragment, you can assert that price <= 1000 when Statement 3 executes.

```
IF price > 2000 THEN
    Statement 1
ELSIF price > 1000 THEN
    Statement 2
ELSE
    Statement 3
END
```

This code fragment executes exactly the same as the previous one, but without the extra test. The redundant test should not be included. ∎

★ The guarded command if statement

The guarded command **if** statement can have more than just two guards. For example an **if** statement with four guards has the form

if $B1 \rightarrow S1$
  ▯ $B2 \rightarrow S2$
  ▯ $B3 \rightarrow S3$
  ▯ $B4 \rightarrow S4$
fi

Each one of the B's is a boolean guard that must be true for the corresponding statement sequence S to execute. The behavior of the GCL **if** statement is quite different from the CP IF statement in two respects.

First, the CP IF statement has an optional ELSE part. Suppose the IF statement does not have an ELSE part, the condition in the IF part is not true, and none of the conditions in any of the ELSIF parts are true either. Then each condition will be tested, none of the statement sequences will execute, and execution will continue with the statement sequentially following the IF statement. However, suppose that the above GCL **if** statement executes when none of the guards are true. Then the statement aborts, which is the equivalent of a program crash or a trap in CP. In other words, GCL has nothing equivalent to the ELSE part, and requires at least one of the guards to be true to avoid a program abort.

The if statement aborts when none of the guards are true.

Example 8.7   Suppose you want to put the values of *x* and *y* in order so that *x* is guaranteed to be less than or equal to *y*. The GCL statement

if $x > y \rightarrow x, y := y, x$
fi

works correctly if, for example, the initial state is $(x, 7)$, $(y, 3)$. In that case, the guard $x > y$ is true and the values are exchanged making the final state $(x, 3)$, $(y, 7)$. However, if the initial state is $(x, 4)$, $(y, 9)$ then no guards are true when the **if** statement executes and the program aborts. ∎

A second difference between IF and **if** is the order in which the conditions are evaluated. In CP, the conditions are evaluated in order starting with the condition of the IF, then the condition of the first ELSIF if necessary, then the condition of the second ELSIF if necessary, and so on. In GCL, however, you should visualize *all* the guards being evaluated at the same time. If no guard is true the statement aborts. If one guard is true its corresponding statement sequence executes. But if more than one guard is true the computer randomly picks the statement sequence of a true guard to execute. In this case, it may be impossible to predict the exact outcome of the computation.

The if statement selects at random when more than one guard is true.

Example 8.8   Suppose you write the processing of Example 8.6 in GCL as

if $price > 2000 \rightarrow S1$
  ⫾ $price > 1000 \rightarrow S2$
  ⫾ $price \leq 1000 \rightarrow S3$
fi

This translation from CP to GCL may seem plausible, but it is not correct. There is no problem if the initial state is $(price, 500)$, which guarantees that *S3* will execute. Nor is there a problem if the initial state is $(price, 1500)$, which guarantees that *S2* will execute. With both initial states exactly one guard is true so that the corresponding statement sequence can be determined. Suppose, however, the initial state is $(price, 2500)$, when the CP statement in Example 8.6 guarantees that *Statement 1* will execute. The problem is that the above GCL statement has both guards $price > 2000$ and $price > 1000$ true and so will randomly pick either *S1* or *S2* to execute. ∎

So how do you translate a CP IF statement to a GCL **if** statement? You simply use the strongest invariant as the guard.

To translate from CP to GCL use the strongest invariant as the guard.

Example 8.9   The processing of Example 8.6 is correctly written in GCL as

if $price > 2000 \rightarrow S1$
  ⫾ $1000 < price \leq 2000 \rightarrow S2$
  ⫾ $price \leq 1000 \rightarrow S3$
fi ∎

Exercises

1. **(a)** What is an assertion? **(b)** Name two kinds of assertions. **(c)** What is dead code?

2. Draw the flowcharts for the following code fragments.

(a)
```
IF Condition 1 THEN
    IF Condition 2 THEN
        Statement 1
    ELSE
        Statement 2
    END
ELSE
    Statement 3
END
```

(b)
```
IF Condition 1 THEN
    IF Condition 2 THEN
        Statement 1
    ELSE
        Statement 2
    END ;
    Statement 3
ELSE
    Statement 4
END
```

(c)
```
IF Condition 1 THEN
    Statement 1 ;
    IF Condition 2 THEN
        Statement 2
    END
ELSE
    Statement 3
END
```

(d)
```
IF Condition 1 THEN
    Statement 1
ELSE
    IF Condition 2 THEN
        Statement 2
    END ;
    Statement 3
END
```

3. Rewrite the following code fragments with the correct indentation and draw their flowcharts.

(a)
```
IF Condition 1 THEN
IF Condition 2 THEN
Statement 1
ELSE
Statement 2
END
END
```

(b)
```
IF Condition 1 THEN
IF Condition 2 THEN
Statement 1
END
ELSE
Statement 2
END
```

4. Rewrite the following code fragments with the correct indentation and draw their flowcharts.

(a)
```
IF Condition 1 THEN
IF Condition 2 THEN
IF Condition 3 THEN
Statement 1
ELSE
Statement 2
END
ELSE
Statement 3
END
END
```

(b)
```
IF Condition 1 THEN
IF Condition 2 THEN
IF Condition 3 THEN
Statement 1
ELSE
Statement 2
END
END
ELSE
Statement 3
END
```

(c)
```
IF Condition 1 THEN
Statement 1
END ;
IF Condition 2 THEN
Statement 2
ELSE
Statement 3
END
```

(d)
```
IF Condition 1 THEN
Statement 1
ELSIF Condition 2 THEN
Statement 2
ELSE
Statement 3
END
```

5. Rewrite the following code fragment with only one IF statement. Your revised code fragment must perform the same processing as the original one.

```
IF Condition 1 THEN
    IF Condition 2 THEN
        Statement 1
    END
END;
Statement 2
```

6. The following code fragment makes four comparisons. Simplify it so that only two comparisons are needed. age is a variable of type INTEGER.

```
IF age > 64 THEN
    Statement 1
END;
IF age < 18 THEN
    Statement 2
END;
IF (age >= 18) & (age < 65) THEN
    Statement 3
END
```

7. Determine the output, if any, of the following code fragment. h, m, and w are variables of type INTEGER. Hint: Rewrite with correct indentation first.

```
IF h > m THEN
IF w > m THEN
StdLog.Int(m)
ELSE
StdLog.Int(h)
END
END
```

(a) Assume h = 10, m = 3, and w = 4.
(b) Assume h = 10, m = 20, and w = 15.
(c) Assume h = 10, m = 5, and w = 3.

8. Determine the output, if any, of the following code fragment. x, y, z, and q are variables of type INTEGER. Hint: Rewrite with correct indentation first.

```
IF x > y THEN
StdLog.Int(y)
ELSIF x > z THEN
IF x > q THEN
StdLog.Int(q)
ELSE
StdLog.Int(x)
END
END
```

(a) Assume x = 10, y = 5, z = 0, and q = 1.
(b) Assume x = 10, y = 20, z = 5, and q = 1.
(c) Assume x = 10, y = 10, z = 12, and q = 5.
(d) Assume x = 10, y = 5, z = 20, and q = 15.

9. Write the strongest possible invariants just before each statement in the following code fragments. Assume that num is a variable of type INTEGER.

(a)
```
IF num < 23 THEN
    IF num >= 15 THEN
        Statement 1
    ELSE
        Statement 2
    END
ELSE
    Statement 3
END
```

(b)
```
IF num >= 50 THEN
    Statement 1
ELSIF num >= 25 THEN
    Statement 2
ELSE
    Statement 3
END
```

(c)
```
IF num >= 60 THEN
    Statement 1
ELSIF num < 80 THEN
    Statement 2
END
```

(d)
```
IF (num < 30) OR (num > 40) THEN
    Statement 1
ELSIF num < 35 THEN
    Statement 2
ELSE
    Statement 3
END
```

10. Write the strongest possible invariant just before each statement in the code fragment. Use the HALT procedure just before each statement that is dead code. Assume that num is a variable of type INTEGER.

(a)
```
IF num < 70 THEN
    IF num >= 80 THEN
        Statement 1
    ELSE
        Statement 2
    END
ELSE
    Statement 3
END
```

(b)
```
IF num >= 45 THEN
    Statement 1
ELSIF num <= 35 THEN
    Statement 2
ELSIF num >= 55 THEN
    Statement 3
ELSE
    Statement 4
END
```

(c)
```
IF num > 35 THEN
    Statement 1
ELSIF num > 45 THEN
    Statement 2
ELSE
    Statement 3
END
```

(d)
```
IF (num < 5) OR (num > 9) THEN
    Statement 1
ELSIF (5 < num) & (num < 9) THEN
    Statement 2
ELSE
    Statement 3
END
```

(e)
```
IF (num < 40) OR (num > 50) THEN
    Statement 1
ELSIF num > 30 THEN
    Statement 2
ELSE
    Statement 3
END
```

(f)
```
IF (40 <= num) & (num <= 50) THEN
    Statement 1
ELSIF (num < 42) OR (num > 48) THEN
    Statement 2
ELSE
    Statement 3
END
```

11. Write the **if** statement in Example 8.7 so that it executes correctly with any initial state.

12. For the GCL **if** statement

> **if** $age < 18 \rightarrow S1$
> ▯ $age \leq 21 \rightarrow S2$
> ▯ $age < 65 \rightarrow S3$
> **fi**

tell which statements could possibly execute for each of the following initial states.

(a) $(age, 10)$ **(b)** $(age, 19)$ **(c)** $(age, 21)$ **(d)** $(age, 40)$ **(e)** $(age, 70)$

13. For the GCL **if** statement

> **if** $j < 40 \rightarrow S1$
> ▯ $20 \leq j < 60 \rightarrow S2$
> **fi**

tell whether the statement will abort and if not, which statements could possibly execute for each of the following initial states.

(a) $(j, 10)$ **(b)** $(j, 30)$ **(c)** $(j, 50)$ **(d)** $(j, 70)$

14. Translate each code fragment in Exercise 9 into a single GCL **if** statement.

Problems

15. Write a program to input three integers in a dialog box and print them in descending order on the Log. Your program must contain no local or global variables other than the ones for input in the dialog box. It must use no more than five comparisons and must work correctly even if some of the integers are equal.

16. Write a program to input three integers in a dialog box and output the number that is neither the smallest nor the largest in an output field of the dialog box. If two or more of the numbers are equal output that number.

17. Write a program to input two integers in a dialog box and output to the dialog box either the larger integer or a message stating that they are equal.

18. A salesperson gets a 5% commission on sales of $1000 or less, and a 10% commission on sales in excess of $1000. For example, a sale of $1300 earns him $80; that is, $50 on the first $1000 of the sale and $30 on the $300 in excess of the first $1000. Write a program that inputs a sales figure in a dialog box and outputs the commission to the dialog box. Output an error message if the user enters a negative sales figure.

19. The fine for speeding in a 45 MPH zone is $10 for every mile per hour over the speed limit for speeds from 46 to 55 MPH. It is $15 for every additional mile per hour between 56 and 65 MPH. It is $20 for every additional mile per hour over 65 MPH. For example, the fine for driving 57 MPH is $100 for the first 10 MPH plus $30 for the 2 MPH in excess of 55 MPH, for a total of $130. Write a program that inputs the speed in a dialog box as an integer and outputs the fine, or a message that there is no fine, to the dialog box. Output an error message if the user enters a negative speed. Use the smallest possible number of comparisons.

Temperature T	Message
$90 \leq T$	Go swimming
$80 \leq T < 90$	Play tennis
$70 \leq T < 80$	Study
$60 \leq T < 70$	Go to sleep
$T < 60$	Go to Hawaii

Figure 8.11
The table for Problem 21.

20.   Design a dialog box that has two input fields—an integer field for the temperature and a check box labeled Humid—and one output field. If the temperature is greater than 85 output the message "It is muggy" if the check box is checked or "Dry heat" if the box is not checked. Otherwise output "Cool man".

21.   Write a program to input the temperature (integer value) in a dialog box, then output the appropriate message for a given value of temperature to the dialog box, as the table in Figure 8.11 shows. Use the smallest possible number of comparisons.

22.   The price per Frisbee depends on the quantity ordered, as the table in Figure 8.12 indicates. Write a program to input the quantity requested from a dialog box and output the total cost of an order, including a 6.5% sales tax, to the dialog box. Output an error message if a negative quantity is entered.

Quantity	Price per Frisbee
0 – 99	$5.00
100 – 199	3.00
200 – 299	2.50
300 or more	2.00

Figure 8.12
The price schedule for Problem 22.

23.   You are eligible for a tax benefit if you are married and have an income of $30,000 or less, or unmarried and have an income of $20,000 or less. Design a dialog box that asks for the user's marital status (check box) and income (real), then outputs a message in the dialog box stating whether the user is eligible for the tax benefit. Output an error message if negative input is entered.

24.   A year is a leap year if it is divisible by 4 but not by 100. The only exception to this rule is that years divisible by 400 are leap years. Design a dialog box that asks the user to enter a positive integer for the year and displays a message that states whether the year is a leap year.

25.   The following statements are from the United States Department of Internal Revenue Form 1040 for 1997:

Enter on line 35 the larger of your itemized deductions or the standard deduction shown below for your filing status.

■ Single—$4,150
■ Married filing jointly or Qualifying widow(er)—$6,900
■ Head of household—$6,050
■ Married filing separately—$3,450.

Write a program that implements the dialog box of Figure 8.13 to output the value for line 35. Note that the first radio button is labeled 1 for the user, but should have a level number of 0 in your program. Output an error message on Line 35 if the amount entered for the standard deduction is negative.

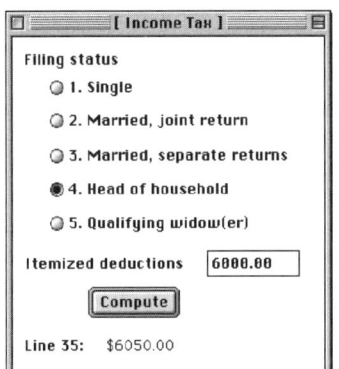 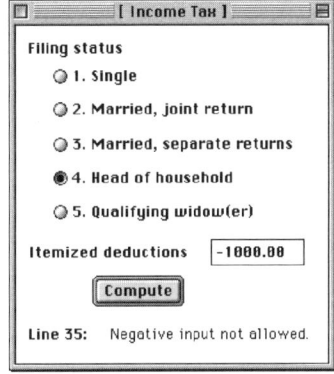

Figure 8.13
The dialog box for Problem 25.

26. Rewrite module **Pbox08B** in Listing 8.5 using a CASE statement instead of an IF statement. The dialog box should appear as in Figure 8.4 without any radio buttons. Use the fact that if d.score is in the range 70–79, for example, then d.score DIV 10 is 7.

 Chapter *9*

The MVC Design Pattern

With most of the examples up to this point, the input of a program comes from a dialog box. The output usually goes to a dialog box, but occasionally it goes to the Log. Although input/output via a dialog box is common, it is by no means the only way to get information into or out of a program. Input can come from the focus window, assumed to have been created before the program executes. Also, the program can create a new window in which to display the output.

This chapter shows how a program can get information from the focus window and how it can create a new window on which to write its output. BlackBox uses an effective technique for window I/O called the MVC design pattern. The MVC design pattern is in turn based on a modern software design methodology called object-oriented programming (OOP). OOP and the MVC design pattern are also the underlying foundations of dialog boxes. For simple programs like those we have encountered thus far, BlackBox has hidden the details of OOP and the MVC design pattern. To program I/O with windows, however, requires a bit more knowledge of both OOP and the MVC design pattern.

Objects

Recall that the difference between an abstract data structure (ADS) and an abstract data type (ADT) is that a server module that supplies a client with an ADS supplies only one data structure, while a server module that supplies an ADT exports a type. The client can then declare more than one variable to have that type. An object is a variable that has a type similar to an ADT. In object-oriented terminology, the type is called a *class*, and the variable with that type is called an *object*. *Classes and objects*

The Pbox project has an implementation of a stack designed to show the difference between an ADT and a class. In this chapter, there appears to be no advantage of the class over the ADT. The two primary advantages of using a class instead of an ADT are the object-oriented features of *inheritance* and *class composition*. Later chapters show how to program with each of these advanced techniques. Both techniques are pervasive throughout the BlackBox framework. For now, rather than incorporating these techniques into your programs, you will use some objects provided by BlackBox to program window I/O. A few details of the interfaces examined below will not be clear to you until you learn how to program with class composition and inheritance. You can easily learn the recipe of how to use the objects to program window I/O without understanding all the concepts behind OOP. *Inheritance and class composition*

But, it will be better if you try to understand as many of the OOP concepts as you can, because they are the basis of most modern software development efforts.

The remainder of this section illustrates a few object-oriented principles by comparing a stack class with the stack ADT from Chapter 6. Figure 9.1 is a listing of the interface of PboxStackObj. The interface of PboxStackADT from Chapter 6 is shown with it for comparison.

```
DEFINITION PboxStackObj;

    CONST
        capacity = 8;

    TYPE
        Stack = RECORD
            (VAR s: Stack) Clear, NEW;
            (IN s: Stack) NumItems (): INTEGER, NEW;
            (VAR s: Stack) Pop (OUT val: REAL), NEW;
            (VAR s: Stack) Push (val: REAL), NEW
        END;

END PboxStackObj.


DEFINITION PboxStackADT;

    CONST
        capacity = 8;

    TYPE
        Stack = RECORD  END;

    PROCEDURE Clear (VAR s: Stack);
    PROCEDURE NumItems (IN s: Stack): INTEGER;
    PROCEDURE Pop (VAR s: Stack; OUT val: REAL);
    PROCEDURE Push (VAR s: Stack; val: REAL);

END PboxStackADT.
```

Figure 9.1
The interface for PboxStackObj and PboxStackADT for comparison.

In both interfaces, Stack is a record type, which is exported. In the stack ADT, the formal parameter list of every procedure must include a variable s of type Stack, because, for example, when a client calls the Pop procedure it must specify not only the item to get the popped value but also the stack from which to pop it. After all, the client can declare more than one stack, so it must have a way to specify the one on which to operate. In the stack class, the specification of the data structure s is not included with the other formal parameters *following* the name of the procedure, but stands alone enclosed in parentheses *before* the name of the procedure. In Component Pascal, the formal parameter before the procedure name is called the *receiver*. *Receivers*

Another difference between the ADT and the class is the physical location of the procedures. In the ADT, the procedures are located outside the Stack record. In the class, the procedures are located within the record. As with the stack ADT, there are additional items in the record of the stack class that are not visible because they are not exported. In object-oriented terminology, procedures that have receivers, and are therefore contained within a record type, are called *methods*.

Methods

Another difference between the procedures of PboxStackADT and the methods of PboxStackObj is the presence of the method attribute NEW. Because inheritance is possible with methods, Component Pascal requires the NEW method attribute to be specified on all newly declared methods. The example in this section does not use inheritance. You will not see the utility of this requirement until you study examples in later chapters of the book that illustrate inheritance.

Example 9.1 In PboxStackObj, Stack is a class, and Pop is a method. In the declaration of Pop

(VAR s: Stack) Pop (OUT val: REAL), NEW;

the receiver is (VAR s: Stack). ∎

Figure 9.2 shows a dialog box that is implemented with PboxStackObj. It is indistinguishable from the dialog box of Figure 7.9. Behind the scenes, however, this dialog box is implemented with PboxStackObj instead of PboxStackADT as is the dialog box in Figure 7.9.

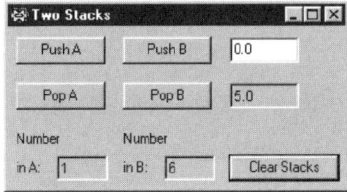

Figure 9.2
The dialog box for manipulating two stacks. It is implemented with PboxStackObj.

The listing in Figure 9.3 uses PboxStackObj to implement the dialog box of Figure 9.2. As in Chapter 3, this chapter names the modules as if the assigned two-digit number of a student in a course is 99, and her homework folder is named Hw99. The structure of the module is identical to the program in Figure 7.10 that uses PboxStackADT to implement the same dialog box. In both programs, there are two global variables, stackA and stackB. They are declared to have type Stack, which is exported from the server module.

The only significant difference between these two programs is how a method is called compared to how a procedure is called. With the ADT, to push a value onto stackB you write

PboxStackADT.Push(d.valuePushed, stackB)

With the class, to perform the same operation you write

stackB.Push(d.valuePushed)

```
MODULE Hw99Pr0980;
  IMPORT Dialog, PboxStackObj;

  VAR
    d*: RECORD
      valuePushed*, valuePopped-: REAL;
      numItemsA-, numItemsB-: INTEGER;
    END;
    stackA, stackB: PboxStackObj.Stack;

  PROCEDURE PushA*;
  BEGIN
    stackA.Push(d.valuePushed);
    d.numItemsA := stackA.NumItems();
    Dialog.Update(d)
  END PushA;

  PROCEDURE PushB*;
  BEGIN
    stackB.Push(d.valuePushed);
    d.numItemsB := stackB.NumItems();
    Dialog.Update(d)
  END PushB;

  PROCEDURE PopA*;
  BEGIN
    stackA.Pop(d.valuePopped);
    d.numItemsA := stackA.NumItems();
    Dialog.Update(d)
  END PopA;

  PROCEDURE PopB*;
  BEGIN
    stackB.Pop(d.valuePopped);
    d.numItemsB := stackB.NumItems();
    Dialog.Update(d)
  END PopB;

  PROCEDURE ClearStacks*;
  BEGIN
    stackA.Clear;
    stackB.Clear;
    d.valuePushed := 0.0; d.valuePopped := 0.0;
    d.numItemsA := 0; d.numItemsB := 0;
    Dialog.Update(d)
  END ClearStacks;

BEGIN
  ClearStacks
END Hw99Pr0980.
```

Figure 9.3
A program that uses a stack class to implement the dialog box of Figure 9.2.

The difference in syntax between these two calls illustrates a significant difference in viewpoint between a procedure and a method. With the stack ADT, the procedure belongs to the module. You must, therefore, prefix the procedure name with the name of the *module*, separated by a period. The procedure call is PboxStack-ADT.Push. With the stack class, the method belongs to the data structure. You must, therefore, prefix the procedure name with the name of the *object*, separated by a period. The method call is stackB.Push.

Procedures belong to modules and methods belong to objects.

A curious feature of object-oriented syntax is that the actual parameter corresponding to the receiver is not enclosed in parentheses. Because the receiver comes before the method name, it seems natural that the actual parameter would come before the method name in the call. However, a receiver contains a pair of parentheses that are not included in the call. In this call to Pop, stackB is an actual parameter along with d.valuePushed. It is not enclosed with parentheses and is separated from Pop by a period.

The table in Figure 9.4 shows the difference in terminology between the items associated with an ADT and those with a class. Unfortunately, terminology in the object-oriented community is not consistent from language to language. The latest Component Pascal language report uses the word "method" as we have here. However, it does not use the words "class" or "object" in the same way as in this text.

Procedure-oriented	Object-oriented
type	class
procedure	method
variable	object

Figure 9.4
Object-oriented terminology.

Models, views, and controllers

The MVC design pattern was developed at the Xerox Palo Alto Research Center in conjunction with an object oriented language called Smalltalk, and was adopted by the designers of BlackBox. The meaning of the letters in the MVC acronym is:

- M model

- V view

- C controller

A *model* is a data structure that stores data. An example of a model is the text model in BlackBox. Text consists of more than just an array of characters. It also includes the font, the size of the font usually measured in points, and various attributes such as whether a letter is bold, italic, or underlined. All this information must be stored for each character in the model.

Models

Another example of a model is a dialog box in the BlackBox forms subsystem. The user constructs a dialog box containing command buttons, radio buttons, text fields for input and output, and captions. The forms model for a dialog box would store data for the width and height of each control and the *x*- and *y*-coordinates for the position of the control in the dialog box. It also stores the font information for any text that appears in the control.

A *view* is the visual representation of a model in a window. In the example of a text model, the view is the image of the characters. Depending on the attributes stored in the text model, the image of a character on the screen would be displayed in one font or another, large or small, bold or not bold, italic or not italic, underlined or not underlined, and so on. In the example of a form, the view is the rendering of the various control objects in the dialog box. For the text field for input or output, depending on the values of the data stored in the model, it will be rendered as tall or

Views

short, wide or narrow, near the top of the dialog box or near the bottom, and so on.

It is clear from the meaning of models and views that a view usually does not exist without a model. Because a view is the visual rendering of a model on an output device, either screen or hardcopy, it must have something to render. From a programming perspective, you must create a model first before you can display it.

A view cannot exist without a model.

A *controller* is an object that controls the interaction between the user and the view to manipulate the model. In the example of the text model, the user might want to insert a word at a particular point in a sentence. She would position the cursor at the insertion point with the mouse, click the mouse, then type the word to insert. The controller changes the shape of the cursor when it is positioned over a text view, and locates the position in the text model when the mouse button is clicked.

Controllers

In the example of the forms model, the user might want to lengthen a text field. She would position the cursor over the field and click the mouse to select the field, which would then be displayed with handles for resizing. Dragging the cursor to the rightmost handle, clicking on the handle and dragging the mouse to the right would lengthen the field. The controller senses where the mouse is when it is clicked over the rightmost handle. As the user drags the handle, the controller sends a message to the model informing it to change the dimensions of the field accordingly.

The primary design concept in the MVC design pattern is that the view is separate from the model. One advantage of separating a view from its model is that you can have more than one view for a given model. Figure 9.5 shows one text model with two views, one of which displays the first part of the model and one of which displays the last part.

The primary design concept in the MVC design pattern

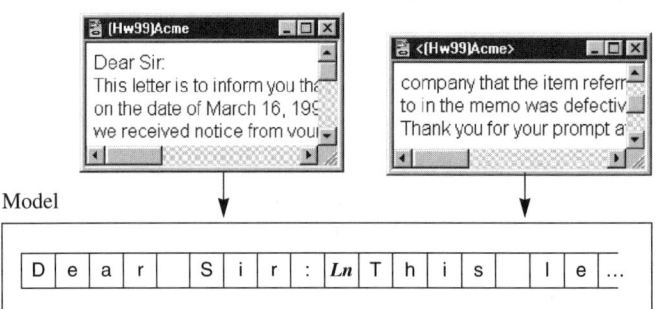

Figure 9.5
The relationship between a view and its model.

The first row of boxes in the model represent the character values. One box contains **Ln**, which represents the line character. There are no lines in computer memory. Instead, the line character is stored in the model when the user presses the <return> key just as any other character is stored when the user presses its key. The second row of boxes represents the fact that each character in the text model must have associated with it a set of attributes. Because the precise way in which this is accomplished need not concern us now, the boxes appear empty.

The BlackBox framework lets you open two views of one text model. You can do this by selecting Edit→View In Window (MacOS) or Window→New Window

(MSWindows). This feature is handy when you have written a long module and you are working on a part near the end and you want to see a part near the beginning. With two views, you do not need to continually scroll back and forth from the beginning of your document to the end.

UML class diagrams

Models, views, and controllers are all objects. That is, they are variables that contain data structures and methods (procedures) that operate on the data. The programs in the remainder of this chapter call the methods of several objects within the MVC system. Because the MVC design pattern is an object-oriented system, the objects are related by the two relationships of inheritance and class composition. Both relationships are conveniently represented by a kind of blueprint called a Unified Modeling Language (UML) class diagram. Figure 9.6 is a UML class diagram for most of the classes that are accessed to perform window I/O.

Figure 9.6
A UML diagram for some classes in the MVC system for text and forms.

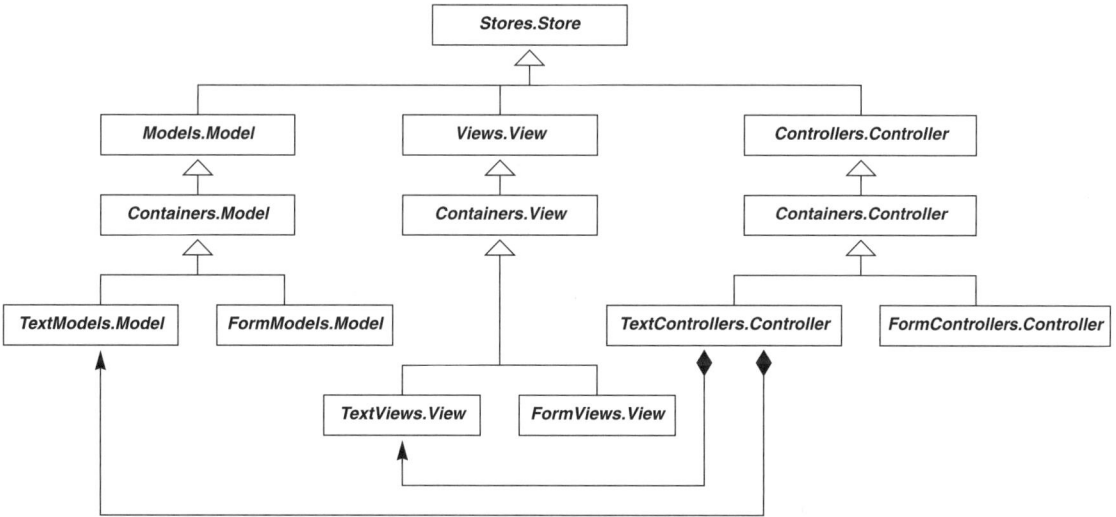

The figure includes classes for the forms subsystem even though you do not need to access them directly to create the dialog boxes in this book. They are included to show that the MVC design pattern applies to containers other than text. The word before the period in each box is the name of a module, and the word after the period is the name of a class (type). For example, in the box labeled Containers.Model, Containers is a module and Model is a class exported by the module. To perform window I/O you will need to access only four of the modules from Figure 9.6— Views, TextModels, TextViews, and TextControllers—and one module not shown in the figure—PboxMappers.

In a UML diagram, the triangle ⟁ is the symbol for inheritance. Figure 9.6 shows that classes Models.Model, Views.View, and Controllers.Controller all inherit

The triangle is the symbol for inheritance.

from Stores.Store. Stores.Store is called the superclass, and each of the other three is called a subclass. When you inherit a characteristic from a parent, the copy of your parent's genes give you similar characteristics and abilities as your parent. In the same way, when a subclass inherits from its superclass, the superclass gives it a characteristic or ability. The important ability that Stores.Store provides to its subclasses is the ability to be saved on disk, that is, to be stored.

For example, after you design a dialog box and you want to save it in your Rsrc folder, you select File→Save As to store it on disk. The fact that a dialog box is part of the forms subsystem, with its model, view, and controller all being subclasses of Stores.Store, gives it the ability to be stored on disk.

In a UML diagram, the arrow with a diamond tail ◆───► is the symbol for class composition. Figure 9.6 shows that class TextControllers.Controller is composed of a link to TextModels.Model and another link to TextViews.View. You can imagine why a controller needs to be composed of links to a model and a view. Recall that a controller is an object that controls the interaction between the user and the view to manipulate the model. Because the controller interacts with both a view and its model, it has links to both.

The arrow with diamond tail is the symbol for class composition.

The iterator design pattern

Besides models, views, and controllers, one additional kind of object is required for window I/O—iterators. Like models, views, and controllers, iterators are objects. That is, they are variables that contain data and methods that operate on the data. Most data structures are storage containers for a collection of values. For example, the list data structure in Chapter 6 stores a collection of strings. An iterator for a data structure is an object that traverses, or iterates over, the collection of values. (The list ADT of Chapter 6 does not have an iterator.)

Iterators

The iterators in BlackBox that are necessary for window I/O are designed to iterate over the character values stored in a text model. There are two kinds of iterators for text—one for inserting text into the model, called a *formatter*, and one for extracting values from the model, called a *scanner*. Formatters are used for window output and scanners are used for window input. Each of these iterators has a relationship with a text model and not with any of its views.

Formatters and scanners

The BlackBox framework supplies powerful iterators for its text model. Unfortunately, the iterators are rather complicated and are difficult for beginning programmers to use. Consequently, the Pbox project supplies its own version of text iterators in the module PboxMappers. Mappers is BlackBox terminology for what are usually known as iterators. Figure 9.7 is the interface for PboxMappers.

In PboxMappers, Formatter and Scanner are both classes (types). The methods that are included in their records have receivers. The first method in each is a procedure called ConnectTo that requires as its parameter a text model. Before you can use a formatter or a scanner you must connect it to a text model. Once it is connected, any operation you perform with that iterator will affect the text model to which it is connected.

Several of the methods for the formatter are similar to the procedures in module StdLog that you use to send output to the Log. WriteInt is similar to StdLog.Int, WriteReal is similar to StdLog.Real, WriteChar is similar to StdLog.Char, WriteString is similar to StdLog.String, and WriteLn is similar to StdLog.Ln. In each case the method of the formatter does the same thing as the corresponding procedure in Std-Log, but it sends the output to a text model instead of to the Log. The only other difference is that WriteReal allows you to specify the number of digits to insert past the decimal point, and StdLog.Real does not.

```
DEFINITION PboxMappers;

    IMPORT TextModels;

    TYPE
        Formatter = EXTENSIBLE RECORD
            (VAR f: Formatter) ConnectTo (text: TextModels.Model), NEW;
            (VAR f: Formatter) WriteInt (n, minWidth: INTEGER), NEW;
            (VAR f: Formatter) WriteReal (x: REAL; minWidth, dec: INTEGER), NEW;
            (VAR f: Formatter) WriteChar (ch: CHAR), NEW;
            (VAR f: Formatter) WriteString (str: ARRAY OF CHAR), NEW
            (VAR f: Formatter) WriteLn, NEW;
            (VAR f: Formatter) WriteIntVector (IN v: ARRAY OF INTEGER; numItm, minWidth: INTEGER), NEW;
            (VAR f: Formatter) WriteRealVector (IN v: ARRAY OF REAL; numItm, minWidth, dec: INTEGER), NEW;
            (VAR f: Formatter) WriteIntMatrix (IN mat: ARRAY OF ARRAY OF INTEGER;
                numR, numC, minWidth: INTEGER), NEW;
            (VAR f: Formatter) WriteRealMatrix (IN mat: ARRAY OF ARRAY OF REAL;
                numR, numC, minWidth, dec: INTEGER), NEW;
        END;

        Scanner = EXTENSIBLE RECORD
            eot-: BOOLEAN;
            (VAR s: Scanner) ConnectTo (text: TextModels.Model), NEW;
            (VAR s: Scanner) Pos (): INTEGER, NEW;
            (VAR s: Scanner) ScanInt (OUT n: INTEGER), NEW;
            (VAR s: Scanner) ScanReal (OUT x: REAL), NEW;
            (VAR s: Scanner) ScanChar (OUT ch: CHAR), NEW;
            (VAR s: Scanner) ScanPrevChar (OUT ch: CHAR), NEW;
            (VAR s: Scanner) ScanString (OUT str: ARRAY OF CHAR), NEW
            (VAR s: Scanner) ScanIntVector (OUT v: ARRAY OF INTEGER; OUT numItm: INTEGER), NEW;
            (VAR s: Scanner) ScanRealVector (OUT v: ARRAY OF REAL; OUT numItm: INTEGER), NEW;
            (VAR s: Scanner) ScanIntMatrix (OUT mat: ARRAY OF ARRAY OF INTEGER;
                OUT numR, numC: INTEGER), NEW;
            (VAR s: Scanner) ScanRealMatrix (OUT mat: ARRAY OF ARRAY OF REAL;
                OUT numR, numC: INTEGER), NEW;
        END;

END PboxMappers.
```

Figure 9.7
The interface for PboxMappers.

The factory design pattern

An interesting characteristic of some objects, particularly those in the MVC design pattern, is how they come into existence. You can think of them as products that are manufactured in a factory. The analogy to a factory that creates products is so close, that the object-oriented design pattern that does the same thing for objects is called the factory pattern. The *factory design pattern* is a software design technique in which one object, the factory, creates another object. Although the terminology of a factory to describe objects that create other objects is widespread in the OOP community, BlackBox does not use that terminology. Instead, the factories of BlackBox are called *directories*. When you encounter a directory in a BlackBox interface, you should think of it as a factory that produces other objects. When you want to send output to a new window, your program will need to create a new text model and a new text view to display that model in a window. You will use a factory, that is, a BlackBox directory, to create the new model and the new view.

The factory design pattern

The listing in Figure 9.8 shows the interface of module TextModels. The complete interface is quite large. Only those parts are shown that we will need for the programs in this text. If you are interested, you can view the complete interface on-line.

```
DEFINITION TextModels;
    TYPE
        Directory = POINTER TO ABSTRACT RECORD
            (d: Directory) New (): Model, NEW, ABSTRACT;
        END;
        Model = POINTER TO ABSTRACT RECORD (Containers.Model);
    VAR
        dir-: Directory;
END TextModels.
```

Figure 9.8
The interface for TextModels. Many items from the interface are omitted from this listing.

Module TextModels declares two classes (types) that we will use for window output. One is Model, which is declared as

Model = POINTER TO ABSTRACT RECORD (Containers.Model);

You can see in the UML diagram of Figure 9.6 that TextModels.Model is a subclass of Containers.Model. In Component Pascal, you declare one class to be a subclass of another by enclosing the superclass in parentheses after the word RECORD. That is why Containers.Model is enclosed in parentheses after RECORD. The word ABSTRACT is a record attribute that indicates the nature of the class. It need not concern us at the moment. (You may have noticed that the font for TextModels.Model in Figure 9.6 is bold and slanted. That font style is the UML standard for a class that is abstract.) Also note that a Model is not just a record, but a pointer to a record. The difference between a record and a pointer to a record can be ignored for the time being. Chapter 21 describes pointer types in great detail.

The other class declared in TextModels is Directory, which is defined as

Directory = POINTER TO ABSTRACT RECORD
    (d: Directory) New (): Model, NEW, ABSTRACT;
END;

It is a class, because it has a method New that is bound to it with a receiver (d: Directory). New is a function procedure as opposed to a proper procedure, because the last part of its signature is : Model. It is a function that returns a text model. New is the method of the factory that you call to get a newly created text model. So, it makes sense that it would return Model.

TextModels.dir is an abstract data structure (ADS). It is an object in module Text-Models and is exported read only. There is only one dir, and any program you write is not allowed to modify it. Its type is Directory. Note that the receiver of method New requires a variable of type Directory. When you call New, you will use dir as the actual parameter for the formal parameter d.

The listing in Figure 9.9 is the interface of module TextViews. As in Figure 9.8, only a small part of the interface is shown here. The interface for TextViews is similar to the interface for TextModels. View is a class that has Containers.View as its superclass. dir is an object ADS that cannot be modified by any module that imports TextViews. As with TextModels, dir will serve as the actual parameter for the formal parameter d.

```
DEFINITION TextViews;
    TYPE
        Directory = POINTER TO ABSTRACT RECORD
            (d: Directory) New (text: TextModels.Model): View, NEW, ABSTRACT;
        END;
        View = POINTER TO ABSTRACT RECORD (Containers.View)
    VAR
        dir-: Directory;
END TextViews.
```

Figure 9.9
The interface for TextViews. Many items from the interface are omitted from this listing.

The signature of method New in TextViews, however, is not quite the mirror image of the signature of method New in TextModels. In module TextModels, New returns a text model and has no formal parameters other than its receiver. In module TextViews, New returns a text view, but it requires a text model for its parameter in addition to its receiver. If you have followed the discussion of the MVC design pattern up until now, this difference should appear reasonable. Remember that a text view cannot exist without a model. Before you can create a text view with NEW, you must have previously created a text model. The model must be supplied to the view factory so the factory can manufacture a new view for that model.

Output to a new window

The programs in this section will show how to use a text model, a text view, and a formatter to create a new window containing output. Besides the factory for the model and the factory for the view, the program will require the services of one more procedure that is exported from module Views. Figure 9.10 shows a small part of its interface.

```
DEFINITION Views;
    TYPE
        View = POINTER TO ABSTRACT RECORD (Stores.Store)
        END;
    PROCEDURE OpenView (view: View);
END Views.
```

Figure 9.10
The interface for Views. Many items from the interface are omitted from this listing.

The interface shows that type View is a subclass of Stores.Store, because Stores.Store is contained in parentheses after the word RECORD. This is consistent with the UML diagram in Figure 9.6, because the triangle symbol is between Stores.Store and Views.View.

Procedure OpenView is not a method. It does not have a receiver, nor is it contained within the View record. It does take a view as a parameter. What kind of view? Any kind that has Views.View as a superclass. Figure 9.6 shows that TextViews.View is a subclass of Containers.View, which is a subclass of Views.View. So, it is legal to supply an object of class TextViews.View as the actual parameter for formal parameter view in procedure OpenView. Similarly, you could supply an object of class FormViews.View for the actual parameter. When you call OpenView, it makes a new window appear on the screen and renders the view inside the window.

Figure 9.11 shows a window that is created by the program in Figure 9.12. Procedure PrintAddress creates a new text model and inserts text into the model. It then creates a new view for the model and displays the view in the window.

Figure 9.11
The output for the program in Figure 9.12

```
MODULE Hw99Pr0981;
    IMPORT TextModels, TextViews, Views, PboxMappers;

    PROCEDURE PrintAddress*;
        VAR
            md: TextModels.Model;
            vw: TextViews.View;
            fm: PboxMappers.Formatter;
    BEGIN
        md := TextModels.dir.New();
        fm.ConnectTo(md);
        fm.WriteString("Mr. K. Kong"); fm.WriteLn;
        fm.WriteString("Empire State Building"); fm.WriteLn;
        fm.WriteString("350 Fifth Avenue"); fm.WriteLn;
        fm.WriteString("New York, NY 10118-0110"); fm.WriteLn;
        vw := TextViews.dir.New(md);
        Views.OpenView(vw)
    END PrintAddress;

END Hw99Pr0981.
```

Figure 9.12
A program that creates a text model and displays it in a text view.

Procedure PrintAddress has three variables—a model md, a view vw, and a formatter fm. Each of these variables is an object. What follows is a description of the effect of the statements in procedure PrintAddress. Figure 9.13 shows the relationships between the objects as the program executes.

When the module is first loaded and before the first statement executes as shown in part (a), md, vw, and fm are all automatically initialized to a special pointer value called NIL. NIL is a value that represents nothing. The fact that these objects have NIL values means that they are not connected to, or do not refer to, anything.

The statement

md := TextModels.dir.New()

calls the factory method New to manufacture a new text model. TextModels is a module. TextModels.dir is an object (variable) of type Directory in the module. The receiver for New requires a variable of type Directory. So, TextModels.dir is the actual parameter that corresponds to the formal parameter d. New is a function that returns a newly created model. md gets the new model. Figure 9.13(b) shows the effect of executing the statement.

The statement

fm.ConnectTo(md)

establishes the relationship of the iterator object fm to the new model. ConnectTo is one of the methods of a formatter shown in Figure 9.7. fm is the actual parameter that corresponds to formal parameter f in the receiver, and md is the actual parameter that corresponds to the formal parameter text in the parameter list. Figure 9.13(c) shows the formatter connected to the model.

The statement

fm.WriteString("Mr. K. Kong")

uses formatter fm to insert text into the new model. Because fm was connected to md earlier, any text that is inserted with the WriteString method is inserted into text model md. Method WriteLn inserts the line character into the model. Figure 9.13(d) shows the text inserted into the model.

The statement

vw := TextViews.dir.New(md)

calls the factory method New to manufacture a new text view. TextViews.dir is the actual parameter that corresponds to formal parameter d in the receiver of New, and md is the actual parameter that corresponds to formal parameter text in the parameter list. Note how you must supply a previously created text model as a parameter to New. You cannot create a view without a previously created model. Figure 9.13(e) shows the newly created view.

All the processing thus far has gone on behind the scenes. Nothing appears on the screen until the last statement

Views.OpenView(vw)

executes. OpenView is the procedure that creates a window for view vw, as Figure

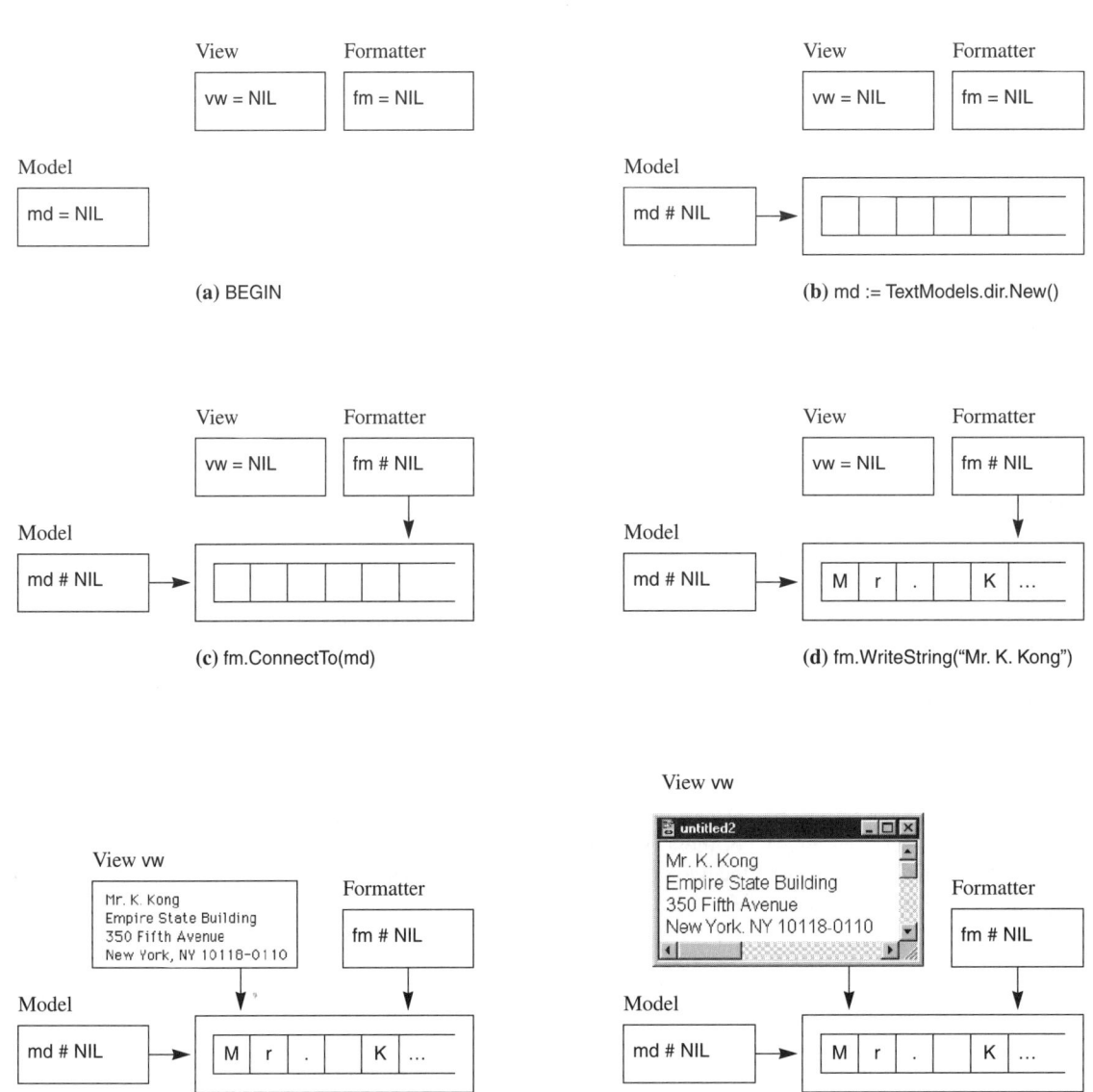

(a) BEGIN

(b) md := TextModels.dir.New()

(c) fm.ConnectTo(md)

(d) fm.WriteString("Mr. K. Kong")

(e) vw := TextViews.dir.New(md)

(f) Views.OpenView(vw)

Figure 9.13
The effect of the MVC
statements in Figure 9.12

9.13(f) shows.

The program in Figure 9.12 uses a text model, a formatter, which is an iterator, and a text view. It does not require the use of a text controller. The program is quite short. You could simply memorize the first two statements and the last two statements in procedure PrintAddress as the pattern to follow when you want your program to send output to a new window. It would be a mistake, however, to ignore the ideas of the MVC design pattern, the factory pattern, iterators, and the object-oriented concepts that these four statements embody. All these concepts are sound software design principles that are beginning to play a large role in modern software development. It is a strength of the BlackBox framework that these powerful ideas can all be provided in a system with a graphical user interface that is so easy for even beginning programmers to use.

The program in Listing 9.14 inserts the values from two real variables into a text model. The output of the program is shown in Figure 9.15. As in the previous program the procedure has a model object, a view object, and an iterator object for processing with text.

```
MODULE Hw99Pr0982;
    IMPORT TextModels, TextViews, Views, PboxMappers;

    PROCEDURE Rectangle*;
        VAR
            md: TextModels.Model;
            vw: TextViews.View;
            fm: PboxMappers.Formatter;
            width: REAL;
            length: REAL;
    BEGIN
        md := TextModels.dir.New();
        fm.ConnectTo(md);
        width := 3.6;
        length := 12.4;
        fm.WriteString("The width is "); fm.WriteReal(width, 1, 2); fm.WriteLn;
        fm.WriteString("The length is "); fm.WriteReal(length, 1, 2); fm.WriteLn;
        vw := TextViews.dir.New(md);
        Views.OpenView(vw)
    END Rectangle;

END Hw99Pr0982.
```

Figure 9.14
A program that inserts real values into a text model.

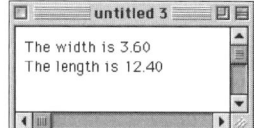

Figure 9.15
The output for the program in Listing 9.14

Besides the objects for the MVC design pattern, procedure Rectangle has local variables width and length. It gives each a real value, then uses method WriteReal to insert their values into the text model. The parameters for PboxMappers.WriteReal are similar to those for PboxStrings.RealToString in Figure 4.12. Namely, in the statement

fm.WriteReal(width, 1, 2)

width is the variable whose value is inserted into the text model, 1 is the field width which will expand to accommodate the complete value if necessary, and 2 is the number of places displayed past the decimal point.

Input from the focus window

All the programs thus far that required input have taken it from a dialog box. One characteristic of these programs is that little input was required. For example, the problem of computing the wage with overtime required only two numbers to be input—the hours worked and the hourly rate. Many problems require processing larger amounts of data, so much data that it would be impractical to ask the user to enter it every time into a dialog box. These problems are solved by storing the information in a document. Typically, the information is created by selecting the File→New menu option and entering it as text. If there is too much information to enter in a single session the data entry person can save the document in a file and continue entering at a later time. When the information needs to be processed, the document is opened so that the information is visible in the focus window. The procedure that processes the information is then invoked by selecting a menu option.

The next program illustrates the above scenario, although the example is shown with a small amount of data to keep things simple. Figure 9.16 shows the result of running the program. Figure 9.16(a) shows the data to be processed in a window titled Data. It was saved previously in file with that name and consists of text that represents two real values. While this window was focused, the user selected the menu option as shown in Figure 9.16(b), which resulted in the output to the Log shown in Figure 9.16(c). The processing simply consists of interpreting the first value as the number of hours worked and the second value as the hourly rate then computing the resulting wage with a possibility of overtime.

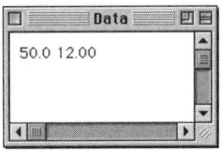   

Figure 9.16
The input and output of the program in Figure 9.18.

(a) The input window.   (b) The menu selection   (c) The output.

To get the values from the focus window requires the use of module TextControllers, whose partial interface is shown in Figure 9.17.

TextControllers.Controller is a class. The UML diagram in Figure 9.6 shows that TextControllers.Controller is a subclass of Containers.Controller because of the triangle between them. Figure 9.17 shows that TextControllers.Controller is a subclass of Containers.Controller because Containers.Controller is contained in parentheses after the Controller record.

```
DEFINITION TextControllers;
    TYPE
        Controller = POINTER TO ABSTRACT RECORD (Containers.Controller)
            view-: TextViews.View;
            text-: TextModels.Model;
        END;
    PROCEDURE Focus (): Controller;
END TextControllers.
```

Figure 9.17
The interface for
TextControllers. Many items
from the interface are omitted
from this listing.

The UML diagram also shows an arrow originating at a diamond symbol on Text-Controllers.Controller and pointing to TextViews.View. That arrow represents class composition. It indicates that TextControllers.Controller is composed of, or contains a reference to, TextViews.View. Figure 9.17 shows that TextControllers.Controller has a field named view in its record with type TextViews.View. That is the meaning of class composition. One class is *composed of* a second class if the first class has a field in its record whose class (type) is that of the second class. Furthermore, a UML diagram illustrates class composition by an arrow originating at a diamond from the box of the first class and terminating at the box of the second class. Similarly, Figure 9.17 shows that TextControllers.Controller is composed of TextModels.Model, because it contains a field of that type as well.

Class composition

Both fields TextViews.Views and TextModels.Model are exported read-only. That means that you cannot change their values by assigning something to them. However, if you have a local variable of type TextModels.Model you can assign the server module's exported field to it. Such an assignment does not change the server mod-ules's exported field. The next program uses that technique to extract a model from a controller.

The following program implements the processing illustrated in Figure 9.16. It has six local variables, three of which are variables for the MVC design pattern—a model md, a controller cn, and a scanner (iterator) sc. Figure 9.19 shows the effect of the MVC statements in procedure ComputeWages.

At the beginning of the procedure, the MVC variables, md, cn, and sc, all have values of NIL. Figure 9.19(a) shows that the values are NIL because there are no arrows that link the three variables to anything. Because there is a view in the focus window, there must be a model that already exists before the program executes. Both the model and its view were created previously by the word processor. The arrow from the view to its model indicates that the view contains a reference to its model.

When function procedure TextControllers.Focus executes in the assignment statement

cn := TextControllers.Focus()

the BlackBox framework detects which window is the focus window. If this window contains the view of a text model, TextControllers.Focus returns a controller for that view and assigns it to cn. Remember that the controller contains a reference (class composition) to both a view and its model. When the controller gets the value from TextControllers.Focus, the field cn.view gets a reference to the focus view, and the field cn.text gets a reference to the view's text model. Figure 9.19(b) shows these values by the arrows from the controller box.

```
MODULE Hw99Pr0983;
   IMPORT TextModels, TextControllers, PboxMappers, StdLog;

   PROCEDURE ComputeWages*;
      VAR
         md: TextModels.Model;
         cn: TextControllers.Controller;
         sc: PboxMappers.Scanner;
         hours, rate: REAL;
         wages: REAL;
   BEGIN
      cn := TextControllers.Focus();
      IF cn # NIL THEN
         md := cn.text;
         sc.ConnectTo(md);
         sc.ScanReal(hours);
         sc.ScanReal(rate);
         IF hours <= 40.0 THEN
            wages := hours * rate
         ELSE
            wages := 40.0 * rate + (hours - 40.0) * 1.5 * rate
         END;
         StdLog.String("Wages:  "); StdLog.Real(wages); StdLog.Ln
      END
   END ComputeWages;

END Hw99Pr0983.
```

Figure 9.18

A program that gets its input from the focus window.

If the window contains the view of some other kind of model such as a graphic of some kind, TextController.Focus returns NIL. Before proceeding, procedure ComputeWages checks the value of cn to verify that the focus window indeed contains the view of a text model.

Now that cn contains a reference to the model, the statement

md := cn.text

extracts the model from cn. After this statement executes, md will be the text model whose view is displayed in the focus window. So, the only purpose of cn is to test if the focus window contains a text view. If so, it gets the view and the model from the focus window. Now that it has given the model to md its job is done. Figure 9.19(c) shows the value given to md by the arrow from the model box.

The statement

sc.ConnectTo(md)

establishes the relationship between the scanner sc and the model md. Now that the

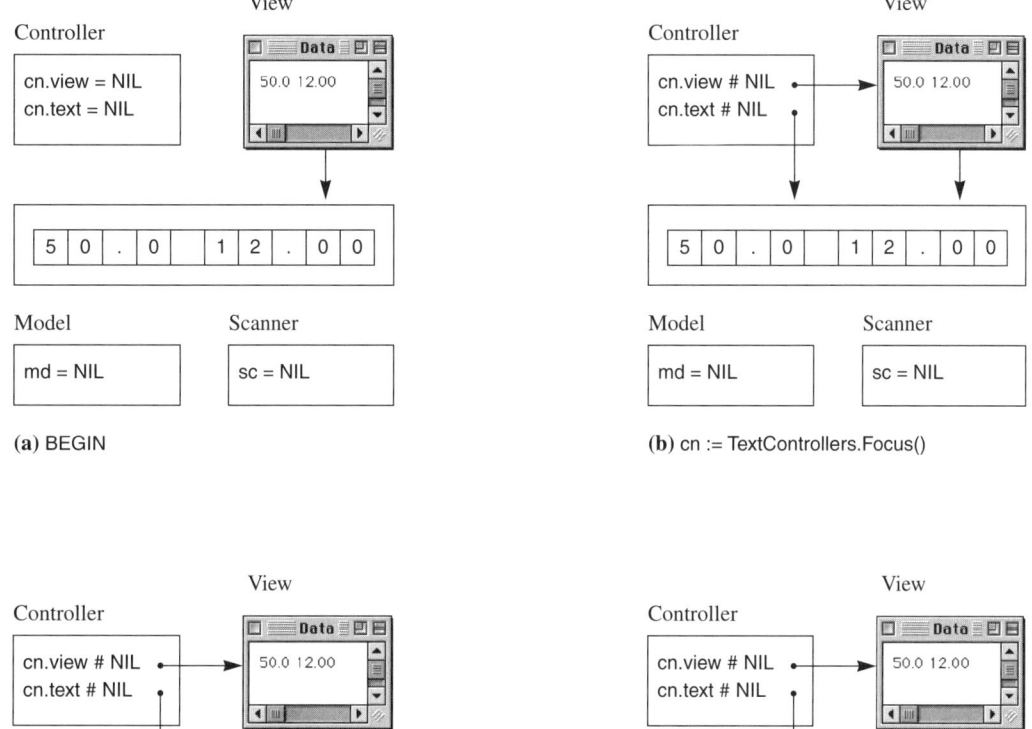

(a) BEGIN

(b) cn := TextControllers.Focus()

(c) md := cn.text

(d) sc.ConnectTo(md)

scanner is connected to the text model, it is ready to scan the values into our variables hours and rate. Figure 9.19(d) shows the connection by the arrow from the scanner box.

When a scanner is connected to a model, it is always positioned at the beginning of the model. Therefore, the statement

sc.ScanReal(hours)

scans from the beginning of the text model. This procedure assumes that the next characters of text in the model represent a real value. If some other character other

Figure 9.19
The effect of the MVC statements in Figure 9.18

than a digit or a decimal point is encountered by the scanner, a trap will occur. The scanner skips over any leading spaces or tabs until it encounters a string of digits containing a single decimal point. It stops scanning when it reaches the first trailing non digit character such as a space or the end of a line. It gives the real value to variable hours.

The next statement

sc.ScanReal(rate)

picks up the scan where the previous scan left off. In this scenario as depicted in Figure 9.16(a), the previous scan gives the variable hours the value 50.0 and this scan gives variable rate the value 12.00.

The remaining statements in procedure ComputeWages compute the wage and output it to the Log.

Creating menu selections

Procedure ComputeTotal is activated by a menu selection as shown in Figure 9.16(b). The menu choices that come standard with BlackBox therefore need to be augmented to allow the user to activate the program. A menu is a resource, in the same way that a dialog box is a resource. You create a menu by writing a BlackBox text document and storing it in your project's Rsrc folder. Figure 9.20 shows the document that created the menu selections in Figure 9.16(b).

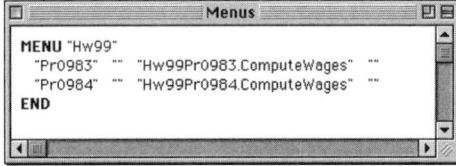

Figure 9.20
The menu document that produced the menu in Figure 9.16(b).

The menu document includes menu selections for the programs in both Figure 9.18 and in Figure 9.22 below. The content of the menu document is

```
MENU "Hw99"
   "Pr0983"    ""    "Hw99Pr0983.ComputeWages"    ""
   "Pr0984"    ""    "Hw99Pr0984.ComputeWages"    ""
END
```

The first line of the menu contains the word MENU followed by the title of the menu enclosed in quotes. In this case, Hw99 is the title that appears on the menu bar at the top of the screen. This title is appropriate if you are using this book in conjunction with a course and your assigned two-digit number is 99. Of course, if you are developing software for another user you would use a title that is more descriptive of the selections that are available for that menu.

Following the menu title is a line for the first selection that contains four strings. The second and fourth strings will not concern us until later. They will always be the empty string for now. The first field is the name of the selection that appears when the user clicks the menu title. The third field is the command that is activated when that selection is made. You can see from Figure 9.16(b) that the user has clicked on the title Hw99 and as a result he may select between Pr0983 and Pr0984. These are the selections that are enumerated in the first strings of the lines in Figure 9.20. When he selects Pr0983, procedure Hw99Pr0983.ComputeWages executes as specified by the third string in the line whose first string is Pr0983.

The last line in the menu document is END. It is possible to have one menu document produce more than one menu on the menu bar. Each menu begins with a line containing MENU and ends with a line containing END.

Your menu document must be saved in your Rsrc folder and must be named Menus. When BlackBox starts up, it scans all the folders named Rsrc contained in all the project folders. If it finds a file named Menus in a Rsrc folder, it interprets the contents as described above and installs the menu in the menu bar at the top of the screen. If you have created or modified a new menu and you wish to install or update it, you do not need to quit BlackBox for the sole purpose of starting it up again to install the menu. After you have saved the menu document in the Rsrc folder simply select Info→ Update All Menus, which will initiate the installation process.

Dialog boxes from programs

Previous chapters showed how to activate a dialog box by providing the user with a commander in the documentation file. Although this is a common technique in the BlackBox environment, commander buttons and documentation files are not common in commercial programs for either MSWindows or MacOS. Sometimes a dialog box is activated by a program to provide information to the user. For example, if you are playing a computer game a dialog box may appear to provide you with information about the progress of the game.

BlackBox provides a way for a program to activate a dialog box. Figure 9.21 shows such a scenario. It is similar to the scenario shown in Figure 9.16, except that the results are displayed in a dialog box instead of on the Log.

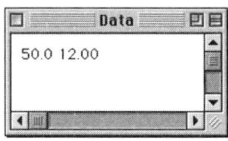

Figure 9.21
The input and output of the program in Figure 9.22.

(a) The input window.   **(b)** The menu selection   **(c)** The output.

The program in Figure 9.22 shows how to activate a dialog box. None of the fields in the dialog box of Figure 9.21(c) allow the user to change the displayed values. Consequently, the corresponding fields in the interactor d are all exported read-only. As in the previous module, this program takes its input from the focus window. It has the usual MVC parameters to scan the input values—a model md, a controller cn, and a scanner sc. Procedure ComputeWages is activated by the menu selection Hw99→ Pr0984.

```
MODULE Hw99Pr0984;
    IMPORT TextModels, TextControllers, PboxMappers,
        PboxStrings, Dialog, StdCmds;
    VAR
        d*: RECORD
            hours-, rate-: ARRAY 16 OF CHAR;
            wages-: ARRAY 16 OF CHAR
        END;

    PROCEDURE ComputeWages*;
        VAR
            md: TextModels.Model;
            cn: TextControllers.Controller;
            sc: PboxMappers.Scanner;
            hours, rate: REAL;
            wages: REAL;
    BEGIN
        cn := TextControllers.Focus();
        IF cn # NIL THEN
            md := cn.text;
            sc.ConnectTo(md);
            sc.ScanReal(hours);
            sc.ScanReal(rate);
            IF hours <= 40.0 THEN
                wages := hours * rate
            ELSE
                wages := 40.0 * rate + (hours - 40.0) * 1.5 * rate
            END;
            PboxStrings.RealToString(hours, 1, 1, d.hours);
            PboxStrings.RealToString(rate, 1, 2, d.rate);
            PboxStrings.RealToString(wages, 1, 2, d.wages);
            StdCmds.OpenAuxDialog('Hw99/Rsrc/Dlg0984', 'Payroll');
            Dialog.Update(d)
        END
    END ComputeWages;

END Hw99Pr0984.
```

Figure 9.22

A program that gets its input from the focus window and puts its output in a dialog box.

The procedure is identical to the one in the previous module except for its output. There are three local variables—hours, rate, and wages—that all have type REAL. The procedure uses the values of hours and rate that are scanned from the focus window to compute the value for wages. Each of these values is converted to a string with the desired number of places past the decimal point for display in the dialog box. The same command that is placed after a commander button in a documentation file is executed directly from the program.

StdCmds.OpenAuxDialog('Hw99/Rsrc/Dlg0984', 'Payroll')

As usual, the first parameter is a string that names the file where the dialog box is stored and the second parameter is a string that gives the title of the dialog box.

When you execute the procedure the first time with given values in the focus window, a new dialog box will appear with the computed values displayed. If you keep the dialog box visible, change the values in the focus window, and select Hw99→ Pr0984 once again, a second dialog box will not appear. Instead, the values in the old dialog box will simply be updated to reflect the new computation.

Exercises

1. Name the two advantages of using a class instead of an ADT.

2. When you program with objects, **(a)** what corresponds to the word type? **(b)** What corresponds to the word procedure? **(c)** What corresponds to the word variable?

3. **(a)** What is a model? **(b)** What is a view? **(c)** What is a controller? **(d)** What is an iterator?

4. What is the primary design concept in the MVC design pattern?

5. In the interface of Figure 9.7, **(a)** is Scanner a module, a type, a constant, a variable, or a procedure? **(b)** Is Scanner a model, a view, a controller, an iterator, or a factory? **(c)** In the line

    (VAR f: Formatter) WriteReal (x: REAL; minWidth, dec: INTEGER), NEW

    is f an actual parameter or a formal parameter? **(d)** Is Formatter a model, a view, a controller, an iterator, or a factory?

6. In the interface of Figure 9.8, **(a)** is dir a module, a type, a constant, a variable, or a procedure? **(b)** Is dir a model, a view, a controller, an iterator, or a factory?

7. In the procedure in Figure 9.12 in the line

    vw := TextViews.dir.New(md)

    (a) is TextViews a module, a type, a constant, a variable, or a procedure? **(b)** Is dir a module, a type, a constant, a variable, or a procedure? **(c)** Is New a module, a type, a constant, a variable, or a procedure? **(d)** Is md a formal parameter or an actual parameter?

Problems

8. Do Chapter 7, Problem 14, to construct an RPN calculator, but use the stack class from PboxStackObj.

9. Do Chapter 7, Problem 16, to construct a full-featured scientific calculator, but use the stack class from PboxStackObj.

10. Do Chapter 7, Problem 20, to construct a dialog box for two stacks with an "A to B" button but use the stack class from PboxStackObj.

11. Write a Component Pascal program to output the following two-line message on a new window:

She said, "Hi there.
What's up?"

Use two WriteString procedure calls for the second line to print both the single and the double quote marks. Test your program by inserting a commander button in a documentation file to execute the exported procedure.

12. Write a Component Pascal program to output to a new window your name and address suitable for use as a mailing label. Test your program by inserting a commander button in a documentation file to execute the exported procedure.

13. Using a procedure that is not exported to output a single pattern, write a Component Pascal program to output the following triple pattern on a new window:

```
+
+++
+++++
+++
+
+
+++
+++++
+++
+
+
+++
+++++
+++
+
```

Test your program by inserting a commander button in a documentation file to execute the exported procedure.

14. Write a program that inputs an integer value for the number of feet and a real value for the number of inches from the focus window. When the user selects a choice from a menu item, compute the equivalent length in meters and output the results of the computation to the Log. One inch is exactly 0.0254 meters and one foot is exactly 12 inches. Here is a sample output to the Log.

```
Feet: 4
Inches: 3.8
Meters: 1.31572
```

15. Work Problem 14, but display the number of feet and inches and the computed value for meters in a dialog box.

16. Write a program that inputs two real values for the lengths of two perpendicular sides of a right triangle from the focus window. When the user selects a choice from a menu item, compute the length of the hypotenuse and show all three lengths on the Log with their values identified appropriately as the values are in Problem 14.

17. Work Problem 16, but display the lengths of the two perpendicular sides and the computed value for the length of the hypotenuse in a dialog box.

18. Write a program to input three real numbers from the focus window. When the user selects a choice from a menu item print them in descending order on the Log.

19. Work Problem 18, but output the three real numbers in a dialog box.

20. Write a program to input three integers from the focus window. When the user selects a choice from a menu item output the number that is neither the smallest nor the largest on the Log. Assume that none of the integers are equal.

21. Work Problem 20, but output the number in a dialog box.

22. Write a program to input two integers from the focus window. When the user selects a choice from a menu item output to the Log either the larger integer or a message stating that they are equal.

23. Work Problem 22, but output the number in a dialog box.

 Chapter *10*

Loops

A powerful feature of all computer systems is their ability to perform repetitious tasks. Most people dislike monotonous, mechanical jobs that require little thought. Computers have the marvelous property of executing monotonous jobs without tiring or complaining. A group of statements that executes repetitively is called a loop. This chapter examines two of Component Pascal's several loop statements—the WHILE statement and the FOR statement.

The WHILE statement

WHILE statements are similar to IF statements because they both evaluate boolean expressions and execute a statement sequence if the boolean expression is true. The difference between them is that after the statement sequence executes in a WHILE statement, control is automatically transferred back up to the boolean expression for evaluation again. Each time the boolean expression is true, the body executes and the boolean expression is evaluated again. Figure 10.1 shows the flowchart for the WHILE statement

```
WHILE C1 DO
    S1
END
```

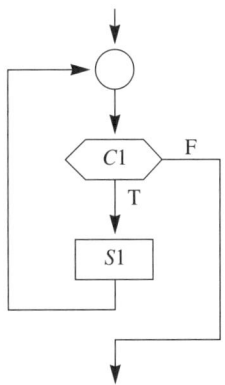

Figure 10.1
The flowchart for the WHILE statement.

The WHILE statement tests condition C1 first. If C1 is false, it skips statement sequence S1. Otherwise, it executes statement sequence S1 and transfers control up through the collector to the test again.

The flowchart shows several important properties of the WHILE statement. First, there are two ways to reach the condition C1—from the statement immediately preceding the WHILE statement or from the body of the loop. If C1 is true the first time, it will be tested again after S1 executes. S1 must eventually do something to change the evaluation of C1. Otherwise, C1 would be true always, and the loop would execute endlessly. Second, Figure 10.1 also shows that it is possible for statement sequence S1 to never execute. It does not execute if C1 is determined to be false the first time.

The eot technique

The first program that illustrates the WHILE statement computes the sum of a list of numbers in the focus window. Each number represents the dollar balance in a customer's account. Figure 10.2 shows the input and output for this program. The input comes from the focus window as the result of a menu selection, and the output is displayed on the Log.

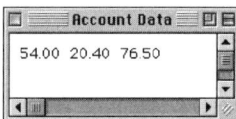

(a) The input window.

(b) The menu selection

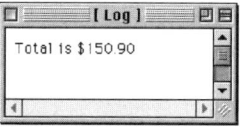

(c) The output to the Log.

Figure 10.2
The input and output of the program in Listing 10.3.

Figure 10.2(a) shows a focus window with three real values. While this window was focused, the user selected the menu option as shown in Figure 10.2(b), which resulted in the output to the Log shown in Figure 10.2(c). The processing simply consists of adding the real values. To keep the analysis short in the following discussion only three numbers were totaled, but the program works equally well with any number of values in the focus window. The program in Listing 10.3 inputs the data from the focus window and produces the output on the Log.

As usual, sc is a variable of type PboxMappers.Scanner. sc is the object that scans the text model for the real values. This program uses the standard pattern for establishing the model from the focus window and linking sc to it.

The statement

```
sum := 0.0
```

initializes variable sum to 0.0. Then the statement

```
sc.ScanReal(balance)
```

scans the first value, which in this example is 54.00. The scan has two effects. First, because the value scanned from the model was 54.00 from the focus window, the effect is the same as the assignment statement

```
balance := 54.00
```

Second, because there was a value that got scanned, the effect is also the same as the assignment statement

```
sc.eot := FALSE
```

```
MODULE Pbox10A;
    IMPORT TextModels, TextControllers, PboxMappers, PboxStrings, StdLog;

    PROCEDURE ComputeTotal*;
        VAR
            md: TextModels.Model;
            cn: TextControllers.Controller;
            sc: PboxMappers.Scanner;
            balance: REAL;
            sum: REAL;
            sumString: ARRAY 16 OF CHAR;
    BEGIN
        cn := TextControllers.Focus();
        IF cn # NIL THEN
            md := cn.text;
            sc.ConnectTo(md);
            sum := 0.0;
            sc.ScanReal(balance);
            WHILE ~sc.eot DO
                sum := sum + balance;
                sc.ScanReal(balance)
            END;
            PboxStrings.RealToString(sum, 1, 2, sumString);
            StdLog.String("Total is $");
            StdLog.String(sumString); StdLog.Ln
        END
    END ComputeTotal;

END Pbox10A.
```

Figure 10.3
A program to find the total of all the data values in the focus window. It uses the eot technique.

You can see from the interface of **PboxMappers** in Figure 9.7 that every scanner has a variable exported read-only called **eot**, which stands for end of text. If your scanner attempts to scan an integer or real value from a text model but there are no more values left to scan, the actual parameter gets some unknown large value and sc.eot is set to true. Otherwise, the actual parameter gets the value scanned and sc.eot is set to false.

The behavior of eot from PboxMappers.Scanner

The next statement to execute is

WHILE ~sc.eot DO

Because sc.eot is false, ~sc.eot is true, and the body of the loop executes. The first statement in the statement sequence of the WHILE body is

sum := sum + balance

giving 0.0 + 54.0 to sum. The second statement in the statement sequence of the WHILE is

sc.ScanReal(balance)

which scans the next group of characters in the text, giving balance the value of 20.40 and s.eot the value of false.

Now, control returns back to the test of the WHILE loop, which is still true. So, the statement sequence executes again. The assignment statement gives sum the value of 54.0 + 20.4, which is 74.4. The sc.ScanReal(balance) statement gives balance the value of 76.5 and sc.eot the value of false.

Control again returns back to the test of the WHILE loop, which is true again. So, the statement sequence executes once more. The assignment statement gives sum the value of 74.4 + 76.5, which is 150.9. This time the sc.ScanReal(balance) statement gives sc.eot the value true because there is no more visible text after the position of the scanner.

When control returns back to the test of the WHILE loop, the condition is false, so the loop terminates, and the statements following the loop END execute. They convert the real value of sum to the corresponding string value of sumString and output the result to the Log.

Execution counts

As consumers, we are familiar with the process of evaluating products. When you choose between two automobiles to purchase, what factors influence your choice? For some people, speed and road handling may be the most important factors. Others may care about fuel economy. Some may be looking for luxury and a smooth ride. Most people are also concerned about price. These factors usually compete with one another in the car buyer's mind. A car with much power and speed typically does not have good fuel economy. One that is luxurious does not come with a low price. In design terminology, that is a trade-off. The buyer may wish to trade off fuel economy to gain speed and power.

The same type of problem emerges when we evaluate algorithms. Several competing factors are present. Usually, a gain of one property in an algorithm comes at the expense of another. Two important properties of an algorithm are the memory space required to store the program and its data, and the time necessary to execute the program. To compare several different algorithms that perform the same computation, we need a method of assessing these two properties. The following discussion presents a method for estimating the time necessary to execute a program.

The space/time trade-off

One way to estimate the time necessary for an algorithm to execute is to count the number of statements that execute. If an algorithm has no IF statements or loops, then the number of statements that execute is simply the number of executable statements in the program listing.

If the algorithm has a loop, however, the number of statements in the listing is not equal to the number of statements executed. This is because the statements in the body may execute many times, even though they appear only once in the program listing.

Procedure ComputeTotal has 12 executable statements shown below. The declarations in the variable declaration part are not executable. Neither are the END reserved words.

Statement number	Executable statement
(1)	cn := TextControllers.Focus()
(2)	IF nc # NIL THEN
(3)	md := cn.text
(4)	sc.ConnectTo(md)
(5)	sum := 0.0
(6)	sc.ScanReal(balance)
(7)	WHILE ~s.eot DO
(8)	sum := sum + balance
(9)	sc.ScanReal(balance)
(10)	PboxStrings.RealToString(sum, 1, 2, sumString)
(11)	StdLog.String("Total is $" + sumString)
(12)	StdLog.Ln

The executable statements of procedure ComputeTotal

Even though the listing contains 12 executable statements, more than 12 statements execute. Statements (8) and (9) are part of a loop and may execute more than once. For the three real values in the focus window, statement (7) executes four times, and statements (8) and (9) each execute three times, as shown by the trace below.

Statement executed	sum	balance	sc.eot	sumString
(1)				
(2)				
(3)				
(4)				
(5)	0.0			
(6)	0.0	54.0	false	
(7)	0.0	54.0	false	
(8)	54.0	54.0	false	
(9)	54.0	20.4	false	
(7)	54.0	20.4	false	
(8)	74.4	20.4	false	
(9)	74.4	76.5	false	
(7)	74.4	76.5	false	
(8)	150.9	76.5	false	
(9)	150.9	?	true	
(7)	150.9	?	true	
(10)	150.9	?	true	"150.90"
(11)	150.9	?	true	"150.90"
(12)	150.9	?	true	"150.90"

A trace of procedure ComputeTotal with three data values in the focus window

So, the total number of executions is one each for statements (1), (2), (3), (4), (5), (6), (10), (11), and (12) for a total of nine, plus four for statement (7), plus three each for statements (8) and (9) for a total of six. The grand total is therefore nine plus four plus six, which is 19 statements executed.

If there were no data values in the focus window, then the trace would be as shown below, and 10 statements would execute.

Statement executed	sum	balance	sc.eot	sumString
(1)				
(2)				
(3)				
(4)				
(5)	0.0			
(6)	0.0	?	true	
(7)	0.0	?	true	
(10)	0.0	?	true	"0.00"
(11)	0.0	?	true	"0.00"
(12)	0.0	?	true	"0.00"

A trace of procedure ComputeTotal with no data values in the focus window

If the focus window contained *n* data values, then a total of $3n + 10$ statements would execute as shown in Figure 10.4.

Statement	No data values	Three data values	*n* data values
(1)	1	1	1
(2)	1	1	1
(3)	1	1	1
(4)	1	1	1
(5)	1	1	1
(6)	1	1	1
(7)	1	4	$n + 1$
(8)	0	3	n
(9)	0	3	n
(10)	1	1	1
(11)	1	1	1
(12)	1	1	1
Total:	10	19	$3n + 10$

Figure 10.4
Statement execution count for the procedure ComputeTotal in Figure 10.3.

Execution time estimates

You can use the general expression for the statement count, $3n + 10$, to estimate the execution time for a large number of data values, given the execution time for a small number of data values.

Example 10.1 Suppose you execute procedure ComputeTotal with 100 data values and it takes 140 μs (140 microseconds, which is 140×10^{-6} seconds). The problem is to estimate how long it would take to execute the program with 1000 data values.

Assuming that each executable statement takes the same amount of time to execute, simply form the ratio

$$\frac{140}{3 \times 100 + 10} = \frac{T}{3 \times 1000 + 10}$$

where T is the time to execute with 1000 data values. Solving for T gives

$$\frac{140}{310} = \frac{T}{3010}$$

or $T = 1359 \ \mu s = 0.001359 \ s$. ∎

The time of 0.00136 seconds is only an estimate. Each statement in procedure ComputeTotal does not execute in the same amount of time. Remember that the compiler must translate the Component Pascal source statements to object statements in machine language before it can execute. Typically, the compiler translates one source statement to more than one object statement. It may translate one source statement into three object statements and another source statement into five object statements. Furthermore, even the object statements do not execute in equal amounts of time. Under these circumstances, it is unreasonable to expect each source instruction to execute in the same amount of time.

The following example shows why the estimate works so well in practice. In dealing with large numbers of data, say hundreds or thousands for the value of n, the additive constants are insignificant to the final result and can be ignored.

Example 10.2 In the previous example, ignoring the additive constant, 10, in the expression can be justified because 310 is about equal to 300, and 3010 is about equal to 3000. Assuming that $3n + 10$ is approximately equal to $3n$, forming the ratio and solving for T then yields

$$\frac{140}{3 \times 100} = \frac{T}{3 \times 1000}$$
$$\frac{140}{100} = \frac{T}{1000}$$

or $T = 1400 \ \mu s = 0.00140 \ s$, which is not too different from our original estimate. ∎

Notice that when you ignore the additive constant, the coefficient of n, which is 3, cancels in the ratio. Why is the coefficient of n unimportant in the estimate of the execution time for 1000 data values? Because for these large amounts of data, namely $n = 100$ and $n = 1000$, the number of statements executed is just about directly proportional to n. That implies that doubling the number of data values will double the number of statements executed, hence it will double the execution time. Or, as in this problem, multiplying the number of data values by 10 multiplies the execution time by 10.

Estimating the execution time by ignoring the additive constant and the coefficients

Although the coefficient of n is unimportant in estimating the execution time for one algorithm with different amounts of data, it is important in comparing two different algorithms for the same job. If one algorithm requires $4n + 5$ statements to execute, and another algorithm to do the same processing requires $7n + 5$ statements to execute, the first will execute faster than the second with the same amount of data.

Loop invariants

A loop invariant is an assertion at the beginning of a loop. Because it is an assertion, it is a statement that is true at a specific point in a program. Figure 10.5 shows the point at which a loop invariant is true.

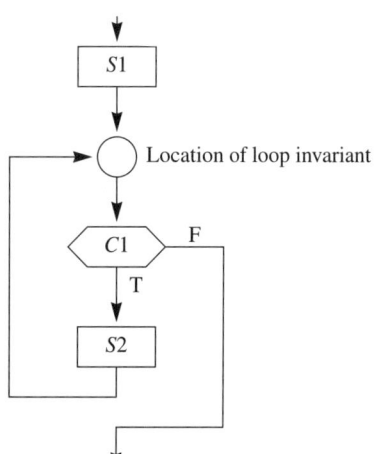

Location of loop invariant

(a) Flowchart.

Figure 10.5
The location of the loop invariant for a WHILE loop.

Statement 1
(* Location of loop invariant *)
(* Loop invariant is true. *)
WHILE *Condition1* DO
    Statement2
END
(* Loop invariant is true and *Condition1* is false. *)

(b) Source code.

You can see from Figure 10.5(a) that there are two ways to get to the loop invariant. You can get to it from above by executing the statement sequence *S1*, or you can get to it from below by executing the statement sequence *S2* in the body of the loop.

In the program of Figure 10.3, the statement sequence *S1* is

```
sum := 0.0;
sc.ScanReal(balance)
```

the condition *C1* is

```
~sc.eot
```

and the statement sequence *S2* is

```
sum := sum + balance;
sc.ScanReal(balance)
```

For this program, the loop invariant is

- sum is the total of all the values scanned, not including the current value scanned into balance.

The loop invariant for Figure 10.3

To prove that a statement is a loop invariant, you must show two things:

- The statement is true initially because of the execution of *S*1.

Proving a loop invariant

- The statement is true at the end of each loop because of the execution of *S*2.

Now consider the proposed loop invariant for Figure 10.3. Because of the execution of *S*1, sum has value 0.0 and balance has value 54.00 assuming the values shown in Figure 10.2. But 0.0 *is* the total of all the values scanned, not including the 54.00 scanned into balance. It follows that the first part of the proof is true. To prove the second part, consider how *S*2 executes. *C*1 must be true at the beginning of *S*2. That is, sc.eot must be false. But regardless of whether you get to the body of the loop from above or from below, the statement

sc.ScanReal(balance)

was just executed. So, you know that you just did a scan into balance, after which sc.eot is false. Therefore, balance contains a valid real number. The statement sequence *S*2 adds the scanned value to sum, then does a scan. So after *S*2 executes, sum is once again the total of all the values scanned, not including the current value scanned into balance. It follows that the second part of the proof is true.

Consider what must be the case when a WHILE loop eventually terminates.

- The loop invariant is true.

When a WHILE loop terminates

- The loop condition is false.

The loop condition must be false, because that is the only way the loop can terminate. For the program of Figure 10.3, you know that after the loop terminates sum is the total of all the values scanned, not including the current value scanned into balance and that sc.eot is true. Because sc.eot is true, you know that the current value of balance should not be added to sum, which now contains the correct value.

This algorithm illustrates a common programming technique. Generally, when you program with loops, you should try to formulate a useful loop invariant. Establish the invariant before the loop executes the first time. Then, design the body of the loop so that each time it executes, the loop invariant becomes true when you reach the condition at the top of the loop from below. That is, you must write the body of the loop in such a way to reestablish the loop invariant.

Using loop invariants

The concept of a loop invariant may seem like much ado about nothing, or it may seem to be making a complicated point about something that appears simple. Using loop invariants to design programs is frequently a useful design technique that you will find aids in reasoning about your loops.

Using the Pbox scanners

Recall the rule for assignment statements that allows you to assign an integer value to a real variable, but does not allow you to assign a real value to an integer variable. A similar rule applies to a Pbox scanner. You can scan an integer value into a real variable, but you cannot scan a real value into an integer variable. Here is the documentation for ScanReal from module PboxMappers.

```
PROCEDURE (VAR s: Scanner) ScanReal (OUT x: REAL), NEW
Pre
s is connected to a text model.   20
Characters scanned represent a real or integer value.   21
Post
~s.eot
    x gets the next real or integer value scanned.
s.eot
    x gets MAX(REAL)
```

It shows that the text scanned can represent integer or real. If it is something else, such as a letter, a trap will be generated with error number 21.

Example 10.3   In Figure 10.2, if the input is

54 20.40 76.50

with the first number written as an integer, the program will execute correctly. However, if the input is

$54.00 $20.40 $76.50

a trap will be generated because of the dollar signs.   ∎

The documentation for ScanInt is

```
PROCEDURE (VAR s: Scanner) ScanInt (OUT n: INTEGER), NEW
Pre
s is connected to a text model.   20
Characters scanned represent an integer value.   21
Post
~s.eot
    n gets the next integer value scanned.
s.eot
    n gets MAX(INTEGER)
```

It shows that the text scanned must represent an integer.

Example 10.4   Suppose numEmp is an integer variable that is supposed to represent the number of employees in a company, and your program executes

sc.ScanInt(numEmp)

with the text

147.0

in the focus window. The program will trap with error number 21 because of the decimal point in the text. ∎

The documentation for both ScanInt and ScanReal shows that when sc.eot is true, that is, when no value is scanned because the end of text has been reached, the actual parameter gets its maximum possible value. See Example 4.15, page 60, for the definition of the MAX function.

If you ever stop doing a scan before the scanner reaches the end of the text model, the remaining values are simply not scanned or processed by your program.

Example 10.5 Suppose score is an integer variable and you execute the loop

```
sc.ScanInt(score);
WHILE ~sc.eot & (score <= 100) DO
   StdLog.String("score = "); StdLog.Int(score); StdLog.Ln;
   sc.ScanInt(score)
END
```

with the input containing the text

```
78  94  85  73  75  200 80  79
```

The program will scan the first five numbers and print them on the Log. Then it will scan the 200, but the condition will be false, because even though ~sc.eot is true, score <= 100 is false. The loop will not print the 200 to the Log, nor will it ever scan the 80 or the 79. ∎

Computing the average

Suppose you want to compute the average of the balances in the accounts. You would need not only their sum, but the number of accounts as well. The algorithm in Figure 10.6 uses another integer variable, numAccts, to count how many data values are in the focus window.

```
sum := 0.0;
numAccts := 0;
sc.ScanReal(balance);
WHILE ~sc.eot DO
   sum := sum + balance;
   INC(numAccts);
   sc.ScanReal(balance)
END;
IF numAccts > 0 THEN
   Output sum / numAccts
ELSE
   Output a no accounts message
END
```

Figure 10.6
An algorithm to find the average of all the data values in the focus window.

This algorithm illustrates a common programming technique. To determine how many times a loop executes, initialize a counting variable, in this algorithm num-Accts, outside the loop to zero. Each time you scan a real value in the statement sequence of the loop, increment the counting variable by one. When the loop terminates, the value of the counting variable will be the number of values scanned by the loop. Before dividing by numAccts to compute the average, you must test to make sure that it is not zero. Otherwise your program may attempt a division by zero, which would cause a program trap by your user.

Finding the largest

The algorithm in Figure 10.7 finds the largest number from the focus window that contains integer values. If the input in the focus window is

73   80   -18   68   92   75

then the output is 92.

The two variables, num and largest, are integers. The algorithm works by scanning the first value from the text model into num. If the text model is empty the boolean sc.eot will be set to true, because a scan was attempted at the end of the text. In that case, the algorithm outputs a message indicating that the focus window is empty.

```
sc.ScanInt(num)
IF sc.eot THEN
    Output empty window message
ELSE
    largest := num
    sc.ScanInt(num)
    WHILE ~sc.eot DO
        IF num > largest THEN
            largest := num
        END
        sc.ScanInt(num)
    END
    Output largest
END
```

Figure 10.7
An algorithm to find the largest value in the focus window.

On the other hand, if sc.eot is false then an integer value has been scanned into num, 73 in this example. The first statement in the ELSE part initializes largest to the first value scanned. So now, both largest and num have the value 73. Then, the sc.ScanInt statement before the WHILE attempts to scan the second value from the text model. In this example, it would scan the 80 into num and set sc.eot false, because the scan was successfully executed before the end of text.

The first time the body of the loop executes, num is greater than largest, because it has the value 80. So, largest gets the value 80 from num. Then, num gets the next value from the focus window, –18. At this point, the WHILE statement is about to execute. You should be able to formulate the loop invariant for this program.

- largest has the largest of all the values scanned, not including the current value scanned into num.

The loop invariant for Figure 10.7

Can you see that this loop invariant is true just before the loop executes even for the first time?

The second time through the loop, the true alternative of the IF statement does not execute, because the value of num, which is now –18, is not greater than the value of largest, which is 80. Had the value of num been greater than 80, largest would have acquired that value and would still be the largest number scanned thus far. When the loop terminates the loop invariant will still be true. That is, variable largest has the largest value scanned so far, except for the last value scanned into variable num. Because no value is scanned into num when the scanner is at the end of text, largest will contain the largest of all the integer values in the focus window.

This algorithm illustrates a common programming technique. To save a value through successive loop iterations, declare a variable and initialize it appropriately. In the body of the loop, update the value with an assignment statement in the alternative of an IF statement as needed.

Real Expressions

You must be careful when you test real expressions in WHILE statements. Unlike integer values, real values have fractional parts, which the computer can store only approximately in main memory. The approximate nature of real values can cause endless loops if you do not design your WHILE tests properly.

Real values are approximate

Example 10.6 The following code fragment, where r is a real variable, is an endless loop:

```
r := 0.6;
WHILE r # 1.0 DO
   r := r + 0.1
END
```

It would seem that after r is initialized to 0.6, the loop would increase it to 0.7, 0.8, 0.9, and 1.0, at which point the loop would terminate. The problem is that r is never exactly 1.0 after those calculations. After four executions of the loop the value of r will be approximately one, not exactly one. ∎

The problem in Example 10.6 is that r was tested for strict inequality. In general, you should use the following rule for testing real values:

- Never test a real expression for strict equality, =, or strict inequality, #.

Tests for real values should always contain a less than or a greater than part.

Example 10.7 The previous example could be coded

```
r := 0.6;
WHILE r <= 0.95 DO
   r := r + 0.1
END
```

which would increase r to 0.7, 0.8, 0.9, and 1.0, at which point the loop would terminate. ∎

The Component Pascal language does not have an operator that raises a value to a
power. However, the Math library module has the function

Minimizing the number of multiplications

```
PROCEDURE IntPower (x: REAL; n: INTEGER): REAL
```

For example, the expression $7x^3$ where x is a real variable can be written

```
7 * Math.IntPower (x, 3)
```

Without the function, the expression would be written 7 * x * x * x, which requires
three multiplications. With the function, three multiplications are necessary inside
the function itself. Multiplication of real values is one of the most time-consuming
operations that the CPU can do. Polynomial expressions, which are sums of terms
such as $7x^3$, are especially time consuming when they occur in loops that execute
repeatedly. A common technique to minimize the computation time is to completely
factor such expressions to reduce the number of real multiplications required. This
technique will be used in the program in Figure 10.11.

Example 10.8   Suppose you need to evaluate $7x^3 + 2x^2 + 8x + 5$. Without factoring, the corresponding Component Pascal expression is

```
7 * x * x * x + 2 * x * x + 8 * x + 5
```

which requires six multiplications and three additions. On the other hand, if you
completely factor the expression as $((7x + 2)x + 8)x + 5$ then the corresponding
Component Pascal expression is

```
((7 * x + 2) * x + 8) * x + 5
```

which requires only three multiplications and three additions. ∎

The bisection algorithm

A numerical method is an algorithm that calculates a value or set of values that
approximates the solution of a mathematical problem. The program in Figure 10.11
is a numerical method that computes one root of the cubic equation
$x^3 - x^2 - 4x + 2 = 0$ with the bisection algorithm.

Figure 10.8 is a graph of the function $f(x) = x^3 - x^2 - 4x + 2$. The roots of the
cubic equation are the values of x for which $f(x) = 0$. Figure 10.8 shows that $f(x)$
is zero for three different values of x: (a) between –2.0 and –1.0, (b) between 0.0 and

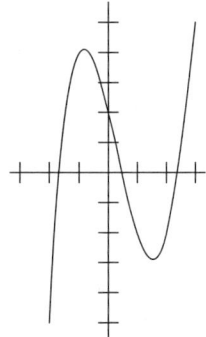

Figure 10.8
A graph of the function
$f(x) = x^3 - x^2 - 4x + 2$

1.0, and (c) between 2.0 and 3.0. Although this cubic equation has three roots, cubic equations in general can have from one to three roots. The program will determine the root of the equation that lies between $x = 2$ and $x = 3$.

In the bisection algorithm, the variable left is a value of x that lies to the left of the root and the variable right is a value of x that lies to the right of the root. This algorithm initializes left to 2.0 and right to 3.0. Then, as Figure 10.9(a) shows, it calculates the variable fLeft as

fLeft := f(left)

The next step is to compute the value of x that is the midpoint between left and right. As Figure 10.9(b) shows, the algorithm gives that value of x to the variable mid and computes fMid as

fMid := f(mid)

The value of fMid determines whether the root lies to the left or right of mid. If fLeft and fMid have the same sign, then the root lies to the right of mid. Otherwise, the root lies to the left of mid. In the figure, fLeft and fMid have the same sign, because both are negative. Therefore, the root lies to the right of mid.

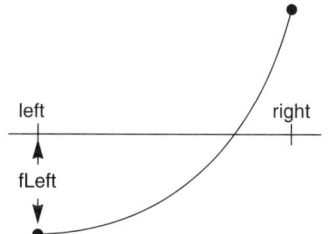
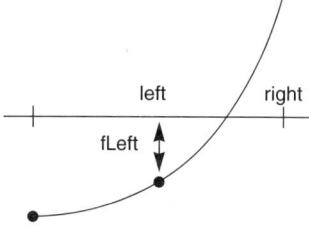

(a) Before the loop executes the first time.

(b) Computation of mid and fMid.

(c) Updating left and fLeft.

If the root lies to the right of mid, the algorithm changes the value of left and fLeft by

Figure 10.9
The bisection algorithm to find a root of $f(x)$.

left := mid
fLeft := fMid

as Figure 10.9(c) shows. The root is still between left and right. Had the root lain to the left of mid, the algorithm would have changed the value of right by

right := mid

so that the root would still be between left and right.

The bisection algorithm continues to find the midpoint between left and right.

Each time it updates left or right, it decreases the interval between them such that the root is still in the interval. The loop invariant is the assertion that *the root is between* left *and* right. The loop terminates when left and right get close enough to satisfy a tolerance limit set by the user.

The loop invariant for the bisection algorithm

Figure 10.10 shows three executions of a program that implements the bisection algorithm. When the user enters 0.1, the bisection method calculates the root as 2.34375. It is accurate to the nearest tenth, so the last four digits, 4375, may not be significant. When the user enters 0.01, the loop executes more times and calculates the root as 2.33984375, a more accurate value for the root than 2.34375. The smaller the tolerance, the more times the loop executes and the more accurate is the value for the root. But then the program runs longer. So there is a trade-off between the accuracy of the solution and the execution time.

Figure 10.10
Three executions of the bisection algorithm of Listing 10.11.

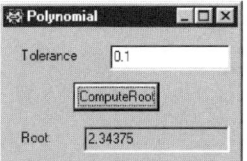
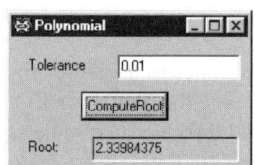
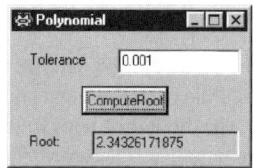

Procedure ComputeRoot in Listing 10.11 implements the bisection algorithm in Component Pascal. The real value for the tolerance entered by the user is stored in d.tolerance. As long as the length of the interval is greater than the tolerance entered by the user, the loop executes. Each time the loop executes, the program halves the interval, which guarantees that the loop will eventually terminate.

If the user enters zero for the tolerance, the loop will execute endlessly, because continually halving the interval never permits it to reach zero. If the user enters a negative tolerance, the loop will execute endlessly because the boolean expression in the WHILE statement will always be true. The program could be improved by testing the tolerance for negative or zero values and not allowing them.

```
MODULE Pbox10B;
  IMPORT Dialog;
  VAR
    d*: RECORD
      tolerance*: REAL;
      root-: REAL
    END;

  PROCEDURE ComputeRoot*;
    CONST
      a3 = 1.0; a2 = -1.0; a1 = -4.0; a0 = 2.0;
    VAR
      left, fLeft: REAL;
      mid, fMid: REAL;
      right: REAL;
  BEGIN
    left := 2.0;
    fLeft := ((a3 * left + a2) * left + a1) * left + a0;
    right := 3.0;
    (* Assert: root is between left and right *)
    WHILE ABS(left - right) > d.tolerance DO
      mid := (left + right) / 2.0;
      fMid := ((a3 * mid + a2) * mid + a1) * mid + a0;
      IF fLeft * fMid > 0.0 THEN
        (* Assert: root is between mid and right *)
        left := mid;
        fLeft := fMid
      ELSE
        (* Assert: root is between left and mid *)
        right := mid
      END
    END;
    d.root := (left + right) / 2.0;
    Dialog.Update(d)
  END ComputeRoot;

BEGIN
  d.tolerance := 1.0;
  d.root := 0.0
END Pbox10B.
```

Figure 10.11
Computation of the root of a polynomial equation with the bisection algorithm.

Stepwise refinement

The next example of the WHILE loop illustrates a software development technique known as stepwise refinement. The data for this problem consists of a focus window containing an employee ID number followed by two real values that represent the number of hours worked per week and the hourly pay rate for that employee. The program must output to the Log a table with the employee ID number, hours worked, and weekly pay with the possibility of overtime. It must also determine the average salary of all the employees as well as the number of employees who earned overtime. For example, if the focus window contains the text

```
"123-A6002"  35.0  13.00
"123-A6517"  45.0  10.00
"561-B3882"  40.0  12.50
"561-B4559"  40.0  11.00
"561-B7384"  50.0  10.00
```

then the output to the Log should be

```
123-A6002  35.0    455.00
123-A6517  45.0    475.00
561-B3882  40.0    500.00
561-B4559  40.0    440.00
561-B7384  50.0    550.00
Average wages: 484.00
Number with overtime: 2
```

Stepwise refinement is based on the concept of abstraction. The idea is to not be concerned with all the details that are necessary for the final Component Pascal program, but instead to focus on the logic at a higher level of abstraction. The process consists of a number of steps or passes at the problem. At each pass, you get to a lower level of abstraction until you reach the final pass which produces the complete program. What follows is a description of the passes for a stepwise refinement solution for the above problem.

The first step is to determine the variables in the VAR section. Remember that input, processing, and output are the three major parts of a program. That gives a hint of the variables required.

Input—The input consists of a sequence of lines, each one of which contains a string and two real values. Hence you will need an array of characters, say empID, and two real variables, say hours and rate, for the input. You will need a scanner sc to input their values. While it is true that you will need a model and a view to get the input from the window, you should not be concerned with those details until the very last pass.

Processing—To compute the average, you must compute each wage and divide the total wages by the number of employees. Hence you will need real variables, wages and totalWages, to store the computed wage for an individual and for the total of all the wages. An integer variable, numEmp, will count the number of employees. The integer variable numOvertime will keep track of the number of employees who worked overtime.

Output—The three variables, hours, rate, and wages, will be used to output a single line in the report. aveWages will be a real variable for outputting the average wage at the bottom of the report. The value of numOvertime will also appear at the bottom.

The tentative variable declaration part now looks like this:

```
VAR
    sc: PboxMappers.Scanner;
    empID: ARRAY 16 OF CHAR;
    hours, rate: REAL;
    wages, totalWages, aveWages: REAL;
    numEmp, numOvertime: INTEGER;
```

In this problem, the number of variables and their types were fairly easy to determine before writing the logic of the program. With some problems it is not always possible to determine the variables beforehand. In general, you should determine the principal variables of the program at an early stage of the stepwise refinement. Then, augment the variable declaration part with new variables as refinement progresses.

First pass—The program in Figure 10.3 showed the technique of processing a set of values using the eot technique. The coding pattern is to perform a scan before the loop. In the body of the loop, process the data that was just read. After processing, scan the model for the next values as the last statements in the loop. Using this pattern, the first pass is the following:

Initialize variables
Input empID, hours, rate
WHILE ~sc.eot DO
    Process empID, hours, rate
    Input empID, hours, rate
END
Compute the average
Output aveWages, numOvertime

Second pass—Each pass in a stepwise refinement solution should concentrate on one aspect of the problem. This problem requires a table with a list of values and summary information at the bottom. The second pass will solve the table output part of the problem. Two kinds of lines appear in the body of the report, one for those who worked overtime and one for those who did not. This requires an IF statement in the body of the loop. The summary information appears once at the bottom of the report. The output statements for the summary must therefore be after the END of the WHILE loop. Here is the second pass:

Initialize variables
Input empID, hours, rate
WHILE ~sc.eot DO
    IF *employee did not work overtime* THEN
        Compute wages without overtime
    ELSE
        Compute wages with overtime
    END
    Output empID, hours, wages
    Input empID, hours, rate
END
Compute the average
Output aveWages, numOvertime

Third pass—This pass will solve the problem of computing the average and the number who worked overtime. The average is the sum of the wages divided by the number of employees. You can compute the sum by the technique of Figure 10.6. That example initialized the variable sum to 0.00 before the WHILE loop. Each time the loop executed, sum increased by the value input from the file. In this problem, you can initialize and increase totalWages the same way.

You can compute the number of employees using numEmp as a counting variable. Initialize numEmp to zero before the WHILE loop. Each time the body of the loop executes, increment numEmp by one. After the loop has terminated, the value of numEmp will equal the number of times the loop was executed, which equals the number of times a line was processed, which equals the number of employees.

Similarly, you can initialize numOvertime to zero before the loop. But now you only want to increment numOvertime by one if the employee worked overtime. The third pass is

```
totalWages := 0.0
numEmp := 0
numOvertime := 0
Input empID, hours, rate
WHILE ~s.eot DO
    IF employee did not work overtime THEN
        wages := hours * rate
    ELSE
        wages := 40.0 * rate + (hours - 40.0) * 1.5 * rate
        INC(numOvertime)
    END
    totalWages := totalWages + wages
    INC(numEmp)
    Output empID, hours, wages
    Input empID, hours, rate
END
IF numEmp > 0 THEN
    aveWages := totalWages / numEmp
ELSE
    aveWages := 0.00
END;
Output aveWages, numOvertime
```

Fourth Pass—This pass is the complete Component Pascal program shown in Figure 10.12.

This program shows several common stepwise refinement characteristics. In every pass except the last one, all the irrelevant details of input and output should be suppressed. The first three passes of this example used the pseudocode statements *Input* and *Output*. Only on the last pass were they converted to Component Pascal scans and StdLog procedures with formatting details.

```
MODULE Pbox10C;
    IMPORT TextModels, TextControllers, PboxMappers, PboxStrings, StdLog;

    PROCEDURE ProcessPayroll*;
        VAR
            md: TextModels.Model;
            cn: TextControllers.Controller;
            sc: PboxMappers.Scanner;
            empID: ARRAY 16 OF CHAR;
            hours, rate: REAL;
            wages, totalWages, aveWages: REAL;
            numEmp, numOvertime: INTEGER;
            outString: ARRAY 32 OF CHAR;
    BEGIN
        cn := TextControllers.Focus();
        IF cn # NIL THEN
            md := cn.text;
            sc.ConnectTo(md);
            totalWages := 0.0; numEmp := 0; numOvertime := 0;
            sc.ScanString(empID); sc.ScanReal(hours); sc.ScanReal(rate);
            WHILE ~sc.eot DO
                IF hours <= 40 THEN
                    wages := hours * rate
                ELSE
                    wages := 40.0 * rate + (hours - 40.0) * 1.5 * rate;
                    INC(numOvertime)
                END;
                StdLog.String(empID);
                PboxStrings.RealToString(hours, 8, 1, outString); StdLog.String(outString);
                PboxStrings.RealToString(wages, 12, 2, outString); StdLog.String(outString);
                StdLog.Ln;
                totalWages := totalWages + wages;
                INC(numEmp);
                sc.ScanString(empID); sc.ScanReal(hours); sc.ScanReal(rate)
            END;
            IF numEmp > 0 THEN
                aveWages := totalWages / numEmp
            ELSE
                aveWages := 0.00
            END;
            StdLog.String("Average wages: ");
            PboxStrings.RealToString(aveWages, 1, 2, outString); StdLog.String(outString); StdLog.Ln;
            StdLog.String("Number with overtime: ");
            PboxStrings.IntToString(numOvertime, 1, outString); StdLog.String(outString); StdLog.Ln;
        END
    END ProcessPayroll;

END Pbox10C.
```

Figure 10.12

A payroll report with summary information

Each pass should isolate and solve one specific part of the problem. In this program, the parts solved by each pass were the following:

- *First pass* input from the focus window
- *Second pass* output of the table
- *Third pass* computation of summary values
- *Fourth pass* Component Pascal details

The strategy here is to divide and conquer. If you have a large problem that you do not know how to solve, divide it into smaller subproblems that you can solve. Stepwise refinement gives you a framework for dividing a problem into smaller parts.

Another tip with stepwise refinement is to work it out on your text editor, not on paper. With each pass you can expand one pseudocode statement into several statements that are closer to Component Pascal, a job more easily accomplished on a screen than on a piece of paper. At the end of the last pass, the Component Pascal program will be on your disk ready to compile.

The structured programming theorem

Component Pascal provides several loop statements other than the WHILE statement, one of which is the FOR statement. Theoretically, there is no reason to provide any loop other than the WHILE. An important computer science theorem about the power of the WHILE statement coupled with the IF statement is known as the structured programming theorem, proved by Corrado Bohm and Guiseppe Jacopini in 1966. They proved mathematically that any algorithm, no matter how large or complicated, can be written with only three control statements—sequence, which is one statement following another, the IF statement, and the WHILE statement.

The structured programming theorem was proved by Bohm and Jacopini.

According to the structured programming theorem, Component Pascal really does not need to provide the CASE statement, for example. You can imagine that any program with a CASE statement could be written to perform the identical processing using an IF statement with several ELSIF parts. By the same token, any program with a FOR statement can be written to perform the identical processing using a WHILE statement. Nevertheless, statements like CASE and FOR are provided, not because of any additional power they give to the programmer, but because they are convenient.

The FOR statement

Suppose you want to compute the sum of all the integers from 1 to 100. You could use a WHILE loop, as in Figure 10.13. sum and i are variables of type INTEGER. i is called the control variable of the loop because its value controls when the loop terminates.

```
sum := 0
i := 1
WHILE i <= 100 DO
    sum := sum + i
    INC(i)
END
```
Output sum

Figure 10.13
An algorithm for the sum of
consecutive integers with a
WHILE loop.

If you execute the above algorithm, it will output 5050, which is the sum $1 + 2 + 3 + ... + 100$.

The sequence of steps

- Initialize a variable.

- Test the variable at the beginning of a loop.

- Execute the body of the loop.

- Increment the variable.

occurs frequently in programs. The FOR statement automatically initializes a control variable, tests it at the beginning of the loop, and increments it after executing the body of the loop. The program in Listing 10.14 is the above algorithm written in Component Pascal. It finds the sum of consecutive integers between one and an ending value entered by the user, but it is written with a FOR loop in place of the WHILE loop. Figure 10.15 shows the dialog box for this program.

When procedure ComputeSum executes, sum gets 0. Then, the statement

FOR i := 1 TO d.num DO

executes. The words FOR, TO, and DO are Component Pascal reserved words. The assignment statement between the reserved words FOR and TO gives an initial value to the control variable of the FOR statement. In this statement, i, the control variable, gets the initial value of 1.

The FOR statement then compares the current value of i with the expression after the reserved word TO. If the value of the control variable is greater than the expression, the loop terminates. Otherwise, the loop body executes. In this statement, the value of the control variable, 1, is not greater than the value of the expression, 100. The loop body executes, which adds 1 to sum.

Control returns to the top of the loop. The FOR statement automatically increments the value of i with the equivalent of INC(i). It then compares the value of i with the expression after the reserved word TO. Because the current value of i, which is 2, is not greater than the value of the expression, which is 100, the body of the loop executes again. The loop continues executing, with i getting the values 1, 2, 3, and so on, to 100. After it executes with i having the value 100, the loop terminates.

```
MODULE Pbox10D;
   IMPORT Dialog, PboxStrings;
   VAR
      d*: RECORD
         num*: INTEGER;
         message-: ARRAY 64 OF CHAR
      END;

   PROCEDURE ComputeSum*;
      VAR
         sum, i: INTEGER;
         intString: ARRAY 16 OF CHAR;
   BEGIN
      sum := 0;
      FOR i := 1 TO d.num DO
         sum := sum + i
      END;
      PboxStrings.IntToString(d.num, 1, intString);
      d.message := "Sum from 1 to " + intString + " is: ";
      PboxStrings.IntToString(sum, 1, intString);
      d.message := d.message + intString;
      Dialog.Update(d)
   END ComputeSum;

BEGIN
   d.num := 0;
   d.message := ""
END Pbox10D.
```

Figure 10.14
Computing the sum of the first d.num integers with a FOR loop.

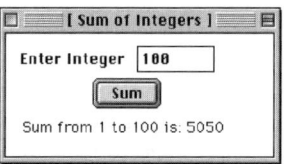

Figure 10.15
The dialog box for the program of Figure 10.14.

You should be able to determine the statement execution count for this program. A total of $2n + 7$ statements execute, where n is the value input for d.num. That is $2(100) + 7$, or 207 statement executions for the computation of the sum of the first 100 integers.

The algorithm of Figure 10.14 may be a good illustration of the **FOR** statement, but it is not a good solution to the problem. The formula, $m(m + 1)/2$, gives the sum of the first m integers directly, as will be shown later. The following simpler algorithm solves the same problem. Assuming that the *Output* statement requires the same five statements as in Figure 10.14, this algorithm requires only six statement executions regardless of the value input for d.num.

```
sum := d.num * (d.num + 1) / 2
Output sum
```

Figure 10.16
A better algorithm for the sum of consecutive integers.

Using FOR Statements

The EBNF definition of the **FOR** statement is

FOR Ident " := " Expr TO Expr [BY ConstExpr] DO StatementSeq END

If you use the [BY ConstExpr] option, the value of the control variable is changed by ConstExpr instead of by one.

The control variable can have steps other than 1.

Example 10.9 The following code fragment

```
FOR i := 1 TO d.num DO
    StdLog.Int(i); StdLog.String(" ")
END
```

where d.num and i are variables of type integer, outputs

1 2 3 4 5

to the Log if the value of d.num is 5. But the code fragment

```
FOR i := d.num TO 1 BY -1 DO
    StdLog.Int(i); StdLog.String(" ")
END
```

outputs

5 4 3 2 1

The Component Pascal language report defines the FOR statement

```
FOR v := beg TO end BY step DO
    statements
END
```

to be equivalent to

```
temp := end;
v := beg;
IF step > 0 THEN
    WHILE v <= temp DO
        statements;
        v := v + step
    END
ELSE
    WHILE v >= temp DO
        statements;
        v := v + step
    END
END
```

where temp has the same type as v, and step must be a nonzero constant expression. If step is not specified, it is assumed to be 1. As is the case for the WHILE statement, it is possible for the body of the FOR statement to never execute.

It is possible for the body of the FOR statement to never execute.

Example 10.10   In the two code fragments of the previous example, if the value of d.num is zero, neither fragment will produce any output.   ∎

In the EBNF definition of the FOR statement, either expression Expr can have any value—positive, negative, or zero.

Example 10.11   The code fragment

```
FOR i := d.num TO 5 DO
    StdLog.Int(i); StdLog.String(" ")
END
```

outputs

-3 -2 -1 0 1 2 3 4 5

if the value of d.num is –3. It outputs

3 4 5

if the value of d.num is 3.   ∎

It is frequently useful to use the control variable in an expression. Although it is legal to change the value of the control variable in the body of a FOR loop, it is extremely bad practice to do so. If you are ever tempted to change the value of the control variable in a FOR loop, you should redesign your algorithm using a WHILE loop instead of a FOR loop.

Do not change the value of the control variable in the body of a FOR statement.

Example 10.12   This code fragment

```
FOR i := 1 TO d.num DO
    j := 2 * i - 1;
    StdLog.Int(j); StdLog.String(" ")
END
```

is legal and produces the output

1 3 5 7 9

if the value of d.num is 5. It is both legal and good practice to use i in the expression on the right side of the assignment statement.   ∎

Example 10.13   The code fragment

```
FOR i := 1 TO d.num DO
    StdLog.Int(i); StdLog.String(" ")
    INC(i)
END
```

is legal but is extremely bad practice because the value of i is changed by the INC procedure. Never do this, even though the compiler allows it! ▌

The control variable is limited to integer or character type. Specifically, it cannot be of type real.

The control variable cannot be real.

Example 10.14 The following code fragment

```
FOR level := 0.5 to 6.5 DO
    StdLog.Real(level)
END
```

where level is a real variable is illegal because the control variable cannot be real. ▌

Example 10.15 The code fragment

```
FOR ch := 'a' TO 'z' DO
    StdLog.Char(ch)
END
```

where ch is a variable of type CHAR is legal and produces the following output on the Log

abcdefghijklmnopqrstuvwxyz ▌

★ The guarded command do statement

The statement that corresponds to the CP WHILE statement is the **do** statement in GCL. As with the **if** statement, the **do** statement uses a guarded command. The CP statement

```
WHILE C1 DO
    S1
END
```

is written in GCL as

do $C1 \rightarrow S1$ **od**

Example 10.16 The algorithm of Figure 10.6 to find the average is written in GCL as

$s := 0.0$; $nA := 0$; sc.ScanR(b);
do ¬sc.eot $\rightarrow$ $s := s + b$; $nA := nA + 1$; sc.ScanR(b) **od**
if $nA > 0 \rightarrow$ *Output s/nA*
  ▯ $nA \leq 0 \rightarrow$ *Output a no accounts message*
fi ▌

Exercises

1. **(a)** What is a loop invariant? **(b)** What two things must you show to prove that a statement is a loop invariant? **(c)** What must be the case when a WHILE loop terminates?

2. For the algorithm in Figure 10.6 that computes the average of the accounts do the following: **(a)** Draw a flowchart. **(b)** Determine the total statement execution count if there are three data values. Include only the statements in the figure and ignore any statements that would be in a complete Component Pascal procedure. **(c)** Determine the total statement execution count if there are n data values. **(d)** If the algorithm executes in 50 μs for 200 data values, estimate the execution time for 10,000 data values from (c). Use both the exact computation and the approximate computation and compare how close they are by computing their percentage difference.

3. For the algorithm in Figure 10.7 that finds the largest value, do the following: **(a)** Draw a flowchart. **(b)** Determine the total statement execution count if there are three data values. Include only the statements in the figure and ignore any statements that would be in a complete Component Pascal procedure. **(c)** Determine the total statement execution count if there are n data values, assuming that the body of the nested IF statement executes every time. This is called the "worst case" time. **(d)** Determine the execution count assuming that the first number in the list is the largest. This is called the "best case" time. **(e)** If the algorithm executes in 120 μs for 80 data values, estimate the execution time for 5000 data values assuming the count in part (c). Use the exact computation. **(f)** Work part (e) assuming the count in part (d). **(g)** Give the percentage difference between the worst case and the best case times.

4. State the loop invariant for the WHILE loop in procedure ComputeTotal in Figure 10.3. The loop invariant will be a statement about the state of sum.

5. State the loop invariant for the WHILE loop in the algorithm to compute the average in Figure 10.6. The loop invariant will include statements about the states of both sum and numAccts.

6. Tell how many multiplication and addition steps are required to evaluate

$$ax^4 + bx^3 + cx^2 + dx + e$$

Factor the expression so that it requires only four multiplication and four addition steps.

7. Determine the output to the Log of the code fragment.

```
sum := 0;
WHILE i < 9 DO
    sum := sum + i;
    INC(i)
END;
StdLog.String("sum = "); StdLog.Int(sum)
```

for the following initial values of i.

(a) 5   **(b)** 8   **(c)** 9   **(d)** 0

8. Answer these questions for each of the Component Pascal code fragments. (1) What is the first value added to sum? (2) What is the last value added to sum? (3) What is the value of a at the termination of the loop? (4) How many times does the body of the loop execute?

(a)
```
sum := 0;
a := 50;
WHILE a < 100 DO
    INC(a, 2);
    sum := sum + a
END
```

(b)
```
sum := 0;
a := 50;
WHILE a < 100 DO
    sum := sum + a;
    INC(a, 2)
END
```

(c)
```
sum := 0;
a := 50;
WHILE a <= 100 DO
    INC(a, 2);
    sum := sum + a
END
```

9. What is the value of count after the statements are executed?

```
i := 15;
count := 0;
WHILE i <= 1000 DO
    INC(i, 2);
    INC(count)
END
```

10. Determine the output to the Log of the following code fragment.

```
sum := 0;
FOR i := 5 to d.num DO
    sum := sum + i
END;
StdLog.String("sum = "); StdLog.Int(sum)
```

for the following values of d.num.

(a) 10   **(b)** 6   **(c)** 5   **(d)** 4

11. Determine the total statement execution count of the code fragment in the previous exercise if d.num has the value n. Assume that n is greater than or equal to 5.

12. Determine the output to the Log of the following code fragment.

```
sum := 0;
FOR i := 10 TO d.num BY -1 DO
    sum := sum + i
END;
StdLog.String("sum = "); StdLog.Int(sum)
```

for the following values of d.num.

(a) 5   **(b)** 9   **(c)** 10   **(d)** 11

13. If procedure ComputeSum in Figure 10.14 takes 40 μs to execute when d.num has the value of 100, how long does it take to execute if d.num has the value of 150? Use both the exact computation and the approximate computation and compare how close they are by computing their percentage difference.

14. The Component Pascal language report defines the FOR statement in terms of an equivalent WHILE statement. **(a)** Using the definition, predict the output of the following code fragment.

```
last := 10;
FOR i := 0 TO last BY 2 DO
    StdLog.String("i = "); StdLog.Int(i); StdLog.Ln;
    StdLog.String("last = "); StdLog.Int(last); StdLog.Ln;
    INC(last)
END
```

(b) Execute the code fragment. Was your prediction correct?

15. Write the algorithm of Figure 10.7 to find the largest value in GCL.

16. Write the algorithm of Figure 10.13 to find the sum of consecutive integers in GCL.

Problems

17. Write a Component Pascal program that outputs to the Log the average of a list of values that are displayed in the focus window, or a statement that there are no values in the window.

18. Write a Component Pascal program that outputs to the Log the maximum integer value from a list of integers in the focus window. Output an appropriate message if no integer values are in the focus window.

19. Modify the program in Figure 10.11 so that it also outputs the number of times the WHILE loop executes. Run the modified program five times with the following tolerances: 1e–2, 1e–3, 1e–4, 1e–5, 1e–6. Graph the number of times the loop executes (y-axis) versus the tolerance (x-axis). What mathematical relationship did you discover between these two quantities? Hint: Use semilog graph paper or, equivalently, let each x-axis division be 10 times greater than the previous x-axis division. For what values of the tolerance, if any, will the loop never execute?

20. Modify the program in Figure 10.11 to always print the solution to four places past the decimal point and to print an error message if the user enters a negative number or zero for the tolerance.

21. Write a program to compute and output to a dialog box the sum of all positive even integers less than or equal to a value entered by the user in the dialog box.

22. Write a program to compute and output to a dialog box the sum of all positive odd integers less than or equal to a value entered by the user in the dialog box.

23. The focus window contains a list of integers. Write a program that counts how many even integers there are in the window. For example, if the focus window contains

5   38   1   -45   21   -7   12   5

the program should display a dialog box that says "There are 2 even integers in the window". You can test if an integer n is even with ~ODD(n).

24. The focus window contains a list of integers. Write a program that counts how many positive integers are in the window. For example, if the focus window contains

    5   38   1   -45   21   -7   12   5

    the program should display a dialog box that says "There are 6 positive integers in the window".

25. A linear sequence is a list of integers, each of which is a constant integer increment of the previous integer. For example,

    3   6   9   12   15   18

    is a linear sequence because each number is three plus the previous one. The constant increment need not be three, however. Write a program that inputs a list of numbers from the focus window and displays on a dialog box whether the sequence is linear, and the constant increment if it is. For example, the dialog box for the above list should state, "The sequence is linear with an increment of 3." The message for the sequence,

    3   6   9   12   16   19

    should state, "The sequence is not linear." Consider the empty list and any list with only one integer to be not linear.

26. A geometric sequence is a list of integers, each of which is a constant integer multiple of the previous integer. For example,

    3   6   12   24   48   96

    is a geometric sequence because each number is two times the previous one. The constant multiple need not be two, however. Write a program that inputs a list of numbers from the focus window and displays on a dialog box whether the sequence is geometric, and the integer multiple if it is. For example, the dialog box for the above list should state, "The sequence is geometric with a multiple of 2." The message for the sequence,

    3   6   12   24   46   92

    should state, "The sequence is not geometric." Consider the empty list and any list with only one integer to be not geometric.

27. A salesperson gets a 5% commission on sales of $1000 or less, and a 10% commission on sales in excess of $1000. For example, a sale of $1300 earns him $80—that is $50 on the first $1000 of the sale and $30 on the $300 in excess of the first $1000. The focus window contains a salesperson's ID number (string) and his sales amount (real) on each line. Write a program that outputs to the Log a report containing the ID number, the amount of sales, and the commission for each salesperson. At the bottom of the report, print the ID number of the salesperson who sold the most. For example, if the focus window contains

```
"EM-00134"    580.00
"EM-01209"    600.00
"EM-00030"   1000.00
"EM-02238"   1200.00
"EM-09411"    800.00
"EM-02344"   1150.00
```

the report on the Log should be

```
EM-00134       580.00      29.00
EM-01209       600.00      30.00
EM-00030      1000.00      50.00
EM-02238      1200.00      70.00
EM-09411       800.00      40.00
EM-02344      1150.00      65.00
Highest sales ID: EM-02238
```

28.   The price per Frisbee depends on the quantity ordered, as indicated in Figure 10.17. The focus window contains a list of numbers that represent order quantities of Frisbees. Write a program that outputs to the Log a report of order quantities and the cost per order. At the bottom of the report print the total cost of all the orders. For example, if the focus window contains

```
50   150   20   200   300   1   250   100
```

the report on the Log should be

```
      50       250.00
     150       450.00
      20       100.00
     200       500.00
     300       600.00
       1         5.00
     250       625.00
     100       300.00
Total: 2830.00
```

Quantity	Price per Frisbee
0 – 99	$ 5.00
100 – 199	3.00
200 – 299	2.50
300 or more	2.00

Figure 10.17
The price schedule for Problem 28.

29.   An instructor determines the total score for each student according to the weights of Figure 10.18. A total of 90 to 100 is a grade of A, 80 to 89 is a B, and so on for C, D, and F. Each line of the focus window contains four real values that are the homework, exam, and final exam scores in that order. Write a program that outputs to the Log a table, each line of which contains

- The four values of each score
- The weighted total
- The letter grade

At the bottom of the report print the average of the weighted totals.

Score item	Percent toward total
Homework	15
Exam 1	25
Exam 2	25
Final exam	35

Figure 10.18
The grading weights for Problem 29.

30. The number of runs for each team in each inning of a Dodgers versus Giants baseball game is in the focus window. The Dodgers bat first. A complete game lasts nine innings. After the last Dodger out in the top of the ninth inning, if the Giants are ahead they do not bat in the bottom of the ninth. The game is over and the Giants win. In that case, no value is in the focus window for the number of Giants runs in the bottom of the ninth, not even a zero.

If it is a tie game or if the Dodgers are ahead after their last out, the Giants bat in the bottom of the ninth. After the last Giant out, whoever is ahead wins. If it is a tie, the game goes into extra innings, after which the same termination conditions apply as in the ninth inning.

Write a program that continues to input the runs for each inning until one team wins. Announce the winner, the score, and the number of innings played. Assume there are no input errors in the focus window. The program must not attempt to read past the end of text. Do not use the scanner eot variable.

The loop termination condition for this problem cannot be conveniently written as a single expression. Declare a boolean variable named over that indicates when the game is over. Initialize it to false before entering your WHILE loop, which should execute once for each inning. The test for termination should be on ~over. The processing at the bottom of the loop body should be a computation for determining if the game is over.

31. If a volleyball team serves the ball and wins the volley, they get 1 point and they get to serve again. If they serve the ball and lose the volley, the opposing team does not get a point. But the opposing team does win the right to serve next. The first team to get 15 points wins the game, except that they must win by at least 2 points. If the score is 15 to 14, play continues until one team is ahead by 2.

The focus window contains a sequence of 1's and 0's for a volleyball team that serves first in a game. A 1 represents winning the volley and a 0 represents losing the volley. For example, the sequence at the beginning of the file

1 1 0 1 0 0

represents

- Winning a volley and a point
- Winning a volley and a point
- Losing the serve
- Winning the serve back
- Losing the serve
- Losing the volley and a point

after which the team is ahead, 2 to 1.

Write a program that continues to scan the 1's and 0's until the game is over. Output the score and state whether the team won or lost. Assume there are no input errors in the focus window. The program must not attempt to read past the end of text. Do not use the scanner eot variable.

The loop termination condition for this problem cannot be conveniently written as a single expression. Declare a boolean variable named over that indicates when the game is over. Initialize it to false before entering your WHILE loop, which should execute once for each input value. The test for termination should be on ~over. The processing at the bottom of the loop body should be a computation for determining if the game is over.

32. A businessman wants to claim depreciation of an asset with the straight line method. If the asset has a useful life of n years, then $1/n$ of its original value is subtracted each year. Write a program that asks for the asset's value and its useful life span in a dialog box, and outputs a depreciation schedule to the Log using the straight line method. For example, if the user enters 1000.00 for the value of the asset and 5 years for the lifesaving the report on the Log should be

```
0    1000.00
1     800.00
2     600.00
3     400.00
4     200.00
5       0.00
```

33. A businessman wants to claim depreciation of an asset with the double declining balance method. If the asset has a useful life of n years, then $2/n$ times its current value is subtracted each year. Write a program that asks for the asset's value and its useful life-span, and outputs a depreciation schedule using the double declining balance method. For example, if the user enters 1000.00 for the value of the asset and 5 years for the lifesaving the report on the Log should be

```
0    1000.00
1     600.00
2     360.00
3     216.00
4     129.60
5      77.76
```

34. The factorial of an integer n is

$$n! = n \cdot (n-1) \cdot (n-2) \cdot \ldots \cdot 3 \cdot 2 \cdot 1$$

For example, the factorial of 4 is 24, because $4 \cdot 3 \cdot 2 \cdot 1 = 24$. Zero factorial is defined to be one. Write a program that asks the user to input a nonnegative integer in a dialog box, then computes and outputs the factorial of that number in the dialog box. Use an integer field in the dialog box to output the factorial. If the number entered is negative, compute nothing and do not change any fields in the dialog box.

35. Suppose that x is a real nonzero number and n is an integer. Then x raised to the nth power, written mathematically as x^n, means

$$
\begin{array}{ll}
x \cdot x \cdot \ldots \cdot x & \text{if } n > 0 \\
1.0 & \text{if } n = 0 \\
1.0/(x \cdot x \cdot \ldots \cdot x) & \text{if } n < 0
\end{array}
$$

where there are n x's in the first and last expressions. Without using the Math module, write a program that inputs a real number and an integer in a dialog box and raises the real number to the power indicated by the integer. For example, if the user enters 2.0 for the real number and -3 for the power, the dialog box should display 0.125 for the power. Use a real field in the dialog box to output the power.

36. The base of the natural logarithms, e, is approximated with four terms as

$$\frac{1}{1} + \frac{1}{1(1)} + \frac{1}{1(1)(2)} + \frac{1}{1(1)(2)(3)}$$

Notice that the fourth term is $1/3$ times the previous term. In general, the nth term is $1/(n-1)$ times the previous term. Write a program that asks the user to input the number of terms in a dialog box and outputs the approximation of e. Use two variables in additional to your control variable—sum, which represents the sum computed so far, and term, which represents the value of the current term. Initialize sum to the first term outside the loop, and start the loop with the second term. For example, if the user enters 4 for the number of terms, the value 2.6666... should be output. Use a real field in the dialog box to output the approximation of e. If the number entered is negative or zero, compute nothing and do not change any fields in the dialog box.

37. The average or mean of n numbers, $x_1, x_2, \ldots, x_n$, is

$$\bar{x} = \frac{x_1 + x_2 + \ldots + x_n}{n}$$

$$= \frac{1}{n} \sum_{i=1}^{n} x_i$$

The standard deviation, a measure of how scattered the n numbers are, is defined as

$$s = \sqrt{\frac{\sum\limits_{i=1}^{n}(x_i - \bar{x})^2}{n-1}}$$

when the numbers are a random sample of a population. If the numbers are all close to each other, they will all be close to the mean, their differences from the mean will be small, and the standard deviation will be small.

(a) The focus window contains a sequence of real values. Write a program that computes and outputs to a dialog box the standard deviation of the real numbers from the definition. Display the result with four places past the decimal point, and write an error message if there is only one value or no values in the focus window. You will need one loop to compute the mean, followed by a second execution of ConnectTo to position the scanner at the beginning of the text model again, followed by another loop for the squares of the differences from the mean.

(b) A mathematically equivalent formula for the standard deviation is

$$s = \sqrt{\frac{\sum\limits_{i=1}^{n} x_i^2 - n\bar{x}^2}{n-1}}$$

(Can you derive this formula from the definitions of the mean and standard deviation?) This formula only requires one loop, because you can accumulate the sum of the squares at the same time you are accumulating the sum for the mean. Write a program that computes and outputs to a dialog box the standard deviation from this formula using only one loop. Display the result with four places past the decimal point, and write an error message if there is only one value or no values in the focus window.

38. An integer greater than 1 is prime if the only positive integers that divide it are 1 and the number itself. For example, 13 is prime because it is divisible only by 1 and 13, while 15 is not prime because it is divisible by 1, 3, 5, and 15. Write a Component Pascal program that asks the user to input a positive integer in a dialog box and then outputs a message to the dialog box indicating whether the integer is prime.

39. Write a program that asks the user to enter a positive integer in a dialog box, then outputs to the Log all the positive factors of that number. If the number entered is less than 1, compute nothing and output an appropriate message to the Log. For example, if the input is 15 then the output should be

1 3 5 15

40. The first two Fibonacci numbers are 0 and 1. The third Fibonacci number is the sum of the first pair, 0 plus 1, which is 1. The fifth is the sum of the previous pair, 1 plus 2, which is 3. The first seven Fibonacci numbers are

0 1 1 2 3 5 8

each number being the sum of the two previous numbers. Write a program that asks the user to enter an integer in a dialog box, and outputs to the Log that many Fibonacci numbers. If the number entered is less than 2, compute nothing and output an appropriate message to the Log. For example, if the user enters 7 the program should output the seven numbers listed above.

41. Implement a dialog box that looks and behaves like Figure 7.9, but with one additional button labeled "A Gets B". When the user presses this button Stack A should be cleared and then given a copy of Stack B. The text fields for Push and Pop should not change. Only the field for the number of items in stack A should change. Use a temporary stack variable called tempStack in your procedure AGetsB to first store the value of Stack B in reverse order by popping all the items from Stack B into it. Then, clear Stack A and copy all the items from tempStack into it and back into Stack B. Import module PboxStackADT.

42. Work Problem 41, but import module PboxStackObj.

43. Implement a dialog box that looks and behaves like Figure 7.19, but with one additional button labeled "A Gets B". When the user presses this button List A should be cleared and then given a copy of List B. All the text fields for the dialog box should not change. Only the field for the number of items in List A should change. Import module PboxListADT. Use a temporary variable called temp of type PboxListADT.T in your procedure AGetsB to store the value between the retrieve and insert operations.

44. Implement a dialog box that looks and behaves like Figure 7.3, but with one additional button labeled "Top To Bottom". If the stack contains two or more items when the user presses this button, the top item on the stack should be moved to the bottom of the stack. Otherwise, the stack should remain unchanged. The text fields for Push and Pop should not change, nor should the field for the number of items change. Use a temporary variable called temp to store the top value of the stack and another temporary variable called tempStack to store the remainder of the stack in your procedure TopToBottom. Import module PboxStackADS.

45. Work Problem 44, but import module PboxStackObj.

46. Implement a dialog box that looks and behaves like Figure 7.19, but with one additional button labeled "A Append B". If the length of List A plus the length of List B is greater than the capacity of a list when the user presses this button, nothing should happen. Otherwise, a copy of List B should be appended to the end of List A. All the text fields for the dialog box should not change. Only the field for the number of items in List A should change. Import module PboxListADT. Use a temporary variable called temp of type PboxListADT.T in your procedure AAppendB to store the value between the retrieve and insert operations.

47. Implement a dialog box that looks and behaves like Figure 7.16, but with one additional button labeled "Reverse". When the user presses this button, all the items of the list should be rearranged in reverse order. All the text fields for the dialog box should not change. Import module PboxListADS. Use two local variables, i initialized to 0 and j initialized to Length() - 1. While i is less than j, switch the items at positions i and j followed by INC(i) and DEC(j). Use a temporary variable called temp of type PboxListADS.T in your procedure ReverseA to store the value between the retrieve, remove, and insert operations

48. Work Problem 47, but import module PboxListADT.

Chapter *11*

Nested Loops

Any structured statement can be nested in any other structured statement. In the same way that an IF statement can be nested inside another IF, a loop statement can be nested inside another loop. Such a configuration is called a nested loop.

Printing a box of characters

Procedure DrawBox in Listing 11.2 uses a nested loop to draw a box of @ symbols with the same number of rows and columns. It prompts the user for the number of rows in a dialog box, then creates a window that displays the box of @s. Figure 11.1 shows the input and output for the program.

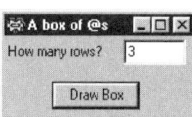

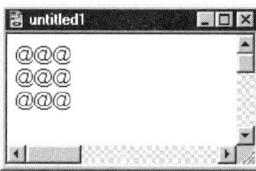

Figure 11.1
The input and output for the program in Figure 11.2.

In Figure 11.2, the FOR loop with control variable i is called the outer loop, and the nested loop with control variable j is called the inner loop. The first time the outer FOR statement executes, it initializes i to 1. Then the inner loop gives the values 1, 2 and 3 in turn to j, causing the body of the inner loop to execute three times. Each time the body of the inner loop executes, it inserts a single @ symbol into the text model. The fourth time the inner FOR statement executes, it detects that the loop should terminate.

Then fm.WriteLn executes, which inserts the line character into the text model. If the line character were omitted in the model, all the @ symbols would be displayed on the same line in the view. The fm.WriteLn statement is outside the body of the inner loop, but inside the body of the outer loop.

The second time the outer FOR statement executes, it increments i to 2. The inner loop executes exactly as before, producing another sequence of three @ symbols in the text model. The same thing happens after i gets the value of 3.

Figure 11.2
A procedure that prints a box of @ characters with nested loops.

```
MODULE Pbox11A;
   IMPORT Dialog, TextModels, TextViews, Views, PboxMappers;
   VAR
      d*: RECORD
         numRows*: INTEGER;
      END;

   PROCEDURE DrawBox*;
      VAR
         md: TextModels.Model;
         vw: TextViews.View;
         fm: PboxMappers.Formatter;
         i, j: INTEGER;
   BEGIN
      md := TextModels.dir.New();
      fm.ConnectTo(md);
      FOR i := 1 TO d.numRows DO
         FOR j := 1 TO d.numRows DO
            fm.WriteChar("@")
         END;
         fm.WriteLn
      END;
      vw := TextViews.dir.New(md);
      Views.OpenView(vw)
   END DrawBox;

BEGIN
   d.numRows := 0
END Pbox11A.
```

Statement execution count

What is the statement execution count for this program? Procedure DrawBox has eight executable statements:

Statement number	*Executable statement*
(1)	md := TextModels.dir.New()
(2)	fm.ConnectTo(md)
(3)	FOR i := 1 TO d.numRows DO
(4)	FOR j := 1 TO d.numRows DO
(5)	fm.WriteChar("@")
(6)	fm.WriteLn
(7)	vw := TextViews.dir.New(md)
(8)	Views.OpenView(vw)

The executable statements of procedure DrawBox

If you trace the algorithm as described above for d.numRows having a value of 3, you will find that statements (1), (2), (7), and (8) each execute once. The outer FOR statement (3) executes four times, and the inner **FOR** statement (4) executes 12 times. The body of the inner loop (5) executes nine times. Statement (6), which is in the body of the outer loop but not in the body of the inner loop, executes three times. A total of 32 statements execute.

What if the value of d.numRows is n in general? Statements in a nested loop are a little more difficult to count than those in a single loop. Consider the statements in the inner loop as if they were not nested in the outer loop.

```
FOR j := 1 TO d.numRows DO
    fm.WriteChar("@")
END;
fm.WriteLn
```

(a) The **FOR** statement would execute $n + 1$ times, (b) the body would execute n times, and (c) the WriteChar statement would execute 1 time. But these statements are, in fact, the body of a loop that executes n times. So each one executes n times the amounts just mentioned. Namely, (a) the first statement executes $n(n + 1)$ times, (b) the body executes n^2 times, and (c) the WriteChar statement executes n times. The **FOR** statement of the outer loop

```
FOR i := 1 TO d.numRows DO
```

executes $n + 1$ times. Adding these terms together plus the four statements outside the loop that each execute once, yields a total of $2n^2 + 3n + 5$ for the whole program. Totals for the statement execution counts when d.numRows has values of zero, three, and n in general are summarized in Figure 11.3.

Statement	d.numRows $= 0$	d.numRows $= 3$	d.numRows $= n$
(1)	1	1	1
(2)	1	1	1
(3)	1	4	$n + 1$
(4)	0	12	$n(n + 1)$
(5)	0	9	n^2
(6)	0	3	n
(7)	1	1	1
(8)	1	1	1
Total:	5	32	$2n^2 + 3n + 5$

Figure 11.3
Statement execution count for the procedure **DrawBox** in Figure 11.2.

The squared term in the expression for the number of statements executed is typical for nested loops. It causes an estimate for the execution time that is quite different from the case where the statement count is proportional to the first power of n.

Example 11.1 Suppose it takes 400 μs to execute procedure DrawBox when d.numRows has the value of 35. If you double the value to 70, how long will it take to execute?

Setting up the precise ratio gives

$$\frac{400}{2(35)^2 + 3(35) + 5} = \frac{T}{2(70)^2 + 3(70) + 5}$$

As before, however, we can approximate by neglecting the lower-order terms in the statement execution count.

$$\frac{400}{2(35)^2} = \frac{T}{2(70)^2}$$

Again, the coefficient cancels, but this time solving for T yields $400(70/35)^2$, which is $400(4)$. That is 1600 μs, which is four times the original execution time, not just double the execution time. ∎

Such a result is expected when you think of the output. When you double the value given to d.numRows, you quadruple the number of @ symbols that need to be output, because the program prints a figure in the shape of a box with an equal number of rows and columns.

Printing a triangle

It is possible for the upper or lower limit of the control variable of the inner loop to depend on the control variable of the outer loop. Suppose you change the loops of procedure DrawBox as in Figure 11.4.

```
FOR i := 1 TO d.numRows DO
   FOR j := 1 TO i DO
      fm.WriteChar("@")
   END;
   fm.WriteLn
END;
```

Figure 11.4
An algorithm for printing a triangle of @ characters.

The control variable of the inner loop, j, now goes from 1 to i, where i is the control variable of the outer loop. When i has the value 1, the inner loop gives j values from 1 to 1. That makes the inner loop execute once. When i has value 2, the inner loop gives j values from 1 to 2, for two executions of the inner loop. The last time, j goes from 1 to 3 for three executions. The effect is to print a triangle of @ symbols. If d.numRows has a value of 3, the output will be

```
@
@ @
@ @ @
```

A trace of the program for d.numRows having a value of 3 is shown below, assuming that statement (4) has been modified as Figure 11.4. The trace does not show the values of i or j that are irrelevant outside their loops.

Statement executed	i	j
(1)		
(2)		
(3)	1	
(4)	1	1
(5)	1	1
(4)	1	2
(6)	1	
(3)	2	
(4)	2	1
(5)	2	1
(4)	2	2
(5)	2	2
(4)	2	3
(6)	2	
(3)	3	
(4)	3	1
(5)	3	1
(4)	3	2
(5)	3	2
(4)	3	3
(5)	3	3
(4)	3	4
(6)	3	
(3)	4	
(7)		
(8)		

A trace of the algorithm in Figure 11.4 with an input of 3

You can see by simply counting this trace that the number of statements executed is 26.

determine the statement execution count of the modified program that prints the triangle for the general case when d.numRows has the value n, is a bit more difficult than with the previous nested loop we analyzed. The problem is that the statements in the inner loop do not simply execute n times more than they would execute if they were not nested. Figure 11.5 shows how to count the number of statements executed when d.numRows has the value zero, three, and n in general.

Statement	d.numRows = 0	d.numRows = 3	d.numRows = n
(1)	1	1	1
(2)	1	1	1
(3)	1	4	$n + 1$
(4)	0	$2 + 3 + 4$	$2 + 3 + 4 + \dots + (n + 1)$
(5)	0	$1 + 2 + 3$	$1 + 2 + 3 + \dots + n$
(6)	0	3	n
(7)	1	1	1
(8)	1	1	1

Figure 11.5
Counting individual statements for the algorithm to draw a triangle.

Notice that the body of the inner FOR statement (5) executes once when i is 1, twice when i is 2, and three times when i is 3. Because the body statement prints a single @ symbol, these counts correspond to the fact that the first row has 1 @, the second has 2 @s, and the third has 3 @s. In general, when d.numRows has the value *n*, the number of times statement (5) executes is $1 + 2 + 3 + \dots + n$. The discussion of the procedure in Figure 10.14 in the previous chapter notes that the formula for the sum of the first *m* integers is

$$1 + 2 + 3 + \dots + m = \frac{m(m + 1)}{2}$$

where *m* is positive. So, the number of times statement (5) executes is $n(n + 1)/2$.

Furthermore, the inner FOR statement (4) executes twice when i is 1, three times when i is 2, and four times when i is 3. The reason statement (4) executes more frequently than statement (5) is the extra test it must perform after the last execution of the body of the loop. So, the total number of times statement (4) executes in general is

$$2 + 3 + 4 + \dots + (n + 1)$$

But, this expression is equal to

$$-1 + 1 + 2 + 3 + 4 + \dots + (n + 1)$$

which in turn is equal to

$$-1 + \frac{(n + 1)[(n + 1) + 1]}{2}$$

using the above formula for the sum of the first *m* integers with $m = (n + 1)$. Multiplying the numerator and combining terms gives a count for statement (4) of

$$\frac{1}{2}n^2 + \frac{3}{2}n$$

Figure 11.6 summarizes the statement execution counts for the algorithm to print a triangle in the cases where d.numRows equals zero, three, and *n* in general. The interesting conclusion to this analysis is that the execution time is still quadratic in *n*, just as with the algorithm to print a square.

Statement	d.numRows $= 0$	d.numRows $= 3$	d.numRows $= n$
(1)	1	1	1
(2)	1	1	1
(3)	1	4	$n + 1$
(4)	0	9	$\frac{1}{2}n^2 + \frac{3}{2}n$
(5)	0	6	$\frac{1}{2}n^2 + \frac{1}{2}n$
(6)	0	3	n
(7)	1	1	1
(8)	1	1	1
Total:	5	26	$n^2 + 4n + 5$

Figure 11.6
Statement execution count for the algorithm to print a triangle.

Example 11.2 Suppose it takes 200 μs to execute this program when *n* has the value of 35. If you double the value to 70, how long will it take to execute?

Using the approximate ratio,

$$\frac{200}{(35)^2} = \frac{T}{(70)^2}$$

Solving for *T* yields $200(70/35)^2 = 200(4) = 800$ μs. So the quadratic nature of the statement execution count again predicts that the execution time is four times the original execution time when *n* is doubled. ∎

A multiplication table

Our last program in this chapter is a stepwise refinement problem that requires nested loops. The problem is to input two numbers and output a multiplication table for the values between the two numbers. The input will be taken from a dialog box and the output will be to a new window as Figure 11.7 shows.

First Pass—The input is a pair of numbers. That calls for two integer variables, d.startNum and d.endNum. The output consists of five rows for the inputs 5 and 8. The first row is different from the next four rows because it is the heading of the table. The other four rows contain the actual products. Regardless of the specific values input, the output will be one heading row and several rows of products. The integer variable, i, will represent the row number and will vary from startNum to endNum.

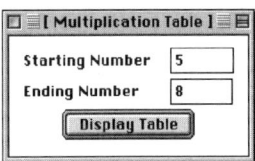

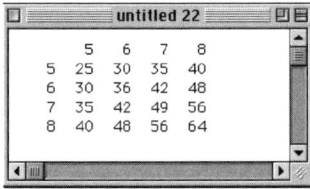

Figure 11.7
The input and output for a program that displays a multiplication table.

Input d.startNum, d.endNum
Output the first row
FOR i := d.startNum TO d.endNum DO
    Output row with i *as first number*
END

Second Pass—The first row is a list of numbers from d.startNum to d.endNum. However, it contains some extra space before the first number, which must be output before the numbers in the first row are output. Otherwise the numbers in the first row will not be aligned over the columns properly. The numbers themselves can be output with a single **FOR** statement.

Each row in the body of the multiplication table starts with the single value of i. The rest of the row is the product of the number, i, with another number, j, that varies from d.startNum to d.endNum. Expanding on the first pass, the second pass is

Input d.startNum, d.endNum
Output the space at the beginning of the first row
FOR j := d.startNum TO d.endNum DO
    Output j
END
FOR i := d.startNum TO d.endNum DO
    Output i
    FOR j := d.startNum TO d.endNum DO
        Output i * j
    END
END

Third Pass—The third pass is the complete Component Pascal module in Figure 11.8. It has several output details not in the previous passes to make the numbers in the table line up properly. It prints each number in a field width of four. Four spaces must precede the first heading line so the numbers in the heading will line up with the proper columns. There is a special character constant named digitspace that you can import from module TextModels. The amount of space occupied by a TextModels.digitspace is exactly equal to the amount of space occupied by a decimal digit. Unless the font is monospaced, as Courier is, the normal space character may not occupy the same amount of space as a decimal digit.

```
MODULE Pbox11B;
   IMPORT Dialog, TextModels, TextViews, Views, PboxMappers;
   VAR
      d*: RECORD
         startNum*, endNum*: INTEGER;
      END;

   PROCEDURE MakeMultiplicationTable*;
      VAR
         md: TextModels.Model;
         vw: TextViews.View;
         fm: PboxMappers.Formatter;
         i, j: INTEGER;
   BEGIN
      md := TextModels.dir.New();
      fm.ConnectTo(md);
      FOR j := 1 TO 4 DO
         fm.WriteChar(TextModels.digitspace)
      END;
      FOR j := d.startNum TO d.endNum DO
         fm.WriteInt(j, 4)
      END;
      fm.WriteLn;
      FOR i := d.startNum TO d.endNum DO
         fm.WriteInt(i, 4);
         FOR j := d.startNum TO d.endNum DO
            fm.WriteInt(i * j, 4)
         END;
         fm.WriteLn
      END;
      vw := TextViews.dir.New(md);
      Views.OpenView(vw)
   END MakeMultiplicationTable;

BEGIN
   d.startNum := 0; d.endNum := 0
END Pbox11B.
```

Figure 11.8
A program that produces the multiplication table shown in Figure 11.7.

This program uses a common programming convention for naming integer variables that are used to process a table. i is usually used as the control variable for the row loop, and j is usually used for the column loop. Later chapters continue this convention, and you should adopt it as well.

A convention for naming integer variables

Exercises

1. Plot the total statement execution counts for procedure DrawBox (Figure 11.2) and its modification to print a triangle (Figure 11.4) on the same graph for values of *n* from 0 to 6. What shape does each graph have?

2.   What is the total statement execution count of the code fragment

```
Statement 1 ;
FOR i := 1 TO d.num DO
    Statement 2 ;
    FOR j := 1 TO i DO
        Statement 3 ;
        Statement 4
    END
END
```

if d.num has the following values? Show the count for each statement in a table similar to Figure 11.6.

(a) 0   **(b)** 3   **(c)** n

3.   What is the total statement execution count of the code fragment

```
Statement 1 ;
FOR i := 2 TO d.num DO
    Statement 2 ;
    FOR j := 1 TO i DO
        Statement 3
    END
END
```

if d.num has the following values? Show the count for each statement in a table similar to Figure 11.6. It may help you to first write the statement counts similar to the way they are written in Figure 11.5.

(a) 1   **(b)** 4   **(c)** n

4.   What is the total statement execution count of the code fragment

```
Statement 1 ;
FOR i := 1 TO d.num DO
    Statement 2
    FOR j := -i TO i DO
        Statement 3
    END
END
```

if d.num has the following values? Show the count for each statement in a table similar to Figure 11.6. It may help you to first write the statement counts similar to the way they are written in Figure 11.5.

(a) 0   **(b)** 3   **(c)** n

You may need to use this formula for the sum of odd integers.

$$1 + 3 + 4 + \ldots + (2n - 1) = n^2 \text{ for positive } n$$

Problems

5. Write a program that asks the user to enter in a dialog box the number of rows and columns of a block of @s to be printed. Display the box in a new window. For example, if the user enters 3 for the number of rows and 5 for the number of columns, the new window should contain the following text:

```
@ @ @ @ @
@ @ @ @ @
@ @ @ @ @
```

6. Write a program that asks the user to enter in a dialog box the number of rows and columns of an empty block of zeros to be printed. Display the box in a new window. For example, if the user enters 5 for the number of rows and 9 for the number of columns, the new window should contain the text shown below. You will need to output the Text-Models.digitspace character inside the box for the right side of the box to line up properly.

```
000000000
0       0
0       0
0       0
000000000
```

7. Write a program that asks the user to enter in a dialog box the number of zeros on the base of a triangle, then prints a right triangle of zeros with a vertical right side. For example, if the user enters 5 for the number of rows, the new window should contain the text shown below. The leading spaces must be the TextModels.digitspace character for the right side of the triangle to be vertical.

```
    0
   00
  000
 0000
00000
```

8. Write a program that asks the user to enter in a dialog box the number of zeros on the base of a triangle, then prints a symmetric triangle. For example, if the user enters 7 for the number of zeros on the base the new window should contain the text

```
   0
  000
 00000
0000000
```

and if the user enters 8 the new window should contain the text

```
   00
  0000
 000000
00000000
```

The leading spaces must be the TextModels.digitspace character for the triangle to be symmetric.

9. Write a program that asks the user to enter in a dialog box a positive one-digit integer and prints a triangle of digits from one up to the digit entered. For example, if the user enters 4 the new window should display

```
1
22
333
4444
```

If the user enters a number other than a positive one-digit integer the new window should display an appropriate error message.

 Chapter *12*

Proper Procedures

The purpose of a called procedure is to perform a task for the calling procedure. Procedure PrintTriangle in Figure 3.13 prints a single pattern and illustrates the flow of control for procedures. Each time the calling procedure calls PrintTriangle, the pattern is printed, then control is passed back to the statement after the calling statement. When a procedure has parameters, its flow of control is identical to that of procedure PrintTriangle. The computer executes the correct flow of control by saving the address of the statement that made the call. When the called procedure terminates, the computer uses the saved address to know where to pass control back to the calling procedure.

PrintTriangle in Figure 3.13 executes in response to the user clicking a button in the graphical user interface. Like all procedures that execute in response to a button click, it has no parameters. Most programs in previous chapters use procedures from other modules that have parameters. This chapter shows how to write procedures with parameters. It also shows the mechanism by which the computer saves the return address when a procedure is called.

The run-time stack

To allocate a resource is to reserve it for someone's use. For example, you may allocate $30 from your paycheck to go to dinner with a friend on the weekend. When you call a procedure, Component Pascal allocates on a stack a portion of main memory for the procedure's use. It is called a run-time stack because the allocation takes place during program execution, that is, during the time the program is running as opposed to when the program is translated.

When a procedure is called, one of the items stored on the run-time stack is the *return address*. The return address contains information about the location of the statement in the calling procedure. When the called procedure finishes its execution, control is returned back to the calling procedure. The computer uses the return address to determine which statement in the calling procedure to execute after it executes the last statement in the called procedure. *The return address*

In addition to the return address, the computer allocates storage for the parameters and for the local variables in the called procedure. Because the allocation takes place at the time of the procedure call, neither the parameters nor the local variables exist before the procedure is called.

Allocation takes place on the run-time stack in the following order when you call a proper procedure:

- Push the parameters.
- Push the return address.
- Push storage for the local variables.

Allocation for a proper procedure

We know from Chapter 6 that a stack has the LIFO property—last in, first out. We will see that this property is especially significant for allocation on the run-time stack.

Parameters called by value

Module Pbox12A in Figure 12.2 has a programmer-defined procedure, PrintLine, which the calling procedure calls twice to print two lines of asterisks. Figure 12.1 shows the commander to activate the exported procedure PrintLines and the resulting output.

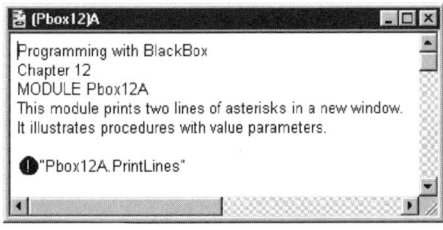
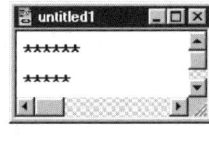

Figure 12.1
The output for the procedure of Figure 12.2.

The first statement of procedure PrintLines creates a new model md, and the second statement attaches formatter fm to it. The next statement

PrintLine(6, fm)

is the procedure call. The actual parameters are 6 and fm, and they match the formal parameters n and f. When the procedure is called, Component Pascal first allocates storage for the two parameters. It gives the value of the actual parameter 6 to the formal parameter n, and a reference to the actual parameter fm to the formal parameter f. Then, it allocates storage for the return address and puts the value of the return address, indicated by ra1 in Figure 12.2, in the storage allocated for it. Finally, it allocates storage for the local variable i. Unlike the parameters and the return address, no values are stored on the run-time stack for the local variables at the time of the procedure call.

The procedure executes the FOR statement to print the first row of six asterisks. The value of i on the run-time stack changes as the FOR statement executes. At the end of the procedure execution, the storage for n, f, the return address, and i is deallocated. Unlike a function, control does not return to the calling statement. Instead, control returns to the statement after the calling statement. In this case, that is the procedure call

```
MODULE Pbox12A;
    IMPORT TextModels, TextViews, Views, PboxMappers;

    PROCEDURE PrintLine (n: INTEGER; IN f: PboxMappers.Formatter);
    (* Inserts a line of n asterisks to a text model with formatter f *)
        VAR
            i: INTEGER;
    BEGIN
        FOR i := 1 TO n DO
            f.WriteChar("*")
        END;
        f.WriteLn
    END PrintLine;

    PROCEDURE PrintLines*;
        VAR
            md: TextModels.Model;
            vw: TextViews.View;
            fm: PboxMappers.Formatter;
    BEGIN
        md := TextModels.dir.New();
        fm.ConnectTo(md);
        PrintLine(6, fm);
        (* ra1 *)
        PrintLine(5, fm);
        (* ra2 *)
        vw := TextViews.dir.New(md);
        Views.OpenView(vw)
    END PrintLines;

END Pbox12A.
```

Figure 12.2
A procedure that prints a row of asterisks. The parameter specifies the number of asterisks in the row.

PrintLine(5, fm)

which calls the procedure again. Storage is reallocated for n, f, the return address, and i. This time the return address ra2, which is the address of

vw := TextViews.dir.New(md)

is stored on the run-time stack. The procedure prints a row of five asterisks. When procedure PrintLine terminates control returns to that statement. A new view is created and opened using the now familiar MVC paradigm.

Figure 12.3 shows the details of the allocation process on the run-time stack for Module12A. It illustrates a prominent feature of frameworks in contrast to those development environments that are based on libraries of procedures. Older development environments require that the programmer write what is known as a main program that always starts first when the application is launched. The main program calls other procedures, some of which are in the library and some of which are written by the programmer. Because BlackBox is a framework, however, there is no

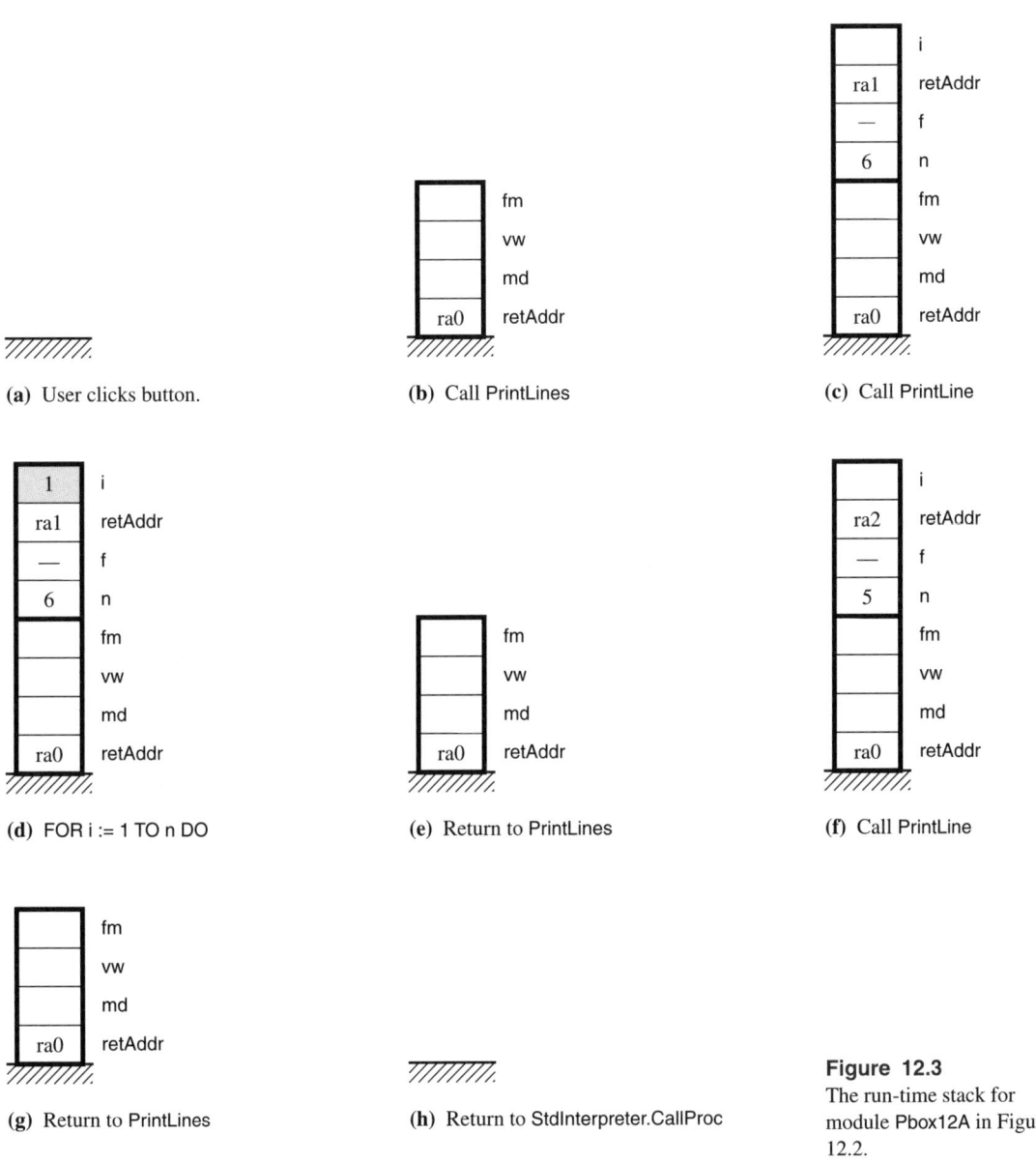

(a) User clicks button.

(b) Call PrintLines

(c) Call PrintLine

(d) FOR i := 1 TO n DO

(e) Return to PrintLines

(f) Call PrintLine

(g) Return to PrintLines

(h) Return to StdInterpreter.CallProc

Figure 12.3
The run-time stack for module Pbox12A in Figure 12.2.

main program that must be written by the programmer. The framework itself is the main program. The programmer writes procedures that are executed in response to user actions within the graphical user interface. In Module12A, procedure PrintLines executes in response to the click of a button by the user. The framework includes a module named StdInterpreter, which in turn contains a procedure named CallProc. StdInterpreter.CallProc is the framework's procedure that calls Module12A.Print-Lines when the user clicks the button.

Figure 12.3(a) shows the top part of the run-time stack before the user clicks the button. A large part of the run-time stack exists below the figure and is not shown.

Figure 12.3(b) shows the run-time stack when procedure StdInterpreter.CallProc calls procedure Pbox12A.PrintLines. Remember that when one proper procedure calls another the items pushed onto the stack are the parameters, followed by the return address, followed by storage for the local variables. Because PrintLines has no parameters, the only items pushed onto the run-time stack are the return address, indicated by retAddr, followed by storage for the local variables md, vw, and fm. The figure shows retAddr below the local variables because retAddr was pushed onto the stack first. It shows the value for retAddr as ra0, which indicates the address of some instruction in StdInterpreter.CallProc that need not concern us.

The collection of all the items pushed onto the run-time stack when a procedure is called is known as the *stack frame*. In this procedure call, the stack frame consists of the return address and storage allocated for the three local variables. The figure indicates the stack frame by the rectangle with the thick border.

The stack frame

After PrintLines is called, the MVC statements

```
md := TextModels.dir.New();
fm.ConnectTo(md)
```

execute. They give values to the cells on the stack. Because we are not concerned with the details of those values, the figures for the run-time stack do not indicate what those values are.

Figure 12.3(c) shows the effect of the first call to PrintLine. Unlike the previous call, this call has parameters as well as local variables. First, parameters n and f are pushed onto the stack. The formal parameter is the label for the memory cell and the value pushed is the content of the cell. Because n is called by value, the value 6 of the corresponding actual parameter is pushed. Because f is called by constant reference, indicated by IN in the formal parameter list, a reference to the corresponding actual parameter fm is pushed. For reasons not described here, formatters must always be called by constant reference. Chapter 15 describes the concept of call by constant reference. For now, we will ignore the formatter calling mechanism and simply put a hyphen in the cell for f on the run-time stack. Second, the return address is pushed onto the stack. Its value is ra1, which Figure 12.2 shows to be the instruction following the one that made the call. Third, storage for the local variable i is allocated. The stack frame in this call consists of all three kinds of items— parameters, return address and local variables.

Formatters are called by constant reference.

Following the call to PrintLine, its statements execute, the first of which is

```
FOR i := 1 TO n DO
```

Whenever assignments are made to local variables or to parameters called by value, they always change the content of the memory cells on the run-time stack. When this statement first executes, it sets i to 1. Figure 12.3(d) shows the content of the cell on the run-time stack labeled i changed to 1. As the loop progresses through the values 2, 3, 4, 5, and 6, the value in the cell changes accordingly. Each time the loop executes an asterisk is inserted into the text model.

Execution of the last line in PrintLine triggers a return from the procedure. The computer uses the stored value for the return address to know which statement to execute next. It deallocates the top stack frame and returns flow of control to the calling procedure. In this case, ra1 is the return address. Figure 12.3(e) shows the stack after the deallocation of the frame just before the statement at ra1 is about to execute.

The statement at ra1 is yet another procedure call. Figure 12.3(f) shows allocation on the run-time stack. This time the value of the actual parameter is 5, and the return address is ra2, which is the address of

```
vw := TextViews.dir.New(md)
```

the instruction following the call. Procedure PrintLine executes again, this time inserting 5 asterisks into the text model.

Figure 12.3(g) shows the deallocation from this procedure call. Following execution of the MVC statements to give the text model a view and display it in a window, control returns to StdInterpreter.CallProc as Figure 12.3(h) shows.

A bar chart program

The next program uses the above technique for printing a row of asterisks to print a bar chart of data values. The input is from the focus window, which contains a list of real values shown in Figure 12.4. Processing is initiated by a menu selection not shown in the figure. The output is to a new window and consists of a single row for each real value containing the real value, followed by the vertical bar character | followed by a row of asterisks equal to the real value rounded off to the nearest integer.

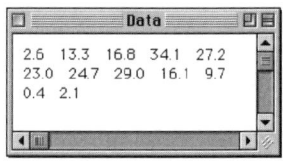
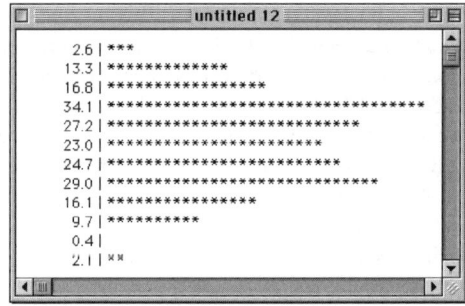

Figure 12.4
The input and output for the program of Listing 12.2.

Figure 12.5 shows the module that creates the output of Figure 12.4. Procedure PrintLine uses the standard function SHORT, which is a type conversion function. If n is a variable of type INTEGER and m is a variable of type LONGINT, then the assignment statement

```
m := n
```

```
MODULE Pbox12B;
    IMPORT TextModels, TextViews, Views, TextControllers, PboxMappers;

    PROCEDURE PrintLine (x: REAL; IN f: PboxMappers.Formatter);
        VAR
            i, n: INTEGER;
    BEGIN
        ASSERT(x >= 0.0, 20);
        f.WriteReal(x, 8, 1);
        f.WriteString(" | ");
        n := SHORT(ENTIER(x + 0.5));
        FOR i := 1 TO n DO
            f.WriteChar("*")
        END;
        f.WriteLn
    END PrintLine;

    PROCEDURE PrintHistogram*;
        VAR
            cn: TextControllers.Controller;
            sc: PboxMappers.Scanner;
            dataValue: REAL;
            md: TextModels.Model;
            vw: TextViews.View;
            fm: PboxMappers.Formatter;
    BEGIN
        cn := TextControllers.Focus();
        IF cn # NIL THEN
            md := TextModels.dir.New();
            fm.ConnectTo(md);
            sc.ConnectTo(cn.text);
            sc.ScanReal(dataValue);
            WHILE ~sc.eot DO
                PrintLine(dataValue, fm);
                (* ra1 *)
                sc.ScanReal(dataValue)
            END;
            vw := TextViews.dir.New(md);
            Views.OpenView(vw)
        END
    END PrintHistogram;

END Pbox12B.
```

Figure 12.5
A program that prints a bar chart from data values in a file. The procedure prints a single bar.

is legal, but the assignment statement

n := m

is not legal. The purpose of SHORT is to convert a long integer to the equivalent integer value. because long integers have a greater range than integers, it is possible that SHORT will truncate the value of the long integer. The assignment statement

n := SHORT(m)

is legal because SHORT(m) has type INTEGER.

In procedure PrintLine, the statement

n := SHORT(ENTIER(x + 0.5));

rounds off the value of real variable x and assigns it to integer variable n. The ENTIER function returns a long integer value. The SHORT function converts it to an integer value so the value can be assigned to n.

Example 12.1   If x has the value 2.6, then x + 0.5 has the value 3.1, ENTIER(x + 0.5) has the long integer value 3, and SHORT(ENTIER(x + 0.5)) has the integer value 3. The real value of 2.6 has been properly rounded up.   ∎

Example 12.2   If x has the value 13.3, then x + 0.5 has the value 13.8, ENTIER(x + 0.5) has the long integer value 13, and SHORT(ENTIER(x + 0.5)) has the integer value 13. The real value of 13.3 has been properly rounded down.   ∎

The program reads the first value from the focus window into the real variable dataValue. If the focus window is empty, then sc.eot will be true and the body of the WHILE loop will never execute. Otherwise, the variable dataValue will get the first real value in the focus window. With each loop execution the procedure PrintLine is called. After it executes and prints a line of the histogram, the next real value from the focus window is input into the real variable dataValue. The loop continues to execute while real values remain to be scanned in the focus window.

Figure 12.6 shows memory allocation for the procedure. Figure 12.6(a) shows the stack frame after the call to PrintHistogram. To keep the figure simple, the local MVC variables in the procedure are not shown. Other than the MVC variables, data-Value is the only local variable.

With the first scan, dataValue gets 2.6 from the focus window as Figure 12.6(b) shows. When PrintHistogram calls PrintLine, the computer allocates a new stack frame. As usual, parameters x and f are first pushed onto the stack, followed by the return address retAddr followed by local variables i and n as Figure 12.6(c) shows.

PrintLine converts the real value of 2.6 from x by rounding up to the integer value 3, which it gives to n. After proceeding through the FOR loop 3 times, the final value of i is 4 as Figure 12.6(d) shows. Termination of procedure PrintLine triggers a return to PrintHistogram. The top stack frame is deallocated as usual and the return address ra1 specifies the instruction in the calling procedure to be executed next. The result is the stack frame in Figure 12.6(e).

The scanner scans the next real value 13.3 from the focus window into local variable dataValue. The scan sets sc.eot to false because a real value was scanned into the variable. The test in the WHILE loop is true, which causes the body to execute again. So, PrintLine is called once again. Figure 12.6(f) shows the state of the run-time stack just before the call. The cell for dataValue contains the scanned value

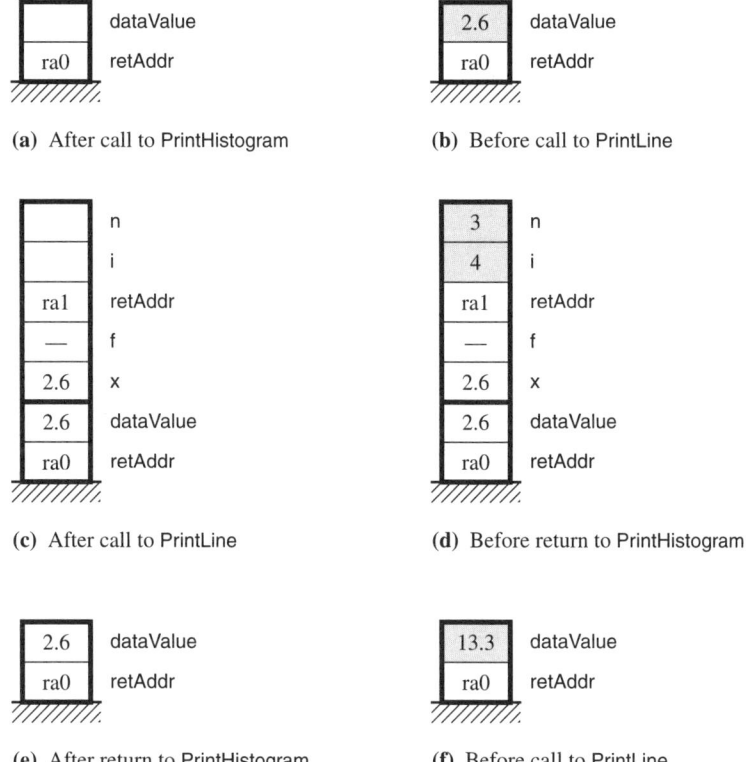

Figure 12.6
Memory allocation for
Listing 12.5. Many MVC
variables are not shown.

(a) After call to PrintHistogram

(b) Before call to PrintLine

(c) After call to PrintLine

(d) Before return to PrintHistogram

(e) After return to PrintHistogram

(f) Before call to PrintLine

13.3. When the procedure is called, a stack frame identical to the top frame in Figure 12.6(c) is allocated except that the value of the formal parameter x is 13.3 instead of 2.6.

It is important to understand that between executions of PrintLine its parameters and local variables do not exist. It would be illegal to write a statement like INC(n) in the body of procedure PrintHistogram. It should be clear that such a statement would be impossible to execute because n would not exist at that point in time. The error would be detected by the compiler, which would not generate any object code.

Implementing preconditions

Procedure PrintLine can only print a bar for the histogram if the value that the calling procedure gives it for x is not negative. It has no mechanism for printing a histogram bar that extends to the left of the numbers in the text view. For the results to be meaningful the user should be restricted to providing nonnegative real numbers.

One approach to solving the problem of invalid input is to have an IF statement in procedure PrintLine that checks if x is negative and prints a histogram bar only if it is not. The problem is, what should the procedure do if the variable is negative? Should it do nothing and simply skip that line in the graph? Should it print a line with no asterisks? Should it send an error message to the Log? The problem of how to deal with input errors is an important one that you should always consider when you design software.

The BlackBox framework promotes a particularly effective philosophy on how to deal with errors. For this problem, the philosophy states that the IF statement to guard against errors should not be in procedure PrintLine but should be in the calling procedure instead. Procedure PrintLine should perform only one task, that of printing a histogram bar with valid data. To program it to also handle the error conditions is not considered good design because those two tasks are not similar. Programs are easier to read, understand, and maintain if each procedure concentrates on one primary task.

The first executable statement in PrintLine

ASSERT(x >= 0.0, 20)

implements a precondition for the procedure and guarantees that the value for x to be processed will not be negative. If it is, a trap will occur as shown in Figure 12.7 where the second number in the focus window is negative. The precondition makes it the caller's responsibility to guard against the possibility of meaningless input. The delegation of that responsibility to the caller allows the called procedure to concentrate on one primary task, namely inserting one line of the histogram bar into the text model.

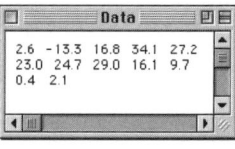

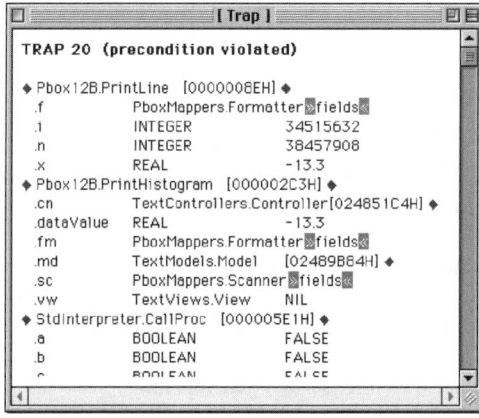

Figure 12.7
The trap generated by violation of the precondition of procedure PrintLine in Figure 12.5.

You should compare the trap window in Figure 12.7 with the figure of the run-time stack in Figure 12.6(c). The trap window is essentially a view of the run-time stack, except that the return address is not shown explicitly, and the local variables and parameters are shown in alphabetic order preceded by a period instead of in the order in which they actually occur on the stack. Figure 12.6(c) shows storage for x, f, i, and n on the top stack frame in the order in which they are allocated (bottom up), while Figure 12.7 shows storage for .f, .i, .n, and .x in alphabetic order. The trap window shows the type of each parameter and local variable as well as its value when the trap occurred. As expected, the trap window shows dataValue in PrintHistogram and x in PrintLine to have value -13.3.

Figure 12.6(c) shows that n and i have not received any values, but the trap window shows some huge random values for both .n and .i. This state is typical for variables that have not been assigned values. It is impossible for a variable to not have a value. If the program has not assigned a value to a variable, it will have some random value left over by the memory cell from the last time it was allocated or from its random state when the computer was first turned on.

Random values before the first assignment

Procedure PrintLine in Figure 12.5 is an illustration of good design philosophy for establishing preconditions with your procedures. Of course, procedure PrintHistogram is not an illustration of good design for user-friendly software because it allows the user to experience a program trap. A bulletproof program will never crash with a program trap. Problem 10 in this chapter challenges you to make procedure PrintHistogram bulletproof.

A bulletproof program does not crash with a program trap.

In practice, procedures that are not exported do not usually contain preconditions that are implemented by ASSERT statements. In that sense, procedure PrintLine in Figure 12.5 is not too typical. A single module is rarely written by more than one person. Because the same programmer who writes a nonexported procedure also writes the procedure that calls it, the programmer does not usually need to safeguard the called procedure against misuse. However, procedures that are exported are frequently used by programmers who did not write them. In those cases, the precondition is the formalization of a contract between the sever module and the client module. The ASSERT statement is frequently used to establish the precondition, and the corresponding error message number is documented in the Docu file. The client module then has the responsibility to ensure that the precondition is met before calling the procedure. This software development practice is known as Design by Contract and is described in Chapter 7, page 144.

Design by contract

Call by value

In Figure 12.5, procedure PrintLine passes its parameters by value. The program in Figure 12.8 illustrates the fact that in call by value, the formal parameter gets a copy of the value of the actual parameter. If a subsequent statement in the procedure changes the value of the formal parameter, it does not affect the actual parameter.

Figure 12.10 shows the memory allocation for Figure 12.8. In procedure CallByValue, variable i gets the value of 6, which is verified by the output statement. Then the program calls procedure PassVal with the actual parameter, i. The formal parameter, j, gets a copy of the value of i. When the statement

In call by value, the formal parameter gets the value of the actual parameter.

INC(j)

executes in procedure PassVal, it changes the copy of the value to 7. The original value of 6 for i in the main program does not change. The output of the program on the log is

i = 6
j = 7
i = 6

When parameters are called by value, the called procedure has access to the values of the formal parameters. If the value of the formal parameter is changed, the change is not reflected in the calling procedure. Information flows from the calling procedure to the called procedure—not in the other direction—via the value of the parameter.

```
MODULE Pbox12C;
   IMPORT StdLog;

   PROCEDURE PassVal (j: INTEGER);
   BEGIN
      INC(j);
      StdLog.String("j = "); StdLog.Int(j); StdLog.Ln;
   END PassVal;

   PROCEDURE CallByValue*;
      VAR
         i: INTEGER;
   BEGIN
      i := 6;
      StdLog.String("i = "); StdLog.Int(i); StdLog.Ln;
      PassVal(i);
      (* ra1 *)
      StdLog.String("i = "); StdLog.Int(i); StdLog.Ln
   END CallByValue;

END Pbox12C.
```

Figure 12.8
A procedure with a parameter called by value.

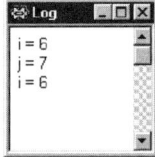

Figure 12.9
The output for Figure 12.8.

(a) Before call to PassVal

(b) After call to PassVal

Figure 12.10
Memory allocation for Figure 12.8.

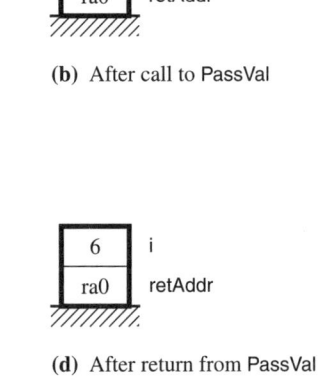

(c) After INC(j)

(d) After return from PassVal

Call by reference

This section introduces the concept of call by reference, a technique by which a procedure can not only get values from the calling statement, but can give values back to it as well.

The program in Figure 12.11 is identical to the program in Figure 12.8 except for one important detail. The programmer placed reserved word VAR before formal parameter j in the formal parameter list. The reserved word VAR in a formal parameter list has a different meaning from its meaning in a local variable declaration. Outside a parameter list, VAR indicates the start of the variable declaration part. In a formal parameter list, VAR indicates that the parameter is called by reference instead of called by value. In Component Pascal, parameters that are called by reference are known as variable parameters.

```
MODULE Pbox12D;
   IMPORT StdLog;

   PROCEDURE PassRef (VAR j: INTEGER);
   BEGIN
      INC(j);
      StdLog.String("j = "); StdLog.Int(j); StdLog.Ln;
   END PassRef;

   PROCEDURE CallByReference*;
      VAR
         i: INTEGER;
   BEGIN
      i := 6;
      StdLog.String("i = "); StdLog.Int(i); StdLog.Ln;
      PassRef(i);
      (* ra1 *)
      StdLog.String("i = "); StdLog.Int(i); StdLog.Ln
   END CallByReference;

END Pbox12D.
```

Figure 12.11
A procedure with a parameter called by reference.

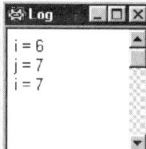

Figure 12.12
The output for Figure 12.11.

Figure 12.13 shows the memory allocation for Listing 12.11. When Component Pascal allocates memory for j, it does not give a copy of the value of the actual parameter, i, to j. Instead, it gives a reference to i. The figure indicates the reference to i by the arrow that points from the cell allocated for j to the cell allocated for i.

When j is used in the procedure, it is as though i has temporarily taken its place. The statement

In call by reference, the formal parameter gets a reference to the actual parameter.

INC(j)

has the effect of

INC(i)

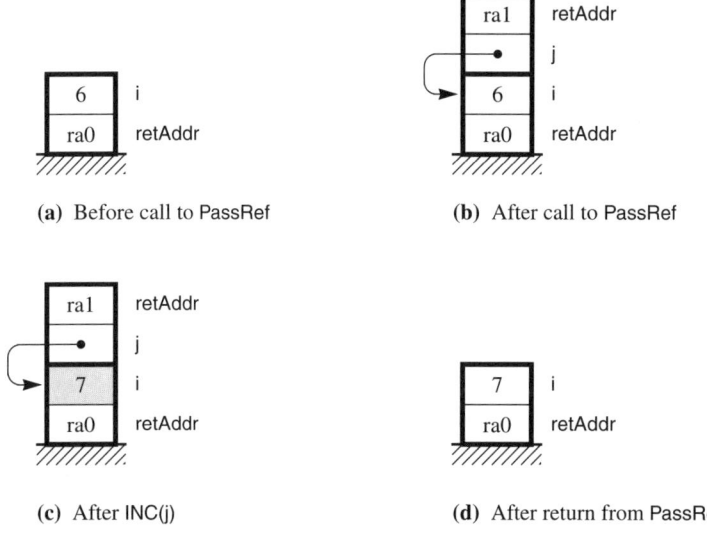

Figure 12.13
Memory allocation for Figure 12.11.

(a) Before call to PassRef

(b) After call to PassRef

(c) After INC(j)

(d) After return from PassRef

because j, during execution of the procedure, refers to i. When control returns back to the calling program, the value of i has been modified. The purpose of call by reference is to change the value of the actual parameter in the calling statement. The output of this program is

```
i = 6
j = 7
i = 7
```

When parameters are called by reference, the procedure has access to the values of the variables in the calling program referred to by the parameters. In this program, procedure PassRef had access to the value, 6, of i in the calling program. In that sense, information can flow from the calling program to the procedure.

When the procedure changes the value of a variable parameter, the value of a variable in the calling program changes. In this program, when procedure PassRef assigned a value to j, the value of i in the calling program changed. In that sense, information can flow from the procedure to the calling program.

In call by value, the actual parameter could be an arbitrary expression. But in call by reference, the actual parameter must be a single variable.

Example 12.3 The procedure call

```
PassVal(i + 2)
```

where PassVal is declared as in Listing 12.8, is legal. The formal parameter, j, is called by value and can take the expression i + 2 as an actual parameter. ∎

Example 12.4   The procedure call

PassRef(i + 2)

where PassRef is defined in Listing 12.11, is not legal, because i + 2 is not a single variable. ∎

Call by result

In Figure 12.11, procedure PassRef uses the value 6 supplied by actual parameter i. It increments the value and gives the incremented value of 7 back to i. So, not only does it use the initial value of j, it also changes the actual parameter that is linked to j.

```
MODULE Pbox12E;
   IMPORT Dialog;
   VAR
      d*: RECORD
         width*, height*: REAL;
         area-, perim-: REAL
      END;

   PROCEDURE CalcRectSize (wid, ht: REAL; OUT ar, per: REAL);
   BEGIN
      ASSERT(wid > 0.0, 20);
      ASSERT(ht > 0.0, 21);
      ar := wid * ht;
      per := 2.0 * (wid + ht)
   END CalcRectSize;

   PROCEDURE Rectangle*;
   BEGIN
      IF (d.width > 0.0) & (d.height > 0.0) THEN
         CalcRectSize(d.width, d.height, d.area, d.perim);
         (* ra1 *)
      ELSE
         d.width := 0.0; d.height := 0.0;
         d.area := 0.0; d.perim := 0.0
      END;
      Dialog.Update(d)
   END Rectangle;

BEGIN
   d.width := 0.0; d.height := 0.0;
   d.area := 0.0; d.perim := 0.0
END Pbox12E.
```

Figure 12.14
Computing the area and perimeter of a rectangle with a procedure.

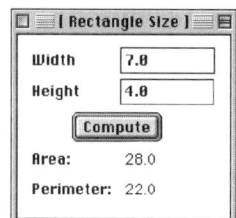

Figure 12.15
The dialog box for the procedure of Figure 12.14.

It frequently happens that the called procedure does not need the initial value of the formal parameter. In these situations, the initial value of the formal parameter can be considered undefined. The passing mechanism is known as call by result, and formal parameters are so designated by the reserved word OUT in the formal parameter list.

The program in Figure 12.14 is a case in point. Figure 12.15 shows the corresponding dialog box. The module uses a procedure to calculate the area and perimeter of a rectangle from its width and height. Procedure CalcRect has four formal parameters. Two of the parameters are called by value and two are called by result.

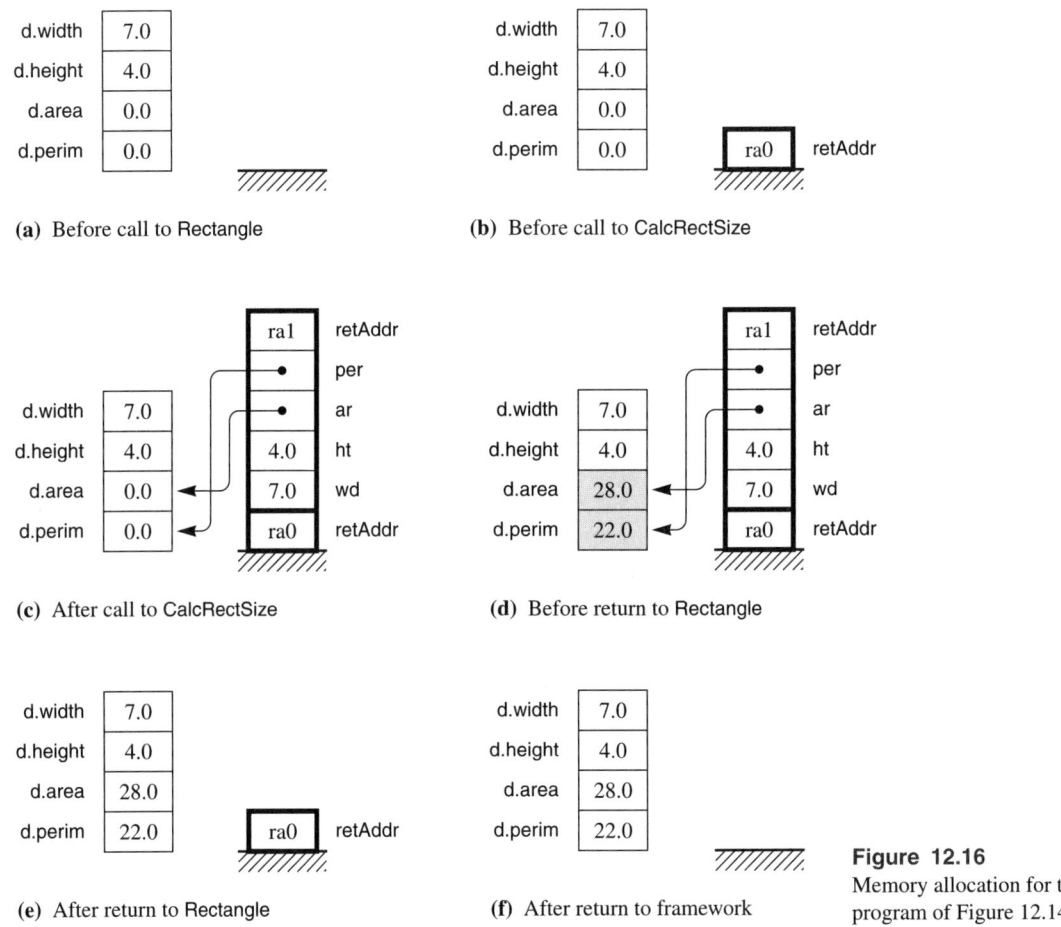

(a) Before call to Rectangle

(b) Before call to CalcRectSize

(c) After call to CalcRectSize

(d) Before return to Rectangle

(e) After return to Rectangle

(f) After return to framework

Figure 12.16
Memory allocation for the program of Figure 12.14.

Because module Pbox12E implements a dialog box, it contains an interactor d, which is a global variable. Unlike local variables and parameters, global variables are not allocated on the run-time stack. They occupy a region of memory set aside for the module apart from its procedures. Memory for global variables is allocated when the module is loaded and remains in place while the stack frames are allocated and deallocated for procedure calls and returns. As long as the dialog box in Figure

12.15 is visible in the graphical user interface, storage for the values in Pbox12E.d is available.

Figure 12.16 is a trace of program execution. Storage for the global variables is shown to the left of the run-time stack. The module gets values for d.width and d.height from the dialog box. When the user presses the compute button, procedure Rectangle executes, which tests to make sure that d.width and d.height are both non-negative then calls procedure CalcRectSize. The actual parameters—d.width, d.height, d.area, and d.perim—correspond to the formal parameters—wid, ht, ar, and per. wid and ht are called by value. ar and per are called by result. wid gets the value from d.width, and ht gets the value from d.height. As with call by reference, ar refers to d.area, and per refers to d.perim. The same arrow notation is used in the figure to indicate call by result as was used previously to indicate call by reference. Another similarity with call by reference is that the actual parameter in call by result must be a variable.

In call by result, the formal parameter gets a reference to the actual parameter.

Procedure CalcRect uses the values of wid and ht in its computation. That information flows from the calling procedure to the called procedure. When CalcRect assigns values to ar and per, it changes the values of d.area and d.perim in procedure Rectangle. That information flows from the called procedure to the calling procedure. In general, information flows from the calling procedure to the called procedure when parameters are called by value, from the called procedure to the calling procedure when parameters are called by result, and both ways when parameters are called by reference. Figure 12.17 shows the flow of information for these three calling mechanisms.

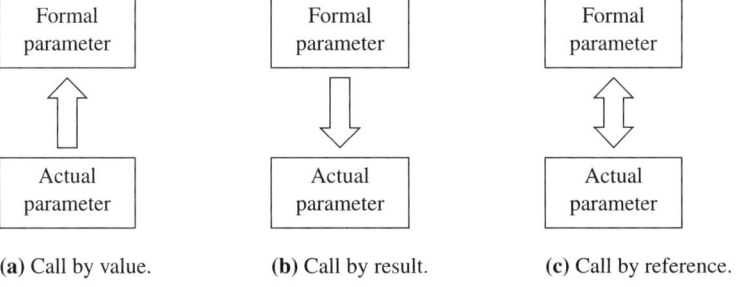

(a) Call by value. **(b)** Call by result. **(c)** Call by reference.

Figure 12.17
The flow of information for three different calling mechanisms.

The key question to ask in deciding whether a parameter should be called by value, called by result, or called by reference is, Which way does the information flow between the actual parameter and the formal parameter? If the purpose of the formal parameter is to receive a value from the actual parameter use call by value. If the purpose of the formal parameter is to change the value of the actual parameter, use call by result. In this case, the initial value of the actual parameter can be considered undefined. If the purpose of the formal parameter is both to receive a value from the actual parameter and to change the value of the actual parameter, use call by reference. In summary:

- Call by value
  - ▲ Default
  - ▲ Use when the actual parameter should not change.
  - ▲ The actual parameter can be an expression.
- Call by result
  - ▲ OUT
  - ▲ Use when the actual parameter should change and its initial value is undefined.
  - ▲ The actual parameter must be a variable.
- Call by reference
  - ▲ VAR
  - ▲ Use when the actual parameter should change and the called procedure uses its initial value.
  - ▲ The actual parameter must be a variable.

Summary of call by value, call by result, and call by reference

Using parameters

Any number of parameters can be in the parameter list of a procedure. The number of parameters in the actual parameter list must equal the number of parameters in the formal parameter list. The types must correspond as well. The violation of these rules is a syntax error.

Example 12.5 The statement

PrintLine(6.0, fm)

where PrintLine is declared as in Figure 12.2, is illegal because the formal parameter, n, is an integer and the actual parameter, 6.0, is a real value. ∎

Example 12.6 With PrintLine declared as before, the function call

PrintLine(6)

is illegal, because there is only one actual parameter but two formal parameters. ∎

Remember that if x is a real variable, the assignment x := 7 is legal. The integer value, 7, is converted to a real value, 7.0, before being assigned to x. But if i is an integer variable, then i := 2.7 is illegal. Similarly, integer values can be actual parameters for real formal parameters.

Example 12.7 The procedure call

CalcRectSize(42, 10, d.area, d.perim)

where CalcRectSize is defined as in Figure 12.14, is legal. The integer value, 42, is automatically converted to the real value, 42.0, before being given to the formal parameter, wid. Similarly, 10 is automatically converted to 10.0. ∎

It is legal to have the actual parameter be a variable with the same name as the formal parameter. But you should realize that there are separate memory locations for each. To keep the distinction clear between the formal parameters and actual parameters, this book will generally avoid using the same name for both. The usual convention will have the formal parameter serve as an abbreviation of the actual parameter.

Example 12.8 If a procedure has a declaration with formal parameters as

PROCEDURE PrintLine (num: INTEGER; f: PboxMappers.Formatter);

and the calling procedure has a variable declared as

VAR
   num: INTEGER

then the procedure call

PrintLine(num, fm)

would be legal even though the first formal parameter has the same name as the actual parameter. ∎

Using global variables

The modules in this book that implement dialog boxes, such as the one in Figure 5.9 that computes the coins required for a given amount of change, use global variables to link to the dialog box. The variable declaration from Figure 5.9

VAR
   d*: RECORD
     change*: INTEGER;
     dimes-, nickels-, pennies-: INTEGER
   END;

is nested within module Pbox05B but not within procedure MakeChange. Therefore, it is a global variable.

Figure 9.3 shows another example of global variables. The declaration

stackA, stackB: PboxStackObj.Stack;

is nested within module Hw99Pr0980 and not within any of the procedures PushA, PushB, PopA, PopB, or ClearStacks. Therefore, stackA and stackB are global variables.

```
MODULE Pbox12F;
   IMPORT TextModels, TextViews, Views, TextControllers, PboxMappers;

   VAR (* WARNING-Unnecessary global variables. Bad design. *)
      cn: TextControllers.Controller;
      sc: PboxMappers.Scanner;
      dataValue: REAL;
      md: TextModels.Model;
      vw: TextViews.View;
      fm: PboxMappers.Formatter;

   PROCEDURE PrintLine;
      VAR
         i, n: INTEGER;
   BEGIN
      ASSERT(dataValue >= 0.0, 20);
      fm.WriteReal(dataValue, 8, 1);
      fm.WriteString(" | ");
      n := SHORT(ENTIER(dataValue + 0.5));
      FOR i := 1 TO n DO
         fm.WriteChar("*")
      END;
      fm.WriteLn
   END PrintLine;

   PROCEDURE PrintHistogram*;
   BEGIN
      cn := TextControllers.Focus();
      IF cn # NIL THEN
         md := TextModels.dir.New();
         fm.ConnectTo(md);
         sc.ConnectTo(cn.text);
         sc.ScanReal(dataValue);
         WHILE ~sc.eot DO
            PrintLine;
            sc.ScanReal(dataValue)
         END;
         vw := TextViews.dir.New(md);
         Views.OpenView(vw)
      END
   END PrintHistogram;

END Pbox12F.
```

Figure 12.18

A procedure whose computation is the same as that in Figure 12.5, but without parameters for PrintLine.

There is nothing to prevent you from declaring as many global variables as you would like, and using them for whatever purpose you desire. You could even use global variables in place of parameters to achieve the same effect. Figure 12.18 shows a module that does the same computation as the one in Figure 12.5, but without any parameters in procedure PrintLine. There is no real parameter x or formatter f, and the variables dataValue and fm (along with a host of other variables) are global. Instead of having the actual parameter dataValue being mapped to parameter x and using x in the procedure, the procedure simply does its computation directly on dataValue. Similarly, instead of having the actual parameter fm being mapped to parameter f and using f in the procedure, the procedure simply does its computation directly on fm.

Which program do you think is better—the one in Figure 12.5 or the one in Figure 12.18? Most beginning programmers think that the one in Figure 12.18 is better. After all, it is shorter, and when you write it you do not need to bother with a parameter list. Why use a parameter list if you can do the same job without one?

Most software designers would contend that the program in Figure 12.5 is better. The general design rule for procedures is that you should avoid unnecessary use of global variables. For small programs, such as the ones in this book, the problems created by using global variables are not as evident as they are with large programs. The advantage of using parameters and local variables in a procedure is that the procedure is self-contained. Therefore, when compared to a procedure that uses global variables, it is

Design rule for global variables

- Easier to read

- Easier to modify

- Easier to use in other programs

Look at the two procedures from these programs, when they are isolated from their environments.

```
PROCEDURE PrintLine (x: REAL; VAR f: PboxMappers.Formatter); PROCEDURE PrintLine;
   VARVAR
   i, n: INTEGER;i, n: INTEGER;
BEGINBEGIN
   ASSERT(x >= 0.0, 20);ASSERT(dataValue >= 0.0, 20);
   f.WriteReal(x, 8, 1);fm.WriteReal(dataValue, 8, 1);
   f.WriteString(" | ");fm.WriteString(" | ");
   n := SHORT(ENTIER(x + 0.5));n := SHORT(ENTIER(dataValue + 0.5));
   FOR i := 1 TO n DOFOR i := 1 TO n DO
   f.WriteChar("*")fm.WriteChar("*")
   END;END;
   f.WriteLnfm.WriteLn
END PrintLine;END PrintLine;
```

Suppose the program listing were 30 pages long, and these procedures are pages away form their calling programs. You are in the process of reading the code to find a bug and you come across these procedures.

The first PrintLine is completely self-contained. Its statements refer only to local variables. You can see from reading it that whatever the calling procedure supplies for the first parameter this PrintLine procedure rounds off that value to an integer and writes that number of asterisks to a text model to which the second parameter is connected. But the second PrintLine is not self-contained. What is dataValue? What is fm? What are their types? You cannot tell for sure unless you scroll back many pages to search for their declarations.

Furthermore, the first PrintLine is more general than the second PrintLine. You can copy it out of this module and paste it into another module with the assurance that it will work correctly. The second PrintLine is not general-purpose. Its correctness depends on its environment. You cannot place it in another module with different global variables and expect it to work. You would need to change its environment to make sure that dataValue and fm are declared consistently and used properly with the procedure. Or, you would need to rename dataValue and f to match the global variables of the environment.

An important skill for you to develop now is the ability to design good procedures. You should always rely on local variables with parameters to pass information between the calling and the called procedure unless there is reason not to. When must you resort to a global variable? When its value must be persistent between invocations of the module's exported procedures.   *When to use a global variable*

Consider the dialog box for Figure 12.14, which computes the area and perimeter of a rectangle. The interactor d for the dialog must be global because the dialog box persists between invocations of the exported procedure Rectangle. Before the procedure executes, the dialog box exists on the screen with values entered by the user. After the procedure executes, the dialog box persists on the screen displaying the results of the computation. Figure 12.16 shows the values linked to the dialog box. The local variables are deallocated when Rectangle terminates, but the dialog box remains on the screen. Therefore, the interactor d must be global.

Another example of the proper use of global variables is the program of Figure 9.3, which manipulates two stacks. The variables stackA and stackB are not linked directly to a dialog box. Nevertheless, the data that they store must be persistent between invocations of PushA, PushB, PopA, PopB, and ClearStacks. After the user pushes a value onto a stack, the stack itself with all its data should not be deallocated. If the stack were deallocated the value that was just pushed would be lost.

Exercises

1.   Determine the outputs to the Log of Exr1a and Exr1b.

<table>
<tr><td>

(a)
```
PROCEDURE Pass1a (n: INTEGER);
BEGIN
    n := n * 2;
    StdLog.Int(n); StdLog.String(" ")
END Pass1a;

PROCEDURE Exr1a*;
    VAR
        num: INTEGER;
BEGIN
    num := 5;
    Pass1a(num);
    StdLog.Int(num) (* ra1 *)
END Exr1a;
```
</td><td>

(b)
```
PROCEDURE Pass1b (VAR n: INTEGER);
BEGIN
    n := n * 2;
    StdLog.Int(n); StdLog.String(" ")
END Pass1b;

PROCEDURE Exr1b*;
    VAR
        num: INTEGER;
BEGIN
    num := 5;
    Pass1b(num);
    StdLog.Int(num) (* ra1 *)
END Exr1b;
```
</td></tr>
</table>

2.   For Exercise 1(a), draw the memory allocation as in Figure 12.10 for the following times:

(a) Just before the call to Pass1a (b) Just after the call to Pass1a
(c) Just before the return from Pass1a (d) Just after the return from Pass1a

3. For Exercise 1(b), draw the memory allocation as in Figure 12.13 for the following times.

(a) Just before the call to Pass1b (b) Just after the call to Pass1b
(c) Just before the return from Pass1b (d) Just after the return from Pass1b

4. Determine the outputs to the Log of Exr4a and Exr4b.

(a)   (b)
```
PROCEDURE Pass4a (OUT n, m: INTEGER)PROCEDURE Pass4b (OUT m, n: INTEGER);
BEGINBEGIN
    n := 1;n := 1;
    m := 2m := 2
END Pass4a;END Pass4b;

PROCEDURE Exr4a*;PROCEDURE Exr4b*;
    VARVAR
    n, m: INTEGER;n, m: INTEGER;
BEGINBEGIN
    Pass4a (n, m);Pass4b (n, m);
    (* ra1 *)(* ra1 *)
    StdLog.String('n = '); StdLog.Int(n); StdLog.Ln;StdLog.String('n = '); StdLog.Int(n); StdLog.Ln;
    StdLog.String('m = '); StdLog.Int(m); StdLog.Ln StdLog.String('m = '); StdLog.Int(m); StdLog.Ln
END Exr4a;END Exr4b;
```

5. For Exercise 4(a), draw the memory allocation as in Figure 12.16 for the following times.

(a) Just before the call to Pass4a (b) Just after the call to Pass4a
(c) Just before the return to Exr4a (d) Just after the return to Exr4a

6. For Exercise 4(b), draw the memory allocation as in Figure 12.16 for the following times.

(a) Just before the call to Pass4b (b) Just after the call to Pass4b
(c) Just before the return to Exr4b (d) Just after the return to Exr4b

7. Suppose a calling procedure declares variables

a, b, c: REAL;

and procedure Exr7 has the heading

PROCEDURE Exr7 (d: REAL; OUT e: REAL; VAR f: REAL)

State whether each of the procedure calls is legal. For those that are not legal, explain why.

(a) Exr7(a, b, c)   (b) Exr7(a, b)   (c) Exr7(7.0, b, c)
(d) Exr7(a, 7.0, c)   (e) Exr7(a, b, 7.0)   (f) Exr7((a + b) / 2.0, b, c)
(g) Exr7(7, b, c)   (h) Exr7(a, 7, c)

8.   Suppose a calling procedure declares variables

p, q, r: INTEGER

and procedure Exr8 has the heading

PROCEDURE Exr8 (s: INTEGER; OUT t: INTEGER, u: INTEGER)

State whether each of the procedure calls is legal. For those that are not legal, explain why.

(a) Exr8(p, q, r)	**(b)** Exr8(p, q)	**(c)** Exr8(5, q, r)
(d) Exr8(p, 5, r)	**(e)** Exr8(p, q, 5)	**(f)** Exr8((p + q) DIV 2, q, r)
(g) Exr8(5.0, q, r)	**(h)** Exr8(p, 5.0, r)	

9.   **(a)** What are the advantages of using local variables and parameters instead of global variables? **(b)** When is it justified to use a global variable?

Problems

10.   Make the program in Figure 12.5 bulletproof by continuing the loop only if the scanner is not at the end of text and dataValue is not negative. After terminating the loop, check sc.eot to determine how the loop terminates. If it terminates without reaching the end of text you know a negative value was encountered. In that case, insert an appropriate error message in the text model. Otherwise do nothing and terminate normally.

11.   Declare

PROCEDURE PrintRow (numSpace, numChr: INTEGER; ch: CHAR; VAR f: PboxMappers.Formatter)

that inserts into a text model to which f is connected one line with numSpace spaces followed by numChr occurrences of ch. For example, PrintRow (5, 3, 'a', fm) should insert one line with five spaces followed by three 'a's. Use your procedure to print the pattern shown below to a new window. Activate your program with a commander in your Docu file. After your program creates the window you will need to display the pattern in Courier or some other monospaced font to have the characters aligned properly.

```
   *
  ***
 *****
*******
  : : :
  : : :
```

12.   For Chapter 11, Problem 5, write a program to display a solid box of @ symbols in a new window. Use a procedure called PrintPattern with three parameters—one that specifies how many rows to print, one that specifies the number of columns to print, and one that specifies the formatter to use. Assert as a precondition that the number of rows and columns must be positive. Insure in the calling procedure that the precondition is not violated by not changing anything in the dialog box and not opening a new window if a nonpositive value is entered.

13. For Chapter 11, Problem 6, write a program to display a hollow box of zeros in a new window. Use a procedure called PrintPattern with three parameters—one that specifies how many rows to print, one that specifies the number of columns to print, and one that specifies the formatter to use. Assert as a precondition that the number of rows and columns must be greater than 1. Insure in the calling procedure that the precondition is not violated.

14. For Chapter 11, Problem 7, write a program to display a right triangle of zeros with a vertical right side in a new window. Use a procedure called PrintPattern with a parameter that specifies how many rows to print and a parameter that specifies the formatter to use. Assert as a precondition that the number of rows must be positive. Insure in the calling procedure that the precondition is not violated.

15. For Chapter 11, Problem 8, write a program to display symmetric triangle of zeros in a new window. Use a procedure called PrintPattern with a parameter that specifies how many rows to print and a parameter that specifies the formatter to use. Assert as a precondition that the number of rows must be positive. Insure in the calling procedure that the precondition is not violated.

16. A rectangular box has width, length, and height. Write a program that inputs these dimensions from a dialog box and calls a procedure that calculates the volume and total surface area of the box. Your procedure should have five formal parameters, each of which you should determine whether to call by value, call by result, or call by reference.

17. Implement a dialog box that looks and behaves like Figure 7.3, but with one additional button labeled "Reverse Stack". When the user presses this button, all the items on the stack should be rearranged in reverse order with the item originally at the top of the stack on the bottom and the item originally at the bottom on the top. The text fields for Push and Pop should not change, nor should the field for the number of items change. Use two temporary variables called tempStack1 and tempStack2 for intermediate storage of stack values in your exported procedure ReverseStack. Write another procedure, not exported, named CopySourceToDest

PROCEDURE CopySourceToDest (source: PboxStackADS.Stack; OUT dest: PboxStackADS.Stack)

that clears Dest then copies source to dest in reverse order by successively popping items from source and pushing them to dest. Use a temporary variable called temp to store an individual value from the stack between the pop and push operations. Note that source is called by value so that its actual parameter will not change. Procedure ReverseStack can simply call CopySourceToDest three times, copying Stack A to tempStack1, then tempStack1 to tempStack2, then tempStack2 back to Stack A, which will be in reverse order. Import module PboxStackADS.

18. Do Problem 17 but import PboxStackObj.

 Chapter *13*

Function Procedures

Component Pascal provides both native and programmer-defined procedures. For example, the module in Figure 12.5 contains the statement

n := SHORT(ENTIER(x + 0.5))

Both the ENTIER function, which truncates a real value and returns a long integer, and the SHORT function, which converts a LONGINT value to an INTEGER value, are native. That is, they are provided by the Component Pascal language, and do not need to be imported from another module or defined by the programmer. If you need a function procedure that is not provided by the language or the framework, you must define your own. This chapter shows how to define function procedures that contain parameter lists.

Function procedures have some characteristics in common with proper procedures and some characteristics that differ. One common characteristic is that a calling procedure makes a procedure call, the called procedure executes, then control is passed back to the calling procedure. The details of the procedure call and return differ, however. Another common characteristic is that storage is allocated on the runtime stack with both proper and function procedures. Again, however, the details differ.

The bisection algorithm

Procedure ComputeRoot in Figure 10.11 computed one root of a cubic equation with the bisection algorithm. The following program improves procedure Compute-Root in several ways. Figure 10.8 shows that the cubic equation has three real roots—one between –2 and –1, one between 0 and 1, and one between 2 and 3. But the original version of ComputeRoot found only the root between 2 and 3. One improvement would be to allow the user to enter the starting values of left and right, which would permit finding any of the roots.

Another shortcoming of the original version of ComputeRoot is that it permits the user to enter a value of 0.0 for the tolerance. The problem is that the loop will execute endlessly if d.tolerance has the value 0.0. It would be better if the program guarded against this possibility. Figure 13.1 shows the dialog box for an improved version of ComputeRoot. The dialog box has additional input fields for the user to enter starting values for left and right. You can see from the figure that the program must be able to prove to itself that a root must lie between the two values entered by the user before it will proceed.

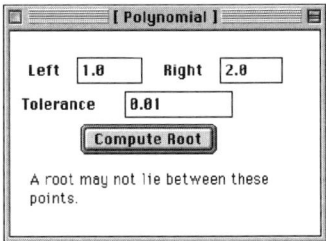 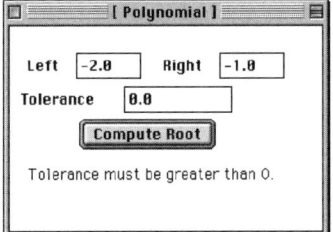 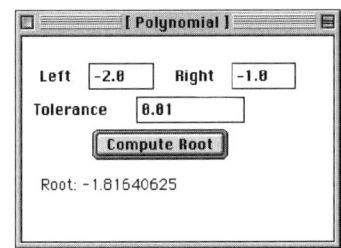

The module in Figure 13.2 uses two procedures to implement these improvements to the program. The first procedure, ComputeRoot, is the same kind of procedure we have always used to link to a button in a dialog box. The second procedure, F, is a programmer defined function procedure. The procedure declaration part of F is

Figure 13.1
Three executions of the bisection algorithm of Listing 13.2.

```
PROCEDURE F (x: REAL): REAL;
    CONST
        a3 = 1.0; a2 = -1.0; a1 = -4.0; a0 = 2.0;
BEGIN
    RETURN ((a3 * x + a2) * x + a1) * x + a0
END F;
```

These are the statements that define the function. The parameter x in this declaration is the formal parameter. You can tell that F is a function procedure by the type ": REAL" that follows the formal parameter, which indicates that the function returns a real value.

```
MODULE Pbox13A;
    IMPORT Dialog, PboxStrings;
    VAR
        d*: RECORD
            left*, right*: REAL;
            tolerance*: REAL;
            message-: ARRAY 64 OF CHAR;
        END;

    PROCEDURE F (x: REAL): REAL;
        CONST
            a3 = 1.0; a2 = -1.0; a1 = -4.0; a0 = 2.0;
    BEGIN
        RETURN ((a3 * x + a2) * x + a1) * x + a0
    END F;
```

Figure 13.2
The bisection algorithm with a programmer-defined function.

```
PROCEDURE ComputeRoot*;
    VAR
        left, mid, right: REAL;
        fLeft, fMid: REAL;
        rootString: ARRAY 32 OF CHAR;
BEGIN
    IF d.tolerance <= 0.0 THEN
        d.message := "Tolerance must be greater than 0."
    ELSIF F(d.left) * F(d.right) > 0 THEN (* ra1 *)
        d.message := "A root may not lie between these points."
    ELSE
        left := d.left; right := d.right; fLeft := F(left); (* ra2 *)
        (* Assert: root is between left and right *)
        WHILE ABS(left - right) > d.tolerance DO
            mid := (left + right) / 2.0;
            fMid := F(mid); (* ra3 *)
            IF fLeft * fMid > 0.0 THEN
                (* Assert: root is between mid and right *)
                left := mid;
                fLeft := fMid
            ELSE
                (* Assert: root is between left and mid *)
                right := mid
            END
        END;
        PboxStrings.RealToString((left + right) / 2, 1, 0, rootString);
        d.message := "Root: " + rootString
    END;
    Dialog.Update(d)
END ComputeRoot;

BEGIN
    d.left := 0.0; d.right := 0.0; d.tolerance := 1.0;
    d.message := ""
END Pbox13A.
```

Figure 13.2
Continued.

One of the statements that calls the function from the main program is

fLeft := F(left)

F(left) is a function call. In this example, it occurs on the right side of an assignment statement. The EBNF for an assignment statement is

Statement = Designator " := " Expr

which shows that an expression occurs on the right side of an assignment statement. So, a function call is an example of an expression. In general, a function can occur within a more complicated expression.

Advantages of function procedures

One advantage of this version of the bisection algorithm is the ability to easily modify the function. In Figure 10.11, modifying the function would require changing the statement in two different places in the main program. In Figure 13.2, you would only need to modify the function definition once. That one modification affects the computation of the function from all calling points in the main program.

Another advantage of this version is its readability. In the original version, the function was buried in the code of the main program, and the coefficients, a3, a2, a1, and a0, were separated from the function computation. In this version, the coefficients and the code for the function are all together. That makes the program easier to understand.

Function procedure calls

When a proper procedure is called, three items are pushed onto the run-time stack—the parameters, the return address, and storage for the local variables. Because the purpose of a function procedure is to return a value, it must allocate an extra cell on the run-time stack for the value returned. The cell for the returned value is allocated before any of the other items on the stack. Allocation takes place on the run-time stack in the following order when you call a function procedure:

- Push storage for the return value.

- Push the parameters.

- Push the return address.

- Push storage for the local variables.

Allocation for a function procedure

Like storage for the local variables, the cell for the return value has some undefined value when the function is called. This is in contrast to the parameters, which get values of or references to the actual parameters, and the return address, which gets the address of the statement to execute when the function terminates.

Another difference in detail between proper procedures and function procedures is flow of control when the procedure terminates. The difference is:

- When a proper procedure terminates, control is passed to the statement *following* the calling statement.

- When a function procedure terminates, control is passed to the *calling* statement.

Flow of control with proper procedures and function procedures

This difference is related to the difference between the way a proper procedure is called and the way a function procedure is called. When you call a proper procedure, the call is its own statement. For example, the proper procedure call

Proper procedure calls stand alone.

StdLog.String("Mr. K. Kong")

stands alone, apart from any other statement. However, when you call a function procedure, it is always part of another statement. For example, in the function procedure call to ABS

Function procedure calls are part of another statement.

x := ABS(-3.7)

the function call is part of an assignment statement, while in the call

StdLog.Real(ABS(-3.7))

the function call is part of a procedure call. You can see from the proper procedure call that when the call terminates, there is nothing left for the calling statement to do. The next statement to execute will be the one following the procedure call. Also, from the function call you can see that when the call terminates, the value 3.7 is returned. The statement that makes the call must do something with this returned value, either assign it to x or output it to the Log. Therefore, control must be returned to the calling statement.

A factorial function

The next program illustrates allocation on the run-time stack. It computes the factorial of an integer entered by the user as shown in Figure 13.3. The factorial function is not defined for values less than zero. If the user enters a number less than zero the program changes the number entered to zero. Also, the factorial function produces very large values even for small parameters. If the number entered is greater than 20, its factorial exceeds the range of a LONGINT, which is 9,223,372,036,854,775,807. If the user enters a number greater than 20, the program guards against numerical overflow by changing it to zero. Otherwise, an overflow trap would occur.

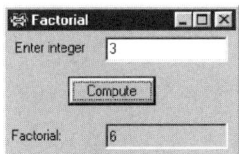
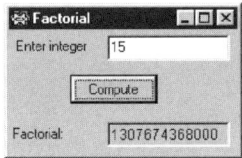

Figure 13.3
The dialog box for the factorial function of Listing 13.4.

The program, which is shown in Figure 13.4, contains two procedures—ComputeFactorial, which is called by the framework when the user clicks the button in the dialog box, and Factorial, which is called by ComputeFactorial.

Figure 13.5 shows the storage allocation for the program in Figure 13.4. The proper procedure ComputeFactorial has no parameters and no local variables. So, when it is called only the return address is stored on the run-time stack. The function procedure Factorial has one parameter and two local variables. So, when it is called five items are stored on the run-time stack—storage for the returned value, one parameter, the return address, and storage for the two local variables.

Figure 13.5(a) shows the storage allocated for global variables d.num and d.factorial when module Pbox13B is loaded. Their values are set by the initialization code for the module. These storage cells remain in memory until the module is unloaded.

Figure 13.5(b) shows what happens when the user enters the value 3 in the dialog box. The text field of the dialog box is linked to the interactor field d.num. So, d.num gets the value 3.

```
MODULE Pbox13B;
  IMPORT Dialog;
  VAR
    d*: RECORD
      num*: INTEGER;
      factorial-: LONGINT
    END;

  PROCEDURE Factorial (n: INTEGER): LONGINT;
    VAR
      i: INTEGER;
      fact: LONGINT;
  BEGIN
    ASSERT((0 <= n) & (n <= 20), 20);
    fact := 1;
    FOR i := 1 TO n DO
      fact := fact * i
    END;
    RETURN fact
  END Factorial;

  PROCEDURE ComputeFactorial*;
  BEGIN
    IF (0 <= d.num) & (d.num <= 20) THEN
      d.factorial := Factorial(d.num)  (* ra1 *)
    ELSE
      d.num := 0;
      d.factorial := 1
    END;
    Dialog.Update(d)
  END ComputeFactorial;

BEGIN
  d.num := 0;
  d.factorial := 1
END Pbox13B.
```

Figure 13.4

A program to compute the factorial of an integer with a function.

Figure 13.5(c) shows what happens when the user clicks the button in the dialog box. The button of the dialog box is linked to procedure ComputeFactorial, so the framework calls ComputeFactorial. The return address ra0 is the location of some instruction within the framework not visible in the program of Figure 13.4. After the IF statement executes, the next statement is

d.factorial := Factorial(d.num); (* ra1 *)

which is a call to the function procedure Factorial.

Figure 13.5(d) shows the storage allocated on the run-time stack immediately after the call to Factorial. Five items are pushed onto the stack in this order: storage for the returned value labeled retVal, the value of the actual parameter labeled n, the

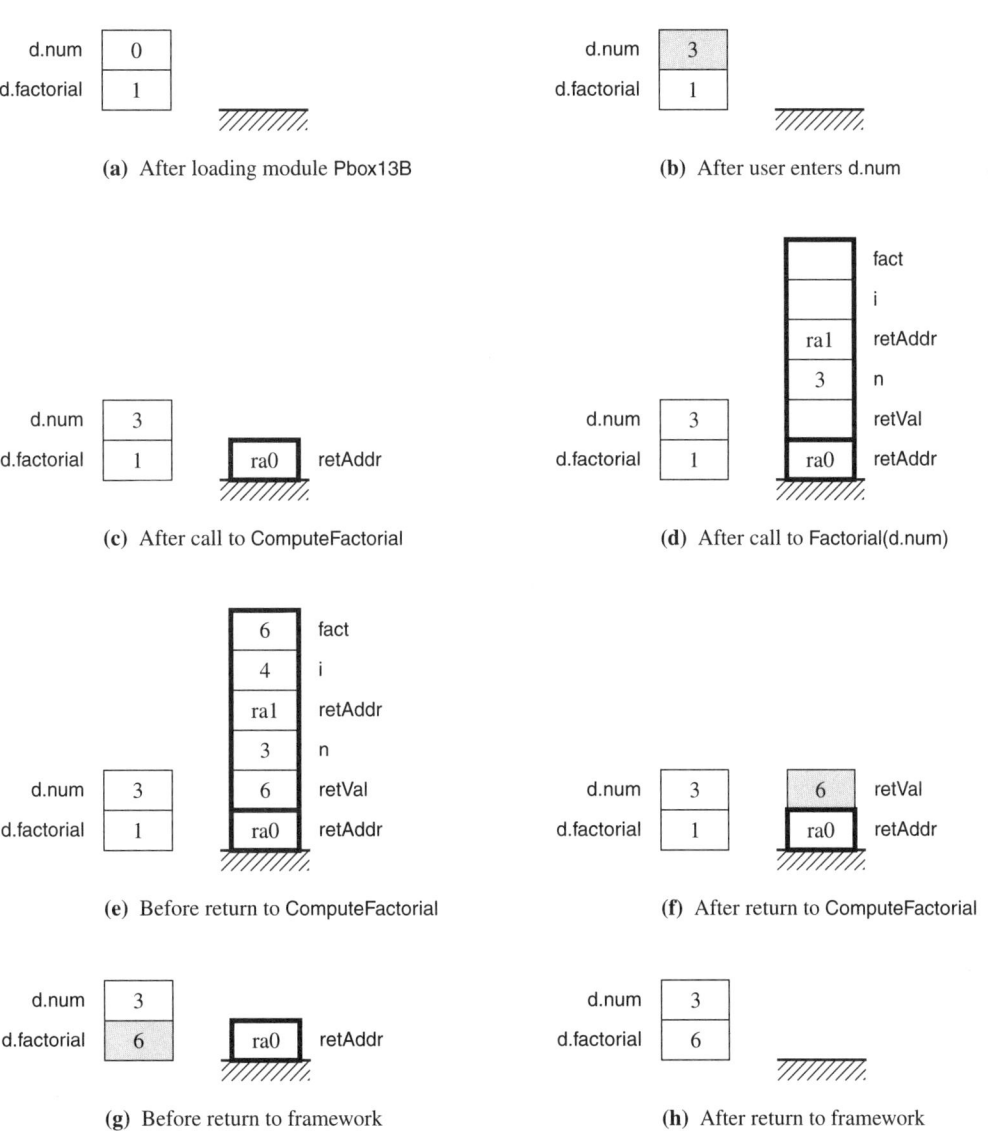

(a) After loading module Pbox13B

(b) After user enters d.num

(c) After call to ComputeFactorial

(d) After call to Factorial(d.num)

(e) Before return to ComputeFactorial

(f) After return to ComputeFactorial

(g) Before return to framework

(h) After return to framework

Figure 13.5
Memory allocation for the
program in Figure 13.4.

return address labeled retAddr, the first local variable labeled i, and the second local variable labeled fact. When you call a function procedure, after the procedure executes control returns to the same statement that called it. Therefore, the return address stored on the stack is the address of the statement that made the call. The program listing has the comment (* ra1 *) on the same line as the calling statement to indicate the return address for the function procedure. As usual, the stack frame is outlined in bold on the stack in the figure.

Figure 13.5(e) shows the values on the stack after Factorial has executed and just before its return to ComputeFactorial. Factorial has used local variable i to compute the value 6 for fact. The statement

RETURN fact

assigns the value of fact to the retVal storage location. Then the return address ra1 is used to determine which instruction to execute next.

Figure 13.5(f) shows the run-time stack immediately after the return from Factorial. The value returned is available to the calling procedure. Control is returned to the instruction at ra1, which is the location of the statement

d.factorial := Factorial(d.num); (* ra1 *)

The entire stack frame is deallocated except for the value returned. This statement now completes its execution by assigning the value returned to d.factorial.

Figure 13.5(g) shows the allocated storage just before the return from ComputeFactorial. The dialog box has been updated so the computed value of d.factorial is visible on the screen.

Figure 13.5(h) shows the run-time stack immediately after the return from ComputeFactorial. Control has returned to ra0, which is the address of some statement in the framework. Storage for variables d.num and d.factorial will remain allocated with their current values until the values are changed by the program or the module is unloaded.

A function to compute wages

The next program is yet another example of computing a wage with possibility of overtime. The computation is performed in a function with preconditions that are guaranteed to be met by the calling procedure. Figure 13.6 shows the dialog box.

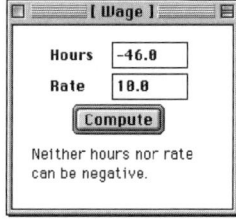

Figure 13.6
The dialog box for the wage function of Figure 13.7.

```
MODULE Pbox13C;
   IMPORT Dialog, PboxStrings;
   VAR
      d*: RECORD
         hours*, rate*: REAL;
         message-: ARRAY 64 OF CHAR
      END;

   PROCEDURE Wages (hrs, rt: REAL): REAL;
   BEGIN
      ASSERT(hrs >= 0.0, 20);
      ASSERT(rt >= 0.0, 21);
      IF hrs <= 40.0 THEN
         RETURN hrs * rt
      ELSE
         RETURN 40.0 * rt + (hrs - 40.0) * 1.5 * rt
      END
   END Wages;

   PROCEDURE ComputeWages*;
      VAR
         wageString: ARRAY 16 OF CHAR;
   BEGIN
      IF (d.hours >= 0.0) & (d.rate >= 0.0) THEN
         PboxStrings.RealToString(Wages(d.hours, d.rate), 1, 2, wageString);  (* ra1 *)
         d.message := "Wage: $" + wageString
      ELSE
         d.message := "Neither hours nor rate can be negative."
      END;
      Dialog.Update(d)
   END ComputeWages;

BEGIN
   d.hours := 0.0; d.rate := 0.0;
   d.message := ""
END Pbox13C.
```

Figure 13.7
A program to compute wages with possible overtime with a function procedure.

Figure 13.7 is the program for the dialog box in Figure 13.6. As usual, the compute button is linked to an exported procedure ComputeWages. The actual computation is performed by the function procedure Wages, which has two formal parameters, hrs and rt. It is typical for the formal parameters to be an abbreviation of the actual parameters. hrs is an abbreviation for d.hours and rt is an abbreviation for d.rate.

Figure 13.8 shows the storage allocation for the program. Figure 13.8(a) assumes the user has entered 46.0 in the dialog box for d.hours and 10.0 in the dialog box for d.rate. When the user clicks the button, the framework calls ComputeWages, which has no parameters and one local variable. The stack frame consists of the return address of some statement in the framework and storage for the one local variable.

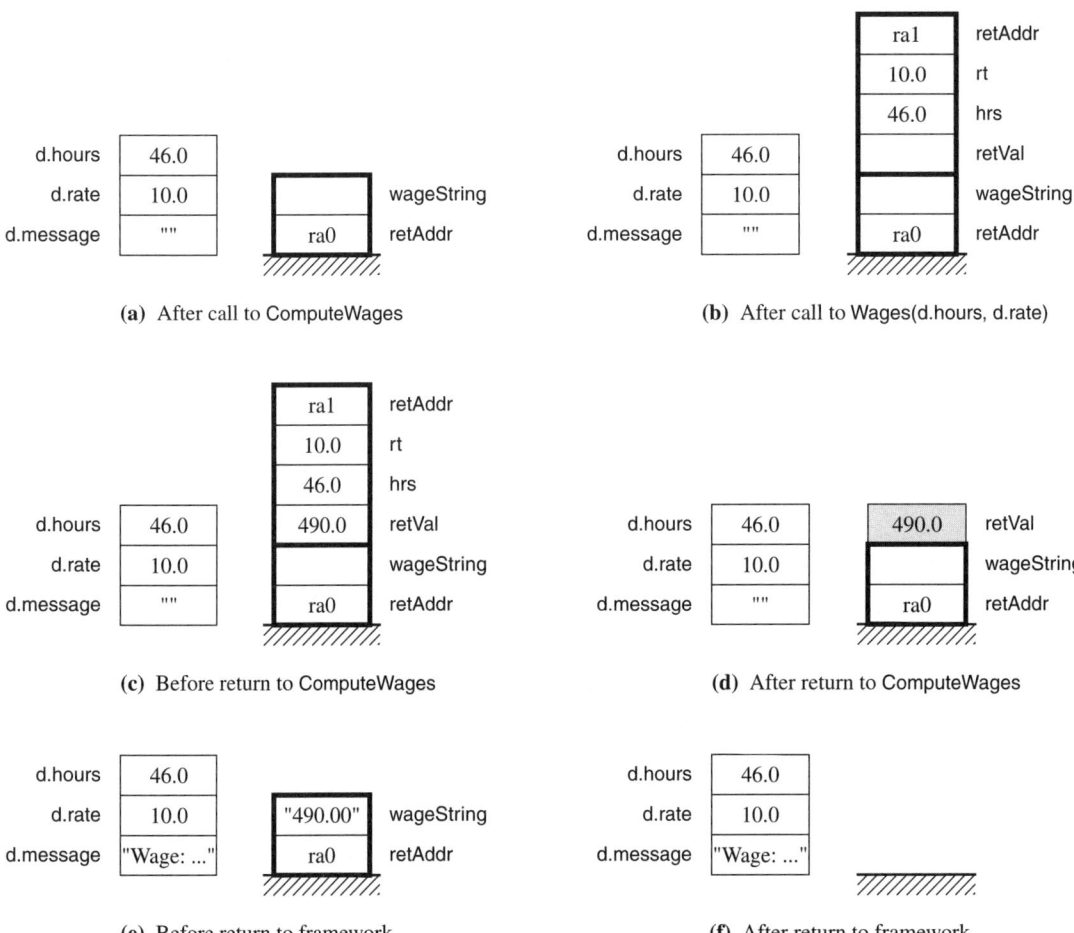

(a) After call to ComputeWages

(b) After call to Wages(d.hours, d.rate)

(c) Before return to ComputeWages

(d) After return to ComputeWages

(e) Before return to framework

(f) After return to framework

Figure 13.8
Memory allocation for the program in Figure 13.7.

Figure 13.8(b) shows allocation on the run-time stack when function procedure Wages is called. First on the stack is storage for the returned value labeled retVal. Then the formal parameters hr and rt are pushed. Because they are called by value, the cells contain the values of the actual parameters d.hours and d.rate. Next on the stack is the return address ra1, which is the address of the calling statement

PboxStrings.RealToString(Wages(d.hours, d.rate), 1, 2, wageString)

Function Wages verifies that the preconditions are met. It tests for the possibility of overtime by comparing hrs with 40.0. There are two RETURN statements within the function, only one of which will execute. When the computer encounters a RETURN within a procedure, the procedure terminates immediately without executing any other statements that may follow the RETURN statement. This program also shows that a RETURN statement can be followed by an arbitrary expression of the correct type. It need not be followed by a single variable as was the RETURN in function Factorial in Figure 13.4. In Figure 13.8(c) the value of the expression to be returned is stored in the cell labeled retVal for the returned value.

Figure 13.8(d) shows the run-time stack after the return to the calling procedure. The returned value of 490.0 is given to the calling statement, which proceeds to use it as the actual parameter in a call to the proper procedure PboxStrings.RealToString. The stack frame for the call to this procedure is not shown in Figure 13.8. The call to the proper procedure give the string value to wageString as shown in Figure 13.8(e). Finally, after the dialog box is updated to show the result, control is returned to the framework in Figure 13.8(f).

Using function procedures

All the examples of call by result and call by reference so far have been with proper procedures instead of function procedures. Component Pascal permits function procedures to use call by result and call by reference. However, such parameters with function procedures are usually inappropriate. The purpose of a function is to return a single value. In mathematics, you give a function a value, x, and it returns a value $f(x)$. The function depends on x but does not change the value of x. Programs are easier to understand if functions behave as they do in mathematics and do not change their actual parameters. This book has no examples of functions with parameters called by result or called by reference.

Do not use call by result or call by reference with functions

Because the formal parameters of function procedures are usually called by value, the actual parameters may be expressions.

Example 13.1   The function call

d.factorial := Factorial(2 * d.num + 1)

where d.factorial, d.num, and Factorial are declared as in Figure 13.4, is legal. If d.num has value 3, then formal parameter n would get the value of 7 at the start of function execution.   ∎

In general, a function call can be placed anywhere an expression is allowed. Figure 13.4 has the function call, Factorial(d.num), on the right side of an assignment statement. The function call can just as easily be part of a larger expression.

Example 13.2   The statement

num := Math.Pi * Math.IntPower(x, 2) / Factorial(i)

is legal, where num and x are real variables, i is an integer variable, and Factorial is declared as in Figure 13.4.   ∎

The RETURN statement for a function can occur anywhere, even within the body of a loop. When it is encountered, the function terminates immediately.

Example 13.3 Suppose that i, max, and testDivisor are integer variables, and the following code executes from within a function procedure with return type BOOLEAN.

```
WHILE i < max DO
   IF i MOD testDivisor = 0 THEN
      RETURN TRUE
   END;
   INC(i)
END;
RETURN FALSE
```

If at any time during execution of the loop i gets a value that makes the test of the IF statement true, the function will terminate immediately and will return true. Otherwise, the loop will terminate because the WHILE test will become false, and the function will return false. ∎

Exercises

1. If the function procedure Exr1 is defined as

    ```
    PROCEDURE Exr1 (a, b: INTEGER): INTEGER;
    BEGIN
       IF a < b THEN
          RETURN 2 * a
       ELSE
          RETURN 2 * b
       END
     END Exr1
    ```

    then what does each of the following code fragments output to the Log?

    (a)
    ```
    i := 12;
    j := 3;
    StdLog.Int(Exr1(i, j))
    ```

    (b)
    ```
    i := 4;
    j := Exr1(2 * i + 1, 10);
    StdLog.Int(j)
    ```

    (c)
    ```
    StdLog.Int(Exr1(Exr1(3, 2), Exr1(4, 5)))
    ```

2. Assume that the user enters 2 for d.a and 3 for d.b. Draw a picture of the memory allocation as in Figure 13.5 produced by the module listed below for the following times.

    (a) After user enters d.a and d.b.   **(b)** After call to ComputeProb2.
    (c) After call to Prob2.   **(d)** Before return to ComputeProb2.
    (e) After return to ComputeProb2.   **(f)** Before return to framework.
    (g) After return to framework.

```
MODULE Pbox13Prob2;
    IMPORT Dialog;
    VAR
        d*: RECORD
            a*, b*: INTEGER;
            c-: INTEGER
        END;

    PROCEDURE Prob2 (e, f: INTEGER): INTEGER;
        VAR
            i, j: INTEGER;
    BEGIN
        i := e; j := f;
        INC(i); INC(j);
        IF i > 2 THEN
            RETURN 2 * i
        ELSE
            RETURN 3 * j
        END
    END Prob2;

    PROCEDURE ComputeProb2*;
    BEGIN
        d.c := Prob2(d.a, d.b);  (* ra1 *)
        Dialog.Update(d)
    END ComputeProb2;

BEGIN
    d.a := 0; d.b := 0;
    d.c := 0
END Pbox13Prob2.
```

Problems

3. For Chapter 6, Problem 13, write the program to find the sales commission. Declare

PROCEDURE Commission (sales: REAL): REAL

to compute the commission from the amount of sales. Implement a precondition for the function that the entered number cannot be less than 0. Insure that the precondition is met in the calling procedure. If it is not met, set the entered sales to $0.00 and the displayed commission to $0.00.

4. Write the bowling prize program of Chapter 6, Problem 14. Declare

PROCEDURE BowlingPrize (scr1, scr2, scr3: INTEGER): REAL

to compute the prize from the three scores, scr1, scr2, and scr3. Implement a precondition for the function that none of the scores can be less than 0 or greater than 300. Insure that the precondition is met in the calling procedure. If it is not met, set the entered scores to 0 and the displayed prize to $0.

5. For Chapter 6, Problem 16, write the program to find the grade point average. Declare

PROCEDURE GPA (numA, numB, numC, numD, numF: INTEGER): REAL

to compute the grade point average from the letter grades. Implement a precondition for the function that none of the entered numbers can be less than 0. Insure that the precondition is met in the calling procedure. If it is not met, set the entered numbers to 0 and the displayed grade point average to a blank field.

6.   For Chapter 8, Problem 19, write the program to determine the traffic fine. Declare

PROCEDURE TrafficFine (speed: INTEGER): REAL

to compute the traffic fine from the speed. Implement a precondition for the function that the entered speed cannot be less than 0. Insure that the precondition is met in the calling procedure. If it is not met, set the entered speed to 0 and the displayed fine to 0.

7.   Write the Frisbee program of Chapter 8, Problem 22. Declare

PROCEDURE OrderCost (numFr: INTEGER): REAL

to compute the cost of the order from the number of Frisbees ordered. Implement a precondition for the function that the entered number of frisbees cannot be less than 0. Insure that the precondition is met in the calling procedure. If it is not met, set the entered numbers to 0 and the displayed cost of the order to $0.00.

8.   Write the schedule program of Chapter 6, Problem 19. Declare

PROCEDURE RegPeriod (lastIntl: CHAR): INTEGER

to compute the registration period from the user's last initial. Allow the user to input uppercase or lowercase letters. Implement a precondition for the function that lastIntl is alphabetic. Insure that the precondition is met in the calling procedure. If it is not met, output an error message in the message field.

9.   For Chapter 8, Problem 24, write the program to determine whether a given year is a leap year. Declare

PROCEDURE IsLeapYear (Year: INTEGER): BOOLEAN

to determine the leap year from the year. Implement a precondition for the function that the year entered cannot be less than 0. Insure that the precondition is met in the calling procedure. If it is not met, set the entered year to 0 and the displayed message to a blank field.

10.   For Chapter 10, Problem 35, write the program to raise a number to a power. Declare

PROCEDURE Power (base: REAL; expon: INTEGER): REAL

to compute the base raised to the exponent. There are no preconditions for the function. If the exponent is 0, return 1 for the function even if the base is 0.0.

11.   For Chapter 10, Problem 36, write the program to estimate the value of the base of the natural logarithms, *e*. Declare

PROCEDURE EstE (numTrm: INTEGER): REAL

to compute the estimate from the number of terms. Implement a precondition for the function that the number of terms numTrm cannot be less than 2. Insure that the precondition is met in the calling procedure. If it is not met, set the entered number to 2 and the displayed estimate to 2.

12. For Chapter 10, Problem 38, write the program to determine if a number is prime. Declare

PROCEDURE IsPrime (n: INTEGER): BOOLEAN

to determine whether the number is prime. Implement a precondition for the function that n cannot be less than 1. Insure that the precondition is met in the calling procedure. If it is not met, set the entered number to 1 and the displayed message to a blank field.

Chapter *14*

Random Numbers

Many events in our lives are random. When you enter a full parking lot, for example, you drive around until someone pulls out of a parking space that you can claim. The event of someone pulling out of a parking space is random. You do not know when or where it will occur. Consequently, you cannot predict exactly how long you will drive before you find a place.

Computers are useful in part because they can behave like the real world. For example, the popular flight-simulator computer programs can give the illusion of piloting an airplane. Large, sophisticated flight simulators are even used to train airline pilots. But how can a computer behave like the real world when some events in the real world are random? Every algorithm you have encountered thus far in this book has no random element. Given the input and the processing statements, you can always predict the output. With random events, you cannot predict the outcome.

A random number module

The solution to the problem of simulating random elements is to design an algorithm whose output appears random, even though it is not. The PboxRandom module contains four procedures that provide the client module the ability to behave in a seemingly random fashion, and thus to simulate random events in the real world. Figure 14.1 is the interface for the random number module PboxRandom.

DEFINITION PboxRandom;
   CONST
     seedLimit = 2147483647;

   PROCEDURE Int (n: INTEGER): INTEGER;
   PROCEDURE Randomize;
   PROCEDURE Real (): REAL;
   PROCEDURE SetSeed (n: INTEGER);

END PboxRandom.

Figure 14.1
The interface of module PboxRandom.

The algorithm that produces seemingly random numbers depends on maintaining an integer value known as a seed. Each time the importing module requests a random number the number is computed from the seed, and the next value of the seed is computed from the current value of the seed. Procedure SetSeed allows the importing module to set the value of the seed before requesting a sequence of random numbers. Its documentation is

```
PROCEDURE SetSeed (n: INTEGER);
Pre
0 < n   20
n < seedLimit   21
Post
The random number seed is initialized to n.
```

A precondition for SetSeed to work correctly is for n to be greater than zero and less than seedLimit. If the seed is set to the same value before requesting a second sequence of random numbers, the second sequence of numbers will be identical to the first sequence.

Procedure Randomize sets the seed to some random number not predictable by the importing module. It gets the value from a clock inside the computer that keeps track of the date to the nearest second. Its documentation is

```
PROCEDURE Randomize
Post
The random number seed is initialized to a value derived from the system clock.
Two calls to Randomize should be separated by more than one second to guarantee
different values of seed.
```

Randomize has no precondition. If you call Randomize twice, the values that the seed is set to will be different, because you will have called the procedure at different times.

Random reals

Figure 14.3 shows the dialog box for a module that illustrates the behavior of procedure PboxRandom.Real(), which is a function procedure. The dialog box has an input field for the user to enter a seed value. When the user clicks the button labeled Set Seed, procedure SetSeed executes with its parameter value equal to the value the user has entered in the dialog box. If the user sets the seed to 4831 as shown in the figure then clicks the button labeled Display, ten real numbers are printed to the Log as shown.

```
MODULE Pbox14A;
   IMPORT Dialog, PboxRandom, PboxStrings, StdLog;
   VAR
      d*: RECORD
         seed*: INTEGER;
      END;
```

Figure 14.2

A procedure that prints ten random real numbers to the Log.

```
PROCEDURE SetSeed*;
BEGIN
   IF (0 < d.seed) & (d.seed < PboxRandom.seedLimit) THEN
      PboxRandom.SetSeed(d.seed)
   ELSE
      StdLog.String("Seed must be greater than 0 and less than 2147483647."); StdLog.Ln
   END
END SetSeed;

PROCEDURE Randomize*;
BEGIN
   PboxRandom.Randomize
END Randomize;

PROCEDURE Display*;
VAR
   i: INTEGER;
   x: REAL;
   realString: ARRAY 8 OF CHAR;
BEGIN
   FOR i := 1 TO 10 DO
      StdLog.String("i = "); StdLog.Int(i);
      x := PboxRandom.Real();
      PboxStrings.RealToString(x, 5, 3, realString);
      StdLog.String("   x = "); StdLog.String(realString); StdLog.Ln
   END;
   StdLog.Ln
END Display;

BEGIN
   d.seed := 1
END Pbox14A.
```

Figure 14.2
Continued.

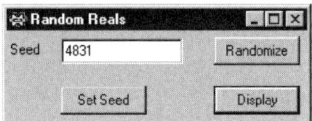

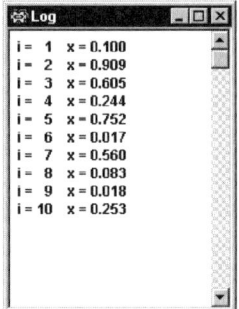

Figure 14.3
The output of procedure Display of Figure 14.2.

If the user clicks the Display button a second time without first setting the seed back to 4831 a different set of ten real values will be displayed as follows:

```
i =   1   x = 0.329
i =   2   x = 0.699
i =   3   x = 0.301
i =   4   x = 0.252
i =   5   x = 0.473
i =   6   x = 0.637
i =   7   x = 0.312
i =   8   x = 0.166
i =   9   x = 0.728
i =  10   x = 0.937
```

The program in Figure 14.2 implements the dialog box of Figure 14.3. The Set Seed and Randomize buttons simply call the corresponding procedures from module PboxRandom, with procedure SetSeed insuring that the precondition for procedure PboxRandom.SetSeed is not violated.

The Display button is linked to a procedure that executes a FOR loop ten times. Each time the body of the loop executes it calls procedure PboxRandom.Real(), which is a function procedure that returns a random real value between zero and one. Its documentation is

```
PROCEDURE Real (): REAL;
Post
Returns a random real between 0.0 and 1.0.
```

PboxRandom.Real has no precondition. Because it is a function, you must use it within another statement. Procedure Display uses it within the assignment statement

```
x := PboxRandom.Real()
```

This function call shows a curious requirement of procedure calls. When you call a proper procedure that has no parameters you omit the parentheses in the call. However, when you call a function procedure that has no parameters you must include the parentheses with nothing between them.

Function procedure calls with no parameters still need parentheses.

Random integers

For simulation purposes it is frequently useful to have a series of random integers rather than random reals. Figure 14.4 shows a dialog box that produces a sequence of ten seemingly random integers. It outputs a different list of random integers depending on the initial value for the seed.

The dialog box has an additional input field labeled Limit. In the figure, the user entered 10 for the limit before clicking on the Display button. That choice caused each random integer to have one of 10 values between 0 and 9.

Module Pbox14B in Figure 14.5 produces the output shown in Figure 14.4. As with the previous module, it consists mostly of simple calls to the procedures of PboxRandom.

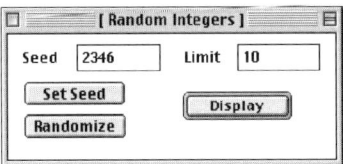

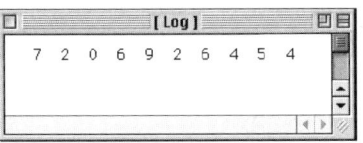

Figure 14.4
The output for the procedure
of Figure 14.5.

Figure 14.5
A procedure that prints ten
random integers to the Log.

```
MODULE Pbox14B;
    IMPORT Dialog, PboxRandom, PboxStrings, StdLog;
    VAR
        d*: RECORD
            seed*: INTEGER;
            limit*: INTEGER;
        END;

    PROCEDURE SetSeed*;
    BEGIN
        IF (0 < d.seed) & (d.seed < PboxRandom.seedLimit) THEN
            PboxRandom.SetSeed(d.seed)
        ELSE
            StdLog.String("Seed must be greater than 0 and less than 2147483647."); StdLog.Ln
        END
    END SetSeed;

    PROCEDURE Randomize*;
    BEGIN
        PboxRandom.Randomize
    END Randomize;

    PROCEDURE Display*;
    VAR
        i: INTEGER;
        m: INTEGER;
    BEGIN
        IF (0 < d.limit) & (d.limit < PboxRandom.seedLimit) THEN
            FOR i := 1 TO 10 DO
                m := PboxRandom.Int(d.limit);
                StdLog.Int(m)
            END;
            StdLog.Ln
        ELSE
            StdLog.String("Limit must be greater than 0 and less than 2147483647."); StdLog.Ln
        END
    END Display;

BEGIN
    d.seed := 1;
    d.limit := 0
END Pbox14B.
```

Procedure PboxRandom.Int is a function that returns an integer. Unlike PboxRandom.Real, it requires a parameter that specifies the range of possible integer values to be returned. The documentation for PboxRandom.Int is

```
PROCEDURE Int (n: INTEGER): INTEGER;
Pre
0 < n    20
n < seedLimit    21
Post
Returns a random integer in the range 0..n-1.
```

The precondition is that n is positive and less than seedLimit, which is checked by the calling procedure.

Example 14.1   Had the user entered 8 for the limit and set the value of seed to 2346 the sequence

6 2 0 5 7 1 5 3 4 3

would be printed on the Log. In this sequence, each random integer has one of eight values between 0 and 7. ∎

The REPEAT statement

When the programs we have written up until now have required loops we were always able to solve the problem at hand with either the WHILE loop or the FOR loop. One characteristic that is common to both of these loops is that the test is at the beginning of the loop. Hence, the body of a WHILE or FOR loop will not execute at all if the first test of the boolean condition is false. It is usually desirable to permit the possibility of the body never executing. For example, if you are processing a list of values in the focus window the body of the loop contains the statements necessary to process one value. Each time the body executes it processes another value. If the focus window has no values, you do not want the body of the loop to execute at all.

Although not as common, the situation sometimes occurs where you always want the body of the loop to execute at least one time. For these cases it would be more convenient to have the test for loop termination be at the end of the loop rather than at the beginning. Component Pascal provides such a loop in the form of the REPEAT statement. It differs from the WHILE statement in two respects. Not only is the test for termination at the end of the loop instead of the beginning, the loop terminates when the test condition is true rather than false. Figure 14.6 is a flowchart for the REPEAT statement

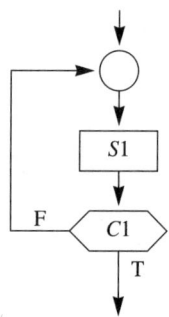

Figure 14.6
The flowchart for the
REPEAT statement.

```
REPEAT
     Statement1
UNTIL Condition1
```

which you should compare with Figure 10.1 for the WHILE statement. Statement1 always executes the first time regardless of Condition1. If Condition1 is false control branches up to the REPEAT and Statement1 executes again. The loop repeats until Condition1 is true.

Rolling a pair of dice

Figure 14.7 shows how module PboxRandom can be used to simulate a random event in the real world. Suppose you are playing a game with a pair of dice. Each die has six sides. When you roll one die, it will come to rest with some random integer between 1 and 6 showing on its top side. The figure shows a simulation of a player who rolls the dice until a total of 7 or 11 appears.

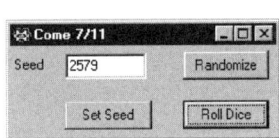

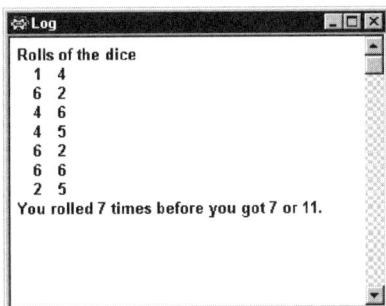

Figure 14.7
The output for the procedure in Figure 14.8.

You can simulate the toss of a single die by calling procedure PboxRandom.Int(6), which will return a random number between 0 and 5. If you add one to that value you will have a random number between 1 and 6. The program in Figure 14.8 simulates the rolls by executing a REPEAT statement. Each time the body of the loop executes it makes two calls to PboxRandom.Int and outputs the result of the rolls on the Log. The loop repeats until the sum of the numbers on the dice equals 7 or 11. You can see how convenient the REPEAT statement is in this situation, because you always want the body to execute at least one time. In the simulation, there is always at least one roll of the dice.

To simulate the toss of a coin, you would need random values with two possibilities, one for heads and one for tails.

Example 14.2 You could call

PboxRandom.Int(2)

and let 0 represent heads and 1 represent tails. The sequence of 20 calls will produce

0 0 1 0 0 0 0 1 0 0 1 1 0 1 1 1 0 1 0 1

with an initial value of 9735 for Seed. ∎

```
MODULE Pbox14C;
   IMPORT Dialog, PboxRandom, PboxStrings, StdLog;
   VAR
      d*: RECORD
         seed*: INTEGER;
      END;

   PROCEDURE SetSeed*;
   BEGIN
      IF (0 < d.seed) & (d.seed < PboxRandom.seedLimit) THEN
         PboxRandom.SetSeed(d.seed)
      ELSE
         StdLog.String("Seed must be greater than 0 and less than 2147483647."); StdLog.Ln
      END
   END SetSeed;

   PROCEDURE Randomize*;
   BEGIN
      PboxRandom.Randomize
   END Randomize;

   PROCEDURE RollDice*;
   VAR
      die1, die2: INTEGER;
      sum, numRolls: INTEGER;
   BEGIN
      numRolls := 0;
      StdLog.String("Rolls of the dice"); StdLog.Ln;
      REPEAT
         die1 := PboxRandom.Int(6) + 1;
         die2 := PboxRandom.Int(6) + 1;
         INC(numRolls);
         sum := die1 + die2;
         StdLog.Int(die1); StdLog.Int(die2); StdLog.Ln
      UNTIL (sum = 7) OR (sum = 11);
      StdLog.String("You rolled "); StdLog.Int(numRolls);
      StdLog.String(" times before you got 7 or 11."); StdLog.Ln
   END RollDice;

BEGIN
   d.seed := 1
END Pbox14C.
```

Figure 14.8
A procedure that simulates rolls of a pair of dice.

Random number generators

The random number generators in the preceding programs are all based on the general computation

$$z_{n+1} = az_n \text{ MOD } m$$

where $z_1, z_2, z_3, \ldots$ are the successive values of the seed, m is the modulus, and a is the multiplier with $2 < a < m$. Generators of this form are called Lehmer generators after the person who proposed them. To design a Lehmer generator you select values of m and a. An (m, a) Lehmer generator is one with a modulus of m and a multiplier of a.

Lehmer generators

Example 14.3 If you select values of $(17, 5)$ for (m, a), and the current value of seed z_n is 11, then the next seed is computed as

$$z_{n+1} = az_n \bmod m$$
$$= 5 \cdot 11 \bmod 17$$
$$= 55 \bmod 17$$
$$= 4$$

The 20 successive seed values from the $(17, 5)$ Lehmer generator are

11 4 3 15 7 1 5 8 6 13 14 2 10 16 12 9 11 4 3 15

with an initial seed of 11. ∎

Example 14.4 The $(17, 13)$ Lehmer generator produces the sequence

4 1 13 16 4 1 13 16 4 1 13

starting from 4. ∎

These examples show an unavoidable feature of all pseudorandom number generators. Because each value is computed from the previous value, once the initial value reappears in the sequence, the sequence must repeat. The period of the generator is the maximum number of values before the sequence begins to repeat. The $(17, 5)$ Lehmer generator has a period of 16, and the $(17, 13)$ generator has a period of 4.

A truly random sequence would contain no repeating cycles. But a pseudorandom sequence must repeat eventually, because there are only a finite number of values less than the modulus. The best you can do is to pick the modulus and multiplier to make the cycle as long as possible and to make the output appear random. The longest possible period with a modulus of m is $m - 1$. A generator with this period is known as a full-period generator.

Full-period generators

Computer scientists have devised a set of statistical tests that measure the randomness of proposed generators. They have investigated the pseudorandom sequences generated by different choices of m and a in an effort to discover the best generators. One standard Lehmer generator that is among the best known has (m, a) values of $(2147483647, 48271)$, which is a full-period generator with good pseudorandom behavior. The modulus m is a Mersenne prime equal to $2^{31} - 1$. This is the generator that is used in module PboxRandom in Figure 14.9.

```
MODULE PboxRandom;
  IMPORT Dates;
  CONST
    multiplier = 48271;
    modulus = 2147483647;
    quotient = modulus DIV multiplier;
    remainder = modulus MOD multiplier;
    seedLimit* = modulus;
  VAR
    seed: INTEGER;

  PROCEDURE ComputeNextSeed;
    VAR
      low, high: INTEGER;
  BEGIN
    low := seed MOD quotient;
    high := seed DIV quotient;
    seed := multiplier * low - remainder * high;
    IF seed <= 0 THEN
      seed := seed + modulus
    END
  END ComputeNextSeed;

  PROCEDURE Int* (n: INTEGER): INTEGER;
  BEGIN
    ASSERT(0 < n, 20);
    ASSERT(n < seedLimit, 21);
    ComputeNextSeed;
    RETURN SHORT(ENTIER(seed / modulus * n))
  END Int;

  PROCEDURE Randomize*;
    VAR
      date: Dates.Date;
      time: Dates.Time;
      i: INTEGER;
  BEGIN
    Dates.GetDate(date); Dates.GetTime(time);
    seed := 86400 * Dates.Day(date) + 3600 * time.hour + 60 * time.minute
      + time.second; (* Elapsed time this year in seconds *)
    FOR i := 0 TO 7 DO
      ComputeNextSeed
    END
  END Randomize;

  PROCEDURE Real* (): REAL;
  BEGIN
    ComputeNextSeed;
    RETURN seed / modulus
  END Real;
```

Figure 14.9
An implementation of the standard (2147483647, 48271) Lehmer random number generator.

```
PROCEDURE SetSeed* (n: INTEGER);
   VAR
      i: INTEGER;
BEGIN
   ASSERT(0 < n, 20);
   ASSERT(n < seedLimit, 21);
   seed := n MOD modulus;
   FOR i := 0 TO 7 DO
      ComputeNextSeed
   END
END SetSeed;

BEGIN
   Randomize
END PboxRandom.
```

Figure 14.9
Continued.

In PboxRandom, the constant multiplier corresponds to a, and the constant modulus corresponds to m in the equation $z_{n+1} = az_n$ MOD m. Module PboxRandom contains a global variable seed, which corresponds to z_n. It must be global, because its value must persist between calls of the procedures. Procedure ComputeNextSeed computes the next seed z_{n+1} from the current seed. A direct translation from the equation to Component Pascal would be one assignment statement,

```
seed := multiplier * seed MOD modulus
```

Instead, module ComputeNextSeed is implemented as

```
low := seed MOD quotient;
high := seed DIV quotient;
seed := multiplier * low - remainder * high;
IF seed <= 0 THEN
   seed := seed + modulus
END
```

where quotient and remainder are defined as the constants

```
quotient = modulus DIV multiplier;
remainder = modulus MOD multiplier;
```

and low and high are local variables. Why is this more complicated algorithm used instead of the more direct translation of a single assignment statement?

The problem is that the range of possible values for a Component Pascal integer is –2147483648 to 2147483647, which not so coincidentally is the modulus of the generator. When z_n gets close to 2147483647 and gets multiplied by 48271 before the MOD operation, the product lies outside the range and an overflow error occurs.

Fortunately, Schrage developed an algorithm (published in 1979) to implement a Lehmer generator in spite of the limited range of the integer type. Instead of multiplying the value of z_n by a, the algorithm computes two intermediate numbers from z_n, each of which is guaranteed to be smaller than m. It then combines these smaller numbers (low and high in procedure ComputeNextSeed) to compute z_{n+1} in a way that is guaranteed mathematically to be equivalent to multiplying z_n by a and then doing the MOD operation. The last section of this chapter provides a more detailed explanation of Schrage's algorithm.

Procedure Real works by computing the next integer value of seed and then converting that value to a real number between 0.0 and 1.0. Because every value of seed is between zero and the modulus, Real simply returns seed divided by the modulus.

Procedure Int is a bit more complicated. Suppose the calling procedure calls Int with value 5 for formal parameter n. Because seed has a value between 1 and the modulus minus 1, the quantity seed / modulus has a value between just above 0.0 and just below 1.0. Therefore, the quantity seed / modulus * n has a value between just above 0.0 and just below 5.0. The ENTIER function truncates this value, producing an integer value between 0 and 4. Figure 14.10 shows the transformation from the real number line to the integer number line.

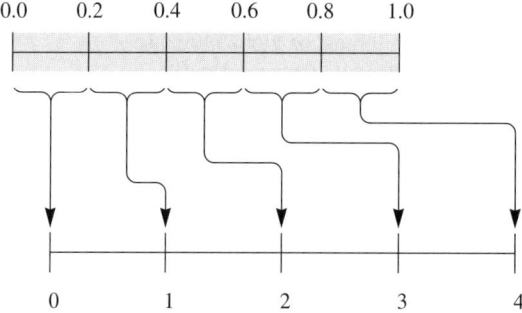

Figure 14.10
The transformation
PboxRandom.Int makes from
the real number line to the
integer number line.

Procedure Randomize sets the value of seed based on the date and time from the system clock. BlackBox provides a module named Dates that links to the clock in your computer. The module provides abstract data types (ADTs) Date and Time. There is a procedure named GetDate that gives the actual parameter the current date and another named GetTime that gives the actual parameter the current time of day. Function Day returns the day of the year, beginning with 1 for the first day of January, 2 for the second of January, and up to 365 for the last day of December (provided the current year is not a leap year). Randomize uses Day together with the current time to compute how many seconds has elapsed since the first of the year. The seed variable is initialized to that number of seconds, and then run through eight cycles of the Lehmer algorithm.

Although you can have fun trying to design your own generator, finding good values of m and a is not an easy task. If the modulus m is a prime number, then zero will never appear in the sequence, a desirable feature indeed. Even so, Example 14.4 shows that a prime modulus is no guarantee of a full-period generator. Actually, making a Lehmer generator full period is the easy part. It is much more difficult to find values of m and a that produce sequences that are sufficiently pseudorandom.

★ Schrage's algorithm

This section uses the following mathematical symbols corresponding to the quantities in module PboxRandom.

z = seed
a = multiplier
m = modulus
q = quotient
r = remainder
l = low
h = high

With these abbreviations, the computation of the quotient and remainder are

q = m div a
r = m mod a

and Schrage's algorithm in GCL is

$l := z$ mod q
$h := z$ div q
$z := a * l - r * h$
if $z \leq 0 \rightarrow z := z + m$
$\quad\text{[\!]}\quad z > 0 \rightarrow$ **skip**
fi

Before describing Schrage's algorithm in general, consider a specific computation of the next seed for the Lehmer generator of Example 14.3.

Example 14.5 For the $(17, 5)$ generator of Example 14.3, the constants q and r are computed as

q = m div a = 17 div 5 = 3
r = m mod a = 17 mod 5 = 2

and the computation of the next seed after 11 from Schrage's algorithm is

$l = z$ mod q = 11 mod 3 = 2
$h = z$ div q = 11 div 3 = 3
$z = a \cdot l - r \cdot h = 5 \cdot 2 - 2 \cdot 3 = 10 - 6 = 4$

The computation for z in Example 14.3 requires the intermediate computation of 5 times 11, which is 55. This computation for the same next seed requires 5 times 2, which is only 10. ∎

Example 14.6 To illustrate how the **if** statement works in Schrage's algorithm, consider the same (17, 5) generator to compute the next seed after 16.

$$l = z \bmod q = 16 \bmod 3 = 1$$
$$h = z \operatorname{div} q = 16 \operatorname{div} 3 = 5$$
$$z = a \cdot l - r \cdot h = 5 \cdot 1 - 2 \cdot 5 = 5 - 10 = -5$$

This time, –5 is less than or equal to 0. So, the **if** statement requires the addition of m as follows.

$$z = -5 + m = -5 + 17 = 12$$

which is the next seed after 16. ∎

The relation between the div and mod operators is based on the fact that x div y is the quotient when you divide x by y, and x mod y is the remainder when you divide x by y. The quotient and remainder are related to x and y by

$$x = y \cdot (\text{quotient}) + \text{remainder} \qquad 0 \le \text{remainder} < y$$

so that

$$x = y \cdot (x \operatorname{div} y) + x \bmod y \qquad 0 \le x \bmod y < y$$

Solving this equation for $x \bmod y$

$$x \bmod y = x - y(x \operatorname{div} y)$$

Schrage's algorithm is an alternate way of computing the quantity $az \bmod m$, which can be manipulated as follows.

$az \bmod m$
$= \quad \langle x \bmod y = x - y(x \operatorname{div} y) \rangle$
$\quad az - m(az \operatorname{div} m)$
$= \quad \langle \text{Add and subtract } m(z \operatorname{div} q) \rangle$
$\quad az - m(z \operatorname{div} q) + m(z \operatorname{div} q) - m(az \operatorname{div} m)$
$= \quad \langle \text{Factor out } m \rangle$
$\quad az - m(z \operatorname{div} q) + m(z \operatorname{div} q - az \operatorname{div} m)$
$= \quad \langle \text{Define } \gamma(z) = az - m(z \operatorname{div} q) \text{ and } \delta(z) = z \operatorname{div} q - az \operatorname{div} m \rangle$
$\quad \gamma(z) + m\delta(z)$

Schrage's algorithm is based on the fact that $\gamma(z)$ is the computation $a \cdot l - r \cdot h$, which is computed just before the **if** statement, and that the quantity $\delta(z)$ is either zero or one. If $\delta(z)$ is zero, the algorithm does not add anything to $\gamma(z)$. If $\delta(z)$ is one, the algorithm adds m to $\gamma(z)$.

To show that $\gamma(z)$ is the computation $a \cdot l - r \cdot h$, use the fact that q is the quotient and r is the remainder when you divide m by a. So, they are related by

$$m = q \cdot a + r \qquad 0 \le r < a$$

Therefore,

$\gamma(z)$

$= \qquad \langle \text{Definition of } \gamma(z) \rangle$

$\quad az - m(z \text{ div } q)$

$= \qquad \langle m = qa + r \rangle$

$\quad az - (qa + r)(z \text{ div } q)$

$= \qquad \langle \text{Algebra} \rangle$

$\quad a[z - q(z \text{ div } q)] - r(z \text{ div } q)$

$= \qquad \langle \text{General relation between div and mod, } x = y \cdot (x \text{ div } y) + x \text{ mod } y \rangle$

$\quad a(z \text{ mod } q) - r(z \text{ div } q)$

$= \qquad \langle \text{Computation from algorithm } l := z \text{ mod } q \text{ and } h := z \text{ div } q \rangle$

$\quad a \cdot l - r \cdot h$

To show that $\delta(z)$ is either zero or one, you must prove both an upper and lower bound, $-1 < \delta(z) < 2$. The lower bound $-1 < \delta(x)$ is straightforward to prove. It depends only on the fact that for positive integers x and y

$$x/y - 1 < x \text{ div } y \le x/y$$

where / represents real division.

Example 14.7 With $x = 25$ and $y = 4$, the inequalities state that

$$25/4 - 1 < 25 \text{ div } 4 \le 25/4$$

which is equivalent to

$$5.25 < 6 \le 6.25$$

With $x = 24$ and $y = 4$, the inequalities state that

$$24/4 - 1 < 24 \text{ div } 4 \le 24/4$$

which is equivalent to

$$5 < 6 \le 6$$ ∎

From the definition of $\delta(z)$, the lower bound is

$$-1 < z \text{ div } (m \text{ div } a) - az \text{ div } m$$

which is equivalent to

$$z \text{ div } (m \text{ div } a) > az \text{ div } m - 1$$

To prove this inequality, start with the left hand side.

$$
\begin{array}{cl}
& z \text{ div } (m \text{ div } a) \\
> & \langle x \text{ div } y > x/y - 1 \rangle \\
& z/(m \text{ div } a) - 1 \\
\geq & \langle x \text{ div } y \leq x/y \rangle \\
& z/(m/a) - 1 \\
= & \langle \text{Algebra} \rangle \\
& az/m - 1 \\
\geq & \langle x/y \geq x \text{ div } y \rangle \\
& az \text{ div } m - 1
\end{array}
$$

The upper bound $\delta(z) < 2$ is not so straightforward to prove and will not be given here. It depends on the fact that $z < m$, which must be true because m is the modulus of the computation for the seed. But, the upper bound also depends on one additional assumption, namely that $r < q$, which is equivalent to $m \bmod a < m \text{ div } a$. This additional assumption is a restriction on Schrage's algorithm. Without it, $\delta(z)$ can be greater than one, and the algorithm would need to add some multiple of m, not just m, to the original computation of $a \cdot l - r \cdot h$. The beauty of Schrage's algorithm is that if you are careful to choose (m, a) for your Lehmer generator so that $m \bmod a < m \text{ div } a$, the computation of $\delta(z)$ is not necessary. By choosing (m, a) so that $\delta(z)$ is zero or one you are guaranteed that the computation $a \cdot l - r \cdot h$ will either be correct or, if it is not positive, will need to be adjusted only by the addition of m.

Exercises

1.   When you toss two dice, the sum is one of the 11 numbers between 2 and 12. Would it be a good idea to simulate the toss of two dice by calling PboxRandom.Int once with a value of 11 for n? Explain.

2.   **(a)** What are the values of r and q for the random number generator in PboxRandom? Do these values satisfy the assumption for the upper bound of $\delta(z)$? **(b)** Answer part (a) for the random number generator of Example 14.3.

3.   Prove the upper bound $\delta(z) < 2$ for Schrage's algorithm for the implementation of the Lehmer random number generator. Send your proof to the author of this book and he

will include it in the next printed revision and credit you in the acknowledgments.

Problems

4. In the child's game of paper/scissors/rock, each child secretly chooses one of the objects. When the choices are revealed, paper loses to scissors, scissors loses to rock, and rock loses to paper. Equal choices are a draw. Design a dialog box that permits the user to set the seed or randomize it. Include a set of three radio buttons for the user to select paper, scissors, or rock. When the user clicks on a button labeled Play, compare her choice with a randomly selected object and print a message on the Log that states what the computer chose and who won, the computer or the user.

5. Add some output fields to the dialog box of Problem 4 to keep track of the score between the user and the computer. Each time the user plays a game, update the score. Include a button to reset the score to zero.

6. In the program of Listing 14.8, it took 8 rolls of the dice to get a 7 or 11. What do you think the average number of rolls would be? Can you calculate the average mathematically? Perform a computational experiment by writing a program to simulate 100 sequences of rolls. Design a dialog box for the user to set the seed or to randomize it. When the user clicks a button, simulate 100 sequences of rolls and output on the Log the fewest number of rolls (integer), the greatest number of rolls (integer) and the average number of rolls (real), to get a 7 or 11.

7. The game of craps is played as follows. Roll a pair of dice. If you get a 7 or 11 on the first roll you win, and if you get 2, 3 or 12 (called craps) you lose. Otherwise, the number you rolled becomes your point. You then keep rolling until you roll your point again, in which case you win, or until you roll a 7, in which case you lose. For example, a roll of 9, then 2, then 10, then 9 is a win, because the point (9 in this case) was rolled again before 7. As another example, a roll of 5, then 2, then 10, then 7 is a loss, because a 7 was rolled before the point (5 in this case).

Write a Component Pascal program to simulate a game of craps. Design a dialog box for the user to set the seed or randomize it. Include one other button for the user to press to play a game of craps. When the user clicks the button, output the result of the sequence of rolls for the game to the Log. In the end, announce if the user won or lost.

8. In the Problem 7, what do you think the probability of winning a game of craps is? Can you calculate it mathematically? Perform a computational experiment by writing a program to simulate 100 games. Design a dialog box that allows the user to set the seed or randomize it. When the user clicks a button, output to the Log the number of wins (integer) and losses (integer), and an estimate of the probability of winning a single game as the ratio (real) of the number of wins divided by the total number of games.

9. The local town drunk gets thoroughly inebriated, climbs to the roof of a skyscraper, steps out onto the center of the ledge, and begins to walk. Each time he takes a step, the probability is 1/3 that he will step to the right, 1/3 that he will step straight ahead, and 1/3 that he will step to the left. If he takes a total of two steps to the left, he will fall safely onto the roof. But if he takes a total of two steps to the right, he will fall to the sidewalk below. Write a program that simulates one walk of the drunk. Design a dialog box that allows the user to set the seed or randomize it. When the user clicks a button, output the random walk to the Log as shown below, with the roof on the left and the sidewalk on the right. At the end of the simulation announce which way he fell. After the program executes you can display the Log in Courier or some other monospaced font to make the spaces next to the x character distinct.

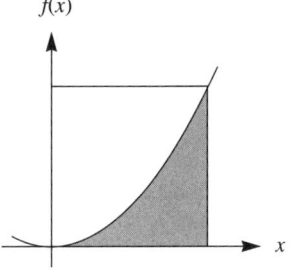

$f(x)$

```
(  x  )
(  x  )
(  x  )
(   x )
(    x )
(    x )
(     x )
(     x )
(      x)
He fell to the sidewalk.
```

(a) The area under the curve.

$f(x)$

10. In Problem 9, suppose a whole army of drunks repeat the walk many times. Guess the average length of a walk. That is, how many steps on the average does a drunk take before he falls off one way or the other? Now perform a computational experiment by writing a program to simulate 100 walks. Design a dialog box that allows the user to set the seed or randomize it. When the user clicks a button, output the number of times he fell to the sidewalk (integer), the number of times he fell onto the roof (integer), and the average number of steps he took (real) before falling. How close is the computed value to your guess?

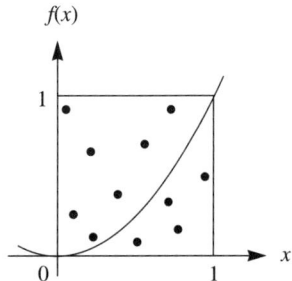

The ideas in this problem form the basis of an important mathematical technique called the Monte Carlo method. The method has application to problems in statistical physics. The "army" of drunks is called an ensemble, and the average is called an ensemble average.

(b) Eleven random points for estimating the area.

Figure 14.11

The function $f(x) = x^2$ for Problem 11.

11. Figure 14.11(a) shows a graph of the equation $y = x^2$ between the points $x = 0.0$ and $x = 1.0$. The square of height 1.0 between these points has area 1.0. You can estimate the area under the curve by picking several points at random inside the square and counting the points that are below the curve. The area is approximately the number of points below the curve divided by the total number of points. For example, the estimate from Figure 14.11(b) is $4/11$ or 0.3636.

Design a dialog box that requests the user to enter a seed and the number of random points, then outputs the estimate of the area in the dialog box. Obtain the coordinates of a single point by calling procedure PboxRandom.Real twice, once for the x-coordinate and once for the y-coordinate. What do you think is the relationship between the number of random points and the accuracy of the estimate? Can you illustrate that relationship with your program?

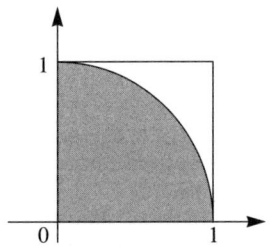

12. You can use a random number generator to compute the value of π based on the fact that the area of a circle is πr^2. Figure 14.12 shows the area of one fourth of a circle with radius 1.0 whose area is $\pi(1.0)^2/4 = \pi/4$. Write a program that asks the user to enter a seed and the number of random points, then computes the estimate of the area using the technique of Problem 11. Output the estimate of π as four times the area. What do you think is the relationship between the number of random points and the accuracy of the estimate? Can you illustrate that relationship with your program?

Figure 14.12

The quarter circle to estimate π for Problem 12.

13. Figure 10.7 shows an algorithm for finding the largest value from a list of values in the focus window. It contains the loop

```
WHILE ~sc.eot DO
   IF num > largest THEN
      largest := num
   END
   sc.ScanInt(num)
END
```

(a) If the numbers in the focus window are random, approximately what percentage of the executions of the loop do you suppose would include the statement largest := num? Explain the reasoning behind your supposition. (b) After answering part (a), write a program in Component Pascal to test your supposition. Modify the algorithm to take the numbers from a random number generator instead of from the focus window. Design a dialog box with seven controls—a field for the user to input a seed, a button to set the seed, a button to randomize the seed, a field for the user to input the number of random integers to process, a button to find the maximum of the random numbers, an output field to display the largest integer found, and an output field to display the percentage of the number of times that execution of the body of the loop includes the statement largest := num. When the user presses the button to find the maximum integer, invoke PboxRandom.Int with an actual parameter of one billion (1,000,000,000). That is, you will be testing to find the maximum of a set of integers, each one of which is between one and one billion. (c) Experiment with your program trying out various values of the seed and of the number of integers to test. Is your supposition from part (a) close to the results from your program? If not, explain how your reasoning must be modified to account for the results of your program.

14. Write a program that outputs to the Log all the values of the multiplier a that will produce a full-period Lehmer generator with a modulus m of 1021. Remember that the multiplier is restricted to $2 < a < m$.

Chapter *15*

One-Dimensional Arrays

Recall that abstraction involves the suppression of detail. The collection of a group of items is generally the first step toward abstraction. The previous chapter presented proper procedures and function procedures, which are collections of program statements executed when one procedure calls another. Declaring a procedure creates a new statement that the calling procedure can use. One advantage of such declarations is that if different people design the calling procedure and the called procedure, the person who writes the calling procedure does not need to know about the collection of statements in the called procedure. This is particularly true when the called procedure is in a different module from the calling procedure. The collection of statements is a step toward program abstraction.

Program abstraction

We have already seen that records are collections of values, each of which may have different types. Arrays are also a collection of values. Unlike records, the values in an array must all be the same type. For example, it is possible for a record to have both an integer field and a real field. However, an array of integer values cannot contain a real value. In this chapter, you will learn how to declare and manipulate arrays. In the same way that the collection of statements is a step towards program abstraction, the collection of values is a step toward data abstraction.

Data abstraction

Array input/output

Figure 15.1 shows the input and output windows of a program that displays the input values in reverse order. Procedure ReverseReals in Figure 15.2 inputs four values from the focus window and outputs them in reverse order in the new window. It declares list to be an array of four real values. The procedure is invoked by a menu selection not shown in the figure.

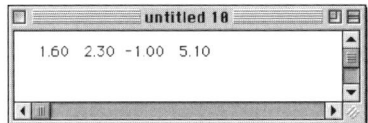

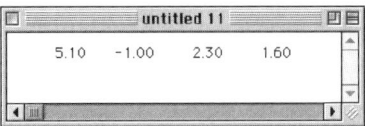

Figure 15.1
The input and output for the procedure of Figure 15.2.

```
MODULE Pbox15A;
   IMPORT TextModels, TextViews, Views, TextControllers, PboxMappers;

   TYPE
      Real4 = ARRAY 4 OF REAL;

   PROCEDURE ReverseReals*;
      VAR
         mdIn: TextModels.Model;
         cn: TextControllers.Controller;
         sc: PboxMappers.Scanner;
         list: Real4;
         i: INTEGER;
         mdOut: TextModels.Model;
         vw: TextViews.View;
         fm: PboxMappers.Formatter;
   BEGIN
      cn := TextControllers.Focus();
      IF cn # NIL THEN
         mdIn := cn.text;
         sc.ConnectTo(mdIn);
         FOR i := 0 TO 3 DO
            sc.ScanReal(list[i])
         END;
         mdOut := TextModels.dir.New();
         fm.ConnectTo(mdOut);
         FOR i := 3 TO 0 BY -1 DO
            fm.WriteReal(list[i], 8, 2)
         END;
         vw := TextViews.dir.New(mdOut);
         Views.OpenView(vw)
      END
   END ReverseReals;

END Pbox15A.
```

Figure 15.2

A program to reverse four real values in the focus window.

You could reverse the four values by declaring four variables, say list1, list2, list3, and list4. You could read them in with four sc.ScanReal statements and write them out with four fm.WriteReal statements. The disadvantage of this approach is that it is not feasible for large data sets. Would you like to write a program with this approach to reverse 100 values?

In this procedure, list is declared to have type Real4, which is declared to be

ARRAY 4 OF REAL

The declaration means that the array variable, list, contains four real values indexed from 0 to 3. The four values are referred to by list[0], list[1], list[2], and list[3]. An element of the array, say list[2], is also called a subscripted variable because of its similarity to subscripted variables in mathematics. In mathematical notation, if a variable

x is subscripted, you refer to its values by x_0, x_1, x_2, and x_3. Component Pascal syntax calls for the subscripts to be enclosed in square brackets. An array variable is also called a vector. An individual compartment that contains a value is called a cell of the array. Figure 15.3 shows the array list and the variable i allocated on the run-time stack. To keep the figure simple, the MVC variables are not shown.

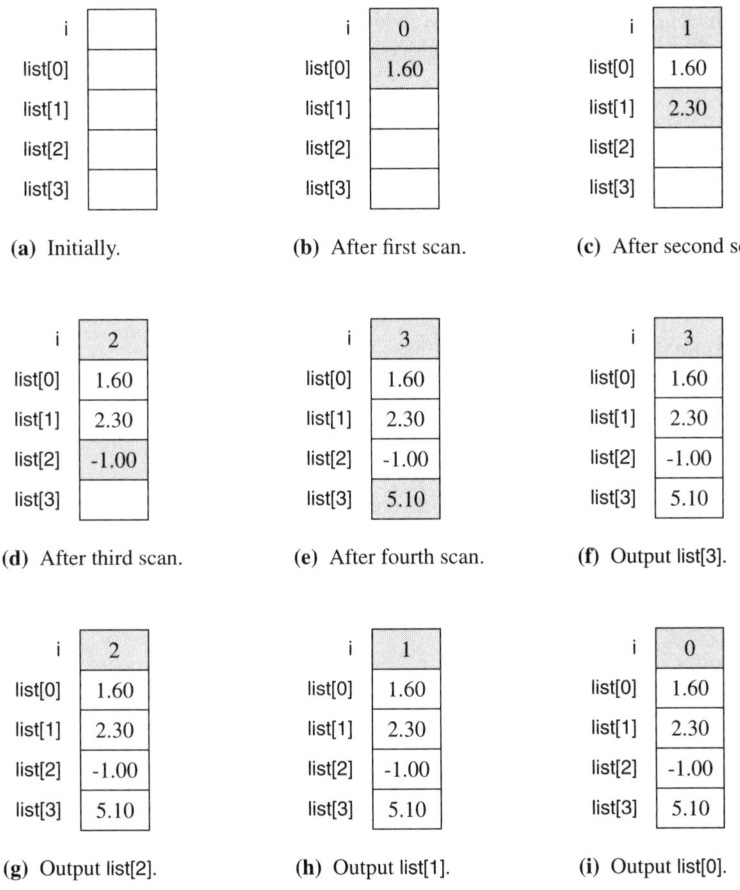
i
list[0]
list[1]
list[2]
list[3]
(a) Initially.
i 0
list[0] 1.60
list[1]
list[2]
list[3]
(b) After first scan.
i 1
list[0] 1.60
list[1] 2.30
list[2]
list[3]
(c) After second scan.
i 2
list[0] 1.60
list[1] 2.30
list[2] -1.00
list[3]
(d) After third scan.
i 3
list[0] 1.60
list[1] 2.30
list[2] -1.00
list[3] 5.10
(e) After fourth scan.
i 3
list[0] 1.60
list[1] 2.30
list[2] -1.00
list[3] 5.10
(f) Output list[3].
i 2
list[0] 1.60
list[1] 2.30
list[2] -1.00
list[3] 5.10
(g) Output list[2].
i 1
list[0] 1.60
list[1] 2.30
list[2] -1.00
list[3] 5.10
(h) Output list[1].
i 0
list[0] 1.60
list[1] 2.30
list[2] -1.00
list[3] 5.10
(i) Output list[0].

Figure 15.3
A trace of procedure ReverseReals in Figure 15.2.

The program works by setting up the usual MVC variables to scan from the model shown in the focus window. The first FOR loop

```
FOR i := 0 TO 3 DO
```

initializes i to 0. Then, the first time through the loop

```
sc.ScanReal(list[i])
```

scans the first value 1.60 from the text model into list[0], because the current value of i is 0. Figure 15.3(b) shows the result of the scan. The next time through the loop i has value 1, so the effect of

sc.ScanReal(list[i])

is to scan the next value from the text model into list[1] as Figure 15.3(c) shows. Similarly, the third and fourth values are scanned into list[2] and list[3].

The second FOR loop outputs the values in reverse order to the text model for the output window. It initializes i to 3 and executes

fm.WriteReal(list[i], 8, 2)

which has the effect of writing list[3] to the output model, because the current value of i is 3. Notice in Figure 15.3(f), that the values maintain their order in the list array. The next time through the loop i has value 2, so the statement

fm.WriteReal(list[i], 8, 2)

has the effect of writing list[2] to the text model as Figure 15.3(g) shows. Similarly, list[1] and list[0] are written without having their order altered in the array.

Using arrays

You must remember that an array like list contains a collection of values, not just one value. To assign a value to a cell of an array you must specify which cell gets the value.

Example 15.1   The statement

list := -1.0

where list is declared as it is in procedure ReverseReals is illegal, even though –1.0 has type real. The problem is that the cell of list is not specified. On the other hand,

list[2] := -1.0

is legal. The assignment statement gives the value of –1.0 to the third cell of list.   ∎

The index of list in procedure ReverseReals has a range of 0 to 3. During execution, the computer checks whether the index is within the allowable range whenever a reference to a cell of an array is made. If it is not, a trap occurs with an appropriate error message.

Example 15.2   If you erroneously change the second FOR statement in Figure 15.2 to

FOR i := 4 TO 0 BY -1 DO

you will get a trap when the statement

fm.WriteReal(list[i], 8, 2)

executes because the first time through the loop i is not between 0 and 3. Figure 15.4 shows the top part of the trap window that results from the error. You can see in part (a) that the values of the list are not visible because they are hidden in the collapsed fold. Expanding the fold as in part (b) shows the value of the array. ∎

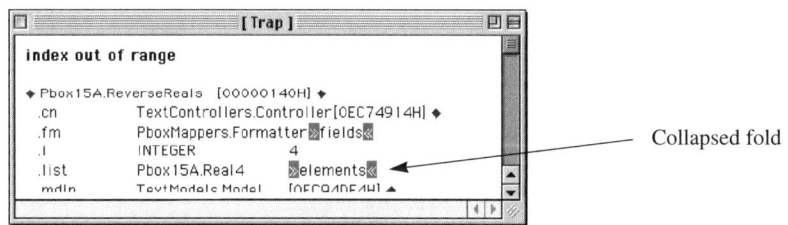

Figure 15.4
The trap window when your index is out of range.

Collapsed fold

(a) The values of list are hidden in the fold.

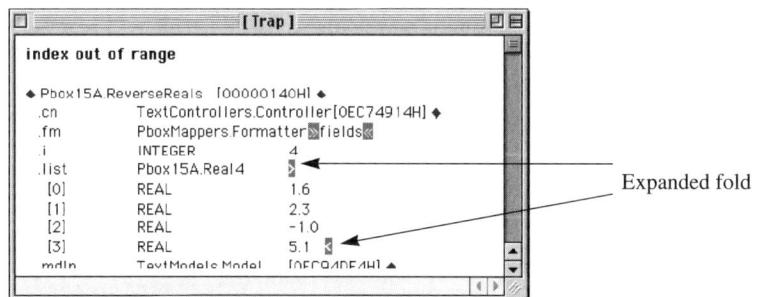

Expanded fold

(b) Expanding the fold to see the values of list.

The index is not limited to a constant or a single variable. It can be any arbitrary expression as long as the expression has type integer.

Example 15.3 The assignment statement

list[3 * i - 5] := 1.6

gives the value of 1.6 to list[1] if i has the value of 2. ∎

Example 15.4 Suppose list gets the values

1.6   2.3   −1.0   5.1

from the model behind the focus window, as in procedure ReverseReals. The code fragment

```
FOR i := 2 TO 5 DO
    fm.WriteReal(list[i MOD 4], 6, 1)
END
```

would output

-1.0 5.1 1.6 2.3

These are the values of list[2], list[3], list[0], and list[1]. ∎

Memory allocation for arrays

If you do not know exactly how many data items will be in the array, you must allocate more space than you would reasonably expect. Figure 15.5 shows the input and output windows for a program that performs processing similar to that in Figure 15.2. The figure shows the output window displaying seven values from the focus window in reverse order, but the program will work for up to 1024 values in the focus window. Procedure ReverseReals in Figure 15.6 shows the technique. It allocates storage for 1024 real values in list, even though the focus window may contain fewer values.

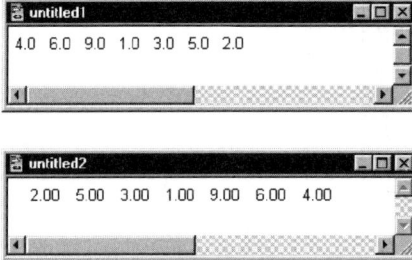

Figure 15.5
The input and output for the procedure of Figure 15.6.

The trace of the run-time stack for this program would be very large indeed. It would have 1024 cells just for list, including list[0], list[1], and so on, to list[1023]. In this example the focus window contained only seven real values. That means that the program did not use 1017 values. They remained undefined throughout the program execution and represent wasted memory.

The program inputs the values into the real array with procedure ScanRealVector from module PboxMappers. The documentation for ScanRealVector is

PROCEDURE (VAR s: Scanner) **ScanRealVector** (OUT v: ARRAY OF REAL; OUT numltm: INTEGER), NEW
Pre
s is connected to a text model.   20
Sequences of characters scanned represent in-range real or integer values.   21
Number of values in text model <= LEN(v).   Index out of range.
Post
v gets all the values scanned up to the end of the text model to which s is connected.
numltm gets the number of integer values scanned.
The values are stored at v[0..numltm - 1].

Both v and numltm are called by result. That means that they each refer to their corresponding actual parameter, and that their initial values when the procedure is called can be considered undefined. You can see that this is the case, because neither list nor numItems has been given any values before the call to ScanRealVector. The effect of the procedure is to change the values of both list and numItems. Scan-RealVector is programmed to scan real values from a text model, skipping over any spaces, tabs, or line characters, until the end of the text is reached. It puts the values in vector v and in the process counts the number of values scanned and puts the value of the count in numltm. In the end, the values have been placed in v[0] to v[numltm - 1].

The type, ARRAY 1024 OF REAL, in the declaration of the array specifies a fixed number of elements in the array. You may be tempted to circumvent the problem of wasted memory by declaring list as

list: ARRAY numItems OF REAL   *An illegal declaration*

but this declaration is illegal because numItems is a variable. You must have a constant expression in the declaration of the size of your array. Storage allocation for variables in the procedure occurs before the first statement executes. The procedure cannot wait until numItems gets a value from

sc.ScanRealVector(list, numItems)

before allocating memory.

Open arrays

It is legal to declare a formal array parameter v with a fixed number of cells. For example, procedure ScanRealVector could have been declared as

(VAR s: Scanner) **ScanRealVector** (OUT v: ARRAY 1024 OF REAL; OUT numltm: INTEGER)

instead of as

(VAR s: Scanner) **ScanRealVector** (OUT v: ARRAY OF REAL; OUT numltm: INTEGER)

Both of these declarations are legal.

```
MODULE Pbox15B;
   IMPORT TextModels, TextViews, Views, TextControllers, PboxMappers;

   TYPE
      Real1024 = ARRAY 1024 OF REAL;

   PROCEDURE ReverseReals*;
      VAR
         mdIn: TextModels.Model;
         cn: TextControllers.Controller;
         sc: PboxMappers.Scanner;
         list: Real1024;
         numItems: INTEGER;
         i: INTEGER;
         mdOut: TextModels.Model;
         vw: TextViews.View;
         fm: PboxMappers.Formatter;
   BEGIN
      cn := TextControllers.Focus();
      IF cn # NIL THEN
         mdIn := cn.text;
         sc.ConnectTo(mdIn);
         sc.ScanRealVector(list, numItems);
         mdOut := TextModels.dir.New();
         fm.ConnectTo(mdOut);
         FOR i := numItems - 1 TO 0 BY -1 DO
            fm.WriteReal(list[i], 6, 2)
         END;
         vw := TextViews.dir.New(mdOut);
         Views.OpenView(vw)
      END
   END ReverseReals;

END Pbox15B.
```

Figure 15.6
A program to reverse any number of real values.

If the server module **PboxMappers** were designed with v having 1024 cells, as in the first declaration above, the program in Figure 15.6 would compile and run with no apparent difference to the user. An array specified without the number of elements it contains, as in the specification of v in the second declaration above, is known as an open array. A formal parameter list is one of the few places you can specify an open array. The advantage of specifying an open array in the formal parameter list of a procedure is that it makes the procedure more general than if you commit to an array of fixed size.

The advantage of open arrays

Example 15.5 Suppose the server module **PboxMappers** were designed with 1024 cells for v, as in the first declaration above. If you wanted the program of Figure 15.6 to process up to 2048 real values by declaring type

Real2048 = ARRAY 2048 OF REAL;

and variable

list: Real2048;

it would not compile. There would be a type conflict between actual parameter list, which would be an ARRAY 2048 OF REAL, and formal parameter v, which would be an ARRAY 1024 OF REAL. Because v is declared as an open array in procedure ScanRealVector, however, the procedure will work correctly regardless of the number of cells allocated for the actual parameter. ∎

One of the preconditions of procedure ScanRealVector is

Number of values in text model <= LEN(v).   Index out of range.

LEN is a built-in Component Pascal function that returns the length of an array regardless of the number of cells that are occupied by meaningful values. It is particularly useful in procedures that have open arrays in their parameter lists.

The LEN function

Example 15.6   The value of LEN(v) in procedure ScanRealVector is 1024 when it is called from procedure ReverseReals in Figure 15.6. ∎

In the program of Figure 15.6, if there are no more than 1024 values in the text model then numItems will get a value less than LEN(v). The program will execute with no ill effects. It will simply have some unused cells in the list array. But, if there are more than 1024 values in the text model the scanner will trap with an "index out of range" error message.

Wasted memory is a common problem in array processing and does not have a simple solution. With some programs you will know ahead of time exactly how much data must be processed and exactly how large to declare your array. With other programs, however, you will not know. In that case, you must decide what is reasonable for the problem at hand and for the main memory size of your computer.

A problem-solving technique

One skill you should develop is the ability to manipulate the elements of an array. Typically you will be confronted with a problem that requires the elements to be rearranged somehow, and you must write the statements that perform the re-arrangement. *Analysis* is determining the manipulation from given program statements, while *design* is determining the program statements from a given desired manipulation.

Analysis versus design

There are two approaches to program design problems. One approach is to go from the specific to the general. This technique involves generalizing from a small number of known patterns to a single general pattern. Another approach is to derive the general pattern using the methods of formal logic. These two approaches are at opposite ends of the inductive/deductive reasoning spectrum. Practitioners of each approach sometimes disparage the opposite approach. Both, however, are valuable and should be mastered by the professional software designer. The usual practice is to use the generalization technique to determine the code initially, then use formal methods to prove that what you have written is correct.

Here are the steps of the generalizing technique:

- *Step 1*—Write some specific initial values for the array in a trace.

- *Step 2*—Perform the manipulation by changing the values in the trace, one at a time.

- *Step 3*—For each change, write a specific assignment statement that will produce the change.

- *Step 4*—Discover a pattern in the indices of the assignment statements you wrote. Generalize from the specific statements to a loop containing arrays with variables in the subscripts.

The last step is usually the hardest.

The following discussion presents a series of problems that require you to design a program or code fragment that manipulates the values of an array. Each problem is developed to show how you might use the generalizing technique.

The rotate left problem

The first illustration of this problem-solving technique is to rotate the elements of an array to the left. The leftmost element will rotate to the rightmost spot. For example, suppose list and numItems are declared as in procedure ReverseReals in Figure 15.6, numItems has the value 4, and list has the values

5.0   –2.3   8.0   0.1

Then, after the rotation, list should have the values

–2.3   8.0   0.1   5.0

Now you apply the four steps of the problem-solving technique.

Steps 1 and 2—In these steps, you write the values in a table and perform the changes one at a time.

	list[0]	list[1]	list[2]	list[3]
Original values	5.0	–2.3	8.0	0.1
Change list[0]	–2.3	–2.3	8.0	0.1
Change list[1]	–2.3	8.0	8.0	0.1
Change list[2]	–2.3	8.0	0.1	0.1
Change list[3]	–2.3	8.0	0.1	5.0

Step 3—For each change, you must write a specific assignment statement that will produce the change.

	list[0]	list[1]	list[2]	list[3]
Original values	5.0	−2.3	8.0	0.1
list[0] := list[1]	−2.3	−2.3	8.0	0.1
list[1] := list[2]	−2.3	8.0	8.0	0.1
list[2] := list[3]	−2.3	8.0	0.1	0.1
list[3] := ?	−2.3	8.0	0.1	?

But here you have a problem. You want list[3] to get the old value of list[0]. But if you write

list[3] := list[0]

then list[3] will get the current value of list[0], which is −2.3, not 5.0. The solution is to employ a temporary real variable, say temp, which saves the old value of list[0]. Here is a revised trace:

	temp	list[0]	list[1]	list[2]	list[3]
Original values		5.0	−2.3	8.0	0.1
temp :=list[0]	5.0	5.0	−2.3	8.0	0.1
list[0] := list[1]	5.0	−2.3	−2.3	8.0	0.1
list[1] := list[2]	5.0	−2.3	8.0	8.0	0.1
list[2] := list[3]	5.0	−2.3	8.0	0.1	0.1
list[3] := temp	5.0	−2.3	8.0	0.1	5.0

Step 4—In this step, you discover a pattern in the indices of the assignment statements you wrote. The pattern in the indices just presented is

```
0   1
1   2
2   3
```

The index on the right of the assignment statement is one more than the index on the left. So the generalization is

```
temp := list[0];
FOR i := 0 TO 2 DO
    list[i] := list[i + 1]
END;
list[3] := temp
```

in the case where the array has four elements. In the more general case where there are numItems values, the statements are

```
temp := list[0];
FOR i := 0 TO numItems - 2 DO
    list[i] := list[i + 1]
END;
list[numItems - 1] := temp
```

```
MODULE Pbox15C;
   IMPORT TextModels, TextViews, Views, TextControllers, PboxMappers;

   TYPE
      Real1024 = ARRAY 1024 OF REAL;

   PROCEDURE RotateLeft (VAR v: ARRAY OF REAL; numItm: INTEGER);
      VAR
         i: INTEGER;
         temp: REAL;
   BEGIN
      ASSERT((0 <= numItm) & (numItm <= LEN(v)), 20);
      IF numItm > 1 THEN
         temp := v[0];
         FOR i := 0 TO numItm - 2 DO
            v[i] := v[i + 1]
         END;
         v[numItm - 1] := temp
      END
   END RotateLeft;

   PROCEDURE ProcessRotation*;
      VAR
         mdIn: TextModels.Model;
         cn: TextControllers.Controller;
         sc: PboxMappers.Scanner;
         list: Real1024;
         numItems: INTEGER;
         mdOut: TextModels.Model;
         vw: TextViews.View;
         fm: PboxMappers.Formatter;
   BEGIN
      cn := TextControllers.Focus();
      IF cn # NIL THEN
         mdIn := cn.text;
         sc.ConnectTo(mdIn);
         sc.ScanRealVector(list, numItems);
         mdOut := TextModels.dir.New();
         fm.ConnectTo(mdOut);
         fm.WriteRealVector(list, numItems, 6, 2);
         RotateLeft(list, numItems);
         fm.WriteLn; fm.WriteLn;
         fm.WriteRealVector(list, numItems, 6, 2);
         vw := TextViews.dir.New(mdOut);
         Views.OpenView(vw)
      END
   END ProcessRotation;

END Pbox15C.
```

Figure 15.7
A program with a procedure to rotate the elements in an array.

Figure 15.7 shows this algorithm implemented in a procedure called RotateLeft. Figure 15.8 shows the input and output windows of the program. It generalizes the problem to work for any number of elements, with seven elements shown in the figure.

Figure 15.8
The input and output for the procedure of Figure 15.7.

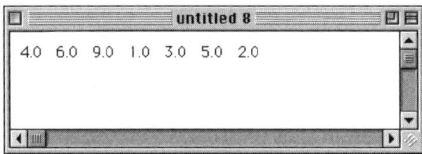

Procedure RotateLeft has formal parameter v that corresponds to actual parameter list and formal parameter numItm that corresponds to actual parameter numItems. The precondition for RotateLeft to work correctly is that numItm have a value between 0 and LEN(v). As is the case with procedure ScanRealVector, v is an open array so that procedure RotateLeft could work with an array of any length.

Example 15.7 Suppose you have two types declared as follows.

```
TYPE
    Real128 = ARRAY 128 OF REAL;
    Real1024 = ARRAY 1024 OF REAL;
```

and two local arrays

```
VAR
    myArray: Real128;
    yourArray: Real1024;
```

If you want to rotate each array and you do not write your procedure with an open array, you must write *two* procedures, one with declaration

PROCEDURE MyRotateLeft (VAR v: Real128; numItm: INTEGER)

that you call with

MyRotateLeft (myArray, myNumItems)

and one with declaration

PROCEDURE YourRotateLeft (VAR v: Real1024; numItm: INTEGER)

that you call with

YourRotateLeft (yourArray, yourNumItems)

However, if you have the open array in the formal parameter list you only need to write *one* procedure as in Figure 15.7 and call it with either array as

```
RotateLeft (myArray, myNumItems);
RotateLeft (YourArray, yourNumItems)
```

It is usually best to not commit to a fixed array length when you design a procedure to process an array. Most server modules provide procedures with open array parameters as does ScanRealVector as shown on page 319. Because v is an open array, your client module can call it with an actual parameter having any length you desire. Because of the advantage of using open arrays you should get in the habit of using them in the formal parameter lists of your procedures.

Call by constant reference

The program uses the procedure WriteRealVector from PboxMappers. Here is its documentation.

```
PROCEDURE (VAR f: Formatter) WriteRealVector (IN v: ARRAY OF REAL; numItm, minWidth, dec: INTEGER),
    NEW
Pre
f is connected to a text model.    20
numItm <= LEN(v).    Index out of range.
Post
The first numItm values of v are written to the text model to which f is connected,
each with a field width of minWidth and dec places past the decimal point. If minWidth
is too small to contain a value of v it expands to accommodate the value.
```

The calling procedure supplies WriteRealVector with the vector to write v, the number of items in v to write numItm, the field width minWidth, and the number of places past the decimal point dec. The designation IN signifies call by constant reference.

The purpose of call by constant reference is identical to the purpose of call by value. Namely, the calling procedure desires to give a value to the called procedure. In that sense we can revise Figure 12.17 to include call by constant reference as shown in Figure 15.9

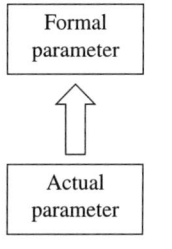

(a) Call by value and call by constant reference.

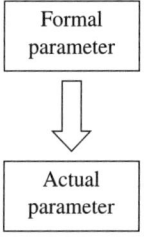

(b) Call by result.

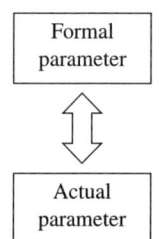

(c) Call by reference.

Figure 15.9
The flow of information for four different calling mechanisms, including call by constant reference.

If call by constant reference has the same effect as call by value, then why does Component Pascal provide both calling mechanisms? The answer is efficiency. In fact, procedure WriteRealVector would work if v were called by value. However, remember that the array corresponding to the actual parameter has 1024 elements. In call by value, the formal parameter gets the value of the actual parameter. Hence, all 1024 elements would be pushed onto the run-time stack when the procedure is called. That action would take much time and would consume much space on the stack. It would be more efficient if v were called by reference. Then only a single cell on the run-time stack would be necessary, and it would contain a reference to the actual parameter.

But the purpose of call by reference is for information to flow in both directions, as shown in Figure 15.9(c). In procedure WriteRealVector, the information is only supposed to flow in one direction as in Figure 15.9(a). So in call by constant reference, Component Pascal pushes a reference to the actual parameter on the run-time stack. At the same time the compiler forbids the called procedure to change the value of the formal parameter. The result is to achieve the effect of call by value but with the efficiency of call by reference.

Now you may be asking, If call by constant reference has the efficiency advantage of call by reference and the effect of call by value, why have call by value in the first place? The answer is twofold. First, call by value has the advantage that the actual parameter can be any expression of the proper type. It need not be a single variable. In call by constant reference the actual parameter must be a single variable.

Figure 15.10
Guidelines for using the four parameter calling mechanisms.

	Integers, reals, booleans, pointers, short arrays and short records	Long arrays and long records
Call by value Default	Common. Use when the actual parameter should *not* change. Actual parameter can be an expression.	Not common. Inefficient procedure call. Use call by constant reference instead.
Call by constant reference IN	Not common (illegal for all types except arrays and records). Inefficient procedure execution. Use call by value instead.	Common. Use when the actual parameter should *not* change. Actual parameter must be a variable.
Call by result OUT	Common. Use when the actual parameter *should* change and its initial value is *undefined*. Actual parameter must be a variable.	
Call by reference VAR	Common. Use when the actual parameter *should* change and its initial value is *defined*. Actual parameter must be a variable.	

Second, the efficiency in call by constant reference is in the procedure call. It is actually less efficient after the procedure call and during execution of the called procedure. It is therefore more efficient in total to use call by value for integers, reals, booleans, pointers (described later in this book), and short arrays and records, and to use call by constant reference for long arrays and records. Figure 15.10 summarizes all these ideas for the four calling mechanisms.

Finding the largest value

The next illustration of this problem-solving technique involves finding the largest value of an array. For example, in the function procedure

PROCEDURE Maximum (IN v: ARRAY OF REAL; numItm: INTEGER): REAL;

if v has the values

5.0   –2.3   8.0   0.1

and numItm has the value 4, then the procedure should return the value 8.0.

The basic idea is the same as the algorithm to find the largest value in the focus window. That algorithm saves the largest value found so far in a variable. Each time the loop executes, the algorithm scans a new value from the model displayed in the focus window. If the value scanned is greater than the largest found to that point, the algorithm updates the variable with the newly scanned value. The algorithm we will now discuss uses the same logic, but it compares largest with the items of the array one at a time.

The first three steps of the problem-solving technique require you to write some specific initial values for the array in a trace table. Then change the values one at a time, and for each change, write a specific assignment statement that will produce the change. The following trace shows one possibility.

	largest	v[0]	v[1]	v[2]	v[3]
Original values		5.0	–2.3	8.0	0.1
largest :=v[0]	5.0	5.0	–2.3	8.0	0.1
IF v[1] > largest THEN	5.0	5.0	–2.3	8.0	0.1
update largest	5.0	5.0	–2.3	8.0	0.1
IF v[2] > largest THEN	5.0	5.0	–2.3	8.0	0.1
update largest	8.0	5.0	–2.3	8.0	0.1
IF v[3] > largest THEN	8.0	5.0	–2.3	8.0	0.1
update largest	8.0	5.0	–2.3	8.0	0.1

You must now discover a pattern in the indices and generalize. The pattern in the indices in the comparisons is

1
2
3

So the statements, one of which is a loop, are

```
largest := v[0];
FOR i := 1 TO 3 DO
    IF v[i] > largest THEN
        largest := v[i]
    END
END;
```

in the case where the array has four elements. In the more general case where there are numItm values, you should replace the constant 4 by numItm - 1. Figure 15.11 is the completed function. A precondition for the function to work is that numItm be strictly greater than zero. Otherwise there is no largest element and it would not make sense to call the procedure. The precondition should be verified in the calling procedure.

```
PROCEDURE Maximum (IN v: ARRAY OF REAL; numItm: INTEGER): REAL;
    VAR
        i: INTEGER;
        largest: REAL;
BEGIN
    ASSERT((0 < numItm) & (numItm <= LEN(v)), 20);
    largest := v[0];
    FOR i := 1 TO numItm - 1 DO
        IF v[i] > largest THEN
            largest := v[i]
        END
    END;
    RETURN largest
END Maximum;
```

Figure 15.11
A function that returns the largest element in an array.

What is the total statement execution count for the algorithm of Figure 15.11? ASSERT statements do not count for execution purposes, because they do no data processing. Their purpose is to specify a procedure, which would execute the same without them. Clearly the initialization of largest executes one time. If numItm has the value n, the FOR statement executes n times. Furthermore, every time the body of the FOR loop executes, the test of the nested IF statement executes. But how many times does the assignment statement

```
largest := v[i]
```

execute? The answer is, It depends. You cannot predict exactly how many times it executes, because you do not know how many times the IF test will be true. In the best case, the IF test will never be true and the assignment will never execute. In the worst case, the IF test will always be true and the assignment will always execute. The average case depends on the original arrangement of the data values in v, and is somewhere between the best case and the worst case. It is an exercise for the student (Exercise 8) to determine the execution count.

Definition of best-case and worst-case execution count

Exchanging the largest with the last

The next problem is to switch the largest value of an array with the last value. For example, if list is declared as before with the same initial values

5.0 −2.3 8.0 0.1

then, after the processing, the values should be

5.0 −2.3 0.1 8.0

For a first attempt, you might try to find the largest number using function Maximum above. Namely, suppose you have computed that largest has the value 8.0. Now, how would you make the exchange? The following trace shows the specific statements.

	temp	largest	v[0]	v[1]	v[2]	v[3]
Original values		8.0	5.0	−2.3	8.0	0.1
temp := v[3]	0.1	8.0	5.0	−2.3	8.0	0.1
v[3] := largest	0.1	8.0	5.0	−2.3	8.0	8.0
v[2] := temp	0.1	8.0	5.0	−2.3	0.1	8.0

How do you generalize the last assignment statement in the trace? Where did the 2 in v[2] come from? The problem is that we have the value of the largest element, when what we really need is the index of the largest element to make the exchange.

So, instead of saving the largest value in the array, we must save the *index* of the largest value in the array. An integer variable, say indexMax, will save the value of the index of the largest element found so far. The following trace shows the specific statements to compute indexMax.

	indexMax	v[0]	v[1]	v[2]	v[3]
Original values		5.0	−2.3	8.0	0.1
indexMax := 0	0	5.0	−2.3	8.0	0.1
IF v[1] > v[indexMax] THEN					
update indexMax	0	5.0	−2.3	8.0	0.1
IF v[2] > v[indexMax] THEN					
update indexMax	2	5.0	−2.3	8.0	0.1
IF v[3] > v[indexMax] THEN					
update indexMax	2	5.0	−2.3	8.0	0.1

The statements in the form of a loop are

```
indexMax := 0;
FOR i := 1 TO 3 DO
   IF v[i] > v[indexMax] THEN
      indexMax := i
   END
END;
```

which is valid when there are four items in the list. In the general case, you must replace the 3 by numItem - 1. The algorithm is shown as the procedure in Figure 15.12. If numItem is not greater than one, there is no need to exchange at all. The procedure works fine even when given an array with one item or an empty array.

```
PROCEDURE LargestLast (VAR v: ARRAY OF REAL; numItm: INTEGER);
    VAR
        i, indexMax: INTEGER;
        temp: REAL;
BEGIN
    ASSERT((0 <= numItm) & (numItm <= LEN(v)), 20);
    IF numItm > 1 THEN
        indexMax := 0;
        FOR i := 1 TO numItm - 1 DO
            IF v[i] > v[indexMax] THEN
                indexMax := i
            END
        END;
        temp := v[numItm - 1];
        v[numItm - 1] := v[indexMax];
        v[indexMax] := temp
    END
END LargestLast;
```

Figure 15.12
A procedure that exchanges the largest element in an array with the last element.

Initializing in decreasing order

The previous problems were rearrangements of existing values in the array. Some problems call for initializing the values in the array. Here is an example. Suppose list is an array of integers. If numItem has the value 5, you must initialize list to

4   3   2   1   0

In general, the values should be in decreasing order, with the first value equal to the number of items minus 1 and the last value equal to 0.

The specific assignment statements for five elements are

v[0] := 4
v[1] := 3
v[2] := 2
v[3] := 1
v[4] := 0

You must discover the general relationship between the pairs

```
0   4
1   3
2   2
3   1
4   0
```

Each time the first integer in the pair increases by one, the second integer decreases by one. If you write the FOR loop

```
FOR i := 0 TO 4 DO
    v[i] := some expression
END
```

the expression must decrease as i increases. An expression with -i satisfies that requirement. As i increases, -i decreases. Namely, the expression 4 - i works for five elements. When i has the value 0, 4 - i has the value 4. When i has the value 4, 4 - i has the value 0.

For four elements the pattern is

```
0   3
1   2
2   1
3   0
```

and the expression is 3 - i. For general values of numItm, the expression is

numItm - i - 1

When i has the value 0, numItm - i - 1 has the value numItm - 1. So, v[0] := numItm - 1. When i has the value numItm - 1, numItm - i - 1 has the value 0. So, v[numItm - 1] := 0. The algorithm in procedure form is in Figure 15.13.

```
PROCEDURE Initialize (OUT v: ARRAY OF INTEGER; numItm: INTEGER);
    VAR
        i: INTEGER;
BEGIN
    ASSERT((0 <= numItm) & (numItm <= LEN(v)), 20);
    FOR i := 0 TO numItm - 1 DO
        v[i] := numItm - i - 1
    END
END Initialize;
```

Figure 15.13
A procedure to initialize the elements of an array to a decreasing sequence.

Another approach to the same problem is to note that the expression always starts with the value of numItem - 1 and decreases by one. You can declare an integer variable, j, and initialize it to numItem - 1. Decrement the value of j each time through the loop and simply give the value of j to v[i]. The algorithm in procedure form is in Figure 15.14.

```
PROCEDURE Initialize (OUT v: ARRAY OF INTEGER; numItm: INTEGER);
    VAR
        i, j: INTEGER;
BEGIN
    ASSERT((0 <= numItm) & (numItm <= LEN(v)), 20);
    j := numItm - 1;
    FOR i := 0 TO numItm - 1 DO
        v[i] := j;
        DEC(j)
    END;
END Initialize;
```

Figure 15.14
A procedure that performs the
identical processing to that in
Figure 15.13.

Character arrays

Recall from Chapter 4 that arrays of characters are terminated with the sentinel value 0X. In that respect they are different from arrays of other types because other arrays are not so terminated. However, like arrays of other types, arrays of characters can be manipulated by subscripting.

The $ symbol denotes the Component Pascal string selector, which affects the processing of arrays of characters, but not arrays of other types. The $ symbol, when it follows the name of a variable of type array of character, signifies all the values from the first up to and including the cell containing the 0X sentinel character. The purpose of the $ string selector is to make string assignments more efficient than would otherwise be the case.

The $ string selector

Example 15.8 Suppose you declare the type

```
TYPE
    String16 = ARRAY 16 OF CHAR;
```

and you have two variables declared as

```
VAR
    d*: RECORD
        stringIn*: String16;
        stringOut-: String16
    END;
```

The value of d.stringIn is "each" and you want to assign it to d.stringOut, so you write

d.stringOut := d.stringIn

Without the $ symbol after d.stringIn, the values represented by d.stringIn include all 16 cells of the array. The assignment statement would cause 16 values to be assigned to d.stringOut as Figure 15.15(a) shows. This is clearly a waste of time, because for an array of characters all the values after the 0X sentinel are irrelevant. With the $

symbol after d.stringIn, the values represented by d.stringIn$ consists of the five values d.stringIn[0], d.stringIn[1], …, d.stringIn[4]. The assignment statement

d.stringOut := d.stringIn$

only needs to give five values to d.stringOut as Figure 15.15(b) shows instead of 16 values. ∎

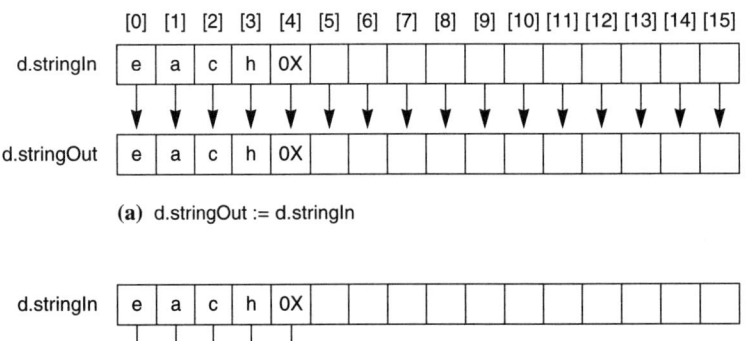

Figure 15.15
The effect of the $ when specifying an array of characters.

(a) d.stringOut := d.stringIn

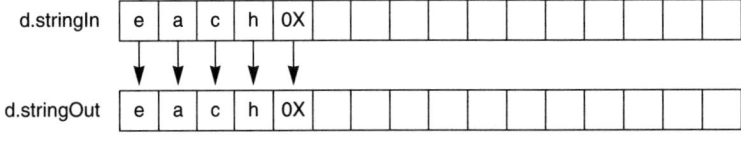

(b) d.stringOut := d.stringIn$

LEN returns the length of an array regardless of the number of cells that are occupied by meaningful values. It works with arrays of characters the same way it works with arrays of other types.

Example 15.9   Within procedure RotateLeft in Figure 15.7, the function call

LEN(v)

would return 1024 because that is the length of the actual parameter, list. It is irrelevant that there may be only seven cells used as in Figure 15.8. The LEN function cannot detect which cells are used and which are not. ∎

Example 15.10   If d.stringIn is declared as in Example 15.8 and has value "each", the function call

LEN(d.stringIn)

returns 16 because that is the number of cells in the array d.stringIn. Again, it is irrelevant that only five cells are used. ∎

When you use the LEN function in conjunction with the $ string selector, the function is able to determine which cells are used, and returns the length of the string, that is the number of characters it contains. LEN is only able to achieve this effect with arrays of characters, because arrays of other types are not terminated with 0X. Another interpretation of LEN when used with the $ string selector is the index of the 0X sentinel.

Using LEN and $ together

Example 15.11   If d.stringIn is declared as in Example 15.8 and has value "each", the function call

LEN(d.stringIn$)

returns 4 because that is the number of characters in the array d.stringIn. You can see from Figure 15.15 that 4 is also the index of the 0X sentinel.   ∎

Here is a program that illustrates string manipulation by subscripting. Figure 15.16 is the dialog box.

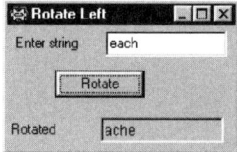

Figure 15.16
The dialog box for a program that rotates an array of characters to the left.

Figure 15.17 shows the program that implements the dialog box. It declares a type String16 to be an array of 16 characters. Although 16 characters are reserved for d.stringIn, the variable can hold a maximum of 15 characters because of the need for the terminal 0X character.

The assignment statement

d.stringOut := d.stringIn$

in procedure ProcessRotation assigns one array to another using the $ string selector to eliminate any unnecessary assignments beyond the 0X sentinel. Procedure RotateLeft uses the function LEN together with the $ string selector to rotate the characters in the actual parameter d.stringOut.

Procedure RotateLeft in Figure 15.17 is similar to the RotateLeft in Figure 15.7. Instead of passing numItm to indicate the number of items in the array, this procedure uses the LEN function to determine the number of characters in the string. The algorithm uses the LEN function three times, which is actually inefficient. Each time you call LEN with an array of characters using the $ symbol, it must execute a loop starting at the beginning of the array and repeating until the 0X sentinel is reached.

```
MODULE Pbox15D;
   IMPORT Dialog, PboxStrings;
   TYPE
      String16 = ARRAY 16 OF CHAR;
   VAR
      d*: RECORD
         stringIn*: String16;
         stringOut-: String16
      END;

   PROCEDURE RotateLeft (VAR str: ARRAY OF CHAR);
      VAR
         i: INTEGER;
         temp: CHAR;
   BEGIN
      IF LEN(str$) > 1 THEN
         temp := str[0];
         FOR i := 0 TO LEN(str$) - 2 DO
            str[i] := str[i + 1]
         END;
         str[LEN(str$) - 1] := temp
      END
   END RotateLeft;

   PROCEDURE ProcessRotation*;
   BEGIN
      d.stringOut := d.stringIn$;
      RotateLeft(d.stringOut);
      Dialog.Update(d)
   END ProcessRotation;

BEGIN
   d.stringIn := "";
   d.stringOut := ""
END Pbox15D.
```

Figure 15.17
A program with a procedure to rotate the elements in an array.

Figure 15.18 shows another version of procedure RotateLeft, which does not use LEN at all. It tests for the 0X symbol directly with a WHILE loop instead of a FOR loop. The algorithm first checks for str[0] equal to the sentinel. If they are equal, str is the empty string and no rotation is necessary. Otherwise str has at least one character and you can do the rotation. Without the IF test, the WHILE loop would execute even if str were the empty string. Eventually the value of i could reach 15, at which point str[i + 1] would be out of range and would generate a trap.

```
PROCEDURE RotateLeft (VAR str: ARRAY OF CHAR);
   VAR
      i: INTEGER;
      temp: CHAR;
BEGIN
   IF str[0] # 0X THEN
      temp := str[0];
      i := 0;
      WHILE str[i + 1] # 0X DO
         str[i] := str[i + 1];
         INC(i)
      END;
      str[i] := temp
   END
END RotateLeft;
```

Figure 15.18
A more efficient version of
RotateLeft.

★ Specifications for arrays

Arrays are frequently processed with FOR statements. Because GCL has no **for** statement, such statements are written with the equivalent **while**. You translate from CP to GCL by making the initialization, test, and increment, which is implicit in the CP FOR statement, explicit.

Example 15.12   The translation of the CP code fragment

```
FOR i := 0 TO numItms - 2 DO
   v[i] := v[i + 1]
END
```

to GCL using n for numItms is

$$i := 0 \, ;$$
$$\textbf{do } i \leq n - 2 \rightarrow$$
$$\quad v[i] := v[i + 1] \, ;$$
$$\quad i := i + 1$$
$$\textbf{od} \qquad\qquad \blacksquare$$

Formal specifications for arrays frequently require universal quantification, ∀, to denote a relationship that is true for all the elements of the array. As an example, consider procedure RotateLeft from Figure 15.7. The body of the procedure is

```
BEGIN
  ASSERT((0 <= numItm) & (numItm <= LEN(v)), 20);
  IF numItm > 1 THEN
    temp := v[0];
    FOR i := 0 TO numItm - 2 DO
      v[i] := v[i + 1]
    END;
    v[numItm - 1] := temp
  END
END RotateLeft;
```

The purpose of the IF statement is to guarantee that numItm is greater than one. To write a specification for the inner code fragment

```
temp := v[0];
FOR i := 0 TO numItm - 2 DO
  v[i] := v[i + 1]
END;
v[numItm - 1] := temp
```

you can use the fact that numItm must be greater than one by making it a precondition. Using *t* as an abbreviation for temp, the above code in GCL is

$$t := v[0];$$
$$i := 0;$$
$$\textbf{do } i \leq n - 2 \rightarrow$$
$$\quad v[i] := v[i + 1];$$
$$\quad i := i + 1$$
$$\textbf{od};$$
$$v[n - 1] := t$$

which we will abbreviate as *S*.

Now, the precondition for the Hoare triple $\{P\}S\{Q\}$ is *P*, and it will contain the conjunct $n > 1$. But how can you specify the postcondition *Q*? The purpose of the procedure is to shift the elements of the array to the left, with the first element moving to the end of the array. You need a rigid variable $\mathbf{V}$ to specify the initial value of the array *v*. The precondition *P* is

$$1 < n \leq len(v) \wedge (\forall i \mid 0 \leq i < n : v[i] = \mathbf{V}[i])$$

For the postcondition, you need to state that all the elements starting from the second are shifted down one slot, and the first is shifted to the end. Using universal quantification again, the postcondition *Q* is

$$(\forall i \mid 0 \leq i < n - 1 : v[i] = \mathbf{V}[i + 1]) \wedge v[n - 1] = \mathbf{V}[0]$$

The complete formal specification in the form of the Hoare triple $\{P\}S\{Q\}$ is

$\{1 < n \le len(v) \land (\forall i \mid 0 \le i < n : v[i] = \mathbf{V}[i])\}$
$v := ?$
$\{(\forall i \mid 0 \le i < n - 1 : v[i] = \mathbf{V}[i + 1]) \land v[n - 1] = \mathbf{V}[0]\}$

To prove that statement S satisfies the specification, you prove using formal methods the validity of the Hoare triple

$\{1 < n \le len(v) \land (\forall i \mid 0 \le i < n : v[i] = \mathbf{V}[i])\}$
$t := v[0];$
$i := 0;$
do $i \le n - 2 \rightarrow$
  $v[i] := v[i + 1];$
  $i := i + 1$
od;
$v[n - 1] := t$
$\{(\forall i \mid 0 \le i < n - 1 : v[i] = \mathbf{V}[i + 1]) \land v[n - 1] = \mathbf{V}[0]\}$

Because so many specifications require you to set up a rigid variable for an array, it is convenient to have an abbreviation for the fully quantified expression. From now on, this book will assume that

$v = \mathbf{V}$

is an abbreviation for

$(\forall i \mid 0 \le i < n : v[i] = \mathbf{V}[i])$

where n is the number of elements in the array. With this abbreviation, the above formal specification is written

$\{1 < n \le len(v) \land v = \mathbf{V}\}$
$v := ?$
$\{(\forall i \mid 0 \le i < n - 1 : v[i] = \mathbf{V}[i + 1]) \land v[n - 1] = \mathbf{V}[0]\}$

Sometimes a rigid variable is not required, particularly if the elements of the array do not change.

Example 15.13 Procedure Maximum in Figure 15.11 does not change the value of v. The ASSERT statement guarantees that numItm is greater than zero, which becomes the precondition. It is an exercise for the student to translate the code fragment

```
largest := v[0];
FOR i := 1 TO numItm - 1 DO
   IF v[i] > largest THEN
      largest := v[i]
   END
END
```

from CP to GCL. Assuming g stands for largest and n stands for numltm, the formal specification states that g is one of the elements of v and that it is the largest element in v as follows.

$$\{0 < n \le len(v)\}$$
$$g := ?$$
$$\{(\exists i \mid 0 \le i < n : g = v[i]) \wedge (\forall i \mid 0 \le i < n : g \ge v[i])\} \qquad \blacksquare$$

The algorithm for putting the largest element at the end of the array assumes that the values in the array after S executes are a rearrangement of the values before S executes. In general, a rearrangement of values is called a permutation.

Example 15.14 If an array of values before S executes is

5 2 7 4

and the values after S executes is

4 2 7 5

then the final value are a permutation of the initial values. $\qquad \blacksquare$

Let f to denote the first index and l the last index in the range $[f..l]$. To specify that the values in array b between $b[f]$ and $b[l]$ are a permutation of the corresponding values in array a, this book will use the predicate $perm(a,b,f,l)$. It takes some care to define this predicate formally. If there are no duplicated values in a or in b, then the definition of the predicate is

$$(\forall i \mid f \le i \le l : (\exists j \mid f \le j \le l : a[i] = b[j]))$$

The definition is more difficult to write if there are duplicated values in a or in b, and will not be given here. It is left as an exercise to use $perm(a,b,f,l)$ to write the formal specification for the algorithm to put the largest element at the end of the array.

Exercises

1. Predict the output of Figure 15.2 if the two loops are modified as follows:

(a)
```
FOR i := 0 TO 3 DO
    sc.ScanReal(list[i])
END;

FOR i := 0 TO 3 DO
    fm.WriteReal(list[i], 8, 2)
END;
```

(b)
```
FOR i := 3 TO 0 BY -1 DO
    sc.ScanReal(list[i])
END;

FOR i := 0 TO 3 DO
    fm.WriteReal(list[i], 8, 2)
END;
```

(Continued on next page.)

(c)
```
FOR i := 0 TO 3 DO
   sc.ScanReal(list[i])
END;

FOR i := 4 TO 7 DO
   fm.WriteReal(list[i MOD 4], 8, 2)
END;
```

(d)
```
FOR i := 5 TO 8 DO
   sc.ScanReal(list[i MOD 4])
END;

FOR i := 0 TO 3 DO
   fm.WriteReal(list[(i + 1) MOD 4], 8, 2)
END;
```

2. Suppose i and n are integers and v is an ARRAY 10 OF REAL in the following code:

```
i := n - 1;
WHILE i >= 0 DO
   StdLog.Real(v[i]); StdLog.String(" ");
   DEC(i, 2)
END
```

(a) What is the output to the Log if n is 6 and the values of v are

4.0   3.0   5.1   1.0   –7.0   8.5

(b) What is the output to the Log if n is 7 and the values of v are

4.0   3.0   5.1   1.0   –7.0   8.5   2.0

3. If i is an integer and v is an array of integers, what is the output of the following code?

```
FOR i := 0 TO 3 DO
   v[i] := 2 * i
END;
FOR i := 3 TO 1 BY -1 DO
   v[i] := v [i - 1] + 1
END;
FOR i := 0 TO 3 DO
   StdLog.Int(v[i]); StdLog.String(" ")
END
```

4. How many statements does procedure RotateLeft of Figure 15.7 execute if the value of numItm is n? Count only the statements in procedure RotateLeft. Do not include the statements in the calling procedure.

5. Your friend writes the following statements in procedure RotateLeft of Figure 15.7.

```
FOR i := 0 TO numItm - 1 DO
   IF i = 0 THEN
      temp := v[0]
   ELSE
      v[i - 1] := v[i]
   END
END;
v[numItm - 1] := temp
```

(a) Does your friend's code work correctly? **(b)** How many statements execute if the value of numItm is n? Compare this count with that of the previous exercise.

6. Your friend writes the following statements in procedure RotateLeft of Figure 15.7.

```
temp := v[numItm - 1];
FOR i := 0 TO numItm - 2 DO
    v[i + 1] := v[i]
END;
v[0] := temp
```

and renames the procedure RotateRight. If the program runs with the values

5.0   –2.3   8.0   0.1

for v, what is the output?

7. Determine the statement execution count for both versions of procedure Initialize in Figure 15.13 and Figure 15.14 if the value of numItm is *n*.

8. Suppose the value of numItm in function procedure Maximum in Figure 15.11 is *n*. Assume that *n* is greater than 1. **(a)** How must the data be arranged initially for the best case to occur? **(b)** What is the total statement execution count for this function in the best case? **(c)** How must the data be arranged initially for the worst case to occur? **(d)** What is the total statement execution count for this function in the worst case?

9. Suppose the value of numItm in procedure LargestLast in Figure 15.12 is *n*. Assume that *n* is greater than 1. **(a)** How must the data be arranged initially for the best case to occur? **(b)** What is the total statement execution count for this procedure in the best case? **(c)** How must the data be arranged initially for the worst case to occur? **(d)** What is the total statement execution count for this procedure in the worst case?

10. The expression $v = V$ where v and V are arrays of n elements is an abbreviation for what quantified expression?

11. **(a)** The predicate $perm(a,b,f,l)$ where a and b are arrays of elements in the range $[f..l]$ is an abbreviation for what quantified expression assuming there are no duplicate values in a or in b? **(b)** Write a list of four integers for a that contains one duplicated value and a list of four integers for b that contains no duplicated values, such that the values in a and b satisfy the quantified expression and such that the values in b are not a permutation of the values in a.

12. Translate the code fragment in Example 15.13 from CP to GCL.

13. **(a)** Translate the code fragment from procedure LargestLast in Figure 15.12

```
indexMax := 0;
FOR i := 1 TO numItm - 1 DO
    IF v[i] > v[indexMax] THEN
        indexMax := i
    END
END;
temp := v[numItm - 1];
v[numItm - 1] := v[indexMax];
v[indexMax] := temp
```

from CP to GCL. You will not need variable temp, because GCL has the multiple assignment statement. **(b)** Write the formal specification for the code fragment. The postcondition will have two conjuncts, one to state that the final values of v are a rearrangement of the initial values, and one to state that the largest element is in the last position. You may use the predicate $perm(a,b,f,l)$.

14. Write the formal specification for the statements S in procedure Initialize in Figure 15.13.

```
PROCEDURE Initialize (OUT v: ARRAY OF INTEGER; numItm: INTEGER)
...
BEGIN
    ASSERT((0 <= numItm) & (numItm <= LEN(v)), 20);
    S
END Initialize
```

Abbreviating n for numItm, S must set the elements of $v[0..n–1]$ to a decreasing sequence of integers, each value one less that the preceding value, and ending with 0.

15. Write the formal specification for the statements S in procedure RotateRight in Problem 20.

```
PROCEDURE RotateRight (VAR v: ARRAY OF REAL; numItm: INTEGER)
...
BEGIN
    ASSERT((0 <= numItm) & (numItm <= LEN(v)), 20);
    IF numItm > 1 THEN
        S
    END
END RotateRight
```

16. Write the formal specification for the statements S in procedure Reverse in Problem 22.

```
PROCEDURE Reverse (VAR v: ARRAY OF REAL; numItm: INTEGER)
...
BEGIN
    ASSERT((0 <= numItm) & (numItm <= LEN(v)), 20);
    IF numItm > 1 THEN
        S
    END
END Reverse
```

17. Write the formal specification for the statements S in procedure FirstOdd in Problem 24. Use the symbol r for the integer value returned. You may need to use existential quantification $\exists$ to state that there does not exist any odd integers before the index returned.

```
PROCEDURE FirstOdd (IN v: ARRAY OF INTEGER; numItm: INTEGER): INTEGER
...
BEGIN
    ASSERT((0 <= numItm) & (numItm <= LEN(v)), 20);
    S
END FirstOdd
```

18. Write the formal specification for the statements S in IsPalindrome in Problem 29. Use the symbol *b* for the boolean value returned and *n* as an abbreviation for LEN(str$).

PROCEDURE IsPalindrome (str: ARRAY OF CHAR): BOOLEAN
...
BEGIN
  S
END IsPalindrome

Problems

19. The focus window contains a list of real numbers. Write a procedure activated from a menu selection that inputs the real numbers into an array and then does the following: outputs every other number starting with the first, outputs every other number starting with the second, outputs every negative number, and outputs how many negative numbers were in the list. If the focus window contains

5.1 23.2 -6.2 1.0 -19.6 -13.0 4.8

Your one procedure should create a new window with all the following output.

Every other one from first:
  5.1   -6.2 -19.6   4.8

Every other one from second:
  23.2   1.0 -13.0

Every negative:
  -6.2 -19.6 -13.0

The list has 3 negative numbers.

You should write a single exported procedure. It is not necessary to have separate procedures for each output.

20. Declare

PROCEDURE RotateRight (VAR v: ARRAY OF REAL; numItm: INTEGER)

with the same parameter list as RotateLeft in Figure 15.7. Your procedure should rotate the numbers to the right instead of to the left. Test the procedure in a program similar to Figure 15.7. Implement the appropriate precondition on numItm.

21. Declare

PROCEDURE Rotate2Left (VAR v: ARRAY OF REAL; numItm: INTEGER)

with the same parameter list as RotateLeft in Figure 15.7 that rotates the items two places to the left instead of only one. For example, if v has the same initial values as in Figure 15.8, its values after the procedure is called should be

9.0   1.0   3.0   5.0   2.0   4.0   6.0

Use only one loop, and do not call RotateLeft. Test the procedure in a program similar to Figure 15.7. Implement the appropriate precondition on numItm, which is the same as the precondition for RotateLeft.

22.   Declare

PROCEDURE Reverse (VAR v: ARRAY OF REAL; numItm: INTEGER)

with the same formal parameter list as procedure RotateLeft in Figure 15.7. The procedure should reverse the elements in the array. Implement the appropriate precondition on numItm. Test the procedure in a program similar to Figure 15.7. Display the values both before and after the call to procedure Reverse. Do not use any output statements in procedure Reverse.

23.   Declare

PROCEDURE Shuffle (IN vIn: ARRAY OF REAL; OUT vOut: ARRAY OF REAL; numItm: INTEGER)

The procedure should shuffle the values like a perfect shuffle of a card deck. Split the deck into two equal stacks and build the shuffled deck by alternately taking cards from the top of each stack. If the list vIn is

1.0   2.0   3.0   4.0   5.0   6.0   7.0   8.0   9.0

then after the shuffle the list vOut should be

1.0   6.0   2.0   7.0   3.0   8.0   4.0   9.0   5.0

Test the procedure in a program similar to Figure 15.7, but with two different lists, one for input and one for output. Implement the appropriate precondition on numItm. Display the values of each list after the call to procedure Shuffle. Do not use any output statements in procedure Shuffle.

24.   Declare

PROCEDURE FirstOdd (IN v: ARRAY OF INTEGER; numItm: INTEGER): INTEGER

The function should return a value that is the index of the first odd integer in the list, or −1 if there are no odd integers. For example, if v contains

8   6   2   7   3   1   4   9   5

the function should return 3, because the first odd integer, 7, is at v[3]. Implement the appropriate precondition on numItm. Test your function by taking the input from the focus window and displaying the result in the Log. Do not use any input or output statements in function FirstOdd.

25.   Declare

PROCEDURE InitOneZero (OUT v: ARRAY OF INTEGER; numItm: INTEGER) that sets the values of v to alternating ones and zeros. For example, if numItm is 7, the values of v should be

1 0 1 0 1 0 1

Implement the appropriate precondition on numItm. Test your procedure with a dialog box that inputs the number of items. When the user clicks the initialize button, initialize the array, then output it to the Log. Do not include any output statements in Init-OneZero.

26. Declare

PROCEDURE InitPairs (OUT v: ARRAY OF INTEGER; numItm: INTEGER)

that sets the values of v to alternating pairs of ones and zeros. For example, if numItm is 7, the values of v should be

1 1 0 0 1 1 0

Implement the appropriate precondition on numItm. Test your procedure with a dialog box that inputs the number of items. When the user clicks the initialize button, initialize the array, then output it to the Log. Do not include any output statements in Init-Pairs. Hint: Because the pattern repeats every four times, consider the MOD 4 operation.

27. The program in Figure 14.5 generates a random sequence of integers between 0 and 9. With a seed of 2346, the integers 4, 6, and 2 each occur twice and the integers 1, 3, and 8 do not appear as Figure 14.4 shows. Write a procedure

InitRandom (OUT v: ARRAY OF INTEGER; numItm: INTEGER)

that puts random integer values between 0 and numItm - 1 in the first numItm cells of v without any repeating values. Initialize the list with sequential integer values, then make one sweep through the list to exchange the content of each cell with the content of another cell chosen at random. For example, if numItm is 7, initialize v to

0 1 2 3 4 5 6

Then interchange v[0] with another cell chosen at random, v[1] with another cell chosen at random, and so on. Implement the appropriate precondition on numItm. Test your procedure with a dialog box that inputs the number of items and gives the user the option to set the seed. When the user clicks the compute button, initialize the array, then output it to the Log. Do not include any output statements in InitRandom.

28. A list of numbers is said to have a run if several identical values are adjacent to each other. For example, the list of numbers

12 3 3 3 3 3 16 3 4 16 9 4 4

has a run of five 3's and another run of two 4's. Declare

PROCEDURE LongestRun (IN v: ARRAY OF INTEGER; numItm: INTEGER): INTEGER that returns the length of the longest run in a list of integers. For example, the function should return 5 if v has the above values. Do not use more than one loop. Be sure to consider the case where the longest run is at the end of the list. Assert as part of your precondition that there is at least one item in the list. Test your procedure by taking the input values from the focus window with a menu selection. Verify in the calling procedure that your precondition is met. Output the length of the longest run on the Log. Do not include any output statements in procedure LongestRun.

29. A palindrome is a word that is the same spelled backward or forward. For example, radar is a palindrome but bulb is not, because in reverse order it would be blub. Declare

PROCEDURE IsPalindrome (str: ARRAY OF CHAR): BOOLEAN

to determine if str is a palindrome. Test it with a dialog box that prompts the user to input a word and outputs whether it is a palindrome. Assume the user will not enter any spaces within or before the word. Consider the empty string to be a palindrome.

30. Declare

PROCEDURE Collapse (VAR str: ARRAY OF CHAR)

that eliminates all the spaces in str. Test it with a dialog box that prompts the user to input a phrase and outputs the modified phrase without the spaces. For example, if the user enters "a head" your procedure should change it to "ahead". Use only one loop, not nested, and collapse all leading and trailing spaces. Do not include any output statements in procedure Collapse. Test your procedure in a program similar to that in Figure 15.17.

31. Write procedure RotateLeft of Figure 15.18 with a REPEAT loop in place of the WHILE loop. Test your procedure in a program similar to that in Figure 15.17 with a dialog box for the user to enter a string. Be sure to test your program for the case where the user enters the empty string, a string with only one character, and a string with several characters.

32. Declare

PROCEDURE MyToUpper (from: ARRAY OF CHAR; OUT to: ARRAY OF CHAR)

that does the identical processing as PboxStrings.ToUpper. Test your procedure in a program similar to that in Figure 15.17 with a dialog box for the user to enter a string. Do not import any module except for Dialog.

33. Figure 15.19(a) shows a funnel that contains a bunch of marbles at the top of a board with rows of pegs. When the door at the bottom of the funnel opens a marble is released and hits the top peg. The probability is 0.5 that it will bounce off the peg to the right and 0.5 that it will bounce to the left. If it bounces to the right, it will hit a peg on the second row, at which time the probability is again 0.5 for bouncing to the left and 0.5 to the right. The marble continues to hit one peg in each row with probability 0.5 of bouncing to the left and 0.5 to the right. After hitting a peg in the bottom row, the marble is caught in one of the buckets below the last row of pegs. Each bucket is so narrow that the marbles are stacked one on top of the other in the bucket.

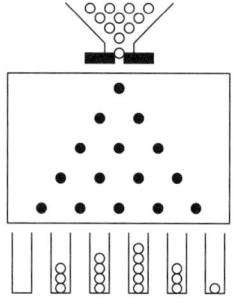

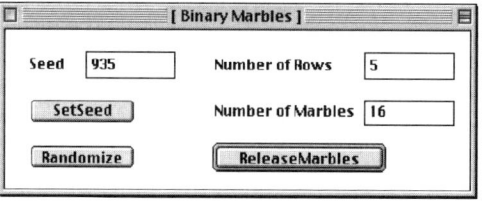

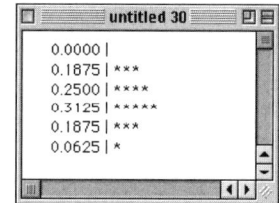

Figure 15.19
Problem 33.

(a) The funnel, marbles, pegs and buckets. **(b)** The dialog box. **(c)** The output.

(a) Write a program that simulates the marbles rolling down the board, hitting the pegs, and landing in the buckets. Implement the dialog box of Figure 15.19(b) to allow the user to input the number of rows of pegs and the number of marbles to release through the funnel. Display the output in a new window like that of Figure 15.19(c) showing the percentage of the number of marbles in each bucket to four places past the decimal point and a histogram with an asterisk symbol for each marble caught in the bucket.

(b) Assuming that the buckets in Figure 15.19(a) are numbered starting with 0 for the leftmost bucket, 1 for the next, and so on up to n for the rightmost bucket, the probability of a single marble landing in bucket number k is

$$P(n, k) = \frac{n!}{k!(n-k)!2^n} \qquad 0 \le k \le n$$

where n is the number of rows of pegs. The percentages that your program computes and displays in the output window should be close to the above theoretical probability. Add to your program a computation of the squared error defined as

$$S(n) = \sum_{i=0}^{n} [P(n, i) - E(n, i)]^2$$

where $E(n, i)$ are the experimental values that you computed as the ratios in the first part of your program. Output the squared error to six places past the decimal point at the bottom of the output window. Experiment with different numbers of marbles for a fixed number of rows. In general, what happens to the squared error as the number of marbles increases?

Chapter *16*

Iterative Searching and Sorting

Probably the most important algorithms in all of computer science are the searching and sorting algorithms. They are important because they are so common. To search for an item is to know a key value and to look it up in a list. For example, when you look up a word in a dictionary or look up a phone number in a phone book based on a person's name you are performing a search. Putting data in order is performing a sort. For example, table entries in many business reports are in some kind of order. The post office wants bulk mailings to be in order by zip code.

Searching

This section presents two basic search algorithms, the sequential search and the binary search. In a search problem, you are given

- An array of values
- The number of values in the array
- A search value

The algorithm must determine whether the array contains a value equal to the search value. If it does, the algorithm must compute the index of the array where the value is located.

For example, suppose you declare the following procedure:

```
PROCEDURE Search (IN v: ARRAY OF INTEGER; numItm, srchNum: INTEGER;
    OUT i: INTEGER; OUT fnd: BOOLEAN);
```

Also, suppose that numItm has the value 4, and the first four values in v are

50   20   70   60

If srchNum has the value 70, then the search algorithm should set fnd to TRUE and i to 2, because v[2] has the value 70. If srchNum has the value 40, the algorithm should set fnd to FALSE. It does not matter what value it gives to i, because v does not contain the value 40.

Parameter v is called by constant reference, because the purpose of Search is not to change the values of v, but to use the values of the actual parameter. It is called by constant reference instead of by value because it could be a long array. Parameters numItm and srchNum are called by value, because the calling procedure gives the values to Search, with information flowing from the calling to the called procedure. Parameters i and fnd are called by result, because their initial values can be considered undefined when the procedure is first called, and Search will change the values of the corresponding actual parameters.

The sequential search

The sequential search algorithm starts at the first of the list. It compares srchNum with v[0], then v[1], and so on until it either finds srchNum in v or it gets to the end of the list. One version of the algorithm follows.

```
PROCEDURE Search (IN v: ARRAY OF INTEGER; numItm, srchNum: INTEGER;
    OUT i: INTEGER; OUT fnd: BOOLEAN);
BEGIN
  ASSERT((0 <= numItm) & (numItm <= LEN(v)), 20);
  i := 0;
  WHILE (i < numItm) & (v[i] # srchNum) DO
    INC(i)
  END;
  fnd := i < numItm
END Search;
```

Figure 16.1
The first version of the sequential search algorithm. This is not the most efficient version.

If you trace this algorithm with a value of 70 for srchNum, you will see that i first gets 0. The WHILE expression is true because 0 is less than 4, and 50 is not equal to srchNum. When i gets 1, the WHILE expression is true again, because 1 is less than 4 and 20 is not equal to srchNum.

When i gets 2, however, the WHILE expression is false, because v[2] equals srchNum. The loop terminates, and fnd gets true. The value of i is the index of v where srchNum was found.

If you trace the algorithm with 40 for the value of srchNum, i will get 0, then 1, then 2, then 3. When i is 3, the WHILE expression will still be true, so i will get 4. Then the expression

(i < numItm) & (v[i] # srchNum)

will be evaluated with i having a value of 4.

At this point in the execution, an interesting feature of Component Pascal comes into play. The first part of the expression is false because i is equal to numItm. The second part of the expression does not need to be evaluated. Regardless of whether it is true or false, the entire expression will be false because of the first part.

There are two evaluation techniques in this situation. One is called full evaluation, and the other is called short-circuit evaluation. The steps of the full evaluation technique are

- Evaluate the first part.

- Evaluate the second part.

- Perform the AND operation.

The steps of the short-circuit evaluation technique are

- Evaluate the first part.

- If it is false, skip the second part.

- Otherwise, evaluate the second part.

Full evaluation of AND expressions

Short-circuit evaluation of AND expressions

With full evaluation, both parts are evaluated, regardless of whether the first part is true or false.

Fortunately, Component Pascal uses the short-circuit evaluation technique. In this example, the second part of the expression

(v[i] # srchNum)

will not be evaluated, with i having the value 4. If it were evaluated, the algorithm would be comparing v[4] with 40. If the array in the actual parameter were an ARRAY 4 OF INTEGER, the comparison would generate a trap. Because Component Pascal uses the short-circuit evaluation technique, such a trap will not occur with this algorithm.

The short-circuit evaluation technique also works with expressions that contain the OR boolean operator. When Component Pascal evaluates the boolean expression in the WHILE statement

WHILE p OR q DO

if it finds that p is true it does not evaluate q, because the entire boolean expression will be true regardless of whether expression q is true or false.

How fast is this algorithm? That depends on several things, namely how many items are in the list, whether the list contains the value of srchNum, and if it does contain srchNum, where it is located. Because the performance depends on these various factors, three categories of performance are commonly specified. They are

- Best-case performance

- Worst-case performance

- Average performance

In this algorithm, the best case is when v[0] contains the same value as srchNum. The worst case is when the value of srchNum is not in the list at all. The average case is somewhat difficult to define because it depends on the probability that srch-Num will be in the list. We will not pursue the problem of determining the average performance of the search algorithms.

Search algorithms are usually evaluated by counting the number of comparisons necessary to find the search item. This algorithm makes two comparisons each time it evaluates the while expression. They are

i < numItm

and

v[i] # srchNum

In the best case, the WHILE expression is false the first time, the body of the loop never executes, and the algorithm makes two comparisons. Let *n* equal the value of numItm. In the worst case, the algorithm searches the entire list, evaluating the WHILE expression *n* times plus one additional comparison to detect the end of the list. So it makes $2n + 1$ comparisons.

Therefore, the performance of this algorithm is

- Best case: 2 comparisons
- Worst case: $2n + 1$ comparisons

If you search a list of 1000 items, then in the best case you will make two comparisons and in the worst case you will make 2001 comparisons.

With a little thought, you can improve this sequential search algorithm substantially. Think about the WHILE expression. Why do you need the comparison of i with numItm? Because, if srchNum is not in the list, i would keep getting bigger and the loop would not terminate. You would not need the first comparison if you knew that srchNum was in the list. You can guarantee that it will be in the list if you put it there yourself, before starting the loop.

```
PROCEDURE Search (VAR v: ARRAY OF INTEGER; numItm, srchNum: INTEGER;
    OUT i: INTEGER; OUT fnd: BOOLEAN);
BEGIN
    ASSERT((0 <= numItm) & (numItm < LEN(v)), 20);
    v[numItm] := srchNum;
    i := 0;
    WHILE v[i] # srchNum DO
        INC(i)
    END;
    fnd := i < numItm
END Search;
```

Figure 16.2
An efficient version of the sequential search algorithm.

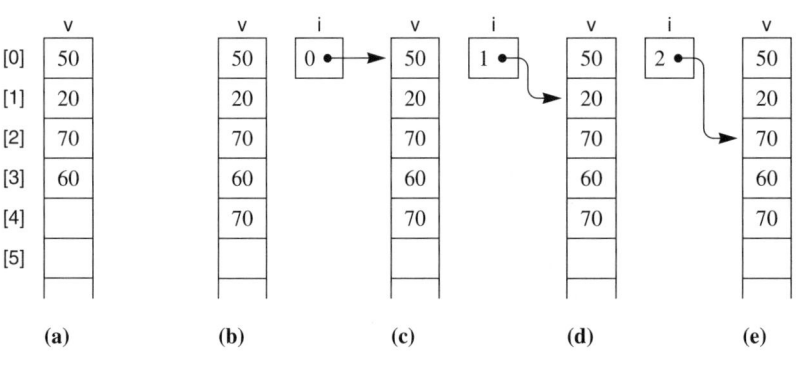

Figure 16.3
A trace of the sequential search algorithm when the value of **srchNum**, 70, is in the list.

Figure 16.2 shows a better version of the sequential search algorithm. The algorithm puts the value of srchNum at the end of the list to act as a sentinel, if necessary. Formal parameter v must be called by reference instead of by constant reference, because the algorithm modifies v. Also, the precondition requires numItm to be strictly less than LEN(v). It cannot be equal to LEN(v) because the algorithm reserves the last spot in the array for the sentinel value.

Figure 16.3 is a trace of the algorithm when the item searched is in the list. i never reaches numItm. Figure 16.4 is a trace when the item is not in the list. This time, i reaches numItm, and the value of srchNum acts like a sentinel.

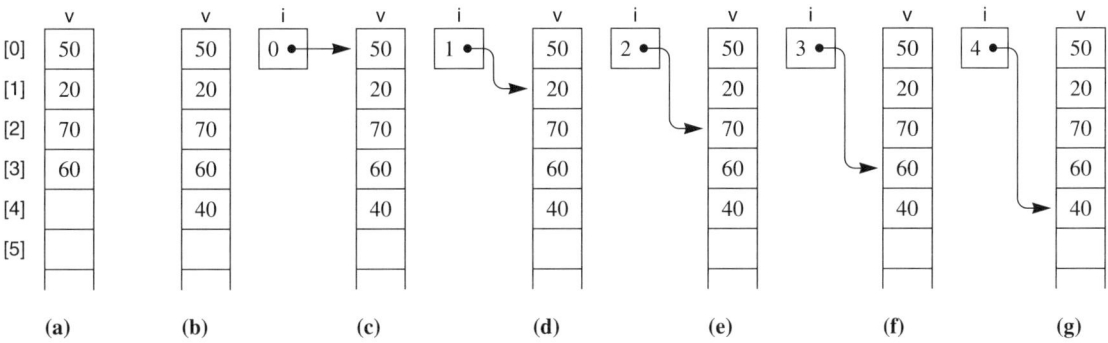

How much better is this version of the sequential search? Counting the comparisons as in the analysis of the previous version gives the following performance figures:

Figure 16.4
A trace of the sequential search algorithm when the value of srchNum, 40, is not in the list.

- Best case: 1 comparison
- Worst case: $n + 1$ comparisons

If you search a list of 1000 items, in the best case you will make 1 comparison instead of 2 and in the worst case you will make 1001 comparisons instead of 2001. This version is substantially better than the first and is the one you should use whenever you need to do a sequential search.

Tool dialog boxes

In practice, you rarely will have to search for a numerical value in a single list of numbers. A more common need is to look up someone's name to retrieve additional information about the person. For example, you may want to search a list of names for a particular name to find the corresponding telephone number.

Figure 16.5 shows a dialog box for such a problem. It consists of two groups of controls, one to load the telephone book and one to perform a query. The figure shows how to load a phone book. A window contains the phone book, which consists of a list of names followed by phone numbers. Each name and number is enclosed in double quotes, but single quotes could be used consistently as well. To load the phone book, the user must first make the phone book window the focus window, then make the dialog box the focus window. With the dialog box the focus window, the user clicks the Load Phone Book button. A procedure then scans the names and numbers from the phone book window into two arrays, one for the names and one for the numbers. The dialog box displays how many entries from the book have been scanned into the phone book.

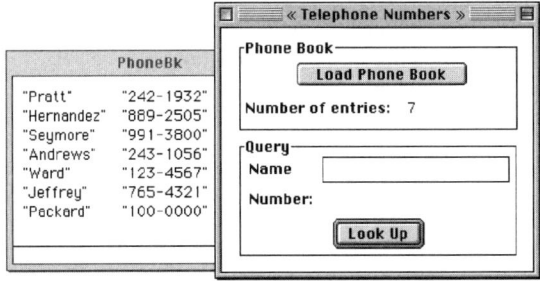

Figure 16.5
A tool dialog box.

You can tell from Figure 16.5 that the dialog box is the focus window because it overlaps with the phone book window and appears on top of it. When the user clicks the Load Phone Book button, how does the BlackBox framework know which window to scan? It cannot scan from the focus window, because when the user clicks the button the dialog box is the focus window. Somehow, the framework must remember which window was the focus window just *before* the dialog box became the focus window.

Tool dialog boxes have the property that they are not considered by the framework to be the focus window. Instead, the framework considers the window that was focused immediately before the tool dialog box is activated to be the focus window. You construct a tool dialog box the same way to construct any dialog box. But instead of opening it as an auxiliary dialog box with procedure StdCmds.OpenAuxDialog, you open it as a tool dialog box with procedure StdCmds.OpenToolDialog.

The framework does not consider a tool dialog box to be the focus window.

One possibility is to have the documentation section provide a commander that when clicked will activate the tool dialog box. Although this technique is convenient for users of the BlackBox framework, a more conventional GUI technique is to provide the user with a menu selection to activate the tool dialog box.

The tool dialog box in Figure 16.5 was opened with the menu script

```
MENU  "Pbox17"
   "A..."   ""   "StdCmds.OpenToolDialog('Pbox17/Rsrc/DlgA', 'Telephone Numbers')"   ""
END
```

When you provide a menu selection to activate a dialog box, you should include the ellipsis ... to give the user a cue that when the menu item is selected a dialog box will appear.

Figure 16.6 shows how the user enters a query by typing a name and clicking the Look Up button. In case the name is not found in the phone book an appropriate message appears in the dialog box.

It is clear from the dialog box that the module will need to export five items for the five controls—a procedure to load the phone book, an output integer for the

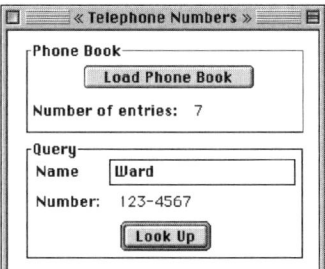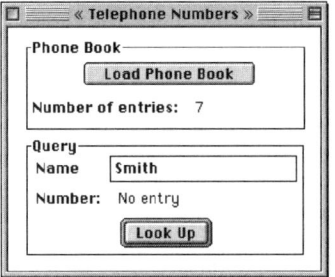

Figure 16.6
Performing a query.

number of items loaded, an input field for the name, an output field for the number, and a procedure for performing the search. In addition, a global data structure is needed for the phone book, which consists of an array of names and an array of numbers. Figure 16.7 shows the array of names and the corresponding array of numbers. They are known as parallel arrays because the number numberList[i] goes with the name nameList[i]. Figure 16.8 shows the module that implements the dialog box.

nameList		numberList	
[0]	Pratt	[0]	242-1932
[1]	Hernandez	[1]	889-2505
[2]	Seymore	[2]	991-3800

Figure 16.7
The parallel arrays for the phone book in Figure 16.8.

```
MODULE Pbox16A;
    IMPORT Dialog, TextModels, TextControllers, PboxMappers;
    TYPE
        Name = ARRAY 32 OF CHAR;
        Number = ARRAY 16 OF CHAR;
    VAR
        d*: RECORD
            numEntries-: INTEGER;
            name*: Name;
            number-: Number
        END;
    CONST
        maxItems = 1024;
    VAR
        nameList: ARRAY maxItems OF Name;
        numberList: ARRAY maxItems OF Number;
```

Figure 16.8
Using the sequential search to look up a phone number.

```
PROCEDURE LoadBook*;
   VAR
      md: TextModels.Model;
      cn: TextControllers.Controller;
      sc: PboxMappers.Scanner;
      i: INTEGER;
BEGIN
   cn := TextControllers.Focus();
   IF cn # NIL THEN
      md := cn.text; sc.ConnectTo(md);
      i := 0;
      sc.ScanString(nameList[i]); sc.ScanString(numberList[i]);
      WHILE ~sc.eot DO
         INC(i);
         sc.ScanString(nameList[i]); sc.ScanString(numberList[i])
      END;
      d.numEntries := i
   END;
   d.number := "";
   Dialog.Update(d)
END LoadBook;

PROCEDURE Search (VAR v: ARRAY OF Name; numItm: INTEGER; IN srchName: Name;
      OUT i: INTEGER; OUT fnd: BOOLEAN);
BEGIN
   ASSERT((0 <= numItm) & (numItm < LEN(v)), 20);
   v[numItm] := srchName$;
   i := 0;
   WHILE v[i] # srchName DO
      INC(i)
   END;
   fnd := i < numItm
END Search;

PROCEDURE LookUp*;
   VAR
      j: INTEGER;
      found: BOOLEAN;
BEGIN
   Search(nameList, d.numEntries, d.name, j, found);
   IF found THEN
      d.number := numberList[j]$
   ELSE
      d.number := "No entry"
   END;
   Dialog.Update(d)
END LookUp;

BEGIN
   d.numEntries := 0; d.name := ""; d.number := ""
END Pbox16A.
```

Figure 16.8
Continued.

The binary search

When you look up a word in a dictionary, you do not use the sequential search. If you want to look up the word walrus, you do not start at the front of the book and look sequentially from the first entry on. Instead, you use the fact that the words are in alphabetical order. You open the book to an arbitrary place and look at a word. If walrus is less than the word you opened to, you know that walrus lies in the section before your place in the book. Otherwise it is in the back part.

This common idea is the basis of the binary search. To perform a binary search the list must be in order. The algorithm makes the initial selection at the midpoint of the list. After the first comparison, the algorithm knows which half of the list the item must be in.

The second comparison is at the midpoint of the proper half. After this comparison the algorithm knows which quarter of the list the item must be in. The algorithm continues to split the known region in half until it finds the value or determines that it is not in the list. It gets the name "binary" from the fact that it divides the list into two equal parts with each comparison.

Figure 16.9 shows the binary search algorithm. The variables for this algorithm are the same as those for the sequential search, except that three local indices are necessary—first, mid, and last—instead of one index, i.

```
PROCEDURE Search (IN v: ARRAY OF INTEGER; numItm, srchNum: INTEGER;
    OUT i: INTEGER; OUT fnd: BOOLEAN);
    VAR
        first, mid, last: INTEGER;
BEGIN
    ASSERT((0 <= numItm) & (numItm <= LEN(v)), 20);
    first := 0;
    last := numItm - 1;
    WHILE first <= last DO
        mid := (first + last) DIV 2;
        IF srchNum < v[mid] THEN
            last := mid - 1
        ELSIF srchNum > v[mid] THEN
            first := mid + 1
        ELSE
            fnd := TRUE; i := mid;
            RETURN
        END
    END;
    fnd := FALSE
END Search;
```

Figure 16.9
The binary search algorithm.

The variables first and last will keep track of the boundaries of the list within which the search value must lie, if it is in the list at all. The algorithm initializes first to zero and last to numItm - 1. At the beginning of the loop, if srchNum is in v then

(v[first] <= srchNum) & (srchNum <= v[last])

will be true. This assertion is the loop invariant. The algorithm works by keeping the loop invariant true each time the loop executes.

The variable mid is the midpoint between first and last. The algorithm compares v[mid] with srchNum. Depending on the test, it updates either first or last such that the value is still between v[first] and v[last]. When the algorithm terminates, mid is the index of the cell of v that contains srchNum. Figure 16.10 is a trace of the algorithm when the values of v are

10   30   40   50   60   70   90

and srchNum is 40, a value in the list. The algorithm initializes first to 0 and last to 6. mid gets (0 + 6) DIV 2, which is 3, the midpoint between 0 and 6.

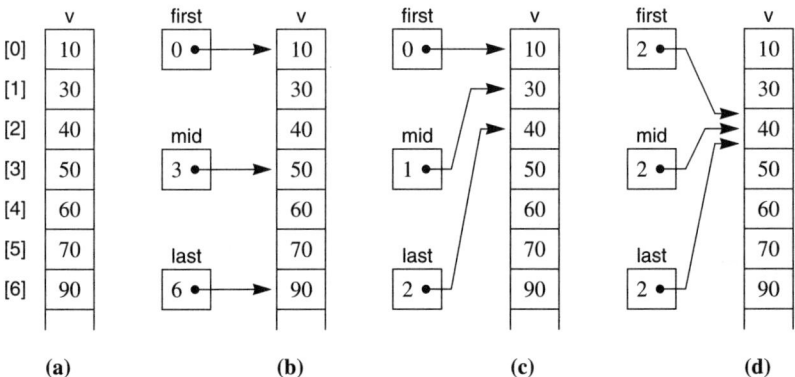

Figure 16.10
A trace of the binary search algorithm when the value of srchNum, 40, is in the list.

The IF statement compares srchNum, 40, with v[mid], 50. Because srchNum is less than v[mid], the algorithm knows that the value cannot be in the bottom half of the list. So it updates last to 1 less than mid, which is 2. Notice how the loop invariant is still true. The search value, if it is in the list, must be between v[0] and v[2].

The next time through the loop mid gets 1, which is the midpoint between 0 and 2. After the comparison, first gets 2. The next time through the loop, mid gets 2 also, and the loop terminates because v[2] has the same value as srchNum.

This algorithm is the first one we have encountered that has the RETURN statement in a proper procedure. Previous examples have always used the RETURN statement in function procedures, where RETURN is followed by an expression for the value to be returned. Because procedure Search in Listing 16.9 is not a function procedure, there is no value to be returned. Therefore, there is no expression following the RETURN statement. The RETURN statement serves to exit the procedure immediately, in this case before reaching the end of the procedure. If the loop terminates because first <= last then fnd will be set to false. On the other hand, if srchNum = v[mid] then fnd will be set to true, and the loop and the procedure will terminate immediately.

The RETURN statement in a proper procedure

Figure 16.11 is a trace with the same values as Figure 16.10 for v, but with a value of 80 for srchNum, which is not in the list. This time first, mid, and last eventually all get 6. Because srchNum, 80, is less than v[mid], 90, the algorithm sets last to mid - 1, which is 5. In the figure, that causes first and last to cross. Mathematically, first > last, which causes the loop to terminate.

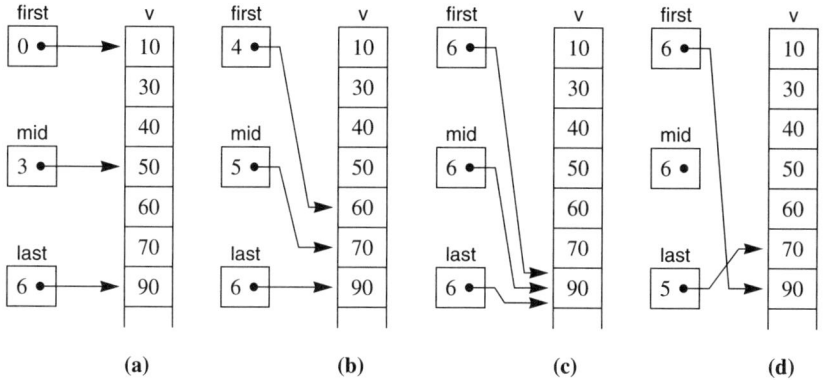

(a) (b) (c) (d)

Figure 16.11
A trace of the binary search algorithm when the value of srchNum, 80, is not in the list.

Does this algorithm look familiar? The bisection algorithm in Chapter 10 for finding the root of an equation was essentially a binary search. Figure 10.9 shows the variables left, mid, and right, which correspond directly to first, mid, and last.

The difference is that the bisection algorithm searches for a real value on the continuous number line, while the binary search algorithm searches for a discrete value in an ordered array. The bisection algorithm updates the real variable mid with

mid := (left + right) / 2.0

while the binary search algorithm updates the integer variable mid with

mid := (first + last) DIV 2

How fast is this algorithm? As with the sequential search, that depends on several factors. The loop will terminate as soon as srchNum equals v[mid]. The best case is when they are equal the first time, which happens if the value is exactly in the middle of the list. The number of comparisons will be 3.

The worst case is when the value is not in the list, the comparison in the test of the WHILE loop is made every time the body executes, and both comparisons in the IF statement are made every time the body executes. That happens if srchNum is always greater than v[mid]. The worst case with the values of v that were just presented occurs with a value of 95 for srchNum.

Each time the loop executes, it makes three comparisons. So the total number of comparisons is three times the number of times the loop executes. If numItm has the value *n*, how many times will the loop execute? The answer to that question is the same as the answer to the question, How many times must you cut an integer, *n*, in half to get to one? After all, each time the loop executes it eliminates half the possible locations for the value.

If you do not know the answer, you can use the problem-solving technique of going from the specific to the general. Let *t* equal the number of times. Here are some specific values of *n* and *t*:

$n = 16, t = 4$ times: 16 8 4 2 1
$n = 32, t = 5$ times: 32 16 8 4 2 1
$n = 64, t = 6$ times: 64 32 16 8 4 2 1

You can see that the general relationship between n and t is $n = 2^t$. This relationship is approximately true even if n is not an exact power of 2. For example, if n is 40, the number of times you must halve it in order to get to 1 is either 5 or 6.

In mathematics, the logarithm to the base 10 is denoted log, and the logarithm to the base e is denoted ln. In computer science, logarithms are usually to the base 2. The logarithm to the base 2 is denoted lg. In mathematical notation, $\log_2 n = \lg n$

lg is the logarithm to the base 2.

The relationship between t and n can be written $t = \lg n$ by the definition of the logarithm. This is the number of times the loop executes in the worst case. Each time the loop executes, it makes three comparisons. So the number of comparisons is $3\lg n$.

Summarizing, the binary search has the following performance figures:

■ Best case: 3 comparisons

■ Worst case: $3\lg n$ comparisons

The average case, however you define it, is somewhere between the best case and the worst case.

The selection sort

Sort algorithms put lists of values in order. For example, if numItm is 9 and the first 9 values of v are

7 3 8 2 1 4 9 5 6

then after the sort, the nine values should be

1 2 3 4 5 6 7 8 9

The selection sort is based on the idea of finding the largest item in the list and putting it at the end. Then it finds the next largest and puts it next to the end. It continues finding the largest item in the top part of the list and putting it at the end of the top part until it gets to the top. Here is the first outline of the algorithm.

```
FOR k := numItm - 1 TO 1 BY -1 DO
    Select the largest element from the top part of the list between v[0] and v[k].
    Exchange it with v[k].
END
```

The first time the loop executes, k gets numItm - 1. So the largest element in the entire list is exchanged with the element at the bottom of the list. After this first execution of the loop, the largest element is in its correct position in the sorted list.

The second time the loop executes, k gets numItm - 2. So the largest element between v[0] and v[numItm - 2] is exchanged with v[numItm - 2]. At this point in the execution, the bottom two elements will be at their correct positions in the list.

Similarly, after the third execution of the loop the bottom three elements will be in their correct positions. The last time, k gets 1, after which the bottom k - 1 elements will be in their correct order. Therefore, the top one must be in its correct order also.

How do you put the largest element between v[0] and v[k] into v[k]? This is precisely the problem solved by procedure LargestLast in Figure 15.12. Inserting the code for that processing into the outer loop yields the algorithm in Figure 16.12 for the selection sort.

```
PROCEDURE Sort (VAR v: ARRAY OF INTEGER; numItm: INTEGER);
   VAR
      i, k: INTEGER;
      maxIndex: INTEGER;
      temp: INTEGER;
BEGIN
   ASSERT((0 <= numItm) & (numItm <= LEN(v)), 20);
   FOR k := numItm - 1 TO 1 BY -1 DO
      maxIndex := 0;
      FOR i := 1 TO k DO
         IF v[i] > v[maxIndex] THEN
            maxIndex := i
         END
      END;
      temp := v[k];
      v[k] := v[maxIndex];
      v[maxIndex] := temp
   END
END Sort;
```

Figure 16.12
The selection sort.

Figure 16.13 is a trace of the outer loop of the selection sort algorithm. Figure 16.13(a) shows the original list. When k has the value 8 the first time the outer loop executes, the inner loop computes maxIndex as 6, the index of the largest element between v[0] and v[8]. The algorithm exchanges v[8] with v[6].

Figure 16.13(b) shows the list after the first exchange. The second time the outer loop executes, maxIndex is computed as 1, after which the algorithm exchanges v[1] with v[7]. At this point in the execution, the last two values are in order. The outer loop executes eight times, after which the entire list is in order.

How fast is the selection sort algorithm? Two criteria are common in the analysis of sort algorithms. One criterion counts the number of comparisons performed by the algorithm. The other counts the number of exchanges. In the selection sort, it is easier to count the number of comparisons.

The inner loop makes one comparison each time it executes. So the number of comparisons is the number of times the inner loop executes. Let n be the value of numItm. The first time the outer loop executes, the inner loop executes $n - 1$ times. The second time the outer loop executes, the inner loop executes one less time, which is $n - 2$. The third time the outer loop executes, the inner loop executes $n - 3$ times, and so on.

Figure 16.13
Eight executions of the outer loop of the selection sort. The shaded cells contain the values of the array that are in order.

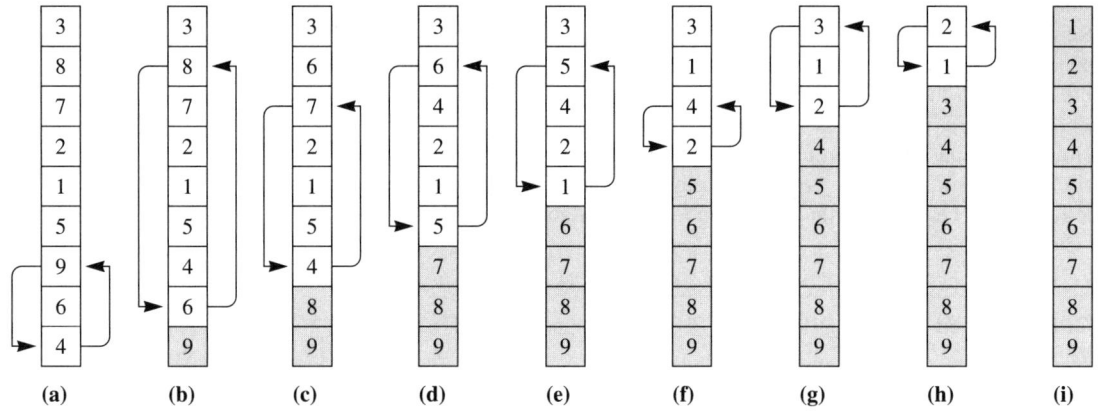

(a) (b) (c) (d) (e) (f) (g) (h) (i)

So, the number of comparisons is

$$(n-1) + (n-2) + (n-3) + \ldots + 3 + 2 + 1$$

which is the sum of the first $n - 1$ integers. You should recognize this problem from the statement execution count for the algorithm that prints a triangle. Remember that the sum of the first m integers is $m(m + 1)/2$. So the sum of the first $n - 1$ integers is $(n-1)(n-1+1)/2$ or $n(n-1)/2$, which is the number of comparisons the selection sort makes to sort n items.

Example 16.1 To sort 100 items requires $100(99)/2 = 4950$ comparisons. If you double the number of items to 200, the algorithm makes $200(199)/2 = 19,900$ comparisons. ∎

So, doubling the number of items more than doubles the number of comparisons. Why? Because the number of comparisons is not linear in n. It is quadratic in n, because $n(n-1)/2$ is the same as $(n^2 - n)/2$. That means doubling the number of items will approximately quadruple the number of comparisons. Four times 4950 is approximately 19,900.

Exercises

1. Determine **(a)** the best case, and **(b)** the worst case execution count of each statement in procedure Search of Figure 16.1 assuming numItm has value n. Calculate the total statement execution count as a polynomial in n. Because there are two tests in the WHILE statement, count that statement as executing twice each time it executes.

2. Determine **(a)** the best case, and **(b)** the worst case execution count of each statement in procedure Search of Figure 16.2 assuming numItm has value n. Calculate the total statement execution count as a polynomial in n.

3. Determine **(a)** the best case, and **(b)** the worst case execution count of each statement in procedure Sort of Figure 16.12 assuming numItm has value n. Calculate the total statement execution count as a polynomial in n.

4. **(a)** For the search algorithm of Figure 16.1, translate the statements

```
i := 0;
WHILE (i < numItm) & (v[i] # srchNum) DO
    INC(i)
END;
fnd := i < numItm
```

from CP to GCL. **(b)** Write a formal specification for the code fragment. Use the fact that if there exists a j in the proper range such that $v[j] = s$ then $s = v[i]$, where s is the search number.

5. **(a)** For the search algorithm of Figure 16.2, translate the statements

```
v[numItm] := srchNum;
i := 0;
WHILE v[i] # srchNum DO
    INC(i)
END;
fnd := i < numItm
```

from CP to GCL. **(b)** Write a formal specification for the code fragment. Use the fact that if there exists a j in the proper range such that $v[j] = s$ then $s = v[i]$, where s is the search number.

6. **(a)** For the binary search algorithm of Figure 16.8, translate the statements

```
first := 0;
last := numItm - 1;
WHILE first <= last DO
    mid := (first + last) DIV 2;
    IF srchNum < v[mid] THEN
        last := mid - 1
    ELSIF srchNum > v[mid] THEN
        first := mid + 1
    ELSE
        fnd := TRUE; i := mid;
        RETURN
    END
END;
fnd := FALSE
```

from CP to GCL. You may assume that GCL has a **return** statement. **(b)** Write a formal specification for the code fragment. Use the fact that if there exists a j in the proper range such that $v[j] = s$ then $s = v[i]$, where s is the search number.

7. **(a)** For the selection sort algorithm of Figure 16.12, translate the statements

```
FOR n := numItm - 1 TO 1 BY -1 DO
   maxIndex := 0;
   FOR i := 1 TO n DO
      IF v[i] > v[maxIndex] THEN
         maxIndex := i
      END
   END;
   temp := v[n];
   v[n] := v[maxIndex];
   v[maxIndex] := temp
END
```

from CP to GCL. **(b)** Write a formal specification for the code fragment. You may use the predicate *perm(a,b,numItm)* to specify that the final values of *v* are a rearrangement of thed initial values of *v*.

Problems

8. Write a procedure

OddFirstSort (VAR v: ARRAY OF INTEGER; numItm: INTEGER)

that rearranges the elements of a list of integers so all the odd integers are before all the even integers. To test it, write a program similar to that in Figure 15.7, with input from the focus window using ScanIntVector from module PboxMappers and OddFirstSort taking the place of RotateLeft. The new window should contain the original list followed by the rearranged list. Activate your procedure with a menu selection.

9. Write a program to input values from a focus window similar to the one titled PhoneBk in Figure 16.5 into the parallel arrays nameList and numberList as defined in Figure 16.8. Declare a procedure

SortBook (VAR nameLst: ARRAY OF Name; VAR numLst: ARRAY OF Number; numItm: INTEGER)

that sorts the parallel arrays based on the values in nameLst. For example, after the sort nameList[0] should be Andrews, and numList[0] should be 243-1056. Output the sorted names with the corresponding numbers next to them on the Log. Activate your procedure with a menu selection.

10. Modify Figure 16.8 so that it uses the binary search instead of the sequential search. Assume the names are in order in the phone book window.

11. The input for this problem is in a focus window that contains a list of up to 1024 integers. Write a program that inputs the list, then outputs to the Log a list of those integers that occur more than once and the number of times each occurs. Activate your procedure with a menu selection. Hint: First sort the list. Also consider the possibility that the last item in the list might be duplicated. Considering that case, you may be able to simplify your code by appending an extra value after the last item of the list, similar to the technique of the sequential search in Figure 16.2.

Sample focus window:
33 -2 25 25 3 7 -2 17 12 25 33 8 17 2 17 20 25

Sample output to the Log:
-2 occurs 2 times
17 occurs 3 times
25 occurs 4 times
33 occurs 2 times

12. Modify procedure Sort in Figure 16.12 so that it sorts with the largest element first. To test it, write a program similar to that in Figure 15.7, with input from the focus window using ScanIntVector from module PboxMappers and Sort taking the place of RotateLeft. The new window should contain the original list followed by the sorted list. Activate your procedure with a menu selection.

13. Modify procedure Sort in Figure 16.12 so that it moves the smallest element to v[0] on the first pass, the next larger to v[1] on the second pass, and so on. To test it, write a program similar to that in Figure 15.7, with input from the focus window using ScanIntVector from module PboxMappers and Sort taking the place of RotateLeft. The new window should contain the original list followed by the sorted list. Activate your procedure with a menu selection.

14. Declare

PROCEDURE Compress (VAR v: ARRAY OF INTEGER; VAR numItm)

which removes duplicate integers from a sorted list of integers. For example, if numItm is 12 and v is

1   4   4   5   9   9   9   14   19   19   19   19

then Compress should change v to

1   4   5   9   14   19

and numItm to 6. To test it, write a program similar to that in Figure 15.7, with input from the focus window using ScanIntVector from module PboxMappers and Compress taking the place of RotateLeft. The new window should contain the original list followed by the compressed list. Activate your procedure with a menu selection. Do not include any output statements in Compress.

15. Anagrams are words that use the same letters. For example, races and acres are anagrams, but car and cat are not. Declare

PROCEDURE IsAnagram (wd1, wd2: ARRAY OF CHAR): BOOLEAN

which determines if wd1 and wd2 are anagrams. Test your function with a dialog box that has two input fields for the words and one output field for a message stating whether the two words are anagrams.

Chapter *17*

Stack and List Implementations

Chapter 6 introduces the concept of an abstract data structure (ADS) and an abstract data type (ADT). It illustrates each of these abstractions with stacks and lists. An ADT differs from an ADS because the server module exports a type. The client module is then able to declare its own variable with that type and can have as many data structures as it needs. The data structures exist in the client module. For example, the module of Figure 7.10 declares two stacks, stackA and stackB. Because an ADS does not export a type, there is only one data structure and it is hidden in the server module. For example, the module of Figure 17.4 does not contain any stack variables. It simply manipulates the one stack contained in PboxStackADS.

Chapter 9 introduces the concept of a class, which is the object-oriented equivalent of an ADT. It introduces classes so you can see how to use the MVC objects provided by the BlackBox framework. The module in Figure 9.3 uses the stack class from PboxStackObj to manipulate two stacks. For now, there is no apparent advantage of using a class instead of an ADT. A demonstration of the advantage of using classes is postponed until a later chapter.

In all the previous chapters you accessed the ADS, the ADT, or the class by inspecting its corresponding interface, which consists of all the items exported by the server module. You then wrote your client modules accessing those items provided by the server. It was not necessary for you to know how the data structure is implemented in order to use the data structure. This chapter shows the implementations of the stack ADS, the stack class, and the list ADT that were previously hidden.

Stack ADS implementation

Figure 17.1 shows the interface for the stack abstract data structure from PboxStack-ADS. The server module exports five items—the constant capacity that specifies the maximum number of values that can be stored in the structure, and the four procedures Clear, NumItems, Pop, and Push. Procedure Push gives the client the ability to store a value in the data structure, and procedure Pop gives the ability to retrieve a value. Stacks are last in, first out (LIFO) structures, so that when a client executes the Pop procedure the value retrieved is the most recent value pushed. Figure 17.2 shows a sequence of push and pop operations on the stack.

DEFINITION PboxStackADS;

   CONST
     capacity = 8;

   PROCEDURE Clear;
   PROCEDURE NumItems (): INTEGER;
   PROCEDURE Pop (OUT val: REAL);
   PROCEDURE Push (val: REAL);

END PboxStackADS.

Figure 17.1
The interface of the stack abstract data structure.

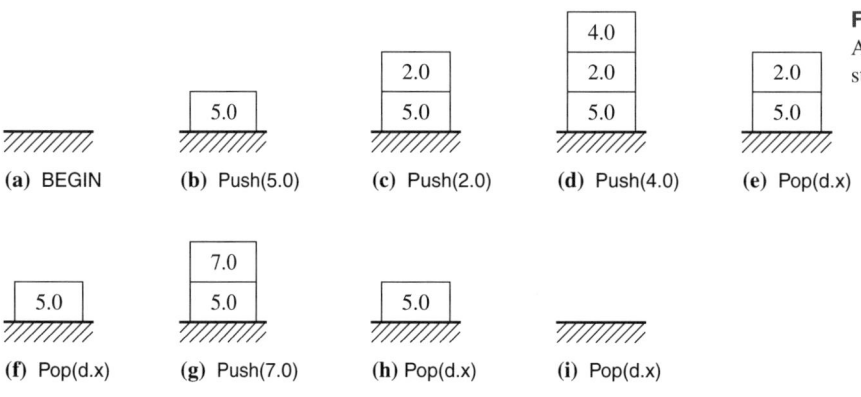

Figure 17.2
A sequence of operations on a stack.

As you might suspect by now, a straightforward implementation of the stack is to use an array to store the values. When the client executes the push operation, you simply store the value in the array. Of course, you need to keep track of where the most recent value was stored so you will know where to store the value pushed. You can use an integer variable whose value will be the index of the most recently stored value. Figure 17.3 is a diagram of the values that the array, named body, and the integer, named top, acquire assuming the same sequence of pushes and pops as in Figure 17.2.

Figure 17.4 is the corresponding implementation of the stack abstract data structure. The module contains two global variables, body and top, that are necessary to maintain the state of the stack between invocations of the procedures. body is an array of eight reals and top is an integer. To clear the stack top is set to –1, which indicates that no items are stored in the array. Procedure Clear performs the operation with the simple assignment

top := -1

You can see from Figure 17.3 that at any point in time, the number of values stored in the stack is one more than the value of top. For example, in part (d) three

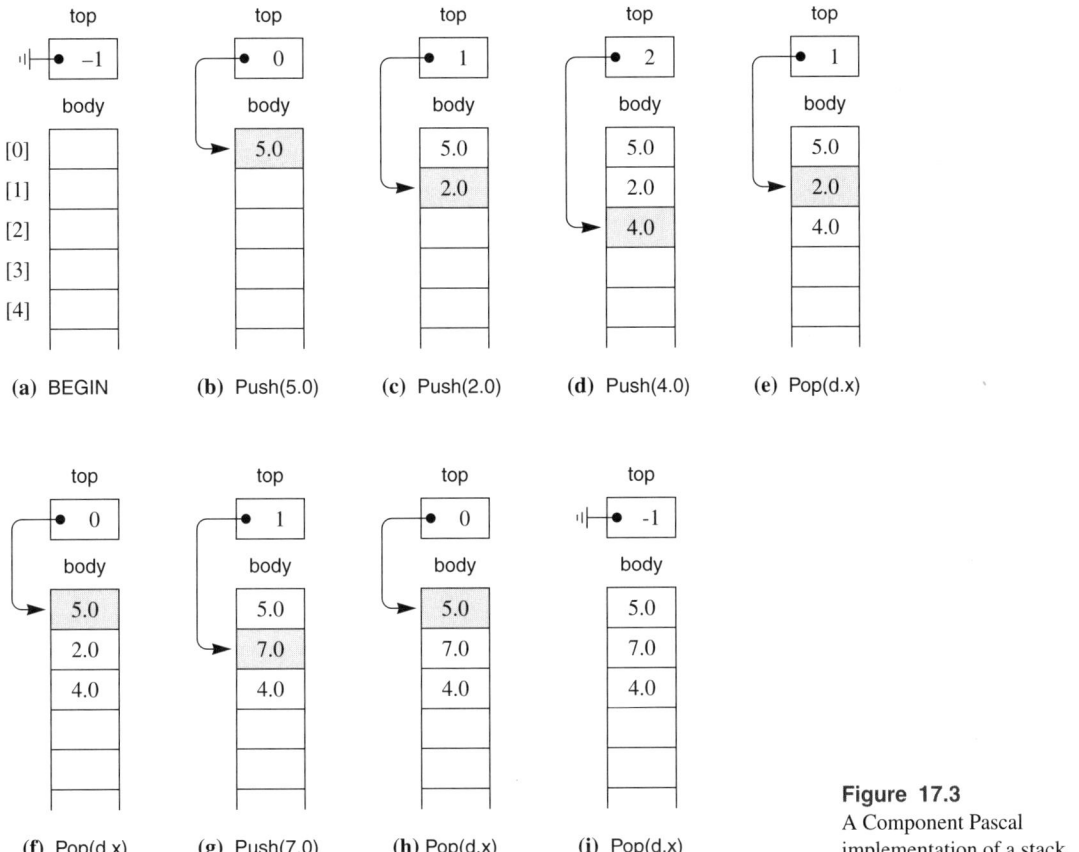

Figure 17.3
A Component Pascal
implementation of a stack.

values are stored and the value of top is two. Therefore, function procedure NumItems simply executes the single statement

RETURN top + 1

The documentation for the push procedure is

PROCEDURE **Push** (val: REAL)
Pre
NumItems() < capacity   20
Post
val is pushed onto the top of the stack.

Procedure Push implements the precondition with the assertion

ASSERT(top < capacity - 1, 20)

Using the ASSERT statement to implement the precondition is consistent with the design-by-contract rule, which states

- IF in the client.
- ASSERT in the server.

The design-by-contract rule

```
MODULE  PboxStackADS;

   CONST
      capacity* = 8;
   VAR
      body: ARRAY capacity OF REAL;
      top: INTEGER;

   PROCEDURE  Clear*;
   BEGIN
      top := -1
   END Clear;

   PROCEDURE  NumItems* (): INTEGER;
   BEGIN
      RETURN top + 1
   END NumItems;

   PROCEDURE  Pop* (OUT val: REAL);
   BEGIN
      ASSERT(0 <= top, 20);
      val := body[top];
      DEC(top)
   END Pop;

   PROCEDURE  Push* (val: REAL);
   BEGIN
      ASSERT(top < capacity - 1, 20);
      INC(top);
      body[top] := val
   END Push;

END PboxStackADS.
```

Figure 17.4
The implementation of the stack abstract data structure.

The value of capacity -1 is the index of the last cell in the array. In this implementation, the capacity of the array is 8, and the index of the last cell is 7. To have room to put another value on the stack, variable top must be less than 7. The push operation is achieved with the assignments

```
INC(top);
body[top] := val
```

where val is the value supplied by the actual parameter from the client module. For example, in Figure 17.3(c) top has value 1. INC(top) gives it value 2, then body[2] gets val, as shown in part (d).

The documentation for procedure Pop is

```
PROCEDURE  Pop (OUT val: REAL)
Pre
0 < NumItems()   20
Post
An item is removed from the top of the stack and val gets its value.
```

The precondition states that you cannot pop a value off the stack unless there is at least one value to be retrieved. Procedure Pop implements the precondition with the assertion

```
ASSERT(0 <= top, 20)
```

A value of zero for top indicates that one value is in the stack, as Figure 17.3(b) shows. Procedure Pop implements the retrieval with the statements

```
val := body[top];
DEC(top)
```

Because top is the index of body where the most recent value was stored, you must make the assignment to formal parameter x before you decrement top. Note how this is consistent with the implementation of procedure Push, in which the INC operation occurs before the assignment to body[top].

Stack class implementation

Figure 17.5 shows the interface of the stack class from module PboxStackObj. It differs from the stack ADS because the type Stack is exported.

```
DEFINITION PboxStackObj;

   CONST
      capacity = 8;

   TYPE
      Stack = RECORD
         (VAR s: Stack) Clear, NEW;
         (IN s: Stack) NumItems (): INTEGER, NEW;
         (VAR s: Stack) Pop (OUT val: REAL), NEW;
         (VAR s: Stack) Push (val: REAL), NEW
      END;

END PboxStackObj.
```

Figure 17.5
The interface of the stack class.

The concept of implementing the stack class with an array is identical to the concept of implementing the stack abstract data structure in the previous section. You have an array named body that stores the values, and you have an integer variable named top that stores the index of the array where the most recent value was pushed. You clear the array by setting top to −1, procedure NumItems returns one plus the value of top, Pop assigns to x then decrements top, and Push increments top then assigns to body[top]. The assertions are implemented as they are with the stack ADS. Figure 17.6 shows the implementation.

```
MODULE PboxStackObj;

    CONST
        capacity* = 8;
    TYPE
        Stack* = RECORD
            body: ARRAY capacity OF REAL;
            top: INTEGER
        END;

    PROCEDURE (VAR s: Stack) Clear*, NEW;
    BEGIN
        s.top := -1
    END Clear;

    PROCEDURE (IN s: Stack) NumItems* (): INTEGER, NEW;
    BEGIN
        RETURN s.top + 1
    END NumItems;

    PROCEDURE (VAR s: Stack) Push* (val: REAL), NEW;
    BEGIN
        ASSERT(s.top < capacity - 1, 20);
        INC(s.top);
        s.body[s.top] := val
    END Push;

    PROCEDURE (VAR s: Stack) Pop* (OUT val: REAL), NEW;
    BEGIN
        ASSERT(0 <= s.top, 20);
        val := s.body[s.top];
        DEC(s.top)
    END Pop;

END PboxStackObj.
```

Figure 17.6
The implementation of the stack class.

Compare the interface of the class in Figure 17.5 with the implementation in Figure 17.6. What is contained between the lines

```
Stack = RECORD

END
```

in each case? The interface does not show body or top in the record for the Stack class, but the implementation does. Furthermore, the interface shows the procedure headings within the record, but the procedures are contained outside the record in the implementation. Why are the interface and the implementation different in these two respects?

One big advantage of the Component Pascal language over many other object-oriented languages is that the interface is generated automatically by the compiler. With other languages, the programmer must write not only the implementation but the corresponding interface as well. So it is the Component Pascal compiler that generates the interface from the implementation. Figure 17.6 shows that Stack is exported with the * export mark but body and top are not. That is why body and top do not appear in the interface. They are both part of class Stack but are hidden from the client.

Automatic generation of the interface is also the reason for the procedure headings appearing inside the Stack record. When the compiler processes the source code, it detects the presence of an exported method by the existence of the receiver in front of the procedure name. The type of the receiver determines the placement of the procedure heading in the interface. For example, when the compiler scans the source line

```
PROCEDURE (VAR s: Stack) Clear*, NEW;
```

it detects the receiver (VAR s: Stack). The type of the receiver is Stack, so the line

```
(VAR s: Stack) Clear, NEW;
```

is inserted in the Stack record in the interface.

Why does the interface display class methods this way? To emphasize that class methods belong to the class record. The style is consistent with the manner in which methods are called. For example, suppose you have a record

```
d*: RECORD
    valuePushed*, valuePopped-: REAL;
    numItemsA-, numItemsB-: INTEGER
END;
```

How do you access one of the fields of the record, say valuePushed? You precede it with the record name with a period between the record name and the field. You refer to the valuePushed field of record d by writing

```
d.valuePushed
```

And how does a client module invoke a method? The style is the same as if the method were a field in the record. For example, if your client module declares

```
VAR
   stackA, stackB: PboxStackObj.Stack;
```

then to call the method to clear stackA, you write

```
StackA.Clear
```

This call is consistent with the interface

```
Stack = RECORD
   (VAR s: Stack) ClearStack, NEW;
END
```

In the same way that valuePushed belongs to the d record, Clear belongs to the Stack record.

The implementation of all the methods in the stack class is similar to the implementations in the stack ADS. Because body and top are part of a record, you simply use the record notation to refer to them. For example, the code for the push procedure with the ADS is

```
INC(top);
body[top] := val
```

where body and top are global variables in the server module. The corresponding code for the push method with the class is

```
INC(s.top);
s.body[s.top] := val
```

where record s is the formal parameter corresponding to the actual parameter in the client module.

List ADT implementation

Figure 17.7 shows the interface of the list ADT. As with the implementation of the stack, an array is a convenient data structure for implementing a list.

```
DEFINITION PboxListADT;

    CONST
        capacity = 8;

    TYPE
        List = RECORD END;
        T = ARRAY 16 OF CHAR;

    PROCEDURE Clear (VAR lst: List);
    PROCEDURE Display (IN lst: List);
    PROCEDURE GetElementN (IN lst: List; n: INTEGER; OUT val: T);
    PROCEDURE InsertAtN (VAR lst: List; n: INTEGER; IN val: T);
    PROCEDURE Length (IN lst: List): INTEGER;
    PROCEDURE RemoveN (VAR lst: List; n: INTEGER);
    PROCEDURE Search (VAR lst: List; IN srchVal: T; OUT n: INTEGER; OUT fnd: BOOLEAN);

END PboxListADT.
```

Figure 17.7
The interface of the list
abstract data type.

Figure 17.8 shows the implementation of the list ADT. The list record contains two fields—body, which is the array itself, and lastIndex, which is the index of the last item in the array.

The array has a capacity of eight, yet the body is declared to be an ARRAY 9 OF T. That is, there are nine cells in the array indexed from 0 to 8. The ninth cell at index 8 cannot be used by the client for storing a value. It is for storing the search value as a sentinel using the efficient version of the search algorithm in Figure 16.2. If the declaration for body did not allocate the extra cell, the algorithm could not do a sequential search when there are eight items in the list, because there would be no room for the sentinel.

```
MODULE  PboxListADT;
    IMPORT StdLog;

    CONST
        capacity* = 8;
    TYPE
        T* = ARRAY 16 OF CHAR;
        List* = RECORD
            body: ARRAY capacity + 1 OF T; (* + 1 necessary for procedure Search *)
            lastIndex: INTEGER
        END;

    PROCEDURE Clear* (VAR lst: List);
    BEGIN
        lst.lastIndex := -1
    END Clear;
```

Figure 17.8
The implementation of the
list abstract data type.

Figure 17.8
Continued.

```
PROCEDURE  Display* (IN lst: List);
   VAR
      i: INTEGER;
BEGIN
   StdLog.Ln;
   FOR i := 0 TO lst.lastIndex DO
      StdLog.Int(i); StdLog.String(" "); StdLog.String(lst.body[i]); StdLog.Ln
   END
END Display;

PROCEDURE  GetElementN* (IN lst: List; n: INTEGER; OUT val: T);
BEGIN
   ASSERT(0 <= n, 20);
   ASSERT(n <= lst.lastIndex, 21);
   val := lst.body[n]
END GetElementN;

PROCEDURE  InsertAtN* (VAR lst: List; n: INTEGER; IN val: T);
   VAR
      i: INTEGER;
BEGIN
   ASSERT(0 <= n, 20);
   ASSERT(lst.lastIndex < capacity - 1, 21);
   IF n > lst.lastIndex + 1 THEN
      n := lst.lastIndex + 1
   END;
   FOR i := lst.lastIndex TO n BY -1 DO
      lst.body[i + 1] := lst.body[i]
   END;
   INC(lst.lastIndex);
   lst.body[n] := val
END InsertAtN;

PROCEDURE  Length* (IN lst: List): INTEGER;
BEGIN
   RETURN lst.lastIndex + 1
END Length;

PROCEDURE  RemoveN* (VAR lst: List; n: INTEGER);
   VAR
      i: INTEGER;
BEGIN
   ASSERT(0 <= n, 20);
   IF n <= lst.lastIndex THEN
      FOR i := n TO lst.lastIndex - 1 DO
         lst.body[i] := lst.body[i + 1]
      END;
      DEC(lst.lastIndex)
   END
END RemoveN;
```

```
PROCEDURE  Search* (VAR lst: List; IN srchVal: T; OUT n: INTEGER; OUT fnd: BOOLEAN);
BEGIN
    lst.body[lst.lastIndex + 1] := srchVal;
    n := 0;
    WHILE lst.body[n] # srchVal DO
        INC(n)
    END;
    fnd := n <= lst.lastIndex
END Search;

END PboxListADT.
```

Figure 17.8
Continued.

Figure 17.9(a) shows an abstract representation of a list containing four items. The first item is at position 0 and the last is at position 3. Figure 17.9(b) shows the implementation. The items are stored in the body part of the data structure. The position of each item corresponds to the index of the array. lastIndex has value 3, because that is the index of the last item in the array.

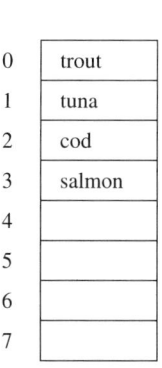

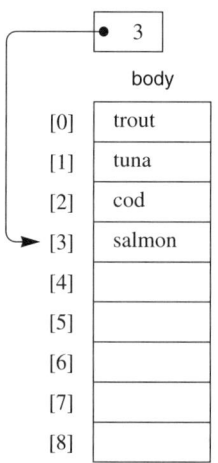

Figure 17.9
The abstract list ADT and its array implementation.

(a) The abstract list　　　**(b)** The array implementation

The procedures for the list ADT are straightforward array manipulations. The Clear procedure simply sets lastIndex with

lst.lastIndex := -1

Any values remaining in the body of the array will be overwritten when the client inserts new values.

The Display procedure outputs lst.body[i] with

StdLog.Int(i); StdLog.String(" "); StdLog.String(lst.body[i]); StdLog.Ln

in the body of a FOR loop, with i ranging from 0 to lst.lastIndex.

Procedure GetElementN implements the preconditions

```
Pre
0 <= n    20
n < Length(lst)    21
```

with the ASSERT statements

```
ASSERT(0 <= n, 20);
ASSERT(n <= lst.lastIndex, 21)
```

Implementation of the second precondition is based on the fact that the index of the last item is one less than the length of the list. In Figure 17.9(b), lastIndex is 3 and the length of the list is 4. n is less than 4 if and only if it is less than or equal to 3. GetElementN has formal parameter val called by result. It sets the value of val by executing the statement

```
val := lst.body[n]
```

Procedure InsertAtN implements the preconditions

```
Pre
0 <= n    20
Length(lst) < capacity    21
```

with the ASSERT statements

```
ASSERT(0 <= n, 20);
ASSERT(lst.lastIndex < capacity - 1, 21)
```

If the preconditions are satisfied, it adjusts the value of n by comparing it with the index of the last item. The procedure allows the client to supply a large value of n, in which case the value gets inserted at the end of the list. The IF statement

```
IF n > lst.lastIndex + 1 THEN
    n := lst.lastIndex + 1
END;
```

adjusts n to the position just after the last item, where the new value will be inserted, if the original value of n is beyond that position. Figure 17.10 shows the effect of

```
FOR i := lst.lastIndex TO n BY -1 DO
    lst.body[i + 1] := lst.body[i]
END;
INC(lst.lastIndex);
lst.body[n] := val
```

for the case of inserting value bass at position 2 for n. The elements of the array must be shifted down to make room for the inserted value.

Figure 17.10
Execution of InsertAtN with 2 for n and bass for val.

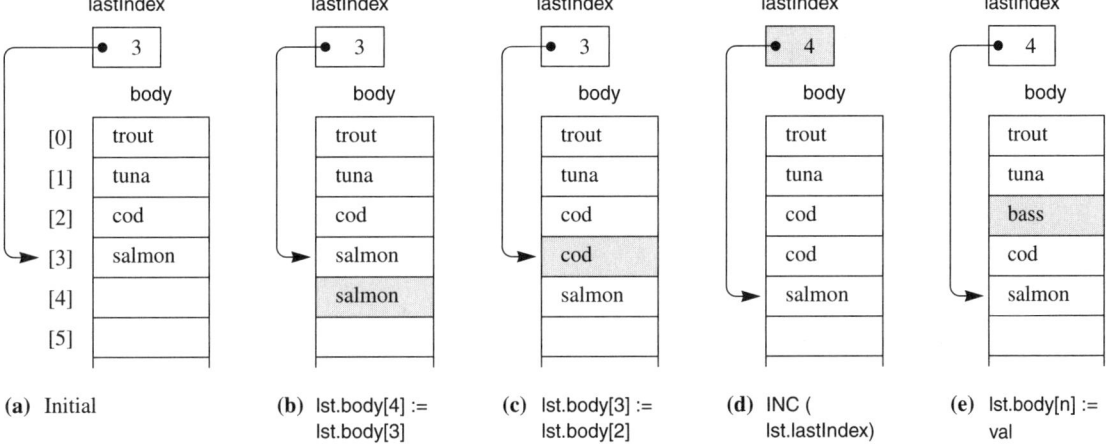

(a) Initial

(b) lst.body[4] := lst.body[3]

(c) lst.body[3] := lst.body[2]

(d) INC (lst.lastIndex)

(e) lst.body[n] := val

The implementation of procedure RemoveN first verifies the precondition that n is nonnegative with an appropriate ASSERT statement. The specification allows a large value of n, in which case the list is unchanged. No processing needs to be done unless n is less than or equal to lastIndex. Consequently, the processing is contained within the IF statement

```
IF n <= lst.lastIndex THEN
```

Figure 17.11 shows the effect of executing

```
FOR i := n TO lst.lastIndex - 1 DO
    lst.body[i] := lst.body[i + 1]
END;
DEC(lst.lastIndex)
```

for the case of removing the item at position 1. This time the items are shifted up and lastIndex is decremented. The garbage value at position 3 will be overwritten when the client inserts a new value later.

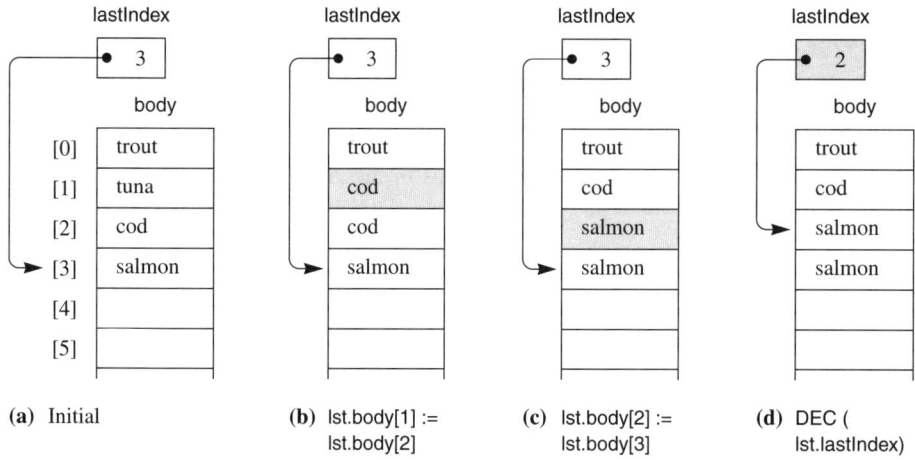

(a) Initial (b) lst.body[1] :=   (c) lst.body[2] :=   (d) DEC (
                  lst.body[2]   lst.body[3]   lst.lastIndex)

Figure 17.11
Execution of RemoveN with 1
for n.

Problems

1. PboxStackADS in Figure 17.4 uses array body and integer top to implement a stack abstract data structure. At any given point in time, top has the index of the item on top of the stack. Modify the corresponding implementation of the abstract data type in PboxStackADT so that at any given point in time top will have the index of the location to push the next item. Hence, when the stack is cleared top will be initialized to 0 instead of to −1. Be sure to modify the ASSERT statements where necessary. Test your program by importing your implementation into a program similar to that in Figure 7.10.

2. Work Problem 1 but test your program by importing your implementation into the program you wrote for Chapter 7, Problem 20.

3. PboxStackObj in Figure 17.6 uses array body and integer top to implement a stack class. At any given point in time, top has the index of the item on top of the stack. Modify PboxStackObj so that at any given point in time top will have the index of the location to push the next item. Hence, when the stack is cleared top will be initialized to 0 instead of to −1. Be sure to modify the ASSERT statements where necessary. Test your program by importing your implementation into a program to construct an RPN calculator as described in Chapter 7, Problem 14. Verify in the calling module that the preconditions are met. If a precondition is not met, the calculator should do nothing and no trap should occur.

4. Work Problem 3, but construct a full-featured scientific calculator as described in Chapter 7, Problem 16.

5. Work Problem 3, but test your program by importing your implementation into a module that implements a dialog box for two stacks with an "A to B" button as described in Chapter 7, Problem 20. Verify in the calling module that the preconditions are met. If a precondition is not met, the dialog box should not change and no trap should occur.

Chapter *18*

Two-Dimensional Arrays

Sometimes you need to store information not as a single list of values, but as a table of values. Tables have rows and columns. The Component Pascal data structure that corresponds to a table is a two-dimensional array. In the same way that vector is another name for a one-dimensional array, matrix is another name for a two-dimensional array.

Matrix input/output

Figure 18.1 shows a tool dialog box for inputting a two-dimensional array of real values from the focus window and outputting the array to a new window. The dialog box is opened as a tool, so the scanner will be attached to the model of the view that was previously the focus window, which is titled "untitled 1" in the figure. When the user clicks the Load Matrix button, the program scans the real numbers into a two-dimensional array. When the user clicks the Display Matrix button a new window appears, which is titled "untitled 2" in the figure, that contains the values previously scanned into the two-dimensional array.

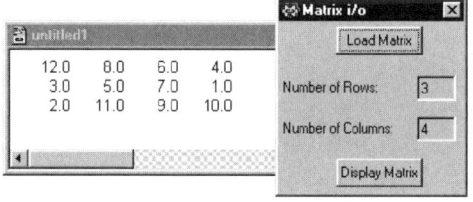
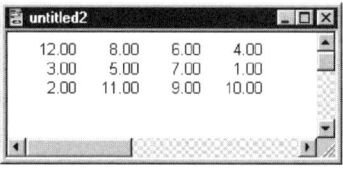

Figure 18.1
Input and output for a two-dimensional array of real values.

Figure 18.2 is the implementation of the dialog box of Figure 18.1. It defines global variable matrix to be a two-dimensional array with the declaration

matrix: ARRAY 32, 32 OF REAL

The two indices, 32 and 32, is what makes the array two-dimensional. The first index numbers the rows and the second index numbers the columns. matrix contains storage for $32 \times 32 = 1024$ values in 32 rows and 32 columns, although the program does not in general use all the storage.

```
MODULE Pbox18A;
   IMPORT Dialog, TextModels, TextViews, Views, TextControllers, PboxMappers;
   TYPE
      Matrix = ARRAY 32, 32 OF REAL;
   VAR
      d*: RECORD
         numRows-, numCols-: INTEGER;
      END;
      matrix: Matrix;

   PROCEDURE LoadMatrix*;
      VAR
         md: TextModels.Model;
         cn: TextControllers.Controller;
         sc: PboxMappers.Scanner;
   BEGIN
      cn := TextControllers.Focus();
      IF cn # NIL THEN
         md := cn.text;
         sc.ConnectTo(md);
         sc.ScanRealMatrix(matrix, d.numRows, d.numCols);
         Dialog.Update(d)
      END;
   END LoadMatrix;

   PROCEDURE DisplayMatrix*;
      VAR
         md: TextModels.Model;
         vw: TextViews.View;
         fm: PboxMappers.Formatter;
   BEGIN
      md := TextModels.dir.New();
      fm.ConnectTo(md);
      fm.WriteRealMatrix(matrix, d.numRows, d.numCols, 8, 2);
      vw := TextViews.dir.New(md);
      Views.OpenView(vw)
   END DisplayMatrix;

BEGIN
   d.numRows := 0; d.numCols := 0;
END Pbox18A.
```

Figure 18.2

A procedure that inputs a matrix and outputs it to a new window.

Figure 18.3 shows how the cells in the matrix are numbered. matrix[2, 3] is the component in row two, column three. In general, matrix[i, j] is the component in row i, column j.

Procedure LoadMatrix in Figure 18.2 contains our usual MVC suspects for connecting to the focus window. It inputs the values by calling the imported procedure ScanRealMatrix from module PboxMappers. Here is the documentaion for Scan-RealMatrix.

matrix[0,0] 12.0	matrix[0, 1] 8.0	matrix[0, 2] 6.0	matrix[0, 3] 4.0
matrix[1, 0] 3.0	matrix[1, 1] 5.0	matrix[1, 2] 7.0	matrix[1, 3] 1.0
matrix[2, 0] 2.0	matrix[2, 1] 11.0	matrix[2, 2] 9.0	matrix[2, 3] 10.0

Figure 18.3
Indices for a two-dimensional
array of real values.

```
PROCEDURE (VAR s: Scanner) ScanRealMatrix (OUT mat: ARRAY OF ARRAY OF REAL;
        OUT numR, numC: INTEGER), NEW
Pre
s is connected to a text model.   20
Sequences of characters scanned represent in-range real or integer values.   21
All nonempty rows have the same number of values.   22
Number of rows in text model <= LEN(mat, 0).   Index out of range.
Number of columns in text model <= LEN(mat, 1).   Index out of range.
Post
mat gets all the values scanned up to the end of the text model to which s is connected.
numR gets the number of rows scanned.
numC gets the number of columns scanned.
The values are stored  at v[0..numR - 1, 0..numC - 1].
```

ScanRealMatrix expects each row of the matrix to be on a separate line. It scans *The operation of* all the values on the first line into the first row of the two-dimensional array mat, *ScanRealMatrix* counting how many values are on the first line of the text model. It then scans each of the other lines in turn, counting the number of values on each line. If it detects a different number of values from the number on the first line, it terminates with a trap. ScanRealMatrix allows you to have any number of leading or trailing blank lines, which it ignores in the scan. You can even have blank lines between two lines of numbers and the embedded blank line will be ignored as well. At the completion of the scan, numR will contain the number of rows in mat, and numC will contain the number of columns.

The Component Pascal function LEN returns the number of elements in a one-dimensional array. You can also use LEN in an array with more than one dimension, *LEN with a two-dimensional* but it requires two parameters instead of just one. The function call LEN(arr, n) *array* returns the number of cells in the nth dimension of array arr starting with $n = 0$ for the first dimension. For a two-dimensional array, LEN(mat, 0) is the number of rows of mat, and LEN(mat, 1) is the number of cells in each row. A precondition for proce-dure ScanRealMatrix is that matrix mat has enough rows and columns to store the values that are in the model to which s is connected.

Procedure DisplayMatrix outputs the values by calling WriteRealMatrix, also from PboxMappers. Here is the documentaion for WriteRealMatrix.

PROCEDURE (VAR f: Formatter) **WriteRealMatrix** (IN mat: ARRAY OF ARRAY OF REAL;
      numR, numC, minWidth, dec: INTEGER), NEW
Pre
f is connected to a text model.   20
numR <= LEN(mat, 0).   Index out of range.
numC <= LEN(mat, 1).   Index out of range.
Post
The first numR rows and numC columns of mat are written to the text model to which f
is connected, each with a field width of minWidth and dec places past the decimal point.
If minWidth is too small to contain a value of mat it expands to accommodate the value.

Parameter mat is called by constant reference, because its values are defined *The operation of* when the procedure is called and its values are not to be changed. To write the *WriteRealMatrix* matrix you must supply the number of rows and columns in numR and numC. You also supply a value for minWidth, the field width for each real value, and for dec, the number of places you want to display past the decimal point.

Printing a column

Figure 18.4 shows the input and output of a program that prints a column of a matrix to a new window. The dialog box allows the user to load the values from the focus window into the matrix as in Figure 18.2. It also contains a text field for the user to enter the column to display.

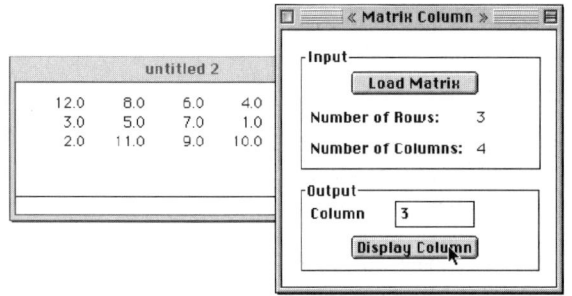
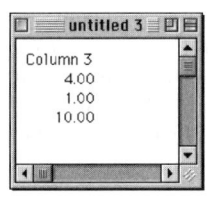

Figure 18.4
Printing a column of a matrix to a new window.

Before looking at the program that implements the dialog box of Figure 18.4, try to solve the problem yourself. Suppose you are given a two-dimensional array matrix with d.numRows rows, and an integer variable, d.column. The problem is to output all the values from matrix in that column. For example, if d.column has the value of 3, the code should output

  4.00
  1.00
10.00

which are all the components in column three. The specific output statements with formatter fm are

```
fm.WriteReal(matrix[0, 3], 8, 2); fm.WriteLn
fm.WriteReal(matrix[1, 3], 8, 2); fm.WriteLn
fm.WriteReal(matrix[2, 3], 8, 2); fm.WriteLn
```

assuming a field width of 8 and two places past the decimal point. In a FOR loop the statements are

```
FOR i := 0 TO 2 DO
    fm.WriteReal(matrix[i, 3], 8, 2); fm.WriteLn
END
```

for an array with values in three rows. Because the value of numRows specifies how many rows of data are in the array, you must replace the 2 with d.numRows - 1. For a general column, you must replace the 3 with d.column. Here is the code for printing the column.

```
FOR i := 0 TO d.numRows - 1 DO
    fm.WriteReal(matrix[i, d.column], 8, 2); fm.WriteLn
END
```

Figure 18.5 shows the module that implements the dialog box of Figure 18.4.

```
MODULE Pbox18B;
    IMPORT Dialog, TextModels, TextViews, Views, TextControllers, PboxMappers;
    TYPE
        Matrix = ARRAY 32, 32 OF REAL;
    VAR
        d*: RECORD
            numRows-, numCols-: INTEGER;
            column*: INTEGER;
        END;
        matrix: Matrix;

    PROCEDURE LoadMatrix*;
        VAR
            md: TextModels.Model;
            cn: TextControllers.Controller;
            sc: PboxMappers.Scanner;
    BEGIN
        cn := TextControllers.Focus();
        IF cn # NIL THEN
            md := cn.text;
            sc.ConnectTo(md);
            sc.ScanRealMatrix(matrix, d.numRows, d.numCols);
            Dialog.Update(d)
        END;
    END LoadMatrix;
```

Figure 18.5
A program to print a column of a matrix. The dialog is activated from a menu selection.

```
PROCEDURE DisplayColumn*;
   VAR
      md: TextModels.Model;
      vw: TextViews.View;
      fm: PboxMappers.Formatter;
      i: INTEGER;
BEGIN
   md := TextModels.dir.New();
   fm.ConnectTo(md);
   IF (0 <= d.column) & (d.column < d.numCols) THEN
      fm.WriteString("Column "); fm.WriteInt(d.column, 1); fm.WriteLn;
      FOR i := 0 TO d.numRows - 1 DO
         fm.WriteReal(matrix[i, d.column], 8, 2); fm.WriteLn
      END
   ELSE
      fm.WriteString("That column is not in the array")
   END;
   vw := TextViews.dir.New(md);
   Views.OpenView(vw)
END DisplayColumn;

BEGIN
   d.numRows := 0; d.numCols := 0; d.column := 0;
END Pbox18B.
```

Finding the largest in a row

The next illustration of a two-dimensional array involves finding the largest element in a row of a matrix. The problem is to complete the statements for the function procedure

```
PROCEDURE MaxInRow (IN mat: ARRAY OF ARRAY OF REAL; row, numCols: INTEGER): REAL;
```

Because mat is called by constant reference, assume its values are defined when the procedure is called. Because row and numCols are called by value, their initial values are also defined. numCols is the number of columns in mat, and row is the row from which we want the maximum value. For example, if the values in mat are again

```
12.0   8.0   6.0   4.0
 3.0   5.0   7.0   1.0
 2.0  11.0   9.0  10.0
```

and if row has the value 2, the function should return the value 11.0. A precondition is that there is at least one row and one column. Otherwise there can be no maximum.

Assume you have a local variable max to store the maximum value found. The specific statements to compute max for row 2 are

```
max := mat[2, 0];
```

```
IF mat[2, 1] > max THEN
    max := mat[2, 1]
END;
IF mat[2, 2] > max THEN
    max := mat[2, 2]
END;
IF mat[2, 3] > max THEN
    max := mat[2, 3]
END
```

After execution, max has the maximum value of 11.0 from row two (the third row). The corresponding FOR statement assuming local integer variable j is

```
max := mat[2, 0];
FOR j := 1 TO 3 DO
    IF mat[2, j] > max THEN
        max := mat[2, j]
    END
END;
```

for an array with values in four columns. For numCols in general, j in the FOR loop ranges from 1 to numCols - 1. And for a general row, the FOR loop is shown in Figure 18.6.

```
PROCEDURE MaxInRow (IN mat: ARRAY OF ARRAY OF REAL;
        row, numCols: INTEGER): REAL;
VAR
    max: REAL;
    j: INTEGER;
BEGIN
    ASSERT((0 <= row) & (row < LEN(mat, 0)), 20);
    ASSERT((0 < numCols) & (numCols <= LEN(mat, 1)), 21);
    max := mat[row, 0];
    FOR j := 1 TO numCols - 1 DO
        IF mat[row, j] > max THEN
            max := mat[row, j]
        END
    END;
    RETURN max
END MaxInRow;
```

Figure 18.6
A function procedure that returns the maximum value in a row of a matrix.

Matrix multiplication

The next illustration deals with multiplication of two matrices, a and b, with the product in c. To multiply matrix a times matrix b, the number of columns of a must equal the number of rows of b. The integer variable numRa is the number of rows in matrix a, numCaRb is the number of columns in matrix a and rows in matrix b, and numCb is the number of columns in b. The product c will have the same number of rows as a and the same number of columns as b.

For example, if a and b have the values

	a				b		
1.0	3.0	−1.0	2.0		−1.0	2.0	5.0
0.0	4.0	1.0	−2.0		−3.0	0.0	4.0
					1.0	−2.0	3.0
					3.0	2.0	−4.0

then the product c should have the values

	c	
−5.00	8.00	6.00
−17.00	−6.00	27.00

With these matrices, numRa is 2, numCaRb is 4, and numCb is 3.

Each value of c comes from multiplying a row of a with a column of b. For example, the element in the second row and third column of c comes from multiplying the second row of a with the third column of b. You multiply a row with a column by multiplying corresponding components from left to right in the row and from top to bottom in the column. Then you add the products. This specific case is

0.0 * 5.0 + 4.0 * 4.0 + 1.0 * 3.0 + (-2.0) * (-4.0)

which is 27.0. In general, the element in row i and column j of c comes from multiplying row i of a with column j of b.

Our problem is to write the proper procedure

PROCEDURE Multiply (IN a, b: ARRAY OF ARRAY OF REAL;
    numRa, numCaRb, numCb: INTEGER; OUT c: ARRAY OF ARRAY OF REAL);

Because a and b are called by constant reference, their initial values are defined. The problem is to compute new values for the matrix product c, which is called by result.

Start with the specific case above. For row one and column two of c, you need to compute

a[1, 0] * b[0, 2] + a[1, 1] * b[1, 2] + a[1, 2] * b[2, 2] + a[1, 3] * b[3, 2]

In a FOR loop, that is

```
sum := 0.0;
FOR k := 0 TO 3 DO
    sum := sum + a [1, k] * b [k, 2]
END;
c [1, 2] := sum
```

where sum is a real variable.

This code is for arrays with four columns in a and four rows in b. For the more general case of numCaRb columns and rows, k in the FOR statement ranges from 0 to numCaRb - 1. Also, this computation is for row one, column two of c. In the more general case of row i and column j of c the code is

```
sum := 0.0;
FOR k := 0 TO numCaRb - 1 DO
   sum := sum + a[i, k] * b[k, j]
END;
c[i, j] := sum
```

This computation must be done for every row and column of c. So, it must be nested in a nested loop with i ranging from 0 to numRa - 1 and j ranging from 0 to numCb - 1. The final code for matrix multiplication is in procedure Multiply in Figure 18.8. Figure 18.7 shows the corresponding dialog box.

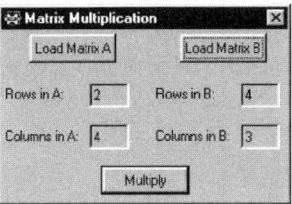
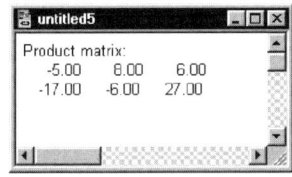

Figure 18.7
Output for the product of two matrices.

```
MODULE Pbox18C;
   IMPORT Dialog, TextModels, TextViews, Views, TextControllers, PboxMappers;
   VAR
      d*: RECORD
         numRowA-, numColA-, numRowB-, numColB-: INTEGER;
      END;
      matrixA, matrixB: ARRAY 32, 32 OF REAL;

   PROCEDURE LoadA*;
      VAR
         md: TextModels.Model;
         cn: TextControllers.Controller;
         sc: PboxMappers.Scanner;
   BEGIN
      cn := TextControllers.Focus();
      IF cn # NIL THEN
         md := cn.text;
         sc.ConnectTo(md);
         sc.ScanRealMatrix(matrixA, d.numRowA, d.numColA);
         Dialog.Update(d)
      END
   END LoadA;
```

Figure 18.8
A program that multiplies two matrices.

Figure 18.8
Continued.

```
PROCEDURE LoadB*;
  VAR
    md: TextModels.Model;
    cn: TextControllers.Controller;
    sc: PboxMappers.Scanner;
BEGIN
  cn := TextControllers.Focus();
  IF cn # NIL THEN
    md := cn.text;
    sc.ConnectTo(md);
    sc.ScanRealMatrix(matrixB, d.numRowB, d.numColB);
    Dialog.Update(d)
  END
END LoadB;

PROCEDURE Multiply (IN a, b: ARRAY OF ARRAY OF REAL;
      numRa, numCaRb, numCb: INTEGER;
      OUT c: ARRAY OF ARRAY OF REAL);
VAR
  sum: REAL;
  i, j, k: INTEGER;
BEGIN
  ASSERT((0 <= numRa) & (numRa <= LEN(a, 0)) & (numRa <= LEN(c, 0))
      & (0 <= numCaRb) & (numCaRb <= LEN(a, 1)) & (numCaRb <= LEN(b, 0))
      & (0 <= numCb) & (numCb <= LEN(b, 1)) & (numCb <= LEN(c, 1)), 20);
  FOR i := 0 TO numRa - 1 DO
    FOR j := 0 TO numCb - 1 DO
      sum := 0.0;
      FOR k := 0 TO numCaRb - 1 DO
        sum := sum + a[i, k] * b[k, j]
      END;
      c[i, j] := sum
    END
  END
END Multiply;
```

```
PROCEDURE Compute*;
   VAR
      md: TextModels.Model;
      vw: TextViews.View;
      fm: PboxMappers.Formatter;
      matrixC: ARRAY 32, 32 OF REAL;
BEGIN
   md := TextModels.dir.New();
   fm.ConnectTo(md);
   IF d.numColA = d.numRowB THEN
      Multiply(matrixA, matrixB, d.numRowA, d.numColA, d.numColB, matrixC);
      fm.WriteString("Product matrix:"); fm.WriteLn;
      fm.WriteRealMatrix(matrixC, d.numRowA, d.numColB, 8, 2)
   ELSE
      fm.WriteString("The number of columns in A must equal the number of rows in B.")
   END;
   vw := TextViews.dir.New(md);
   Views.OpenView(vw)
END Compute;

BEGIN
   d.numRowA := 0; d.numColA := 0; d.numRowB := 0; d.numColB := 0;
END Pbox18C.
```

Figure 18.8
Continued.

To determine the statement execution count of procedure Multiply number the executable statements as follows.

Statement
number	*Executable statement*
(1)	FOR i := 0 TO numRa - 1 DO
(2)	FOR j := 0 TO numCb - 1 DO
(3)	sum := 0.0;
(4)	FOR k := 0 TO numCaRb - 1 DO
(5)	sum := sum + a[i, k] * b[k, j]
(6)	c[i, j] := sum

The executable statements of procedure Multiply

For simplicity, assume that both matrix a and b have n rows and n columns. Then, the test for each for loop executes $n + 1$ times and each statement in the body of the for loop executes n times. Figure 18.9 shows the statement execution count for numRa values of 2, 3, and n in general.

So, the effect of a doubly nested loop is to give a cubic execution time as a function of the size of the matrices to be multiplied. The implication for execution time estimates is that if you double the size of the arrays you multiply the execution time by eight.

Statement	numRa = 2	numRa = 3	numRa = n
(1)	3	4	$n + 1$
(2)	6	12	$(n + 1) \cdot n$
(3)	4	9	n^2
(4)	12	36	$n^2 \cdot (n + 1)$
(5)	8	27	n^3
(6)	4	9	n^2
Total:	37	97	$2n^3 + 4n^2 + 2n + 1$

Figure 18.9
Statement execution count for the procedure Multiply in Figure 18.8.

Using two-dimensional arrays

In Component Pascal, the declaration

ARRAY L1, L2 OF T

is really an abbreviation of

ARRAY L1 OF
    ARRAY L2 OF T

That is, a two-dimensional array is a one-dimensional array of vectors.

Example 18.1   In Figure 18.3, the declaration

Matrix = ARRAY 32, 32 OF REAL;

could be written

Matrix = ARRAY 32 OF ARRAY 32 OF REAL;

Considered in this light, variable matrix has 32 elements from matrix[0] up to matrix[31], each of which is a vector of 32 reals as Figure 18.10 shows. ∎

Consistent with this abbreviation, the notation matrix[i, j], which denotes the element in row i, column j of the matrix, is simply an abbreviation for matrix[i][j], which denotes element j in the vector matrix[i] as Figure 18.10 shows.

Example 18.2   The assignment statement max := mat[row, j] in Figure 18.6 can be written max := mat[row][j]. ∎

matrix[0]	matrix[0][0] 12.0	matrix[0][1] 8.0	matrix[0][2] 6.0	matrix[0][3] 4.0
matrix[1]	matrix[1][0] 3.0	matrix[1][1] 5.0	matrix[1][2] 7.0	matrix[1][3] 1.0
matrix[2]	matrix[2][0] 2.0	matrix[2][1] 11.0	matrix[2][2] 9.0	matrix[2][3] 10.0

Figure 18.10
The matrix of Figure 18.3 considered as an array of vectors.

Exercises

1. Assume that matrices a and b of Figure 18.8 each have n rows and n columns. If it takes 50 μs for procedure Multiply to execute with $n = 25$, how many microseconds will it take to execute with $n = 65$? Use the approximate ratio where you neglect the low-order terms of the polynomial.

2. Assume that matrix a of Figure 18.8 has l rows and m columns, and matrix b has m rows and n columns. Write an expression in terms of l, m, and n for the statement execution count of procedure Multiply.

Problems

3. Write a program that inputs a two-dimensional array of real values from a window, and outputs to a new window the row sum of each row, the column sum of each column, and the grand total. For example if the focus window contains

   ```
   4.0  -6.0   1.0   3.0
  -2.0   3.0   7.0   2.0
   1.0   0.0   4.0   5.0
   ```

   the new window should contain

   ```
   4.0  -6.0   1.0   3.0   2.0
  -2.0   3.0   7.0   2.0  10.0
   1.0   0.0   4.0   5.0  10.0
   3.0  -3.0  12.0  10.0  22.0
   ```

   Hint: If the original matrix contains 3 rows and 4 columns, store the column sums in the 4th row and row sums in the 5th column. Test your program with a dialog box similar to that in Figure 18.1. Activate your dialog box with a menu selection.

4. Write a program to output to the Log the indices of the largest element of a two-dimensional array of real values. For example, if the input is identical to that of Problem 3, the output to the Log should be

Largest value: 7.00
Row: 1
Column: 2

Test your program with a dialog box similar to that in Figure 18.1. Activate your dialog box with a menu selection.

5. Declare

PROCEDURE Normalize (VAR mat: ARRAY OF ARRAY OF REAL; normR, numC: INTEGER)

where normR is a row in mat to be normalized, and numC is the number of columns in mat. Implement appropriate preconditions with the ASSERT statement. To normalize a row, divide every element in that row by the element in the row with the largest absolute value. For example, to normalize row 0 of the matrix in Problem 3, you would call

Normalize (matrix, 0, 4)

which would divide each element in the first row by –6.0, producing

–0.667	1.000	–0.167	–0.500
–2.000	3.000	7.000	2.000
1.000	0.000	4.000	5.000

To normalize row 1, the procedure should divide each element in the second row by 7.0, producing

4.000	–6.000	1.000	3.000
–0.286	0.429	1.000	0.286
1.000	0.000	4.000	5.000

Display the normalized matrix with three places past the decimal point. Test your procedure with a dialog box similar to that of Figure 18.4 with an input field for the user to enter the number of the row to normalize. When the user clicks the compute button, verify that the row number entered in the dialog box is valid. If it is, output the matrix before and after the normalization. Otherwise output an error message. Do not include any output statements in Normalize. Activate your dialog box with a menu selection.

6. Declare

PROCEDURE SwapRow (VAR mat: ARRAY OF ARRAY OF REAL; row1, row2, numC: INTEGER)

where numC is the number of columns in mat. Implement appropriate preconditions with the ASSERT statement. The procedure should exchange row1 with row2. Test your procedure with a dialog box similar to that of Figure 18.4 with input fields for the user to enter two row numbers. When the user clicks the compute button, verify that the row numbers entered in the dialog box are valid. If they are, output the matrix before and after the exchange. Otherwise output an error message. Do not include any output statements in SwapRow. Activate your dialog box with a menu selection.

7. Declare

PROCEDURE Transpose (VAR mat: ARRAY OF ARRAY OF REAL; VAR numR, numC: INTEGER) where numR and numC are the number of rows and columns in mat. Implement appropriate preconditions with the ASSERT statement. The procedure should transpose mat and switch the values of numR and numC. To transpose a matrix, turn its columns into rows and its rows into columns. For example, the transpose of the matrix in Problem 3 is the following matrix with four rows and three columns.

```
 4.0  -2.0   1.0
-6.0   3.0   0.0
 1.0   7.0   4.0
 3.0   2.0   5.0
```

Test your procedure with a dialog box similar to that of Figure 18.1. When the user clicks the compute button, output the matrix before and after the transposition. Do not include any output statements in Transpose. Activate your dialog box with a menu selection.

8. Declare

PROCEDURE InitUnit (OUT mat: ARRAY OF ARRAY OF REAL; numR, numC: INTEGER)

where numR and numC are the number of rows and columns in mat. Implement appropriate preconditions with the ASSERT statement. The procedure should initialize the matrix to all zeros, except for ones on the diagonal. For example, if numR is 3 and numC is 4, mat should get

```
1.0   0.0   0.0   0.0
0.0   1.0   0.0   0.0
0.0   0.0   1.0   0.0
```

Test your procedure with a dialog box that requests the user to enter the number of rows and columns. When the user clicks the compute button, verify that the number of rows and columns are each nonnegative. If they are, initialize the matrix and output it to a new window with one place past the decimal point. Otherwise, output an error message. Your procedure should work with the empty matrix, in which the number of rows or columns is zero. Do not use any output statements in InitUnit. Activate your dialog box with a menu selection.

9. Declare

PROCEDURE InitBand (OUT mat: ARRAY OF ARRAY OF REAL; numR, numC: INTEGER)

where the meanings of the parameters are the same as in Problem 8. Implement appropriate preconditions with the ASSERT statement. The procedure should initialize the matrix to all zeros, except for ones on the diagonal and elements immediately adjacent to the diagonal. For example, if numR is 4 and numC is 5, mat should get

```
1.0   1.0   0.0   0.0   0.0
1.0   1.0   1.0   0.0   0.0
0.0   1.0   1.0   1.0   0.0
0.0   0.0   1.0   1.0   1.0
```

Test your procedure as specified in Problem 8.

10. Generalize Chapter 15, Problem 27 to a two-dimensional array. Declare

PROCEDURE InitRandom (OUT mat: ARRAY OF ARRAY OF INTEGER; numR, numC: INTEGER)

that initializes the array to a random sequence of nonrepeating integers. Implement appropriate preconditions with the ASSERT statement. Test your procedure with a dialog box that inputs the number of rows and columns in a dialog box and gives the user the option to set the seed. When the user clicks the compute button, verify that the number of rows and columns are each nonnegative. If they are, initialize the matrix and output it to a new window. Otherwise, output an error message. For example, if the user enters 3 rows and 4 columns the procedure should initialize mat to

```
0    1    2    3
4    5    6    7
8    9   10   11
```

then exchange mat[0, 0] with another component chosen at random, mat[0, 1] with another component chosen at random, and so on. Output the matrix of nonrepeating random integers to a new window. Do not use any output statements in InitRandom. Activate your dialog box with a menu selection.

11. Each integer of a two-dimensional array of integers represents the elevation at one point of some rugged terrain. A local maximum is a point whose integer value is greater than the values of its surrounding eight neighbors. For example, the integer array

```
20   30   30   43   53   72   83
41   40   53   61   77   95   99
42   62   90   85   71   87   88
30   60   70   50   49   56   58
```

has a local maximum at row two, column two because 90 is greater than 40, 53, 61, 62, 85, 60, 70, and 50. Values on the borders, such as 99, are not candidates for local maxima. Note also that 95 is not a local maximum because 99 is greater than 95. Write a program that inputs a two-dimensional array of integers with a dialog box similar to that of Figure 18.1. When the user clicks the compute button, output the location of all the local maxima, if any, to the Log.

12. A saddle point is a point whose integer value is greater than its two neighbors' values in the same row but smaller than its two neighbors' values in the same column. A point can also be a saddle point if its integer value is smaller than its two neighbors' values in the same row but greater than its two neighbors' values in the same column. For example, the integer array

```
48   52   30   43   67
64   55   50   58   95
61   62   40   51   70
56   60   32   48   49
```

has a saddle point at row one, column two because 50 is greater than 30 and 40, but less than 55 and 58. Values on the borders are not candidates for saddle points. Write a program that inputs a two-dimensional array of integers with a dialog box similar to that of Figure 18.1. When the user clicks the compute button, output the location of all the saddle points, if any, to the Log.

Chapter *19*

Recursion

Did you ever look up the definition of some unknown word in the dictionary only to discover that the dictionary defined it in terms of another unknown word? Then, when you looked up the second word, you discovered that it was defined in terms of the first word! The problem with the dictionary is that you did not know the meaning of the first word to begin with. Had the second word been defined in terms of a third word that you knew, you would have been satisfied.

Definition of recursion

A recursive definition of an item is a definition in terms of that same item. In the dictionary example, the recursion is circular or mutual. In mathematics, a recursive definition of a function is a definition that uses the function itself. For example, suppose a function, $f(n)$, is defined as follows:

$$f(n) = nf(n-1)$$

You want to use this definition to determine $f(4)$, so you substitute 4 for n in the definition.

$$f(4) = 4f(3)$$

But now you do not know what $f(3)$ is. So you substitute 3 for n in the definition and get

$$f(3) = 3f(2)$$

Substituting this into the formula for $f(4)$ gives

$$f(4) = 4(3)f(2)$$

But now you do not know what $f(2)$ is. The definition tells you it is 2 times $f(1)$. So the formula for $f(4)$ becomes

$$f(4) = 4(3)(2)f(1)$$

You can see the problem with this definition. With nothing to stop the process, you will continue to compute $f(4)$ endlessly.

$$f(4) = 4(3)(2)(1)(0)(-1)(-2)...$$

It is as if the dictionary gave you an endless string of definitions, each based on another unknown word.

To be complete, the definition must specify the value of $f(n)$ for a specific value of n. Then the preceding process will terminate, and you can compute $f(n)$ for any n. Here is a complete recursive definition of $f(n)$:

$$\begin{cases} f(0) = 1 \\ f(n) = nf(n-1) \quad \text{for } n > 0 \end{cases}$$

A recursive definition of factorial

This definition says you can stop the previous process at $f(0)$. So $f(4)$ is

$$\begin{aligned} f(4) &= 4f(3) \\ &= 4(3)f(2) \\ &= 4(3)(2)f(1) \\ &= 4(3)(2)(1)f(0) \\ &= 4(3)(2)(1)(1) \\ &= 24 \end{aligned}$$

You should recognize this definition as the factorial function.

A recursive factorial function

A recursive function in Component Pascal is a function that calls itself. There is no special recursion statement with a new recursion syntax to learn. The method of storage allocation on the run-time stack is the same as with nonrecursive functions. The only difference is that a recursive function contains a statement that calls itself.

Figure 19.1 shows a dialog box for the factorial function. It is identical to the dialog box of Figure 14.3, which is linked to a procedure that also calculates the factorial function but using iteration instead of recursion. As far as the user is concerned, there is no difference between the results of the two programs.

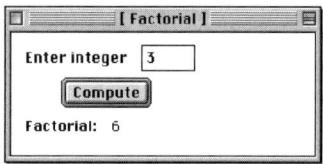
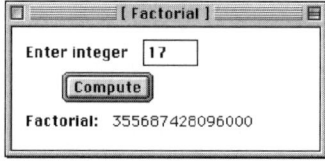

Figure 19.1
The dialog box for the factorial function of Figure 19.2.

The function in Figure 19.2 computes the factorial of a number recursively. It is a direct application of the recursive definition of $f(n)$, which is shown above.

```
MODULE Pbox19A;
    IMPORT Dialog;
    VAR
        d*: RECORD
            num*: INTEGER;
            factorial-: LONGINT
        END;

    PROCEDURE Factorial (n: INTEGER): LONGINT;
    BEGIN
        ASSERT((0 <= n) & (n <= 20), 20);
        IF n = 0 THEN
            RETURN 1
        ELSE
            RETURN n * Factorial(n - 1)  (* ra2 *)
        END
    END Factorial;

    PROCEDURE ComputeFactorial*;
    BEGIN
        IF d.num >= 0 THEN
            d.factorial := Factorial(d.num)  (* ra1 *)
        ELSE
            d.factorial := 0
        END;
        Dialog.Update(d)
    END ComputeFactorial;

BEGIN
    d.num := 0;
    d.factorial := 1
END Pbox19A.
```

Figure 19.2
A program to compute the factorial recursively.

When a function is called, memory allocation on the run-time stack takes place in the following order.

- Push storage for the returned value.

Allocation for function procedures

- Push the parameters.

- Push the return address.

- Push storage for the local variables.

Figure 19.3 is a trace that shows the run-time stack. Figure 19.3(a) shows the values for global variables d.num and d.factorial after the user has entered 3 for d.num in the dialog box. When she clicks the button in the dialog box, the framework calls procedure ComputeFactorial, pushing the return address onto the run-time stack, as shown in Figure 19.3(b). The return address is ra0, which represents the address of some statement in the framework. Figure 19.3(c) shows the stack frame after procedure ComputeFactorial calls Factorial. The return address on the run-time stack is ra1, the address of the statement

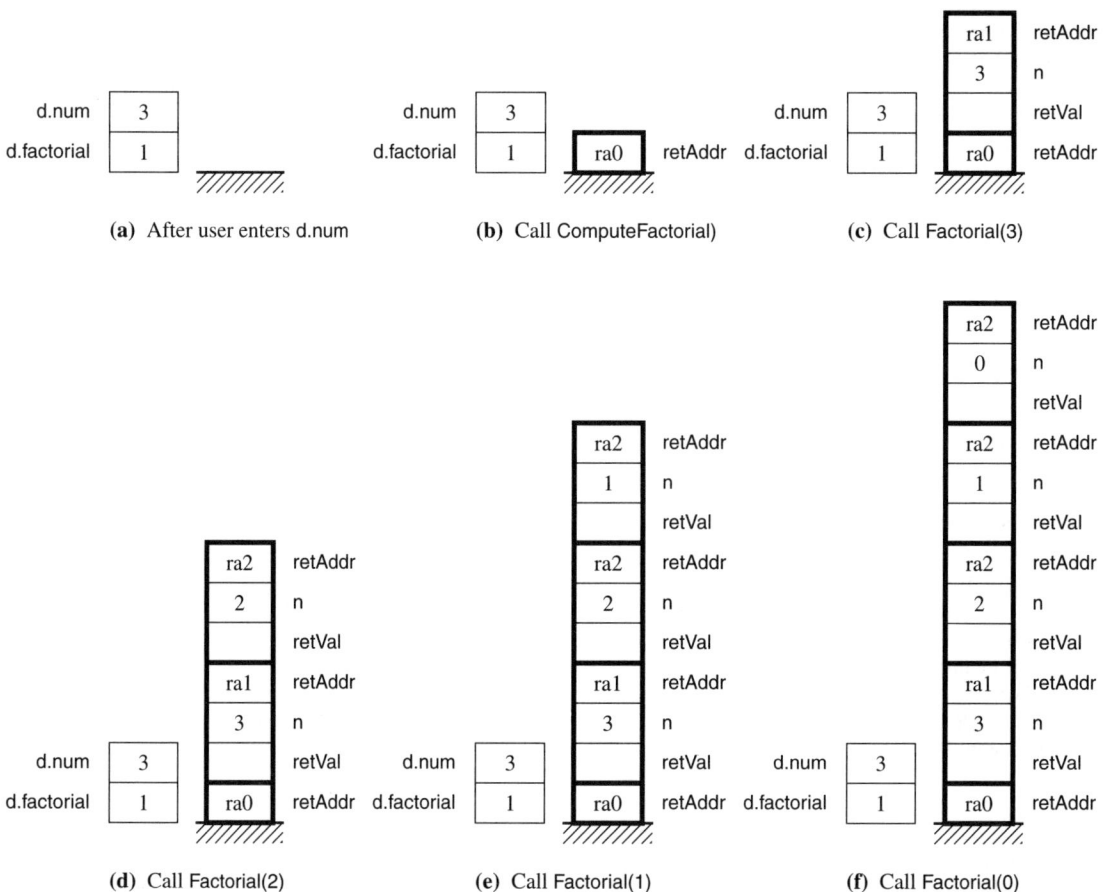

(a) After user enters d.num

(b) Call ComputeFactorial)

(c) Call Factorial(3)

(d) Call Factorial(2)

(e) Call Factorial(1)

(f) Call Factorial(0)

d.factorial := Factorial(d.num); (* ra1 *)

Figure 19.3
The run-time stack for Figure 19.2.

The first statement in the function tests if n equals 0. Because it does not, the ELSE part of the IF statement executes, which causes the first recursive call.

Figure 19.3(d) shows the stack after the first recursive call. Procedure Factorial calls itself. The statement that makes the call is

RETURN n * Factorial(n - 1) (* ra2 *)

so the return address is the address of this statement, ra2. The function is suspended and a new instance of the same function begins executing. The actual parameter is n - 1, and the current value of n is 3. Because the parameter is called by value, the formal parameter n for the new stack frame gets the value 2.

Figure 19.3(d) shows a curious situation that is typical of recursive calls. The program in Listing 19.2 shows only one declaration of n in the formal parameter list of Factorial. But Figure 19.3(d) shows two instances of n. The old instance of n has the

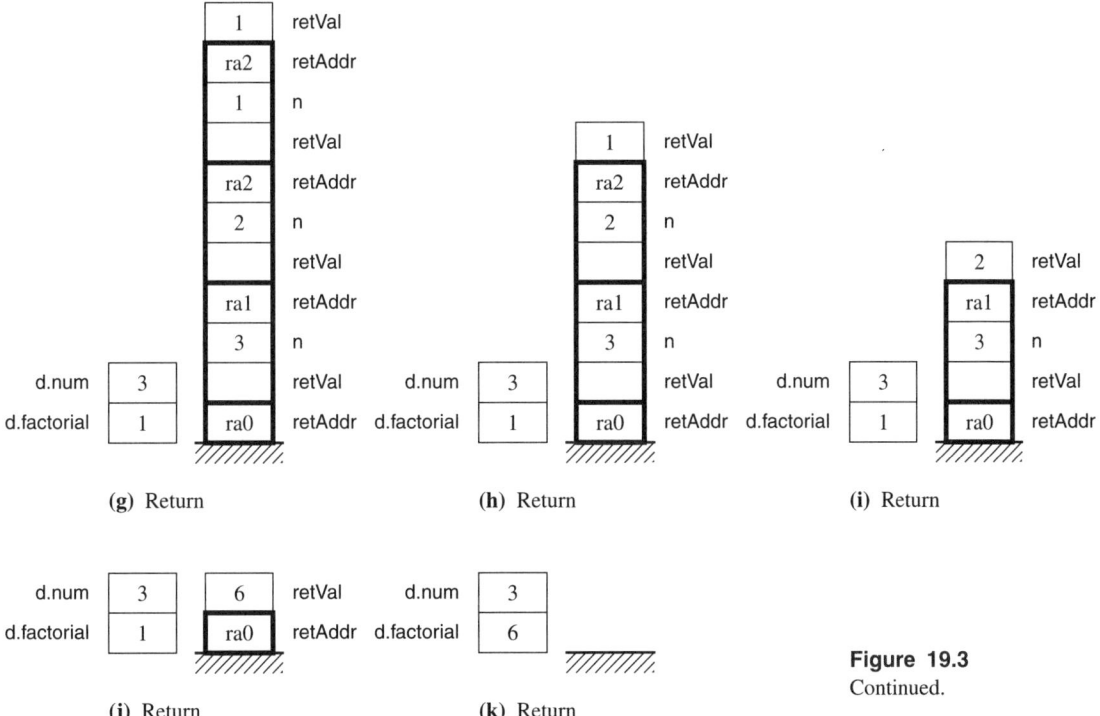

(g) Return

(h) Return

(i) Return

(j) Return

(k) Return

Figure 19.3
Continued.

value 3 from procedure ComputeFactorial. But the new instance of n has the value 2 from the recursive call.

The computer suspends the old execution of the function and begins a new execution of the same function from its beginning. The first statement in the function tests n for 0. But which n? Figure 19.3(d) shows two n's on the run-time stack. The rule is that any reference to a local variable or formal parameter is to the one on the top stack frame. Because the value of n is 2, the ELSE part executes.

But now the function makes another recursive call. It allocates another stack frame as Figure 19.3(e) shows, then another as Figure 19.3(f) shows. Each time, the newly allocated formal parameter gets a value one less than the old value of n because the function call is

Factorial(n - 1)

Finally, in Figure 19.3(f), n has the value 0. The statement

RETURN 1

gives 1 to the cell on the run-time stack allocated for the returned value. The RETURN statement also triggers a return to the calling statement.

The same events transpire with a recursive return as with a nonrecursive return.

The bottom cell of the stack frame gets the returned value, and the return address tells which statement to execute next. In Figure 19.3(f), the bottom cell of the top stack frame gets 1, and the return address is the calling statement in the function. The top frame is deallocated as shown in Figure 19.3(g). The calling statement

RETURN n * Factorial(n - 1) (* ra2 *)

completes its execution. It multiplies its value of n, which is 1, by the value returned, which is 1, and assigns the result to the cell reserved for the returned value. So, the cell for the returned value gets 1, as Figure 19.3(h) shows. A similar sequence of events occurs on each return. Figure 19.3(i) and (j) show that the value returned from the second call is 2 and from the third call is 6.

Figure 19.4 shows the calling sequence for Figure 19.2. The down arrows represent function calls, and the up arrows represent returns. The value returned is next to each up arrow. Procedure ComputeFactorial calls Factorial. Then Factorial calls itself three times. In this example, Factorial is called a total of four times.

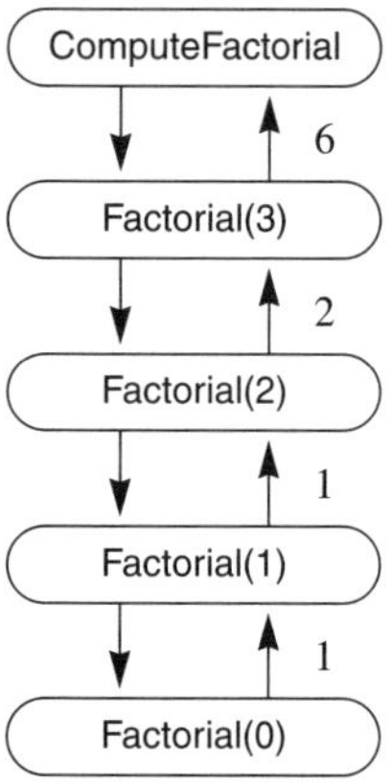

You can see that the program computes the factorial of 3 the same way you would compute $f(3)$ from its recursive definition. You start by computing $f(3)$ as 3 times $f(2)$. Then you must suspend your computation of $f(3)$ to compute $f(2)$. After you get your result for $f(2)$, you can multiply it by 3 to get $f(3)$. Similarly, the program must suspend its execution of the function to call the same function again. The run-time stack keeps track of the current values of the variables so they can be used when that instance of the function resumes.

Figure 19.4
The calling sequence for Figure 19.2.

Thinking recursively

You can take two different viewpoints when dealing with recursion—microscopic and macroscopic. Figure 19.3 illustrates the microscopic viewpoint and shows precisely what happens inside the computer during execution. It is the viewpoint that considers the details of the run-time stack during a trace of the program. The macroscopic viewpoint does not consider the individual trees. It considers the forest as a whole.

The microscopic viewpoint of recursion

You need to know the microscopic viewpoint to understand how Component Pascal implements recursion. The details of the run-time stack are necessary when you study how recursion is implemented at the machine level. But to write a recursive function you should think macroscopically, not microscopically.

The most difficult aspect of writing a recursive function is the assumption that you can call the procedure that you are in the process of writing. To make that assumption, you must think macroscopically and forget about the run-time stack. The two key elements of designing a recursive function are

■ Compute the function for the basis.

■ Assuming the function for n – 1, write it for n.

Imagine you are writing function Factorial. You get to this point:

```
PROCEDURE Factorial (n: INTEGER): LONGINT;
BEGIN
   IF n = 0 THEN
      RETURN 1
   ELSE
```

and wonder how to continue. You have computed the function for the basis, n = 0. But now you must assume that you can call function Factorial, even though you have not finished writing Factorial. You must assume that Factorial(n - 1) will return the correct value for the factorial.

Here is where you must think macroscopically. If you start wondering how Factorial(n - 1) will return the correct value, and if visions of stack frames begin dancing in your head, you are not thinking correctly. In writing Factorial, you must assume you can call Factorial(n - 1), with no questions asked.

The macroscopic viewpoint of recursion

Recursive programs are based on a divide and conquer strategy. It is appropriate when you can solve a large problem in terms of a smaller one. Each recursive call makes the problem smaller and smaller until the program reaches the smallest problem of all, the basis, which is simple to solve.

Recursive addition

Here is another example of a recursive problem. Figure 19.5 shows the input/output for a program that scans a list of integers into an array. It computes their sum and displays it on the Log. Because this problem can be solved much more efficiently using the techniques of earlier chapters without an array, this example serves only to illustrate recursion.

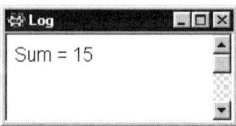

Figure 19.5
The input and output for the module in Figure 19.6.

Suppose v is an array of n integers. You want to find the sum of all n integers in the list recursively. The first step is to formulate the solution of the large problem in terms of a smaller problem. If you knew how to find the sum of the first n-1 integers, you could simply add it to the nth integer in v. You would then have the sum of all n integers.

The next step is to design a function with the appropriate parameters. The function will compute the sum of n integers by calling itself to compute the sum of n-1 integers. So the parameter list must have a parameter that tells how many integers in the array to add. These considerations should lead you to the following function head:

```
PROCEDURE Sum (IN v: ARRAY OF INTEGER; n: INTEGER): INTEGER;
   (* Returns the sum of the first n elements of v *)
```

How do you establish the basis? That is simple. If n is less than 1, there are no numbers left to add, and the function should return 0. Now you can write

```
BEGIN
  IF n < 1 THEN
    RETURN 0
  ELSE
```

Now think macroscopically. You can assume that Sum(v, n - 1) will return the sum of the first n-1 integers. Have faith. All you need to do is add that sum to v[n - 1]. Listing 19.6 shows the function in a finished program. v is called by constant reference because it is an array whose initial values are defined an not changed by Sum.

```
MODULE Pbox19B;
  IMPORT TextControllers, PboxMappers, StdLog;

  PROCEDURE Sum (IN v: ARRAY OF INTEGER; n: INTEGER): INTEGER;
    (* Returns the sum of the first n elements of v *)
  BEGIN
    ASSERT (n >= 0, 20);
    IF n = 0 THEN
      RETURN 0
    ELSE
      RETURN v[n - 1] + Sum(v, n - 1)  (* ra2 *)
    END
  END Sum;

  PROCEDURE ComputeSum*;
    VAR
      cn: TextControllers.Controller;
      sc: PboxMappers.Scanner;
      list: ARRAY 1024 OF INTEGER;
      numItems: INTEGER;
  BEGIN
    cn := TextControllers.Focus();
    IF cn # NIL THEN
      sc.ConnectTo(cn.text);
      sc.ScanIntVector(list, numItems);
      StdLog.String("Sum = ");
      StdLog.Int(Sum(list, numItems));  (* ra1 *)
      StdLog.Ln
    END
  END ComputeSum;

END Pbox19B.
```

Figure 19.6

A recursive function that returns the sum of the first n numbers in an array.

Even though you write the function without considering the microscopic view, you can still trace the run-time stack. Figure 19.7 shows the stack frames for the first two calls to Sum. The stack frame consists of the value returned, the parameters, v and n, and the return address. Because there are no local variables, no storage for them is allocated on the run-time stack. v is called by constant reference. Hence, a reference to its actual parameter is passed on the run-time stack.

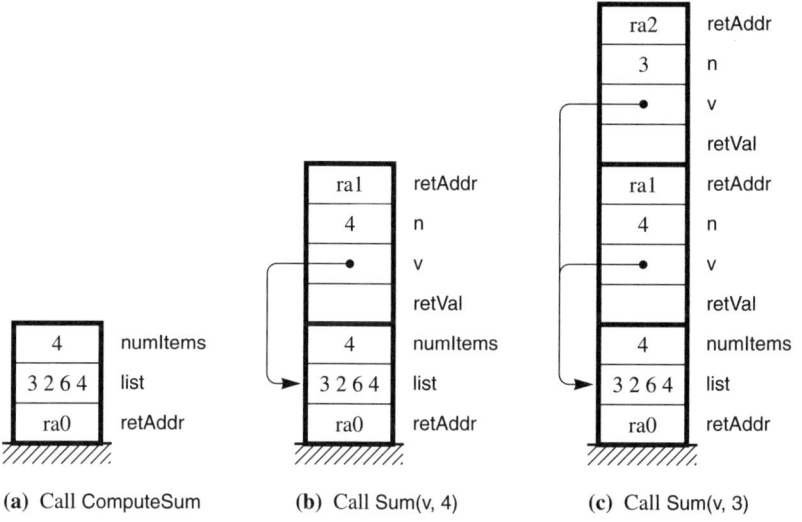

Figure 19.7
The run-time stack for Figure 19.6.

(a) Call ComputeSum   **(b)** Call Sum(v, 4)   **(c)** Call Sum(v, 3)

A recursive greatest common divisor function

To reduce a fraction to lowest terms you must determine the greatest common divisor (*gcd*) of the numerator and denominator, then divide them both by the *gcd*.

Example 19.1 The fraction $24/30$ is not in lowest terms. The divisors of 24, other than 1 and 24 itself, are 2, 3, 4, 6, 8, and 12. The divisors of 30 are 2, 3, 5, 6, 10, and 15. The common divisors of 24 and 30 are 2, 3, and 6. Of these common divisors the greatest is 6. Therefore, to reduce $24/30$ to lowest terms you divide 24 by 6 and 30 by 6 to get $4/5$. ∎

An elegant algorithm for computing the *gcd* of two integers is based on the following mathematical property.

$$gcd(m, n) = \begin{cases} m & \text{if } n = 0 \\ gcd(n, m \text{ mod } n) & \text{if } n > 0 \end{cases}$$

It is a recursive property, because the *gcd* function is defined in terms of itself.

Example 19.2 The recursive property of the *gcd* computes the greatest common divisor of 24 and 30 as follows.

$$gcd(24, 30) = gcd(30, 24 \bmod 30)$$
$$= gcd(30, 24)$$
$$= gcd(24, 30 \bmod 24)$$
$$= gcd(24, 6)$$
$$= gcd(6, 24 \bmod 6)$$
$$= gcd(6, 0)$$
$$= 6 \qquad \blacksquare$$

The algorithm is based on the fact that if an integer k divides both m and n, then it divides m mod n. To see why this is true consider the relationship between div and mod.

- m div n is the quotient of $m \div n$.
- m mod n is the remainder of $m \div n$.

Let

$$q = m \text{ div } n$$
$$r = m \bmod n$$

Then the relationship between div and mod is expressed mathematically as

$$m = q \cdot n + r \qquad 0 \le r < n$$

Example 19.3 For $m = 30$ and $n = 24$,

$$q = m \text{ div } n = 30 \text{ div } 24 = 1$$
$$r = m \bmod n = 30 \bmod 24 = 6$$

The mathematical relationship between div and mod states that

$$30 = 1 \cdot 24 + 6 \qquad 0 \le 6 < 24 \qquad \blacksquare$$

What does it mean for k to divide m? It means that there exists some integer, call it m', such that $m = km'$. So, if k divides both m and n, then

$$m = km'$$
$$n = kn'$$

The mathematical relationship between div and mod becomes

$$km' = q \cdot kn' + r$$

Solving for r and factoring out k yields

$$r = km' - qkn'$$
$$= k \cdot (m' - qn')$$

Because r is k times some integer, the last equation says that k divides r, which is m mod n. So, if k divides both m and n, then it divides m mod n. That is why the *gcd* of m and n is the *gcd* of n and m mod n.

The algorithm terminates by making the second parameter smaller until it reaches zero, at which time the first parameter is the *gcd* of the two numbers. Example 19.2 shows that if $m < n$ the first call to $gcd(m, n)$ simply switches m and n. Thus, the call has made the second parameter smaller. That operation is mathematically justified because the *gcd* of two integers does not depend on their order.

On the other hand, if m is not less than n then the call gives n to the first parameter and computes m mod n as the second parameter. Because the mod operation is the remainder when you divide m by n, that remainder is guaranteed to be between 0 and $n - 1$. It is, therefore, smaller than m as well. Because subsequent calls make the second parameter smaller than both m and n, the algorithm is guaranteed to terminate.

The algorithm terminates when n equals 0. But because n gets its value recursively from m mod n, that can only be possible if n divides m with no remainder. But that implies that n is the *gcd* of m and n. Implementation of the *gcd* function is left as a problem for the student at the end of the chapter.

A recursive binomial coefficient function

The next example of a recursive function has a more complex calling sequence. It is a function to compute the coefficient in the expansion of a binomial expression.

Consider the following expansions:

$$(x + y)^1 = x + y$$
$$(x + y)^2 = x^2 + 2xy + y^2$$
$$(x + y)^3 = x^3 + 3x^2y + 3xy^2 + y^3$$
$$(x + y)^4 = x^4 + 4x^3y + 6x^2y^2 + 4xy^3 + y^4$$

The coefficients of the terms are called binomial coefficients. If you write the coefficients without the terms, they form a triangle of values called Pascal's triangle. Figure 19.8 is Pascal's triangle for the coefficients up to the seventh power.

You can see from Figure 19.8 that each coefficient is the sum of the coefficient immediately above and the coefficient above and to the left. For example, the binomial coefficient in row 5, column 2, which is 10, equals 4 plus 6. Six is above 10, and 4 is above and to the left.

Mathematically, the binomial coefficient $b(n, k)$ for power n and term k is

$$b(n, k) = b(n - 1, k) + b(n - 1, k - 1)$$

	Term number, k							
Power, n	0	1	2	3	4	5	6	7
1	1	1						
2	1	2	1					
3	1	3	3	1				
4	1	4	6	4	1			
5	1	5	10	10	5	1		
6	1	6	15	20	15	6	1	
7	1	7	21	35	35	21	7	1

Figure 19.8
Pascal's triangle.

That is a recursive definition, because it defines the function $b(n, k)$ in terms of itself. You can also see that if k equals 0, or if n equals k, the value of the binomial coefficient is 1. The complete mathematical definition is

$$\begin{cases} b(n, 0) = 1 \\ b(k, k) = 1 \\ b(n, k) = b(n-1, k) + b(n-1, k-1) \qquad 0 < k < n \end{cases}$$

A recursive definition of the binomial coefficient

where the first two equations are the basis for the recursive function.

```
MODULE Pbox19C;
   IMPORT StdLog;

   PROCEDURE BinomCoeff (n, k: INTEGER): INTEGER;
      VAR
         y1, y2: INTEGER;
   BEGIN
      ASSERT((0 <= k) & (k <= n), 20);
      IF (0 = k) OR (k = n) THEN
         RETURN 1
      ELSE
         y1 := BinomCoeff(n - 1, k);  (* ra2 *)
         y2 := BinomCoeff(n - 1, k - 1); (* ra3 *)
         RETURN y1 + y2
      END
   END BinomCoeff;

   PROCEDURE ComputeBinomCoeff*;
   BEGIN
      StdLog.String("BinomCoeff(3, 1) = ");
      StdLog.Int(BinomCoeff(3, 1));  (* ra1 *)
      StdLog.Ln
   END ComputeBinomCoeff;

END Pbox19C.
```

Figure 19.9
A recursive computation of the binomial coefficient.

The program in Figure 19.9 computes the value of a binomial coefficient recursively. It is based directly on the recursive definition of $b(n, k)$. To keep the following figures simple, the program always computes the same coefficient and does not ask the user for an arbitrary coefficient.

Figure 19.10 shows a trace of the run-time stack. Figures 19.10(b), (c), and (d) show the allocation of the stack frames for the first three calls to procedure BinomCoeff. They represent calls to BinomCoeff(3, 1), BinomCoeff(2, 1), and BinomCoeff(1, 1). The first stack frame has the return address ra1 of the calling program in procedure ComputeBinomCoeff. The next two stack frames have the return address ra2 of the y1 assignment statement.

Figure 19.10(e) shows the return from BinomCoeff(1, 1). y1 gets the value 1 returned by the function in Figure 19.10(f). Then the y2 assignment statement calls the function BinomCoeff(1, 0). Figure 19.10(g) shows the run-time stack just after the function call to BinomCoeff(1, 0). Each stack frame has a different return address.

The calling sequence for this program is different from the previous recursive programs. The other programs keep allocating stack frames until the run-time stack reaches its maximum height. Then they keep deallocating stack frames until the run-

Figure 19.10
The run-time stack for Figure 19.9. BC stands for BinomCoeff.

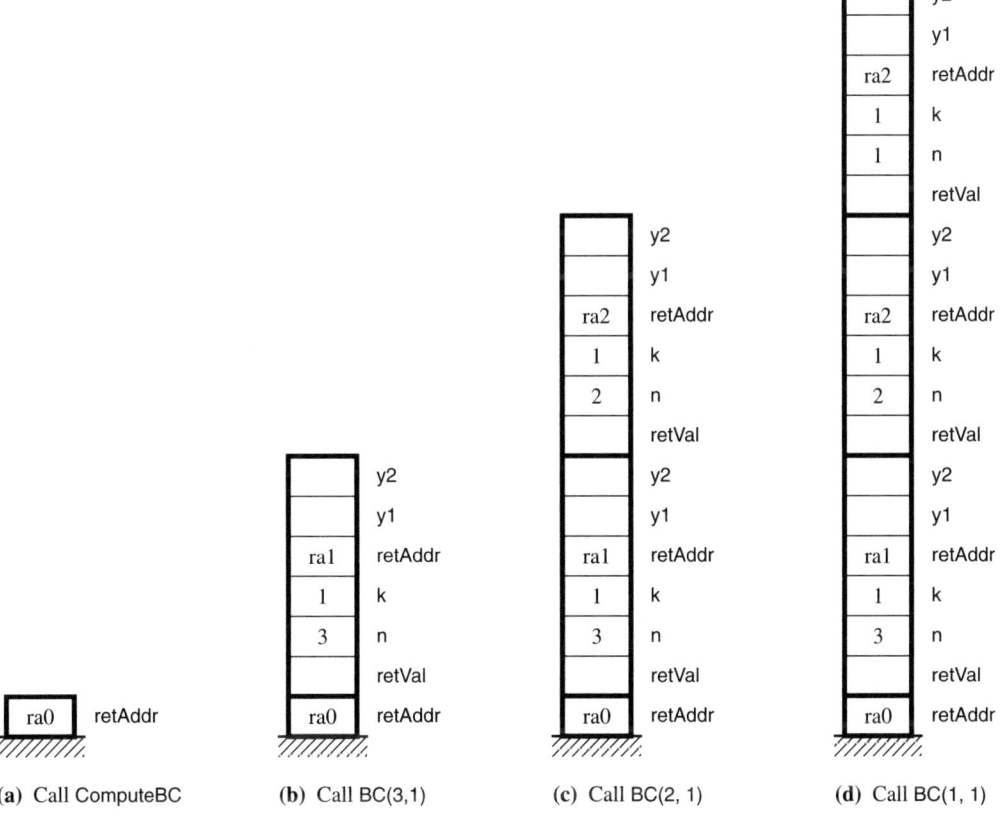

(a) Call ComputeBC   **(b)** Call BC(3,1)   **(c)** Call BC(2, 1)   **(d)** Call BC(1, 1)

Figure 19.10
Continued.

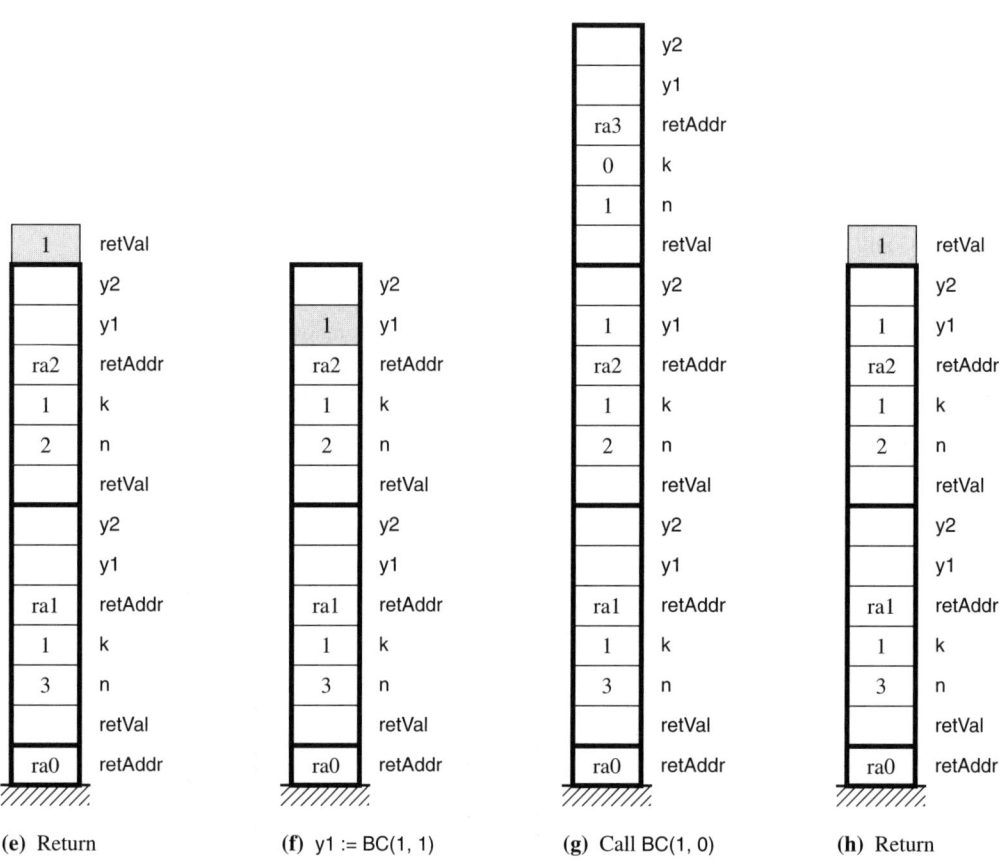

(e) Return   **(f)** y1 := BC(1, 1)   **(g)** Call BC(1, 0)   **(h)** Return

time stack is empty.

This program allocates stack frames until the run-time stack reaches its maximum height. It does not deallocate stack frames until the run-time stack is empty, however. From Figures 19.10(d) to (e) and (f) it deallocates, but from Figure 19.10(f) to (g) it allocates. From Figures 19.10(g) to (h), (i), (j), and (k) it deallocates, but from Figure 19.10(k) to (l) it allocates. Why?

Because this function has two recursive calls instead of one. If the basis step is true, the function makes no recursive call. But if the basis step is false, the function makes *two* recursive calls, one for y1 and one for y2.

Figure 19.10
Continued.

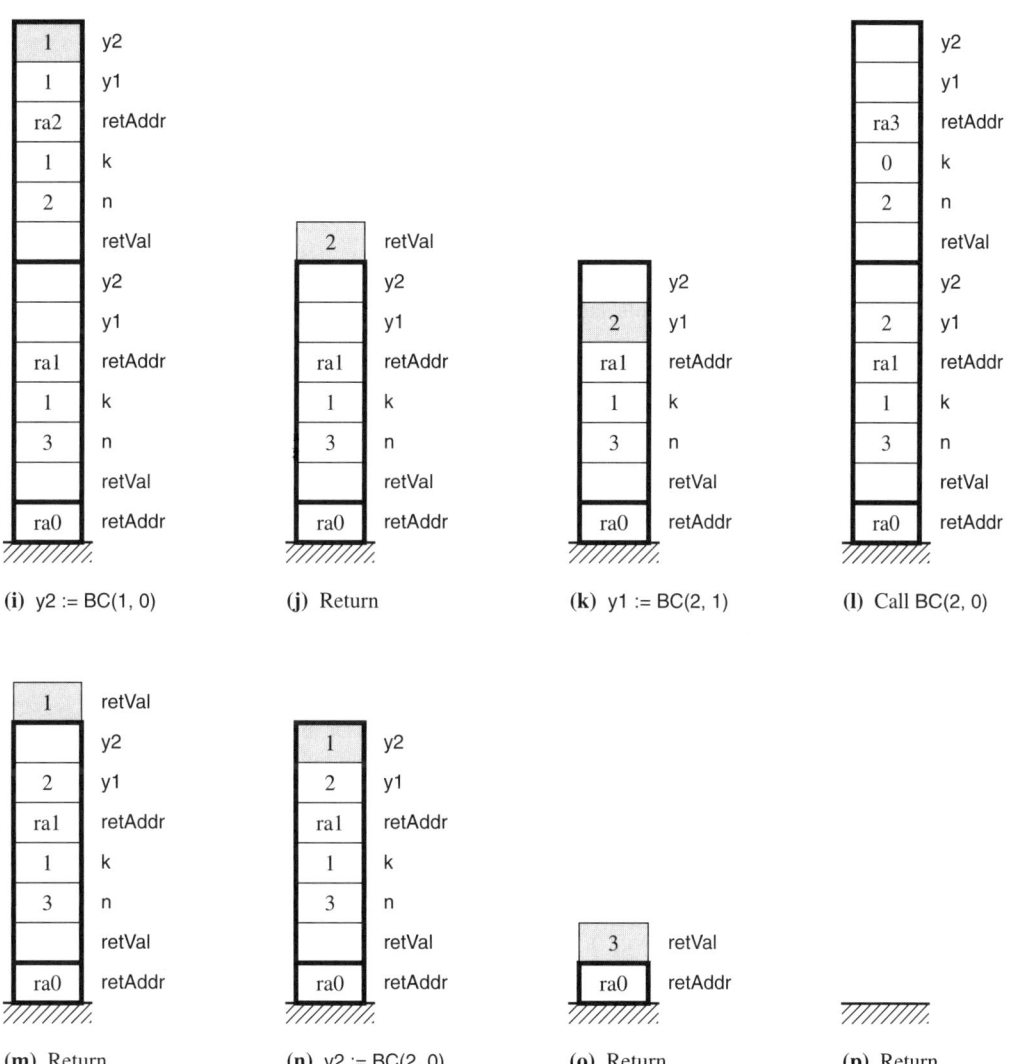

(i) y2 := BC(1, 0)   **(j)** Return   **(k)** y1 := BC(2, 1)   **(l)** Call BC(2, 0)

(m) Return   **(n)** y2 := BC(2, 0)   **(o)** Return   **(p)** Return

Figure 19.11 shows the calling sequence for the program. Notice that it is in the shape of an inverted tree with the root of the tree at the top and the leaves at the bottom. Each node of the tree represents a function call. Except for the main program, a node has either two children or no children, corresponding to two recursive calls or no recursive calls.

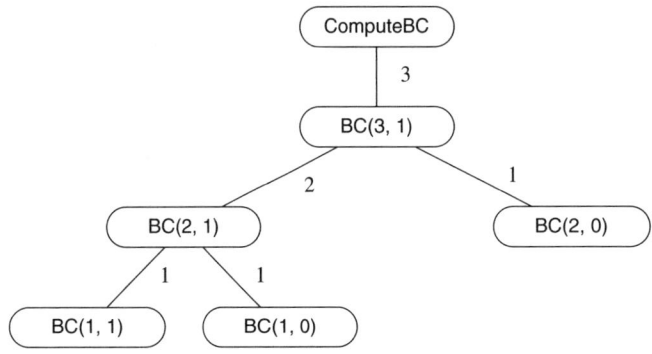

Figure 19.11
The call tree for Figure 19.9.
The numbers next to the
branches represent the value
returned by the function.

Referring to Figure 19.11, the sequence of calls and returns is

```
ComputeBinomCoeff
    Call BC (3, 1)
        Call BC (2, 1)
            Call BC (1, 1)
        Return to BC (2, 1)
            Call BC (1, 0)
        Return to BC (2, 1)
    Return to BC (3, 1)
        Call BC (2, 0)
    Return to BC (3, 1)
Return to ComputeBinomCoeff
```

Figure 19.12 shows how to visualize the execution sequence. You can think of the
call tree as a land mass in an ocean. A boat begins at the left side of the root and sails
along the coastline. It continually moves forward in and out of the bays always keeping the land mass to its left until it arrives back at the right side of the root.

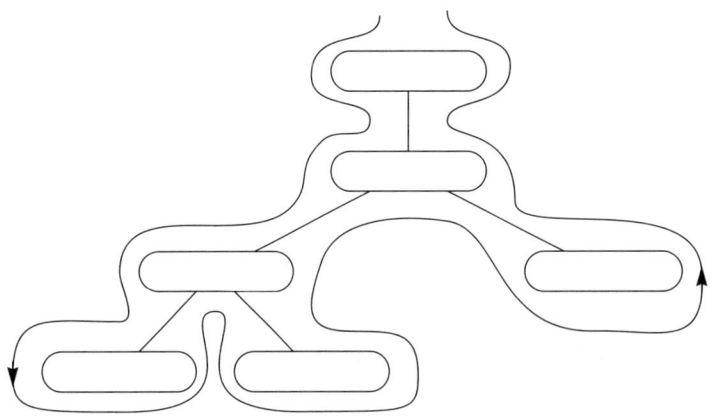

Figure 19.12
A visualization of the calling
sequence for the call tree of
Figure 19.11.

When analyzing a recursive program from a microscopic point of view, it is easier to construct the call tree before you construct the trace of the run-time stack. Once you have the tree, it is easy to see the behavior of the run-time stack. Every time a transition is made to a lower node in the tree, the program allocates one stack frame. Every time a transition is made to a higher node in the tree, the program deallocates one stack frame.

You can determine the maximum height of the run-time stack from the call tree. Just keep track of the net number of stack frames allocated when you get to the lowest node of the call tree. That will correspond to the maximum height of the run-time stack. In this program, the maximum number of stack frames is four, which occurs twice—once with the call to BinomCoeff(1, 1) and once with the call to BinomCoeff(1, 0).

Drawing the call tree in the order of execution is not the easiest way. The previous execution sequence started

ComputeBinomCoeff
   Call BC (3, 1)
      Call BC (2, 1)
         Call BC (1, 1)

You should not draw the call tree in that order. It is easier to start with

ComputeBinomCoeff
   Call BC (3, 1)
      Call BC (2, 1)
      …
      Call BC (2, 0)
      …
   Return to BC (3, 1)
Return to BinomCoeff

recognizing from the program listing that BC (3, 1) will call itself twice—BC(2, 1) once, and BC (2, 0) once. Then you can go back to BC (2, 1) and determine its children. In other words, determine all the children of a node before analyzing the deeper calls from any one of the children.

This is a "breadth first" construction of the tree as opposed to the "depth first" construction that follows the execution sequence. The problem with the depth-first construction arises when you return up several levels in a complicated call tree to some higher node. You might forget the state of execution the node is in and not be able to determine its next child node. If you determine all the children of a node at once, you no longer need to remember the state of execution of the node.

Reversing an array

The module in Figure 19.13 has a recursive proper procedure instead of a function. It reverses the elements in an array of characters. Remember that to solve a problem recursively, you need to think of solving a problem with a large size in terms of the same problem with a smaller size. Suppose you want to reverse the string "Backward" to produce "drawkcaB". This is a problem involving eight characters. But what if you could assume that you had a procedure that would automatically reverse the middle six characters.

Here is the paradox of designing recursive solutions: You need to write a procedure assuming that it is already written. In this problem, you write a procedure that will reverse eight characters by assuming you can call the *same* procedure to reverse the middle six characters. So, the parameter list must include the indices of the first and last positions of the array. To reverse all eight characters in an array, simply exchange the first and last characters, then call the procedure recursively to reverse the middle six characters.

In general the procedure reverses the characters in the array str between str[first] and str[last]. The calling procedure wants to reverse the characters between 'B' and 'd'. So it calls Reverse with 0 for first and 7 for last. The called procedure switches str[first] with str[last] and calls itself recursively to switch all the characters between str[first + 1] and str[last - 1]. If first is ever greater than or equal to last, no switching is necessary and the procedure does nothing.

```
MODULE Pbox19D;
   IMPORT StdLog;

   PROCEDURE Reverse (VAR str: ARRAY OF CHAR; first, last: INTEGER);
      (* Reverses the characters between str[first] and str[last] *)
      VAR
         temp: CHAR;
   BEGIN
      ASSERT((0 <= first) & (last < LEN(str$)), 20);
      IF first < last THEN
         temp := str[first];
         str[first] := str[last];
         str[last] := temp;
         Reverse(str, first + 1, last - 1)
      END  (* ra2 *)
   END Reverse;

   PROCEDURE ComputeReverse*;
      VAR
         word: ARRAY 16 OF CHAR;
   BEGIN
      word := "Backward";
      Reverse(word, 0, LEN(word$) - 1);
      StdLog.String(word);  (* ra1 *)
      StdLog.Ln
   END ComputeReverse;

END Pbox19D.
```

Figure 19.13
A recursive procedure to reverse the elements of an array.

Figure 19.14 shows the beginning of a trace of the run-time stack. In this program, str must be called by reference because the procedure changes the values of the array in the actual parameter list. Even though there are multiple copies of str, one in each stack frame, they all refer to word in the calling procedure.

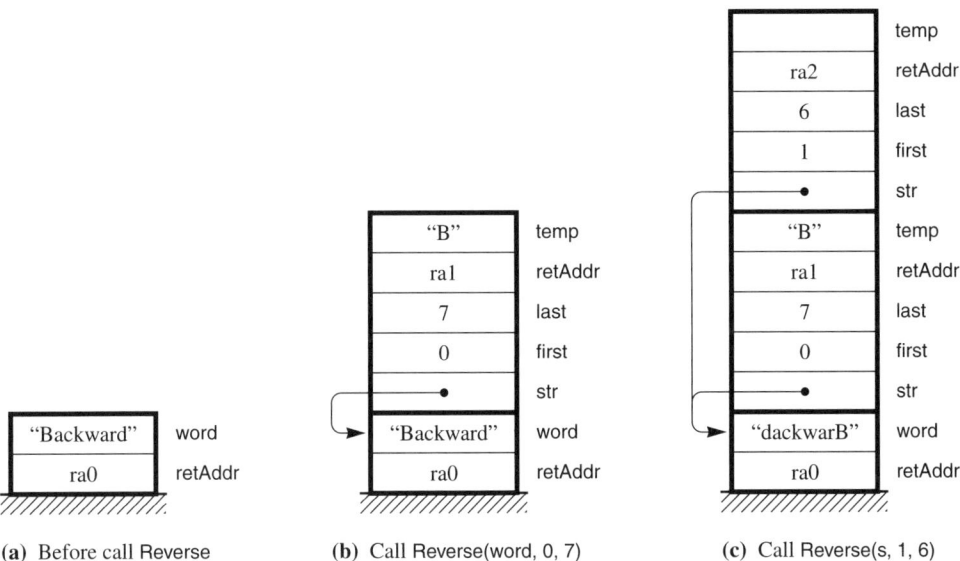

(a) Before call Reverse

(b) Call Reverse(word, 0, 7)

(c) Call Reverse(s, 1, 6)

Permutations

The next example of recursion has the most complex calling sequence yet. The problem is to print all the permutations of a list of characters. For example, the characters abcd have 24 permutations as follows:

abcd	bacd	cabd	dabc
abdc	badc	cadb	dacb
acbd	bcad	cbad	dbac
acdb	bcda	cbda	dbca
adbc	bdac	cdab	dcab
adcb	bdca	cdba	dcba

Figure 19.14
The run-time stack for Figure 19.13.

In general, we need a procedure that will print all the permutations of any number of characters.

Remember, the key to a recursive solution is to solve the large problem assuming you already have the solution to a smaller problem. This problem is to print the permutations of the characters in some array of characters, say str, between str[0] and str[3]. As usual the procedure heading will include the array for which we want the permutation and the limits of the indices.

```
PROCEDURE Permute (str: ARRAY OF CHAR; first, last: INTEGER);
    (* Print the permutations of str between str[first] and str[last] *)
```

In this problem we will call the procedure with str having a value of "abcd", and first and last having values 0 and 3.

What can you assume? You can assume you have a procedure that will print all the permutations between str[1] and str[3]. For example, if you give the procedure the characters "xabc" for str and values 1 and 3 for first and last, you can assume that it will print the following six permutations:

xabc   xacb   xbac   xbca   xcab   xcba

Look at the pattern of permutations for four characters. It is simply four groups of six permutations. Each group starts with one of the four characters and contains the six permutations of the remaining three characters. You can print the permutations of four characters as follows:

Make str[0] 'a'
Print permutations from str[1] to str[3] with str[0] at the beginning
Make str[0] 'b'
Print permutations from str[1] to str[3] with str[0] at the beginning
Make str[0] 'c'
Print permutations from str[1] to str[3] with str[0] at the beginning
Make str[0] 'd'
Print permutations from str[1] to str[3] with str[0] at the beginning

This is obviously a job for a loop. To make the first character of str each letter in turn, simply exchange it with each of the other characters.

```
FOR i := 0 TO 3 DO
    Exchange str[0] with str[i]
    Print all permutations from str[1] to str[3]
END
```

For this scheme to work, the procedure that prints the permutations cannot change any of the values in str. The array of characters must be called by value.

Starting with abcd, the loop exchanges 'a' with 'a' and prints the first group of six permutations starting with abcd. Then it exchanges 'a' with 'b' and prints the group of six permutations starting with bacd. Then it exchanges 'b' with 'c' and prints the group of six permutations starting with cabd. Then it exchanges 'c' with 'd' and prints the group of six permutations starting with dabc.

In general, you want to be able to print the permutations between str[first] and str[last], where first and last are parameters. The loop generalizes to

```
FOR i := first TO last DO
    Exchange str[first] with str[i]
    Print permutations from str[first + 1] to str[last]
END
```

Figure 19.15 shows the completed program.

```
MODULE Pbox19E;
   IMPORT StdLog;

   PROCEDURE Exchange (VAR s: ARRAY OF CHAR; i, j: INTEGER);
      VAR
         temp: CHAR;
   BEGIN
      temp := s[i];
      s[i] := s[j];
      s[j] := temp
   END Exchange;

   PROCEDURE Permute (str: ARRAY OF CHAR; first, last: INTEGER);
      (* Print the permutations of str between str[first] and str[last] *)
      VAR
         i: INTEGER;
   BEGIN
      ASSERT((0 <= first) & (first <= last) & (last < LEN(str$)), 20);
      IF first = last THEN
         StdLog.String(str); StdLog.Ln
      ELSE
         FOR i := first TO last DO
            Exchange(str, first, i);
            Permute(str, first + 1, last)
         END
      END
   END Permute;

   PROCEDURE ComputePermutation*;
   BEGIN
      Permute("abc", 0, 2);
   END ComputePermutation;

END Pbox19E.
```

Figure 19.15

A recursive procedure that prints the permutations of the elements in an array.

Figure 19.16 shows the call tree for the case where procedure Permute is given initial values of "abc" for s, and 0 and 2 for first and last. Procedure ComputePermutation calls the procedure once with first equals 0 and last equals 2. The FOR loop executes three times. Each time it executes it makes a recursive call to Permute. So, the node below the main program has three children.

Each child has first equals 1 and last equals 2. Their FOR loops execute twice, so they each have two children. The bottom nodes have first equals 2 and last equals 2. They have no children. They simply print the value they received in the array. The six leaves on the tree print the six permutations.

Towers of Hanoi

The Towers of Hanoi puzzle is a classic computer science problem that is conveniently solved by the recursive technique. The puzzle consists of three pegs and a set

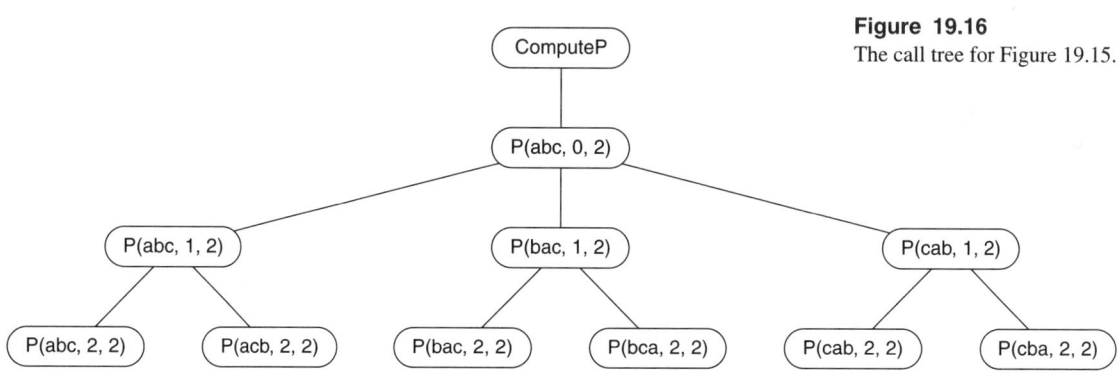

Figure 19.16
The call tree for Figure 19.15.

of disks with different diameters. The pegs are numbered 1, 2, and 3. Each disk has a hole at its center so that it can fit onto one of the pegs. The initial configuration of the puzzle consists of all the disks on one peg in a way that no disk rests directly on another disk with a smaller diameter. Figure 19.17 is the initial configuration for four disks.

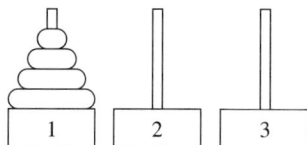

Figure 19.17
The Towers of Hanoi puzzle.

The problem is to move all the disks from the starting peg to another peg under the following conditions:

■ You may only move one disk at a time. It must be the top disk from one peg, which is moved to the top of another peg.

■ You may not place one disk on another disk having a smaller diameter.

The procedure for solving this problem has three parameters, n, i, and j, where

■ n is the number of disks to move

■ i is the starting peg

■ j is the goal peg

i and j are integers that identify the pegs. Given the values of i and j, you can calculate the intermediate peg, which is the one that is neither the starting peg nor the goal peg, as 6 - i - j. For example, if the starting peg is 1 and the goal peg is 3 then the intermediate peg is $6 - 1 - 3 = 2$.

To move the n disks from peg i to peg j, first check to see if n = 1. If it does, then simply move the one disk from peg i to peg j. But if it does not, then decompose the problem into several smaller parts.

- Move n - 1 disks from peg i to the intermediate peg.
- Move one disk from peg i to peg j.
- Move n - 1 disks from the intermediate peg to peg j.

Figure 19.18 shows this decomposition for the problem of moving four disks from peg 1 to peg 3.

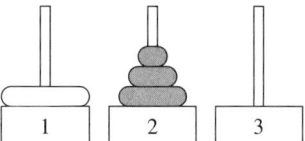 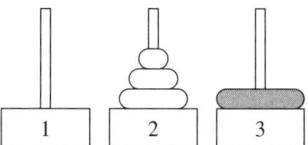 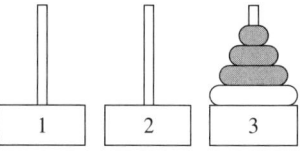

(a) Move three disks from peg 1 to peg 2.

(b) Move one disk from peg 1 to peg 3.

(c) Move three disks from peg 2 to peg 3.

This procedure guarantees that a disk will not be placed on another disk with a smaller diameter, assuming that the original n disks are stacked correctly. Suppose, for example, that four disks are to be moved from peg 1 to peg 3 as in Figure 19.18. The procedure says that you should move the top three disks from peg 1 to peg 2, move the bottom disk from peg 1 to peg 3, and then move the three disks from peg 2 to peg 3.

In moving the top three disks from peg 1 to peg 2, you will leave the bottom disk on peg 1. Remember that it is the disk with the largest diameter, so any disk you place on it in the process of moving the other disks will be smaller.

In order to move the bottom disk from peg 1 to peg 3, peg 3 must be empty. You will not place the bottom disk on a smaller disk in this step either.

When you move the three disks from peg 2 to peg 3, you will place them on the largest disk, now on the bottom of peg 3. So the three disks will be placed on peg 3 correctly.

The procedure is recursive. In the first step, you must move three disks from peg 1 to peg 2. To do that, move two disks from peg 1 to peg 3, then one disk from peg 1 to peg 2, then two disks from peg 3 to peg 2. Figure 19.19 shows this sequence.

Figure 19.18
The solution for moving four disks from peg 1 to peg 3.

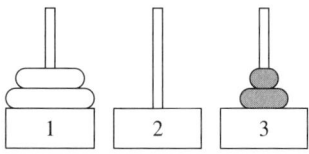 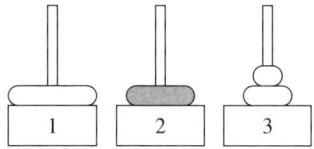 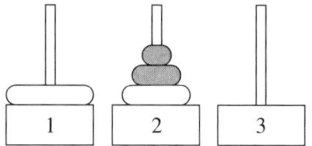

(a) Move two disks from peg 1 to peg 3.

(b) Move one disk from peg 1 to peg 2.

(c) Move two disks from peg 3 to peg 2.

Using the previous reasoning, these steps will be carried out correctly. In the process of moving two disks from peg 1 to peg 3, you may place any of these two disks on the bottom two disks of peg 1 without fear of breaking the rules.

Figure 19.19
The solution for moving three disks from peg 1 to peg 2.

Eventually you will reduce the problem to the basis step where you only need to move one disk. But the solution with one disk is easy. Programming the solution to the Towers of Hanoi puzzle is left as a problem at the end of the chapter.

Mutual recursion

Some problems are best solved by procedures that do not call themselves directly but that are recursive nonetheless. Suppose a procedure calls procedure A, and procedure A contains a call to procedure B. If procedure B contains a call to procedure A, then A and B are mutually recursive. Even though procedure A does not call itself directly, it does call itself indirectly through procedure B.

There is nothing different about the implementation of mutual recursion compared to plain recursion. Stack frames are allocated on the run-time stack the same way, with parameters allocated first, followed by the return address, followed by local variables.

There is one slight problem in specifying mutually recursive procedures in a Component Pascal program, however. It arises from the fact that procedures must be declared before they are used.

If procedure A calls procedure B, the declaration of procedure B must appear before the declaration of procedure A in the listing. But, if procedure B calls procedure A, the declaration of procedure A must appear before the declaration of procedure B in the listing. The problem is that if each calls the other, each must appear before the other in the listing, an obvious impossibility.

For this situation, Component Pascal provides the forward declaration, which allows the programmer to write the first procedure heading without the rest of the procedure. In a forward declaration, you include the heading with the formal parameter list, but you insert the ^ character after the reserved word PROCEDURE. After the forward declaration comes the declaration of the second procedure, followed by the declaration of the first procedure with formal parameters that match the formal parameters of the forward declaration.

Figure 19.20 is an outline of the structure of the mutually recursive procedures A and B as just discussed:

MODULE Alpha;
CONST, TYPE, VAR *of* Alpha

PROCEDURE^ A (x: SomeType);

PROCEDURE B (Y: SomeOtherType);
   Procedure body for B, *including* CONST, TYPE, VAR, *etc.*

PROCEDURE A (x: SomeType);
   Procedure body for A, *including* CONST, TYPE, VAR, *etc.*

BEGIN
  etc.
END Alpha.

Figure 19.20
The structure of a program with mutual recursion.

If B has a call to A, the compiler will be able to verify that the number and types of the actual parameters match the formal parameters of A scanned earlier in the forward declaration. If A has a call to B, the call will be in the procedure body of A. The compiler will have scanned the declaration of B because it occurs before the procedure body of A.

Mutual recursion is rare in practice with one notable exception. Some compilers are based on a technique called recursive descent, which uses mutual recursion heavily. You can get an idea of why this is so by considering the structure of Component Pascal statements. It is possible to nest an IF inside of a WHILE, which is nested in turn inside of another IF. A compiler that uses recursive descent has a procedure to translate IF statements and another procedure to translate WHILE statements. When the procedure that is translating the outer IF statement encounters the WHILE statement, it calls the procedure that translates WHILE statements. But when that procedure encounters the nested IF statement, it calls the statement that translates IF statements; hence the mutual recursion. We will leave complete examples of mutual recursion to the problems following this chapter.

The cost of recursion

The selection of examples in this section was based on only one criterion—the ability of the example to illustrate recursion. You can see that recursive solutions require much storage for the run-time stack. It also takes time to allocate and deallocate the stack frames. Recursive solutions are expensive in both space and time.

If you can solve a problem easily without recursion, the nonrecursive solution will usually be better than the recursive solution. Function procedure Factorial in Figure 13.4, the nonrecursive function to calculate the factorial, is certainly better than the recursive factorial function of Figure 19.2. Both procedure Sum in Figure 19.6 and procedure Reverse in Figure 19.13 can easily be programmed iteratively with a loop. The iterative versions are simpler and more efficient than the recursive versions.

The binomial coefficient $b(n, k)$ has a nonrecursive definition that is based on factorials.

$$b(n, k) = \frac{n!}{k!(n-k)!}$$

If you compute the factorials nonrecursively, a program based on this definition may be more efficient than the corresponding recursive program. Here the choice is a little less clear, because the nonrecursive solution requires multiplication and division but the recursive solution requires only addition. Also, the nonrecursive version overflows with smaller values of n and k compared to the recursive version.

Some problems are recursive by nature and can only be solved nonrecursively with great difficulty. The problems of printing the permutations of n letters and solving the Towers of Hanoi puzzle are recursive by nature. You can try to solve them without recursion to see how difficult it would be.

Exercises

1. The function Sum in Figure 19.6 is called for the first time by procedure ComputeSum. From the second time on it is called by itself. **(a)** How many times is it called altogether assuming the input of Figure 19.5? **(b)** Draw a picture of the run-time stack just after the function is called for the third time. You should have four stack frames, including the one for ComputeSum.

2. For the following call statements from ComputeBinomCoeff

   (a) StdLog.Int(BinomCoeff(4, 1)); (* ra1 *)
   (b) StdLog.Int(BinomCoeff(5, 1)); (* ra1 *)
   (c) StdLog.Int(BinomCoeff(3, 2)); (* ra1 *)
   (d) StdLog.Int(BinomCoeff(4, 4)); (* ra1 *)
   (e) StdLog.Int(BinomCoeff(4, 2)); (* ra1 *)

   (1) Draw the call tree as in Figure 19.11. (2) How many times is procedure BinomCoeff called? (3) What is the maximum number of stack frames (including the frame for ComputeBinomCoeff) on the run-time stack during the execution? (4) Write the sequence of calls and returns using the indentation style as on page 414.

3. For Exercise 2, draw the run-time stack as in Figure 19.10 just before the return from the following function calls.

   (a) BinomCoeff(2, 1)   **(b)** BinomCoeff(3, 1)
   (c) BinomCoeff(1, 1)   **(d)** BinomCoeff(4, 4)
   (e) BinomCoeff(2, 1)

   In part (e), BinomCoeff(2, 1) is called twice. Draw the run-time stack just before the return from the second call of the function.

4. Draw the calling sequence for Figure 19.13. How many times is procedure Reverse called? What is the maximum number of stack frames (including the frame for ComputeReverse) allocated on the run-time stack? Draw the run-time stack just after the third call to procedure Reverse.

5. Answer the three questions below and draw the call tree as in Figure 19.16 for procedure Permute of Figure 19.15 for the following call statements from procedure ComputePermutation.

   (a) Permute ("wxyz", 0, 3)   **(b)** Permute ("wxyz", 1, 3)
   (c) Permute ("wxyz", 1, 2)   **(d)** Permute ("wxyz", 2, 2)

   How many times is procedure Permute called? What is the maximum number of stack frames (including the frame for ComputePermutation) on the run-time stack during the execution? In what order does the program make the calls and returns?

6. For Exercise 5, draw the run-time stack just after the following function calls.

   (a) Permute ("xwyz", 2, 3)   **(b)** Permute ("wyzx", 3, 3)
   (c) Permute ("wyxz", 2, 2)   **(d)** Permute ("wxyz", 2, 2)

7. The mystery numbers are defined recursively as

$$\begin{cases} Myst(0) = 2 \\ Myst(1) = 1 \\ Myst(n) = 2 \times Myst(n-1) + 4 \times Myst(n-2) \qquad \text{for } n > 1 \end{cases}$$

(a) Draw the call tree for $Myst(4)$. **(b)** What is the value of $Myst(4)$?

8. For your solution to Problem 13, draw the call tree as in Figure 19.16 for the following Fibonacci numbers.

(a) $Fib(3)$ **(b)** $Fib(4)$ **(c)** $Fib(5)$

For each of these calls, (1) how many times is Fib called? (2) What is the maximum number of stack frames (including the frame for the procedure linked to the dialog box button) allocated on the run-time stack?

9. For your solution to Problem 15, **(a)** draw the call tree as in Figure 19.16 for the problem to move four disks from peg 1 to peg 3. **(b)** How many times is your procedure called? **(c)** What is the maximum number of stack frames (including the frame for the procedure linked to the dialog box button) on the run-time stack?

10. For your solution to Problem 20, **(a)** draw the call tree as in Figure 19.16 for the example input given in the problem. **(b)** How many times is procedure Comb called? **(c)** What is the maximum number of stack frames (including the frame for the procedure that calls Comb the first time) on the run-time stack?

11. For your solution to Problem 21, **(a)** draw the call tree as in Figure 19.16 for the example input given in the problem. **(b)** How many times is procedure Select called? **(c)** What is the maximum number of stack frames (including the frame for the procedure that calls Select the first time) on the run-time stack?

12. Examine the Component Pascal module that follows. **(a)** Draw the run-time stack just after procedure What is called for the last time. **(b)** What is the output of the program?

```
MODULE Pbox19Exercise12;
   IMPORT StdLog;

   PROCEDURE What (VAR word: ARRAY OF CHAR; j: INTEGER);
   BEGIN
      IF j > 3 THEN
         word[j - 1] := word[6 - j];
         What(word, j - 1)
      END (* ra2 *)
   END What;
```

```
PROCEDURE Mystery*;
   VAR
      string: ARRAY 8 OF CHAR;
BEGIN
   string := 'abcdef';
   What (string, 6);
   StdLog.String(string) (* ra1 *)
END Mystery;

END Pbox19Exercise12.
```

Problems

13.   The Fibonacci sequence is

   0   1   1   2   3   5   8   13   21   ...

   Each Fibonacci number is the sum of the preceding two Fibonacci numbers. The sequence starts with the first two Fibonacci numbers, defined as

$$\begin{cases} Fib(0) \; = \; 0 \\ Fib(1) \; = \; 1 \\ Fib(n) \; = \; Fib(n-1) + Fib(n-2) \qquad \text{for } n > 1 \end{cases}$$

   Design a dialog box with one input field for the value of n and one output field for the Fibonacci number. Use a recursive function to compute $Fib(n)$ and output it. Assert a precondition in your function that n cannot be negative, and do nothing if the user enters a negative value. By experimentation, determine the largest value of n that will cause an overflow. Implement a precondition in the function and a test in the calling procedure to prevent the overflow.

14.   Design a dialog box with two integer input fields, one field that outputs a message, and one button labeled GCD. Use a recursive function to output the greatest common divisor in the message field. Assert a precondition in your function that at least one parameter must be nonzero. If the user enters two negative numbers display an appropriate message in the message field.

15.   Write a program in Component Pascal that prints the solution to the Towers of Hanoi puzzle. It should present the user with a dialog box with three input fields—the number of disks in the puzzle, the peg on which all of the disks are placed initially, and the peg on which the disks are to be moved. Display the solution in a new window. For example, if the user requests the solution for moving three disks from peg 3 to peg 2, your window should display the following solution.

   Move a disk from peg 3 to peg 2.
   Move a disk from peg 3 to peg 1.
   Move a disk from peg 2 to peg 1.
   Move a disk from peg 3 to peg 2.
   Move a disk from peg 1 to peg 3.
   Move a disk from peg 1 to peg 2.
   Move a disk from peg 3 to peg 2.

Assert a precondition in your function that the number of disks must be greater than zero and that the peg numbers must be in 1..3. If the user violates the preconditions write an appropriate error message on the window. Pass the formatter as a parameter as in Figure 12.2.

16. (Silas Smith) Write the recursive function procedure

    PROCEDURE NumDiskMoves (n: INTEGER): LONGINT

    that returns the number of moves it takes to transfer n disks in the Towers of Hanoi puzzle from one peg to another one. Output the number of moves after the instructions for moving the disks in Problem 15. Do not use any global variables in NumDiskMoves, and do not change its parameter list as specified above.

17. Write a recursive version of RotateLeft in Figure 15.7. To rotate n items left, rotate the first n - 1 items left recursively, then exchange items n - 2 and n - 1. For example, to rotate the five items

    5.0   –2.3   7.0   8.0   0.1

    to the left, recursively rotate the first four items to the left,

    –2.3   7.0   8.0   5.0   0.1

    then exchange items four and five.

    –2.3   7.0   8.0   0.1   5.0

    Do not use a loop. Test your procedure with input/output as in Figure 15.7. Your program must work with the empty list.

18. Write a function

    PROCEDURE Maximum (IN v: ARRAY OF INTEGER; last: INTEGER): INTEGER

    that returns the largest value of the integers in v between v[0] and v[last]. Use recursion without a loop. Test your procedure with a tool dialog box containing one button to load an array and another to compute the maximum. Display the maximum in a read-only field in the dialog box. Assert a precondition in your function that v contains at least one value and verify in the calling procedure that the precondition is not violated. Also assert an appropriate precondition on the upper bound of last.

19. Write a recursive version of boolean function IsPalindrome described in Chapter 15, Problem 29. You will need to modify the parameter list. Do not use a loop.

20. Write a program to print all combinations of *n* letters taken *r* at a time. As opposed to permutations, the order of the elements in combinations is irrelevant. For example, the combinations of six letters taken four at a time are the possible sets of four letters from abcdef as follows:

abcd	bcde	cdef
abce	bcdf	
abcf	bcef	
abde	bdef	
abdf		
abef		
acde		
acdf		
acef		
adef		

The solution for selecting four letters from abcdef is to first output 'a' followed by the solution for selecting three letters from bcdef. Then output 'b' followed by the solution for selecting three letters from cdef. Then output 'c' followed by the solution for selecting three letters from def.

The following is the parameter list for a procedure to output the combinations.

```
PROCEDURE Comb (prefix: ARRAY OF CHAR; n, r: INTEGER; suffix: ARRAY OF CHAR);
    (* Prints the prefix string followed by the combination *)
    (* of n characters taken r at a time from the suffix string. *)
    (* Assumes suffix contains n characters. *)
```

To produce the previous list of combinations, the main program called

```
Comb("", 6, 4, "abcdef")
```

The top level recursive calls were

```
Comb("a", 5, 3, "bcdef")
Comb("b", 4, 3, "cdef")
Comb("c", 3, 3, "def")
```

Before each recursive call you will need to concatenate the first character from the suffix onto the last character of the prefix, then strip the first character from the suffix. Test your program with a dialog box for the user to enter a string of up to seven characters and the number of characters from the string to output. Before calling procedure Comb, verify that the number of characters to output is not greater than the length of the string. When the user clicks the compute button, output the combinations to the Log.

21. Write a program to print *n* selections of *m* letters with duplication. As opposed to the elements in combinations of Problem 20, the elements in selections can be duplicated. For example, the two selections of four letters with duplication from abcd are as follows:

aa	ba	ca	da
ab	bb	cb	db
ac	bc	cc	dc
ad	bd	cd	dd

The solution for selecting two letters from abcd is first to output 'a' followed by the solution for selecting one letter from abcd. Then output 'b' followed by the solution for selecting one letter from abcd. Next output 'c' followed by the solution for selecting one letter from abcd. Finally output 'd' followed by the solution for selecting one letter from abcd.

The following is the parameter list for a procedure to output the selections.

```
PROCEDURE Select (prefix: ARRAY OF CHAR; n: INTEGER; IN suffix: ARRAY OF CHAR);
    (*Prints the prefix string followed by the selection *)
    (* of n characters taken from the suffix string. *)
```

To produce the previous list of selections, the main program called

```
Select("", 2, "abcd")
```

The top level recursive calls were

```
Select("a", 1, "abcd")
Select("b", 1, "abcd")
Select("c", 1, "abcd")
Select("d", 1, "abcd")
```

Before each recursive call you will need to concatenate one character from the suffix onto the last character of the prefix. Test your program with a dialog box for the user to enter a string of up to seven characters and the number of characters from the string to output. Before calling procedure Select, verify that the number of characters to output is not negative. When the user clicks the compute button, output the selections to the Log.

22. The determinant of an $n \times n$ matrix is defined recursively in terms of the determinants of $(n-1) \times (n-1)$ matrices. For example, the 3×3 determinant

$$\begin{vmatrix} 6 & 4 & 7 \\ 0 & 2 & 5 \\ 8 & 9 & 1 \end{vmatrix}$$

is defined recursively in terms of the 2×2 determinants as follows:

$$6 \begin{vmatrix} 2 & 5 \\ 9 & 1 \end{vmatrix} - 4 \begin{vmatrix} 0 & 5 \\ 8 & 1 \end{vmatrix} + 7 \begin{vmatrix} 0 & 2 \\ 8 & 9 \end{vmatrix}$$

In general, the coefficients that multiply the smaller determinants come from the first row of the larger determinant and alternate in sign starting with positive. Each smaller determinant comes from the larger one by eliminating the first row and the column of the coefficient. For example, the second determinant comes from eliminating the first row and the second column of the large determinant, because the coefficient, 4, is in the second column. The determinant of a 1×1 matrix is simply the value of the single element. Write a program that inputs a matrix of integer values from the focus window and outputs the value of its determinant to the Log. The determinant value of the above matrix is -210.

23. At the start of any particular day, a machine is either broken down or in operating condition. If the machine is broken at the start of day n, the probability is p that it will be successfully repaired and in operating condition at the start of day $(n+1)$ and $(1-p)$ that it will still be broken. If the machine is in operating condition at the start of day n, the probability is q that it will have a failure causing it to be broken down at the start of day $(n+1)$ and $(1-q)$ that it will still be in operating condition. At the start of day one, the machine is in operating condition.

The problem is to calculate the probability that the machine is in operating condition on day m. That state can occur in two ways, depending on its state the previous day. Either the machine was broken on the previous day and was repaired with probability p, or it was operating on the previous day and remained operating with probability $(1-q)$. Mathematically,

$Prob$(Operating on day m) $= pProb$(Broken on day $(m-1)$) $+ (1-q)Prob$(Operating on day $(m-1)$)

Similarly

$Prob$(Broken on day m) $= (1-p)Prob$(Broken on day $(m-1)$) $+ qProb$(Operating on day $(m-1)$)

Notice that these two relationships are mutually recursive. What is the basis of the recursion?

(a) Declare ProbOperate and ProbBroken, two mutually recursive functions. Use them in a program that inputs the day, m, and probabilities, p and q, and outputs the probability that the machine is operating on day m. **(b)** Draw the call tree for m = 3. **(c)** Use your program to calculate the probability that the machine is operating on days m = 1, 2, 3, 4, 5 if p = 0.4 and q = 0.2. Plot your data. Experiment with different values of p and q and discuss your results.

24. (Gregory Boudreaux) The sum of the first four 1's is

$$\sum_{i=1}^{4} 1 = 1 + 1 + 1 + 1 = 4$$

The sum of the first four integers is

$$\sum_{i=1}^{4} i = 1 + 2 + 3 + 4 = 10$$

The sum of the first four squares is

$$\sum_{i=1}^{4} i^2 = 1 + 4 + 9 + 16 = 30$$

In general, the sum of the first n powers to the j is

$$\sum_{i=1}^{n} i^j = n \sum_{i=1}^{n} i^{j-1} - \sum_{k=2}^{n} \sum_{i=1}^{k-1} i^{j-1}$$

which is a recursive relationship. Defining the function $sum(n, j)$ to be the sum of the first n terms to the power j,

$$sum(n, j) = \sum_{i=1}^{n} i^j$$

the recursive relationship is expressed as

$$\begin{cases} sum(n, 0) = n \\ sum(1, i) = 1 \\ sum(n, j) = n \cdot sum(n, j-1) - \sum_{k=2}^{n} sum(k-1, j-1) \qquad \text{for } n > 1, i > 0 \end{cases}$$

(a) Write a recursive function procedure

PROCECURE Sum (n, j: LONGINT): LONGINT

that returns the sum of the first n terms to the power j. Test your program with a dialog box containing two input fields for n and j, and one output field for the sum. (b) Draw the call tree for the evaluation of Sum(3, 2). Show the value returned for each call on the call tree and verify that the final value returned is the sum of the first three squares.

Chapter *20*

Recursive Searching and Sorting

Any algorithm that uses a loop to perform its processing can be written without a loop using recursion. In particular, the iterative searching and sorting algorithms we learned in Chapter 17 can all be written recursively. This chapter presents a recursive version of the binary search and a taxonomy of sorting algorithms based on recursion.

Recursive binary search

Figure 20.1 shows the input window and dialog box for a program that tests a recursive version of the binary search. As far as the user is concerned, there is no difference between a recursive and an iterative version of the search. The user loads a vector of values into a one-dimensional array, enters a number to search for, and clicks the LookUp button. The dialog box responds with the position of the number in the vector.

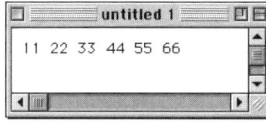

Figure 20.1
The input window and dialog box for testing a binary search algorithm.

   The idea of a recursive solution to a problem is to assume that the procedure can call itself to solve a smaller problem. With the binary search, the smaller problem is the same search carried out on either the first half or second half of the list. The parameter list of the procedure, therefore, must include the indices between which the search for the smaller problem is carried out. The complete procedure heading is

PROCEDURE Search (IN v: ARRAY OF INTEGER; first, last, srchNum: INTEGER;
    OUT i: INTEGER; OUT fnd: BOOLEAN);

v is the array to search, first and last are the indices in v between which the search is to take place, and srchNum is the number to be searched. If srchNum is in the list, the procedure sets fnd to true and i to its location. Otherwise, it sets fnd to false. Figure 20.2 shows the procedure in a module that implements the dialog box in Figure 20.1.

Procedure Search contains no loop. The test for the basis is whether first is greater than last. If it is, the indices have crossed as shown in Figure 16.11(d), and the item is not in the list. Further recursive calls are not needed and fnd can be set to false. Otherwise, the midpoint between first and last is computed, and srchNum is compared to v[mid]. Depending on the result of this comparison, a recursive call is made on the first half of the list, or on the last half of the list, or srchNum was found, in which case fnd is set to true and no further recursive calls are necessary.

```
MODULE Pbox20A;
   IMPORT Dialog, TextModels, TextControllers, PboxMappers, PboxStrings;
   VAR
      d*: RECORD
         numItems-: INTEGER;
         searchNumber*: INTEGER;
         indexString-: ARRAY 16 OF CHAR;
      END;
      list: ARRAY 1024 OF INTEGER;

   PROCEDURE LoadList*;
      VAR
         md: TextModels.Model;
         cn: TextControllers.Controller;
         sc: PboxMappers.Scanner;
   BEGIN
      cn := TextControllers.Focus();
      IF cn # NIL THEN
         md := cn.text;
         sc.ConnectTo(md);
         sc.ScanIntVector(list, d.numItems)
      END;
      Dialog.Update(d)
   END LoadList;
```

Figure 20.2
A recursive version of the binary search algorithm.

```
PROCEDURE Search (IN v: ARRAY OF INTEGER; first, last, srchNum: INTEGER;
    OUT i: INTEGER; OUT fnd: BOOLEAN);
  VAR
    mid: INTEGER;
BEGIN
  ASSERT((0 <= first) & (last < LEN(v)), 20);
  IF first > last THEN
    fnd := FALSE
  ELSE
    mid := (first + last) DIV 2;
    IF srchNum < v[mid] THEN
      Search(v, first, mid - 1, srchNum, i, fnd)
    ELSIF srchNum > v[mid] THEN
      Search(v, mid + 1, last, srchNum, i, fnd)
    ELSE
      fnd := TRUE;
      i := mid
    END
  END
END Search;

PROCEDURE LookUp*;
  VAR
    j: INTEGER;
    found: BOOLEAN;
BEGIN
  Search(list, 0, d.numItems - 1, d.searchNumber, j, found);
  IF found THEN
    PboxStrings.IntToString(j, 1, d.indexString)
  ELSE
    d.indexString := "No entry"
  END;
  Dialog.Update(d)
END LookUp;

BEGIN
  d.numItems := 0;
  d.searchNumber := 0; d.indexString := ""
END Pbox20A.
```

Figure 20.2
Continued.

The Merritt sort taxonomy

The idea of a recursive sort is to sort a large list assuming you can recursively sort a smaller part of the list. Figure 20.3 shows the general approach. Suppose you have a list of elements, L. To sort the list, you split it into two sublists, $L1$ and $L2$. The sublists are each smaller than the original list, L. The recursive idea lets you assume that you have the solution to the problem of sorting the smaller lists. So you recursively sort $L1$, producing the sorted sublist $L1'$. Then you recursively sort $L2$, producing the sorted sublist $L2'$. The last step is to join the two sorted sublists, $L1'$ and $L2'$, into the final sorted list, L'.

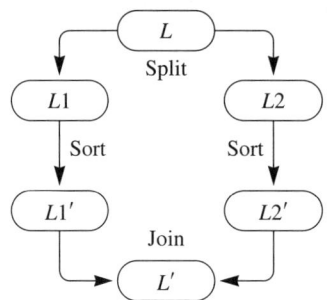

Figure 20.3
The general sort algorithm in the Merritt sort taxonomy.

Merge sort and quick sort

There are two basic sort algorithms, which differ in the methods they use to perform the split and the join. The two are the merge sort algorithm and the quick sort algorithm, shown in Figure 20.4. The classification of sort algorithms into these two families is known as the Merritt taxonomy after Susan Merritt, who proposed it in 1985.

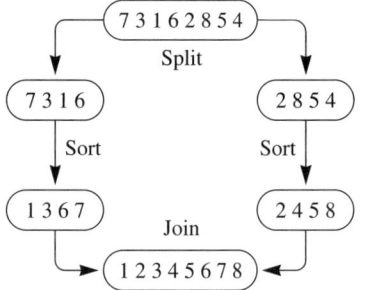

(a) The merge sort algorithm.

(b) The quick sort algorithm.

Figure 20.4
The two basic sort algorithms in the Merritt sort taxonomy.

The figure shows the original unsorted list, *L*, as the eight values

7   3   1   6   2   8   5   4

for both algorithms. The final list for both is

1   2   3   4   5   6   7   8

which is the sorted list, *L'*.

The merge sort algorithm performs a simple split. It takes *L*1 as the first half of the list

7   3   1   6

and *L*2 as the second half of the list

The idea behind merge sort

2   8   5   4

It recursively sorts the sublists, producing the sorted sublist $L1'$ as

1   3   6   7

and the sorted sublist $L2'$ as

2   4   5   8

The last step is to merge these two sublists into a single sorted list, L'. You can see that the split of L into $L1$ and $L2$ is easy. You simply take the left half of L as $L1$ and the right half as $L2$. On the other hand, the join is hard. It requires a loop to cycle through the sublists, selecting the smallest number at each step to place in the merged list.

The quick sort algorithm splits the original list, L, such that every element in the sublist $L1$ is at most the median value, and every element in the sublist $L2$ is at least the median value. It follows that every element in $L1$ will be less than or equal to every element in $L2$. The sublist $L1$ is

The idea behind quick sort

3   1   2   4

and the sublist $L2$ is

7   6   8   5

The algorithm sorts $L1$ recursively into the list $L1'$

1   2   3   4

and $L2$ recursively into the list $L2'$

5   6   7   8

Then it joins $L1'$ and $L2'$ into the final sorted list, L'. You can see that the split of L into $L1$ and $L2$ is hard. It requires a loop that somehow compares the elements in the list with each other and moves the smaller elements to the left and the larger ones to the right. On the other hand, the join is easy. It does not require any further comparisons in a loop, the way the join in the merge sort does.

Insertion sort and selection sort

Figure 20.5 shows the special cases of the merge sort and quick sort when the split of n elements subdivides the list such that $L1$ has $n-1$ elements and $L2$ has one element.

When $L2$ has a single element, the merge sort algorithm simply picks the rightmost element in the list during the split operation. In Figure 20.5(a), the rightmost element is 4 which is split off into *L2*. *L1* is the sublist

7   3   1   6   2   8   5

The algorithm recursively sorts the sublist *L1* into

1   2   3   5   6   7   8

but does not need to sort *L2* because *L2* has only one element. Then, it joins *L1′* and

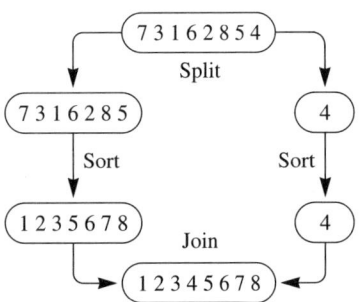

(a) The insertion sort algorithm.

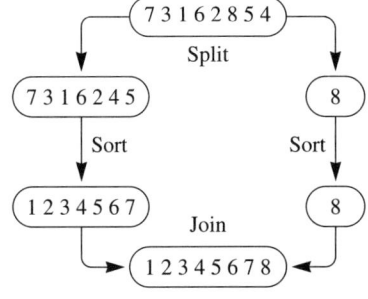

(b) The selection sort algorithm.

Figure 20.5
Sorting with a split of one element.

L2′ by inserting the single element from *L2′* into *L1′*. The insertion process requires a simple loop to shift the lower elements down one slot to make room for the element from *L2*. The merge sort with a split of one element is called the insertion sort. The insert operation is really a merge of two lists where one of the lists has a single element.

When *L2* has a single element, the quick sort algorithm must select the largest value from *L* to put in *L2*. Figure 20.5(b) shows that the largest element from the original list is 8. After it is selected from the original list, *L1* is left as

7   3   1   6   2   4   5

The selection process requires a simple loop to find the index of the largest value. After the index is computed, an exchange puts the largest value in *L2*. In this example, the largest value 8 is exchanged with 4. The algorithm sorts the sublist *L1* into

1   2   3   4   5   6   7

but it does not need to sort *L2* because *L2* has only one element. The quick sort with a split of one element is called the selection sort.

You can program the selection and insertion sorts recursively or nonrecursively. Figure 20.6 is a nonrecursive trace of the single-element sort algorithms with the same original unsorted list, *L*, as in the previous figure. The shaded areas are those regions that are guaranteed to be in order after each pass of the algorithm.

Nonrecursive versions of the insertion sort and selection sort

Initial list	7	3	1	6	2	8	5	4
Pass 1, insert 3	3	7	1	6	2	8	5	4
Pass 2, insert 1	1	3	7	6	2	8	5	4
Pass 3, insert 6	1	3	6	7	2	8	5	4
Pass 4, insert 2	1	2	3	6	7	8	5	4
Pass 5, insert 8	1	2	3	6	7	8	5	4
Pass 6, insert 5	1	2	3	5	6	7	8	4
Pass 7, insert 4	1	2	3	4	5	6	7	8

(a) The insertion sort algorithm.

Initial list	7	3	1	6	2	8	5	4
Pass 1, select 8	7	3	1	6	2	4	5	8
Pass 2, select 7	5	3	1	6	2	4	7	8
Pass 3, select 6	5	3	1	4	2	6	7	8
Pass 4, select 5	2	3	1	4	5	6	7	8
Pass 5, select 4	2	1	3	4	5	6	7	8
Pass 6, select 3	2	1	3	4	5	6	7	8
Pass 7, select 2	1	2	3	4	5	6	7	8

(b) The selection sort algorithm.

The nonrecursive version of the insertion sort begins by inserting 3 into the sublist

Figure 20.6
Nonrecursive traces of the single element sort algorithms.

7

producing the sorted sublist

3   7

Then it inserts 1 into this list, producing the sorted sublist

1   3   7

and so on.

Procedure Sort in Figure 16.12 is a nonrecursive implementation of the selection sort, which is traced in Figure 16.13. Figure 20.6(b) is also a trace of the nonrecursive selection sort, but with the same list as in Figure 20.6(a). The nonrecursive sort begins by selecting 8 and exchanging it with the last element of the list. Then, it selects 7 and exchange it with the penultimate element, and so on.

Figure 20.7 summarizes the four basic sort algorithms. Many other sort algorithms have been invented, but most fall into one of the two basic families, either merge sort or quick sort.

Quick sort

Figure 20.4(b) shows the ideal quick sort split. That figure had an original list, L, of eight items. The algorithm split L exactly in half, with four items in $L1$ and four in $L2$. The median value of a list of items is that value, m, such that there are as many items less than m as greater than m. If you knew the median value, you could split the list exactly in half. Unfortunately, the only way to determine the median value is

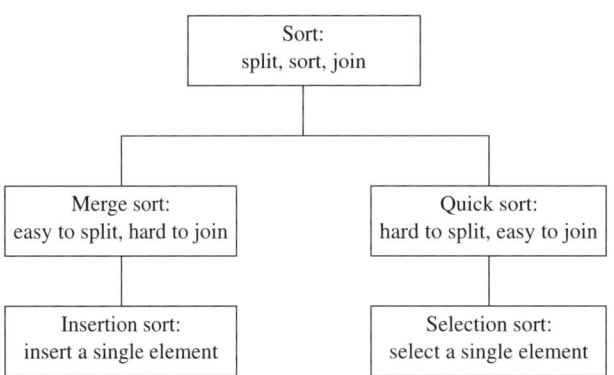

Figure 20.7
Summary of the sort algorithms.

to sort the list and pick the middle item. But you need the median value to sort the list in the first place. The only thing you can do in the face of this dilemma is to be satisfied with a less-than-ideal split.

Figure 20.8 shows the dialog box and input focus window for the quick sort algorithm. As with the recursive version of the binary search, it is impossible for the user to tell whether the sort is done iteratively or recursively. Figure 20.9 is an implementation of the quick sort algorithm.

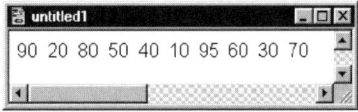

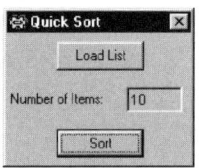

Figure 20.8
The input and output for the quick sort algorithm.

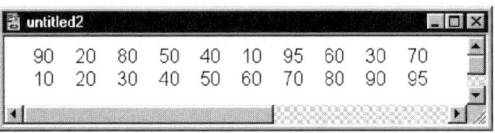

Figure 20.9
An implementation of the quick sort algorithm.

```
MODULE Pbox20B;
    IMPORT Dialog, TextModels, TextViews, Views, TextControllers, PboxMappers;
    VAR
        d*: RECORD
            numItems-: INTEGER;
        END;
        list: ARRAY 1024 OF INTEGER;
```

```
PROCEDURE LoadList*;
    VAR
        md: TextModels.Model;
        cn: TextControllers.Controller;
        sc: PboxMappers.Scanner;
BEGIN
    cn := TextControllers.Focus();
    IF cn # NIL THEN
        md := cn.text;
        sc.ConnectTo(md);
        sc.ScanIntVector(list, d.numItems);
        Dialog.Update(d)
    END;
END LoadList;

PROCEDURE QuickSort (VAR v: ARRAY OF INTEGER; first, last: INTEGER);
    (* Sorts the items of array v between v[first] and v[last]. *)
    VAR
        i, j: INTEGER;
        key: INTEGER;
        temp: INTEGER;
BEGIN
    ASSERT((0 <= first) & (first <= last) & (last < LEN(v)) OR (last < 0) & (0 <= first), 20);
    IF first < last THEN
        key := v[(first + last) DIV 2];
        i := first;
        j := last;
        (* Invariant 1: key <= v[j + 1..last]. *)
        (* Invariant 2: v[first..i - 1] <= key. *)
        (* Invariant 3: if i <= j, there exists k in [first..j] such that v[k] <= key. *)
        (* Invariant 4: if i <= j, there exists k in [i..last] such that key <= v[k]. *)
        WHILE i <= j DO
            WHILE v[i] < key DO
                INC(i)
            END;
            WHILE key < v[j] DO
                DEC(j)
            END;
            IF i <= j THEN
                temp := v[j];
                v[j] := v[i];  (* Establish invariant 4. *)
                v[i] := temp;  (* Establish invariant 3. *)
                INC(i);  (* Establish invariant 2. *)
                DEC(j)  (* Establish invariant 1. *)
            END
        END;
        QuickSort (v, first, i - 1);
        QuickSort (v, i, last)
    END
END QuickSort;
```

Figure 20.9
Continued.

```
PROCEDURE SortList*;
   VAR
      md: TextModels.Model;
      vw: TextViews.View;
      fm: PboxMappers.Formatter;
   BEGIN
      md := TextModels.dir.New();
      fm.ConnectTo(md);
      fm.WriteIntVector(list, d.numItems, 4); fm.WriteLn;
      QuickSort(list, 0, d.numItems - 1);
      fm.WriteIntVector(list, d.numItems, 4); fm.WriteLn;
      vw := TextViews.dir.New(md);
      Views.OpenView(vw)
   END SortList;

BEGIN
   d.numItems := 0
END Pbox20B.
```

Figure 20.9
Continued.

The precondition for procedure QuickSort has two disjuncts. The first disjunct

(0 <= first) & (first <= last) & (last < LEN(v))

is for the case of a nonempty array, and the second disjunct

(last < 0) & (0 <= first)

is for the case of an empty array. If there are no items in the focus window d.numItems gets 0 when list is scanned. Because the call from procedure SortList is

QuickSort(list, 0, d.numItems - 1)

formal parameter first gets 0 and formal parameter last gets −1. The second disjunct is true, which allows procedure QuickSort to handle the case of an empty array.

Procedure QuickSort picks the middle item of the unsorted list and hopes it is close to the median value. The value it picks is called the *key*. If the key is less than the true median, list $L1$ will contain fewer items than list $L2$. If the key is greater than the true median, $L1$ will contain more items.

You could be extremely unlucky and have the key be the smallest value in the list, in which case $L1$ will have only one value. Or if the key is the largest value, $L2$ will have only one value. On the other hand, you could be extremely lucky and have the key be the true median. You must be content to let the key be what it will be, and accept the average behavior of the algorithm.

Figure 20.10 is a trace of the first call to procedure QuickSort in Figure 20.9. Procedure SortList calls the QuickSort with a value of 0 for first and 9 for last. As Figure 20.10(a) shows, QuickSort initializes i to first and j to last. It computes key as 40.

The WHILE loop splits the list into sublists $L1$ and $L2$. The two nested WHILE loops increase j and decrease j until i finds the value 90, which is greater than key, and j finds the value 30, which is less than key. Because i is less than or equal to j, 90

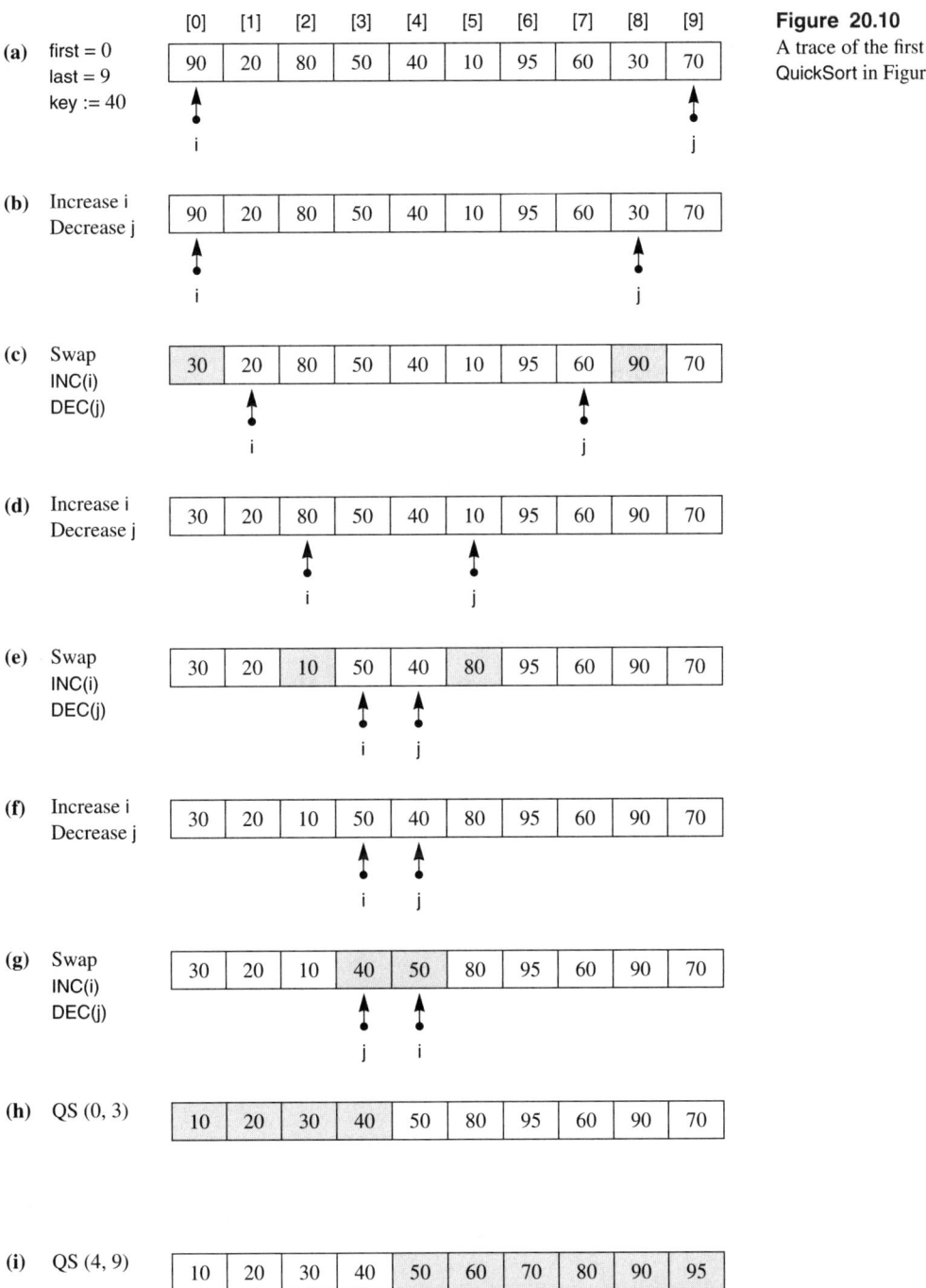

Figure 20.10
A trace of the first call to
QuickSort in Figure 20.9.

is to the left of 30. So they need to be exchanged. Figure 20.10(c) shows the result of the exchange. Afterward, QuickSort increments i by 1 and decrements j by 1.

Because i is still to the left of j, the loop repeats. Figure 20.10(d) shows i increasing to find 80 and j decreasing to find 10. j skips over 60 and 95 because they are greater than key. i is still to the left of j. Figure 20.10(e) shows the exchange of 10 and 80, the increment of i, and the decrement of j.

The algorithm has four loop invariants as shown in the comments. They are described more formally in the next section. The net effect of the four invariants is to establish the single invariant:

- Every element between v[first] and v[i - 1] is less than or equal to every element between v[j + 1] and v[last].

In Figure 20.10(e), the loop invariant means that each of the values (30, 20, 10) is less than or equal to each of the values (80, 95, 60, 90, 70).

The initializing statements make the loop invariant true the first time. Because they initialize i to first, there are no elements between v[first] and v[first - 1]. Because they initialize j to last, there are no elements between v[last + 1] and v[last]. Because there are no elements in the left interval and no elements in the right interval, every element in the left interval is less than or equal to every element in the right interval.

The statements in the body of the WHILE loop keep the invariant true. They increase i and/or decrease j, in effect widening the left and right intervals. When i finds a value greater than or equal to key and j finds a value less than or equal to key, you know that i's value is greater than or equal to j's value. The exchange keeps the invariant true.

Figure 20.10(g) shows the last exchange. QuickSort swaps 50 and 40. After it increments i and decrements j, i has the value 5 and j has the value 4. So j is to the left of i, and the loop terminates.

The assertion in the listing follows from the loop invariant and the termination condition. *L1* is the sublist between v[first] and v[j]. *L2* is the sublist between v[i] and v[last].

Figure 20.10(h) and (i) shows the result of the recursive calls to QuickSort. The abbreviation QS (0, 3) stands for the procedure call

QuickSort (v, first, i - 1)

when first has the value 0 and i has the value 4. Similarly, QS (4, 9) stands for the procedure call

QuickSort (v, i, last)

when i has the value 4 and last has the value 9.

Each recursive call to QuickSort splits a smaller list. The first recursive call splits the list

30 20 10 40

with a first of 0 and a last of 3. The second recursive call splits the list

50 80 95 60 90 70

with a first of 4 and a last of 9. Each of these executions produces a trace like that of
Figure 20.10.

What is the structure of the call tree of QuickSort? The listing shows that the procedure makes either two recursive calls or no recursive calls, depending on the size
of *L*. Therefore, each node in the call tree will have either two children or no children. For the values listed in Figure 20.8, you would need to do a trace of the split at
each call. If you do the traces, you will see that the call tree is structured as shown in
Figure 20.11.

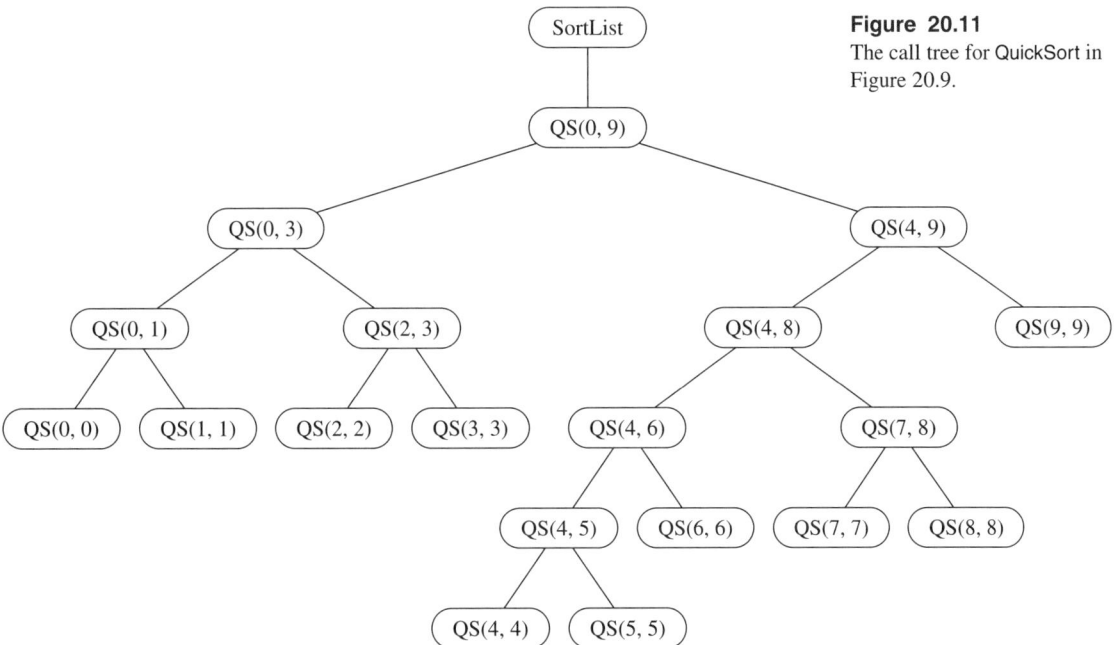

Figure 20.11
The call tree for QuickSort in
Figure 20.9.

The program makes a total of 19 calls to QuickSort, including the initial call from
SortList. The figure shows that QS (4, 9) splits the list of six elements into *L*1, with
five elements, and *L*2, with one element. It does not call itself recursively for *L*2, but
it does for *L*1. QS (4, 8) makes a more even split. Its list *L* has five items, from v[4] to
v[8]. It splits it into sublist *L*1, from v[4] to v[6], and *L*2, from v[7] to v[8].

Using the technique of Figure 19.12, you can determine from the call tree that the
order of calls and returns is as follows:

```
SortList
   Call QS (0, 9)
      Call QS (0, 3)
         Call QS (0, 1)
            Call QS (0, 0)
         Return to QS (0, 1)
            Call QS (1, 1)
         Return to QS (0, 1)
      Return to QS (0, 3)
         Call QS (2, 3)
            Call QS (2, 2)
         Return to QS (2, 3)
            Call QS (3, 3)
         Return to QS (2, 3)
      Return to QS (0, 3)
   Return to QS (0, 9)
      Call QS (4, 9)
         Call QS (4, 8)
            Call QS (4, 6)
               Call QS (4, 5)
                  Call QS (4, 4)
               Return to QS (4, 5)
                  Call QS (5, 5)
               Return to QS (4, 5)
            Return to QS (4, 6)
               Call QS (6, 6)
            Return to QS (4, 6)
         Return to QS (4, 8)
      Return to QS (4, 9)
         Call QS (9, 9)
      Return to QS (4, 9)
   Return to QS (0, 9)
Return to SortList
```

You can also see from Figure 20.11 that the maximum number of stack frames on the run-time stack is seven, including the stack frame for procedure SortList. The maximum occurs twice, once after the call to QS(4, 4) and then again after the call to QS(5, 5).

★ Correctness of quick sort

The quick sort procedure with the outer loop invariant is written in GCL as follows.

procedure *QuickSort*(*v*,*first*,*last*) ;
   if *first* < *last* →
     key := *v*[(*first* + *last*) div 2]; *i* := *first*; *j* := *last*;
     {(∀*k* | *j* + 1 ≤ *k* ≤ *last* : *key* ≤ *v*[*k*]) ∧
     (∀*k* | *first* ≤ *k* ≤ *i* − 1 : *v*[*k*] ≤ *key*) ∧
     (*i* ≤ *j* ⇒ (∃*k* | *first* ≤ *k* ≤ *j* : *v*[*k*] ≤ *key*)) ∧
     (*i* ≤ *j* ⇒ (∃*k* | *i* ≤ *k* ≤ *last* : *key* ≤ *v*[*k*]))}
     do *i* ≤ *j* →
       do *v*[*i*] < *key* → *i* := *i* + 1 **od**;
       do *key* < *v*[*j*] → *j* := *j* − 1 **od**;
       if *i* ≤ *j* → *v*[*i*], *v*[*j*] := *v*[*j*], *v*[*i*]; *i*, *j* := *i* + 1, *j* − 1
       ⫿ *i* > *j* → **skip**
       fi
     od;
     QuickSort(*v*,*first*,*i* − 1) ;
     QuickSort(*v*,*i*,*last*)
   ⫿ *first* ≥ *last* → **skip**
   fi
end *QuickSort*

To prove the correctness of the quick sort algorithm requires several steps. This section outlines the steps and leaves the details of the proof to the exercises.

Step 1: The quick sort algorithm is recursive. Therefore, the proof of its correctness is a proof by mathematical induction. The first step in a proof by mathematical induction is to prove the base case. The base case occurs when the segment of *v* to be sorted is empty or when it has one element. The complete formal specification for *QuickSort* including the precondition from the ASSERT statement in Figure 20.9 is

{(0 ≤ *first* ≤ *last* < *len*(*v*) ∨ *last* < 0 ≤ *first*) ∧ *v* = **V**}
v := ?
{*perm*(*v*,**V**,*first*,*last*) ∧ (∀*i* | *first* ≤ *i* < *last* − 1 : *v*[*i*] ≤ *v*[*i* + 1])}

The first disjunct in the precondition is for the case when the segment has one or more elements. The second disjunct is for the case when the original array to be sorted has no elements. Use the precondition with the base case to prove the postcondition.

Step 2: The second step in a proof by mathematical induction is to show that the correctness for a small number of elements implies the correctness for a larger number of elements. With *QuickSort*, you assume that the recursive call

QuickSort(*v*,*first*,*i* − 1)

will correctly sort *v* between *first* and *i* − 1, and that the recursive call

QuickSort(*v*,*i*,*last*)

will correctly sort *v* between *i* and *last*. For the recursion to terminate, these calls must be for segments that are smaller than the original segment [*first*..*last*]. If

$i = first$ then the second recursive call will be for a segment that is the same length as the original segment, and if $i = last + 1$ then the first recursive call will be for a segment that is the same length as the original segment. The second step is to prove that neither of these cases can happen, that is, that $first < i \leq last$, so the recursion will terminate.

Step 3: The idea behind the quick sort algorithm is to partition the segment $[first..last]$ into two subsegments $[first..i-1]$ and $[i..last]$ such that every element in $[first..i-1]$ is less than or equal to every element in $[i..last]$. Assuming that the recursive calls correctly sort the subsegments the entire segment will be sorted. The third step is to prove that every element in the first subsegment is less than or equal to every element in the second subsegment. That is, you must prove that

$$(\forall k \mid first \leq k < i : (\forall l \mid i \leq l < last : v[k] \leq v[l]))$$

before the recursive calls are made. The recursive calls are made just after the outer **do** loop. So, for this part of the proof you may assume the four loop invariants and the negation of the loop condition.

Step 4: The previous step assumed the loop invariants. The fourth step is to prove the loop invariants from the precondition and the initialization statements just before the outer **do** loop.

Step 5: The fifth step is to prove that one execution of the outer **do** loop maintains the loop invariants.

Step 6: The sixth step is to prove that the outer **do** loop terminates. You can prove that it terminates with the help of the loop invariants.

Merge sort

Unlike the quick sort algorithm, merge sort splits *L* exactly in half every time. Figure 20.12 shows the split part of the merge sort algorithm. The parameters are the same as those for procedure QuickSort and the procedure is called the same way. The merge part of the algorithm is left as a problem for the student.

```
PROCEDURE MergeSort (VAR v: ARRAY OF INTEGER; first, last: INTEGER);
    (* Sorts the items of array v between v[first] and v[last]. *)
    VAR
        i, j, k, mid: INTEGER;
        temp: ARRAY 128 OF INTEGER;
BEGIN
    ASSERT((0 <= first) & (first <= last) & (last < LEN(v)) OR (last < 0) & (0 <= first), 20);
    IF first < last THEN
        mid := (first + last) DIV 2;
        MergeSort(v, first, mid);
        MergeSort(v, mid + 1, last);
        (* Problem for the student to join v[first..mid] and v[mid + 1..last] *)
    END
END MergeSort;
```

Figure 20.12
An implementation of the merge sort algorithm.

Merge sort has a problem that quick sort does not have. To merge two parts of one list into a second list requires storage for the second list. To perform the merge you must allocate storage for the second list as a local array variable, which is the purpose of temp in Figure 20.12. You then merge the two sublists into the second list and copy the second list back into the original.

Figure 20.13 shows a trace of the top-level call to MergeSort of Figure 20.12. The split is the simple computation of local variable mid. The recursive calls are at the beginning of the algorithm in contrast to the recursive calls of QuickSort, which are at the end.

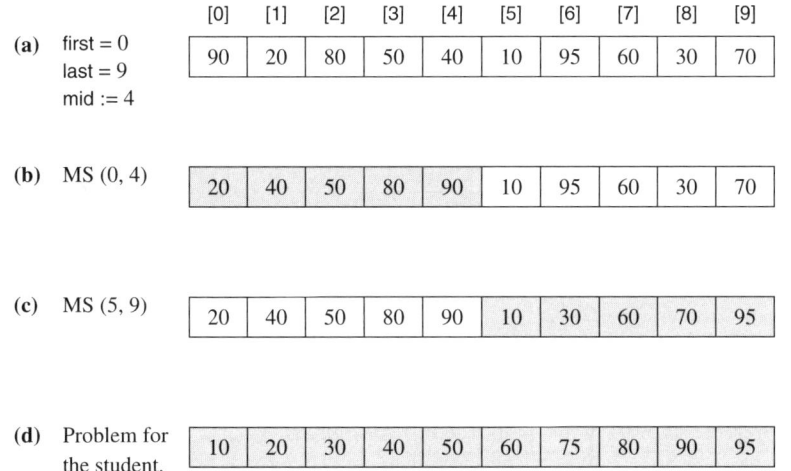

Figure 20.13
A trace of the top-level call to MergeSort in Figure 20.12.

Figure 20.14 shows a trace of the join operation that is left as a problem for the student. Each part of the figure shows the v array located above the temp array. The idea is to have one FOR loop with control variable k that increments from first to last and denotes the index of temp that receives a value from v. At each iteration of the loop, temp[k] will get either v[i], after which i is incremented, or v[j], after which j is incremented. The figure does not show seven steps in the loop that occur between parts (c) and (d). At the conclusion of the merge from array v to array temp, the elements from temp[first] to temp[last] must be copied back into array v from v[first] to v[last].

Figure 20.15 is the call tree for the values in Figure 20.13(a). The values in parentheses are the values of parameters first and last. The leaf nodes have first equal to last, indicating that a subarray of one element needs to be sorted. The algorithm does no processing in those cases, but just returns to the calling procedure.

You should be able to visualize the order in which the merges are performed from Figure 20.15. Figure 20.16 show the merges in the order they occur for the left half of the array.

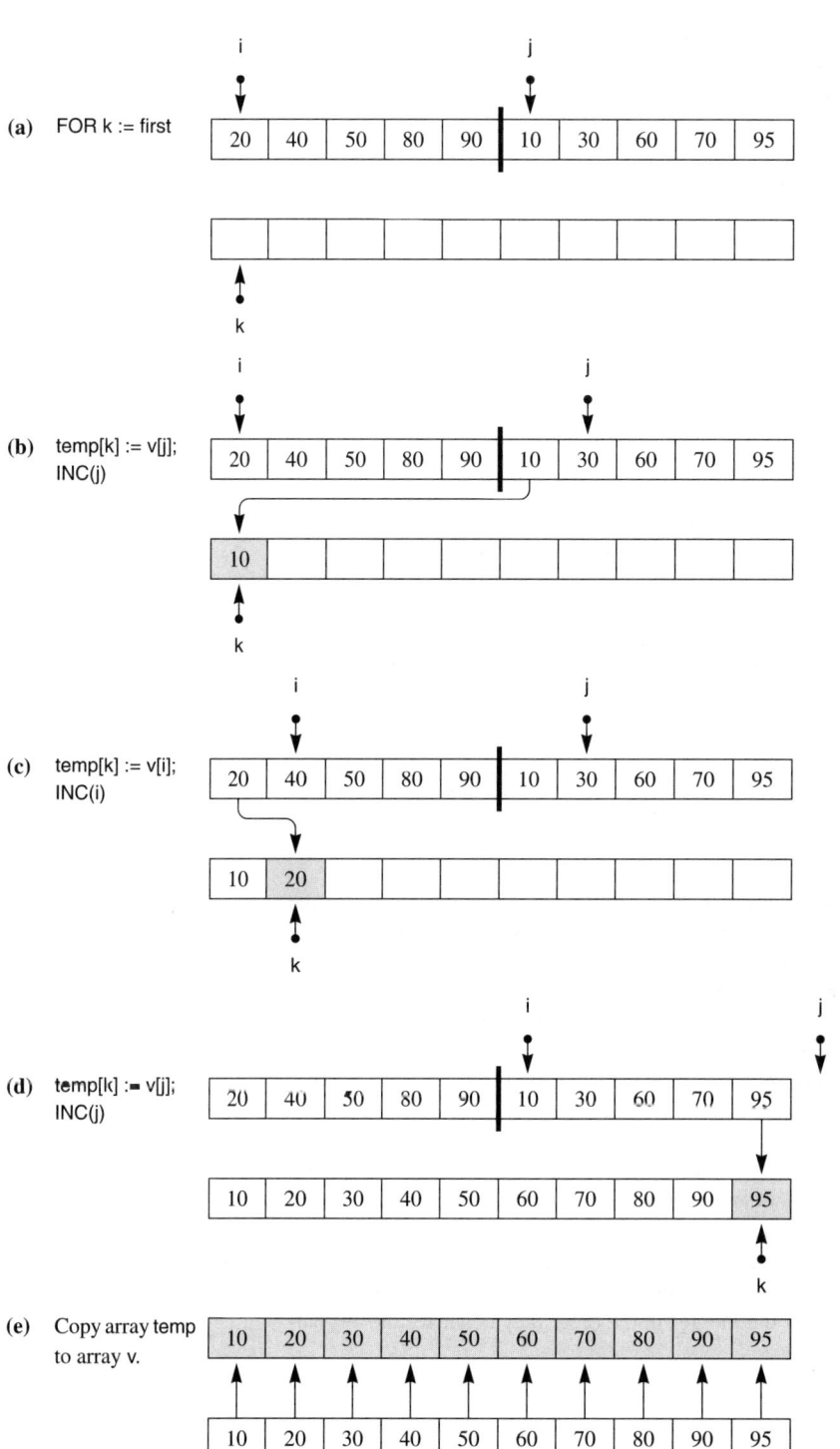

(a) FOR k := first

(b) temp[k] := v[j];
INC(j)

(c) temp[k] := v[i];
INC(i)

(d) temp[k] := v[j];
INC(j)

(e) Copy array temp
to array v.

Figure 20.14
A trace of the top-level call to
MergeSort in Figure 20.12.
Seven steps are not shown
between parts (c) and (d).

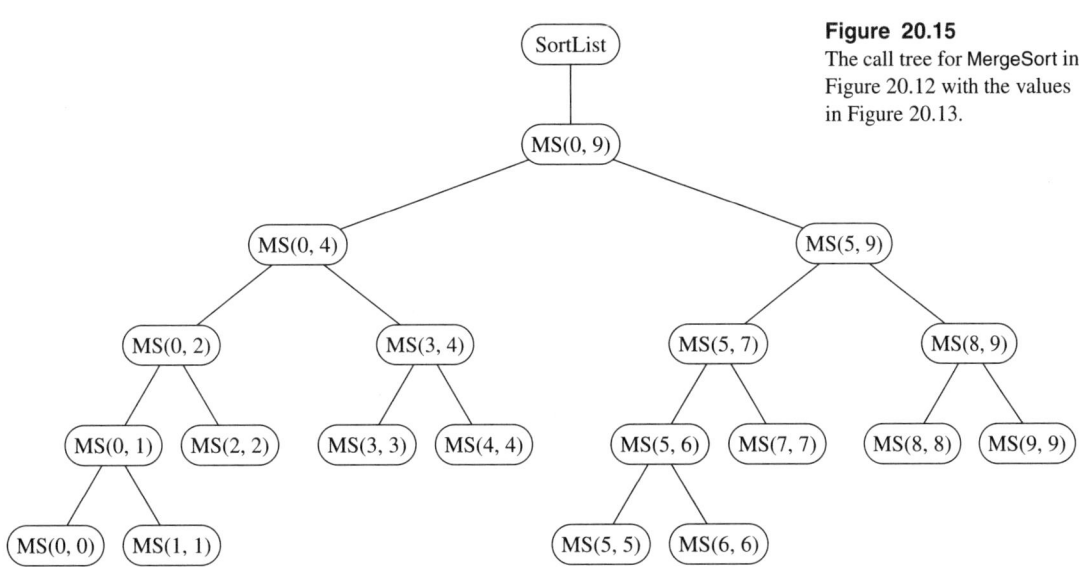

Figure 20.15
The call tree for MergeSort in
Figure 20.12 with the values
in Figure 20.13.

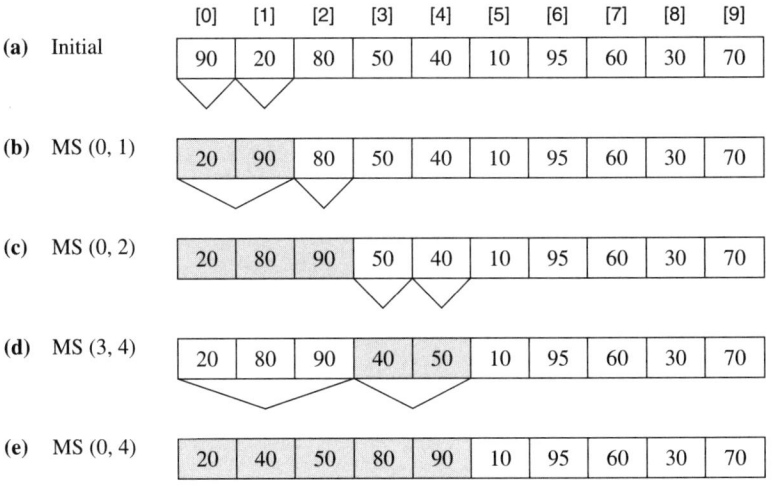

Figure 20.16
The merges in MergeSort in
the order they occur for the
left half of the array.

In-place merge sort

The program in Figure 20.17 is an implementation of the in-place merge sort. It is a more efficient implementation of the algorithm because it does not require extra storage for the second array or extra time for the copy operation in Figure 20.14(e). The program sorts an array of integers. It stores each value in a record with two parts, value and link. The array to be sorted is an array of records. The algorithm does not exchange any records in the array. Instead, it alters the link part of all the records in such a way that you can always determine the next higher number from the link field.

The input and output are identical to that for the quick sort in Figure 20.8. One difference from the previous sort algorithms is that the in-place merge sort cannot work with an empty array. Consequently, its precondition is weaker, and procedure SortList must test for the case of an empty array.

```
MODULE Pbox20C;
   IMPORT Dialog, TextModels, TextViews, Views, TextControllers, PboxMappers;
   TYPE
      Item = RECORD
         value: INTEGER;
         link: INTEGER
      END;
   VAR
      d*: RECORD
         numItems-: INTEGER;
      END;
      list: ARRAY 1024 OF Item;

   PROCEDURE LoadList*;
      VAR
         md: TextModels.Model;
         cn: TextControllers.Controller;
         sc: PboxMappers.Scanner;
         i: INTEGER;
   BEGIN
      cn := TextControllers.Focus();
      IF cn # NIL THEN
         md := cn.text;
         sc.ConnectTo(md);
         i := 0;
         sc.ScanInt(list[i].value); list[i].link := -1;
         WHILE ~sc.eot DO
            INC(i);
            sc.ScanInt(list[i].value); list[i].link := -1
         END;
         d.numItems := i;
         Dialog.Update(d)
      END;
   END LoadList;
```

Figure 20.17
An implementation of the in-place merge sort algorithm.

```
PROCEDURE MergeSort (VAR v: ARRAY OF Item; first, last: INTEGER; OUT start: INTEGER);
    (* Sorts the items of array v between v[first] and v[last]. *)
    VAR
        mid, loStart, hiStart: INTEGER;
        i, j, k: INTEGER;
BEGIN
    ASSERT((0 <= first) & (first <= last) & (last < LEN(v) - 1), 20);
    IF first = last THEN
        start := first
    ELSE
        mid := (first + last) DIV 2;
        MergeSort(v, first, mid, loStart);
        MergeSort(v, mid + 1, last, hiStart);
        i := loStart;
        j := hiStart;
        k := LEN(v) - 1; (* Temporary start of merged list *)
        WHILE (i # -1) & (j # -1) DO
            IF v[i].value <= v[j].value THEN
                v[k].link := i;
                k := i;
                i := v[i].link
            ELSE
                v[k].link := j;
                k := j;
                j := v[j].link
            END
        END;
        IF i = -1 THEN
            v[k].link := j  (* Attach remainder of last list *)
        ELSE
            v[k].link := i  (* Attach remainder of first list *)
        END;
        start := v[LEN(v) - 1].link
    END
END MergeSort;
```

Figure 20.17
Continued.

```
PROCEDURE SortList*;
   VAR
      md: TextModels.Model;
      vw: TextViews.View;
      fm: PboxMappers.Formatter;
      i: INTEGER;
      first: INTEGER;
BEGIN
   md := TextModels.dir.New();
   fm.ConnectTo(md);
   FOR i := 0 TO d.numItems -1 DO
      fm.WriteInt(list[i].value, 4)
   END;
   fm.WriteLn;
   IF d.numItems > 0 THEN
      MergeSort(list, 0, d.numItems - 1, first);
      i := first;
      WHILE i # -1 DO
         fm.WriteInt(list[i].value, 4);
         i := list[i].link
      END
   END;
   vw := TextViews.dir.New(md);
   Views.OpenView(vw)
END SortList;

BEGIN
   d.numItems := 0
END Pbox20C.
```

Figure 20.17
Continued.

Figure 20.18(a) shows the array of records before SortList calls procedure Merge-Sort. Procedure LoadList sets the link field of every record to –1 before the call.

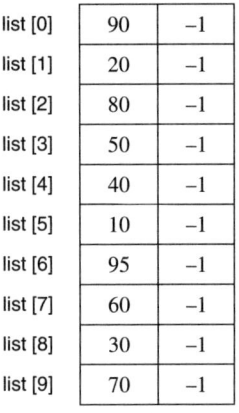 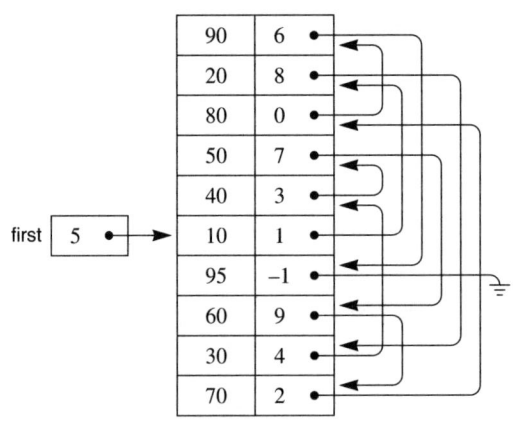

Figure 20.18
The result of a MergeSort call from procedure SortList of Figure 20.17.

(a) Before the first MergeSort call.   (b) After the top-level merge

Figure 20.18(b) shows the array of records after the call to MergeSort. Procedure SortList has an integer variable, first. MergeSort sets first to 5 because list[5].value is the smallest item in the list. It sets list[5].link to 1 because list[1].value is the next larger item in the list. It sets list[1].link to 8 because list[1].value is the next larger item in the list, and so on.

For each record, i, list[i].link is the index of the record whose value part is the next larger item in the list. The second field links each item to the next larger item. The record with the largest value, record 6 in this list, has a Link of −1. That link points to nothing at all, which the figure indicates by the dashed triangle.

The WHILE loop in SortList outputs the list in order. It initializes i to 5 and outputs list[5].value. The assignment

i := list[i].link

gives i the value 1. The next time through the loop the WriteInt procedure outputs list[1].value. The loop continues to advance i through the linked list until it gets the value −1, when the loop terminates. Even though the program exchanged no values, the output is indistinguishable from the QuickSort program. In effect, the program sorted the list.

Procedure SortList calls MergeSort with a value of 0 for first and 9 for last. MergeSort splits the list in half with

mid := (first + last) DIV 2

which gives 4 to mid. It calls itself recursively to sort *L1* as the list between v[0] and v[4], and *L2* as the list between v[5] and v[9]. Figure 20.19 shows the list after these two recursive calls to MergeSort.

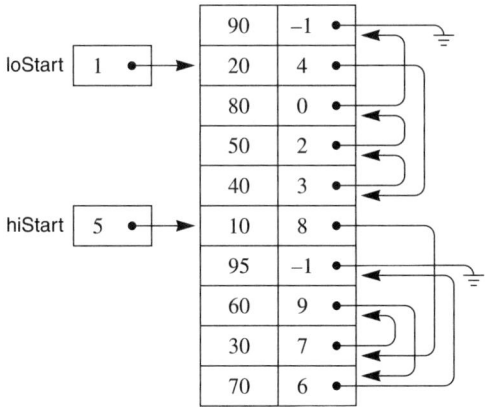

Figure 20.19
The list in the call to MergeSort(v, 0, 9, first) after the recursive calls to MergeSort(v, 0, 4, loStart) and MergeSort(v, 5, 9, hiStart).

The split was easy. The rest of MergeSort, that part in the WHILE loop, is the join. Given the values for loStart and hiStart, which point to the start of two ordered linked lists, the problems is to alter their link fields to make one ordered linked list with start pointing to the smallest element. Figure 20.20 shows a trace of the join operation for two short linked lists.

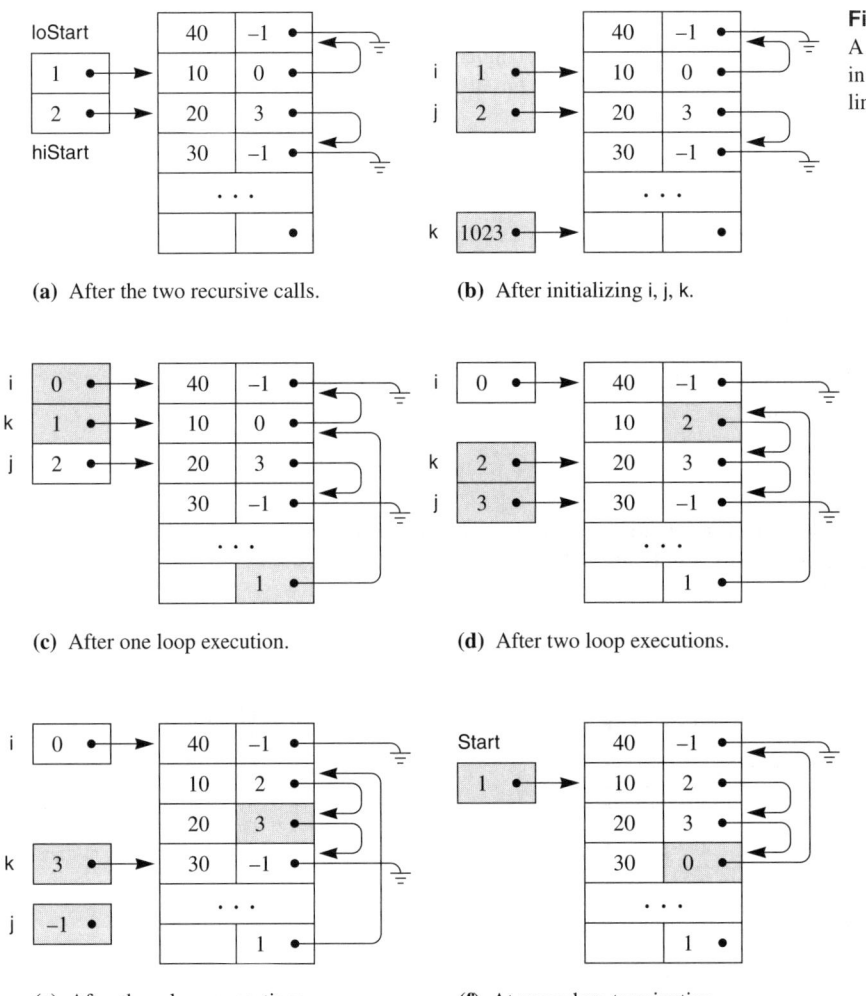

Figure 20.20
A trace of the join operation in MergeSort for two short linked lists.

(a) After the two recursive calls.

(b) After initializing i, j, k.

(c) After one loop execution.

(d) After two loop executions.

(e) After three loop executions.

(f) At procedure termination.

Figure 20.20(b) shows i initialized to loStart and j initialized to hiStart. MergeSort initializes k to LEN(v) - 1. It assumes that the list does not use the entire array and that the last record is available for temporary storage. i advances through the first list, j advances through the second list, and k advances through the merged list.

Each time the loop executes, it finds the next item from lists *L*1 and *L*2 to put in the merged list. It changes the link in the last record of the merged list to point to the newly merged item from *L1* or *L2*. The newly merged item is taken off the sublist. At the conclusion of the loop, all the items will be in one merged list with no physical exchanges.

Figure 20.20(c) shows the operation after one loop execution. The statements

```
v[k].link := i;
k := i;
i := v[i].link
```

link the v[1] record into the new merged list and unlink it from the i list. Figure 20.20(d) and (e) show the same operation with both values from the j list.

When the WHILE loop gets to the end of one of the lists, you know that all the remaining links of the other sublist do not need changing. The last IF statement links the tail of the other sublist to the end of the merged list, as Figure 20.20(f) shows.

Complexity of the sort algorithms

How fast are the sort algorithms that are described in this section? Remember from Chapter 19 that the selection sort is $O(n^2)$. The insertion sort is also $O(n^2)$. You can visualize in Figure 20.6 that each algorithm requires n passes through the list. Each pass requires a loop to do the insertion or selection. The doubly nested loops give the algorithms their $O(n^2)$ behavior.

How do quick sort and merge sort compare with the single-element sorts? In the best case with quick sort, you divide the list in half each time. Figure 20.21 shows the call tree for merge sort and the best case quick sort for a 16-element list.

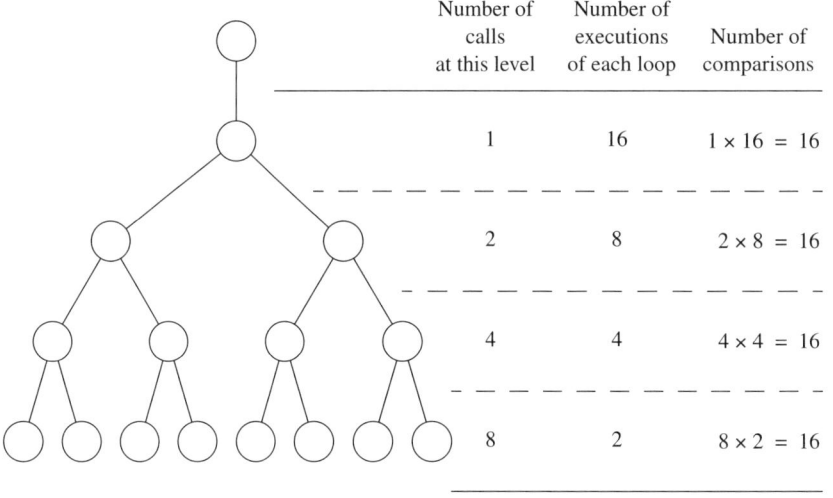

	Number of calls at this level	Number of executions of each loop	Number of comparisons
	1	16	$1 \times 16 = 16$
	2	8	$2 \times 8 = 16$
	4	4	$4 \times 4 = 16$
	8	2	$8 \times 2 = 16$

Total number of comparisons: $4 \times 16 = 64$

Figure 20.21
The call tree for merge sort and the best case quick sort with a 16-element list.

The list at the top level has 16 elements. The lists at the next lower recursive call have 8 elements. The lists at the next lower call have 4 elements, and the bottom level has 2-element lists.

A loop executes at each level. In merge sort, the WHILE loop performs the join. In quick sort, the REPEAT loop performs the split. In both algorithms, the loop passes through the list comparing items. The number of comparisons equals the number of items in the list.

For example, the top level has a list of 16 items, and the algorithm makes 16 comparisons. The next level has lists with 8 items. The loops at this level make 8 comparisons each. Because there are 2 recursive calls at the second level, the total number of comparisons at this level is also 16. Similarly, the number of comparisons at the next lower level is also 16. There are 4 lists, and each list requires 4 comparisons. In general, if the list has n elements, the algorithms make n comparisons at each level. So the total number of comparisons is n times the total number of levels.

How many levels are there for a list of n elements? The number of times you need to divide n in half to get it down to 1. You recognize this answer from the analysis of the binary search algorithm. It is $\lg n$. In Figure 20.21, the logarithm of 16 is 4, which corresponds to the 4 levels of recursive calls. The total number of comparisons is therefore 4 times 16, which is 64.

In general, the total number of comparisons is n times $\lg n$. Merge sort and the best-case quick sort are $O(n\lg n)$ algorithms. In the worst case, quick sort is $O(n^2)$ because in that case it is equivalent to the selection sort. In practice, quick sort is $O(n\lg n)$ on the average.

The five orders encountered thus far, starting with the fastest, are

- $O(\lg n)$ Example: the binary search
- $O(n)$ Example: the sequential search
- $O(n\lg n)$ Example: the merge sort and quick sort
- $O(n^2)$ Example: the single-element sorts
- $O(n^3)$ Example: matrix multiplication

If you are comparing two algorithms with different orders, the algorithm with an order farther down the list will be worse for large amounts of data, regardless of the coefficients. For example, an algorithm with a statement execution count of $5n\lg n$ will be faster than one with $2n^2$. Even though 5 is greater than 2, for large n the first expression will be smaller than the second. On the other hand, the coefficients are important when you compare two algorithms with the same order. If one algorithm has a statement execution count of $5n\lg n$, and the second has a count of $2n\lg n$, the second algorithm will be faster.

Some algorithms, not encountered in this book, are even worse than $O(n^3)$. They are $O(2^n)$, and form a class of difficult problems that computer scientists have spent a great deal of time investigating. They are interesting problems that you will learn about if you take more advanced computer science courses.

Exercises

1. Draw the ideal quick sort and merge sort traces corresponding to Figure 20.4(a) and (b) for the following lists:

   (a) 4 7 5 2 3 8 1 6
   (b) 8 7 6 5 4 3 2 1
   (c) 8 1 2 3 4 5 6 7

2. Work Exercise 1 for the single-element sorts of Figure 20.5(a) and (b).

3. Work Exercise 1 for the nonrecursive single-element sorts of Figure 20.6(a) and (b).

4. Write the list of 10 integer values just after the following calls to QuickSort in Figure 20.11.

   (a) QS (0, 3)   (b) QS (2, 3)   (c) QS (4, 9)
   (d) QS (4, 8)   (e) QS (4, 5)   (f) QS (7, 8)

5. Draw the list and the elements that j and i point to corresponding to Figure 20.10(g), (h), and (i) for the initial lists that follow. Figure 20.10(g) represents the list just before the first recursive call to QuickSort.

   (a) 10 60 40 80 30 90 20 70 25 50
   (b) 10 20 25 30 40 50 60 70 80 90
   (c) 90 80 70 60 50 40 30 25 20 10
   (d) 80 90 50 50 50 50 50 50 10 20

6. Draw the QuickSort call tree as in Figure 20.11 for the following initial lists.

   (a) 30 70 40 20   (b) 80 40 20 90 70
   (c) 40 60 10 70 90 30   (d) 10 20 30 40 50 60 70
   (e) 70 60 50 40 30 20 10

   How many times is QuickSort called? What is the maximum number of QuickSort stack frames on the run-time stack during the execution? In what order does the program make the calls and returns?

7. The section on the correctness of the quick sort algorithm, page 446, gave an eight-step outline of the proof. (a) Prove step 1. (b) Prove step 2. (c) Prove step 3. (d) Prove step 4. (e) Prove step 5. (f) Prove step 6. (g) Prove step 7. (h) Prove step 8.

8. Draw the result of a MergeSort call corresponding to Figure 20.18 for the following lists of numbers.

   (a) 30 50 10 80 40 70 20 60
   (b) 10 20 30 40 50 60 70 80
   (c) 80 70 60 50 40 30 20 10

9. Work Exercise 8 for the two top-level recursive MergeSort calls corresponding to Figure 20.19.

10. What is the total number of comparisons for the merge sort and the best-case quick sort with the following number of elements?

   (a) 32   **(b)** 1024   **(c)** 65,536

   What is the maximum number of stack frames allocated at one time for each of the lists?

Problems

11. Write the recursive version of the sequential search. Use the technique of inserting the number to be searched at the end of the list as shown in Figure 16.3 and Figure 16.4. Declare

```
PROCEDURE RecursiveSearch (VAR v: ARRAY OF INTEGER; numItm, srchNum: INTEGER;
        VAR i: INTEGER; OUT fnd: BOOLEAN);
BEGIN
   (* Problem for the student *)
END RecursiveSearch;

PROCEDURE Search (VAR v: ARRAY OF INTEGER; numItm, srchNum: INTEGER;
        OUT i: INTEGER; OUT fnd: BOOLEAN);
BEGIN
    ASSERT((0 <= numItm) & (numItm < LEN(v)), 20);
    i := 0;
    v[numItm] := srchNum;
    RecursiveSearch(v, numItm, srchNum, i, fnd)
END Search;
```

   Note that i is called by reference in RecursiveSearch. Do not use a loop. Do not compare i with numItm. Test your program with a dialog box identical to that in Figure 20.1.

12. Write the recursive version of the insertion sort algorithm as shown in Figure 20.5(a). Make a recursive call to sort the left part of the list, and use a single loop, starting from the end of the sorted part of the list to insert the single element. Test your algorithm in a program similar to the one in Figure 20.9.

13. Write the recursive version of the selection sort algorithm as shown in Figure 20.5(b). Use a single loop to move the largest element to the end of the list, then make a recursive call to sort the remaining left part of the list. Test your algorithm in a program similar to the one in Figure 20.9.

14. Write the nonrecursive version of the insertion sort algorithm as shown in Figure 20.5(a). Use a nested loop. Test your algorithm in a program similar to the one in Figure 20.9.

15. Suppose an application uses the merge sort, but it needs to have the array elements physically in order, not just linked in order. Modify procedure SortList of Figure 20.17 to put the elements of list physically in order. Declare tempList to be an array of the same type as list. After the call to MergeSort, copy the elements from list into tempList in physical order. Then copy the elements from tempList to list and output list without using the link field to verify that its elements are physically in order.

16. Complete procedure MergeSort of Figure 20.12. Test it in a program identical to Figure 20.9 except that the call is to MergeSort instead of to QuickSort.

Chapter *21*

Linked Lists

Previous chapters show how Component Pascal allocates storage on the run-time stack when a proper procedure is called. First, storage is allocated for the parameters, then for the return address, and finally for the local variables of the procedure. When the program returns from a procedure, it deallocates the storage. When a function procedure is called, storage for the returned value is allocated followed by allocation for the same items as those for a proper procedure.

Component Pascal provides an alternate method for allocating and deallocating storage from main memory. It maintains a region in memory that is called the heap, which is separate from the stack. You do not control allocation and deallocation from the heap during procedure calls and returns. Instead, you allocate from the heap with the help of pointer variables. Allocation that is not triggered automatically by procedure calls is known as dynamic storage allocation.

The heap

Dynamic storage allocation

Pointers are common building blocks for implementing abstract data types and classes. This chapter presents the Component Pascal pointer type and shows how you can use pointers to implement a linked list abstract data type and a linked list class.

Pointer data types

When you declare an array, you must declare it to be an array of some type. For example, you can declare an array of integers or an array of real values. Pointers share this characteristic of arrays. When you declare a pointer, you must declare that it points to some type. The program in Figure 21.1 illustrates the Component Pascal pointer type. It shows how to declare a pointer variable and how to access the values associated with it.

The program declares type Node to be a record that contains an integer field i and a real field x. Local variable a is declared to be a pointer to a Node, that is, a pointer to a record. a is not a record. It is a pointer to a record. If a acquires a value during execution of the program, that value will not be a record. Instead, the value given to a will specify the memory location of where the record is stored, somewhere in the heap.

Figure 21.2 is a trace of the execution of the procedure in Figure 21.1. Figure 21.2(a) shows a after PointerExample1 is called. Because a is a local variable, it is allocated on the run-time stack when the procedure is called. Return address ra0 is the location of some instruction in the framework. Most local variables have undefined values when they are allocated. Pointer variables, however, are initialized to the special value NIL. In Figure 21.2(a) the NIL value is shown as the dashed triangle.

```
MODULE Pbox21A;
    IMPORT StdLog;

    PROCEDURE PointerExample1*;
        TYPE
            Node = RECORD
                i: INTEGER;
                x: REAL
            END;
        VAR
            a: POINTER TO Node;
        BEGIN
            NEW(a);
            a.i := 6;
            a.x := 15.2;
            StdLog.String("a.i = "); StdLog.Int(a.i); StdLog.Ln;
            StdLog.String("a.x = "); StdLog.Real(a.x); StdLog.Ln
        END PointerExample1;

END Pbox21A.
```

Figure 21.1
A program that illustrates the Component Pascal pointer type.

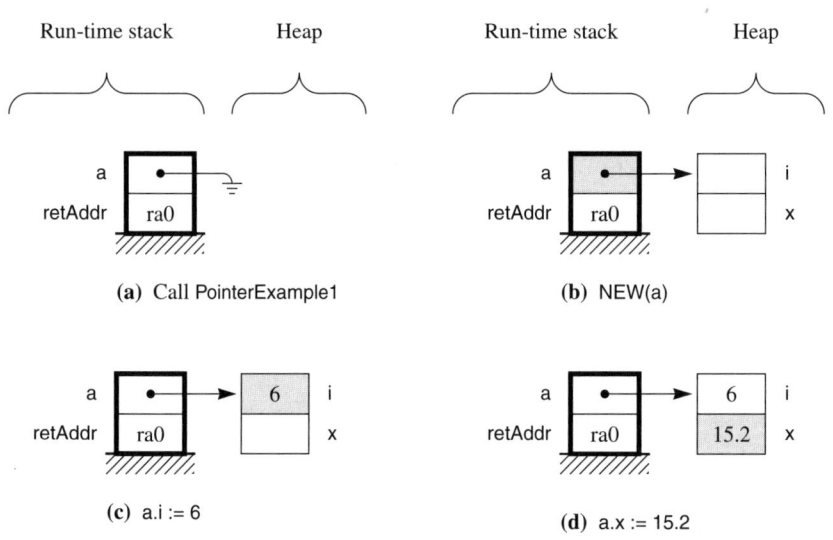

Run-time stack   Heap

(a) Call PointerExample1

(b) NEW(a)

(c) a.i := 6

(d) a.x := 15.2

Figure 21.2
The trace of the procedure in Figure 21.1.

The first statement the program executes is

NEW(a)

The procedure NEW is a standard Component Pascal procedure that does two things:

The two actions of NEW

- It allocates storage from the heap. Because a was previously declared to be a pointer to a record with an integer and a real component, NEW(a) allocates enough memory to store a record with those components.

- It assigns to a the location of this newly allocated storage. So a now points to the location of a record.

Figure 21.2(b) indicates the effect of NEW(a). The box adjacent to the a box represents the storage allocated from the heap. The arrow pointing from the a box to the newly allocated box represents the value that NEW assigns to a.

The next statement the program executes is

a.i := 6

Figure 21.2(c) shows the effect of the assignment. In the same way that you access the field of a record by writing the name of the *record* followed by the field and separated by a period, you access the field of the record to which a pointer points by writing the name of the *pointer* followed by the field and separated by a period. Remember that a is not a record. It is a pointer to a record. Therefore, the integer field of the record to which a points gets 6.

The next statement,

a.x := 15.2

assigns a value to the real field of the record to which a points as shown in Figure 21.2(d).

The last statements

StdLog.String("a.i = "); StdLog.Int(a.i); StdLog.Ln;
StdLog.String("a.x = "); StdLog.Real(a.x); StdLog.Ln

simply output the following text to the Log.

a.i = 6
a.x = 15.2

Pointer assignments

You can assign one pointer to another, but you must be careful to consider the effect of such an assignment. Because a pointer "points to" an item, if you give the pointer's value to a second pointer, the second pointer will point to the same item to which the first pointer points. The program in Figure 21.3 illustrates the effect of the assignment operation on pointers.

```
MODULE Pbox21B;
   IMPORT StdLog;

   PROCEDURE PointerExample2*;
      TYPE
         Node = RECORD
            i: INTEGER
         END;
      VAR
         a, b, c: POINTER TO Node;
      BEGIN
         NEW(a); a.i := 5;
         NEW(b); b.i := 3;
         c := a;
         a := b;
         a.i := 2 + c.i;
         StdLog.String("a.i = "); StdLog.Int(a.i); StdLog.Ln;
         StdLog.String("b.i = "); StdLog.Int(b.i); StdLog.Ln;
         StdLog.String("c.i = "); StdLog.Int(c.i); StdLog.Ln
      END PointerExample2;

END Pbox21B.
```

Figure 21.3

The effect of the assignment operation on pointers.

The program allocates and assigns values to a.i and b.i, as Figure 21.4(a–e) shows. These operations are similar to those of the previous program.

Figure 21.4

A trace of Figure 21.3.

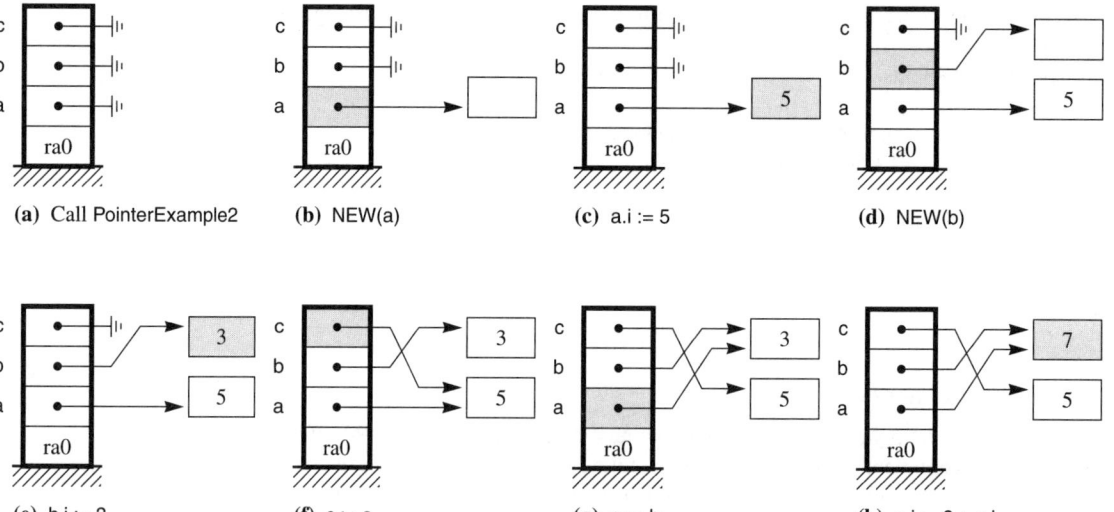

(a) Call PointerExample2   (b) NEW(a)   (c) a.i := 5   (d) NEW(b)

(e) b.i := 3   (f) c := a   (g) a := b   (h) a.i := 2 + c.i

After b.i := 3 in Figure 21.4(e), the statement

c := a

gives the value of a to c, as Figure 21.4(f) shows. a is a pointer. Therefore c will point to the same memory location to which a points. After the assignment, c also points to the record that contains 5. Notice that the statement does not assign to c the value 5. It assigns to c the pointer to the record that contains 5.

The statement

a := b

copies the b pointer into a, as Figure 21.4(g) shows. As in all assignment statements, the previous value of a is destroyed. a no longer points to the record containing 5, but to the same record to which b points, namely the record containing 3.

The last assignment statement

a.i := 2 + c.i

contains the + arithmetic operation. Because a.i and c.i are integer variables and not pointers, the statement is legal. It adds 2 to the integer in the record to which c is pointing, 5, to get 7. The 7 is copied into the record to which a is pointing. As in all assignment statements, the original content of the memory location, 3, is destroyed.

The output statements

```
StdLog.String("a.i = "); StdLog.Int(a.i); StdLog.Ln;
StdLog.String("b.i = "); StdLog.Int(b.i); StdLog.Ln;
StdLog.String("c.i = "); StdLog.Int(c.i); StdLog.Ln;
```

produce

```
a.i = 7
b.i = 7
c.i = 5
```

Because a and b now point to the same record, the record containing 7, its value is printed twice.

Using pointers

Component Pascal allows you to declare a pointer to a record or to an array. It does not allow you to declare a pointer to any other type.

Example 21.1 The declaration

a: POINTER TO INTEGER;

is illegal because you cannot have a pointer to an integer, only to a record or an array. ∎

The period that separates the name of the pointer from the name of the field of the record to which it points is actually an abbreviation for a longer notation. In general, if pointer p points to a record r that contains field f, then

- p   is a pointer
- p^   is the record r to which p points
- p^.f   is field f of the record r to which p points.

The notation p.f is an abbreviation for the longer notation p^.f.

The period abbreviation for pointers to records

Example 21.2   The program statements in Figure 21.1

```
a.i := 6;
a.x := 15.2;
```

can be written in non abbreviated form with the circumflex ^ as

```
a^.i := 6;
a^.x := 15.2;
```
∎

You can output the components of a record to which a pointer points, but you cannot output the value of a pointer variable.

Example 21.3   The statement

```
StdLog.Int(a)
```

is illegal with a declared as in Figure 21.3. ∎

The only operations that are allowed on pointer data types are

```
:= assignment
=  test for equality
#  test for inequality
```

The only operations allowed on pointer data types

Specifically, you cannot test if one pointer is greater than another, and you cannot perform mathematical operations on pointers.

Example 21.4   With a and b declared as in Figure 21.3, the test

```
IF a.i < b.i THEN
```

is legal, because you can test if an integer value is less than another integer value. However, the test

IF a < b THEN

is illegal because a and b are pointers.   ∎

Example 21.5 With a declared as in Figure 21.3, the statement

a.i := a.i * 2

would be legal because a.i is an integer. On the other hand, the statement

a := a * 2

would be illegal, because you cannot multiply a pointer by 2.   ∎

One of the most common errors in programming with pointers is to assume that a pointer points to a record when in fact it does not.

Example 21.6 Suppose a is declared as in Figure 21.3, and you forget to execute the NEW procedure as follows.

```
BEGIN
   a.i := 5;
```

The assignment statement will generate a trap with the error message

NIL dereference

Because a is NIL it does not point to anything, and a.i does not exist. The system protests with the run-time error message, complaining that you are referring to something with a but that a does not refer to anything.   ∎

Linked lists

In practice, you frequently combine a pointer with other variables into a record. Then the pointer part of the record can point to yet another record, linking the two records together. The program in Figure 21.6 constructs a linked list of three real numbers. Each record in the linked list has two parts, a value part, which contains the value of a real number, and a next part, which points to the next record in the linked list. Figure 21.5 shows the structure of a record of type Node as declared in the program. The box labeled value will contain a real value and the box labeled next will contain a pointer value.

Figure 21.7 is a trace of the first part of the program in Figure 21.6, which creates a linked list. The following is a description of each statement executed by the first part of the program.

Figure 21.7(a) shows the allocated memory after the call to LinkedListExample. The program allocates storage for the local variables declared in the variable declaration part on the run-time stack. The variables first and p are not records. They are pointers to records. Initially their values are NIL.

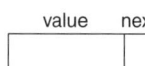

value   next

Figure 21.5
The structure of a record of type Node in Figure 21.6.

```
MODULE Pbox21C;
   IMPORT StdLog;

   PROCEDURE LinkedListExample*;
      TYPE
         List = POINTER TO Node;
         Node = RECORD
            value: REAL;
            next: List
         END;
      VAR
         first, p: List;
      BEGIN
         (* Create linked list *)
         NEW(first); first.value := 4.5;
         p := first;
         NEW(first); first.value := 1.2;
         first.next := p; p := first;
         NEW(first); first.value := 7.3;
         first.next := p;
         (* Output linked list *)
         p := first;
         StdLog.Real(p.value); StdLog.String(" ");
         p := p.next;
         StdLog.Real(p.value); StdLog.String(" ");
         p := p.next;
         StdLog.Real(p.value); StdLog.String(" ")
      END LinkedListExample;

END Pbox21C.
```

Figure 21.6

A program that constructs a linked list of three real numbers.

Figure 21.7(b) shows the effect of the procedure call NEW(first). Procedure NEW does two things. First, it allocates enough storage from the heap for a record of type Node. Then it changes the value of first to point to the record just allocated. It also initializes the value of link to NIL. All pointers are automatically initialized to NIL whenever they are allocated, whether on the stack or from the heap. Then, first.value := 4.5 stores value 4.5 in the value part of the node to which first points.

Creating a linked list

Figure 21.7(c) shows the effect of the statement

p := first

This is a pointer assignment. It makes p point to the same node to which first points. Because first points to the node containing 4.5, p will point to the same node after the assignment.

Figure 21.7(d) shows that procedure call

NEW(first)

allocates another record from the heap and sets first to point to the newly allocated

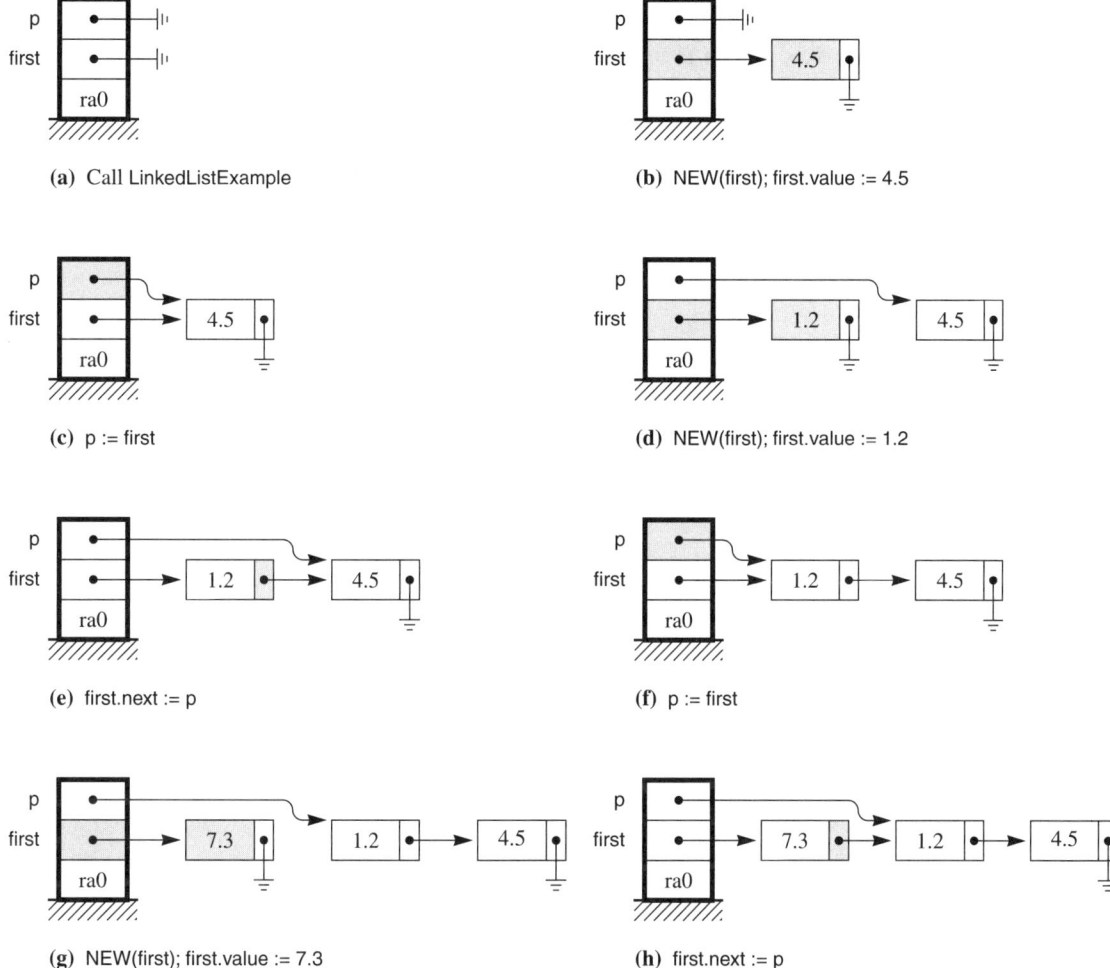

(a) Call LinkedListExample

(b) NEW(first); first.value := 4.5

(c) p := first

(d) NEW(first); first.value := 1.2

(e) first.next := p

(f) p := first

(g) NEW(first); first.value := 7.3

(h) first.next := p

record. Then,

first.value := 1.2

sets the value part of the record to which first points, to 1.2.

Figure 21.7(e) shows the effect of the assignment statement

first.next := p

This is another pointer assignment. It makes first.next point to the same record to which p points. You can see from the figure that this statement is responsible for linking the 1.2 node to the 4.5 node.

Figure 21.7(f) shows the effect of the pointer assignment

Figure 21.7
The trace of Figure 21.6 to create a linked list.

p := first

This assignment statement makes p point to the same thing to which first points, namely, the newly allocated record.

Figure 21.7(g) shows that the procedure call

NEW(first)

allocates another record from the heap and sets first to point to the newly allocated record. Furthermore,

first.value := 7.3

sets the value part of that record to 7.3.

Figure 21.7(h) shows how the statement

first.next := p

links the 7.3 node to the 1.2 node.

Now the linked list is complete. The first record containing 7.3 in its value part is linked to the second record, which contains 1.2 in its value part. The second record is, in turn, linked to the third which contains 4.5 in its value part.

The last part of the program outputs the linked list to the Log. Figure 21.8 is a *Outputting a linked list* trace. The idea is for p to start at the beginning of the list and to advance through it by way of the next field. Following is a description of each statement executed.

Figure 21.8(a) shows the effect of the assignment statement

p := first

Because p and first are both pointers, the assignment makes p point to the same record to which first points, namely the first record of the linked list. It is similar to an initializing statement. Because p.value is the value field of the first record, the StdLog.Real call outputs 7.3.

Figure 21.8(b) shows how the statement

p := p.next

advances p to the next record of the linked list. p.value is now the value of the second record. The StdLog.Real call outputs 1.2.

Figure 21.8(c) shows how the same statement

p := p.next

advances p to the next record of the linked list again. p.value is now the value of the last record. The StdLog.Real call outputs 4.5.

The action of the pointer p is typical of algorithms that must process information from every node in a linked list. You initialize a local pointer variable p to point to the first node in the list. You process all the nodes of the list by putting the statement

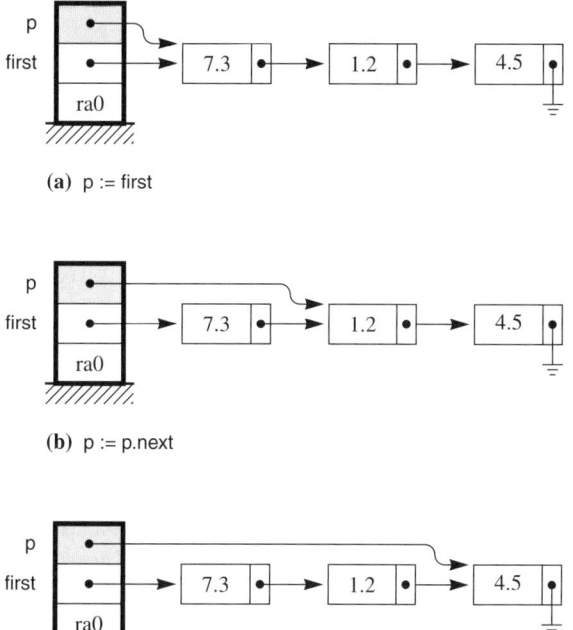

Figure 21.8
The trace of the procedure in Figure 21.6 to output a linked list.

p := p.next in the body of a loop. Each time the loop executes, p advances to the next node of the linked list. Also in the body of the loop are any statements that process the data in the value part of the node. How would such a loop terminate? When p points to the last node of the linked list. That happens when p.next = NIL. The statements to output the linked list could be written with a single loop as follows.

```
p := first;
WHILE p # NIL DO
    StdLog.Real(p.value); StdLog.String(" ");
    p := p.next
END
```

This loop works correctly even if the list is empty, because an empty list would have first equal to NIL. The test for a WHILE statement is at the beginning of the loop, so the test would be false the first time and the body of the loop would never execute.

In Figure 21.6, first and p are local variables that are allocated on the run-time stack. When the procedure terminates, first and p are all deallocated and so no longer point to any of the nodes of the linked list. So how do the nodes of the linked list get deallocated? They stay allocated until the heap runs out of memory and the execution of a NEW statement requires memory from the heap. At that point, the Component Pascal system initiates an operation known as *garbage collection*. The garbage collection algorithm sweeps through all the nodes in the heap and deallocates all

Automatic garbage collection

those that are unreachable from any active pointers. This automatic garbage collection feature is a major advantage of Component Pascal over many other programming languages. Languages that do not have automatic garbage collection require the programmer to deallocate any unused nodes. It is easy to make programming errors in the deallocation of dynamic memory, because the effects of incorrect deallocation frequently do not show up immediately.

Class assignments

There are two basic relationships in object-oriented design—class composition and inheritance. The examples in this section assume that Alpha, Beta, and Gamma are each a record type and are related by the second relationship, inheritance. Specifically, Beta inherits from Alpha, and Gamma inherits from Alpha. The Unified Modeling Language (UML) symbol for inheritance is the triangle. Figure 21.9 illustrates the object-oriented relationship of inheritance between Alpha, Beta, and Gamma in a UML class diagram. The Component Pascal term for inheritance is extension. Beta is an extension of Alpha. Beta is called the subclass, and Alpha is called the superclass.

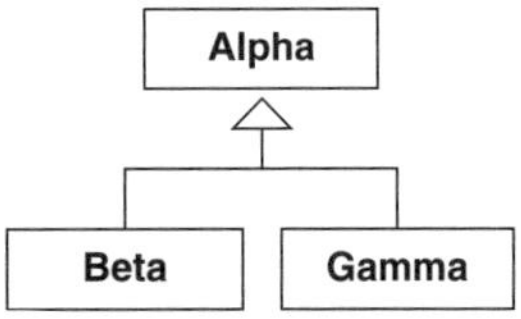

Figure 21.9
The object-oriented relationship of inheritance between Alpha, Beta, and Gamma.

The examples also assume that AlphaPtr, BetaPtr, and GammaPtr are pointers to Alpha, Beta, and Gamma respectively and that alphaPtr, betaPtr, and gammaPtr are variables of type AlphaPtr, BetaPtr, and GammaPtr respectively as follows.

```
TYPE
    AlphaPtr = POINTER TO Alpha;
    BetaPtr = POINTER TO Beta;
    GammaPtr = POINTER TO Gamma;
VAR
    alphaPtr: AlphaPtr;
    betaPtr: BetaPtr;
    gammaPtr: GammaPtr;
```

The word class is object-oriented terminology for type, and the word object is object-oriented terminology for variable. The statement, "Variable alphaPtr has type AlphaPtr", becomes in object-oriented terminology, "Object alphaPtr is an instantiation of class AlphaPtr".

The idea behind inheritance is that Alpha is the more general class and Beta is the more specific class. The fundamental class assignment rule is that you can assign the specific to the general, but you cannot assign the general to the specific.

The fundamental class assignment rule

Example 21.7 With alphaPtr and betaPtr declared as above, and Beta inheriting from Alpha as in Figure 21.9, the assignment

betaPtr := alphaPtr

is *not* legal, but the assignment

alphaPtr := betaPtr

is legal.   ▊

In Example 21.7, what is the type of alphaPtr after the legal assignment? It would appear from its declaration that it has type AlphaPtr, but because it has just been assigned betaPtr, it would appear to have beta's type, which is BetaPtr. In fact, it has both. Its static type is AlphaPtr and its dynamic type is BetaPtr. In computer science terminology, the word static means something that happens or is determined at compile time, and the word dynamic means something that happens or is determined at execution time. The compiler can determine the static type of alphaPtr from its declaration in the VAR section. But, the assignment to alphaPtr does not occur until the program is executing.

The meaning of static and dynamic

It is possible that at some later time alphaPtr could get the value of gammaPtr, at which time its dynamic type would change to GammaPtr. To morph is to change from one object into another object, as in the metamorphosis of a caterpillar into a butterfly. In object-oriented terminology, alpha is polymorphic because it can change from being a beta object to being a gamma object.

Polymorphism

From the fundamental class assignment rule it follows that an object's dynamic type is either the same as its static type or is more specific than its static type. Suppose you have one object with some static type, and another object of a more general static type but whose dynamic type is the same as the static type of the first object. You want to assign the second object to the first. According to the static types the assignment violates the fundamental class assignment rule. But if the dynamic type of the second object is the same as the static type of the first object it seems that you should be able to make the assignment.

Example 21.8   Suppose that betaTwoPtr has declaration

VAR
    betaTwoPtr: BetaPtr;

and the assignment statement

alphaPtr := betaTwoPtr

executes. This assignment statement is legal by the class assignment rule, because alphaPtr is more general than betaTwoPtr. Furthermore, alphaPtr now has dynamic type BetaPtr. It seems as though the assignment

betaPtr := alphaPtr

should now be legal, because the dynamic type of alphaPtr is the same as the static type of betaPtr.   ▊

Component Pascal provides a way. To make the assignment, you must append a type guard to the variable on the right hand side of the assignment statement, which consists of an extension (that is, a subclass) of its static type enclosed in parentheses. The assignment statement will compile correctly only if the type guard is an extension of the expression that it guards.

Type guards

Example 21.9 With the above declarations,

alphaPtr (BetaPtr)

is a valid type guard, because type BetaPtr is a subclass of AlphaPtr, which is the type of alphaPtr. However, the type guard

betaPtr (AlphaPtr)

will not compile, because AlphaPtr is not a subclass of BetaPtr. ∎

Example 21.10 Because a type is a subclass of itself, the type guard

alphaPtr (AlphaPtr)

although not very useful, is legal. ∎

To determine if an assignment statement will compile, the compiler treats the guarded variable as if it had the type of the guard and applies the class assignment rule.

Example 21.11 With alphaPtr and betaPtr declared as above, the assignment statement

betaPtr := alphaPtr (BetaPtr)

will compile, because if alphaPtr had the type BetaPtr it would compile. ∎

If variable v has type guard T, the guarded expression v(T) asserts that the dynamic type of v is T or an extension (that is, a subclass) of T. The program will trap if during execution the dynamic type of v is not T or a subclass of T.

Example 21.12 The assignment statement in Example 21.11 will always compile successfully. If during execution alphaPtr first gets betaTwoPtr as in Example 21.8 the assignment will also execute successfully. However, if during execution alphaPtr first gets gammaPtr (a legal assignment by the class assignment rule) then the assignment statement in Example 21.11 will trap. ∎

Component Pascal has a special record named ANYREC, which is the most gen-   *The ANYREC record*
eral record of all. Any record that does not inherit from any other record automatically inherits from ANYREC. So, even though it is not shown in the UML diagram of Figure 21.9, class Alpha inherits from ANYREC.

Example 21.13 Suppose Alpha and Beta have the inheritance relationship of Figure 21.9, and alphaPtr and betaPtr are declared as above. If you declare

```
VAR
    deltaPtr: POINTER TO ANYREC;
```

then the assignments

deltaPtr := alphaPtr;
deltaPtr := betaPtr

are legal. The second assignment is based on the transitive property of inheritance. That is, because Beta inherits from Alpha, and Alpha inherits from ANYREC, Beta inherits from ANYREC. So, deltaPtr is more general than betaPtr and can get its value. The assignment

alphaPtr := deltaPtr (AlphaPtr)

will compile successfully, but will execute successfully only if the dynamic type of deltaPtr is AlphaPtr or a subclass of AlphaPtr. ▮

A circular linked list ADT

It is possible to package a linked list as an abstract data structure, an abstract data type, or a class. The same advantages and disadvantages apply to any ADS, ADT, and class. Namely, an ADS is appropriate when there is only one data structure. To implement an ADS, you put the data structure in the server module and usually export only the procedures that operate on the data structure. An ADT and a class are appropriate when the client module might want more than one instance of the data structure. The server module exports the type of the data structure so the client module is free to declare as many data structures as needed.

Figure 21.10 shows the interface of a list abstract data type. It has two interesting features. First, it is a circular list in which the next field of the last node is not NIL, but points back to the first node in the list. Second, the value part of each node is not limited to any particular type like REAL or INTEGER. Instead, the value part is a pointer to ANYREC. The client is free to define any record it desires to store in the value part of each node. The ADT maintains a current position in the circular list, which the client can change via the GoNext procedure.

```
DEFINITION PboxCListADT;

    TYPE
        CList = POINTER TO Node;

    PROCEDURE Clear (OUT lst: CList);
    PROCEDURE Empty (lst: CList): BOOLEAN;
    PROCEDURE GoNext (VAR lst: CList);
    PROCEDURE Insert (VAR lst: CList; val: POINTER TO ANYREC);
    PROCEDURE NodeContent (lst: CList): POINTER TO ANYREC;

END PboxCListADT.
```

Figure 21.10
The interface of the circular list abstract data type.

Like all interfaces, the one in Figure 21.10 hides the details of the implementation. A client can use the procedures with the circular list without knowing anything about how they are implemented. Here are the specifications of the procedures.

The documentation of the clear procedure is

PROCEDURE **Clear** (OUT lst: CList)
post
lst is cleared to the empty list.

As an example of what procedure Clear does, suppose you have a variable named myList that has been declared as follows

VAR
   myList: PboxCListADT.CList;

and has the structure shown in Figure 21.11(a) where it contains three items. The clouds in Figure 21.11(a) represent records of some unknown type to which the pointers to ANYREC point. If you execute the statement

PboxCListADT.Clear(myList)

then myList is cleared to the empty list, as shown in Figure 21.11(b).

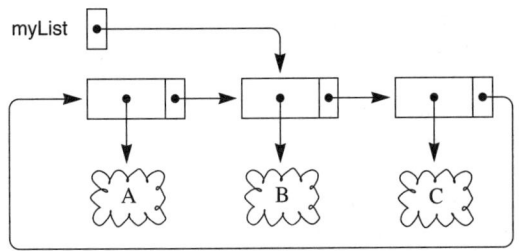

myList   myList

Figure 21.11
The result of calling procedure Clear.

(a) Before PboxCListADT.Clear(myList)   **(b)** After PboxCListADT.Clear(myList)

The documentation of the procedure Empty is

PROCEDURE **Empty** (lst: CList): BOOLEAN
post
Returns TRUE if lst is empty. Otherwise returns FALSE.

If myList has the structure of Figure 21.11(a), then PboxCListADT.Empty(myList) returns FALSE, but if myList has the structure of Figure 21.11(b) it returns TRUE.

Procedure GoNext advances the list to the next node in the list. Its documentation is

PROCEDURE **GoNext** (VAR lst: CList)
pre
lst is not empty.   20
post
The next location in lst is designated as the current item.

Figure 21.12 shows the effect of executing

PboxCListADT.GoNext(myList)

One more execution of GoNext would make myList point to the node whose value part points to the A record.

Figure 21.12
The result of calling procedure GoNext.

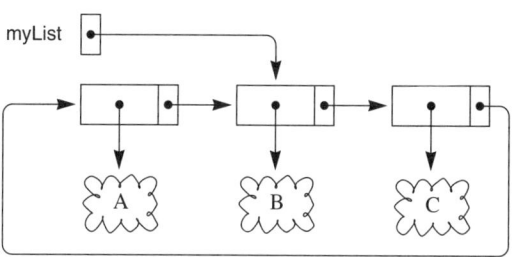

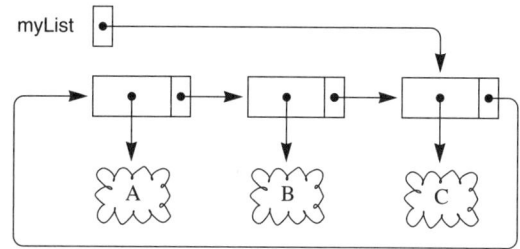

(a) Before PboxCListADT.GoNext(myList)

(b) After PboxCListADT.GoNext(myList)

Procedure Insert assumes that val is a pointer to some record. It inserts a new node into the list whose value part points to the same record that val points to. Its documentation is

PROCEDURE **Insert** (VAR lst: CList; val: POINTER TO ANYREC)
post
Value val is inserted in lst after the current item, and it becomes the current item.

Figure 21.13
The result of calling procedure Insert.

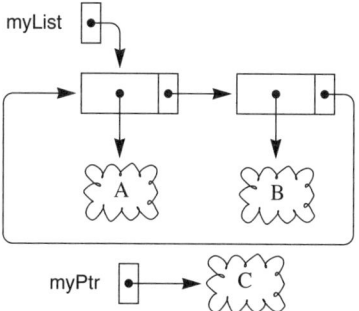

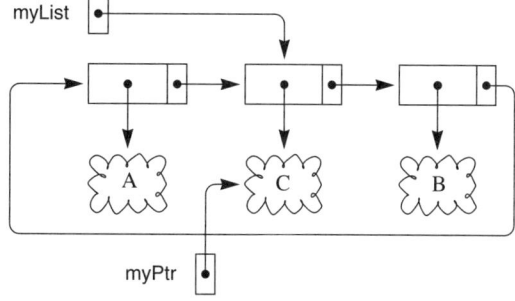

(a) Before PboxCListADT.Insert(myList, myPtr)

(b) After PboxCListADT.Insert(myList, myPtr)

Figure 21.13 shows the effect of executing the statement

PboxCListADT.Insert(myList, myPtr)

Before execution, myPtr points to some record. After execution, myPtr still points to the record but a new node is created and inserted into the circular list. The value part of the new node also points to the record.

The last procedure NodeContent returns the value part of the current node, that is, the node to which lst points. Its documentation is

PROCEDURE **NodeContent** (lst: CList): POINTER TO ANYREC
pre
lst is not empty.   20
post
Returns the content from the current item of lst.

The purpose of NodeContent is for the programmer to retrieve the content of the current node. For example, suppose myPtr is a pointer of type MyPtr with an initial value of NIL as in Figure 21.14(a). After executing the statement

myPtr := PboxCListADT.NodeContent(myList) (MyPtr)

Figure 21.14
The result of calling procedure NodeContent when myList initially has the structure of Figure 21.11(a).

myPtr points to the record to which the value part of the current node in the list points as in Figure 21.14(b). Note the required use of the type guard (MyPtr), because myPtr is more specific than POINTER TO ANYREC. The programmer can then use myPtr to access the various fields of the record.

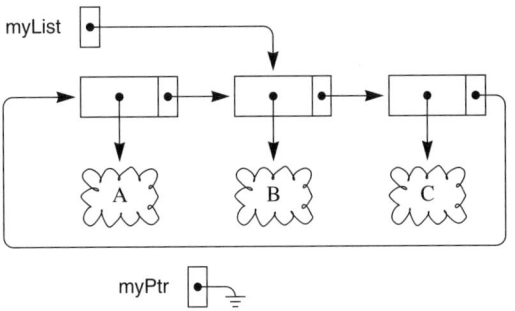

(a) Before
myPtr := PBoxCListADT.NodeContent(myList) (MyPtr)

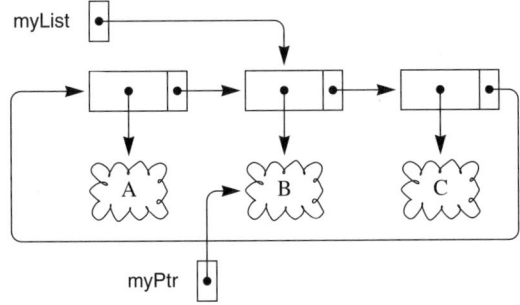

(b) After
myPtr := PBoxCListADT.NodeContent(myList) (MyPtr)

Figure 21.15 is the dialog box for a program that uses the circular list in Pbox-CListADT. The program stores a list of books where the type Book is defined as

```
TYPE
  String64 = ARRAY 64 OF CHAR;
  Book = POINTER TO RECORD
    title: String64;
    author: String64;
    price: REAL
  END;
```

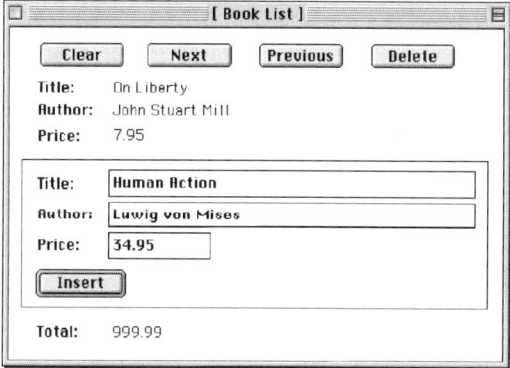

Figure 21.15
The dialog box for a program that uses the circular list from module PboxCListADT.

A book is a pointer to a record with three fields—one for the title of the book, one for the author, and one for the price. The dialog box allows the user to enter information into each of these fields, and then insert the book into the circular list. The dialog box represents a situation where the user has entered the information for the book *Human Action*, inserted it, and then pressed the Next button to display the next book in the list, which is *On Liberty*. Figure 21.16 shows the corresponding structure of the circular list.

Figure 21.16
The circular list corresponding to the dialog box in Figure 21.15.

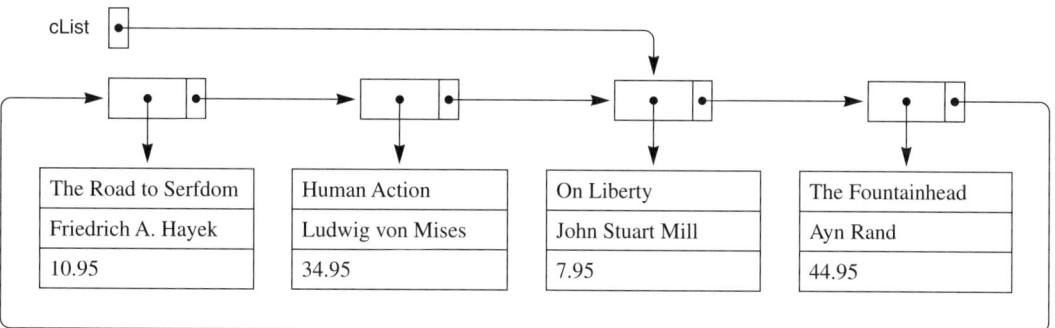

The dialog box has five buttons. The Clear button will obviously execute a procedure that calls PboxCListADT.Clear, the Next button will execute a procedure that calls PboxCListADT.GoNext, and the Insert button will execute a procedure that calls PboxCListADT.Insert. The Previous button allows the user to display the content of the previous node in the list and the Delete button allows the user to delete the current node from the list. These features cannot be implemented directly with the procedures of Figure 21.10. Implementation of additional procedures to provide these capabilities is left as a problem for the student at the end of this chapter. Also left as a problem for the student is computation of the total price of all the books in the linked list, which has a stub value of 999.99 in Figure 21.15.

Figure 21.17 is the program that implements the dialog box of Figure 21.15. The module contains a global variable cList, which is the circular list of books, along with the usual d interactor for the dialog box.

```
MODULE Pbox21D;
   IMPORT Dialog, PboxCListADT;

   TYPE
      String64 = ARRAY 64 OF CHAR;
      Book = POINTER TO RECORD
         title: String64;
         author: String64;
         price: REAL
      END;

   VAR
      d*: RECORD
         titleOut-, authorOut- : String64;
         priceOut-: REAL;
         titleIn*, authorIn* : String64;
         priceIn*: REAL;
         total-: REAL
      END;
      cList: PboxCListADT.CList;

   PROCEDURE ClearDialog;
   BEGIN
      d.titleOut := ""; d.authorOut := ""; d.priceOut := 0.0;
      d.titleIn := ""; d.authorIn := ""; d.priceIn := 0.0;
      d.total := 0.0
   END ClearDialog;

   PROCEDURE SetBookOut (b: Book);
   BEGIN
      d.titleOut := b.title;
      d.authorOut := b.author;
      d.priceOut := b.price
   END SetBookOut;

   PROCEDURE SetTotal;
   BEGIN
      (* A problem for the student *)
      d.total := 999.99
   END SetTotal;
```

Figure 21.17
The program that implements the dialog box of Figure 21.15.

```
PROCEDURE Clear*;
BEGIN
   ClearDialog;
   PboxCListADT.Clear(cList);
   Dialog.Update(d)
END Clear;

PROCEDURE Next*;
   VAR
      book: Book;
BEGIN
   IF ~PboxCListADT.Empty(cList) THEN
      PboxCListADT.GoNext(cList);
      book := PboxCListADT.NodeContent(cList) (Book);
      SetBookOut(book);
      Dialog.Update(d)
   END
END Next;

PROCEDURE Previous*;
BEGIN
   (* A problem for the student *)
END Previous;

PROCEDURE Delete*;
BEGIN
   (* A problem for the student *)
END Delete;

PROCEDURE Insert*;
   VAR
      book: Book;
BEGIN
   NEW(book);
   book.title := d.titleIn;
   book.author := d.authorIn;
   book.price := d.priceIn;
   PboxCListADT.Insert(cList, book);
   SetBookOut(book);
   SetTotal;
   Dialog.Update(d)
END Insert;

BEGIN
   Clear
END Pbox21D.
```

Figure 21.17
Continued.

Execution of the Clear procedure is straightforward. It calls ClearDialog, which clears the fields in the dialog box, then calls the Clear procedure for the circular list to make cList empty. It then updates the dialog box to make the changes visible.

Procedure Clear

Note that procedure Clear is executed when the module is loaded.

*Procedure Next*Procedure Next first checks if cList is empty. If it is, nothing happens. Otherwise, the precondition for GoNext is satisfied, and it executes

PboxCListADT.GoNext(cList)

which makes cList point to the next node in the linked list. Now the procedure needs to access the fields of the book contained in the value part of the node so it can display them on the dialog box. It gets the information by executing

book := PboxCListADT.NodeContent(cList) (Book)

where book is a local variable of type Book. The type guard (Book) is necessary because NodeContent returns a pointer to ANYREC, which is more general than Book. Now that Book has a value the procedure call

SetBookOut(book)

puts its values in the d record, after which time the dialog is updated to make the changes visible.

*Procedure Insert*Procedure Insert also has a local variable book of type Book. First it executes

NEW(book)

which creates a new record with three fields—title, author, and price—and sets book to point to the newly allocated record. Then, the statements

```
book.title := d.titleIn;
book.author := d.authorIn;
book.price := d.priceIn
```

transfer the data from the input fields of the dialog box to the newly allocated record. The procedure call

PboxCListADT.Insert(cList, book)

inserts the new book into the list as shown in Figure 21.13, and

```
SetBookOut(book);
SetTotal
```

sets the output fields in the dialog box, after which they are updated to make the changes visible.

Figure 21.18 shows the implementation of the circular linked list. The exported type CList is a pointer to Node where Node has a value field and next field as does the node in Figure 21.5, page 469. The difference here is that the value part is a pointer to ANYREC.

```
MODULE  PboxCListADT;

    TYPE
        CList* = POINTER TO Node;
        Node = RECORD
            value: POINTER TO ANYREC;
            next: CList
        END;

    PROCEDURE Clear* (OUT lst: CList);
    BEGIN
        lst := NIL
    END Clear;

    PROCEDURE Empty* (lst: CList): BOOLEAN;
    BEGIN
        RETURN lst = NIL
    END Empty;

    PROCEDURE GoNext* (VAR lst: CList);
    BEGIN
        ASSERT (lst # NIL, 20);
        lst := lst.next
    END GoNext;

    PROCEDURE NodeContent* (lst: CList): POINTER TO ANYREC;
    BEGIN
        ASSERT (lst # NIL, 20);
        RETURN lst.value
    END NodeContent;

    PROCEDURE Insert* (VAR lst: CList; val: POINTER TO ANYREC);
        VAR
            temp: CList;
    BEGIN
        IF lst = NIL THEN
            NEW(lst);
            lst.value := val;
            lst.next := lst
        ELSE
            temp := lst.next;
            NEW(lst.next);
            lst := lst.next;
            lst.value := val;
            lst.next := temp
        END
    END Insert;

END PboxCListADT.
```

Figure 21.18
Implementation of the circular list PboxCListADT.CList.

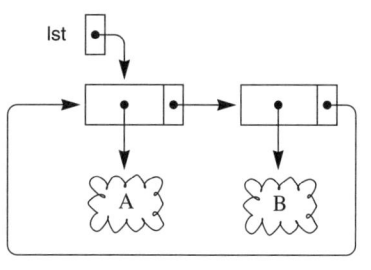
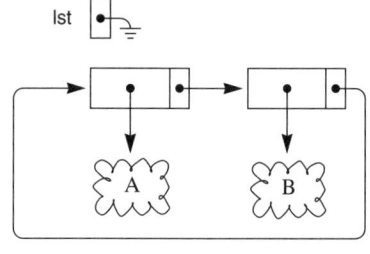
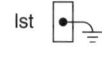

(a) Before lst := NIL

(b) Immediately after lst := NIL

(c) After automatic garbage collection.

Procedure Clear simply sets lst to NIL. Something important is going on behind the scenes here—the process known as automatic garbage collection. Figure 21.19 shows the effect of automatic garbage collection. Immediately after execution of lst := NIL, the nodes of the circular list are still allocated from the heap. However, there is no way they can be used, because there are no pointers from any program that link to them. Periodically the BlackBox framework detects every allocated piece of memory in the heap that cannot be reached from any active pointers, and automatically returns each one to the heap so the storage can be reused. If Component Pascal did not provide for automatic garbage collection, procedure Clear would be more complicated. It would require a loop to advance a pointer through the list, individually returning each unused node to the heap. Most modern programming languages have automatic garbage collection, but a few older programming languages still in widespread use do not.

Procedure Empty simply executes

RETURN lst = NIL

If list lst is empty, lst equals NIL and the boolean expression lst = NIL is true. Procedure GoNext implements its precondition with the ASSERT statement, and then executes

lst := lst.next

in the usual manner. Formal parameter lst is called by reference because the actual parameter must change. Procedure NodeContent is another one-liner. After its precondition test it simply returns lst.value. See Figure 21.14 for the effect.

Procedure Insert takes a pointer to an existing record, creates a new node in the circular list, and sets the value part of the new node to point to the same record. There are two cases depending on whether lst is empty. Figure 21.20 shows the non-empty case with the pointers labeled with their formal parameters. It corresponds to Figure 21.13 where the pointers are labeled with the corresponding actual parameters.

Here is how procedure Insert works. Figure 21.20(a) shows the initial configuration with lst pointing to one of the nodes in the circular list and val pointing to a record that needs to be inserted. The first statement

Figure 21.19
Implementation of procedure Clear with automatic garbage collection.

Procedure PboxCListADT.Empty

Procedure PboxCListADT.GoNext

Procedure PboxCListADT.NodeContent

Procedure PboxCListADT.Insert

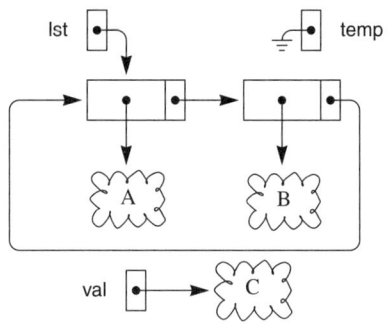

(a) Initial.

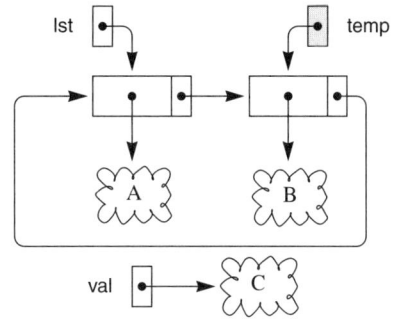

(b) temp := lst.next.

Figure 21.20
Execution of procedure
PboxCListADT.Insert with a
nonempty list.

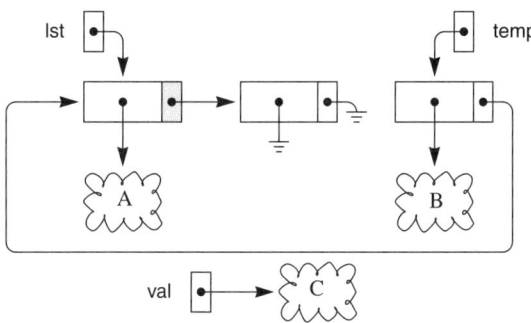

(c) NEW(lst.next).

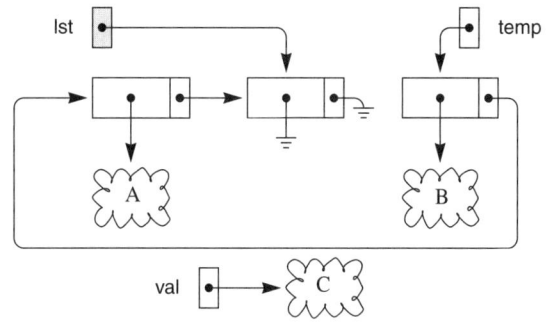

(d) lst := lst.next.

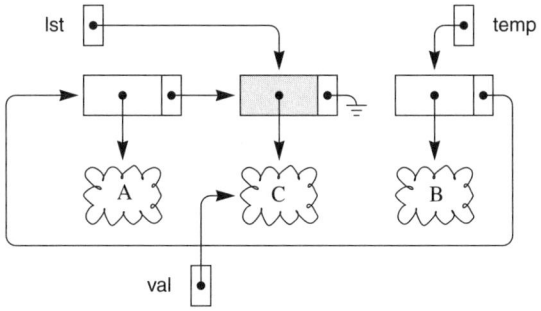

(e) lst.value := val.

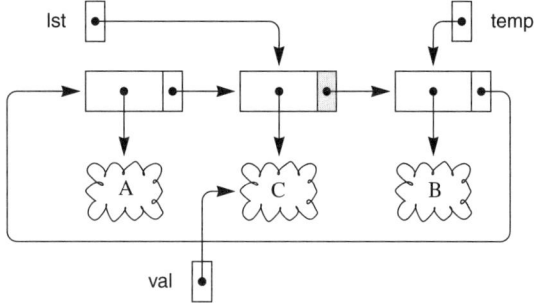

(f) lst.next := temp.

temp := lst.next

sets the temporary pointer to point to the node after the current one as in Figure 21.20(b). It is necessary to have a pointer to this node, because the link between it and the original one will be broken. Figure 21.20(c) shows the effect of

NEW(lst.next)

As always, NEW does two things—allocates storage from the heap and makes its parameter point to allocated storage. In this case, lst.next is the parameter. Its type is Node, so storage for a Node is allocated and lst.next points to it. The newly allocated node has two pointer fields that Component Pascal initializes to NIL. You can see from the figure that lst.next no longer points to the node to which temp points. The next statement

lst := lst.next

brings lst over to the new node as in Figure 21.20(d). Figure 21.20(e) shows the effect of

lst.value := val

which is yet another pointer assignment. It makes lst.value point to the same record to which val points. This is how the record is placed into the list. Figure 21.20(f) shows how

lst.next := temp

links the new current node to the next node. It now becomes clear why you need temp to be able to link up the new node to the next one.

A circular doubly-linked list

To implement the Previous and Delete buttons on the dialog box of Figure 21.15 you will need to modify module PboxCListADT. To change the current position to the previous node it is convenient for each node to have a link not only to the next node but to the previous one as well. The definition of a node is augmented to

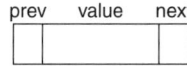

```
Node = RECORD
    prev: CList;
    value: POINTER TO ANYREC;
    next: CList
END;
```

Figure 21.21
The structure of a record of type Node for a doubly-linked list.

as in Figure 21.21. Figure 21.22 shows the doubly linked version of the circular list in Figure 21.11.

Because of the extra prev link in each node you will need to add some processing to procedure PboxCListADT.Insert. The prev link of the next node must be made to

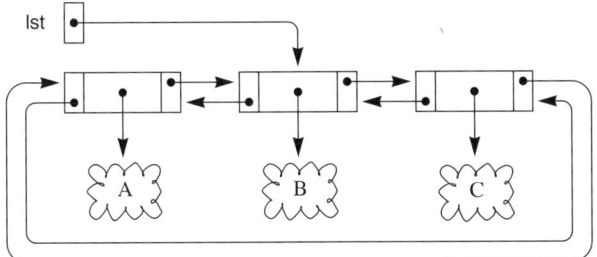

Figure 21.22
A circular doubly-linked list that corresponds to the singly-linked list of Figure 21.11

point to the newly inserted node, and the prev link of the newly inserted node must be made to point to the old current node.

With the prev link it is simple to implement a procedure that changes the current position to the previous node. Use the technique as in PboxCListADT.GoNext but with the prev link instead of the next link. It is more complicated but possible to implement the Previous button of the dialog box in Figure 21.15 without modifying PboxCListADT at all. You can find the previous node by looping all the way around the list until you get to the node just before the current one. Implementation of the Previous button with this approach is a problem for the student at the end of the chapter.

A procedure that deletes the current node should have as its precondition that the list is not empty, because it is impossible to delete a node from an empty list. There is a special case if the list contains a single node, because after the deletion the list is empty. Figure 21.23 shows what you must do to the nonempty list of Figure 21.22 to delete the current node. Make the links of the previous and the next node bypass the current node, and set lst to the previous node. After automatic garbage collection, the node will be reclaimed. It is not necessary to change the links of the deleted node. The fact that it is possible to get *from* the deleted node *to* the list is irrelevant. What matters is that it is impossible to get *to* the deleted node from any accessible pointer. The inaccessibility of the deleted node is a sufficient condition for automatic garbage collection. The garbage collector will not necessarily collect the nodes to which the deleted pointers point. In Figure 21.23, record B is also inaccessible and will be garbage collected along with its list node.

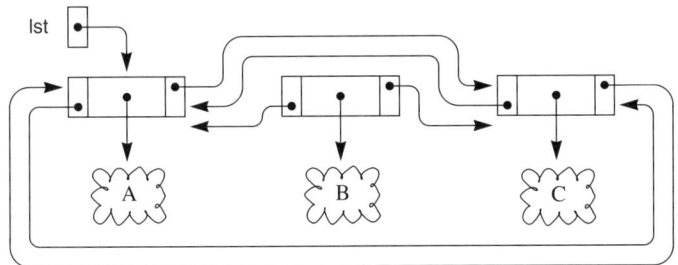

Figure 21.23
Deleting a node from a doubly linked circular list with the list initially as in Figure 21.22.

Record assignment

Both arrays and records are collections of values. With arrays, the values must all be of the same type but with records they need not be. If you have two array variables of the same type, say a and b, and you make an assignment between them, say a := b, then every element of b gets copied to the corresponding element of a. Figure 4.17(a), page 68, shows such a copy for arrays of characters.

It is possible to assign a whole record to another one, provided they have the same type. In the same way that assignment of one array to another causes every element of the array to be copied, assignment of one record to another causes every field to be copied.

All fields get copied in a record assignment

Example 21.14 Suppose type Composer is a record with two fields, and composerA and composerB are declared as follows.

```
TYPE
   Composer = RECORD
      name: ARRAY 32 OF CHAR;
      birthYear: INTEGER
   END;
VAR
   composerA, composerB: Composer;
```

If composerA and composerB have the values in Figure 21.24(a), and you make the assignment

```
composerA := composerB
```

then both fields of composerB get copied to composerA as in Figure 21.24(b). That is, the assignment is equivalent to

```
composerA.name := composerB.name;
composerA.birthYear := composerB.birthYear▮
```

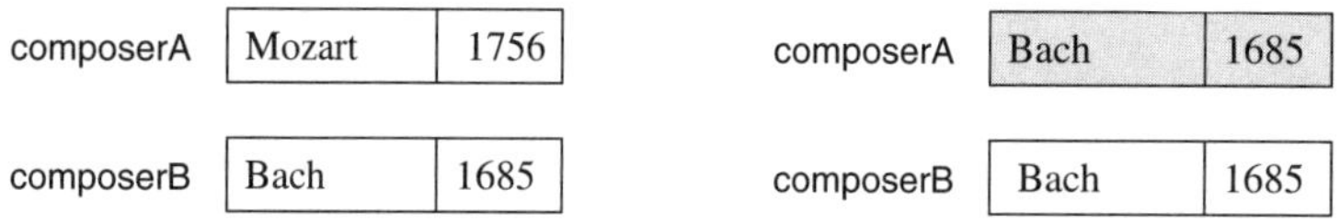

composerA	Mozart	1756		composerA	Bach	1685
composerB	Bach	1685		composerB	Bach	1685

(a) Before composerA := composerB. (b) After composerA := composerB.

Figure 21.24
Record assignment.

The declaration of CList in PboxCListADT defines CList to be a pointer to a node. The following section declares List from module PboxLListObj to be a linked list that has the same interface as the list presented in Chapter 7 (whose implementation is shown in Chapter 17). Rather than implement List as an ADT like CList, the following section implements List as a class. Because it is implemented as a class, List is not defined to be a pointer, but a record. Here is the declaration.

List* = RECORD
   head: POINTER TO Node
END;
Node = RECORD
   value: T;
   next: List
END;

Type List is a record containing only one field named head, which is a pointer to a Node. As usual, a Node is a record with two fields—value and next—and next has type List. With this setup, List is not a pointer. It is a record that contains a pointer. Furthermore, the next field is not a pointer. It is also a record that contains a pointer. That makes next a record inside of a record. Figure 21.25(a) shows the structure of a node for List assuming that myList is a variable of type List. To keep the diagrams simple, the abbreviation in part (b) will be used to represent the structure in part (a) throughout the remainder of this book.

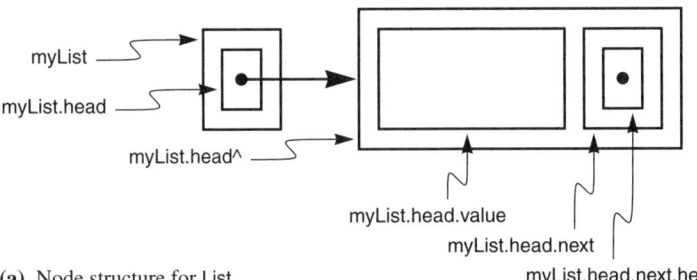

(a) Node structure for List.

Figure 21.25
Diagrams for the node structure of List.

(b) Abbreviated diagram of the same structure as in (a).

Suppose myList and yourList are both variables of type List. The assignment statement

myList := yourList

is a record assignment. Therefore, every field of record yourList gets copied to the corresponding field of myList. But there is only one field in the record, namely head, which is a pointer. Therefore, the above record assignment is equivalent to the pointer assignment

myList.head := yourList.head.

A linked list class

The remainder of this chapter describes how a linked list can be implemented as a class. Recall from Chapter 9 that the two primary advantages of using a class instead of an ADT are the object-oriented features of *inheritance* and *class composition*. Chapters 23 and 24 describe these object-oriented features. In this chapter, there is no direct advantage to implementing the linked list as a class because those features of the class are not used.

Inheritance and class composition

The purpose for introducing the linked list as a class is to learn some of the details of how to program with objects. The culmination of our study of object-oriented programming is a design pattern known as the state pattern presented in Chapter 24. That chapter presents yet another implementation of the linked list based on an object-oriented property of inheritance known as polymorphism. The state pattern design technique is a modification of the class implementation of this chapter. So, you may view this class implementation as an opportunity to learn some more details of how to program with objects. It is a preliminary step in the direction of more advanced object-oriented programming. Figure 21.26 shows the interface of PboxLLListObj, a linked list packaged as a class.

```
DEFINITION PboxLLListObj;

   TYPE
      T = ARRAY 16 OF CHAR;
      List = RECORD
         (VAR lst: List) Clear, NEW;
         (IN lst: List) Display, NEW;
         (IN lst: List) GetElementN (n: INTEGER; OUT val: T), NEW;
         (VAR lst: List) InsertAtN (n: INTEGER; IN val: T), NEW;
         (IN lst: List) Length (): INTEGER, NEW;
         (VAR lst: List) RemoveN (n: INTEGER), NEW;
         (IN lst: List) Search (IN srchVal: T; OUT n: INTEGER; OUT fnd: BOOLEAN), NEW
      END;

END PboxLLListObj.
```

Figure 21.26
The interface of the linked list class PboxLLListObj.

Compare Figure 21.26 with Figure 7.18, page 139, which is the interface of PboxListADT, a list abstract data type. Because PboxListADT implements its list with an array it has a capacity, which the linked implementation does not have. This is a major advantage of a linked data structure compared to an array-based data structure. With an array, you must declare the maximum amount of storage you will need even if you do not use all the storage. With a linked structure, you need not commit to a maximum size. The data structure can grow to fit the data as long as storage is available in the heap. Heap storage is, in turn, limited only by the amount of physical storage available on your computer.

A major advantage of a linked implementation over an array implementation

The procedures for PboxLLListObj in Figure 21.26 perform the same operations as the procedures for PboxListADT in Figure 7.18. Procedure Clear initializes a list to the empty list. Display displays the content of the list on the Log. GetElementN returns the element at position *n* in a list assuming that the first element is at position

0. InsertAtN provides a value and a location of where to insert the value into a list. Length returns the number of elements in a list. RemoveN supplies a position in a list and removes the element at that position from the list. Search supplies a search value and sets fnd to false if the value is not in the list. Otherwise it sets fnd to true and n to the position of the first occurrence of that value in the list. Figure 21.27 is the documentation for PboxLListObj.

TYPE **List**
The linked list class supplied by PboxLListObj.

TYPE **T**
The type of each element in the list, a string of at most 15 characters.

PROCEDURE (VAR lst: List) **Clear**
Post
List lst is initialized to the empty list.

PROCEDURE (IN lst: List) **Display**
Post
List lst is output to the Log, one element per line with each element preceded by its position.

PROCEDURE (IN lst: List) **GetElementN** (n: INTEGER; OUT val: T)
Pre
0 <= n   20
n < lst.Length()   21
Post
val gets the data value of the element at position n of list lst.
Note: 0 is the position of the first element in the list.

PROCEDURE (VAR lst: List) **InsertAtN** (n: INTEGER; IN val: T)
Pre
0 <= n   20
Post
val is inserted at position n in list lst, increasing lst.Length() by 1.
If n > lst.Length(), val is appended to the list.

PROCEDURE (IN lst: List) **Length** (): INTEGER
Post
Returns the number of elements in list lst.

PROCEDURE (VAR lst: List) **RemoveN** (n: INTEGER)
Pre
0 <= n   20
Post
If n < lst.Length(), the element at position n in list lst is removed.
Otherwise, the list is unchanged.

Figure 21.27
The documentation of the linked list class PboxLListObj.

PROCEDURE (IN lst: List) **Search** (IN srchVal: T; OUT n: INTEGER; OUT fnd: BOOLEAN)
Post
If srchVal is in list lst, fnd is set to TRUE and n is set to the first position where srchVal is found.
Otherwise, fnd is set to FALSE and n is undefined.

Figure 21.28 shows the dialog box of a program that uses the linked list class of
Figure 21.26. It is identical to the dialog box of Figure 7.19 except that the number
of items in each list (999) is not correct. It is your job to complete the implementation of the linked list class to display the correct number of items in the list.

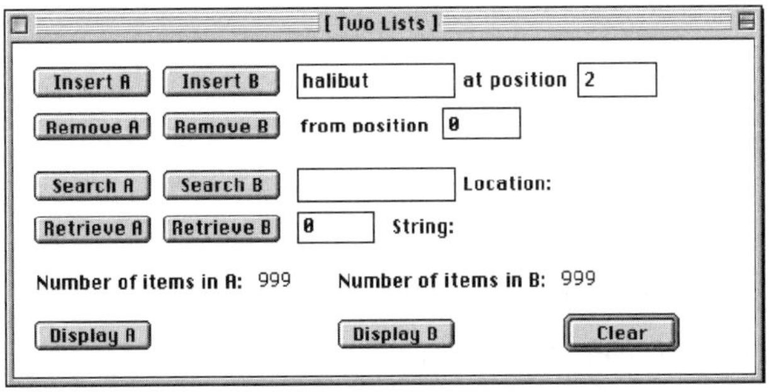

Figure 21.28
The dialog box for
manipulating two lists.

Figure 21.29 shows the module that produces the dialog box of Figure 21.28. The
interface in Figure 21.26 shows that two types are exported by the linked list class—
List, which corresponds to the linked list, and T, which corresponds to the type of the
value that is stored in each cell of the list. In this linked list, the type stored in each
cell is a string of up to 15 characters. You can see this type PboxLListObj.T for the
fields in the d record that correspond to the controls of the dialog box used for input
and output of values with this type.

Figure 21.29
The program for the dialog
box of Figure 21.28.

```
MODULE Pbox21E;
    IMPORT Dialog, PboxLListObj, PboxStrings;

    TYPE
        String32 = ARRAY 32 OF CHAR;

    VAR
        d*: RECORD
            insertT*: PboxLListObj.T; insertPosition*: INTEGER;
            removePosition*: INTEGER;
            searchT*: PboxLListObj.T; searchPosition-: String32;
            retrievePosition*: INTEGER; retrieveT-: PboxLListObj.T;
            numItemsA-, numItemsB-: INTEGER;
        END;
        listA, listB: PboxLListObj.List;
```

Figure 21.29
Continued.

```
PROCEDURE InsertAtA*;
BEGIN
   listA.InsertAtN(d.insertPosition, d.insertT);
   d.numItemsA := listA.Length();
   Dialog.Update(d)
END InsertAtA;

PROCEDURE InsertAtB*;
BEGIN
   listB.InsertAtN(d.insertPosition, d.insertT);
   d.numItemsB := listB.Length();
   Dialog.Update(d)
END InsertAtB;

PROCEDURE RemoveFromA*;
BEGIN
   listA.RemoveN(d.removePosition);
   d.numItemsA := listA.Length();
   Dialog.Update(d)
END RemoveFromA;

PROCEDURE RemoveFromB*;
BEGIN
   listB.RemoveN(d.removePosition);
   d.numItemsB := listB.Length();
   Dialog.Update(d)
END RemoveFromB;

PROCEDURE SearchForA*;
VAR
   found: BOOLEAN;
   position: INTEGER;
BEGIN
   listA.Search(d.searchT, position, found);
   IF found THEN
      PboxStrings.IntToString(position, 1, d.searchPosition);
      d.searchPosition := "At position " + d.searchPosition + "."
   ELSE
      d.searchPosition := "Not in list."
   END;
   Dialog.Update(d)
END SearchForA;
```

```
PROCEDURE SearchForB*;
VAR
   found: BOOLEAN;
   position: INTEGER;
BEGIN
   listB.Search(d.searchT, position, found);
   IF found THEN
      PboxStrings.IntToString(position, 1, d.searchPosition);
      d.searchPosition := "At position " + d.searchPosition + ".";
   ELSE
      d.searchPosition := "Not in list."
   END;
   Dialog.Update(d)
END SearchForB;

PROCEDURE RetrieveFromA*;
BEGIN
   listA.GetElementN(d.retrievePosition, d.retrieveT);
   Dialog.Update(d)
END RetrieveFromA;

PROCEDURE RetrieveFromB*;
BEGIN
   listB.GetElementN(d.retrievePosition, d.retrieveT);
   Dialog.Update(d)
END RetrieveFromB;

PROCEDURE DisplayListA*;
BEGIN
   listA.Display()
END DisplayListA;

PROCEDURE DisplayListB*;
BEGIN
   listB.Display()
END DisplayListB;

PROCEDURE ClearLists*;
BEGIN
   listA.Clear; listB.Clear;
   d.insertT := ""; d.insertPosition := 0;
   d.removePosition := 0;
   d.searchT := ""; d.searchPosition := "";
   d.retrievePosition := 0; d.retrieveT := "";
   d.numItemsA := 0; d.numItemsB := 0;
   Dialog.Update(d)
END ClearLists;

BEGIN
   ClearLists
END Pbox21E.
```

Figure 21.29

Continued.

The two lists processed by the module are the global lists declared as

listA, listB: PboxLLListObj.List;

This client module can have more than one data structure because the type of the data structure PboxLLListObj.List is exported by the server module. The lists are global because they must persist between the clicks of the buttons in the dialog box.

To invoke a method for the linked list the client module uses the syntax appropriate for objects. For example, in procedure InsertAtA, listA is an object. The relevant method exported by the server module is InsertAtN, whose documentation specifies

PROCEDURE (VAR lst: List) **InsertAtN** (n: INTEGER; IN val: T)

The receiver is (VAR lst: List), which acts like one of the formal parameters, except that it is placed before the method name instead of after it along with the other formal parameters. The corresponding method call as shown in Figure 21.29 is

listA.InsertAtN(d.insertPosition, d.insertT)

In the same way that d.insertPosition is the actual parameter that corresponds to formal parameter n, and d.insertT is the actual parameter that corresponds to formal parameter val, listA is the actual parameter that corresponds to formal parameter lst. Unlike the other actual parameters, the object listA comes before the name of the method, it is not enclosed by parentheses, and it is separated from the method name by a period.

Figure 21.30 is a partial implementation of the linked list class. Most of the methods are left as problems for the student. The statements in the procedures that are not completed are known as *stubs*. Their purpose is to allow the module to be compiled *The purpose of a stub* before all the procedures are completed. For example, the statement

(* A problem for the student *)
RETURN 999

in method Length is a stub. The RETURN statement is necessary for the module PboxLLListObj to compile. Placing stubs in some of the procedures allows the other procedures in the module to be compiled and tested. When you complete procedure Length you should delete its stub.

```
MODULE  PboxLLListObj;
    IMPORT StdLog;

    TYPE
        T* = ARRAY 16 OF CHAR;
        List* = RECORD
            head: POINTER TO Node
        END;
        Node = RECORD
            value: T;
            next: List
        END;

    PROCEDURE (VAR lst: List) Clear*, NEW;
    BEGIN
        lst.head := NIL
    END Clear;

    PROCEDURE (IN lst: List) Display*, NEW;
        VAR
            p: List;
            i: INTEGER;
    BEGIN
        i := 0;
        p := lst;
        WHILE p.head # NIL DO
            StdLog.Int(i); StdLog.String(" "); StdLog.String(p.head.value); StdLog.Ln;
            INC(i);
            p := p.head.next
        END
    END Display;

    PROCEDURE (IN lst: List) GetElementN* (n: INTEGER; OUT val: T), NEW;
        VAR
            p: List;
            i: INTEGER;
    BEGIN
        ASSERT(0 <= n, 20);
        p := lst;
        FOR i := 1 TO n DO
            ASSERT(p.head # NIL, 21);
            p := p.head.next
        END;
        ASSERT(p.head # NIL, 21);
        val := p.head.value
    END GetElementN;
```

Figure 21.30
Implementation of the linked
list class that is used in Figure
21.29.

```
PROCEDURE (VAR lst: List) InsertAtN* (n: INTEGER; IN val: T), NEW;
  VAR
    prev, p: List;
    i: INTEGER;
BEGIN
  ASSERT(0 <= n, 20);
  IF (n = 0) OR (lst.head = NIL) THEN (* Insert at beginning *)
    p := lst;
    NEW(lst.head);
    lst.head.value := val;
    lst.head.next := p
  ELSE
    i := 1;
    prev := lst;
    p := lst.head.next;
    WHILE (i < n) & (p.head # NIL) DO
      INC(i);
      prev := p;
      p := p.head.next
    END;
    NEW(prev.head.next.head);
    prev.head.next.head.value := val;
    prev.head.next.head.next := p
  END
END InsertAtN;

PROCEDURE (IN lst: List) Length* (): INTEGER, NEW;
BEGIN
  (* A problem for the student *)
  RETURN 999
END Length;

PROCEDURE (VAR lst: List) RemoveN* (n: INTEGER), NEW;
BEGIN
  (* A problem for the student *)
END RemoveN;

PROCEDURE (IN lst: List) Search* (IN srchVal: T; OUT n: INTEGER; OUT fnd: BOOLEAN), NEW;
BEGIN
  (* A problem for the student *)
  fnd := FALSE
END Search;

END PboxLListObj.
```

Figure 21.30
Continued.

The declaration of the linked list from module PboxLListObj in Figure 21.30 is

```
List* = RECORD
   head: POINTER TO Node
END;
Node = RECORD
   value: T;
   next: List
END;
```

which is shown in Figure 21.25. Enclosing the head pointer within a record is necessary because the linked list is implemented as a class, and some of the methods for the class would be impossible to implement otherwise. Like the declaration for CList, however, the type of the next field of the Node is a List.

Why not structure the node for the class the same way as for CList? Because of restrictions that Component Pascal puts on the receiver of a method. The type of the receiver must be either

- a pointer to a record called by value (default),
- a record called by reference (VAR), or
- a record called by constant reference (IN).

Restrictions on the receiver of a method

It would be legal to declare the linked list class as follows

```
List* = POINTER TO Node;
Node = RECORD
   value: T;
   next: List
END;
```

which is similar to the way it is declared in Figure 21.18 for CList. The problem is with the implementation of some of the methods, such as procedure Clear. This procedure clears a list by setting the pointer to NIL. To change the value of the pointer requires the pointer be called by reference in procedure Clear, as Figure 21.30 shows. It would be impossible to call the pointer by reference in the receiver, because pointers are restricted to call by value in the receiver.

Method PboxLListObj.Clear works just like its counterpart PboxCListADT.Clear. The CList procedure sets

Method PboxLListObj.Clear

```
lst := NIL
```

while the corresponding List method sets

```
lst.head := NIL
```

In both cases, automatic garbage collection reclaims any inaccessible nodes resulting from the NULL assignment.

Method GetElementN takes as input an integer n and list lst, and retrieves the element val from the node at position n in lst. Figure 21.31(a) shows listA before execution of procedure GetElementN. Figure 21.31(b) shows the usual memory allocation

Method PboxLListObj.GetElementN

on the run-time stack when a call to listA.GetElementN(d.retrievePosition, d.retrie-veT) executes assuming that the user has entered 1 for d.retrievePosition. Formal parameter lst is called by constant reference, and so gets a reference to listA. val is called by result, so it gets a reference to its actual parameter d.retrieveT, which is not shown in the figure.

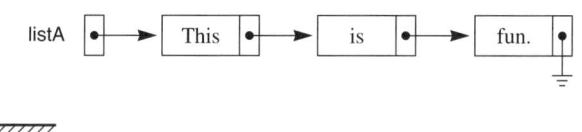

Figure 21.31
Memory allocation when method GetElementN is called.

(a) Before call to GetElementN

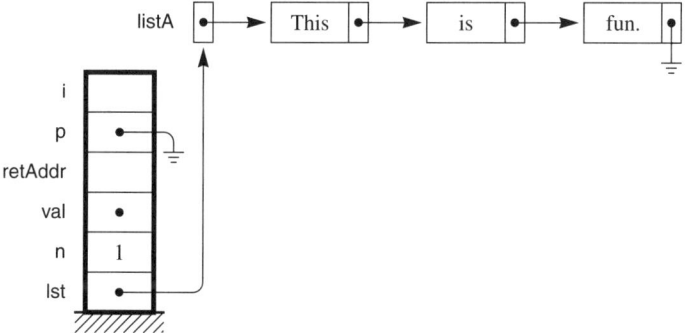

(b) Call listA.GetElementN(d.retrievePosition, d.retrieveT)

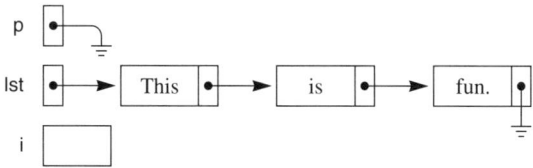

(c) Abbreviated version of (b)

To keep things simple, the following diagrams will frequently show only the relevant formal parameters and local variables as in Figure 21.31(c). Even though formal parameters and local variables are allocated on the run-time stack, the structure of the stack itself is not shown. The receiver lst is a record that contains the single link head. Rather than show the actual parameter, the figures will show the formal parameter lst, and label the pointer to the first node as lst.head as in Figure 21.31(c). Likewise, the label for the formal parameter p will be the pointer that is in the one field of the record, p.head.

The preconditions of procedure GetElementN as specified in the documentation are

```
0 <= n   20
n < lst.Length()   21
```

The first statement in the implementation of the procedure

```
ASSERT(0 <= n, 20)
```

insures that n is greater than zero. If it is not, a trap will execute with the appropriate message that a precondition was violated and will display the identifying number 20.

The technique for retrieving the element at position n is to initialize List variable p to list lst, and then advance it through the list n times. Figure 21.32 shows the sequence of steps to retrieve the element at position 1. The record assignment

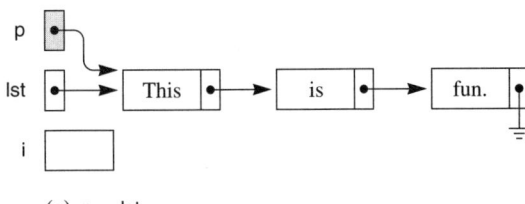

(a) p := lst

Figure 21.32
A trace of procedure GetElementN.

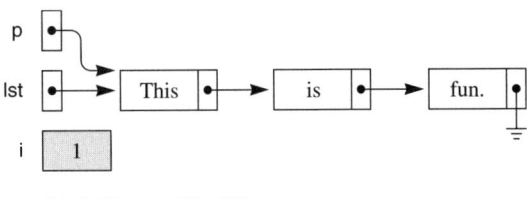

(b) FOR i := 1 TO n DO

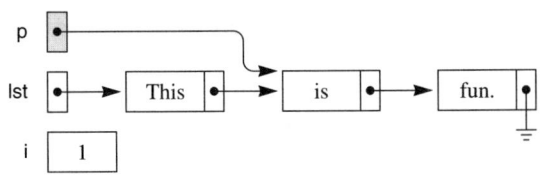

(c) p := p.head.next

```
p := lst
```

in Figure 21.32(a) is equivalent to

```
p.head := lst.head
```

and initializes p.head to point to the first element of the list. The first execution of

```
FOR i := 1 TO n DO
```

in Figure 21.32(b) initializes i to 1 and causes the body of the loop to execute. The first statement in the body of the loop is the assertion

ASSERT(p.head # NIL, 21)

which will trigger a trap if p.head equals NIL. If n is less than the length of the list, then p will eventually get the NIL value from the last node in the list, producing the trap. The ASSERT statement implements the precondition n < lst.Length(). The second statement in the body of the loop

p := p.head.next

in Figure 21.32(c) advances p.head through the linked list. In this example, p.head only advances once to get to the node at position 1, but in general it will advance n times to get to position n. The assertion preceding this statement guarantees that p.head is not NIL and, therefore, that p.head.value exists. The last statement in the procedure

val := p.head.value

gives the value part of the node pointed to by p.head to formal parameter val.

It is important to be aware of the types involved when dealing with linked structures. In the assignment statement

p := p.head.next

the relevant types are

- p   is a record (which is also a List)
- p.head   is a pointer to a Node
- p.head.next   is a record (which is also a List)

So, the assignment is a record assignment, or, equivalently, a List assignment. Because the record contains a single field named head, which is a pointer, you could write the same assignment as

p.head := p.head.next.head

However, an assignment statement such as

p := p.head

would be illegal due to type conflict, because you would be trying to assign a pointer to a record.

Method InsertAtN takes as input an integer n and a string value val, and inserts a new node with val into list lst at position n. Figure 21.33 is a trace of the procedure call to insert the word "such" at position 2. The figure uses the abbreviated style without showing the run-time stack for simplicity.

The first statement

Method PboxLListObj.InsertAtN

ASSERT(0 <= n, 20)

corresponds directly to the precondition 0 <= n of the procedure. Unlike procedure GetElementN, which requires n to be less than the length of the list, InsertAtN permits n to be greater than or equal to the length of the list. If it is, the new node is appended to the end of the list.

The processing for the case of the empty list or when n has the value of zero is different from the case when the list has at least one node and n is greater than zero. Figure 21.33 shows a list with three elements and an insertion at position 2. A trace of the procedure for the other case is left as an exercise for the student.

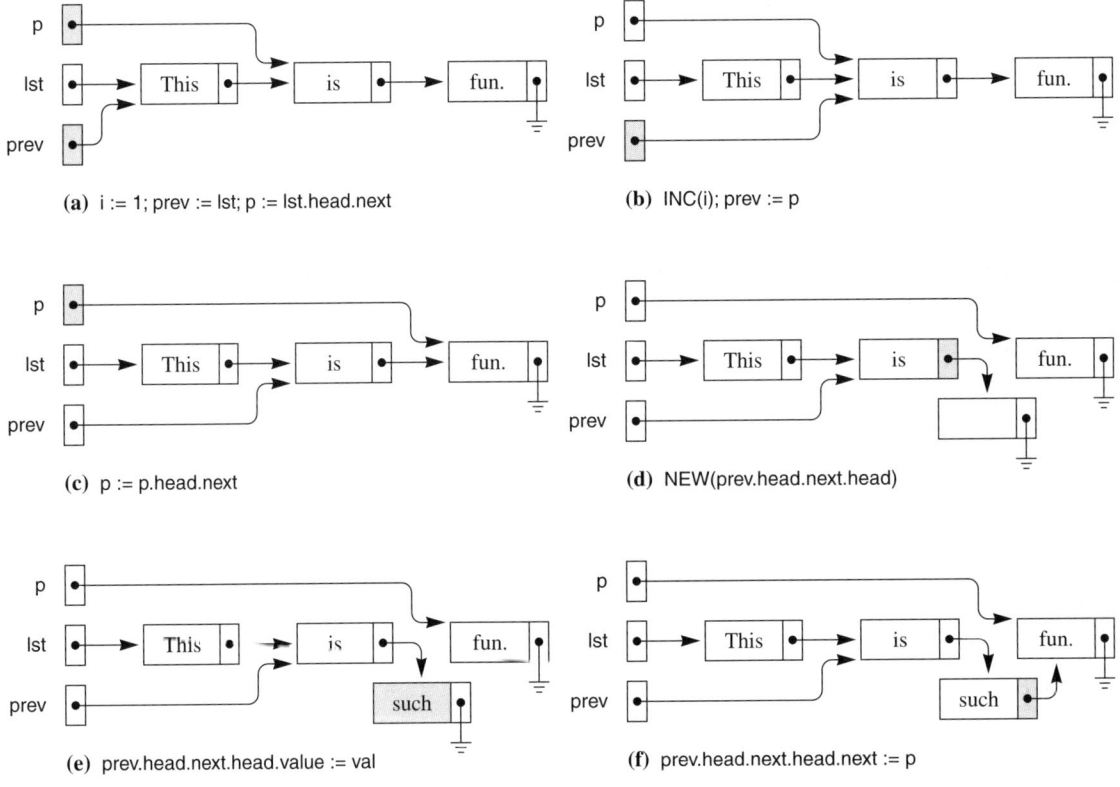

(a) i := 1; prev := lst; p := lst.head.next

(b) INC(i); prev := p

(c) p := p.head.next

(d) NEW(prev.head.next.head)

(e) prev.head.next.head.value := val

(f) prev.head.next.head.next := p

Figure 21.33(a) shows the list after the first three statements in the ELSE part of the procedure execute. To keep the figure simple, storage for local variable i is not shown. The statement

prev := lst

makes pointer prev.head point to the same node to which lst.head points, namely the

Figure 21.33
Execution of procedure InsertAtN to insert the word "such" at position 2.

node that contains "This". The statement

p := lst.head.next

makes pointer p.head point to the same node to which lst.head.next.head points, namely the node that contains "is". The program is guaranteed to not produce a trap from a NIL pointer reference with this assignment, because the IF part of the test must be false, which implies that lst.head is not NIL. Therefore, lst.head points to a node and the next part of that node exists. It is true that if the list consists of a single node that p.head would get NIL from this assignment, but such an assignment would not produce a trap.

These statements set up the loop invariant, which is that p.head points to the node at position i, and prev.head points to the previous node. Specifically, the value of i is 1, p.head points to the node at position 1, and prev.head points to the previous node at position 0. The body of the loop processes the variables by increasing i while maintaining the loop invariant.

Establish the loop invariant

The test at the beginning of the loop is

WHILE (i < n) & (p.head # NIL) DO

By De Morgan's law the loop will terminate when (i >= n) OR (p.head = NIL). In fact, because the loop increments i only by one each time through the loop, the loop will terminate when (i = n) OR (p.head = NIL).

Figure 21.33(b) and (c) show the effect of one execution of the loop body. The statements

INC(i);
prev := p

increment i by one and advance prev.head to point to the next node. Then, the assignment statement

p := p.head.next

makes p.head point to the next node in the list. As with the initialization statements before the loop, you are guaranteed that this assignment will not produce a NIL reference trap. This time it is the WHILE test that guarantees no trap because you can execute the body only if (p.head # NIL). So, you know that p.head points to a node and that p.head.next exists.

Figure 21.33(c) shows that the loop invariant is maintained. Specifically, the value of i is 2, p.head points to the node at position 2, and prev.head points to the previous node at position 1. At this time the loop terminates because i equals n. Because the loop body maintains the invariant, you know that when the loop terminates that (i = n) OR (p.head = NIL) and that p.head points to the node at position i, and prev.head points to the previous node. The remaining task is to allocate a new node and splice it into the linked list between the nodes pointed to by prev.head and p.head.

Reestablish the loop invariant

Figure 21.33(d) shows the effect of the statement

NEW(prev.head.next.head);

to allocate a new node from the heap. Figure 21.33(e) shows how

prev.head.next.head.value := val;

sets the value part of the node to the string entered by the user. The next statement illustrated in Figure 21.33(f)

prev.head.next.head.next := p

links the new node to the remainder of the list.

With these pointer manipulations you can see why the algorithm needs to keep track of the previous node prev and the next node p. The link of prev must be changed to point to the newly allocated node. And the link of the newly allocated node must be set to point to the node to which p.head points.

Figure 21.34 shows the sequence of events that must transpire to implement RemoveN. In Figure 21.34(a) the algorithm initializes prev.head to point to the node at position 0 in the list and p.head to point to the node at position 1. A loop is required to search for the node that contains the search word. The body of the loop contains statements to advance p and prev.

Method
PboxLLListObj.RemoveN

prev := p;
p := p.head.next

When p.head points to the node to be removed, prev.head points to the node before it, as shown in Figure 21.34(b). Figure 21.34(c) shows how to remove the node from the list. The algorithm merely changes the link part of the preceding node to point to the node after the one to be deleted. Implementation of the procedure to delete a node is a problem for the student at the end of this chapter.

Design trade-offs with linked lists

What are the advantages of using linked lists with pointers? After all, Figure 17.8 shows all the operations on the list data structure implemented with arrays. The linked implementation of lists has two advantages over the array implementation. The first advantage is the flexibility of dynamic storage allocation. With arrays you must allocate enough memory for the maximum problem size you expect to encounter. With dynamic storage allocation you always have the entire heap from which to allocate another element.

Flexibility of storage
allocation

This advantage is particularly important in problems with many lists. Suppose you have three lists—a, b, and c. One time when you run the program, list a may have 10,000 elements, and lists b and c only a few. The next time, list b may have 10,000, and lists a and c only a few. If you implement the lists with arrays, you would need to allocate 10,000 elements for a, b, and c, for a total of 30,000 elements, to account for the possibility of any of the three lists having a maximum of 10,000 elements. Your computer would need storage for 30,000 elements to run the program.

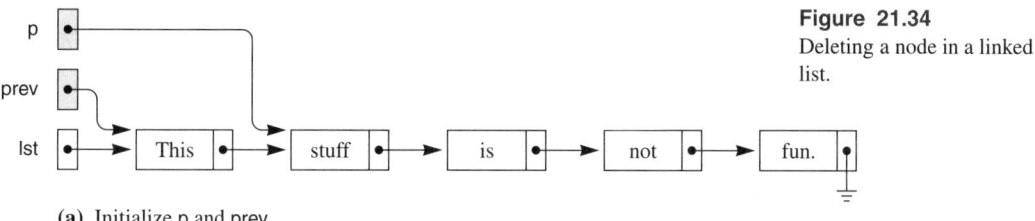

(a) Initialize p and prev.

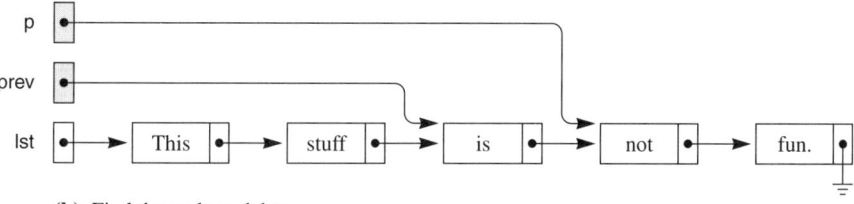

(b) Find the node to delete.

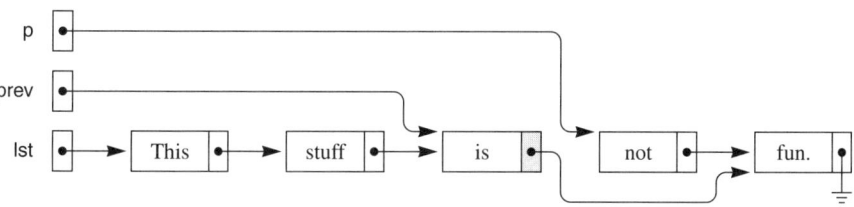

(c) Unlink the node from the list.

Figure 21.34
Deleting a node in a linked list.

But if you implement the lists with dynamic storage allocation, you do not need to declare the maximum size of each list. Your computer would need storage for only a few more than 10,000 elements regardless of which list used most of them. Using pointers, different lists use storage from the same heap. The net result is that the linked list implementation can require less storage because of the flexibility of dynamic storage allocation from the heap.

The second advantage of a linked implementation is the speed of insertions and deletions in long lists. To delete item 10 in a 100-item array, a, requires you to shift a[11] to a[10], a[12] to a[11], a[13] to a[12], and so on. But to delete item 10 in a 100-item linked list only requires you to change the link field of item 9 to point to item 11. You need not make any shifts.

Speed of insertions and deletions

The disadvantage of linked lists is their sequential nature. The only way to access an element in the middle of a list is to start at the beginning and sequentially advance a pointer through all the intermediate nodes. Arrays, however, are random access data structures. That is, you can access the element at position i of array a directly by subscripting a[i]. Direct access with subscripting is what allows for efficient searching and sorting. For example, you cannot do a binary search of a linked list because you cannot access the middle of the list in one step the way you can with

Sequential access

an array.

So, whether to use an array implementation or a linked implementation of a list depends on the use to which it will be put. If speed of insertions and deletions is important and if flexibility of memory allocation is important use a linked implementation. If speed of searching and sorting is important use an array implementation. Such considerations arise frequently in the study of data structures. You typically have more than one implementation at your disposal and the implementation you choose will involve trade-offs that require you to take into account the use to which the data structure will be put.

Trade-offs with data structures

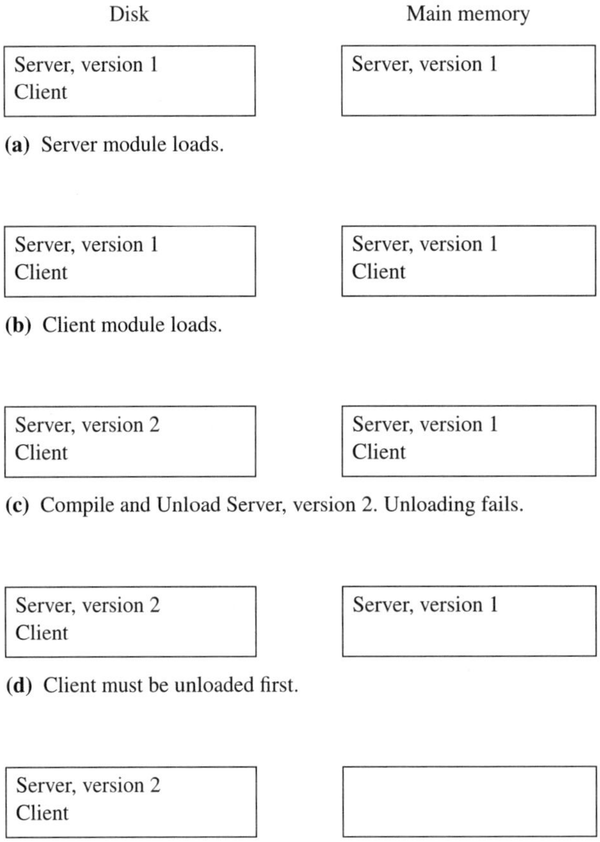

Disk   Main memory

| Server, version 1 | | Server, version 1 |
| Client | | |

(a) Server module loads.

| Server, version 1 | | Server, version 1 |
| Client | | Client |

(b) Client module loads.

| Server, version 2 | | Server, version 1 |
| Client | | Client |

(c) Compile and Unload Server, version 2. Unloading fails.

| Server, version 2 | | Server, version 1 |
| Client | | |

(d) Client must be unloaded first.

| Server, version 2 | | |
| Client | | |

(e) Then Server, version 1 can be unloaded.

Figure 21.35
Developing a server module.

Unloading

The problems at the end of this chapter require you to program a server module that is imported by a client module. Usually, the client module will be written or modified only once, and you will spend most of your program development effort on the server module. Because the BlackBox framework is based on dynamic linking and loading, you must take care with the unloading process. Suppose you write some code in a server module, call it version 1, and test it with the client module. Figure 21.35 shows a likely scenario.

Figure 21.35(a) and (b) show that before a client module can be loaded from disk to main memory, all modules that it imports, that is, the server modules, must be loaded first. The framework cannot allow a module to be loaded without the modules that it uses (that is, imports) to also be loaded. Therefore, when you test a server module, the server loads first followed by the client that uses it.

Figure 21.35(c) shows what happens if you make a change to your server module, call it version 2, and select Dev→Compile And Unload. The compile may be successful, but the unload will fail because the system cannot unload the server module while the client is still in main memory. To unload a server you must first unload all the clients that import it.

There are several ways to unload a module. If the focus window contains the source code for the module you want to unload, you can simply select Dev→Unload and that module will be unloaded. Alternatively, you can type the name of the module in the Log or in some other text window and highlight it with your mouse. Then select Dev→Unload Module List.

How to unload a module

If you ever want to see which modules are currently loaded you can select Info→Loaded Modules. A window will appear that contains a list of all the currently loaded modules, the number of bytes each one occupies in main memory, the number of clients for each server module, and the date and time of the compile and of the load. Because the list of modules in the window has every client listed before its servers, you can even highlight the list in the window in order to execute Dev→Unload Module List.

Exercises

1. Suppose the variable declaration part of a Component Pascal program declares a, b, c, and d to each be a pointer to a record as in Figure 21.3. What does each of the following code fragments output to the Log?

(a)	**(b)**	**(c)**	**(d)**
NEW(a);	NEW(a);	NEW(a);	NEW(a);
NEW(b);	a.i := 7;	a.i := 9;	a.i := 2;
a.i := 5;	NEW(b);	b := a;	NEW(b);
b.i := 6;	b.i := 2;	a.i := b.i + a.i;	b.i := 3;
a := b;	c := a;	StdLog.Int(a.i);StdLog.Ln;	c := a;
StdLog.Int(a.i);StdLog.Ln;	d := b;	StdLog.Int(b.i);StdLog.Ln;	a := b;
StdLog.Int(b.i);StdLog.Ln;	a := b;		b := c;
	StdLog.Int(a.i);StdLog.Ln;		StdLog.Int(a.i);StdLog.Ln;
	StdLog.Int(b.i);StdLog.Ln;		StdLog.Int(b.i);StdLog.Ln;
	StdLog.Int(c.i);StdLog.Ln;		StdLog.Int(c.i);StdLog.Ln;
	StdLog.Int(d.i);StdLog.Ln;		

2. Suppose p, q, r, and last have type List as in Figure 21.6 and have the values in Figure 21.36. Draw the figure after execution of the following instructions.

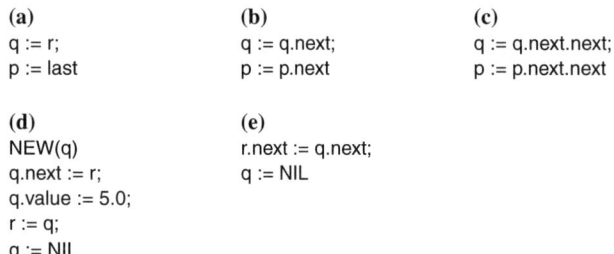

(a)
q := r;
p := last

(b)
q := q.next;
p := p.next

(c)
q := q.next.next;
p := p.next.next

(d)
NEW(q)
q.next := r;
q.value := 5.0;
r := q;
q := NIL

(e)
r.next := q.next;
q := NIL

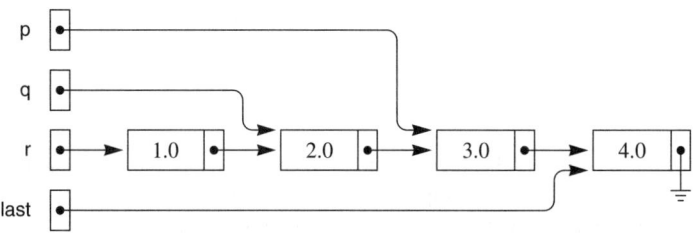

Figure 21.36
The linked list for Exercises 2, 3, and 6.

3. Suppose p, q, r, and last have type List as in Figure 21.6 and have the values in Figure 21.36. State whether each of the following instructions produces a NIL pointer reference error. For those that do, explain why.

(a)
p := NIL;
p := p.next

(b)
p := p.next;
p := p.next

(c)
last := last.next;
last := last.next

4. In computer science terminology, **(a)** what is the meaning of the word static? **(b)** What is the meaning of the word dynamic?

5. Assuming the declarations of the types and variables in the section Class assignments, page 474, state whether each of the following assignments will or will not compile correctly. For those that will not compile correctly, explain why not.

(a) alphaPtr := gammaPtr
(b) alphaPtr := gammaPtr (GammaPtr)
(c) alphaPtr := gammaPtr (AlphaPtr)
(d) gammaPtr := alphaPtr
(e) gammaPtr := alphaPtr (GammaPtr)
(f) gammaPtr := alphaPtr (AlphaPtr)
(g) betaPtr := gammaPtr
(h) betaPtr := gammaPtr (BetaPtr)
(i) deltaPtr := gammaPtr
(j) gammaPtr := deltaPtr (GammaPtr)

6. Suppose p, q, r, and last have type List as in Figure 21.30 and have the values in Figure 21.36 assuming the abbreviation of Figure 21.25(b). Draw the figure after execution of the following instructions.

(a)
q.head := r.head;
p := last

(b)
q := q.head.next;
p := p.head.next

(c)
q := q.head.next.head.next;
p := p.head.next.head.next

(d)
NEW(q.head)
q.head.next := r;
q.head.value := 5.0;
r := q;
q.head := NIL

(e)
r.head.next := q.head.next;
q.head := NIL

7. Suppose p and q have type List as in Figure 21.30. State whether each of the following statements will or will not compile correctly. For those that will not compile correctly, explain why not.

(a) p := q
(b) p.head := q.head
(c) p^.head := q^.head
(d) p := q.head
(e) p.next := q.next
(f) p.head.next := q
(g) p.head^.next := q
(h) NEW(p)
(i) NEW(p.head)

8. **(a)** What types are receivers restricted to in Component Pascal? **(b)** For each of the types in (a), which parameter calling mechanisms are allowed?

Problems

9. Modify the PboxStackADT to implement the stack with a linked list instead of an array. The interface for your modified stack should be similar to the interface in Figure 7.8 except that it should not export a capacity, because you will be able to allocate as many nodes as you wish from the heap. Define a stack to be a pointer to a node as follows.

```
Stack* = POINTER TO Node;
Node = RECORD
    value: REAL;
    next: Stack
END;
```

Your interface should have the following specifications.

```
PROCEDURE Clear (VAR s: Stack);
PROCEDURE NumItems (s: Stack): INTEGER;
PROCEDURE Pop (VAR s: Stack; OUT x: REAL);
PROCEDURE Push (VAR s: Stack; x: REAL);
```

In each of these procedures, s will point to the node at the top of the stack. The next field of the node will point to the node that is second from the top, and so on. Test your implementation with the program of Figure 7.10.

10. It is possible for the user to generate a trap when she executes module Pbox21E, Figure 21.29. Rewrite the module to make it bulletproof so that no trap will be generated regardless of the user input. If an input value would generate a trap, program the module to do nothing.

11. Implement procedure SetTotal in Figure 21.17 to compute the total price for all the books in the circular list. The empty list is a special case, for which the total is 0.00. If there is at least one book in the list you should initialize a local variable, say p, of type CList to cList. Leaving cList unchanged, progress around the circular list with p using GoNext(p) to advance through the circular list until p equals cList. At each position in the circular list accumulate the total from the price of the current book. You will need to use a local variable book of type Book as in PROCEDURE Next on page 483 to access the price field of the book record.

12. Implement the Previous button of the dialog box in Figure 21.15 by completing procedure Previous in Figure 21.17. Do not modify PboxCListADT.

13. Implement the Delete button of the dialog box in Figure 21.15 by completing procedure Delete in Figure 21.17. Add a procedure to PboxCListADT also named Delete, which is called by procedure Delete in Figure 21.17. The precondition for procedure Delete is that the list is not empty. The postcondition is for the new current position to be the old previous one. Do not change the declaration for Node in PboxCListADT.

14. Implement the Previous button of the dialog box in Figure 21.15 by completing procedure Previous in Figure 21.17. Add a prev link to the PboxCListADT node as described in the section, A circular doubly-linked list, page 488. Add a procedure to Pbox-CListADT named GoPrev, which is called by procedure Previous. The precondition for GoPrev is that the list is not empty.

15. Implement the Delete button of the dialog box in Figure 21.15 by completing procedure Delete in Figure 21.17. Do this problem only after you have completed Problem 14 for the doubly-linked list. Add a procedure to PboxCListADT also named Delete, which is called by procedure Delete in Figure 21.17. The precondition for procedure Delete is that the list is not empty. The postcondition is for the new current position to be the old previous one as shown in Figure 21.23.

16. This problem is for you to complete the following methods for the linked list class in module PboxLListObj. Test your procedures with the program in Figure 21.29 using the dialog box of Figure 21.28. For each of the following procedures, implement any preconditions with the appropriate ASSERT or HALT procedure. Do not use recursion in any of your implementations.

    (a) (VAR lst: List) RemoveN (n: INTEGER), NEW
    (b) (IN lst: List) Search (IN srchVal: T; OUT n: INTEGER; OUT fnd: BOOLEAN), NEW
    (c) (IN lst: List) Length (): INTEGER, NEW

17. Change the implementation of procedure Display in PboxLListObj as follows.

```
PROCEDURE (IN lst: List) Display*, NEW;
BEGIN
    lst.DisplayRecursive(0)
END Display;
```

    Then, define DisplayRecursive as

PROCEDURE (IN lst: List) DisplayRecursive (n: INTEGER), NEW

which recursively outputs a list starting with its first element numbered n. Do not use a loop.

18. Work Problem 17, but output the list in reverse order.

19. Work Problem 16(b) to write the method Search for the linked list class, but do it recursively without a loop. Define SearchN as

PROCEDURE (IN lst: List) SearchN (IN srchVal: T; VAR n: INTEGER; OUT fnd: BOOLEAN), NEW;

whose signature differs from that of Search only by n being called by reference (VAR) instead of called by result (OUT). The programmer of the client in Figure 21.29 must see the same interface for your recursive version of PboxLLListObj and must not need to initialize the value of n before it calls the server method. In the implementation of Search, initialize n to 0 then call SearchN, which assumes that the initial value of n is defined. If lst is not empty and the value field of its first node does not equal srchVal, then SearchN must call itself recursively. If srchVal is at position n in the next list of the first node of lst, then it is at position n + 1 in lst. In that case, SearchN must increment n.

20. Work Problem 16(c) to write the method Length for the linked list class, but do it recursively without a loop. The base case is for the empty list.

21. This problem requires you to add the following methods to module PboxLLListObj in Figure 21.30. Test your procedures by importing them into the module of Figure 21.29. Augment the dialog box of Figure 21.28 to test the procedures.

(a) PROCEDURE (VAR lst: List) **Copy*** (listB: List), NEW
Create a new list, lst, which is a copy of listB. You must allocate new copies of all the nodes of listB. You are not allowed to simply set lst.head to point to the same head node that listB.head points to.

(b) PROCEDURE (VAR lst: List) **Append*** (listB: List), NEW
Append a copy of ListB to the end of ListA. You must allocate new copies of all the nodes of listB. You are not allowed to simply set the head field of the last node of lst to point to the same head node that listB.head points to.

(c) PROCEDURE (VAR lst: List) **Merge*** (listB: List), NEW
Merge a copy of listB with lst starting with the first word in lst. For example, if lst is the list

Now the for

and listB is the list

is time action

then after the procedure is called, lst should be the list

Now is the time for action

Be sure your procedure works correctly if lst has more words than listB or if listB has more words than lst. You must allocate new copies of all the nodes of listB. You are not allowed to alter the original nodes of listB.

Chapter *22*

Binary Trees

Like stacks and lists, binary trees are structures that store values. Stacks and lists are linear. That is, you can visualize them as consisting of a sequential row of values, one after the other. Each data structure has operations for storing and retrieving values. With a stack, to store an item you push it onto the top of the stack, while a list allows you to insert a value at an arbitrary location.

Binary trees have more of a two-dimensional structure compared to stacks and lists. Like all data structures, however they have operations for storing and retrieving values. This chapter begins by defining the characteristics of an abstract binary tree. It concludes by showing how pointers can be used to implement the data structure.

Abstract binary trees

The definition of an abstract binary tree is recursive. It is defined in terms of itself. An abstract binary tree is

- an empty tree

or

- a nonempty tree consisting of a root cell containing
  - ▲ a left child, which is a binary tree
  - ▲ a value
  - ▲ a right child, which is a binary tree.

The definition of an abstract binary tree

You can see the recursive nature of the definition, because the root cell of a nonempty tree contains a left child, which is in turn a tree. Similarly to programming with recursion, a recursive definition must have a base case that stops the recursion. In this definition, the empty tree is the base case, because it is not defined in terms of another tree.

Figure 22.1 illustrates this definition of an abstract binary tree for a tree of integers. The root of the tree is the node that contains 5. The leaves—6, 1, and 7—are those nodes whose left and right children are both empty. The structure in Figure 22.1(a) is a binary tree because its root, 5, has a left child that is a binary subtree, as shown in (b), and a right child that is a binary subtree, as shown in (c).

The definition of a leaf

Figure 22.2 shows why the structure in Figure 22.1(b) is a binary tree. The root of this tree contains 4, its left child in Figure 22.2(b) is empty, and its right child, shown in Figure 22.2(c), consists of a single node. You can see from this line of rea-

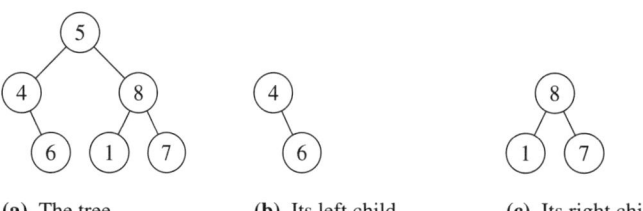

Figure 22.1
An abstract binary tree.

(a) The tree.   **(b)** Its left child.   **(c)** Its right child.

soning that each child of a node in the original structure of Figure 22.1(a) can be shown to be a binary tree. The basis of the definition is the fact that a binary tree can be empty.

Figure 22.2
Another abstract binary tree.

(a) The tree.   **(b)** Its left child.   **(c)** Its right child.

Every node in a tree has a depth. The depth of the root node is always zero. The depth of any child of the root is one. In general, the depth of any node is one plus the depth of its parent node. The height of a tree is the maximum value of the depths of all its nodes. Figure 22.3 shows a binary tree having nine nodes with the depth of each node labeled. Node 42 has a depth of 2. Node 7 has the maximum depth, 4, of all the nodes. Therefore, 4 is the height of the tree

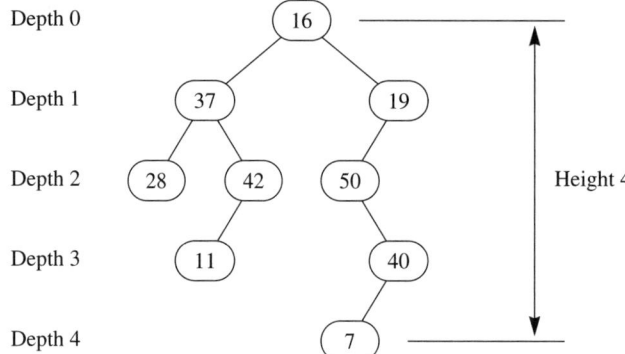

Figure 22.3
The depth of the nodes and the height of the tree.

The values in the binary tree of Figure 22.3 have no particular order associated with them. This binary tree is said to be unordered. In practice, binary trees usually are ordered in a way that makes retrieving a value efficient. Such a tree is called a *binary search tree*. A binary search tree satisfies four criteria:

- every value in the left subtree of the root is less than the value of the root

- the left subtree is a search tree

- every value in the right subtree of the root is greater than the value of the root

- the right subtree is a search tree

It is possible to construct a binary tree in which the left and right children of the root are search trees, but the tree itself is not a search tree. It is also possible to construct a binary tree in which every value in the left subtree is less than the root and every value in the right subtree is greater than the root, but the tree itself is not a search tree. For a binary tree to be a search tree, all four criteria must hold.

Example 22.1 In Figure 22.1(a), the fact that 1 is in the right subtree of root 5, shows that the tree is not a search tree. Another node out of order is 6, which is in the left subtree of the root. ∎

Example 22.2 The binary tree of Figure 22.4 is a search tree. All the nodes in the left subtree of the root (20, 10, 30) are less than the root value, and all the nodes in the right subtree (60, 50) are greater than the root value. Furthermore, the subtree with 20 as a root is itself a search tree, because 10 is less than 20, and 30 is greater than 20. Similarly, the subtree with 60 as a root is itself a search tree, because 50, the value in the left child of 60, is less than 60. ∎

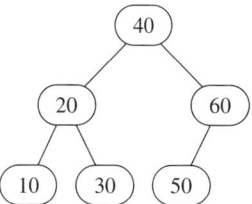

Figure 22.4
A binary search tree.

In their abstract form, binary trees are usually written on paper or displayed on the screen as two-dimensional drawings. It is frequently necessary, however, to output the values from the tree in a single list as opposed to a flat drawing. To print all the values requires a procedure that somehow travels around the tree, visiting the various nodes and outputting their values. Such a trip is called a *traversal*. Three common traversals of a binary tree are:

- Preorder traversal

- Inorder traversal

- Postorder traversal

The definition of each traversal is recursive and is related to the recursive nature of the definition of a binary tree.

The definition of a preorder traversal is

- Visit the root.

- Make a preorder traversal of the left subtree, if any.

- Make a preorder traversal of the right subtree, if any.

This definition is recursive because the preorder traversal requires two other preorder traversals.

Figure 22.5(a) shows the preorder traversal of the binary tree of Figure 22.1. The line that enters from the upper left and exits to the upper right traces the path. The definition says to first visit the root, which the figure indicates by the solid box to the left of the root. Then do a preorder traversal of the subtree whose root is 20, followed by a preorder traversal of the subtree whose root is 60.

Now apply the preorder traversal to the tree whose root is 20. First visit 20, then

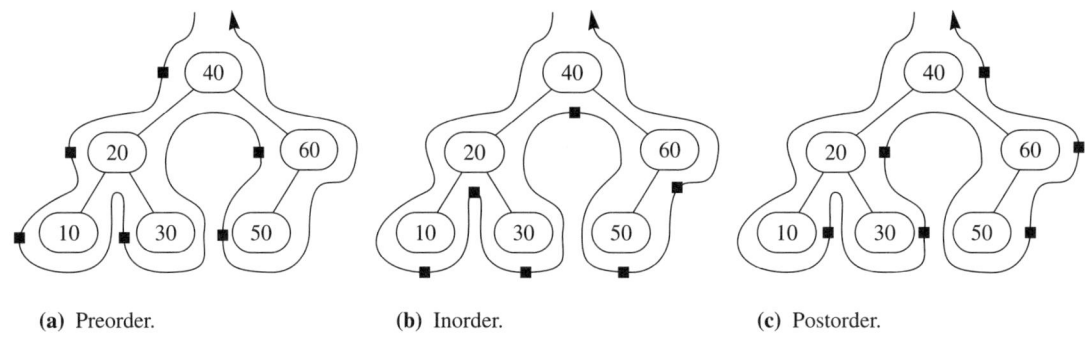

(a) Preorder.　　　　　　　　**(b)** Inorder.　　　　　　　　**(c)** Postorder.

do a preorder traversal with 10 as the root, followed by a preorder traversal with 30 as the root. Similarly, the preorder traversal of the tree whose root is 60 consists of a visit to 60, followed by a visit to 50. The net result is

Figure 22.5
The visits to the nodes in the tree traversal algorithms.

40　20　10　30　60　50

The definition of an inorder traversal is

- Make an inorder traversal of the left subtree, if any.

The inorder traversal

- Visit the root.

- Make an inorder traversal of the right subtree, if any.

Figure 22.5(b) shows the corresponding inorder visitation on the same tree. This time the incoming path does not first visit the root. Instead, it waits until the left subtree has been traversed. Then the root is visited as indicated by the solid box on the path just under the root. After the root is visited, the path traverses the right subtree. The net result is

10　20　30　40　50　60

The definition of a postorder traversal is

- Make a postorder traversal of the left subtree, if any.

The postorder traversal

- Make a postorder traversal of the right subtree, if any.

- Visit the root.

Figure 22.5(c) shows the postorder traversal. The path does not show a visit to the root until both the left and right subtrees have been traversed. This time the output is

10　30　20　50　60　40

Remember that the tree in Figure 22.5 is a binary search tree. The example of an inorder traversal of a binary search tree shows that it outputs the values in order, as if they were sorted. In fact, one of the primary uses of binary trees is to maintain lists of elements in sorted order.

To build a binary search tree requires an insert operation. Insert assumes that a given binary tree is a search tree and inserts a new node with some value to the tree, maintaining its ordered state. Figure 22.6 shows the structure of an abstract tree of integers that is initially empty and is constructed with the sequence of inserts 40, 20, 60, 50, 10, 30.

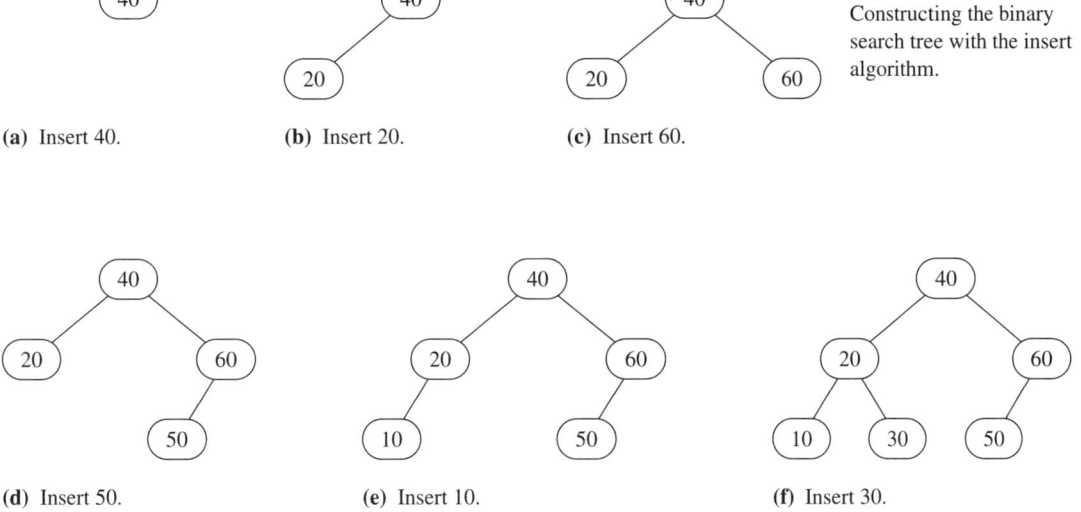

Figure 22.6
Constructing the binary search tree with the insert algorithm.

(a) Insert 40.   **(b)** Insert 20.   **(c)** Insert 60.

(d) Insert 50.   **(e)** Insert 10.   **(f)** Insert 30.

With each insert operation, the newly created node takes the place of an empty left child or an empty right child of some node in the tree. The node that is inserted becomes a leaf. If the node to which it is attached was previously a leaf, that node becomes an *internal node*, that is, a node that is not a leaf.   *Definition of an internal node*

When a given value is inserted to a given ordered binary tree, the attachment point is unique. For example, to insert 10 to the tree of Figure 10.18(d) it must take the place of the left child of 20. Placing 10 at any other available location would produce a tree that is not ordered.

A binary search tree ADT

In the same way that a linked list can be packaged as an ADT or as a class, a binary search tree can be packaged both ways. Figure 22.7 shows the interface for a binary search tree ADT.

DEFINITION PboxTreeADT;

    TYPE
      Tree = POINTER TO Node;
      T = ARRAY 16 OF CHAR;

    PROCEDURE Clear (OUT tr: Tree);
    PROCEDURE Contains (tr: Tree; IN val: T): BOOLEAN;
    PROCEDURE Insert (VAR tr: Tree; IN val: T);
    PROCEDURE NumItems (tr: Tree): INTEGER;
    PROCEDURE PreOrder (tr: Tree);
    PROCEDURE InOrder (tr: Tree);
    PROCEDURE PostOrder (tr: Tree)

END PboxTreeADT.

Figure 22.7
The interface for the binary search tree ADT.

As with the list ADT in Chapter 21, type T is the type of the values that are stored in the data structure. The tree itself is a pointer. The documentation for Tree and T is

TYPE **Tree**
The binary search tree ADT supplied by PboxTreeADT.

TYPE **T**
The type of each element in the tree, a string of at most 15 characters.

The documentation for procedure Insert shows that it has a precondition.

PROCEDURE **Insert** (VAR tr: Tree; IN val: T)
Pre
Tree tr does not already contain val.   20
Post
val is inserted in tree tr, maintaining its ordered property.

If you try to insert an element in the tree that already contains the same value, a trap will be generated with error number 20.

Procedure Contains returns true iff tr contains element val, and function NumItems returns the number of items in tr. Neither of these methods has a precondition. The next three procedures output the tree in preorder, inorder, and postorder. Because the operation of outputting a tree to the Log does not change the tree, tr in these methods is called by value. The Clear procedure clears an existing tree to the empty tree. Because this method will change the tree, tr is called by reference.

As with the linked list interface in Chapter 21, no capacity is specified, indicating that the only limit on the size of a binary search tree is the amount of available memory. It is apparent from this fact that this binary tree is implemented as a linked structure with dynamic storage allocation as opposed to being implemented with an array. While the previous examples showed binary search trees that stored integers, this interface is for an ordered binary tree that stores strings.

Figure 22.8 shows one possible data structure for the binary search tree ADT. As

with the list ADT, type Tree is a pointer to Node. Node, however, contains two links
to the left and right subtree rather than just one link to the next element in a list.
Rather than describe the implementation of the binary search tree ADT, this chapter
concludes with the corresponding implementation of the binary search tree class.

```
TYPE
    T* = ARRAY 16 OF CHAR;
    Tree* = POINTER TO Node;
    Node = RECORD
        leftChild: Tree;
        value: T;
        rightChild: Tree
    END;
```

Figure 22.8
The data structure for the
binary search tree ADT.

A binary search tree class

Module PboxTreeObj implements an ordered binary tree as a class. Figure 22.9
shows its interface. The methods have the same names and operations as the corresponding procedures in the ADT of Figure 22.7. In particular, the only method that
has a precondition is Insert, which does not allow the insertion of a duplicate item.

Figure 22.10 shows the dialog box for a program that uses the binary search tree
class of Figure 22.9. The user does not specify a position for an insertion. Instead,
the insert algorithm inserts an element into the one place that will maintain the
ordered property of the tree. The result of a search is simply a statement of whether
a tree contains a given element. No position is associated with the result as it is with
the locate option in the dialog box of Figure 21.28 for the linked list. Completion of
method Contains, which performs the search, is left as a problem for the student.
Also left as a problem are methods NumItems, InOrder, and PostOrder. The numbers
999 in the dialog box are produced by a stub in method NumItems.

```
DEFINITION PboxTreeObj;

    TYPE
        T = ARRAY 16 OF CHAR;
        Tree = RECORD
            (VAR tr: Tree) Clear, NEW;
            (IN tr: Tree) Contains (IN val: T): BOOLEAN, NEW;
            (VAR tr: Tree) Insert (IN val: T), NEW;
            (IN tr: Tree) NumItems (): INTEGER, NEW;
            (IN tr: Tree) PreOrder, NEW;
            (IN tr: Tree) InOrder, NEW;
            (IN tr: Tree) PostOrder, NEW
        END;

END PboxTreeObj.
```

Figure 22.9
The interface for the binary
search tree class.

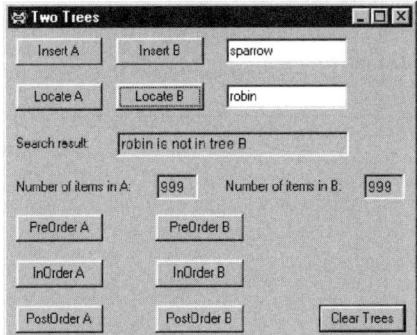

Figure 22.10
The dialog box for manipulating two binary search trees.

The program in Figure 22.11 shows how to use the ordered binary tree class. The interactor is linked to the dialog box of Figure 22.10. Corresponding to the 11 buttons in the dialog box are 11 procedures in module Pbox22A.

Figure 22.11
A program that uses the binary search tree class.

```
MODULE Pbox22A;
   IMPORT Dialog, PboxTreeObj, StdLog;

   VAR
      d*: RECORD
         insertT*: PboxTreeObj.T;
         searchT*: PboxTreeObj.T;
         resultString-: ARRAY 64 OF CHAR;
         numItemsA-, numItemsB-: INTEGER;
      END;
      treeA, treeB: PboxTreeObj.Tree;

   PROCEDURE InsertA*;
   BEGIN
      treeA.Insert(d.insertT);
      d.numItemsA := treeA.NumItems();
      Dialog.Update(d)
   END InsertA;

   PROCEDURE InsertB*;
   BEGIN
      treeB.Insert(d.insertT);
      d.numItemsB := treeB.NumItems();
      Dialog.Update(d)
   END InsertB;
```

```
PROCEDURE SearchA*;
BEGIN
   IF treeA.Contains(d.searchT) THEN
      d.resultString := d.searchT + " is in tree A"
   ELSE
      d.resultString := d.searchT + " is not in tree A"
   END;
   Dialog.Update(d)
END SearchA;

PROCEDURE SearchB*;
BEGIN
   IF treeB.Contains(d.searchT ) THEN
      d.resultString := d.searchT + " is in tree B"
   ELSE
      d.resultString := d.searchT + " is not in tree B"
   END;
   Dialog.Update(d)
END SearchB;

PROCEDURE PreOrderA*;
BEGIN
   StdLog.Ln;
   treeA.PreOrder
END PreOrderA;

PROCEDURE PreOrderB*;
BEGIN
   StdLog.Ln;
   treeB.PreOrder
END PreOrderB;

PROCEDURE InOrderA*;
BEGIN
   StdLog.Ln;
   treeA.InOrder
END InOrderA;

PROCEDURE InOrderB*;
BEGIN
   StdLog.Ln;
   treeB.InOrder
END InOrderB;

PROCEDURE PostOrderA*;
BEGIN
   StdLog.Ln;
   treeA.PostOrder
END PostOrderA;
```

Figure 22.11
Continued.

```
PROCEDURE PostOrderB*;
BEGIN
    StdLog.Ln;
    treeB.PostOrder
END PostOrderB;

PROCEDURE ClearTrees*;
BEGIN
    treeA.Clear; treeB.Clear;
    d.insertT := "";
    d.searchT := ""; d.resultString := "";
    d.numItemsA := 0; d.numItemsB := 0;
    Dialog.Update(d)
END ClearTrees;

BEGIN
    ClearTrees
END Pbox22A.
```

Figure 22.11
Continued.

---

treeA and treeB are the two global variables whose states are maintained between clicks of the buttons of the dialog box. Most of the procedures simply use the user input from the dialog box as actual parameters in a call to the corresponding method from the class. The procedures for outputting the tree traversals include a call of Std-Log.Ln before calling on the class so that the output for a traversal will begin on a new line.

The implementation of a binary tree is closely related to the recursive definition of an abstract binary tree. From an abstract perspective, a binary tree is either empty or is a cell containing a value and two binary trees. In the same way that a list is implemented as a pointer to the *head* node of the list, a binary tree is implemented as a pointer to the *root* node of a tree. Each node in the tree contains a value part to hold the data and two other parts to hold its left child and its right child. The data part obviously has type T, but what is the type of the left child and right child? From the recursive definition of a binary tree, they should each have type Tree. Figure 22.12 shows the structure of a record for a node in the implementation of a binary tree.

The abstract binary tree of strings in Figure 22.13(a) has three elements with robin as the root of the tree, finch as its left child and sparrow as its right child. The links are simply drawn as lines between the nodes. Figure 22.13(b) shows the nodes in the tree as it would be implemented with the record of Figure 22.12. treeA is a pointer to the node record that represents its root. The value part of the root node contains the string robin. The leftChild is a tree. That is, it is a pointer to the root of the left subtree, a record containing finch in its value part. Because the node containing finch has no left child, the pointer in its leftChild part is NIL. Likewise, the pointer in its rightChild part is NIL.

Figure 22.14 shows the implementation using the structure of the nodes as shown in the previous figures. The type declarations define type Tree to be a record, which contains a pointer to the tree's root node. The root node, in turn, contains a left subtree, a value to store the data at the node, and a right subtree. Subtrees leftChild and

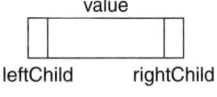

Figure 22.12
The structure of a record for a node in the implementation of a binary tree.

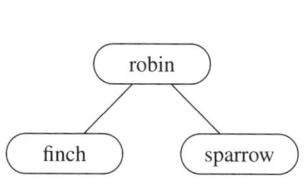

(a) An abstract binary tree.

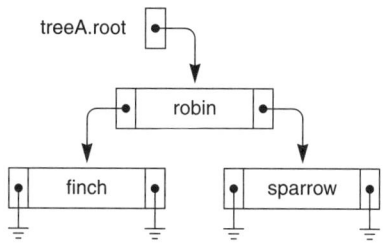

treeA.root

robin

finch   sparrow

(b) Its linked implementation.

Figure 22.13
An abstract binary tree and its
implementation as a class.

rightChild have type Tree. That is, they are records with a single pointer to the roots
of the left and right subtrees.

Because a tree is a pointer to its root node, and an empty tree has no nodes, an
empty tree is represented by a pointer whose value is NIL. Method Clear makes a
tree empty by setting to NIL the pointer to its root node. The nodes that comprised
the tree are later reclaimed by the automatic garbage collector.

```
MODULE PboxTreeObj;
   IMPORT StdLog;

   TYPE
      T* = ARRAY 16 OF CHAR;
      Tree* = RECORD
         root: POINTER TO Node
      END;
      Node = RECORD
         leftChild: Tree;
         value: T;
         rightChild: Tree
      END;

   PROCEDURE (VAR tr: Tree) Clear*, NEW;
   BEGIN
      tr.root := NIL
   END Clear;

   PROCEDURE (IN tr: Tree) Contains* (IN val: T): BOOLEAN, NEW;
   BEGIN
      (* A problem for the student *)
      RETURN FALSE
   END Contains;
```

Figure 22.14
Implementation of the
ordered binary tree class that
is used in Figure 22.11.

Figure 22.14
Continued.

```
PROCEDURE (VAR tr: Tree) Insert* (IN val: T), NEW;
   VAR
      parent: Tree;
      p: Tree;
BEGIN
   (* Find insertion point *)
   parent.root := NIL;
   p := tr;
   WHILE p.root # NIL DO
      parent := p;
      ASSERT(p.root.value # val, 20);
      IF val < p.root.value THEN
         p := p.root.leftChild
      ELSE
         p := p.root.rightChild
      END
   END;
   (* Attach new node to parent *)
   NEW(p.root);
   p.root.value := val;
   IF parent.root = NIL THEN (* tr is empty *)
      tr := p
   ELSIF val < parent.root.value THEN
      parent.root.leftChild := p
   ELSE
      parent.root.rightChild := p
   END
END Insert;

PROCEDURE (IN tr: Tree) NumItems* (): INTEGER, NEW;
BEGIN
   (* A problem for the student *)
   RETURN 999
END NumItems;

PROCEDURE (IN tr: Tree) PreOrder*, NEW;
BEGIN
   IF tr.root # NIL THEN
      StdLog.String(tr.root.value); StdLog.String(" ");
      tr.root.leftChild.PreOrder;
      tr.root.rightChild.PreOrder
   END
END PreOrder;

PROCEDURE (IN tr: Tree) InOrder*, NEW;
BEGIN
   (* A problem for the student *)
END InOrder;
```

```
PROCEDURE (IN tr: Tree) PostOrder*, NEW;
BEGIN
    (* A problem for the student *)
END PostOrder;

END PboxTreeObj.
```

Figure 22.14
Continued.

PboxTreeObj implements method PreOrder directly from the definition of a preorder traversal. If a tree is empty, it has no preorder traversal and the method simply returns to the calling procedure. Otherwise, the steps in the algorithm are to first visit the root, then to do a preorder traversal of the left subtree followed by a preorder traversal of the right subtree. To indicate that the root is visited, the method outputs the data from the current node. It then recursively calls for a preorder traversal of the left subtree followed by a recursive call for a preorder traversal of the right subtree. Implementation of procedures InOrder and PostOrder are similar and are left as a problem for the student.

Figure 22.15 shows the action of procedure Insert when it is called to insert the value pat into an ordered binary tree. The procedure has two parts. First, it must find the position in the tree to attach the new node. Then, it must allocate the new node and attach it.

To find the position, the procedure maintains two local variables, p and parent, which are both trees. Variable p advances through the tree starting from the root, and makes its way to the correct insertion point. Each time p advances one level down the tree, variable parent points to the node from which p advances. When p finally gets NIL, parent will point to the node to which the new node must be attached. Figure 22.15(a) through (d) shows the sequence of events of the first part of the procedure to find the position in the tree.

Each time through the loop the procedure must decide whether to advance p to the left or to the right. Recall from Figure 22.9 the precondition that duplicate values are not allowed. The assertion in the body of the WHILE loop in procedure Insert guarantees that if v is not less than p.value it will be greater than p.value.

Figure 22.15(e) shows the effect of the call to procedure NEW. Figure 22.15(f) shows how the new node is attached to its parent. In the figure, the original tree tr is not empty. If it were, variable parent would be NIL, and procedure Insert would simply point tr to the newly allocated node.

Implementation of procedure Contains is left as a problem for the student. It is best programmed recursively. If tree tr is empty it obviously does not contain v and can return false. Otherwise, tr is not empty and its root must contain some value. If that value equals v, the procedure can return true with no further recursive calls necessary. Otherwise, the procedure must determine whether v might be contained in the left subtree or the right subtree. Your implementation should not search the entire tree, but should use the fact that every value in the left subtree is less than the value in the root and every value in the right subtree is greater than the root.

Procedure NumItems is also left as a problem for the student, and is also best programmed recursively. If tree tr is empty, it obviously has zero elements. Otherwise, it contains one element, its left subtree contains some number of elements, and its right subtree contains some number of elements. The integer it must return is, therefore, one plus the number of elements in its left subtree plus the number of elements in its right subtree.

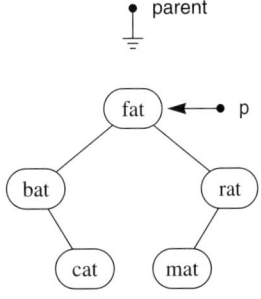

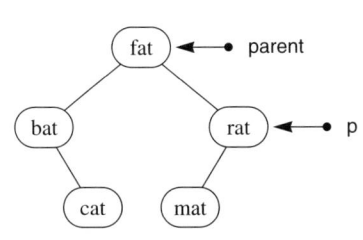

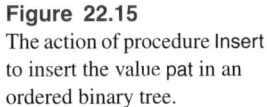

Figure 22.15
The action of procedure Insert to insert the value pat in an ordered binary tree.

(**a**) parent.root := NIL; p := tr

(**b**) parent := p; p := p.root.rightChild

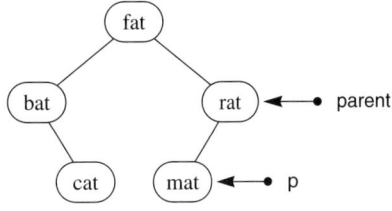

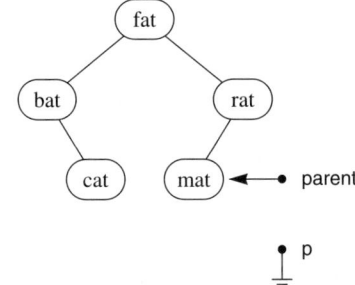

(**c**) parent := p; p := p.root.leftChild

(**d**) parent := p, p := p.root.rightChild

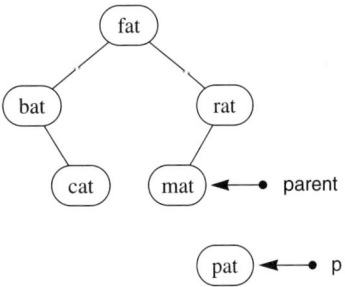

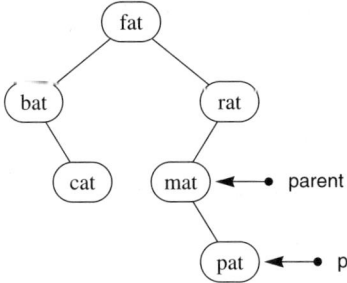

(**e**) NEW(p.root); p.root.value := val

(**f**) parent.root.rightChild := p

Exercises

1. Draw the final binary search tree as in Figure 22.6(f) for each of the following sequences of the insert operation.

   (a) 50 30 80 60 40 20 10   **(b)** 50 30 80 60 40 10 20
   (c) 50 60 70 80 10 20 30 40   **(d)** 10 20 30 40 50
   (e) 50 40 30 20 10

2. For each of the binary search trees of Exercise 1, write the preorder sequence.

3. For each of the binary search trees of Exercise 1, write the postorder sequence.

4. For each binary tree in Figure 22.16, (1) state whether the tree is a search tree, (2) write the preorder traversal, (3) write the inorder traversal, and (4) write the postorder traversal.

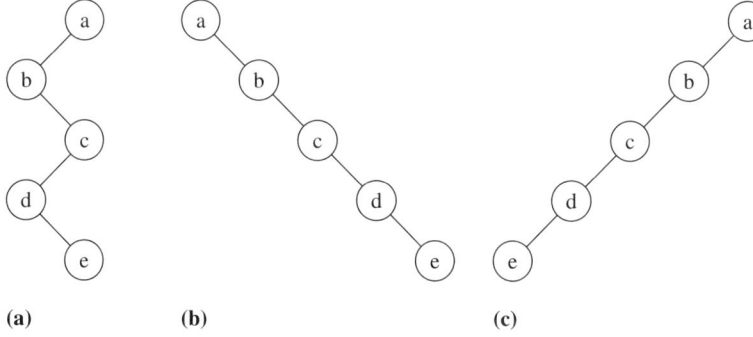

(a)   (b)   (c)

Figure 22.16
The binary trees for Exercise 4.

5. A binary search tree contains a set of integers. Assume that each of the following sequences is the preorder sequence. From the preorder sequence and the known inorder sequence, draw the ordered binary tree.

   (a) 40 20 60   **(b)** 60 40 20
   (c) 60 20 40   **(d)** 20 40 60 80
   (e) 60 30 10 80 70 90

6. A binary search tree contains a set of integers. Assume that each of the following sequences is the postorder sequence. From the postorder sequence and the known inorder sequence, draw the ordered binary tree.

   (a) 40 20 60   **(b)** 20 60 40
   (c) 20 40 60   **(d)** 80 60 40 20
   (e) 30 10 80 90 70 60

Problems

7. This problem is for you to complete the procedures for the binary search tree ADT in module PboxTreeADT. Test your procedures with a program similar to the one in Figure 22.11 using the dialog box of Figure 22.10. For each procedure, access the documentation and implement any preconditions with the appropriate ASSERT or HALT procedure.

(a) PROCEDURE Insert (VAR tr: Tree; IN val: T)
(b) PROCEDURE Contains (tr: Tree; IN val: T): BOOLEAN
(c) PROCEDURE NumItems (tr: Tree): INTEGER
(d) PROCEDURE PreOrder (tr: Tree)
(e) PROCEDURE InOrder (tr: Tree)
(f) PROCEDURE PostOrder (tr: Tree)
(g) PROCEDURE Clear (OUT tr: Tree)

8. Implement the following methods in module PboxTreeObj.

(a) PROCEDURE (IN tr: Tree) Contains (IN val: T): BOOLEAN, NEW
Write a nonrecursive version.

(b) PROCEDURE (IN tr: Tree) Contains (IN val: T): BOOLEAN, NEW
Write a recursive version without a loop. Use the fact that the tree is a search tree to avoid unnecessary comparisons. For example, if val is not in the tree, do not search the entire tree.

(c) PROCEDURE (IN tr: Tree) NumItems (): INTEGER, NEW
(d) PROCEDURE (IN tr: Tree) InOrder, NEW
(e) PROCEDURE (IN tr: Tree) PostOrder, NEW

9. This problem requires you to add the following methods to Figure 22.14. Test your methods by importing them into the module of Figure 22.11. Augment the dialog box of Figure 22.10 to test the procedures.

(a) PROCEDURE (IN tr: Tree) NumLeaves (): INTEGER, NEW
Return the number of leaves of tree tr. A leaf is a node that has no children.

(b) PROCEDURE (IN tr: Tree) NumInternals (): INTEGER, NEW
Return the number of internal nodes of tree tr. An internal node is a node that is not a leaf.

(c) PROCEDURE (IN tr: Tree) OutLeaves, NEW
Output the leaves of tree tr to the Log.

(d) PROCEDURE (VAR tr: Tree) StripLeaves, NEW
Remove all the leaves from binary tree tr.

(e) PROCEDURE (IN tr: Tree) ReverseOrder, NEW
Output the values from binary tree tr to the Log in the reverse of inorder.

(f) PROCEDURE (IN tr: Tree) Height (): INTEGER, NEW

Return the height of the binary tree tr. The definition of the height is recursive. If the tree is empty, its height is −1. Otherwise its height is 1 plus the larger of the height of the left and right subtrees.

(g) PROCEDURE (VAR tr: Tree) Copy (trB: Tree), NEW

Create a new tree tr, which is a copy of trB. tr must contain the same values as trB and must also have the same shape as trB. This is best done recursively. If trB is empty then tr should be made empty. Otherwise, a copy of trB's root node should be created for tr's root, and copies should be made recursively for the left and right children.

(h) PROCEDURE (VAR tr: Tree) Equal (trB: Tree): BOOLEAN, NEW

Return true iff tr is equal to trB. Two trees are equal if they have the same number of equal values and if they have the same shape. This is best done recursively. The base cases are (1) both trees empty, (2) one tree empty and the other not, and (3) both trees not empty but with unequal values in their roots.

Chapter *23*

Inheritance and Polymorphism

The history of computer science shows a steady progression from lower levels of abstraction to higher levels. When the electronic computer was first invented in the mid twentieth century, there was no assembly language much less the higher level languages with which we are familiar today. It is no accident that the historic evolution is toward progressively higher levels of abstraction instead of the other way around. Human intellectual progress shows that generalities are usually discovered from many specific observations. It is only with hindsight that you can start with the general case and deduce specific consequences from it.

This chapter describes six levels of abstraction.

- Data abstraction, encompassing
  - ▲ Type abstraction, and
  - ▲ Structure abstraction
- Control abstraction, encompassing
  - ▲ Statement abstraction, and
  - ▲ Procedure abstraction
- Class abstraction
- Behavior abstraction

Six abstraction processes

Previous chapters show programs that use the first five abstraction processes—type, structure, statement, procedure, and class. This chapter reviews these five abstraction processes and introduces the sixth—behavior abstraction.

Data abstraction

Plato, in his theory of forms, claimed that reality ultimately lies in the abstract form that represents the essence of individual objects we sense in the world. In the *Republic*, written in the form of a dialogue between Socrates and a student, he writes:

> Well then, shall we begin the enquiry in our usual manner: Whenever a number of individuals have a common name, we assume them to have also a corresponding idea or form: do you understand me?
>
> I do.
>
> Let us take any common instance; there are beds and tables in the world—

Plato's abstraction

plenty of them, are there not?

Yes.

But there are only two ideas or forms of them—one the idea of a bed, the other of a table.

True.

And the maker of either of them makes a bed or he makes a table for our use, in accordance with the idea—that is our way of speaking in this and similar instances—but no artificer makes the ideas themselves: how could he?

Impossible.

Plato's consideration between the specific and the general exemplifies the abstraction process. Another example of the abstraction process is the concept of type in programming languages. Consider all the possible real values, such as 2.0, 5.2, –43.7, 0.8, and so on. In the same way that Plato considered many different instances of a table to be representations of a single abstract table, from a computation point of view the collection of all possible real values defines a single abstract type REAL. Figure 23.1 shows the abstraction process, known as *type abstraction*, for type REAL. A type is defined by a collection of values. Each value, such as 5.2 in the box on the left, is specific, while the type REAL is general.

Type abstraction

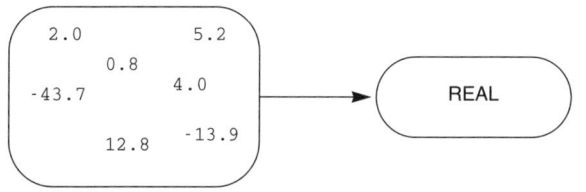

Figure 23.1
Type abstraction for type REAL.

In the history of computing languages, types emerged as one of the first steps toward higher levels of abstraction. At the machine level, which must be programmed with machine language or its equivalent assembly language, there are no types other than the bit patterns of pure binary. With assembly language, you have unlimited freedom to interpret a bit pattern any way you choose. The same bit pattern in a specific memory location can be interpreted as an integer and processed with the addition circuitry of the processor. It can be interpreted as a character and sent to a Web page as such. It can even be interpreted as an instruction and executed.

In Component Pascal, every variable has a name, a type, and a value. The name is an identifier, defined by the syntax rules of the language. The type is supplied by the language. Both the name and the type of a variable are determined when the software designer writes and compiles the program. The value of a variable, on the other hand, is stored in the main memory of the computer as the program is executing. The value stored is one of the values that defines the type.

Every variable has a name, a type, and a value.

The compiler enforces type compatibility, which is a restriction on the freedom of programmers that they do not have with assembly language. The abstraction process frequently imposes a loss of freedom because the nature of abstraction is the hiding of detail. Programmers then have no access to the details that are hidden. With the advent of types to restrict the value that a variable can have to some mathematical entity like a real number comes the inability to consider the bit pattern behind the value. But the restriction of freedom to access low-level details is also liberation from the necessity to do so. Abstraction is powerful because the limitation it places on the programmer's ability to access low level details at the same time frees the programmer from that requirement.

Advantages and disadvantages of abstraction

The abstraction process permits the grouping together of specific real values into a type because each value shares certain characteristics with all the other values. For example, each value has a sign and a magnitude. Any value can be combined with any other value with the arithmetic operators like multiplication. And any value can be compared with any other value to determine whether the first is less than, equal to, or greater than the second. If it were not for these common properties among individual values, the grouping together of them to define a type would not be useful.

Furthermore, the collection of many specific numeric values to make a general type is useful in a programming language because it models the same process in the real world. For example, the type REAL in Component Pascal corresponds to the notion of a real number in mathematics. All computer applications exist to solve problems in the human world. The first step toward solving any problem is to model it with the machine. There are usually approximations to the model, which may make the solution approximate. For example, there are only a finite number of real values that a computer can store while there are an infinite number of real values in mathematics. Nevertheless, one source of power of the abstraction process in computing is that it can mirror the same process in the human world and so serve as a model to compute the desired solution.

The next step toward higher levels of abstraction in programming languages occurred when languages gave programmers the ability to create new types as combinations of primitive types. Collections of primitive types are known as records or structures in most programming languages. The corresponding abstraction process is called *structure abstraction*.

Structure abstraction

For example, suppose you need to process several different shapes—rectangles and circles. Figure 23.2 shows geometrically how the collection of all possible rectangles and circles define a single shape type. The abstraction process parallels the process of defining a type as a collection of values. An individual rectangle is characterized by its length, say 2.0, and width, say 5.2. An individual circle is characterized by its diameter, say 4.1. A shape is a collection of values—each one having a type—to store its dimensions.

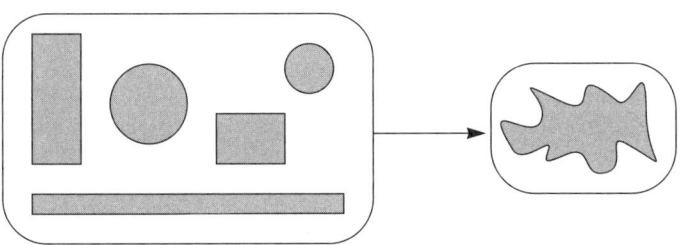

Figure 23.2
Structure abstraction to abstract from specific shapes of many different sizes to a single shape with a general size.

In Component Pascal, you declare a new type as a record structure, which is a collection of fields, each one of which is a primitive type supplied by the language or a previously declared type. To store the information about a shape you need to distinguish between rectangles and circles. You can do that with an integer field called kind. If kind has value 0 then the shape is a rectangle. If kind has value 1 then the shape is a circle. To store the dimensions of a rectangle you need real fields named length and width. To store the dimensions of a circle you need a real field named diameter. The type could be declared

```
MODULE ...ShapeADT;
   TYPE
      Shape* = POINTER TO RECORD
         kind: INTEGER;
         length, width: REAL;
         diameter: REAL
      END
```

You could then declare an individual shape as a variable of type Shape.

```
VAR
   myShape: ...ShapeADT.Shape
```

To initialize myShape to be a 2×3 rectangle you use the usual period notation to separate the variable name from the record field name as follows.

```
myShape.kind := 0;
myShape.length := 2.0;
myShape.width := 3.0
```

Programmer-defined types are powerful because they allow the programmer to conveniently model the problem to mirror the situation in the problem domain. For example, an airline reservation system might need to store a collection of information for each ticket it sells, say the passenger's name, address, flight date, flight number, and price of the ticket. Collecting all these types into a single programmer-defined type allows the program to process a ticket variable as a single entity.

Computation abstraction

Abstraction of data is only one side of a two-sided coin. The other side is abstraction of computation. At the lowest level between programming languages and the machine is *statement abstraction*.

Statement abstraction

All computers consist of a central processing unit (CPU) that has a set of instructions wired into it. The instruction set varies from one computer chip maker to another, but all commercial CPUs have similar instructions. CPUs contain cells called registers that store values and perform operations on them. The collection of the operations specifies a computation.

Typical instructions are load, add, mul, and store. The load instruction gets a value from main memory and stores it in a register of the CPU. The add instruction adds the content of two registers. The mul instruction multiplies the content of two registers. The store instruction puts a value from a register of the CPU into main memory.

Before the advent of high-level languages, programmers wrote their programs using the individual instructions of the instruction set of the particular CPU on which the program was designed to run. Figure 23.3 shows an example of a sequence of instructions for some hypothetical CPU that computes the perimeter of a rectangle. The first two instructions load the value of length into register r1 and the value of width into register r2. The next instruction adds the content of r1 to r2 and puts the sum in register r3. Then, 2.0 is multiplied by the content of r3 with the result placed back in r3, after which it is stored in main memory in the location reserved for variable perim.

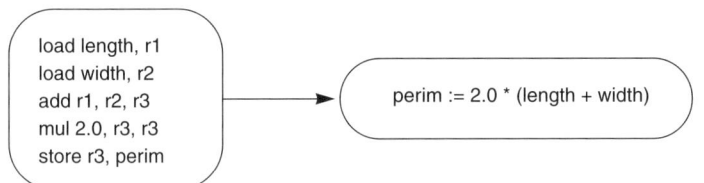

Figure 23.3
Statement abstraction for the assignment statement.

The language illustrated by this sequence of instructions is called assembly language. When you program in assembly language you must consider the details of the CPU—how many registers it has, how to access them, and which values you want to store in which registers. In a high-level language, however, all those details are hidden. The compiler abstracts them away from the view of the programmer, so that the programmer need only write the single assignment statement

perim := 2.0 * (length + width)

With statement abstraction, even the structure of the CPU is hidden. The programmer does not need to know about registers or hardware instruction sets. A single assignment statement in Component Pascal is a collection of several instructions in assembly language. One statement in a high-level language is defined by many statements at the machine level, in the same way that one type in a high-level language is defined by many possible values at the machine level.

Corresponding to structure abstraction on the data side of the coin is procedure abstraction on the computation side. In the same way that high-level languages allow you to collect variables into structures to create a new data type, they allow you collect statements into procedures to create a new computation. The corresponding abstraction process is *procedure abstraction*.

Procedure abstraction

Figure 23.4 shows procedure abstraction for the computation of the perimeter of a shape. The Component Pascal computation of the perimeter of an arbitrary shape is encapsulated in a function with formal parameter s whose type is Shape. Any time the programmer needs to compute the perimeter, for example to output it with StdLog.Real, a simple call to the function is all that is required. The computation need only be done once, freeing the programmer from having to remember those details whenever the computation is required. For example, if you have two vari-

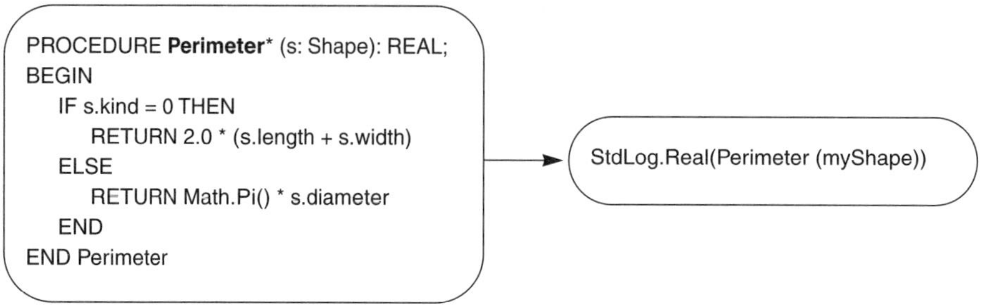

PROCEDURE **Perimeter*** (s: Shape): REAL;
BEGIN
   IF s.kind = 0 THEN
      RETURN 2.0 * (s.length + s.width)
   ELSE
      RETURN Math.Pi() * s.diameter
   END
END Perimeter

StdLog.Real(Perimeter (myShape))

Figure 23.4

Procedure abstraction for the computation of the perimeter of a rectangle

ables—myShape and yourShape—both of type Shape, you can output their perimeters with

StdLog.Real(Perimeter (myShape)); StdLog.Ln;
StdLog.Real(Perimeter (yourShape)); StdLog.Ln

It would not matter if myShape is a circle and yourShape is a rectangle. The procedure takes care of determining what kind of shape the parameter is and returns the appropriate value. The details of the computation are hidden in the function procedure calls. As with statement abstraction in Figure 23.3, one procedure call at a high level causes the execution of several statements at a low level.

Class abstraction

The next step in the evolution of programming languages toward higher levels of abstraction was the combination of data abstraction with computation abstraction to produce class abstraction. Consider again the shapes in Figure 23.2 and imagine what sort of processing might be required for such geometric figures. A rectangle might represent part of a building like the interior wall of a room or a door. If the walls and doors are to be painted your program would need to compute the area of each rectangle to determine the amount of paint required. Or a circle might represent a corral around which a fence is to be erected. Your program would then need to compute the perimeter to determine the amount of material required for the fence.

Before the advent of object-oriented programming, the function to compute the area or the perimeter of a shape would exist separately from its dimensions. For example, you might have functions to compute the area and perimeter of a shape, which is passed as a parameter in the parameter list of the function. The interface for the server module providing ShapeADT might look something like

DEFINITION ...ShapeADT;
   TYPE
      Shape = POINTER TO RECORD END;
   PROCEDURE Area (s: Shape): REAL;
   PROCEDURE Perimeter (s: Shape): REAL;

where the kind field and the dimensions are not exported, and so do not appear in the interface.

With class abstraction, however, you bind the procedures with the type resulting in type-bound procedures, also called methods, having the interface

```
DEFINITION ...ShapeObj;
    TYPE
        Shape = POINTER TO RECORD
            (s: Shape) Area (): REAL, NEW;
            (s: Shape) Perimeter (): REAL, NEW
        END;
```

The procedures belong to the type rather than belonging to the module. As before, values for the kind field and the dimensions are not exported and have an implementation like

```
MODULE ...ShapeObj;
    TYPE
        Shape* = POINTER TO RECORD
            kind: INTEGER;
            length, width: REAL;
            diameter: REAL
        END
```

Figure 23.5 shows the process of class abstraction with this shape example. In the figure, the data part on the top left combines with the control part on the bottom left to produce the class on the right. The box in the right part of the figure is the Unified Modeling Language (UML) class diagram for the class named Shape. It shows all the fields of the record, whether exported or not, and also includes the head of each method.

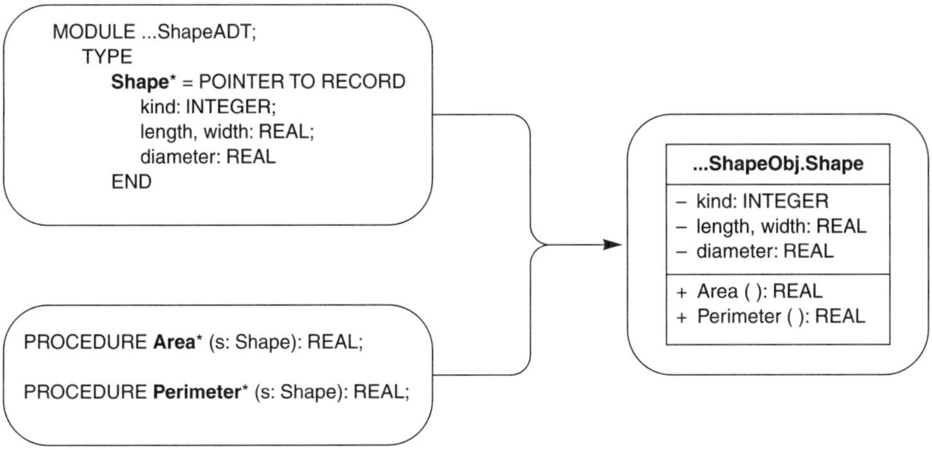

Figure 23.5
Class abstraction that combines the structure abstraction of Figure 23.2 with the procedure abstraction of Figure 23.4.

A class diagram has three parts. The top box contains the name of the class, in this diagram ...ShapeObj.Shape. The UML standard is for the class name to be in a

bold typeface. The middle box contains the data fields of the record, which are *Attributes*
known as *attributes*. In this diagram the attributes are kind, length, width, and diameter. In UML, an item that is not exported is preceded by a – sign and an item that is exported is preceded by a + sign. All of the attributes are preceded by a – sign because none of them are exported. The bottom box contains the methods, which are *Operations*
known as *operations*. There are slight differences in syntax between Component Pascal and UML. The receiver of the methods is not shown before the name of the operation, because it can be inferred by the name of the class in the top box of the UML diagram.

Example 23.1   The heading for the Perimeter procedure would be written in Component Pascal as

PROCEDURE (s: Shape) **Perimeter*** (): REAL, NEW

The corresponding UML entry in the class diagram for the operation is

+ Perimeter ( ): REAL   ∎

Object orientation is a viewpoint that shifts the focus from an external operation *The object orientation shift in*
that requires the input of data about the shape, to an internal operation that is part of *focus*
the shape itself. This is a significant shift in focus. Computing the perimeter is no longer something that you do to a shape. It is something the shape does for you.

In Figure 23.2, each individual shape on the left has an area and a perimeter in addition to its dimensions. The area and perimeter are not data values that are independent from the dimensions. So, their values should not be stored the same way the dimensions are stored, but they should be computed from the dimensions. In object-oriented design, the functions to compute the area and perimeter are no longer external to the type, but are internal. They literally become part of the type.

To emphasize the shift in focus when a function is bound to a type, object-oriented designers established a new set of terminology. Roughly speaking, in object-oriented terminology

- *class* corresponds to *type*

- *object* corresponds to *variable*

- *method* corresponds to *procedure* or *function*

That is, an object has a class, like a variable has a type. It is more usual to state that an object is an instance of a class rather than to state that an object has a class.

A shape class

Although the true power of object orientation requires behavior abstraction, this section presents a program that illustrates class abstraction without it. The purpose of the program is to show how to solve a problem without behavior abstraction, so it can be contrasted with the program in the following section, which does use it. Figure 23.6 shows the abstraction process for class abstraction without behavior abstraction.

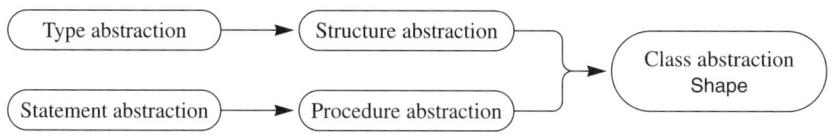

Figure 23.6
Using class abstraction
without behavior abstraction
to process data for several
different kinds of shapes.

Figure 23.7 is the complete interface of the Shape class alluded to in the previous section. Like type Book in Figure 21.17, page 482, type Shape is defined to be a pointer to a record instead of a record. That way, an instance of a Shape can be stored in a circular list CList, which is a list whose nodes have value parts that are pointers to ANYREC.

```
DEFINITION PboxShapeObj;

    TYPE
        Shape = POINTER TO RECORD
            (s: Shape) GetIDString (OUT str: ARRAY OF CHAR), NEW;
            (s: Shape) GetDimensionString (OUT str: ARRAY OF CHAR), NEW;
            (s: Shape) Area (): REAL, NEW;
            (s: Shape) Perimeter (): REAL, NEW;
            (s: Shape) SetRectangleState (length, width: REAL), NEW;
            (s: Shape) SetCircleState (diameter: REAL), NEW
        END;

END PboxShapeObj.
```

Figure 23.7
The interface for a Shape
class without behavior
abstraction.

Method GetIdString sets parameter str to a string that can be displayed in a dialog box. For example, if s is a rectangle the method sets str to "Rectangle". Method GetDimensionString sets parameter str to a string that displays the dimensions of the shape to three places past the decimal point. For example, if s is a rectangle with a length of 2 and a width of 3 the method sets str to "Length = 2.000, Width = 3.000". Method Area is a function procedure that returns the area of shape s, and method Perimeter returns the perimeter of s.

The first four methods do not change the state of s. They simply report back information about its state. The last two methods, however, change the state of s. If you supply SetRectangleState with actual parameters 2.0 and 3.0 corresponding to formal parameters length and width, the method will change the state of s to be a rectangle having length 2.0 and width 3.0 regardless of the kind of shape that it was before. Similarly, if you supply SetCircleState with actual parameter 6.0 corresponding to formal parameter diameter, the method will change the state of s to be a circle having diameter 6.0.

Figure 23.8 shows a sequence of screen shots of a user manipulating a list of shapes. Part (a) shows the dialog box for the first time. The bottom part of the dialog box gives the user the option to enter data for a rectangle, circle, or triangle. As with the circular list for books in Figure 21.15, page 481, the dialog box allows the user to enter data about a shape and store the shape in a circular list. Figure 23.9 is a listing of the program that implements the dialog box of Figure 23.8.

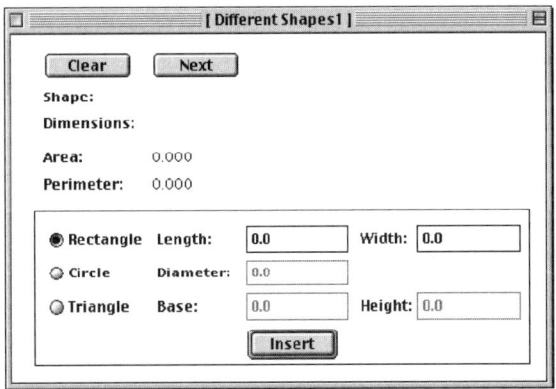

(a) Initial.

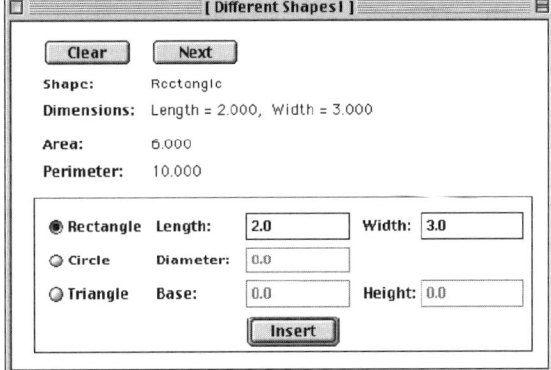

(b) Insert a rectangle.

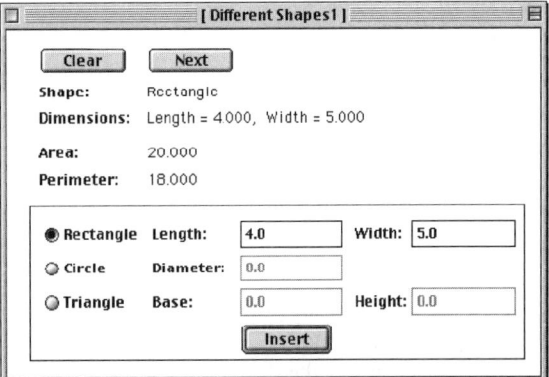

(c) Insert a rectangle.

(d) Insert a circle.

(e) Press Next.

Figure 23.8
A sequence of screen shots for execution of a program to process shapes.

```
MODULE Pbox23A;
   IMPORT Dialog, C := PboxCListADT, S := PboxShapeObj;

   VAR
      d*: RECORD
         idString-, dimensionString- : ARRAY 64 OF CHAR;
         area-, perimeter-: REAL;
         shapeNumber*: INTEGER;
         length*, width*: REAL; (* for rectangle *)
         diameter*: REAL; (* for circle *)
         base*, height*: REAL (* for triangle *)
      END;
      cList: C.CList;

   PROCEDURE ClearDialog;
   BEGIN
      d.idString := ""; d.dimensionString := "";
      d.area := 0.0; d.perimeter := 0.0;
      d.length := 0.0; d.width := 0.0;
      d.diameter := 0.0;
      d.base := 0.0; d.height := 0.0
   END ClearDialog;

   PROCEDURE SetDialog (s: S.Shape);
   BEGIN
      s.GetIDString(d.idString);
      s.GetDimensionString(d.dimensionString);
      d.area := s.Area();
      d.perimeter := s.Perimeter()
   END SetDialog;

   PROCEDURE Clear*;
   BEGIN
      ClearDialog;
      C.Clear(cList);
      Dialog.Update(d)
   END Clear;

   PROCEDURE Next*;
      VAR
         shape: S.Shape;
   BEGIN
      IF ~C.Empty(cList) THEN
         C.GoNext(cList);
         shape := C.NodeContent(cList) (S.Shape);
         SetDialog(shape);
         Dialog.Update(d)
      END
   END Next;
```

Figure 23.9

A program that produces the sequence of screen shots in Figure 23.8.

```
PROCEDURE Insert*;
  VAR
    shape: S.Shape;
BEGIN
  NEW(shape);
  CASE d.shapeNumber OF
  0:
    shape.SetRectangleState(MAX(0.0, d.length), MAX(0.0, d.width)) |
  1:
    shape.SetCircleState(MAX(0.0, d.diameter)) |
  2:
    (* Problem for the student *)
    HALT(100)
  END;
  C.Insert(cList, shape);
  SetDialog(shape);
  Dialog.Update(d)
END Insert;

PROCEDURE RectangleGuard* (VAR par: Dialog.Par);
BEGIN
  par.disabled := d.shapeNumber # 0
END RectangleGuard;

PROCEDURE CircleGuard* (VAR par: Dialog.Par);
BEGIN
  par.disabled := d.shapeNumber # 1
END CircleGuard;

PROCEDURE TriangleGuard* (VAR par: Dialog.Par);
BEGIN
  par.disabled := d.shapeNumber # 2
END TriangleGuard;

BEGIN
  Clear
END Pbox23A.
```

Figure 23.9
Continued.

The import list

IMPORT Dialog, C := PboxCListADT, S := PboxShapeObj;

sets up a convenient abbreviation scheme. Component Pascal allows you to rename
an imported module using the alias symbol :=. This import list renames module
PboxCListADT as simply C. Everywhere in this module that you would normally
place the name PboxCListADT, you can now place the abbreviation C. The same substitution applies to PboxShapeObj with its abbreviation S. Once you redefine
imported module names like this you cannot revert back to the long form.

The import abbreviation

Example 23.2 In Figure 23.9, the procedure heading

PROCEDURE SetDialog (s: S.Shape);

would be written

PROCEDURE SetDialog (s: PboxShapeObj.Shape);

if the import list had not defined the abbreviation S. If you write the procedure heading the second way with the abbreviation defined, however, the module will not compile. ∎

Buttons Clear, Next, and Insert are obviously linked to exported procedures Clear, Next, and Insert. Procedure Clear operates the same way the corresponding procedure does in Figure 21.17.

Procedure Clear

Procedure Next has a local variable shape of type PboxShapeObj.Shape. The procedure checks if cList is empty, and if it is not calls GoNext to advance it to the next entry. Then it sets shape to the content of the current node by calling NodeContent. Now that shape has the content of the current node the procedure calls SetDialog, passing shape as the actual parameter that corresponds to formal parameter s. The first statement in SetDialog

Procedure Next

s.GetIDString(d.idString)

changes d.IdString to the name of shape s. The dimensions, area, and perimeter fields get set similarly. Finally, after the return to procedure Next, the dialog is updated so the changes in the d interactor will be made visible.

Procedure Insert also has a local variable shape of type PboxShapeObj.Shape. To insert a new shape into the linked list based on the user's request, the procedure executes

Procedure Insert

NEW(shape)

to allocate a new shape from the heap. The interactor field d.shapeNumber is linked to the set of radio buttons in the dialog box. The level of the button for a rectangle is set to 0, for a circle is set to 1, and for a triangle is set to 2. Procedure Insert uses a CASE statement, testing the value of d.shapeNumber, to determine what shape the user wants to store. If the user wants to store a rectangle as in Figure 23.8(b) d.shapeNumber will have the value 0 and procedure Insert will execute

shape.SetRectangleState(MAX(0.0, d.length), MAX(0.0, d.width))

The first MAX function returns the maximum of the two real values 0.0 and d.length. Method SetRectangleState has a precondition that neither of its formal parameters can be negative. The purpose of MAX is guarantee that the precondition will be met. If the user enters a negative value for the length or width of the rectangle, zero will be stored instead. Procedure Insert concludes by calling the Insert procedure for the circular list, setting the output fields in the d interactor, and updating the dialog box to make the changes visible.

Control guards

In Figure 23.8(c), the radio button for the rectangle is on, and fields to input the length and width are available, while those to input the diameter of a circle or the base and height of a triangle are not. An important user-interface design principle is that the user should have a visual cue of those actions which can and cannot be performed on a dialog box. The cue is usually the dimming of those elements that cannot be selected. Figure 23.8(c) has the circle and triangle input fields dimmed while the user can input information about a rectangle. Figure 23.8(d) has the rectangle and triangle fields dimmed while the user can input information about a circle.

A user-interface design principle

The ease with which the programmer can implement this user-interface design principle is a testament to the power of the BlackBox framework. The technique is based on the fact that BlackBox is a true framework and not just a collection of server modules. Consider the dialog box in Figure 23.8(c). There are three buttons labeled Clear, Next, and Insert. The program to implement the dialog box has three corresponding procedures that are executed when the buttons are pressed. The radio buttons correspond to d.shapeNumber, which will have the value 0 with the Rectangle button pressed. Furthermore, the input and output fields correspond to fields in the d interactor record.

If the user presses the Circle radio button, the effect on the dialog box will be to dim the rectangle input and allow input for the circle as is done in Figure 23.8(d). But, it seems that the only effect of pressing the Circle button is to change the value of d.shapeNumber from 0 to 1. How can you program the dialog box to dim the rectangle input when d.shapeNumber gets the value 1? After all, pressing the radio button does not cause any of your procedures to execute.

The answer is that the BlackBox framework continually monitors the appearance of the dialog box. It can automatically detect the change in d.shapeNumber the instant it occurs. Somehow you need to inform the framework when a field should be dimmed. But you cannot do that by calling a procedure, because the event of pressing a radio button does not cause any of your procedures to execute. The solution is for you to write a procedure that the *framework* calls. Such a procedure is known as a control guard.

Every forms control has a potential control guard that you can link to with the Inspector. You write a guard, which is an exported procedure, in your module. Then use the Inspector to link to the guard. For example, in Figure 23.8(c) one of the forms controls is the input field for the length of a rectangle. The user has entered 4.0 in the field. This control is linked to d.length in the d interactor. Figure 23.10 shows the Inspector for this control. You can see from the Link field of the Inspector that this is indeed the Inspector for d.length. There is a Guard field in the Inspector, in which the programmer has entered Pbox23A.RectangleGuard. This is the control guard, which is an exported procedure in Figure 23.9.

The presence of procedure RectangleGuard may seem strange in Figure 23.9, because nowhere in the module is a call to it. You do not call procedure Rectangle-Guard; the framework does. When does the framework call the control guard?

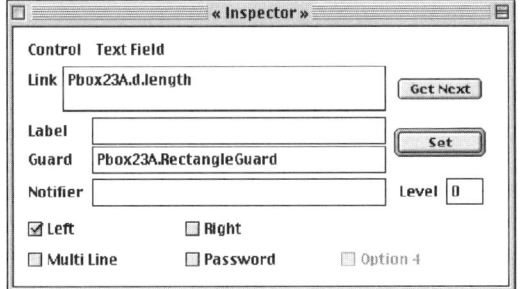

(a) MacOS.

(b) MSWindows.

Whenever it needs to, namely when you call Dialog.Update and when the user changes the state of the dialog box, like when she presses a radio button. You, as an applications programmer, do not need to concern yourself with those details of when and how the framework calls your guard. All you need to do is provide the entry in the Inspector for the control guard. The framework will see to it that the guard is called at the appropriate times. This arrangement is not that different from the programs you have been writing in BlackBox from the beginning. Most programs implement a dialog box with buttons for the user to click on to initiate an action. Your programs simply supply exported procedures that the framework calls at the appropriate time.

The guard for the rectangle's length input field is

```
PROCEDURE RectangleGuard* (VAR par: Dialog.Par);
BEGIN
    par.disabled := d.shapeNumber # 0
END RectangleGuard;
```

The rectangle's width input field is linked to the same guard. The guard procedure has one formal parameter par whose type is Dialog.Par. It is called by reference, meaning that if this procedure modifies par, the corresponding actual parameter in the calling program will be modified. What is the actual parameter? Some variable in the framework that you do not see, because the framework calls RectangleGuard instead of you calling it.

To investigate the type Dialog.Par you can consult the documentation of Dialog, part of which is shown in Figure 23.11. From the documentation, a variable of type Par has five fields, the first four of which are boolean. The first boolean field is named disabled. If par.disabled is set to false, the corresponding control in the dialog box will not be disabled. That is, it will be available for the user to access. If par.disabled is set to true, the control will be dimmed to show that the user cannot access it. Any attempt at accessing the control will result in no action. The rectangle guard sets par.disabled to the boolean expression

Figure 23.10
Links that must be entered in the Inspector to enable the guards for dimming controls in the dialog box.

d.shapeNumber # 0

which will disable the rectangle's width input field if d.shapeNumber is not equal to 0. Because the rectangle's width input field is linked to the same guard it will be disabled under the same circumstances.

```
DEFINITION Dialog;

   TYPE
      Par = RECORD
         disabled: BOOLEAN;
         checked: BOOLEAN;
         undef: BOOLEAN;
         readOnly: BOOLEAN;
         label: String
      END;
```

Figure 23.11
A partial listing of the documentation for the Dialog module.

The arrangement between BlackBox and the application programmer where the framework calls the programmer's procedures is what distinguishes a true framework from a library of server modules. It is known as the Hollywood Principle, "Don't call us. We'll call you." The ability to program a graphical user interface with so much power and yet so much simplicity from the application programmer's perspective is due to the BlackBox framework as much as it is due to the power and simplicity of the Component Pascal language.

The Hollywood Principle

A shape class implementation

Figure 23.13 is the implementation of the shape class whose interface is in Figure 23.7. The exported type Shape is a pointer to a record with four fields as shown in Figure 23.12. The first field is an integer kind, which indicates what kind of shape is stored—0 for rectangle and 1 for circle. The second and third fields are length and width for storing the length and width of a rectangle when kind has value 0. The fourth field is diameter for storing the diameter of a circle when kind has value 1. Modification of the Shape structure to accommodate triangles is left as a problem for the student.

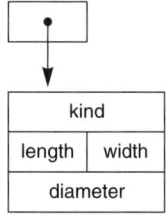

Figure 23.12
The structure of type Shape in Figure 23.13.

```
MODULE  PboxShapeObj;
   IMPORT PboxStrings, Math;

   TYPE
      Shape* = POINTER TO RECORD
         kind: INTEGER;
         length, width: REAL;
         diameter: REAL
      END;
```

Figure 23.13
Implementation of the shape class with class abstraction only. Figure 23.7 shows the interface for this class.

```
PROCEDURE (s: Shape) GetIDString* (OUT str: ARRAY OF CHAR), NEW;
BEGIN
    CASE s.kind OF
    0:
        str := "Rectangle" |
    1:
        str := "Circle"
    END
END GetIDString;

PROCEDURE (s: Shape) GetDimensionString* (OUT str: ARRAY OF CHAR), NEW;
    VAR
        temp: ARRAY 16 OF CHAR;
BEGIN
    CASE s.kind OF
    0:
        PboxStrings.RealToString(s.length, 1, 3, temp);
        str := "Length = " + temp + ", ";
        PboxStrings.RealToString(s.width, 1, 3, temp);
        str := str + "Width = " + temp |
    1:
        PboxStrings.RealToString(s.diameter, 1, 3, temp);
        str := "Diameter = " + temp
    END
END GetDimensionString;

PROCEDURE (s: Shape) Area* (): REAL, NEW;
BEGIN
    CASE s.kind OF
    0:
        RETURN s.length * s.width |
    1:
        RETURN Math.Pi() * s.diameter * s.diameter / 4.0
    END
END Area;

PROCEDURE (s: Shape) Perimeter* (): REAL, NEW;
BEGIN
    CASE s.kind OF
    0:
        RETURN 2.0 * (s.length + s.width) |
    1:
        RETURN Math.Pi() * s.diameter
    END
END Perimeter;
```

Figure 23.13
Continued.

```
PROCEDURE (s: Shape) SetRectangleState* (length, width: REAL), NEW;
BEGIN
    ASSERT((length >= 0.0) & (width >= 0.0), 20);
    s.kind := 0;
    s.length := length;
    s.width := width
END SetRectangleState;

PROCEDURE (s: Shape) SetCircleState* (diameter: REAL), NEW;
BEGIN
    ASSERT(diameter >= 0.0, 20);
    s.kind := 1;
    s.diameter := diameter
END SetCircleState;

END PboxShapeObj.
```

Figure 23.13
Continued.

Methods SetIdString, GetDimensionString, Area, and Perimeter all have a similar control structure. Each method first determines what kind of shape is stored using a CASE statement on s.kind. If s.kind has value 0, the method processes the data assuming that a rectangle is stored and uses s.length and s.width accordingly. If s.kind has value 1, the method processes the data assuming that a circle is stored and uses s.diameter accordingly.

Methods SetRectangleState and SetCircleState, unlike the previous methods, change the state of s. Each method has a precondition that does not allow the dimensions of the state to be negative. The precondition is implemented with the usual ASSERT statement. The input of the set state methods are values of the dimensions of the shape. The method simply sets the kind field to the integer code for that state and transfers the dimension values to the corresponding fields in the shape's record.

The program of Figure 23.9 stores the shapes in the circular list provided by PboxCListADT. The dialog box in Figure 23.8(e) shows a dialog box where the user has entered a circle of diameter 6.0 and pressed the Next button so that the current shape is a rectangle of length 2.0 and width 3.0. Figure 23.14 shows the corresponding data structure.

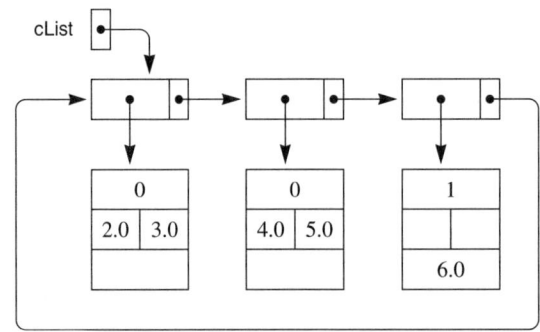

Figure 23.14
The data structure that corresponds to the screen shot of Figure 23.8(e) with the shape of PboxShapeObj.

The difference in syntax for defining and calling a method with class abstraction compared to a procedure with procedure abstraction does not illustrate the power of object-oriented design. After all, there is no inherent benefit to putting an actual parameter in front of a method name instead of enclosing it in parentheses after a function name. The only thing the object-oriented syntax does is to emphasize that functions are bound to classes along with the data. The real power of object-orientation comes with yet another level of abstraction—behavior abstraction.

Behavior abstraction

The program in the previous section processed different shapes using class abstraction. The class Shape in PboxShapeObj is a pointer to a record that contains a kind field to specify what kind of shape is stored in the record. The methods for Shape test the kind field with a CASE statement to determine the appropriate processing to perform. Instead of adopting the viewpoint of class abstraction, where a shape is simply a collection of data and methods that correspond to some specific shape, suppose you take a further step towards abstraction and collect several different shapes together to form an abstract shape. What is common that can be abstracted out?

That is, what do rectangles, circles, and right triangles have in common? They are certainly not all specified by length and width as is the rectangle. A circle, for example, is specified by its diameter. Because dimensions for different objects are specified differently, you cannot include the dimensions in the abstract shape. However, all closed shapes have an area and a perimeter. So, you can at least include those. You must be careful, however, because the algorithm for computing the area of a circle is not the same as the algorithm for computing the area of a right triangle. Even though the abstract shape will specify a method for computing the area and perimeter, it cannot implement it because the algorithm depends on the specific object. Furthermore, each shape has a method to set its ID string and its dimension string.

Figure 23.15
Behavior abstraction that combines class abstraction for two different classes into a single abstract class.

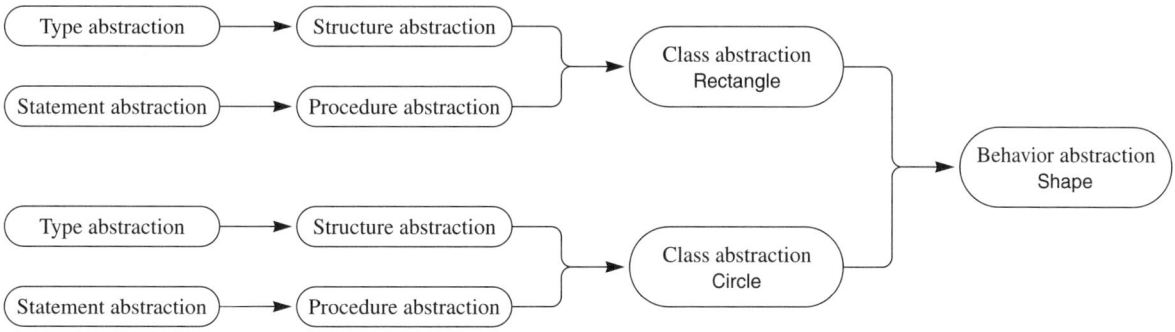

Figure 23.15 is a representation of the behavior abstraction process. The figure shows the abstraction processes for data and control culminating in class abstraction for Rectangle and the same abstraction processes culminating in class abstraction

for Circle. Behavior abstraction combines the specific shapes Rectangle and Circle into the abstract class Shape.

Compare Figure 23.15, which shows the abstraction process for a shape using behavior abstraction, with Figure 23.6, which shows the abstraction process using only class abstraction. In Figure 23.6, the concepts of rectangle and circle are merged with the concept of shape. Class Shape is a kind of hybrid, whose data is a combination of fields that must accommodate information for both rectangles and circles and a field kind to tell them apart. However, Figure 23.15 uses class abstraction for each individual shape and behavior abstraction for the abstract shape. This is a significant difference that has major consequences in the program.

Inheritance

In Figure 23.15, the object-oriented relation between class Rectangle and class Shape is that of inheritance. Rectangle inherits from Shape. Similarly, Circle inherits from Shape. The Component Pascal terminology for the inheritance relation is type extension. Type Rectangle is an extension of Shape, which is called the base type. Circle is also an extension of Shape. Figure 23.16 is the interface for Pbox-ShapeAbs, which implements the inheritance relationship between the classes.

Type extension and the base type

```
DEFINITION PboxShapeAbs;

    TYPE
        Shape = POINTER TO ABSTRACT RECORD
            (s: Shape) GetIDString (OUT str: ARRAY OF CHAR), NEW, ABSTRACT;
            (s: Shape) GetDimensionString (OUT str: ARRAY OF CHAR), NEW, ABSTRACT;
            (s: Shape) Area (): REAL, NEW, ABSTRACT;
            (s: Shape) Perimeter (): REAL, NEW, ABSTRACT
        END;

        Rectangle = POINTER TO RECORD (Shape)
            (r: Rectangle) GetIDString (OUT str: ARRAY OF CHAR);
            (r: Rectangle) GetDimensionString (OUT str: ARRAY OF CHAR);
            (r: Rectangle) Area (): REAL;
            (r: Rectangle) Perimeter (): REAL;
            (r: Rectangle) SetState (length, width: REAL), NEW
        END;

        Circle = POINTER TO RECORD (Shape)
            (c: Circle) GetIDString (OUT str: ARRAY OF CHAR);
            (c: Circle) GetDimensionString (OUT str: ARRAY OF CHAR);
            (c: Circle) Area (): REAL;
            (c: Circle) Perimeter (): REAL;
            (c: Circle) SetState (diameter: REAL), NEW
        END;

END PboxShapeAbs.
```

Figure 23.16
The interface for a general geometric shape. that uses behavior abstraction.

In the declaration of the Shape type

Shape = POINTER TO ABSTRACT RECORD

the word ABSTRACT is a record attribute. It indicates that the class Shape is an abstract class, which means it cannot be instantiated. No variables or fields of such a record can ever exist.

Example 23.3 Suppose Shape is declared as in Figure 23.16 and you have a local variable myShape declared as

VAR
    myShape: Shape;

The instantiation

NEW(myShape)

is illegal and will not compile, because Shape is abstract.   ▌

Why declare a type if you can never instantiate it? Because an abstract type is not used by itself. Instead, it is a form to be used as a guide for creating concrete types that are extensions of it. You can think of a superclass as a blueprint for the sub- *Superclass and subclass* classes that inherit from it.

The first method in the abstract shape is

(s: Shape) GetIDString (OUT str: ARRAY OF CHAR), NEW, ABSTRACT

It has two method attributes, NEW and ABSTRACT. In the same way that an abstract class can never be instantiated, an abstract method can never contain any executable statements and can never be called. Why declare a method if it can never be called? Again, because it is not used by itself. Instead, it is a blueprint for the corresponding method of the subclass. In this case, the blueprint says that the method of the sub- class must be named GetIDString and must have one parameter called by result of type ARRAY OF CHAR. A record containing abstract methods must be abstract. The *Rules for abstract records* attribute NEW must be used on all newly introduced methods. *and abstract methods*

The remaining methods of Shape—GetDimensionString, Area, and Perimeter— each have method attributes NEW and ABSTRACT. It is the responsibility of the sub- classes to implement the methods using the same method names and signatures, that is, the same number and types of the formal parameters.

In the declaration of type Rectangle

Rectangle = POINTER TO RECORD (Shape)

the base type is enclosed in parentheses after the reserved word RECORD. The dec- laration states that Rectangle inherits from Shape; or, Rectangle is the subclass and Shape is the superclass; or, Rectangle is an extension of Shape. The idea of inherit- ance is that the specific inherits from the general. Shape is general, and Rectangle is specific. The fundamental class assignment rule is that you can assign the specific to the general, but you cannot assign the general to the specific.

The fundamental class assignment rule

Example 23.4   If myShape is a formal paramter of type Shape and myRectangle is a local variable of type Rectangle, then the assignment

myShape := myRectangle

is legal, but the assignment

myRectangle := myShape

is not legal.   ▉

The first method of class Rectangle is

(r: Rectangle) GetIDString (OUT str: ARRAY OF CHAR)

It has the same name as the first method of class Shape and the same signature. The only difference is that the type Rectangle in the receiver (r: Rectangle) is a subclass of the type Shape in the receiver (s: Shape). Furthermore, the method GetIDString for Rectangle is neither ABSTRACT nor NEW. Because it is not ABSTRACT, it has statements and can be called. Because it is not NEW, it is based on a previously declared method. All these characteristics indicate that GetIDString for Rectangle is a concrete implementation of GetIDString for Shape. Methods GetDimensionString, Area, and Perimeter have the same characteristics as GetIDString. They are all concrete implementations of the corresponding methods of Shape.

The last method of class Rectangle, however,

(r: Rectangle) SetState (length, width: REAL), NEW

is not an implementation of a previously declared method. It is NEW but not ABSTRACT. There is no corresponding method in the superclass of Rectangle.

The declaration of class Circle mirrors that of class Rectangle. Circle is a subclass of Shape. It implements the four methods declared in Shape—GetIDString, GetDimensionString, Area, Perimeter—and declares its own fifth method SetState that is not an implementation of a previously declared abstract method.

Comparing the interface in Figure 23.16 with that in Figure 23.7 it should be obvious that each method of PboxShapeAbs does the same processing as that in the corresponding method of PboxShapeObj. Namely, GetIDString gives str a string value that describes the name of the shape, GetDimensionString gives str a string value that describes the dimensions of the shape with three places past the decimal, Area returns the area of the shape, and Perimeter returns the perimeter of the shape. SetState for Rectangle sets the state to a rectangle and SetState for Circle sets the state for a circle. You can see that the SetState methods cannot be specified by the abstract class Shape, because the parameter lists are different for rectangles and circles. Signatures must be identical between superclass and subclass methods, which would be impossible for SetState.

Polymorphism

Figure 23.17 is a program that implements the same dialog box as that shown in Figure 23.8. From the user's perspective, there is no difference in the behavior of the dialog box between the two versions. However, the program of Figure 23.17 uses behavior abstraction with polymorphism.

```
MODULE Pbox23B;
   IMPORT Dialog, C := PboxCListADT, S := PboxShapeAbs;

   VAR
      d*: RECORD
         idString-, dimensionString- : ARRAY 64 OF CHAR;
         area-, perimeter-: REAL;
         shapeNumber*: INTEGER;
         length*, width*: REAL; (* for rectangle *)
         diameter*: REAL; (* for circle *)
         base*, height*: REAL (* for triangle *)
      END;
      cList: C.CList;

   PROCEDURE ClearDialog;
   BEGIN
      d.idString := ""; d.dimensionString := "";
      d.area := 0.0; d.perimeter := 0.0;
      d.length := 0.0; d.width := 0.0;
      d.diameter := 0.0;
      d.base := 0.0; d.height := 0.0
   END ClearDialog;

   PROCEDURE SetDialog (s: S.Shape);
   BEGIN
      s.GetIDString(d.idString);
      s.GetDimensionString(d.dimensionString);
      d.area := s.Area();
      d.perimeter := s.Perimeter()
   END SetDialog;

   PROCEDURE Clear*;
   BEGIN
      ClearDialog;
      C.Clear(cList);
      Dialog.Update(d)
   END Clear;
```

Figure 23.17

A program that produces the same output as the one in Figure 23.9 but that uses behavior abstraction.

Figure 23.17
Continued.

```
PROCEDURE Next*;
  VAR
    shape: S.Shape;
BEGIN
  IF ~C.Empty(cList) THEN
    C.GoNext(cList);
    shape := C.NodeContent(cList) (S.Shape);
    SetDialog(shape);
    Dialog.Update(d)
  END
END Next;

PROCEDURE Insert*;
  VAR
    rectangle: S.Rectangle;
    circle: S.Circle;
BEGIN
  CASE d.shapeNumber OF
  0:
    NEW(rectangle);
    rectangle.SetState(MAX(0.0, d.length), MAX(0.0, d.width));
    C.Insert(cList, rectangle);
    SetDialog(rectangle) |
  1:
    NEW(circle);
    circle.SetState(MAX(0.0, d.diameter));
    C.Insert(cList, circle);
    SetDialog(circle) |
  2:
    (* Problem for the student *)
  END;
  Dialog.Update(d)
END Insert;

PROCEDURE RectangleGuard* (VAR par: Dialog.Par);
BEGIN
  par.disabled := d.shapeNumber # 0
END RectangleGuard;

PROCEDURE CircleGuard* (VAR par: Dialog.Par);
BEGIN
  par.disabled := d.shapeNumber # 1
END CircleGuard;

PROCEDURE TriangleGuard* (VAR par: Dialog.Par);
BEGIN
  par.disabled := d.shapeNumber # 2
END TriangleGuard;
```

BEGIN
  Clear
END Pbox23B.

Figure 23.17
Continued.

A comparison of modules Pbox23A in Figure 23.9 and Pbox23B in Figure 23.17 shows little apparent difference except for procedure Insert. Pbox23B.Insert has two local variables—rectangle with type PboxShapeABS.Rectangle and circle with type PboxShapeAbs.Circle. Suppose the user enters information about a rectangle and clicks the Insert button. The CASE statement determines that the value of d.ShapeNumber is 0 and executes

NEW(rectangle)

In Pbox23A, the corresponding statement is NEW(shape) where shape has type PboxShapeObj.Shape. But in Pbox23B, that would be impossible because PboxShapeAbs.Shape is abstract and you cannot instantiate an abstract class. That is why Pbox23B.Insert needs two local variables each with a concrete type instead of one local variable with an abstract type.

The next statement

rectangle.SetState(MAX(0.0, d.length), MAX(0.0, d.width))

calls method SetState. But two SetState methods are imported from PboxShapeAbs—one for a rectangle and one for a circle. How does Component Pascal know which one to call? By the type of the receiver. With this call, the actual parameter rectangle has type Rectangle. So, Component Pascal calls the SetState method whose receiver has the same type. The effect of the call is to set the dimensions of rectangle according to the user input.

Then the call

C.Insert(cList, rectangle)

executes procedure PboxCListADT.Insert. Actual parameter rectangle is a pointer to a record extended from PboxShapeAbs.Shape while the corresponding formal parameter val is a pointer to ANYREC. This is an example of the fundamental class assignment rule applied to parameters. The formal parameter can be general and the actual parameter specific, but the formal parameter cannot be specific and the actual parameter general. In this example, Shape inherits from ANYREC, and Rectangle inherits from Shape. Therefore, Rectangle, which is specific, inherits from ANYREC, which is general.

The fundamental class assignment rule applied to parameters

The next statement in Pbox23B.Insert

SetDialog(rectangle)

calls procedure Pbox23B.SetDialog. Here again the fundamental class assignment rule applied to parameters comes into play. The formal parameter s has type Shape, which is general, and the actual parameter rectangle has type Rectangle, which is specific. As it is with class assignments, formal parameter s now has two types. Its static type is Shape, while its dynamic type is Rectangle.

The first statement in Pbox23B.SetDialog is

s.GetIDString(d.idString)   *Polymorphism*

which illustrates behavior abstraction with polymorphism. The question is, How does Component Pascal know which GetIDString to call? The situation is different from the call to SetState. In that case, the actual parameter is rectangle, which has type Rectangle. Component Pascal can determine from the interface in Figure 23.16 that there is a method with a Rectangle receiver and call that one. But in this case, the actual parameter is s, which has type Shape. The interface shows that the GetID-String with a Shape receiver is abstract.

(s: Shape) GetIDString (OUT str: ARRAY OF CHAR), NEW, ABSTRACT

Therefore, it has no statements and cannot be called.

The solution to this problem is at the heart of polymorphism. The only methods that can be called are the concrete ones

(r: Rectangle) GetIDString (OUT str: ARRAY OF CHAR)

and

(c: Circle) GetIDString (OUT str: ARRAY OF CHAR)

which are the methods that implement the corresponding abstract method. But the question remains, How does Component Pascal know which of the concrete methods to call? It knows, not from the *static* type of s at compile time, but from its *dynamic* type at execution time. In this scenario, because the dynamic type of s is Rectangle it calls the GetIDString whose receiver has type Rectangle. The selection of one method among several identically named methods based on the dynamic type of the actual parameter for the receiver is called polymorphic dispatch.   *Polymorphic dispatch*

The remaining method calls in PBox23B.SetDialog are all based on polymorphic dispatch. The formal parameter s has static type Shape, but dynamic type Rectangle. Therefore, the corresponding method implemented for Rectangle gets called. Suppose the user were entering data for a circle. In that case Pbox23B.Insert would execute

NEW(circle)

followed by setting the state of circle and inserting it into cList. Then, the procedure call

SetDialog(circle)

would give formal parameter s in procedure SetDialog the dynamic type Circle. The method calls would all be to the ones with a Circle receiver.

An abstract shape class implementation

Figure 23.19 is the implementation of the shape class whose interface is in Figure 23.16. The exported type Shape is a pointer to an abstract record with no fields. Figure 23.18(a) depicts the abstraction as a cloud. Class Rectangle inherits from Shape. Its record has two fields, length and width, for storing the length and width of a rectangle as Figure 23.18(b) shows. Class Circle also inherits from Shape. Its record has one field, diameter, for storing the diameter of a circle. Compare Figure 23.18 with Figure 23.12 where only class abstraction is used without behavior abstraction. With behavior abstraction there is no need for the kind field to determine what kind of shape is being processed.

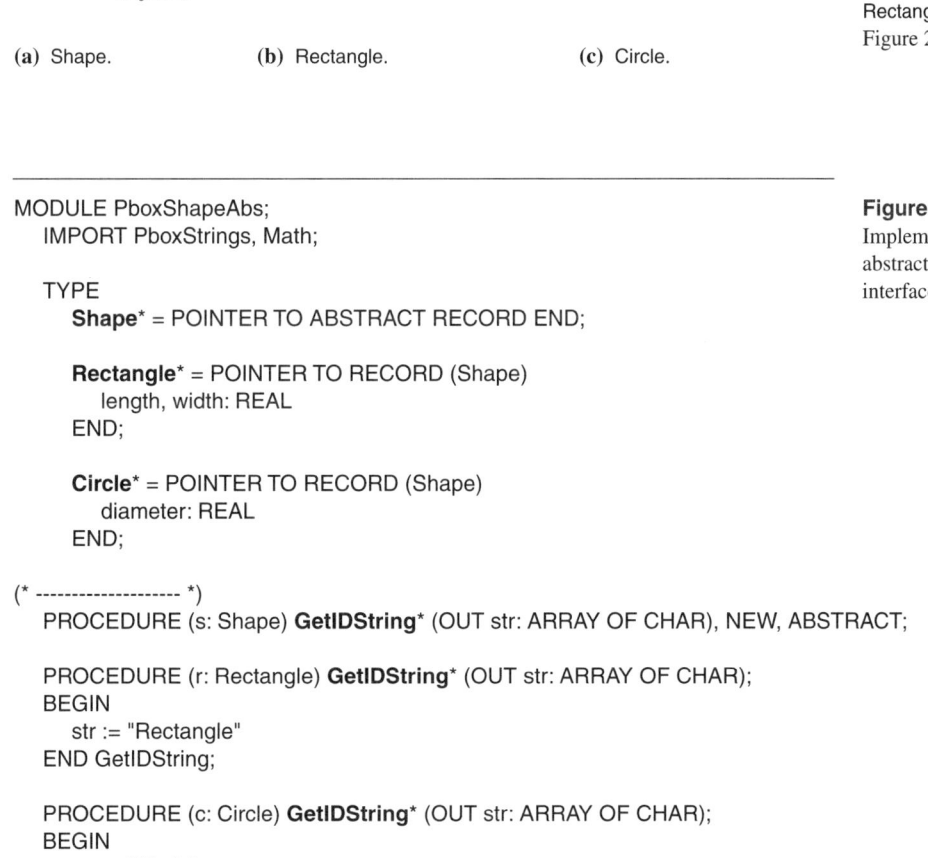

length	width

diameter

(a) Shape. **(b)** Rectangle. **(c)** Circle.

Figure 23.18
The structure of type Shape, Rectangle, and Circle in Figure 23.19.

```
MODULE PboxShapeAbs;
   IMPORT PboxStrings, Math;

   TYPE
      Shape* = POINTER TO ABSTRACT RECORD END;

      Rectangle* = POINTER TO RECORD (Shape)
         length, width: REAL
      END;

      Circle* = POINTER TO RECORD (Shape)
         diameter: REAL
      END;

(* ------------------- *)
   PROCEDURE (s: Shape) GetIDString* (OUT str: ARRAY OF CHAR), NEW, ABSTRACT;

   PROCEDURE (r: Rectangle) GetIDString* (OUT str: ARRAY OF CHAR);
   BEGIN
      str := "Rectangle"
   END GetIDString;

   PROCEDURE (c: Circle) GetIDString* (OUT str: ARRAY OF CHAR);
   BEGIN
      str := "Circle"
   END GetIDString;
```

Figure 23.19
Implementation of the abstract class Shape whose interface is in Figure 23.16.

```
(* ------------------- *)
   PROCEDURE (s: Shape) GetDimensionString* (OUT str: ARRAY OF CHAR), NEW, ABSTRACT;

   PROCEDURE (r: Rectangle) GetDimensionString* (OUT str: ARRAY OF CHAR);
      VAR
         temp: ARRAY 16 OF CHAR;
   BEGIN
      PboxStrings.RealToString(r.length, 1, 3, temp);
      str := "Length = " + temp + ",  ";
      PboxStrings.RealToString(r.width, 1, 3, temp);
      str := str + "Width = " + temp
   END GetDimensionString;

   PROCEDURE (c: Circle) GetDimensionString* (OUT str: ARRAY OF CHAR);
      VAR
         temp: ARRAY 16 OF CHAR;
   BEGIN
      PboxStrings.RealToString(c.diameter, 1, 4, temp);
      str := "Diameter = " + temp
   END GetDimensionString;

(* ------------------- *)
   PROCEDURE (s: Shape) Area* (): REAL, NEW, ABSTRACT;

   PROCEDURE (r: Rectangle) Area* (): REAL;
   BEGIN
      RETURN r.length * r.width
   END Area;

   PROCEDURE (c: Circle) Area* (): REAL;
   BEGIN
      RETURN Math.Pi() * c.diameter * c.diameter / 4.0
   END Area;

(* ------------------- *)
   PROCEDURE (s: Shape) Perimeter* (): REAL, NEW, ABSTRACT;

   PROCEDURE (r: Rectangle) Perimeter* (): REAL;
   BEGIN
      RETURN 2.0 * (r.length + r.width)
   END Perimeter;

   PROCEDURE (c: Circle) Perimeter* (): REAL;
   BEGIN
      RETURN Math.Pi() * c.diameter
   END Perimeter;
```

Figure 23.19
Continued.

```
(* -------------------- *)
   PROCEDURE (r: Rectangle) SetState* (length, width: REAL), NEW;
   BEGIN
      ASSERT((length >= 0.0) & (width >= 0.0), 20);
      r.length := length;
      r.width := width
   END SetState;

   PROCEDURE (c: Circle) SetState* (diameter: REAL), NEW;
   BEGIN
      ASSERT(diameter >= 0.0, 20);
      c.diameter := diameter
   END SetState;

END PboxShapeAbs.
```

Figure 23.19
Continued.

Method GetIDString for PboxShapeAbs.Rectangle has only one assignment statement

```
str := "Rectangle"
```

and GetIDString for PboxShapeAbs.Circle also has only one assignment statement

```
str := "Circle"
```

Contrast this state of affairs with the GetIDString for PboxShapeObj.Shape in Figure 23.13

```
CASE s.kind OF
0:
   str := "Rectangle" |
1:
   str := "Circle"
END
```

which uses the kind field to determine which shape is being processed. Without behavior abstraction, you need a CASE statement to process a shape. With behavior abstraction you do not.

The basic characteristic of abstraction is hidden detail. With behavior abstraction, the details of selecting what kind of shape to process are hidden. Rather than use a CASE statement to select the processing within a single method, the processing for specific shapes is separated into different methods, one for each kind of shape, which are then called with polymorphic dispatch. Of course, hiding the detail in a lower level of abstraction does not eliminate the detail. Component Pascal must maintain the equivalent of a kind field behind the scenes. It stores data to identify the specific concrete class each time the program executes the NEW procedure to instantiate an object. The object's internal "kind" data is consulted during execution time to determine the dynamic type of the object.

Now, consider the implications of polymorphism in a software project with dozens of modules and thousands of lines of code. The software is always in a state of flux with updates and revisions carried out continuously to satisfy the customers and keep up with the competition. Without behavior abstraction in PboxShapeObj, what does it take to add another shape like a triangle? The answer is that you must modify every method in PboxShapeObj that processes a general shape by adding an additional case for the triangle to the CASE statement. In a large software project, the required modifications for a similar revision could be extensive.

With behavior abstraction in PboxShapeAbs, what does it take to add another shape like a triangle? The answer is, You do not need to modify PboxShapeAbs at all! You can simply package your additional shape in its own module, which imports PboxShapeAbs. There is nothing in Component Pascal to prevent you from declaring a subclass in one module whose superclass is in another module. So, with behavior abstraction you do not modify existing code. You simply add code for additional features. The ability to extend an application by adding code instead of modifying existing code is probably the most important benefit of object-oriented programming. It permits a company to design an abstract class with a few concrete classes and have third-party developers write their own concrete classes to enhance the product. The plug-ins for Web browsers are implemented with this idea. For this approach to software development to be effective, the original abstract classes must be well designed.

The most important benefit of object-oriented programming

Another benefit of behavior abstraction over simple class abstraction is the savings in space for the attributes of a object. Figure 23.20 shows the data structure for the circular linked list that corresponds to Figure 23.14. With class abstraction only, you must allocate unused space for a diameter even if the shape is a rectangle, or you must allocate unused space for a width and length even if the shape is a circle. With behavior abstraction, you allocate only enough space for the attributes that are required for the object.

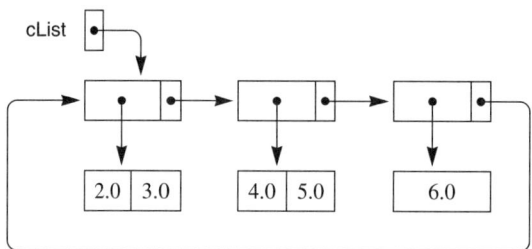

cList

2.0 | 3.0   4.0 | 5.0   6.0

Figure 23.20
The data structure that corresponds to Figure 23.14, but with the abstract shape of PboxShapeABS.

Unified Modeling Language

Figure 23.21 is a Unified Modeling Language (UML) class diagram of the classes declared in PboxShapeAbs. The UML standard specifies several diagrams other than class diagrams. Each box in a class diagram represents a class. A box has three compartments. The name of the class is always in the top compartment in a bold typeface as in **Rectangle**. The name of an abstract class is slanted as in ***Shape***. The second compartment contains the attributes, and the third compartment contains the operations. The names of abstract methods are slanted as in *GetIDString* in class Shape.

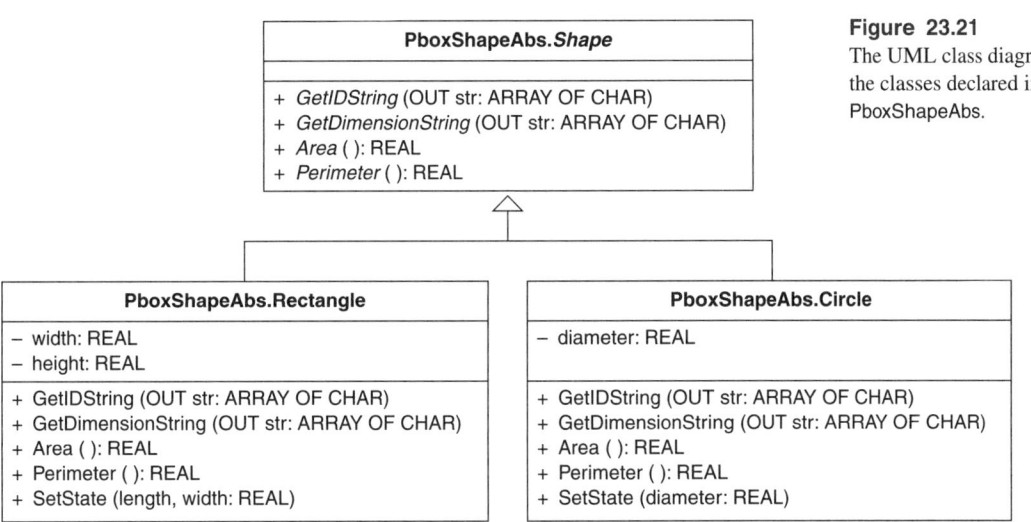

(a) The full version of the class diagram.

Figure 23.21
The UML class diagram for the classes declared in PboxShapeAbs.

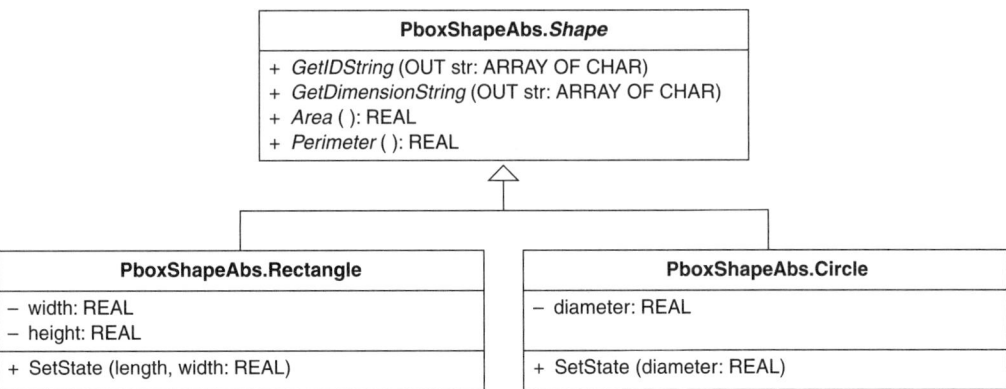

(b) The abbreviated version of the class diagram.

In UML, the receiver of a method is not shown, because it can be inferred from the class. Nor are the method attributes listed. The ABSTRACT attribute can be inferred from the slanted type. In UML terminology, items that are exported read/ write are called public and are preceded by the plus symbol +. Items that are not exported are called private and are preceded by the minus symbol −. There is no UML standard for items that are exported read-only.

Example 23.5 The method heading for GetIDString in Component Pascal is

PROCEDURE (s: Shape) **GetIDString*** (OUT str: ARRAY OF CHAR), NEW, ABSTRACT;

The receiver is (s: Shape). The method attributes are NEW and ABSTRACT. The corresponding heading in the UML class diagram is

+ *GetIDString* (OUT str: ARRAY OF CHAR)

The receiver is missing, but its type can be inferred in Figure 23.21 because it is in the Shape class box. The plus sign indicates that the method is exported. The slanted type for the name implies that the method is abstract. ∎

The triangle symbol △ is the UML notation for inheritance. The tip of the triangle points to the superclass and the other end of the triangle is connected to the subclasses. In this book, the superclass will always be an abstract class with abstract methods. Each concrete class will implement its own version of each abstract method. Figure 23.21(a) shows the full UML class diagram. The abstract class Shape has four abstract methods—GetIDString, GetDimensionString, Area, and Perimeter. Both class Rectangle and Circle implement each of these methods. Rather than repeat the abstract methods in each concrete class, this book will use an abbreviated version of the UML class diagram where the corresponding concrete methods are omitted as in Figure 23.21(b). It will be assumed that each abstract method of the superclass is implemented by each concrete subclass.

Class composition

Object-oriented design consists of defining several objects and establishing the relationships between them. Inheritance is one way that objects can be related and class composition is another. Inheritance is frequently described as the "is-a" relationship because the subclass "is a" superclass. For example, in the previous section a circle is a shape. In contrast to inheritance, class composition is described as the "has-a" relationship.

The is-a relationship

The has-a relationship

The program in this section illustrates class composition with a Pizza class. There are two kinds of pizzas, rectangular and circular. Because Shape is a class, and Pizza is a class, and a pizza has a shape, the relationship between the two is one of class composition. The Pizza class is composed of the Shape class.

An arrow with a diamond tail ◆—→ is the UML symbol for class composition. In a UML class diagram, the diamond tail touches the containing class, and the arrowhead touches the class that it contains. There is no new Component Pascal syntax to learn for class composition. Because a class is a record with various fields, to use class composition you simply put the contained class in the field of the class that you want to contain it.

Example 23.6 Suppose you want to define a class named Pizza that contains a Shape class. In Component Pascal, you would declare

Pizza* = POINTER TO RECORD
   shape*: PboxShapeAbs.Shape
END;

Figure 23.22 shows the corresponding UML class diagram. The shape field of class Pizza is in the attribute box of the Pizza class. The Pizza class contains the Shape class. So, the diamond tail in the UML class diagram touches the Pizza class box, and the arrowhead touches the Shape class box. ∎

Figure 23.22
The UML class diagram for a Pizza class that has a Shape.

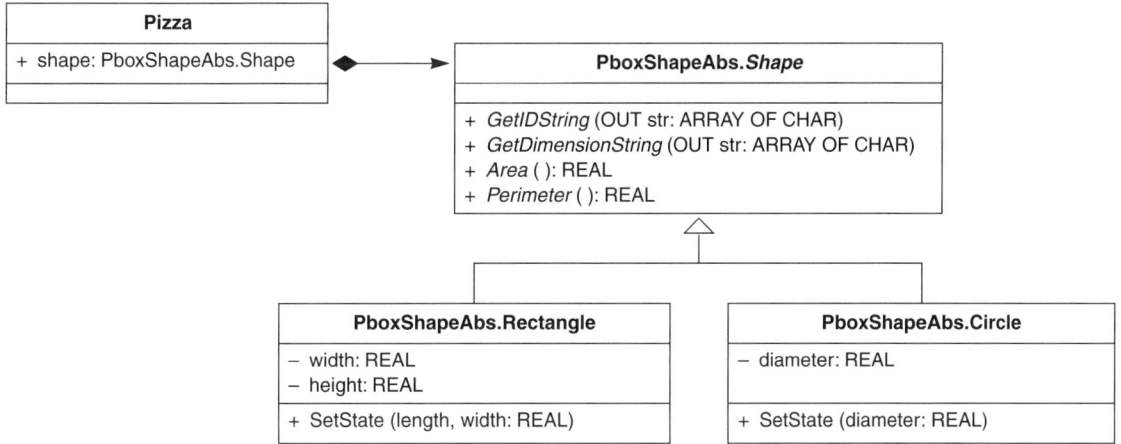

To access an element of a composed class, use the standard period "." notation for accessing the field of a record.

Example 23.7 Suppose you have a variable myPizza of type Pizza as in Figure 23.22 and an output text field in your dialog box linked to d.dimensionString. You want to display the dimensions of your pizza in your dialog box. Then, myPizza.shape is a Shape with method GetDimensionString. The statement

myPizza.shape.GetIDString(d.dimensionString)

calls the GetIDString method polymorphically to set d.dimensionString to the dimensions of the shape of myPizza. ∎

A Pizza class

In real life, a pizza has more than just a shape. It also has a crust, a topping, and a price. The crust for the Pizza class in this section can be thick or thin. The topping can be vegetarian or pepperoni, and either topping can have extra cheese. The price of the pizza depends on all these characteristics. Figure 23.23 shows a dialog box for a program that implements a Pizza class that has a shape, a topping with possible extra cheese, and a crust. It is for a restaurant where you can order a custom pizza with any shape, any size, any topping, and any crust. The program computes the price according to the pizza specification. The figure shows an order that has been entered for a rectangular pizza, 20 × 30 cm, vegetarian, thick crust. The price is computed as 7.63. The user is about to enter an order for a circular pizza, 25 cm diameter, pepperoni, thick crust with extra cheese.

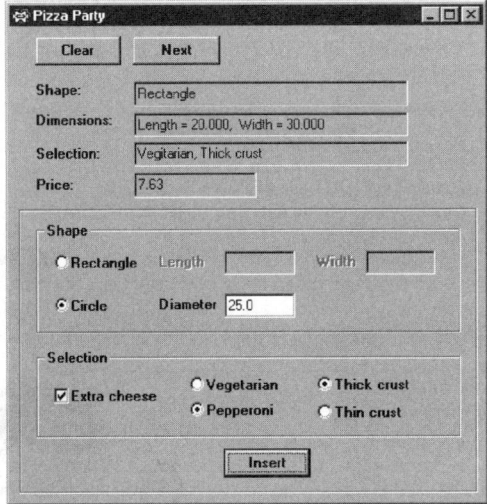

Figure 23.23
The dialog box for a program that uses the Pizza class.

The price of a pizza is determined by a fixed cost of 2.50 regardless of the shape or selection plus a variable cost that depends on the ingredients. A vegetarian pizza has a variable cost of 0.0045 per square cm, and a pepperoni pizza has a variable cost of 0.0065 per square cm. An order with extra cheese adds 0.0010 per square cm, so that the vegetarian and pepperoni toppings are 0.0055 and 0.0075 respectively. Thick crust costs 0.0030 and thin crust 0.0020. The final price is determined by adding a tax of 0.09 to the fixed plus variable cost.

Example 23.8 In Figure 23.23, the area of the rectangular pizza is

$$20 \times 30 = 600 \text{ cm}^2$$

So, the price is computed as

$$(2.50 + 0.0045 \times 600 + 0.0030 \times 600) \times 1.09 = 7.63$$

If the order had been with extra cheese the Selection would display "Vegetarian, Extra cheese, Thick crust", and the price would be computed as

$$(2.50 + 0.0055 \times 600 + 0.0030 \times 600) \times 1.09 = 8.28$$

Figure 23.24 is the UML class diagram for class Pizza in module PboxPizza. Because a pizza "has a" shape, and a pizza has a topping, and a pizza has a crust, class composition is used to include each of these three constituents in class Pizza. In the same way that Shape is an abstract class with concrete subclasses Rectangle and Circle, Topping is an abstract class with concrete subclasses Vegetarian and Pepperoni. Inheritance is the relation between class Pepperoni and class Topping, because pepperoni "is a" topping. Similarly, Crust is an abstract class with concrete subclasses Thick and Thin.

The abstract class Topping has boolean attribute extraCheese, which is true if the customer wants extra cheese on his topping and false otherwise. It is possible to duplicate the extraCheese attribute in classes Vegetarian and Pepperoni and not have it in Topping. It is usually best, however, to have those characteristics that are common to a set of classes appear only once in a more general class. Accordingly, the extraCheese attribute appears only once in class Topping.

When any subclass inherits from any superclass, the subclass inherits all the attributes of the superclass. An object of the subclass accesses the attributes of the superclass as if they were all declared as fields of the subclass. That is, you use the period "." between the name of the object and the field to access the field.

A subclass inherits the attributes of its superclass.

Example 23.9 Suppose you declare

VAR
   myPepperoni: Pepperoni;

where the classes are declared as in the UML class diagram of Figure 23.24. You have allocated myPepperoni from the heap with

NEW(myPepperoni)

and you want to set the field extraCheese in the Topping superclass to FALSE. The statement

myPepperoni.extraCheese := FALSE

performs the assignment. It is as if extraCheese is an attribute of myPepperoni directly, even though it is an attribute of the Topping superclass. ∎

Example 23.10 Suppose you declare

VAR
   myPizza: Pizza;

where the classes are declared as in the UML class diagram of Figure 23.24. If you want to set extraCheese to FALSE for myPizza, use the usual technique for class composition. Assuming a concrete topping has been allocated from the heap, the following statement performs the assignment.

myPizza.topping.extraCheese := FALSE ∎

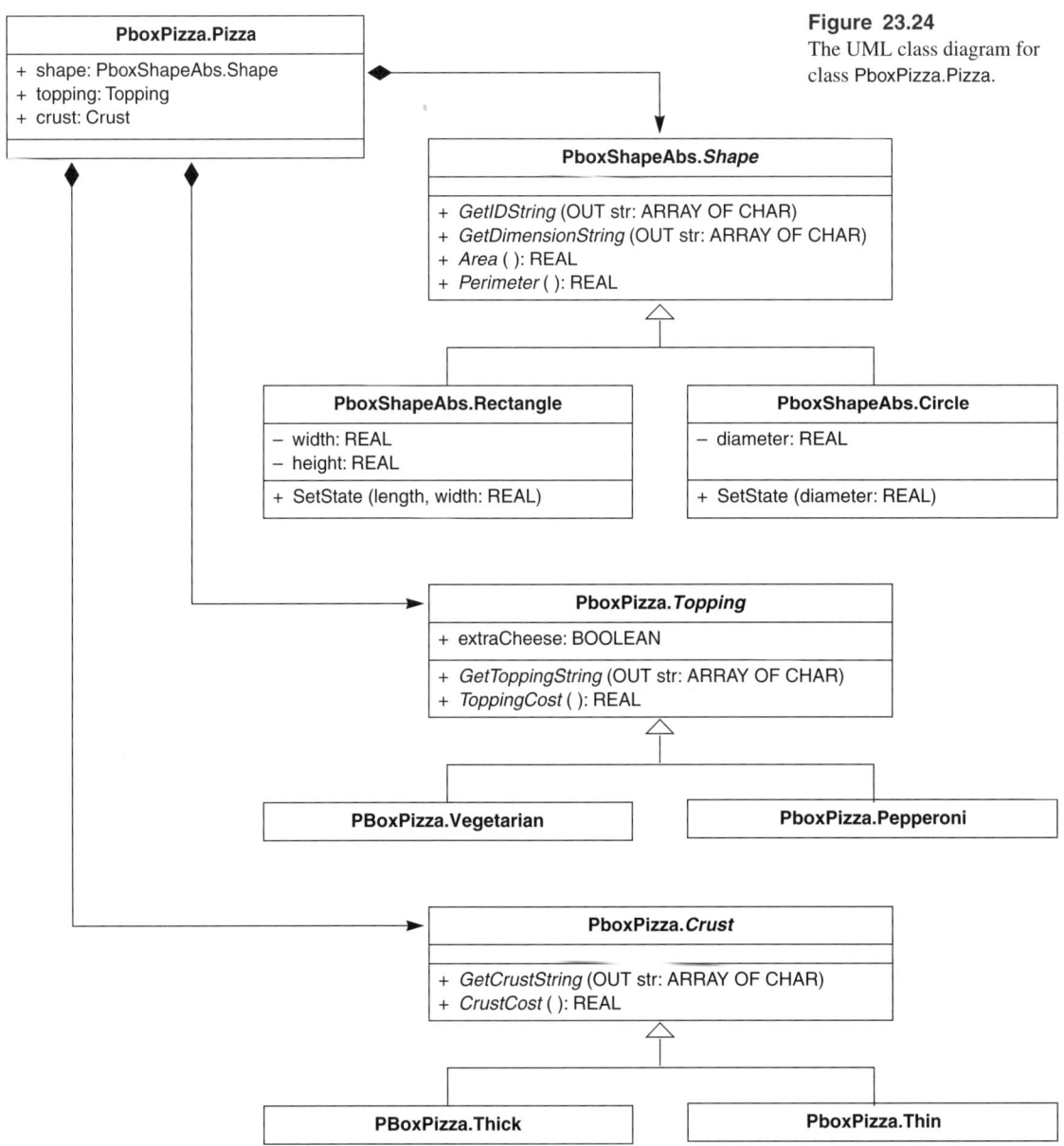

Figure 23.24
The UML class diagram for class PboxPizza.Pizza.

Classes Vegetarian and Pepperoni each implement abstract method GetTopping-String. The Vegetarian version of GetToppingString sets str to "Vegetarian" if extra-Cheese is false, and to "Vegetarian, Extra cheese" otherwise. Similarly, the Pepperoni version sets str to "Pepperoni" or "Pepperoni, Extra cheese". Method ToppingCost returns the variable cost per square cm for each topping, taking into account whether extra cheese is ordered. For the Vegetarian class, ToppingCost returns 0.0065 without extra cheese or 0.0075 with extra cheese.

The Thick and Thin classes are simpler because their methods do not depend on any attributes. The Thick version of GetCrustString always sets str to "Thick crust" and the Thin version always sets it to "Thin crust". The Thick version of CrustCost always returns 0.0030 and the Thin version always returns 0.0020.

Figure 23.25 shows the implementation of the PboxPizza.Pizza class. Most of the implementation is left as a problem for the student. Your solution should translate the UML design of Figure 23.24 into Component Pascal code.

```
MODULE PboxPizza;
   IMPORT PboxShapeAbs;

   TYPE
      Topping* = POINTER TO ABSTRACT RECORD
         (* Problem for the student. *)
      END;

      (* Topping subclasses, Problem for the student. *)
      (* Crust class and subclasses, Problem for the student. *)

      Pizza* = POINTER TO RECORD
         shape*: PboxShapeAbs.Shape;
         topping*: Topping;
         (* Problem for the student *)
      END;

(* -------------------- *)
   PROCEDURE (t: Topping) GetToppingString* (OUT str: ARRAY OF CHAR), NEW, ABSTRACT;

   (* GetToppingString, Problem for the student. *)

(* -------------------- *)
   PROCEDURE (t: Topping) ToppingCost* (): REAL, NEW, ABSTRACT;

   (* ToppingCost, Problem for the student. *)

(* -------------------- *)

   (* GetCrustString, Problem for the student *)

(* -------------------- *)

   (* CrustCost, Problem for the student *)

END PboxPizza.
```

Figure 23.25
Implementation of the Pizza class whose UML class diagram is in Figure 23.24.

Figure 23.26 shows the program for the dialog box of Figure 23.23. It imports, among other modules, PboxPizza. As with PboxPizza, parts of the module are left as a problem for the student at the end of the chapter. Procedure setDialog requires a local temporary array of characters to set the selection string, because it is the concatenation of the topping string, the string ", ", and the crust string. In the same way that procedure Insert requires local concrete classes for a rectangle and a circle, it requires local concrete classes for vegetarian and pepperoni toppings, and thick and thin crusts.

Figure 23.26

The program for the dialog box of Figure 23.23.

```
MODULE Pbox23C;
   IMPORT Dialog, C := PboxCListADT, S := PboxShapeAbs, P := PboxPizza;

   CONST
      basePrice = 2.50;
      tax = 0.09;

   VAR
      d*: RECORD
         shapeString-, dimensionString-, selectionString-: ARRAY 64 OF CHAR;
         price-: REAL;
         shapeNumber*: INTEGER;
         length*, width*: REAL; (* for rectangle *)
         diameter*: REAL; (* for circle *)
         extraCheese*: BOOLEAN;
         toppingNumber*, crustNumber*: INTEGER
      END;
      cList: C.CList;

   PROCEDURE ClearDialog;
   BEGIN
      d.shapeString := ""; d.dimensionString := ""; d.selectionString := "";
      d.price := 0.0;
      d.shapeNumber := 0;
      d.length := 0.0; d.width := 0.0;
      d.diameter := 0.0;
      d.extraCheese := FALSE;
      d.toppingNumber := 0; d.crustNumber := 0
   END ClearDialog;

   PROCEDURE SetDialog (pz: P.Pizza);
      VAR
         tempStr: ARRAY 32 OF CHAR;
   BEGIN
      pz.shape.GetIDString(d.shapeString);
      pz.shape.GetDimensionString(d.dimensionString);
      (* Problem for the student *)
   END SetDialog;

   PROCEDURE Clear*;
   BEGIN
      ClearDialog;
      C.Clear(cList);
      Dialog.Update(d)
   END Clear;
```

```
PROCEDURE Next*;
   VAR
      pizza: P.Pizza;
BEGIN
   IF ~C.Empty(cList) THEN
      C.GoNext(cList);
      pizza := C.NodeContent(cList) (P.Pizza);
      SetDialog(pizza);
      Dialog.Update(d)
   END
END Next;

PROCEDURE Insert*;
   VAR
      pizza: P.Pizza;
      rectangle: S.Rectangle;
      circle: S.Circle;
      (* Problem for the student. *)
BEGIN
   NEW(pizza);
   CASE d.shapeNumber OF
   0:
      NEW(rectangle);
      rectangle.SetState(MAX(0.0, d.length), MAX(0.0, d.width));
      pizza.shape := rectangle |
   1:
      NEW(circle);
      circle.SetState(MAX(0.0, d.diameter));
      pizza.shape := circle
   END;
   (* CASE d.toppingNumber, Problem for the student *)
   (* d.extraCheese, Problem for the student *)
   (* CASE d.crustNumber, Problem for the student *)
   C.Insert(cList, pizza);
   SetDialog(pizza);
   Dialog.Update(d)
END Insert;

PROCEDURE RectangleGuard* (VAR par: Dialog.Par);
BEGIN
   par.disabled := d.shapeNumber # 0
END RectangleGuard;

PROCEDURE CircleGuard* (VAR par: Dialog.Par);
BEGIN
   par.disabled := d.shapeNumber # 1
END CircleGuard;

PROCEDURE TriangleGuard* (VAR par: Dialog.Par);
BEGIN
   par.disabled := d.shapeNumber # 1
END TriangleGuard;
```

Figure 23.26
Continued.

BEGIN
  Clear
END Pbox23C .

Figure 23.26
Continued.

An alternate design of the Pizza class

Behavior abstraction with polymorphic dispatch allows you to eliminate IF or CASE statements. The design of the Pizza class in the previous section requires an IF statement in the implementation of GetToppingString, because the topping string depends on whether the boolean field extraCheese is true or false. The design also requires an IF statement in the implementation of ToppingCost for the same reason. The cost of the topping depends on the value of the extraCheese attribute. The design in Figure 23.27 uses behavior abstraction to eliminate all IF statements in the methods for the Pizza class.

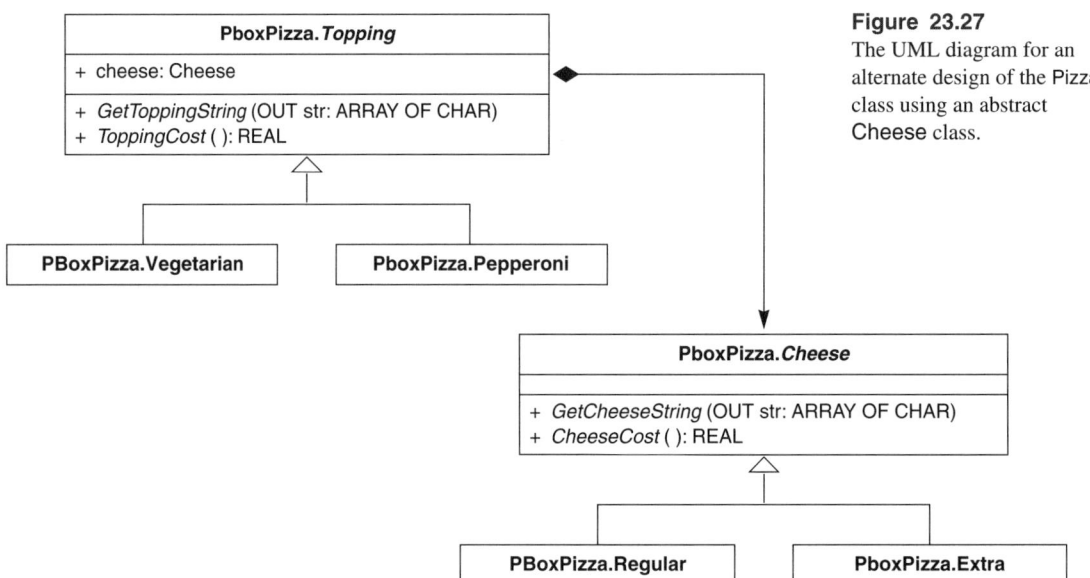

Figure 23.27
The UML diagram for an alternate design of the Pizza class using an abstract Cheese class.

In this design, extraCheese is not a boolean attribute of Topping. Instead, class Topping is composed of class Cheese, which is abstract. The Cheese class specifies methods GetCheeseString and CheeseCost, which are implemented by the concrete subclasses Regular and Extra.

The Regular version of GetCheeseString sets str to the empty string "". The Extra version of GetCheeseString sets str to the string ", Extra cheese" with a leading comma and space. The implementation of the Vegetarian version of GetTopping-String simply concatenates "Vegetarian" with the string for the cheese. If cheese is instantiated as Regular, then "Vegetarian" concatenated with the empty string is simply "Vegetarian". If cheese is instantiated as Extra, then "Vegetarian" concatenated with ", Extra cheese" is "Vegetarian, Extra cheese".

The same idea is used to eliminate the IF statements from the implementation of ToppingCost. The Regular version of CheeseCost returns 0.0, and the Extra version returns the price difference between regular and extra cheese. ToppingCost can simply add the price difference to the cost for the topping without extra cheese.

Class composition versus inheritance

When object-oriented (OO) design was first invented there was no history of design experience on which to draw to develop programs. In the early days, programmers concentrated on inheritance and the power of polymorphism. With the hindsight that comes with experience, many designs from that era are now known to be less than sound because the designers did not have an appreciation of the utility of class composition. Most of OO design consists of modeling the problem to be solved with an optimum mixture of class composition and inheritance. UML class diagrams are useful because they capture these two aspects of OO structure in a standard form that does not depend on the programming language used for the implementation.

As with any design process, there is always more than one way to solve a problem. The choice of a particular solution depends on the trade-offs that the designer makes according to the goals of the project. Figure 23.28 shows another way to model the relationship between a pizza and a crust. Suppose the application is for a bakery where the crust is the important object. The bakery may make crusts for pies as well as pizzas. You might choose to have classes Pie and Pizza inherit from Crust, reasoning that crust is common to both pies and pizzas and should therefore be abstracted out to the superclass.

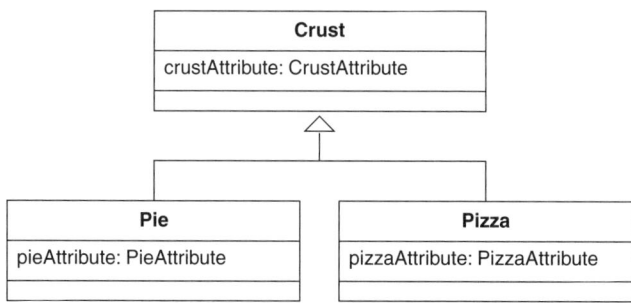

Figure 23.28
A possible design with a different relationship between Pizza and Crust.

Most OO designers would object (!) to this design. Remember that inheritance is the "is-a" relationship and class composition is the "has-a" relationship. The design of Figure 23.28 implies that a pizza *is* a crust, whereas the design of Figure 23.24 implies that a pizza *has* a crust. In this example, the real world nature of pizza provides a guide for the proper model to use. In some situations the problem is not so clear even after considering the so-called real world. For example, what is the relationship between a square and a rectangle? Mathematically, a square is a rectangle with equal sides. Would you therefore make a square a subclass of a rectangle? The problem with that implementation is that a square object would inherit both the length and width of the rectangle when it only needs the length of one side. The square versus rectangle design problem has provoked much debate in OO circles. The upshot is that many solutions to any given problem are possible, and good OO design can be difficult.

Records versus pointers

Figure 23.19 shows that Shape, Rectangle, and Circle are all declared to be pointers to records.

```
Shape* = POINTER TO ABSTRACT RECORD END;
Rectangle* = POINTER TO RECORD (Shape)
   length, width: REAL
END;
Circle* = POINTER TO RECORD (Shape)
   diameter: REAL
END;
```

With these declarations, you can allocate local pointer variables on the run-time stack with

```
myShape: Shape;
myRectangle: Rectangle;
myCircle: Circle;
```

You can allocate rectangle and circle records from the heap with

```
NEW(myRectangle);
NEW(myCircle)
```

because myRectangle and myCircle are pointers. It is the records that are allocated from the heap, and the pointers on the stack that point to them. However, you cannot allocate a shape from the heap with

```
NEW(myShape)
```

because Shape is abstract. The usual class assignment rule applies. The assignment

```
myShape := myRectangle
```

is legal, but the assignment

```
myRectangle := myShape
```

is not.

There is nothing in Component Pascal to prevent you from declaring classes and subclasses to be records instead of pointers to records. For example, Component Pascal permits the following declarations, which differ from the previous declarations only by the omission of POINTER TO.

ShapeR* = ABSTRACT RECORD END;
RectangleR* = RECORD (Shape)
   length, width: REAL
END;
CircleR* = RECORD (Shape)
   diameter: REAL
END;

You can allocate local variables for the rectangle and circle records on the run-time stack, such as

yourRectangle: RectangleR;
yourCircle: CircleR

But, the declaration of a local variable of type Shape such as

yourShape: ShapeR;

is not allowed, because it attempts to allocate an abstract record. The class assignment rule

yourShape := yourRectangle

cannot apply here, because it is impossible to have yourShape in the first place.

    Component Pascal provides the record attribute EXTENSIBLE to allow the programmer to declare a superclass that is not abstract as follows.

Extensible records

ShapeE* = EXTENSIBLE RECORD END;
RectangleE* = RECORD (Shape)
   length, width: REAL
END;
CircleE* = RECORD (Shape)
   diameter: REAL
END;

The local variable allocations on the run-time stack

herShape: ShapeE;
herRectangle: RectangleE;
herCircle: CircleE;

are all legal. The allocation for herShape is legal, because herShape is not abstract. Now that you have a superclass with subclasses you might think that the class assignment rule would permit the assignment

herShape := herRectangle

But, it does not! These variables are not assignment compatible, even though you can assign myRectangle to myShape in the pointer version.

Class assignment rule

    Object-oriented programming languages in general and Component Pascal in particular rely on the characteristics of pointers and allocation from the heap to pro-vide polymorphism. Some pure OO languages do not have explicit pointers at all. In these languages, every variable is automatically a pointer to a record, even though the pointer is hidden. The only assignment that is possible is a pointer assignment. The phrase "pointer to" is usually not part of the terminology in these languages. Instead, a variable is said to be a "reference to" an object. But apart from the termi-nology, such languages are identical to Component Pascal in their OO capabilities and their underlying structure. Most pure OO languages provide automatic garbage collection because of the prevalence of heap allocation.

Other OO languages are similar to Component Pascal in that they are not pure OO. These languages provide procedure abstraction as well as class and behavior abstraction and usually have pointers as an explicit primitive type. An advantage of such mixed-paradigm languages is that you are not forced to use OO techniques when they are not appropriate. These languages also tend to be more efficient than pure OO languages. Component Pascal is rather unique in that pointers are an explicit primitive type, yet the language still provides automatic garbage collection.

Extensible records have a place in OO design. However, the most important OO design patterns are based on abstract records instead. An abstract record cannot be instantiated. Its purpose is to be a kind of blueprint for the subclasses that are extended from it. The design patterns presented in this book use abstract records for inheritance together with class composition.

Private versus public

Items that are not exported are called private, and items that are exported are called public. An important OO design issue is whether to export an attribute, making it public, and if so, whether it should be exported read/write or read-only.

Consider class Rectangle in Figure 23.21 where attributes length and width are private. Because they are private, they are not accessible to any client module, including module Pbox23C in Figure 23.26. But, procedure Pbox23C.Insert needs to give values to length and width from the input dialog box. It does so by executing the call

```
rectangle.SetState(MAX(0.0, d.length), MAX(0.0, d.width))
```

Method SetState is public, and so can be called from Pbox23C.Insert. An alternate design would be to make length and width public. Then, you would not even need the SetState method. To set the length and width of the rectangle, Pbox23C.Insert would simply make the assignments

```
rectangle.length := MAX(0.0, d.length);
rectangle.width := MAX(0.0, d.width)
```

Now, consider attribute shape in class Pizza in Figure 23.24. Because it is public, Pbox23C.Insert can access it directly with the assignment

```
pizza.shape := rectangle
```

An alternate design would be to make shape private and supply the public method

```
PROCEDURE (p: PboxPizza) SetShape* (s: PboxShape.Shape), NEW;
BEGIN
   p.shape := s
END SetShape;
```

Procedure Pbox23C.Insert would then make the call

```
pizza.SetShape(rectangle)
```

to set the shape attribute of pizza to rectangle.

What is the difference between these two design decisions? Why are Rectangle.length and Rectangle.width private, which requires a public method to change them, while Pizza.shape is public, which requires no such method? Why not make every attribute public and dispense with methods to change their values? After all, your program would be shorter and would also run faster because of the time it takes to call a method.

The programs in this book are small enough to be written by a single individual. You typically write both the client module, like that in Figure 23.26, and the server module, like that in Figure 23.25. It is common, however, in a large project for the programming effort to include a team of programmers, so that the person who writes the client module is not the person who writes the server module. Indeed, it is even possible for the server programmer to provide the module to many different customers who write their own clients. In such an environment, protection is the key concept. If you write a server and you do not know who will write the client you should program defensively, making sure that the data in your data structures are consistent and meaningful. You should not allow clients to corrupt your data structures.

BlackBox provides design by contract to ensure that clients cannot violate the preconditions of any methods. The Component Pascal ASSERT statement enforces the preconditions stated in the specification of each procedure. Rectangle.length and Rectangle.width are private to enforce the invariant that they cannot be negative. If one of these dimensions were set negative, then its value would be meaningless as would be the computations of the area and perimeter of the rectangle. The public method to set the state of the rectangle ensures with an ASSERT statement that the values will never be set negative. This implementation is consistent with the design-by-contract rule, which states

Design by contract

- IF in the client.
- ASSERT in the server.

The design-by-contract rule

There is no corresponding reason to protect Pizza.shape beyond the protection provided by the language itself. Component Pascal is a strongly typed language. The compiler will allow an assignment to pizza.shape only if the right side of the assignment has the same type or an extension of the same type as the left side. Method SetShape above adds no protection value to the server. Whatever damage a client could do with a direct assignment to the public attribute it could do with a call to the public method that changes the private attribute.

You should be aware that some OO designers adhere to a blanket rule that attributes should always be private and only accessed through public methods. The philosophy in this book, however, is to not provide superfluous methods. If a method to access the state of a private variable does not add protection value to the server, then the method can be dispensed with and the attribute made public.

The read-only export feature of public attributes is unique to Component Pascal. For example, class PboxMappers.Scanner has the attribute

```
eot-: BOOLEAN
```

exported read-only. When you write a statement like

```
WHILE ~sc.eot DO
```

where sc is an instance of class Scanner, you are accessing the value of a public attribute. Because it is not exported read/write, however, Component Pascal does not allow you to change its value with an assignment like

```
sc := FALSE
```

Such an assignment would corrupt the scanner's data structure. Most OO languages do not provide public read-only attributes. They would maintain eot as a private attribute and provide the function

```
PROCEDURE (s: PboxMappers.Scanner) Eot* (): B OOLEAN, NEW;
BEGIN
    RETURN s.eot
END Eot;
```

You would then include the function call in the WHILE statement as

```
WHILE ~sc.Eot() DO
```

This design is less efficient than the one permitted by Component Pascal, because a function must be called with each execution of the loop. It is necessary, however, when the language does not provide read-only access.

Abstract objects and methods

A curious restriction on abstract objects and methods are the following two rules.

- You cannot instantiate an abstract object with NEW.
- You cannot implement an abstract method with BEGIN..END.

Restrictions on abstract objects and methods

If you cannot allocate a new abstract object from the heap, to what use could you ever put such an object? Similarly, if you cannot give any instructions to an abstract method, you certainly can never call it. So, why have an abstract method at all if it can never be called?

The answer is that abstract objects and methods are necessary blueprints for the implementation of behavior abstraction with polymorphism. Procedure SetDialog in

Figure 23.17 shows an example of how an abstract object and method can be useful. Formal parameter s is an abstract object. When the compiler translates the SetDialog procedure, it cannot determine the dynamic type of s. That is, the compiler only knows that the static type of s is an abstract Shape. The statement

NEW(s)

would be a compile error because of the restriction that you cannot instantiate an abstract object with NEW. During execution, however, formal parameter s might correspond to actual parameter rectangle as in the call to SetDialog from procedure Insert. In that situation, the dynamic type of s would be Rectangle. On the other hand, the dynamic type could just as easily be circle as in another call to SetDialog from the same procedure. The general object s can morph between these two specific classes during execution. When the compiler translates SetDialog it must take into account that s could be either. It is the specific objects that are instantiated with NEW in procedure Insert.

When the compiler translates

s.GetDimensionString(d.dimensionString)

in procedure SetDialog, it must translate the method call for the general case, because s is general. There are three headings for GetDimensionString in Figure 23.19. Only the concrete versions for a Rectangle and a Circle are implemented with BEGIN..END. The version of GetDimensionString for a Shape cannot be implemented. Its purpose is for the compiler to verify that any specific object that inherits the general method will have the same signature, that is, the same number and types of parameters. It also allows the compiler to verify that the signature of the above call to GetDimensionString from SetDialog matches the signature in the heading for the general case.

Exercises

1. **(a)** What is the fundamental class assignment rule? **(b)** What is the fundamental class assignment rule applied to parameters?

2. What is the most important benefit of object-oriented design?

3. **(a)** What object-oriented relationship is the "has-a" relationship? **(b)** What object-oriented relationship is the "is-a" relationship?

4. What is the Hollywood Principle? What does it have to do with BlackBox?

5. Draw the abbreviated version of the UML class diagram for the following classes.

```
TYPE
   Alpha* = RECORD
      rho: POINTER TO Beta
   END;

   Beta = ABSTRACT RECORD END;
   Gamma = RECORD (Beta) END;
   Delta = RECORD (Beta)
      value: T;
      omega: Alpha
   END;

PROCEDURE (IN b: Beta) Phi (n: INTEGER; OUT val: T), NEW, ABSTRACT;
PROCEDURE (IN a: Alpha) Phi* (n: INTEGER; OUT val: T), NEW;
PROCEDURE (IN g: Gamma) Phi (n: INTEGER; OUT val: T);
PROCEDURE (IN d: Delta) Phi (n: INTEGER; OUT val: T);
```

Problems

6. Modify PboxShapesObj in Figure 23.13 to include a right triangle shape containing two fields named base and height. Test your program by modifying the program in Figure 23.9.

7. Modify the program in Figure 23.17 to include a right triangle shape containing two fields named base and height. Do not modify PboxShapesAbs in Figure 23.19. Instead, implement the Triangle class in a new module without changing any code in module PboxShapeAbs.

8. Complete the PboxPizza implementation of Figure 23.25 according to the design of the UML class diagram of Figure 23.24. Test your implementation by completing the program of Figure 23.26.

9. Complete the PboxPizza implementation of Figure 23.25 according to the design of the UML class diagram of Figure 23.24 with the modification of Figure 23.27 where class Cheese is abstract. None of the methods of any of the classes are allowed to have IF or CASE statements or any local variables. Test your implementation by completing the program of Figure 23.26, which should be unchanged from that of Problem 8.

Chapter *24*

The State Design Pattern

The state design pattern is an object-oriented technique that uses inheritance and class composition. It is applicable to a variety of software design problems where an object needs to alter its behavior when its internal state changes. This chapter illustrates the state design pattern with implementations of a binary tree and a linked list.

Binary trees and linked lists have several things in common. Both structures are based on links between nodes. The state of each structure is defined as a pointer to its first node. That is, the state of a binary tree is defined as a pointer to its root node, while the state of a linked list is defined as a pointer to its head node. Furthermore, the definition of each data structure is inherently recursive. A binary tree is either empty or a pointer to a node that contains a value, a left tree, and a right tree. A list is either empty or a pointer to a node that contains a value and a list. These common properties are the basis of the state pattern implementation of the data structures.

Binary search trees

Figure 24.1 is the interface for a binary search tree implemented with the state design pattern. The methods should look familiar, as they are identical to the methods of the binary search tree class of Figure 22.9, which is also shown in the figure. Examine the interfaces for these two classes and you will find that they are identical in every detail except that the name of the module for the tree with the state design pattern is PboxTreeSta while that for the tree in Chapter 22 is PboxTreeObj.

Because the interfaces are identical, the programs that use them are identical as well. Rather than showing the dialog box that uses the tree with the state design pattern see Figure 22.10, which is identical. Rather than showing the program that implements the dialog box see Figure 22.11, which is identical except for the substitution of PboxTreeSta for every occurrence of PboxTreeObj. In all respects, a client module that uses the binary search tree implemented with the state design pattern is not aware of any difference between its behavior and that of the binary search tree as implemented in Chapter 22.

Figure 24.1
The interfaces for a binary search tree implemented with the state design pattern and as it is implemented in Chapter 22.

```
DEFINITION PboxTreeSta;

   TYPE
      T = ARRAY 16 OF CHAR;
      Tree = RECORD
         (VAR tr: Tree) Clear, NEW;
         (IN tr: Tree) Contains (IN val: T): BOOLEAN, NEW;
         (VAR tr: Tree) Insert (IN val: T), NEW;
         (IN tr: Tree) NumItems (): INTEGER, NEW;
         (IN tr: Tree) PreOrder, NEW;
         (IN tr: Tree) InOrder, NEW;
         (IN tr: Tree) PostOrder, NEW
      END;

END PboxTreeSta.


DEFINITION PboxTreeObj;

   TYPE
      T = ARRAY 16 OF CHAR;
      Tree = RECORD
         (VAR tr: Tree) Clear, NEW;
         (IN tr: Tree) Contains (IN val: T): BOOLEAN, NEW;
         (VAR tr: Tree) Insert (IN val: T), NEW;
         (IN tr: Tree) NumItems (): INTEGER, NEW;
         (IN tr: Tree) PreOrder, NEW;
         (IN tr: Tree) InOrder, NEW;
         (IN tr: Tree) PostOrder, NEW
      END;

END PboxTreeObj.
```

Figure 24.2 shows the UML diagram for the state design pattern applied to a binary search tree. The declarations of Tree and Node are

The data structure for a binary tree using the state design pattern

```
TYPE
   T* = ARRAY 16 OF CHAR;
   Tree* = RECORD
      root: POINTER TO Node
   END;

   Node = ABSTRACT RECORD END;
   EmptyNode = RECORD (Node) END;
   NonEmptyNode = RECORD (Node)
      leftChild: Tree;
      value: T;
      rightChild: Tree
   END;
```

The relation between a tree and an abstract node is class composition. A tree has a node. The relation between an empty node and an abstract node is inheritance. An empty node is an abstract node. The relation between a nonempty node and an abstract node is also inheritance. A nonempty node is an abstract node. The relation between a nonempty node and a tree is class composition. A nonempty node has two trees.

Figure 24.2
The UML diagram for a state design pattern implementation of a binary search tree.

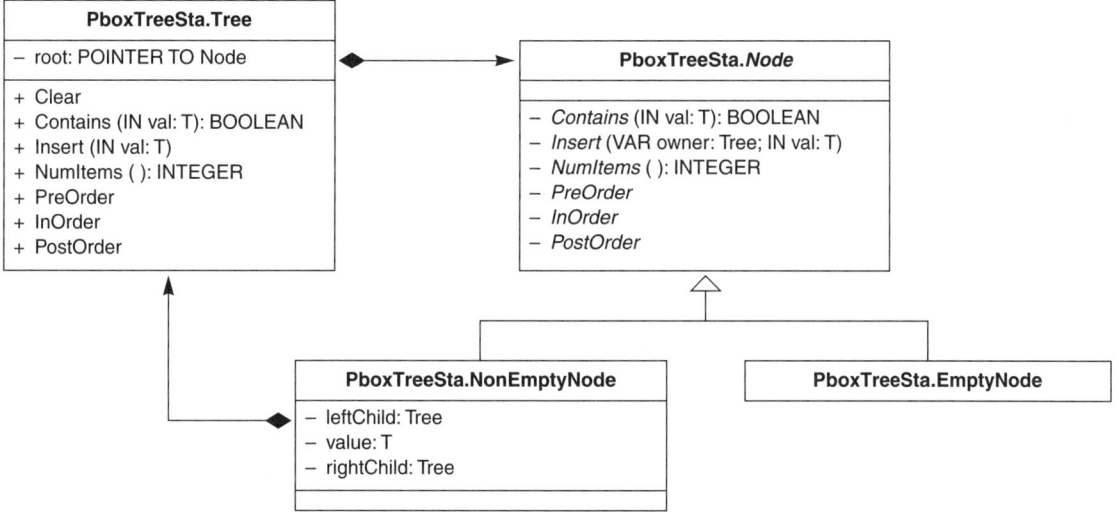

The module for the binary search tree contains the class for the tree as well as the class for the abstract node and each of its two subclasses. The details of the node structure are hidden from the client module by virtue of the fact that none of the node declarations are exported. In Figure 24.1, none of the details of the node or even the pointer to the head node are visible to the client. Unfortunately, many object-oriented languages are not based on the module concept, which is one of the great strengths of Component Pascal compared to them. If you had no way of packaging several classes into one module, you would need to export the methods of the abstract Node, making them public, so the Tree class could have access to them.

Class abstraction unifies attributes and operations. Because an instance of a class has both, it becomes an autonomous entity. You should think of OO design as a collection of cooperating objects, each one of which is autonomous. It sometimes helps to have an anthropomorphic view of the design in which each object is like an independent person who cooperates with the other people objects. Figure 24.3 is such a view for the state design pattern of the binary search tree.

Object-oriented design is a collection of cooperating objects.

Figure 24.3(a) shows the viewpoint of a tree object. As far as the tree is concerned, he owns an abstract node. The tree looks through a window, represented by the dashed vertical line, and sees an abstract node, represented by the amorphous shape on the right side of the window. The tree does not know what kind of node he owns, that is, whether his node is empty or nonempty. The state of the tree is defined by its root. Figure 24.2 shows that root is a pointer to a Node. But type Node is abstract. That is, it can never be allocated. The only nodes that can be allocated are

The viewpoint of a tree

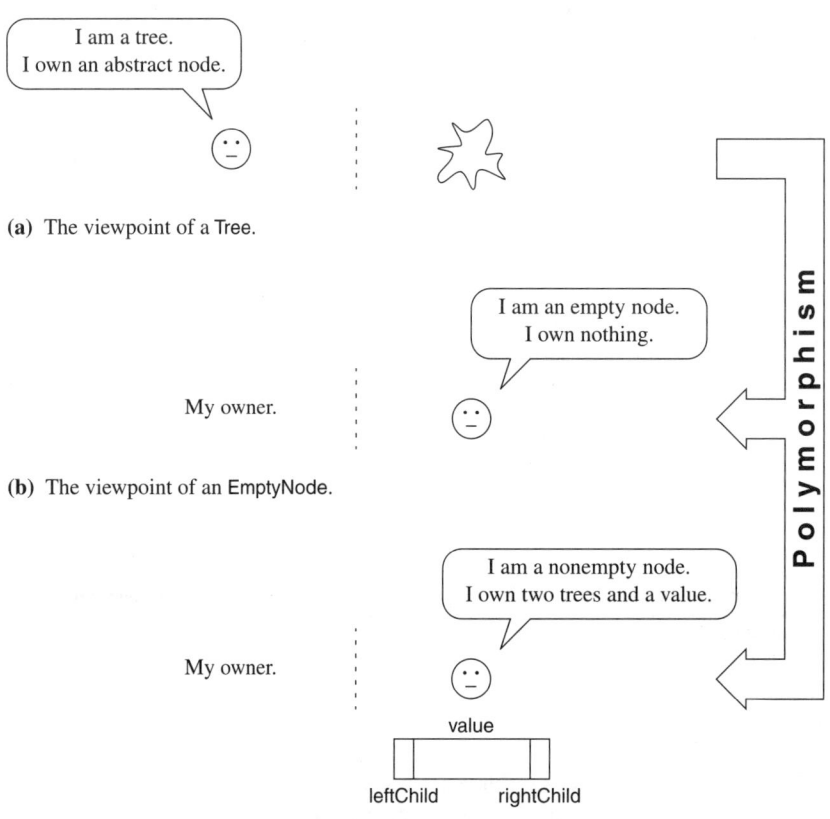

(a) The viewpoint of a Tree.

(b) The viewpoint of an EmptyNode.

(c) The viewpoint of a NonEmptyNode.

Figure 24.3
The cooperating objects in the state design pattern for the binary search tree.

its concrete subclasses, EmptyNode and NonEmptyNode.

The viewpoint of an empty node

Now consider the viewpoint of an empty node in Figure 24.3(b). An empty node has no attributes. Every node has an owner, but not in the same sense that the owner has a node. If myTree is a tree, then it can always refer to the node it owns by the expression myTree.root. But if myEmptyNode is an EmptyNode, there is no corresponding myEmptyNode.owner. Consequently, the empty node cannot look through the window directly to see his owner.

The viewpoint of a nonempty node

The viewpoint of a nonempty node is similar to that of the empty node. He cannot see his owner directly. However, he owns something that an empty node does not own, namely two trees and a value.

Delegation

The system of these three cooperating objects—trees, empty nodes, and nonempty nodes—works by delegation. Each autonomous object either knows how to perform a simple task itself or, if it cannot perform the task, delegates all or part of the task to another object. Typically, the client module gives a tree a task to perform by calling one of the tree's methods. The tree then delegates the task to its node.

For example, the PboxTree.Sta box in Figure 24.2 shows that a tree object has method NumItems(), which returns the number of items in the tree. Imagine that you are the tree in Figure 24.3(a). You are instructed to return the number of nodes contained in yourself. The problem is that you do not even know whether you are empty or not! The only thing you know is that you have an abstract node. When you look through the window at your node, you cannot tell what kind of node it is. You only see that abstract blob. Fortunately, the PboxTreeSta.Node box in Figure 24.2 shows that an abstract node also has a method named NumItems(). You own an abstract node, and your abstract node provides a method that will return the number of items in the tree. So, you simply call the method for your node.

NumItems for a tree

Now, which method executes? Certainly not the abstract method NumItems(), because an abstract method cannot be implemented. Figure 24.2 shows that EmptyNode and NonEmptyNode are concrete subclasses of the abstract class Node. They inherit from Node and each one implements its own version of NumItems(). The double-headed arrow on the right of Figure 24.3 indicates that polymorphic dispatch determines which of these two versions of NumItems() executes. You can see that polymorphism eliminates an IF statement here. As a tree, you do not know what kind of node you own, whether empty or nonempty. But you do not need to know or even to test what kind of tree you are with an IF statement. You simply delegate to your node the task of computing the number of items with a single call, which is polymorphically dispatched.

Polymorphism

Consider the implementation of the empty node's version of NumItems(). If you are the empty node in Figure 24.3(b), and you are the root of a tree, how many items do you contain? The answer should be obvious—none. Your version of NumItems() simply returns 0.

NumItems for an empty node

What about the implementation of the nonempty node's version of NumItems()? If you are the nonempty node in Figure 24.3(c) what do you return? That is, if you are the root of a tree, how many nodes does your tree contain? Remember, you own a value and two subtrees. So, the answer is one (yourself) plus the number of nodes in your left child plus the number of nodes in your right child.

NumItems for a nonempty node

Figure 24.4 shows the implementation of the binary search tree with the state design pattern. Implementation of some of the methods are left as problems for the student. Compare this tree class with that in Figure 22.14. As with that implementation, a Tree is a record that contains a single pointer to a node. With the state design pattern, however, the root of a tree is never NIL. It always points to something, either an empty node if the tree is empty or a nonempty node if it is not.

```
MODULE PboxTreeSta;
   IMPORT StdLog;

   TYPE
      T* = ARRAY 16 OF CHAR;
      Tree* = RECORD
         root: POINTER TO Node
      END;
```

Figure 24.4
The implementation of the binary search tree with the state design pattern.

```
Node = ABSTRACT RECORD END;
EmptyNode = RECORD (Node) END;
NonEmptyNode = RECORD (Node)
   leftChild: Tree;
   value: T;
   rightChild: Tree
END;
```

Figure 24.4
Continued.

```
(* ------------------- *)
   PROCEDURE (VAR tr: Tree) Clear*, NEW;
     VAR
        p: POINTER TO EmptyNode;
   BEGIN
     NEW(p);
     tr.root := p
   END Clear;

(* ------------------- *)
   PROCEDURE (IN tr: Tree) Contains* (IN val: T): BOOLEAN, NEW;
   BEGIN
     (* A problem for the student *)
     RETURN FALSE
   END Contains;

(* ------------------- *)
   PROCEDURE (IN node: Node) Insert (VAR owner: Tree; IN val: T), NEW, ABSTRACT;

   PROCEDURE (VAR tr: Tree) Insert* (IN val: T), NEW;
   BEGIN
     tr.root.Insert (tr, val)
   END Insert;

   PROCEDURE (IN node: NonEmptyNode) Insert (VAR owner: Tree; IN val: T);
   BEGIN
     ASSERT(node.value # val, 20);
     IF node.value < val THEN
        node.rightChild.Insert(val)
     ELSE
        node.leftChild.Insert(val)
     END
   END Insert;

   PROCEDURE (IN node: EmptyNode) Insert (VAR owner: Tree; IN val: T);
     VAR
        p: POINTER TO NonEmptyNode;
   BEGIN
     NEW(p);
     p.leftChild.Clear;
     p.value := val;
     p.rightChild.Clear;
     owner.root := p (* Change the state of owner *)
   END Insert;
```

```
(* ------------------ *)
    PROCEDURE (IN tr: Tree) NumItems* (): INTEGER, NEW;
    BEGIN
        (* A problem for the student *)
        RETURN 999
    END NumItems;

(* ------------------ *)
    PROCEDURE (IN node: Node) PreOrder, NEW, ABSTRACT;

    PROCEDURE (IN tr: Tree) PreOrder*, NEW;
    BEGIN
        tr.root.PreOrder
    END PreOrder;

    PROCEDURE (IN node: EmptyNode) PreOrder;
    BEGIN
        (* Do nothing *)
    END PreOrder;

    PROCEDURE (IN node: NonEmptyNode) PreOrder;
    BEGIN
        StdLog.String(node.value); StdLog.String(" ");
        node.leftChild.PreOrder;
        node.rightChild.PreOrder
    END PreOrder;

(* ------------------ *)
    PROCEDURE (IN tr: Tree) InOrder*, NEW;
    BEGIN
        (* A problem for the student *)
    END InOrder;

(* ------------------ *)
    PROCEDURE (IN tr: Tree) PostOrder*, NEW;
    BEGIN
        (* A problem for the student *)
    END PostOrder;

END PboxTreeSta.
```

Figure 24.4
Continued.

Compare Figure 24.4 with Figure 22.14 and you will see that with the state design pattern there is no setting of any pointer to NIL, nor is there a comparison of any pointer to NIL. The concept of NIL is hidden at a lower level of abstraction with the state design pattern. There are fewer IF statements because polymorphic dispatch takes their place.

For example, method Clear from PboxTreeSta in Figure 24.4 declares p to be a local pointer to an empty node as p: POINTER TO EmptyNode;

It clears tree tr by setting its root to a pointer to an empty node as follows.

NEW(p);
tr.root := p

Compare this with the corresponding implementation of Clear from PboxTreeObj in Figure 22.14.

tr.root := NIL

This version of Clear clears tree tr by setting its root to NIL. In contrast, there is no concept of NIL in the PboxTreeSta version. Figure 24.5 shows the difference between empty trees in these two versions. There is really nothing in the oval box labeled EmptyNode in Figure 24.5(b), because an empty node has no attributes.

treeA.root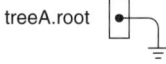

treeA.root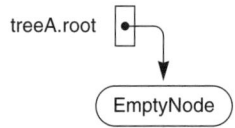

Figure 24.5
The empty tree in PboxTreeObj and PboxTreeSta.

(a) The empty tree from PboxTreeObj in Figure 22.14.

(b) The empty tree from PboxTreeSta in Figure 24.4.

To see how the state design pattern eliminates the IF statement and the NIL value, consider the implementation of method PreOrder. In PboxTreeObj, the implementation of method PreOrder in Figure 22.14 begins with the statement

IF tr.root # NIL THEN

followed by the recursive calls to PreOrder in the body of the IF statement. But, the PreOrder implementation in PboxTreeSta has no IF statement and no reference to NIL. Imagine you are the tree in Figure 24.3(a). You do not know what kind of tree you are, whether empty or nonempty. Only your root node knows. But you cannot tell by looking at your root node, because it is abstract. All you see is that abstract blob. So, you delegate. The implementation of PreOrder for a tree is the one liner

tr.root.PreOrder   *PreOrder for a tree*

which is a call to the PreOrder method of a node. Which version of PreOrder gets called—the one for an empty node or the one for a nonempty node? Polymorphism decides with no IF statement or NIL test. The implementation of the empty node version is simply the comment

(* Do nothing *)   *PreOrder for an empty node*

The implementation of the nonempty version is an output of the nonempty node's value with

StdLog.String(node.value); StdLog.String(" ")

followed by the usual recursive calls to PreOrder for the left and right children. In the first recursive call,

PreOrder for a nonempty node

node.leftChild.PreOrder

node is the current nonempty node, and node.leftChild is its left child, which is a tree. Therefore, node.leftChild.PreOrder is a method call for a tree, not for a node.

The implementation of method Insert in PboxTreeSta shows the power of object-oriented programming with polymorphism. Consider implementation of the method from PboxTreeObj in Figure 22.14. It has a WHILE loop to determine the leaf where the new value is to be attached and tests for NIL all over the place. Contrast the complexity of that implementation with the simplicity of the one from PboxTreeSta in Figure 24.4. There are no loops, and there is only one simple IF statement that compares the value to be inserted with the value of the current nonempty node. Here is how it works.

The heading for the Insert method for a tree is

PROCEDURE (VAR tr: Tree) **Insert*** (IN val: T), NEW;

Formal parameter tr is the tree into which the value is to be inserted, and val is the formal parameter of the value to insert. Imagine you are the tree in Figure 24.3(a). You have a value val to insert into yourself, but you do not even know what kind of tree you are, whether empty or nonempty. So, you delegate the task to your root node, which knows what kind of node it is. If your root node is nonempty, it will simply pass the request down to one of its children.

Insert for a tree

But, there is a slight complication if your root node is empty. In that case, your root node must change your state (hence, the name *state* design pattern). Your current state is empty, but after the insertion your state will be changed to nonempty. That is, your root attribute will need to point to a new nonempty node after the insertion rather than the empty node to which it currently points. Your empty node will need to change your root. So, you the owner of the node must pass yourself to your node so it can change your state. The heading for the Insert method for an abstract node is

Insert for an abstract node

PROCEDURE (IN node: Node) Insert (VAR owner: Tree; IN val: T), NEW, ABSTRACT;

Not only must the tree pass the value via parameter val to its node, it must also pass itself via parameter owner to its node. Formal parameter owner is passed by reference, because the method may use its value and change the corresponding actual parameter.

The heading for the Insert method for a nonempty node is

PROCEDURE (IN node: NonEmptyNode) Insert (VAR owner: Tree; IN val: T);

Figure 24.6 shows the perspective of a nonempty node object who owns a value and two children. The value it owns is robin. It does not know what kind of children it owns, because each child contains a root that points to an abstract node. It has access to its owner and to val through its parameter list. The figure assumes that sparrow is passed as val. The implementation of Insert for the nonempty node is simple. First, the statement

ASSERT(node.value # val, 20)

verifies that a duplicate value is not being inserted into the tree. Then,

```
IF node.value < val THEN
    node.rightChild.Insert(val)
ELSE
    node.leftChild.Insert(val)
END
```

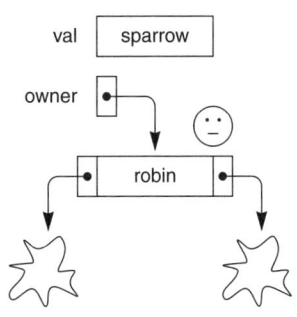

Figure 24.6
The viewpoint of a nonempty node in the environment of an

executes, which tests if robin is less than sparrow. Because robin is indeed less than sparrow in alphabetical order, the nonempty node simply delegates the insertion task by passing sparrow to be inserted into its right child with the call

node.rightChild.Insert(val)

Because node.rightChild is a tree, the method call is for a tree with no owner in the parameter list.

The heading for the Insert method for an empty node is

PROCEDURE (IN node: EmptyNode) Insert (VAR owner: Tree; IN val: T);

Because the node is empty, a new nonempty node must take its place with the value from val in the new node's value field. Also, the left and right children of the new node must be empty trees. The code is straightforward as Figure 24.7 shows. Initially the empty node is in an environment that provides access to its owner, the value passed to it in parameter val, and the local variable p, as Figure 24.7(a) shows. When the statement

NEW(p)

executes in Figure 24.7(b), a nonempty node is allocated because p is declared to be a pointer to a nonempty node. Then,

p.leftChild.Clear

clears the left child in Figure 24.7(c),

p.value := val

puts the value from the parameter into the value part of the new nonempty node in Figure 24.7(d), and

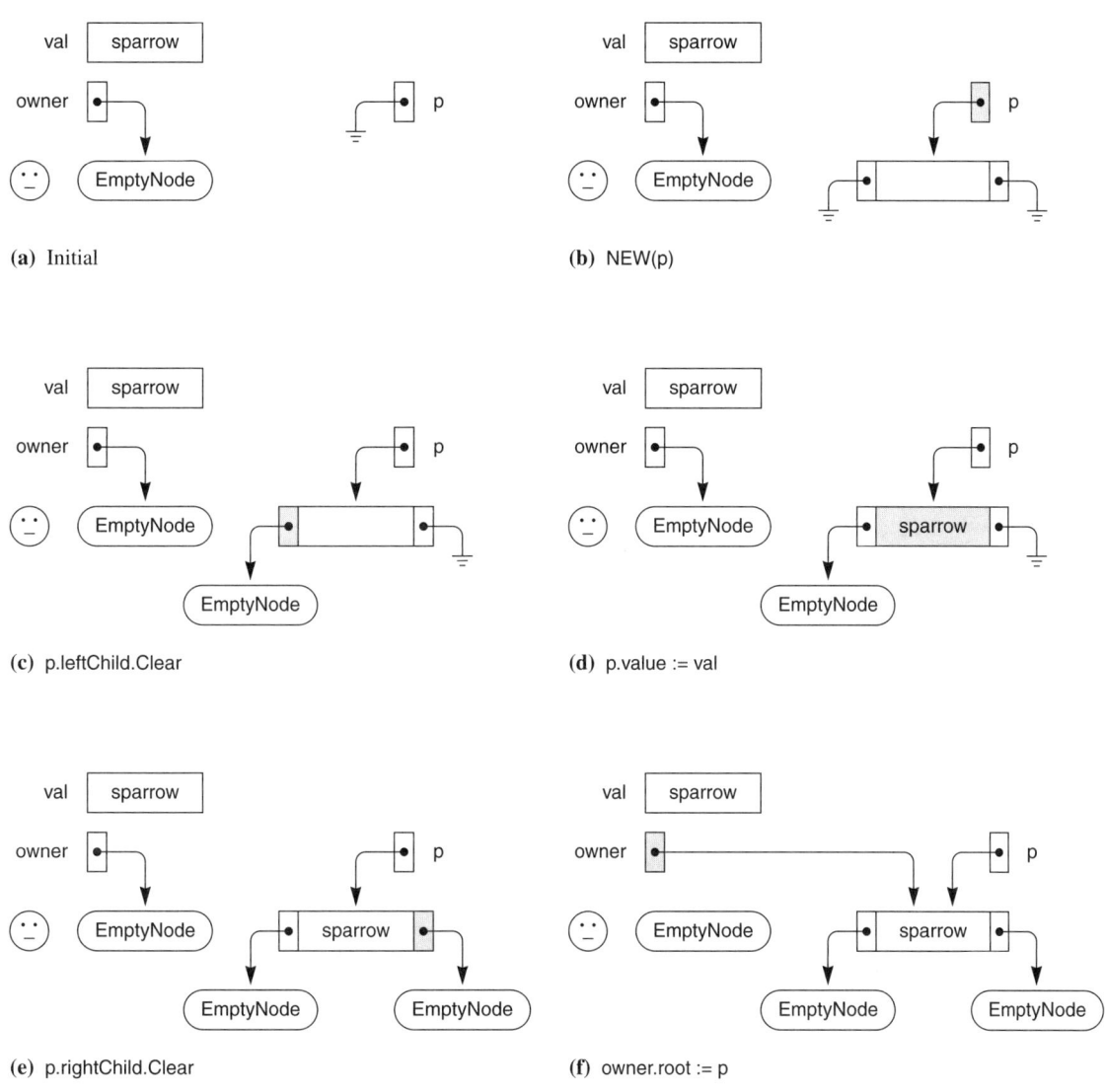

(a) Initial

(b) NEW(p)

(c) p.leftChild.Clear

(d) p.value := val

(e) p.rightChild.Clear

(f) owner.root := p

p.rightChild.Clear

clears the right child in Figure 24.7(e). The last statement in the method

owner.root := p

shown in Figure 24.7(f) changes the state of the owner. Whereas the owner used to be an empty tree, it is now a nonempty tree.

A striking feature of method Insert for the state design pattern in Figure 24.7 compared to the original method illustrated in Figure 22.15 is the locality of the

Figure 24.7
The viewpoint of an empty node in the environment of an Insert call.

environment. Figure 22.15 shows how that algorithm must view the entire tree, keeping track of the parent of each node as it works its way to the proper leaf. But, the algorithm with the state design pattern is separated into three parts—one for the tree, one for a nonempty node, and one for an empty node. Each part is a separate method. The implementation of the tree method is a single line. The simplicity of the method is due to the fact that the environment of the tree is local. The tree does not even know what kind of tree it is because it cannot see past its abstract root. There is no larger picture of the tree as a whole. The implementation of the non-empty node method is a single IF statement. It cannot see past its children, because their roots are abstract. The nonempty node cannot see past its owner above or past its children below. The environment in which it accomplishes its task is strictly local. The same can be said for the empty node. It works in a local environment without even the concept of a parent.

Locality of the environment

In effect, the original insertion algorithm is distributed among three kinds of objects—one tree and two nodes—each acting in its own local environment. In each environment, abstraction hides the details from the other environments. The problem is subdivided into smaller problems in a natural way. Each smaller problem is easier to solve that the larger problem of which it is a part. A distributed algorithm using polymorphism in a system of cooperating objects is the hallmark of object-oriented thinking. An example of the utility of such an approach is programming for a net-work of computers. It is possible to have the different objects of the system exist on different computers in the network. In such an environment, the distribution of the algorithm is not just a logical construction among objects executing on the same computer, but is a literal distribution of objects executing on physically different computers.

Distributed algorithms

Linked lists

The state design pattern is a general technique not limited to binary trees. Figure 24.8 shows the interfaces for a linked list implemented with the state design pattern and for the linked list implemented in Chapter 21.

```
DEFINITION PboxLListSta;

    TYPE
        T = ARRAY 16 OF CHAR;
        List = RECORD
            (VAR lst: List) Clear, NEW;
            (IN lst: List) Display, NEW;
            (IN lst: List) GetElementN (n: INTEGER; OUT val: T), NEW;
            (VAR lst: List) InsertAtN (n: INTEGER; IN val: T), NEW;
            (IN lst: List) Length (): INTEGER, NEW;
            (VAR lst: List) RemoveN (n: INTEGER), NEW;
            (IN lst: List) Search (IN srchVal: T; OUT n: INTEGER; OUT fnd: BOOLEAN), NEW
        END;

END PboxLListSta.
```

Figure 24.8
The interfaces for a linked list implemented with the state design pattern and as it is implemented in Chapter 21.

DEFINITION PboxLLListObj;

Figure 24.8
Continued.

```
    TYPE
        T = ARRAY 16 OF CHAR;
        List = RECORD
            (VAR lst: List) Clear, NEW;
            (IN lst: List) Display, NEW;
            (IN lst: List) GetElementN (n: INTEGER; OUT val: T), NEW;
            (VAR lst: List) InsertAtN (n: INTEGER; IN val: T), NEW;
            (VAR lst: List) Length (): INTEGER, NEW;
            (VAR lst: List) RemoveN (n: INTEGER), NEW;
            (IN lst: List) Search (IN srchVal: T; OUT n: INTEGER; OUT fnd: BOOLEAN), NEW
        END;

END PboxLLListObj.
```

There is no difference between these two interfaces other than the name of the module. Consequently, the program that uses PboxLLListSta is identical in all respects to the program that uses PboxLLListObj except for the textual substitution of the name of one module for the other. Refer to Figure 21.28 for a dialog box that uses the linked list and Figure 21.29 for a program that implements the dialog box.

The state design pattern for the linked list uses the same kind of abstract node that is used in the state design pattern for the binary tree. The state of a list is defined as a pointer to a head node, which is abstract. An empty node and a nonempty node are type extensions of an abstract node. An empty node contains no attributes. A nonempty node contains a field for the value and a field named next, which is a list. Here is the declaration of a list and its associated nodes.

```
TYPE
    T* = ARRAY 16 OF CHAR;
    List* = RECORD
        head: POINTER TO Node
    END;

    Node = ABSTRACT RECORD END;
    EmptyNode = RECORD (Node) END;
    NonEmptyNode = RECORD (Node)
        value: T;
        next: List
    END;
```

The data structure for a linked list using the state design pattern

Figure 24.9 is the UML diagram for the state design pattern of the linked list, which you should compare with Figure 24.2 for the binary tree. Figure 24.9 shows that seven public methods are exported by PboxLLListSta, corresponding to the seven methods provided by the interface in Figure 24.8. As usual, all the methods for the nodes, as well as the nodes themselves, are private. The user of the module has no concept of the internal workings of the list. Unlike the binary tree, however, Figure 24.9 shows that List has two private methods that are helpers for their corresponding public methods. Method DisplayN is a helper for Display and SearchN is a helper for

Search. The abstract node provides six methods that correspond to six of the seven methods provided by the list. Clear is the one method that List can implement without delegating the task to a corresponding Node method. As usual, each concrete node implements all the abstract methods inherited from the abstract node.

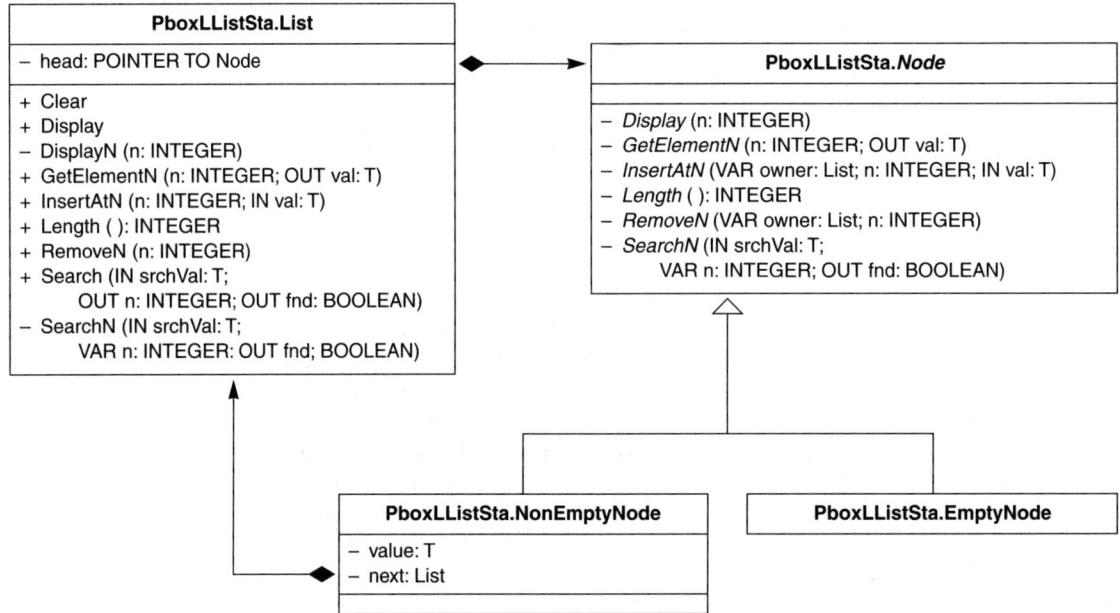

The viewpoint of each object in the state design pattern for the linked list is identical to the viewpoint of the corresponding object in the state design pattern for the binary tree in Figure 24.3. A List is an owner of an abstract head node. Because the node is abstract, the list cannot see past it and does not know whether it is an empty list or a nonempty list, similar to the tree in Figure 24.3(a). An empty node does not own anything, similar to the empty node in Figure 24.3(b). A nonempty node owns a value and a next list, similar to the way the nonempty node in Figure 24.3(c) owns a value and two children.

As with a tree, the system of cooperating objects works by delegation. A client module typically calls a method for the list. Because the list does not know what kind of list it is, it simply delegates the task to its head node by calling the corresponding method for the node. Polymorphism determines whether the method for an empty node or for a nonempty node executes, with no recourse to an IF statement to determine which. For two methods—Display and Search—the list delegates the task to its helper function. The helper function then delegates the task polymorphically to the corresponding method for the node. As with the binary tree, usually the method for the empty node can execute without further calls, and the method for the nonempty node makes a further call to a method of its next list.

Figure 24.10 is the implementation of the linked list with the state design pattern.

Figure 24.9
The UML diagram for a state design implementation of a linked list.

Methods Length, RemoveN, and Search are left as problems for the student.

```
MODULE  PboxLListSta;
    IMPORT StdLog;

    TYPE
      T* = ARRAY 16 OF CHAR;
      List* = RECORD
         head: POINTER TO Node
      END;

      Node = ABSTRACT RECORD END;
      EmptyNode = RECORD (Node) END;
      NonEmptyNode = RECORD (Node)
         value: T;
         next: List
      END;

(* -------------------- *)
    PROCEDURE (VAR lst: List) Clear*, NEW;
      VAR
         p: POINTER TO EmptyNode;
    BEGIN
      NEW(p);
      lst.head := p
    END Clear;

(* -------------------- *)
    PROCEDURE (IN node: Node) DisplayN (n: INTEGER), NEW, ABSTRACT;

    PROCEDURE (IN lst: List) DisplayN (n: INTEGER), NEW;
    BEGIN
      lst.head.DisplayN(n)
    END DisplayN;

    PROCEDURE (IN lst: List) Display*, NEW;
    BEGIN
      lst.DisplayN (0)
    END Display;

    PROCEDURE (IN node: EmptyNode) DisplayN (n: INTEGER);
    BEGIN
      (* Do nothing *)
    END DisplayN;

    PROCEDURE (IN node: NonEmptyNode) DisplayN (n: INTEGER);
    BEGIN
      StdLog.Int(n); StdLog.String(" "); StdLog.String(node.value); StdLog.Ln;
      node.next.DisplayN(n+1)
    END DisplayN;
```

Figure 24.10
The implementation of the linked list with the state design pattern.

```
(* -------------------- *)
    PROCEDURE (IN node: Node) GetElementN (n: INTEGER; OUT val: T), NEW, ABSTRACT;

    PROCEDURE (IN lst: List) GetElementN* (n: INTEGER; OUT val: T), NEW;
    BEGIN
        ASSERT(0 <= n, 20);
        lst.head.GetElementN(n, val)
    END GetElementN;

    PROCEDURE (IN node: EmptyNode) GetElementN (n: INTEGER; OUT val: T);
    BEGIN
        HALT(21)
    END GetElementN;

    PROCEDURE (IN node: NonEmptyNode) GetElementN (n: INTEGER; OUT val: T);
    BEGIN
        IF n = 0 THEN
            val := node.value
        ELSE
            node.next.GetElementN(n - 1, val)
        END
    END GetElementN;

(* -------------------- *)
    PROCEDURE (VAR node: Node) InsertAtN (VAR owner: List; n: INTEGER; IN val: T), NEW, ABSTRACT;

    PROCEDURE (VAR lst: List) InsertAtN* (n: INTEGER; IN val: T), NEW;
    BEGIN
        ASSERT(n >= 0, 20);
        lst.head.InsertAtN(lst, n, val)
    END InsertAtN;

    PROCEDURE (VAR node: EmptyNode) InsertAtN (VAR owner: List; n: INTEGER; IN val: T);
        VAR
            p: POINTER TO NonEmptyNode;
    BEGIN
        NEW(p);
        p.value := val;
        p.next.Clear;
        owner.head := p (* Change the state of owner *)
    END InsertAtN;
```

Figure 24.10
Continued.

```
PROCEDURE (VAR node: NonEmptyNode) InsertAtN (VAR owner: List; n: INTEGER; IN val: T);
  VAR
    p: POINTER TO NonEmptyNode;
BEGIN
  IF n > 0 THEN
    node.next.InsertAtN(n - 1, val)
  ELSE
    NEW(p);
    p.value := val;
    p.next := owner; (* Change the state of p.next *)
    owner.head := p (* Change the state of owner *)
  END
END InsertAtN;

(* -------------------- *)
  PROCEDURE (IN lst: List) Length* (): INTEGER, NEW;
  BEGIN
    (* A problem for the student *)
    RETURN 999
  END Length;

(* -------------------- *)
  PROCEDURE (VAR lst: List) RemoveN* (n: INTEGER), NEW;
  BEGIN
    (* A problem for the student *)
  END RemoveN;

(* -------------------- *)
  PROCEDURE (IN lst: List) Search* (IN srchVal: T; OUT n: INTEGER; OUT fnd: BOOLEAN), NEW;
  BEGIN
    (* A problem for the student *)
    fnd := FALSE
  END Search;

END PboxLListSta.
```

Figure 24.10
Continued.

As with the binary tree, the implementation of a linked list with the state design pattern relegates NIL to a lower level of abstraction. Nowhere is there any test for NIL in the implementation of Figure 24.10. Nor does the implementation contain any loops, all of which are replaced by recursion. There are also fewer IF statements, many of which are replaced by polymorphic dispatch.

The implementation of method Clear for the linked list is identical to its counterpart for the binary tree. The method has a local pointer, which it uses to allocate a new empty node. It sets its head pointer to point to the new empty node as does the tree in Figure 24.5.

Display requires a helper function because each item of a list is printed on the Log prefixed by its position in the list. For example, a list of items might be displayed as

0 trout
1 tuna
2 cod
3 salmon

So, a nonempty node needs to know its position in the list so it can display the position before it displays its value. The idea is for the helper method DisplayN to contain an additional parameter n that signifies the position of the first item in the current list. When the client module calls Display for a list, the list simply calls the helper function DisplayN with an actual parameter of 0 corresponding to formal parameter n.

lst.DisplayN (0)   *Display for a list*

The 0 indicates that the first item in the client's list is at position 0. The helper method delegates the display task polymorphically to the list's head node, passing along the current position.

lst.head.DisplayN(n)   *DisplayN for a list*

If the head node is an empty node, there is nothing to print and no more processing to be done. DisplayN for an empty node is simply

(* Do nothing *)   *DisplayN for an empty node*

If the head node is a nonempty node, it prints the value of n followed by the value it owns. Then, it delegates the task of printing the rest of the list by calling the helper method for its next list. Because the position of the first item in the next list is the position of the current item plus 1, it supplies n + 1 for the actual parameter.

StdLog.Int(n); StdLog.String(" "); StdLog.String(node.value); StdLog.Ln;   *DisplayN for a nonempty*
node.next.DisplayN(n+1)   *node*

You should compare this implementation of Display with the implementation of Display in Figure 21.30 for PboxLLListObj. This implementation divides the algorithm into four methods, two of which consist of a single statement and one of which contains no statements! It is necessary to have an implementation for the empty node even if it does nothing, because the method does get called polymorphically. The implementation for PboxLLListSta exhibits the object-oriented features of locality of environments in a system of cooperating objects.

When a client calls InsertAtN for a list it supplies n, the position in the list to insert, and val, the value to be inserted. The implementation for the list version implements the precondition with an ASSERT statement, then delegates as usual.

ASSERT(n >= 0, 20);   *InsertAtN for a list*
lst.head.InsertAtN(lst, n, val)

A third parameter is included in the corresponding method for a node. lst is the actual parameter and owner is the formal parameter. A head node needs to have access to its owner, because the owner's state will change if n is 0.

The implementation of InsertAtN for a nonempty node must first decide if the value is to be inserted at the current position or at a position further down the list. If n is greater than 0, it belongs further down the list. So, the method delegates with

node.next.InsertAtN(n - 1, val)

Because node.next is a list, the method call is for the list version of InsertAtN, which has only two parameters. The implementation supplies n - 1 for the actual parameter, because the position of the first item in the next list is one less than the current position.

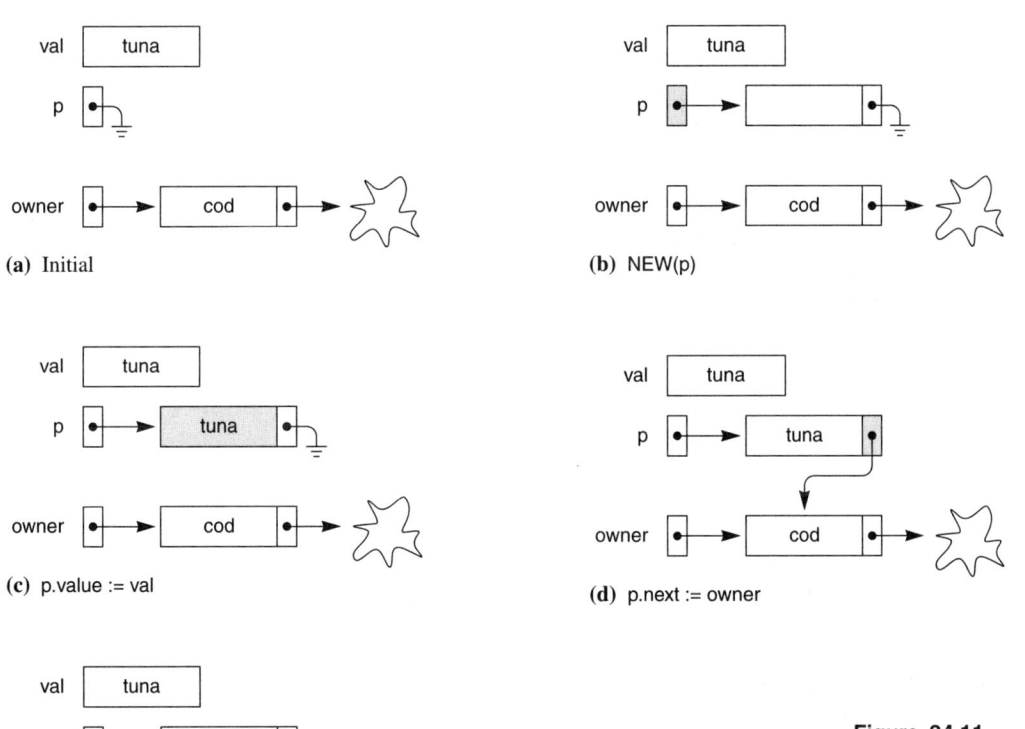

(a) Initial

(b) NEW(p)

(c) p.value := val

(d) p.next := owner

(e) owner.head := p

Figure 24.11
Method InsertAtN for a nonempty node.

If n equals 0, the four statements in Figure 24.11 execute. Figure 24.11(a) shows the initial environment for a nonempty node who owns value cod and next, which is a list. The nonempty node has access to its owner as a formal parameter. The figure assumes that tuna is passed in parameter val from the list. Figure 24.11(b) shows the effect of

NEW(p)

where p is a local variable that points to a nonempty node. Storage for the node is allocated from the heap. The statement

p.value := val

sets the value field of the new node to tuna from parameter val. Figure 24.11(d) shows the effect of

p.next := owner

which changes the state of p.next to point to the same nonempty node to which owner points. Finally, Figure 24.11(e) shows the effect of

owner.head := p

which changes the state of owner to point to the inserted node.

The implementation of InsertAtN for an empty node is similar to the above implementation for a nonempty node. No IF statement is required, because the specification requires the value to be inserted at the end of the list if the position supplied exceeds the length of the list. The empty node simply executes

```
NEW(p);
p.value := val;
p.next.Clear;
owner.head := p
```

where p is a local nonempty node. The only difference between this sequence of statements and the sequence for a nonempty node is that p.next is cleared instead of being set to point to the following node. There is no following node that must be linked to the inserted node.

You should compare this algorithm to the implementation of InsertAtN in Figure 21.30 for PboxLLListObj. This version for PboxLLListSta with polymorphism exhibits the object-oriented locality of environment for its distributed system of cooperating objects. Because the environment is local, the code for each method is easier to write and to understand compared to the version for PboxLLListObj.

Method Search for a list is implemented with the help of method SearchN also for a list, whose signature differs from that of Search only by n being called by reference (VAR) instead of called by result (OUT).

PROCEDURE (IN lst: List) SearchN (IN srchVal: T; VAR n: INTEGER; OUT fnd: BOOLEAN), NEW;

The programmer of the client sees the same interface for PboxLLListSta as for PboxLLListObj and does not need to initialize the value of n before she calls the server method. Inside the PboxLListSta server, Search initializes n to 0 then calls SearchN, which assumes that the initial value of n is defined. The idea is for SearchN to delegate to its head node the request to search for srchVal. The head node executes SearchN for an empty node or for a nonempty node with polymorphic dispatch. The nonempty node reasons that if srchVal is not equal to its value field, it must further delegate the task to the list in its next field. If srchVal is at position n in the next list, then it is at position $n + 1$ in the nonempty node's owner's list. In that case, the nonempty node must increment n for its owner. The details are a problem for the student.

Problems

1.   Complete the methods for the binary search tree of Figure 24.4. You will need to write the methods for the abstract node, and the corresponding implementations for the concrete empty node and nonempty node. Test your implementation with a client program identical to that in Figure 22.11 but importing your server module instead of Pbox-TreeObj.

   (a) PROCEDURE (IN tr: Tree) **Contains*** (IN val: T): BOOLEAN, NEW
   (b) PROCEDURE (IN tr: Tree) **NumItems*** (): INTEGER, NEW
   (c) PROCEDURE (IN tr: Tree) **InOrder***, NEW
   (d) PROCEDURE (IN tr: Tree) **PostOrder***, NEW

2.   Complete the methods for the linked list of Figure 24.10. You will need to write the methods for the abstract node, and the corresponding implementations for the concrete empty node and nonempty node. Test your implementation with a client program identical to that in Figure 21.29 but importing your server module instead of PboxLListObj.

   (a) PROCEDURE (IN lst: List) **Length*** (): INTEGER, NEW
   (b) PROCEDURE (VAR lst: List) **RemoveN*** (n: INTEGER), NEW
   (c) PROCEDURE (IN lst: List) **Search*** (IN srchVal: T; OUT n: INTEGER; OUT fnd: BOOLEAN), NEW

Appendix *A*

Component Pascal Syntax

The lexical rules of Component Pascal are:

Ident	=	(Letter	" _ ") {Letter	" _ "	Digit}.
Letter	=	" A " .. " Z "	" a " .. " z "	" À " .. " Ö "	" Ø " .. " ö "	" ø " .. " ÿ ".
Digit	=	" 0 "	" 1 "	" 2 "	" 3 "	" 4 "	" 5 "	" 6 "	" 7 "	" 8 "	" 9 ".
Number	=	Integer	Real.
Integer	=	Digit {Digit}	Digit {HexDigit} (" H "	" L ").
Real	=	Digit {Digit} " . " {Digit} [ScaleFactor].
ScaleFactor	=	" E " [" + "	" - "] Digit {Digit}.
HexDigit	=	Digit	" A "	" B "	" C "	" D "	" E "	" F ".
Character	=	Digit {HexDigit} " X ".
String	=	" " " {Char} " " "	" ' " {Char} " ' ".

The start symbol for a valid Component Pascal program is Module. The syntax rules of Component Pascal are:

Module	=	MODULE Ident " ; " [ImportList] DeclSeq [BEGIN StatementSeq] [CLOSE StatementSeq] END Ident " . ".
ImportList	=	IMPORT [Ident " := "] Ident {" , " [Ident " := "] Ident} " ; ".
DeclSeq	=	{CONST {ConstDecl " ; "}	TYPE {TypeDecl " ; "}	VAR {VarDecl " ; "}} {ProcDecl " ; "	ForwardDecl " ; "}.
ConstDecl	=	IdentDef " = " ConstExpr.
TypeDecl	=	IdentDef " = " Type.
VarDecl	=	IdentList " : " Type.
ProcDecl	=	PROCEDURE [Receiver] IdentDef [FormalPars] [" , " NEW] [" , " (ABSTRACT | EMPTY | EXTENSIBLE)] [" ; " DeclSeq [BEGIN StatementSeq] END Ident].
ForwardDecl	=	PROCEDURE " ^ " [Receiver] IdentDef [FormalPars].
FormalPars	=	" (" [FPSection {" ; " FPSection}] ") " [" : " Type].
FPSection	=	[VAR	IN	OUT] Ident {" , " Ident} " : " Type.
Receiver	=	" (" [VAR | IN] Ident " : " Ident ") ".
Type	=	Qualident
			ARRAY [ConstExpr {" , " ConstExpr}] OF Type
			[ABSTRACT	EXTENSIBLE	LIMITED] RECORD [" (" Qualident ") "] FieldList {" ; " FieldList} END
			POINTER TO Type
FieldList	=	[IdentList " : " Type].
StatementSeq	=	Statement {" ; " Statement}.

Statement	=	[Designator " := " Expr
		| Designator [" (" [ExprList] ") "]
		| IF Expr THEN StatementSeq {ELSIF Expr THEN StatementSeq}
		[ELSE StatementSeq] END
		| CASE Expr OF Case {" | " Case} [ELSE StatementSeq] END
		| WHILE Expr DO StatementSeq END
		| REPEAT StatementSeq UNTIL Expr
		| FOR Ident " := " Expr TO Expr [BY ConstExpr] DO StatementSeq END
		| LOOP StatementSeq END
		| WITH Guard DO StatementSeq {" | " Guard DO StatementSeq}
		[ELSE StatementSeq] END
		| EXIT
		| RETURN [Expr]
		].
Case	=	[CaseLabels {" , " CaseLabels} " : " StatementSeq].
CaseLabels	=	ConstExpr [" .. " ConstExpr].
Guard	=	Qualident " : " Qualident.
ConstExpr	=	Expr.
Expr	=	SimpleExpr [Relation SimpleExpr].
SimpleExpr	=	[" + " | " - "] Term {AddOp Term}.
Term	=	Factor {MulOp Factor}.
Factor	=	Designator
		| Number
		| Character
		| String
		| NIL
		| Set
		| " (" Expr ") "
		| " ~ " Factor.
Set	=	" { " [Element {" , " Element}] " } ".
Element	=	Expr [" .. " Expr].
Relation	=	" = " | " # " | " < " | " <= " | " > " | " >= " | IN | IS.
AddOp	=	" + " | " - " | OR.
MulOp	=	" * " | " / " | DIV | MOD | " & ".
Designator	=	Qualident {" . " Ident | " [" ExprList "] " | " ^ " | " $ "
		| " (" Qualident ") " | " (" [ExprList] ") "}.
ExprList	=	Expr {" , " Expr}.
IdentList	=	IdentDef {" , " IdentDef}.
Qualident	=	[Ident " . "] Ident.
IdentDef	=	Ident [" * " | " - "].

Index